Wild Turkey Management:
Accomplishments, Strategies, and Opportunities

Proceedings of the
Ninth National Wild Turkey Symposium

Grand Rapids, Michigan
10–14 December, 2005

Edited by

C. ALAN STEWART AND VALERIE R. FRAWLEY
Michigan Department of Natural Resources
Lansing, Michigan

Sponsored by

**Michigan Department
of Natural Resources**

**Hal & Jean Glassen
Memorial Foundation**

**National Wild
Turkey Federation**

**Michigan State University,
Department of Fisheries and
Wildlife**

**Michigan Chapter of
The Wildlife Society**

**U.S. Department of Agriculture,
Forest Service**

**Wisconsin Department of
Natural Resources**

Published by

Michigan Department of Natural Resources

Copyright © 2007 by Michigan Department of Natural Resources

Published by

Michigan Department of Natural Resources
Stevens T. Mason Building
P.O. Box 30444
Lansing, MI 48909-7944

Printed by

Allen Press, Inc. 810 East Tenth Lawrence, KS 66044

Printed in the United States of America
10   9 8 7 6 5 4 3 2 1

First edition

Illustrations by Ed Sutton

Library of Congress Cataloging-in-Publication Data

National Wild Turkey Symposium (9th : 2005 : Grand Rapids, Mich.)
  Wild Turkey management : accomplishments, strategies, and opportunities : proceedings of the Ninth National Wild Turkey Symposium, Grand Rapids, Michigan, 10–14 December, 2005 / edited by C. Alan Stewart and Valerie R. Frawley ; sponsored by Michigan Department of Natural Resources ... [et al.]
    p. cm.
  Includes bibliographical references and index.
ISBN 1-891276-59-X (alk. paper)
  1. Wild turkey--Congresses. 2. Upland game bird management--Congresses. I. Stewart, C. Alan, 1952- II. Frawley, Valerie R., 1974- III. Michigan. Dept. of Natural Resources. IV. Title.
QL696.G27N39 2005
598.6'45--dc22
                    2007038811

Proceedings available from:

National Wild Turkey Federation
Post Office Box 530
Edgefield, SC 29824–0530
www.nwtf.org
1-800-The-NWTF

Wild Turkey Management:
Accomplishments, Strategies, and Opportunities
——————— Grand Rapids, Michigan ———————

NWTF State Chapter Sponsors

Alabama
Illinois
Indiana
Kansas
Maryland
Michigan
Minnesota
Missouri
New Jersey
New Mexico
North Carolina
Oklahoma
Ontario, Canada
Pennsylvania
Rhode Island
Vermont
Virginia
West Virginia
Wisconsin
Wyoming

Corporate Sponsors

Advanced Tex
Hunter's Specialties
Nighthawk Publications
Quaker Boy
Rapid River Knifeworks
Wolverine Power Cooperative

Individual Sponsors

Denny Grinold
Tom Karsten
Bob LeBlanc
Chad Lehman
Charlie Reynar
Steve Sharp
Pete Squibb

Ninth National Wild Turkey Symposium Acknowledgments

Many people helped make this symposium a success.
It is through their dedication and attention to detail that
this symposium has come to fruition.

Program Committee Members and Manuscript Reviewers

Roger D. Applegate
Steven E. Backs
Jeff J. Beringer
Stephen M. Beyer
Valerie R. Frawley

Todd E. Gosselink
Richard O. Kimmel
Jennifer L. Kleitch
Chad P. Lehman
Michael W. Malhiot

Darren A. Miller
Gary W. Norman
Thomas E. Oliver
William F. Porter
Brent A. Rudolph

C. Alan Stewart
Brian C. Tefft
Brian F. Wakeling
D. Keith Warnke

Additional Manuscript Reviewers

Ted A. Benzon
Dean E. Beyer
Peter A. Bull
Bryan J. Burhans
John D. Burk
Michael J. Chamberlain
Karen T. Cleveland
David T. Cobb
Bret A. Collier
L. Mike Conner
Thomas M. Cooley
Dennis C. Daniel
Stephen J. DeMaso
Randy W. DeYoung
James G. Dickson
Michael L. Donovan

Shelli A. Dubay
Richard D. Earle
Dwayne R. Etter
Jean S. Fierke
Lester D. Flake
Brian E. Flock
Brian J. Frawley
K. David Godwin
Fred S. Guthery
Kurt J. Haroldson
Mark A. Hatfield
William M. Healy
David G. Hewitt
Michael W. Hubbard
Fred G. Kimmel
William P. Kuvlesky

Bruce D. Leopold
Douglas A. Little
R. Scott Lutz
Sarah L. Mayhew
James E. Miller
Richard A. Morschek
Dave G. Neu
Daniel J. O'Brien
William L. Palmer
John J. Paskus
Joel A. Pedersen
Peter J. Pekins
Larry S. Perrin
R. Ben Peyton
Harold H. Prince
David J. Reid

Marco Restani
Raymond A. Rustem
Sanford D. Schemnitz
Joel A. Schmutz
T. Wayne Schwertner
Randy J. Showalter
Nova J. Silvy
Rod W. Smith
David E. Steffen
Marshall L. Strong
John A. Thiebes
John W. Urbain
Larry D. Vangilder
Lovett E. Williams, Jr.
Scott R. Winterstein
Brian M. Zielinski

Additional Program Committee Members

Mark R. Bishop
Vicki P. Brown
Kelly Siciliano Carter
James L. Dexter
Robert E. Eriksen
Chad A. Fedewa

Troy A. Hopkins
Thomas W. Hughes
Kent W. Kurtz
Phil and Jan Kuhtic
Dan W. Potter
Mark S. Sargent

H. William Scullon
Steve J. Sharp
Lou Ann Shaw
Alice L. Stimpson
Robert J. Stout
David A. Swanson

William W. Taylor
Bruce E. Warren
Jill K. Zimmerman-Todd

Wild Turkey Management:
Accomplishments, Strategies and Opportunities

"If facts are the seeds that later produce knowledge and wisdom, then the emotions and the impressions of the senses are the fertile soil in which the seeds must grow."

Rachel Carson

The Michigan Department of Natural Resources, in cooperation with many partners, hosted the Ninth National Wild Turkey Symposium in December 2005 in Grand Rapids, Michigan. In addition to the scientific papers presented at the symposium, there was a rocket-net safety training ·workshop and a field trip to areas in southwestern Michigan where wild turkey restoration has been successful. The symposium was held in conjunction with the 66th Midwest Fish and Wildlife Conference.

The theme for the Ninth National Wild Turkey Symposium was *Wild Turkey Management: Accomplishments, Strategies and Opportunities.* Authors submitted papers on a variety of topics associated with biology, ecology, behavior, conservation, research methods, and management for wild turkeys. Manuscripts, which were peer-reviewed, contribute toward a greater understanding of the wild turkey. Nearly 90 referees contributed to the quality of the manuscripts contained in these proceedings. Their expertise and ability to offer a constructive critique were paramount to the success of the review process. The professionalism of authors and referees during proceedings development was greatly appreciated by the editors.

The National Wild Turkey Symposia provide a venue for researchers, biologists, and land managers to present and share the results of their current research. The symposia offer valuable opportunities for professionals to discuss current topics, confer about challenges they face, and reflect on successes that they have had regarding turkey management. The symposia are also valuable settings for hunters and other conservationists to learn more about wild turkeys and to interact with individuals that have an obsession for this magnificent bird.

The first symposium was held in Memphis, Tennessee, in 1959. Since the first meeting, the symposium has been hosted in Missouri (1970), Texas (1975), Arkansas (1980), Iowa (1985), South Carolina (1990), South Dakota (1995), and Georgia (2000). Michigan is the northernmost state to hold this symposium to date.

With each consecutive symposium, the content of the proceedings has expanded in depth and scope. This has led to improved wild turkey management and has helped us shift wild turkeys from a species of scarcity to an animal of abundance.

The contributors to this symposium have a passion for natural resources and wild turkeys. This passion is nurtured by their sense of awe for the wild turkey as they strive to provide facts for the future. In a quest for understanding, these scientists amass information in a professional format as they continue to strengthen and expand the foundation of our wisdom about these remarkable birds.

Wildlife research and management are activities that encourage individuals to learn more about themselves, their outdoor surroundings, and the ways of their quarry. Renowned turkey biologists know this better than anyone. These resource professionals attempt to "think like a turkey" in an effort to understand the behavior and life requisites of their research samples. These biologists demonstrate patience as they sit motionless awaiting birds to approach their rocket-net location. In an effort to monitor wild turkeys, they work to improve their woodsmanship skills and seek to blend with their surroundings with chameleon-like concealment. They can visualize the presence of a turkey track in hard-packed soil, or inspect a chromosome allele under the concentrated light of a microscope. They operate with a self-imposed code of scientific ethics that rise above the most stringent of other wildlife exploration activities. These specialists crave the dynamics of discussion that expand their knowledge about natural resources and the wild turkeys they manage. They strive to understand turkey language and the subtle nuances of a cluck or yelp, and strain to hear a distant gobble or a pulsing beep from a radio-telemetry transmitter. These disciplined biologists know that studying wild turkeys has a way of humbling the experienced professional and awakening a child's sense of wonder and amazement. They live to share this awe and admiration with others while working to pursue emerging issues that affect wild turkeys. I am indebted to and salute these professionals for their contributions to this symposium.

Many people contributed significant time and energy to the success and quality of this symposium and subsequent proceedings. My gratitude goes to each and every one of them. Special thanks to co-editor Val Frawley for her assistance. Val always gave more than she was asked to give, and her grace and style are admired by everyone around her. Val and I are indebted to our families (Brian, Seth and Shawn; Pat, Chris and Tom) for their support during the symposium publication process. We also acknowledge the encouragement and understanding of our supervisors Michael Bailey and William Moritz. We hope that these proceedings provide fertile soil for future generations to grow their passion for natural resource stewardship.

C. Alan Stewart, Editor

Symposium Welcome

Good Morning! It's a great morning for the wild turkey and the many people who revere and hunt this great game bird. It's great to be here at the ninth symposium and a thrill for me since I've been to every one since I began employment with the National Wild Turkey Federation (NWTF) 28 years ago. First, on behalf of the NWTF's more than 500,000 members, I want to thank the Michigan Department of Natural Resources, headed up by Rebecca Humphries, for hosting this conference. I would also like to give a special thank you to Al Stewart, who has worked tirelessly to pull all of the details together.

It's your presence at this symposium, though, that is the key to its success. Your work has been important to restoring and managing wild turkeys and the Federation is proud to have supported these efforts. You and your work have been, are, and always will be vital to the future of the wild turkey. You have made a difference.

We've made progress together. The NWTF, our volunteers, and this country's wildlife professionals have set a standard for partnership excellence that could serve as a model for all teams. We've pooled our resources—money, manpower, and professional expertise—and have accomplished more for wild turkeys and other wildlife than was ever dreamed possible. Since 1985, the Federation and its cooperators have spent $224 million for the benefit of the wild turkey and our hunting heritage. During that time, the NWTF has contributed more than $3.5 million to research efforts in 34 states, Mexico, and Guatemala. In the Federation's early days, I know there was some concern about the role we would play. However, 32 years later, now that the dust has settled, we're proud of how you've worked with us, what our volunteers have contributed, and what we've accomplished together.

Vern Ross, Pennsylvania Game Commission's executive director, who will retire at the end of the year, spoke last month at a turkey release about how the Federation's volunteers have helped the agency. He shared information about the agency's turkey management efforts dating back to the infancy of the Game Commission. He acknowledged that since the formation of the NWTF in the 1970s, the Federation has been a major presence in Pennsylvania. He stated that the NWTF has remained committed for decades to help support the Game Commission's wild turkey management program, turkey hunting safety, habitat improvement, and land acquisitions.

We've tried to be that kind of partner in all 50 states and Canada. Thanks to the strength of these partnerships, we have been able to clear plenty of hurdles since the early years of wild turkey restoration. Whether it was pulling together the Technical Committee to improve cooperation and communications between the agencies, developing the concept of replacement dollars so agencies could be reimbursed for trapping costs, or working with our forest industry partners to provide turkey transport boxes—we've been with you, every step of the way.

With restoration largely complete east of the Rockies and nearly 7 million birds across North America, today we're working on many other projects with you: habitat restoration, law enforcement efforts, hunter safety education, expanding hunting opportunities, sharing the outdoors with youth, women, and people with disabilities and, of course, research. When we partner with you, we bring more to the table than us. You benefit from the relationships we've built with others, whether it's the U.S. Sportsmen's Alliance, National Assembly of Sportsmen's Caucuses, National Shooting Sports Foundation, or a multitude of federal, corporate and industry partners.

Many times non-governmental organizations can do things and say things that the agencies may not be able to address. Organizations such as the National Wild Turkey Federation can help with problem solving and speak on behalf of our hunting traditions, wildlife, or habitat management. When there's an issue you can't jump into, there's a good chance the Federation and our partners can.

We've always supported the concept of science-based management and championed funding that would benefit your work. We have helped tell the story to the media about your great accomplishments. A good example of how we're preaching OUTSIDE of the choir is the wild turkey releases we do each year before Thanksgiving. During this time, the media is looking for a turkey story. By hosting a wild turkey release, we give them a story they love and one we want to tell—how hunters, wildlife professionals such as yourself and our volunteers worked to restore populations. Conservation and communications must have equal footing. Some of the agencies we've worked with were concerned at first about holding a release just for media purposes; however, that disappeared when they saw the positive light shined on their work.

We have a great conference ahead of us. I'm excited to hear what you have learned through your research. As we kick off this symposium, I want to issue you a challenge—reach out beyond the scientific community and communicate your good work to the millions of lay conservationists in North America. The papers you're presenting and the work you've embraced is of tremendous value and interest to the non-scientific members of the Federation and beyond. Many of you are their heroes and this country's hunters and conservationists want to fund and support you in even bigger ways than they are presently doing. They want to understand what you do. It's critical that we communicate your achievements to them in a popular and graphic way. It's also important that we consider research that will help us answer today's pressing questions about the wild turkey and its management. I challenge you to communicate your efforts and achievements to those volunteers and chapters that helped you achieve your goals. Encourage them to support your continued work. Five years from now, it's my hope that our lay conservationists will be attending the tenth symposium, giving them the knowledge, understanding, and wisdom to raise even more dollars for your quality research. Ultimately, we're all winners and your valuable research benefits this great natural resource—the wild turkey.

Thank you for answering the call.

Rob Keck, NWTF CEO

Dedicated to the Memory of
George A. Wright
1943–2005

George A. Wright is the undisputed architect of Kentucky's wild turkey restoration, management and research program. He retired from the Kentucky Department of Fish and Wildlife Resources (KDFWR) in 2002 after 27 years. He suffered a massive heart attack while turkey hunting with his wife in Mexico in March 2005 and died a few days later in a Nashville hospital. He was 62.

George A. Wright was born in Pensacola, Florida, and graduated from Treadwell High School in Memphis in 1961. He served in the U.S. Navy from 1961 through 1969. He received his B.S. in Wildlife Management from Tennessee Technological University in 1972, and his M.S. in Wildlife Management from Auburn University in 1974.

He was employed by the KDFWR from 1974 through 2002 and as the state's first turkey program coordinator from 1978 through 2002.

George was hired by KDFWR in September 1974 to conduct a raccoon study in east Kentucky. In 1978, requests from dedicated turkey enthusiasts in western Kentucky resulted in George being transferred to western Kentucky to spend full time on turkey restoration.

He supervised modern-day turkey restoration efforts in Kentucky, which lasted from 1978 to 1998, and watched the Kentucky turkey population grow from almost none to 230,000 birds. George used turkeys trapped in Mississippi and turkeys obtained from Missouri through a river otter trade to build his own supply source, transplanting them into prime locations with good natural habitat and with landowners who promised to protect them. The transplants took root and soon he and other KDFWR employees were trapping turkeys in state and transplanting them all over Kentucky.

After restoration efforts were essentially complete, George concentrated his efforts on understanding the impacts of spring harvest on gobblers. George used his great turkey trapping skills to catch and put radio transmitters on almost 600 gobblers over the course of 5 years in and around Caldwell County, Kentucky.

Wild turkeys were George's passion. If you ever sat in a turkey blind with him or hunted with him you would know that George never stopped being 'torn up' (George's words) when wild turkeys came in to the bait or in to the call. George worked very hard at his job and spent many long hours trying to trap turkeys in the winter or trying to "make deals" with other states for animals that he could trade for turkeys.

When spring or fall turkey season arrived, however, George worked just as hard at hunting turkeys. He was one of the best turkey hunters on the planet, not because of his superior calling ability, but because he just knew what turkeys were going to do even before the turkeys did.

George was presented the National Wild Turkey Federation's Henry Mosby Award in 2002 for his work with wild turkeys in Kentucky. The Mosby award is given only to those few biologists who have made significant contributions to wild turkey restoration, research and/or management.

George Wright left this world too soon, but he left while doing what he loved most and with the person he loved most. We should all be so lucky.

HENRY S. MOSBY AWARD
presented to
Dr. James Earl Kennamer

As part of the Ninth National Wild Turkey Symposium, Dr. James Earl Kennamer received the highly coveted Henry S. Mosby Award. Dr. Kennamer is the senior vice president for conservation programs with the National Wild Turkey Federation (NWTF). The Mosby Award is named for Dr. Henry S. Mosby, whose research with wild turkeys in the early 1900s set the standard for their management. Dr. Mosby also helped found The Wildlife Society and was the recipient of its highest honor—the Aldo Leopold Award. The Mosby Award acknowledges individuals who have dedicated their careers and lives to conservation and wild turkeys.

"This award recognizes an outstanding lifetime commitment to wild turkey research and conservation," said Dr. Bill Porter, professor of wildlife ecology at the State University of New York, Environmental Science and Forestry. "It is given to people who, over a career, have made outstanding contributions regarding wild turkeys, and we couldn't think of a better person to receive the award than Dr. Kennamer."

Dr. Kennamer came to the NWTF from a tenured professorship at Auburn University in 1980. His leadership in wild turkey research and management has garnered respect throughout the conservation community. Dr. Kennamer has been responsible for providing input about wild turkey management by coordinating NWTF programs with state and federal agencies, private organizations and companies throughout the United States, Canada and Mexico. Not only has Dr. Kennamer led the NWTF's conservation programs department, he has also edited, reviewed and contributed to past National Wild Turkey Symposia.

"We thought it only fitting Dr. Kennamer receive this honor," said Al Stewart, upland game bird specialist with the Michigan Department of Natural Resources and co-chairman of the Ninth National Wild Turkey Symposium. "We are proud to present this award to Dr. Kennamer because of his past involvement in turkey symposia and his dedication to turkey management."

"This award came as a great surprise," Kennamer said. "I'm grateful to have had the opportunity over my career to watch the advancement in wild turkey research and populations. I've seen great strides in wild turkey populations and research throughout my career and I hope I continue to see progress. I believe that participation in symposia such as this are important to the advancement of our knowledge about wild turkeys."

Dr. Kennamer continues to represent the conservation community and to lead the NWTF's conservation programs. He was one of eight experts asked to testify before the U.S. Senate's Subcommittee on Forestry, Conservation and Rural Revitalization on the Review of Implementation of the Healthy Forest Restoration Act of 2003. He was the only representative from a nonprofit conservation organization. In pursuing his responsibilities, Dr. Kennamer has consistently demonstrated dependability, vigor, enthusiasm, and professional competence and integrity.

Contents

CHAPTER III. HABITAT ECOLOGY OF WILD TURKEYS

CHAPTER IV. TURKEYS ON THEIR NORTHERN RANGE

CHAPTER V. HARVEST MANAGEMENT

Ninth National Wild Turkey Symposium

Wild Turkey Management: Accomplishments, Strategies and Opportunities

CHANGES, OPPORTUNITIES, AND CHALLENGES

William M. Healy[1]

USDA Forest Service (Retired), Northeastern Forest Experiment Station,
Amherst, MA 01003, USA

Abstract: Changes in ecosystem function and human demography will present unique challenges and opportunities to natural resource managers in the near future. The function of North American forest ecosystems has been altered by introduced pathogens, loss of key species, and changed fire regimes. Management is required to sustain ecosystem function and the abundance of wildlife we enjoy. Effective management will require an interdisciplinary approach and unprecedented cooperation among management agencies. A wave of retirements will significantly reduce senior staffing of all natural resource agencies by 2010. By 2050 the United States population will be older, more urbanized, and more ethnically and racially diverse. Effective communication of resource needs and policies will require understanding public attitudes. The North American model of conservation is characterized by the wise consumptive use of wildlife. Conservation efforts would be severely weakened without the continued support of hunters, anglers, and trappers, and public support for these activities. Current hunting traditions fail to meet the social and ethical standards of the non-hunting majority. Natural resource professionals must lead in creating a new hunting ethic that is both socially acceptable and capable of meeting ecosystem management goals.

Proceedings of the National Wild Turkey Symposium 9:1–6

Key words: conservation, ethics, hunting, management, *Meleagris gallopavo,* opportunities, wild turkey.

The restoration of wild turkeys (*Meleagris gallopavo*) is a well-known story, having been told in both the popular and technical literature. Changes in the abundance and distribution of turkeys have been documented in past symposia, and Tapley et al. (*this volume*) describe the current status and distribution of turkeys at this Symposium. Lewis (2001) provided an excellent history of the restoration process and the technical advances that made restoration possible. Lewis noted that in Missouri, the impetus for restoration was a request made in 1952 by the Conservation Federation of Missouri to the Department of Conservation asking for immediate action to restore the wild turkey. Hunters and conservation organizations played a key role in turkey restoration, and their continued support is essential for future management.

As turkey populations have expanded during the past 50 years, so has our knowledge of their behavior, biology, and population dynamics. Dickson (2001) highlighted advances in research at the Eighth National Wild Turkey Symposium. In his concluding remarks about the challenges ahead, Dickson indicated that the loss of understanding and support of wildlife management and hunting from a public increasingly removed from the land, both physically and philosophically, would become more important than habitat loss for the turkey's future. I agree.

There is a sound scientific basis for protecting the wild turkey and its habitat and providing a sustainable harvest. The challenging issues will be social, political, and economic changes driven by growth and demographic changes in the human population. The most likely biological challenges, climate change and introduced species, are directly linked to human activity and much less tractable than the issues the wildlife profession faced in the past (Jenkins 2003).

In this paper I will take a broad view of the challenges and opportunities facing the wildlife profession. I will start with a model of forest dynamics that provides an ecological perspective for current management issues. Then, I will describe demographic changes that are affecting our profession and hunting. Finally, I will share some thoughts about hunting and its future.

FOREST DYNAMICS: PAST AND PRESENT

To put current management issues in context, it is useful to examine changes that have occurred in North American forests over the past 3 centuries. For convenience, I will use the eastern deciduous forest

[1] Present address: Owl Run Farm, P.O. Box 187, Smithville, WV 26178.

(Braun 1950) as an example. Note, however, that the factors that have most changed the eastern forest—loss of habitat, loss of key endemic species, introduction of foreign species and pathogens, and altered fire regimes—affect all North American ecosystems, and most ecosystems world-wide.

In 1700, North American forests were expansive. Disturbance patterns varied by region and disturbance factors included hurricanes, other storms with strong winds and ice or snow, fire, beaver (*Castor canadensis*), and death of individual canopy trees (Runkle 1990). Land clearing by Europeans was still confined to the edges of this great forest. Fire was a strong ecological force shaping tree species composition of mixed hardwood, pine, and oak forests. Most of the forest was mature, but young stands and early successional habitats were common, often occupying 10–20% of the landscape.

The most common and widespread tree genera were oak (*Quercus*), beech (*Fagus*), maple (*Acer*), basswood (*Tilia*), hickory (*Carya*), ash (*Fraxinus*), elm (*Ulmus*), birch (*Betula*), yellow poplar (*Liriodendron*), and chestnut (*Castanea*) (Braun 1950). Tree seeds were the most abundant and energy-rich plant food available for wildlife during the dormant season, and probably through most of the year. Wildlife was abundant. These forests supported the passenger pigeon (*Ectopistes migratorius*), formerly one of the world's most abundant birds (Bucher 1992). Pigeons fed primarily on beechnuts and acorns and to a lesser extent on chestnuts (Schorger 1955). The flocks nested in early spring, and successful breeding was dependent on locating abundant mast crops that had persisted over winter. John J. Audubon estimated the pigeon population at 1.1 billion and their daily mast consumption at 8.7 million bushels (about 307,000 m³/day) (Schorger 1955). The consumption figures cannot be verified, but considering the long list of mast-consuming species in eastern forests, an enormous mast crop must have been necessary to support pigeon populations (Bucher 1992).

Predators were abundant and predation exerted a top-down control of deer (*Odocoileus* spp.) and elk (*Cervus elaphus*) populations. The suite of large predators included humans, mountain lions (*Puma concolor*), wolves (*Canis* spp.), black bears (*Ursus americanus*), bobcats (*Lynx rufus*), and coyotes (*Canis latrans*). Because predation was a strong force, herbivorey was a relatively weak force at the forest level and there was little competition among herbivores for food. The forests were self-sustaining through natural regeneration.

In 1700, the European population was confined to the eastern seaboard, but the process of introducing foreign species was well underway. The grasses and weeds of England were introduced into the colonies early in the 17th century and they spread rapidly. By 1700 blue grass (*Poa* L.) and white clover (*Trifolium repens* L.) were considered indigenous (Edwards 1948). The rates of forest clearing and species introductions increased rapidly after 1700.

The most obvious landscape change between 1700 and 2005 is the reduction in forest area and the increase in agricultural and developed lands. Several less obvious,

but equally important, changes have occurred in the remaining forest due to the introduction of pathogens, the exclusion of fire, and the elimination of large predators.

Mast production potential has been reduced, primarily by introduced pathogens. The chestnut blight fungus (*Cryphonectria parasitica*) has eliminated American chestnut as a dominant species throughout its 200 million-acre range (Brewer 1995). American chestnut was the most prolific and consistent of our nut-producing trees. American beech has also been greatly reduced in importance as a canopy tree due to introduced insects and pathogens (Tubbs and Houston 1990).

Acorns and other seeds are still the most valuable and energy-rich plant food available in the dormant season (Robbins 1993). Once oak forests reach seed-bearing age, the supply of seeds usually exceeds that of browse and forage (Liscinsky 1984). The annual acorn crop often exceeds 100 kilograms per hectare and can be as large as 800 kilograms per hectare in good seed years (Christisen and Kearby 1984, McShea and Schwede 1993). Where acorns and browse have been measured on the same sites, mean annual acorn production has been 3 to 10 times greater than browse production (Segelquist and Green 1968, Rogers et al. 1990). On these sites acorns accounted for more than 80% of the total seed crop. It is only in years of complete mast failure that forage abundance exceeds that of mast.

The suppression of fire in eastern forests has resulted in the loss of early successional habitats, grasslands and savannas, and poor regeneration of oak on mesic sites. On these sites oaks are being replaced by more shade-tolerant species, and the prognosis for maintaining oak as a dominant component is not good (Healy et al. 1997, McShea and Healy 2002).

The elimination of wolves and mountain lions from eastern forests has had profound, and largely unappreciated, effects (Terborgh et al. 2001). Predation has become a relatively weak ecological force while herbivory has become a strong force. In 1700, predation controlled deer numbers, but today, competition among deer for food limits many deer populations. Whenever deer compete for food, palatable plant species decline in abundance and unpalatable ones increase, and plant species composition and forest structure gradually change. When competition for food is severe, stands cannot be regenerated, either naturally or with silvicultural techniques. Mature stands cannot progress to an old-growth condition because the understory reinitiation phase is interrupted by herbivory. Canopy trees that die are not replaced, and there is a gradual conversion of forest habitat to openings dominated by ferns and other plants that are unpalatable to deer. Habitat structure is simplified, biodiversity is reduced, and forest management is not sustainable (Healy 1997).

There are two points that I would like you to retain from this overview of past and current forest ecosystem function. First, management is essential for maintaining biodiversity and sustaining our forest ecosystems. Second, interagency cooperation and interdisciplinary communication will have to improve to accomplish the job. For example, foresters have recognized a widespread problem with oak regeneration for about 40 years. The profession has worked diligently to understand the ecological factors influencing oak regeneration and to develop silvicultural techniques to regenerate oak. Unfortunately, the techniques that are most effective at regenerating oak, the clearcutting method of regeneration, shelterwood regeneration, and shelterwood with burning, are unacceptable to the public when done for timber management. In my experience in Massachusetts, the same techniques were acceptable when done for wildlife management or ecosystem restoration. The difference was in the message and perceived motivation of the manager. The timber harvest message is narrow, and the motivation is perceived as selfish—profit at the expense of nature. The wildlife message is more complex and interesting, and the motive appears selfless—helping nature.

I encourage all natural resource professionals to be active, enthusiastic advocates of habitat management. The natural history of wildlife species and ecological relationships within communities can be used to sell habitat management to most audiences. Advocate active land management within your agency. Encourage private landowners to take advantage of professional help and state and federal programs available to them.

HUMAN DEMOGRAPHY AND NATURAL RESOURCES MANAGEMENT

Demographic changes will cause a large turnover in the senior staffing of natural resource agencies by 2010, and may result in reduced public support for wildlife management. All of the nation's environmental and natural resource agencies are facing a crisis due to an impending wave of retirements (Colker and Day 2004). For example, one-half of the Senior Executive Service (SES) members at the Department of Interior (DOI), USDA Forest Service, and Environmental Protection Agency (EPA) will retire by 2007. Within the same period, DOI will lose 61% of its program managers, the Forest Service will lose 81% of its entomologists and 49% of its foresters, and EPA will lose 45% of its toxicologists and about 30% of its environmental specialists.

This wave of retirements is an opportunity for a new generation of leaders, but it will be a challenge for the agencies to maintain core scientific and managerial skills and to sustain public and political support. Unfortunately, if recent history holds, many positions will go unfilled due to budgetary constraints.

The same demographic changes will affect the general population (Cohen 2003). By 2050, fertility in the United States will have fallen to unprecedented low levels, and the population will be older, more urban, and more racially and ethnically diverse. Although global population will continue to increase beyond 2050, the populations of the rich countries, including the United States, will have been declining for 20 years. Growth in the United States population will come from international migration, so we will continue to be a melting pot of cultures. Urbanization will continue, rising from 75% of population in 2000 to 83% in 2030. The rural population peaked around 1950 and has declined slowly since then. Slowly growing populations have a high elderly dependency ratio—the ratio of the number of people aged 65 and older to the number of people aged 15 to 64. After 2010 the elderly dependency ratio will increase sharply.

Family structure will change. The ties between men and women based on parenthood and the ties between fathers and children are weakening. Non-marital births increased as percentage of all births in the United States from 5.3% in 1960 to 33.0% in 1999. By 1994, about 40% of children in the United States did not live with their biological father. Declining fertility rates, by themselves, change family structure. In a population with one child per family, no children have siblings. In the next generation, the children of those children have no cousins, aunts, or uncles. Urbanization and changes in family structure will make it more difficult for people to have direct, personal contact with living nature. It will also be more difficult to pass hunting, angling, and trapping traditions and skills along family social networks.

It is unclear how these changes in demography and family structure will influence public support for conservation and wildlife management. Surveys of American attitudes towards scientific wildlife management and human use of fish and wildlife reveal the following relationships among demography and attitudes (Duda and Young 1998). Disapproval of hunting increased as population density of place of residence increased. The likelihood to strongly approve of hunting decreased as level of education increased. White Americans were more likely than minority Americans to approve of hunting. Americans who were raised in single-parent households were less likely to strongly approve and more likely to strongly disapprove of hunting when compared with those who were raised by two parents. Duda and Young (1998) emphasize that public opinion is not fixed, and that resource managers can develop appropriate messages if they identify core issues through research.

Contemplating these impending social changes may be disquieting, until one thinks of the social milieu of the early 1900s from which today's conservation movement emerged. Then, there were waves of international immigration, migration to cities, disregard for the environment, and overexploitation of wildlife resources. Yet, dedicated individuals were able to sell a conservation message. The demography and social dynamics of the United States have never been stable. Each generation of conservationists has faced its own challenges and each generation has been better equipped to understand the attitudes of our diverse publics. I am confident that the current generation of natural resource professionals will develop a conservation message that is effective in the 21st century.

HUNTING AND THE NORTH AMERICAN MODEL OF CONSERVATION

Natural resource professionals need to define the knowledge and skills that hunters will need in the 21st century. Current hunting traditions fail to meet the social and ethical standards of the non-hunting majority. However, I cannot conceive of a future where wildlife is abundant and biodiversity is protected without a vibrant hunting culture. The North American Model of Conservation has produced an incredible abundance of wildlife and it is characterized principally by a policy of wise consumptive use (Mahoney 1998, Organ et al. 1998). Wildlife management, and conservation in general, would be severely weakened without the economic and social support of hunters, anglers, and trappers (Peterson 2004).

In a thoughtful review of the social legitimacy of hunting, Peterson (2004) concludes that the three dominant hunting ethics fail to justify hunting or place it in a shared context with modern society. Peterson (2004) suggests an alternative ethic that combines Aldo Leopold's vision of an expanding community with traditional utilitarian and rights-based evaluations of ethical criteria. Hunting will remain socially acceptable if it can be demonstrated that the ethics of hunters and non-hunters broadly overlap, and that hunting provides an array of social and economic benefits to society. Many professionals have expressed apprehension about the future of hunting and the North American model of conservation in the face of declining trends in hunter participation and changing attitudes among hunters, natural resource professionals, and non-hunters (Hamilton and Organ 1998, Organ and Fritzel 2000, Peyton 2000).

Non-governmental conservation organizations (NGCOs), such as Ducks Unlimited, the National Wild Turkey Federation, Rocky Mountain Elk Foundation, and Ruffed Grouse Society, may hold the key to the future of hunting. The popularity of turkey hunting illustrates some of the advantages of collaboration among NGCOs and state conservation agencies. At this Symposium, Tapley et al. (*this volume*) report that numbers of turkey hunters increased again during the past five years. Beringer et al. (*this volume*) will show how the Missouri Department of Conservation has used youth turkey hunts to increase hunter recruitment and retention. Despite declines in license sales and rates of graduation from hunter education programs, there is a large pool of people who have positive associations with hunting although they do not hunt themselves (Enck et al. 2000). That fact is obvious at NGCO social functions. Many people at these events do not hunt, but do derive some social benefit from hunting, and they provide social support for hunters and financial and political support for conservation agencies. NGCOs can advocate hunting and policies that support hunting when wildlife agencies must remain value neutral.

Part of the need for a new hunting ethic arises from a fundamental change in the mission of state and federal conservation agencies. During the 1990s, the core mission of the USDA Forest Service changed from one of multiple use, sustained yield management to the protection and enhancement of biodiversity (Thomas 2004). That policy change came about unintentionally through the interaction of the Endangered Species Act and other federal legislation. The consequences of this policy change have yet to be formally recognized by politicians, professionals, or the public. I contend that all state natural resource agencies are now also in the business of protecting biodiversity, and that ecosystem management is the dominant paradigm. Many biologists will argue this point. I see no alternative given the state of scientific knowledge and the public expectation that resource agencies protect all species within their jurisdiction. Today, most hunting programs incorporate the concept of maintaining populations in balance with the available habitat, and many management programs are explicit in their ecological goals.

Hunters have not been prepared for the agency change from recreation provider to ecosystem manager. There was little support among Pennsylvania hunters for efforts to manage white-tailed deer to protect the ecological integrity of forests (Diefenbach et al. 1997). Forty-four percent of hunters agreed that antlerless permits should be reduced, and 19% believed they should be eliminated. A majority of hunters agreed that controlling deer populations was necessary (87%) and that deer populations should be kept in balance with natural food supplies (89%), but 57% of hunters did not think that damage to Pennsylvania's forests by deer was a problem. Legally required harvest reporting rates by Pennsylvania deer hunters were low (Rosenberry et al. 2004), and hunter behavior and effort in the field appeared inadequate to manage deer numbers (Stedman et al. 2004).

Natural resource professionals must define the knowledge and skills that hunters need to meet our changing mission. The American hunting ethic has not kept pace with the growth in scientific knowledge and management capabilities that have occurred in the past 50 years. State and federal agencies need to work with NGCOs to promote a socially acceptable hunting ethic. NGCO staff and other independent experts may be more effective at promoting change than wildlife agency staff would be. My credibility with hunters seems to be greater when I speak as a member of the West Virginia Trappers Association than when I speak as a Ph.D., USDA Forest Service biologist. State biologists who work closely with NGCOs also gain stature and credibility with hunters. There are tremendous opportunities to promote an acceptable hunting ethic if management agencies work with NGCOs and other independent experts. But, professionals need to define the new ethic and agree on the message.

Social and economic support from hunters, anglers, and trappers and their families and friends is essential if the North American model of conservation is to be carried into the 21st century. Hunter behavior and attitudes need to change (Williams 2005). American hunters hold the key to public opinion on hunting. Overall, public attitudes towards and opinion on hunting are being damaged because of poor hunter behavior, rather than outside influences (Duda and Young 1998). I am optimistic that an acceptable hunting ethic can emerge, especially when I consider the changes in hunter behavior that occurred at the start of the last century. A new hunting ethic will emerge only if professionals can decide what we expect hunters to contribute and what hunters need to know within the context of ecosystem management to enhance biodiversity.

LITERATURE CITED

Beringer, J., J. J. Millspaugh, R. A. Reitz, and M. Hubbard. *This volume*. A youth turkey season in Missouri: implications towards recruitment and retention. Proceedings of the National Wild Turkey Symposium 9:*This volume*.

Braun, E. L. 1950. Deciduous forests of eastern North America. Hafner, New York, New York, USA.

Brewer, L. G. 1995. Ecology of survival and recovery from blight in American chestnut trees (*Castanea dentata* (Marsh.) Borkh.) in Michigan. Bulletin of the Torrey Botanical Club 122(1):40–57.

Bucher, E. H. 1992. The causes of extinction of the passenger pigeon. Current Ornithology 9:1–36.

Christisen, D. M., and W. H. Kearby. 1984. Mast measurement and production in Missouri (with special reference to acorns). Missouri Department of Conservation, Terrestrial Series 13.

Cohen, J. E. 2003. Human population: The next half century. Science 302(5648):1172–1175.

Colker, R. M., and R. D. Day, editors. 2004. Conference on personnel trends, education policy, and evolving roles of federal and state natural resources agencies. Renewable Resources Journal 21(4):1–31.

Dickson, J. G. 2001. Summary of the important findings of the Eighth National Wild Turkey Symposium. Proceedings of the National Wild Turkey Symposium 8:1–4.

Diefenbach, D. R., W. L. Palmer, and W. K. Shope. 1997. Attitudes of Pennsylvania sportsmen towards managing white-tailed deer to protect the ecological integrity of forests. Wildlife Society Bulletin 25(2):244–251.

Duda, M. D., and K. C. Young. 1998. American attitudes towards scientific wildlife management and human use of fish and wildlife: Implications for effective public relations and communication strategies. Transactions of the North American Wildlife and Natural Resources Conference 63:589–603.

Edwards, E. E. 1948. The settlement of grasslands. 1969 Reprint. Pages 272–287 *in* H. Borland, editor. Our natural world. J. B. Lippincott, Philadelphia, Pennsylvania, USA.

Enck, J. W., D. J. Decker, and T. L. Brown. 2000. Status of hunter recruitment and retention in the United States. Wildlife Society Bulletin 28(4):817–824.

Hamilton, D. A., and J. F. Organ. 1998. Responsible human use of fish and wildlife: Challenges to professional management. Transactions of the North American Wildlife and Natural Resources Conference 63:525–639.

Healy, W. M. 1997. Influence of deer on the structure and composition of oak forests in central Massachusetts. Pages 249–266 *in* W. J. McShea, H. B. Underwood, and J. H. Rappole, editors. The science of overabundance: deer ecology and management. Smithsonian, Washington, D.C., USA.

———, K. W. Gottschalk, R. P. Long, and P. M. Wargo. 1997. Changes in eastern forests: Chestnut is gone, are the oaks far behind? Transactions of the North American Wildlife and Natural Resources Conference 62:249–263.

Jenkins, M. 2003. Prospects for biodiversity. Science 302(5648):1175–1177.

Lewis, J. B. 2001. A success story revisited. Proceedings of the National Wild Turkey Symposium 8:7–13.

Liscinsky, S. 1984. Tree seed production. Pennsylvania Game News 55(8):23–25.

Mahoney, S. P. 1998. The animal/human interface: A journey toward understanding our views of nature and our use of animals. Transactions of the North American Wildlife and Natural Resources Conference 63:628–639.

McShea, W. J., and W. M. Healy, editors. 2002. Oak forest ecosystems, ecology and management for wildlife. Johns Hopkins University Press, Baltimore, Maryland, USA.

———, and G. Schwede. 1993. Variable acorn crops: responses of white-tailed deer and other mast consumers. Journal of Mammalogy 74(4):999–1006.

Organ, J. F., and E. K. Fritzel. 2000. Trends in consumptive recreation and the wildlife profession. Wildlife Society Bulletin 28:780–787.

———, R. M. Muth, J. E. Dizard, S. J. Williamson, and T. A. Decker. 1998. Fair chase and humane treatment: balancing the ethics of hunting and trapping. Transactions of the North American Wildlife and Natural Resources Conference 63:528–543.

Peterson, M. N. 2004. An approach for demonstrating the social legitimacy of hunting. Wildlife Society Bulletin 32(2):310–321.

Peyton, R. B. 2000. Wildlife management: cropping to manage or managing to crop. Wildlife Society Bulletin 28:774–779.

Robbins, Charles T. 1993. Wildlife feeding and nutrition. Academic Press, Harcourt Brace Jovanovich, San Diego, California, USA.

Rogers, M. J., L. K. Halls, and J. G. Dickson. 1990. Deer habitat in the Ozark forests of Arkansas. U.S. Forest Service, Southern Forest Experiment Station Research Paper SO-259.

Rosenberry, C. S., D. R. Diefenbach, and B. D. Wallingford. 2004. Reporting-rate variability and precision of white-tailed deer harvest estimates in Pennsylvania. Journal of Wildlife Management 68(4):860–869.

Runkle, J. R. 1990. Gap dynamics in an Ohio *Acer-Fagus* forest and speculations on the geography of disturbance. Canadian Journal of Forest Science 20:632–641.

Schorger, A. W. 1955. The passenger pigeon, its natural history and extinction. University of Wisconsin Press, Madison, Wisconsin, USA.

Segelquist, C. A., and W. E. Green. 1968. Deer food yields in four Ozark forest types. Journal of Wildlife Management 32(2):330–337.

Stedman, R. S., D. R. Diefenbach, C. B. Swope, J. C. Finley, H. C. Zinn, G. J. San Julian, and G. A. Wang. 2004. Integrating wildlife and human-dimensions research methods to study hunters. Journal of Wildlife Management 68:762–773.

Tapley, J. L., R. K. Abernathy, and J. E. Kennamer. *This volume*. Status and distribution of the wild turkey in 2004. Proceedings of the National Wild Turkey Symposium. 9: *This volume*.

Terborgh, J. L. Lopez, V. P. Nunez, M. Rao, G. Shahabuddin, G. Orihuela, M. Riveros, R. Ascanio, G. H. Adler, T. D. Lambert, and L. Balbas. 2001. Ecological meltdown in predator-free forest fragments. Science 294(5548):1923–1926.

Thomas, J. W. 2004. The Journals of a Forest Service Chief. Forest History Society and University of Washington Press, Seattle, Washington, USA, and London, UK.

Tubbs, C. H., and D. R. Houston. 1990. American beech. Pages 325–332 *in* R. M. Burns and B. H. Honkula, technical coordinators. Silvics of North America. Volume 2. Hardwoods. Agricultural Handbook 654, U.S. Forest Service, Washington, D. C., USA.

Williams, T. 2005. Public menace. Audubon 107(4):20–27.

William M. Healy retired from the U.S. Forest Service in 2000 after a 33 year career as a research wildlife biologist. He received degrees in Forestry and Wildlife Management from Penn State University, and his Ph.D. from West Virginia University where he studied relationships among turkey poult feeding activity, insect abundance, and vegetation structure. To accomplish this in depth study, he pioneered an imprinting technique used widely to study behavior of precocial birds. After being transferred to Massachusetts, he continued studies of forest wildlife habitat relationships, including effects of deer browsing on forest vegetation, and the relationship between acorn crops and small mammal abundance. Bill now applies his research experience and knowledge on his 200 acre farm in West Virginia. He remains active in professional societies as well as in local chapters of various conservation organizations.

9th National Wild Turkey Symposium

Wild Turkey Management:
Accomplishments, Strategies, and Opportunities
———— Grand Rapids, Michigan ————

SYMPOSIUM SUMMARY

James Earl Kennamer
National Wild Turkey Federation, 770 Augusta Road,
Edgefield, SC 29824, USA

Thank you for your attention over the 3 days of the symposium, and thank you, Al Stewart, for all your hard work.

Earlier you heard Bob Eriksen say he'd missed the first symposium because he was in the third grade at the time. I, too, missed the first symposium, because I was in the eleventh grade in 1959. However, my father, who was an Extension Fish and Wildlife specialist in Alabama, was there. Since then, I have been in attendance at every symposium and have had one or more papers in each one.

Al asked me to give the closing remarks for this Ninth National Wild Turkey Symposium, which I consider a real honor for me, but also a big challenge to cover 3 days of papers and discuss in 20 minutes where we came from and where I see us needing to go in the future.

Before I go further, I want to challenge each of you to think ahead. Will there be a Tenth National Wild Turkey Symposium in 2010? Will there be a need? I'm reminded of an article published in a British medical journal that said we have reached the limit of medical breakthroughs, with no more advance possible. The date I think was somewhere around 1640. So yes, there will be a need for a tenth symposium, but probably not in the sense we think. For example, can we learn more about wild turkey productivity? The answer is yes, but first we need to determine if that is the best use of our money. A look at the history of what we did in 1959 compared to 2005 may help give us a perspective. In 1959, the wild turkey population in this country was about 468,000 and the total harvest was 66,000. The number of hunters was unknown, 8 states had a spring season, and 12 had a fall season. Research priorities included life history, restoration, population dynamics and management techniques. In 2005, the situation is vastly different. Today the wild turkey population is about 7 million birds, and the harvest last year was 920,000—almost twice the total population in 1959. In 2005, there were 2.8 million turkey hunters, 49 states held a spring season, and 42 held a fall season. In addition, 4 Canadian provinces held a spring season, and one had a fall season, too. Priorities have changed as well. Today, our focus is on the wild turkey's expanding range into what was not thought to be turkey habitat, on "overabundance" issues, and on habitat loss and fragmentation. Today's technology has come a long way since 1959, too. Who'd have thought then that we'd have radio collars with transmitters that really work? Who could have foreseen geographic information systems (GIS) and

data loggers, satellite images, computer modeling and infrared surveillance cameras?

We have the tools, but tools alone are not enough. Fortunately for the wild turkey, this relatively small but very dedicated group of wildlife biologists continues to push the boundaries of knowledge about this unique species. The papers presented at the Ninth National Wild Turkey Symposium are a collection of the latest and best research available on the wild turkey. I'm honored to be able to provide the following brief summary of the 46 manuscripts included in this proceedings. The manuscripts are divided among 5 categories, and many reflect new trends in turkey research, while others address gaps in our knowledge in more conventional areas.

Habitat Ecology

The 10 manuscripts that comprise the category on wild turkey habitat range from research at the landscape level to specific ecosystems. Again, there is a large component of research on western subspecies, reflecting our need for more knowledge of these turkeys and their habitat use and requirements.

Fleming and Porter investigated the effect of landscape features and landscape fragmentation on dispersal patterns for a New York wild turkey population and found that average dispersal cost was negatively correlated with edge density of the landscape. In Arkansas, Goetz and Porter used satellite imagery and GIS technology to identify habitat characteristics that allow assessment of the potential of landscapes to support wild turkey harvest. Wakeling developed models to describe roosting, nesting, winter, and summer habitat use on a landscape level for Merriam's wild turkeys in Arizona. In Mississippi, Jones and coworkers investigated the effects of red-cockaded woodpecker management on wild turkey brood habitat. They report that mature pine stands managed for woodpeckers made good nesting habitat but were not used in proportion to their occurrence for brood-rearing, and suggest providing for interspersed brood-rearing habitat as a mitigating technique. Jackson and colleagues investigated active forest management components as they compared the results of silvicultural techniques including prescribed burning and several thinning options. They found increases in understory vegetation after shelterwood and wildlife retention cuts, and enhanced nesting and brooding cover after several techniques, but determined that additional treatments were necessary to increase herbaceous growth.

Nest success comparisons between declining and stable wild turkey populations by Randel and coworkers showed no differences, failing to support the hypothesis that low nest success was responsible for the decline. However, Schapp and coworkers found supporting evidence for the importance of spatial distribution of nests.

Keegan and Crawford found that Rio Grande wild turkey hens in southwestern Oregon selected nest sites in regenerating mixed-conifer stands that were ≤10 years old. Nest sites were characterized by dense horizontal screening, understory vegetation >20 cm tall, and widespread low shrub cover. Roost site selection may be very specific, too. In Kansas, Holdstock and his associates found that Rio Grande wild turkey gobblers selected eastern cottonwoods over 70% of the time, whereas display areas were categorized by low visual obstruction and low shrub density. However, Rio Grande wild turkeys will adapt to other tree species for roost sites. Keegan and Crawford found a preference by Rio Grande wild turkeys for Douglas fir in Oregon, comprising 77% of identified roost trees.

Turkeys on Their Northern Range

Turkey restoration and stocking has not only restored populations in historic turkey range, but has also resulted in range expansions to the north of previously occupied habitat. This expansion has resulted in new hunting opportunities and, in some cases, new management issues. The 7 manuscripts in this category represent a full range of topics concerning northern wild turkeys, ranging from bioenergetics to winter roost activity.

Kimmel and Kruger, in Minnesota, reviewed research on tolerance of wild turkeys for severe winter weather conditions. In addition, they surveyed northern state and provincial wildlife agency biologists, finding that most agencies have successfully translocated wild turkeys north of the ancestral limit. Primary management concerns were weather, food availability, and habitat limitations. Pekins investigated winter bioenergetics of eastern wild turkeys in New Hampshire and found that nutritional value of winter diets is inversely related to snow depth, with ground diets dominated by acorns or corn of highest metabolizable energy. He also determined that the persistence and stability of many northern populations of wild turkeys may depend on their use of supplemental food during winter. Porter confirmed these finding as he explored the ecology of wild turkeys in northern latitudes. He also reported that spring weather conditions were more important than winter to long-term fluctuations in population abundance and that forest cover in the region was sufficient and agriculture proved to be a major asset to wild turkeys because of the food it provided. In Michigan, Chadwick determined that northern range expansion by wild turkeys may also be as least partially attributed to the alteration of Michigan's native habitats and to human activities that promote turkey survival throughout the year.

In addition to the importance of food to winter

survival of wild turkeys, roost site selection may be very important. Ermer and coworkers, in Minnesota, found that selection of winter microhabitats that minimize heat loss from wind and radiation can potentially reduce thermoregulatory energy requirements and increase survival of wild turkeys. Wild turkeys were found to use roost sites characterized by a higher canopy, larger diameter and stem density than adjacent sites. Conifers were used for roost sites much more than expected by their percentage of occurrence.

In South Dakota, Lehman and colleagues investigated survival and cause-specific mortality for Merriam's wild turkeys. They found lowest seasonal survival for females during the spring, with mammalian predators accounting for the highest percentage of mortality.

In Ontario, Bellamy and Pollard used knowledge gained from an experimental assessment of habitat suitability, and by overlaying the best available information on historic distribution, factoring in land-use change and a consideration of prevailing weather patterns to define the spatial extent of their wild turkey restoration program. They consider the Mixedwood Plain Ecozone to represent a biologically suitable and ecologically appropriate framework for wild turkey program delivery in Ontario.

Managing Wild Turkey Populations

The 9 manuscripts that make up this category encompass a number of different directions for wild turkey research. Western subspecies continued to be covered, as they were in the previous categories. As restoration of the Gould's wild turkey continues, new procedures and techniques have evolved, many due to the complexities uniquely presented by the location of this subspecies. Because most of these turkeys had to be brought into the United States from Mexico, and kept for 30 days in quarantine before release into the wild, quarantine and recapture techniques had to be refined. In their manuscript, Maddrey and Wakeling described the process, which resulted in the eventual release of over 85% of the captured turkeys. Disease testing during the quarantine period made recapture of the turkeys necessary. Past recapture attempts resulted in considerable stress and mortality for the turkeys. During this project, Bergman and coworkers successfully used alpha-chloralose as a turkey sedative. Based on this study and a review of published literature, they recommended that alpha-chloralose be considered for inclusion on the current Investigative New Animal Drug label for alpha-chloralose.

In the last few years, more attention has turned to census by remote camera. For the first time, this has been tested on the Gould's wild turkey. In southeastern Arizona, Dubay and her coworkers used a combination of telemetry and patagial markers in conjunction with remote cameras to estimate the Huachuca Mountain population. They found this method to be more precise than ground surveys, but also more time-consuming.

For wild turkeys, subspecies identification has traditionally been dependent on morphological characteristics, many of which are subjective in nature. With the continued development of DNA analysis techniques, we now have definitive methods to differentiate the subspecies. Latch and associates described the molecular markers available for wild turkeys, and reviewed their applications in wild turkey management.

Capture-related mortality has been an issue since turkey trapping began, and Brunjes and his colleagues, in a long-term and large-scale investigation of Rio Grande wild turkeys in north Texas, have been uniquely situated to evaluate the problem. They report that 8.5% of the nearly 700 turkeys captured died ≤14 days post capture, with male mortality > female mortality. Additionally, afternoon captures caused more mortalities than morning capture. Illegal kill has long been a concern, too, especially in the East. Norman and his associates in Virginia and West Virginia found average illegal fall mortality for wild turkey females to be 5%. Mast abundance influenced illegal mortality rates during fall hunting seasons.

Public concerns about crop depredation by wild turkeys is a growing issue. However, Humberg and his coworkers in Indiana found that allegations of turkey damage to corn and soybeans were unfounded; raccoons and white-tailed deer were the actual species responsible for the damage.

Tapley and associates, continuing the wild turkey status and distribution report begun in 1970 and updated in each subsequent symposium, reported that wild turkey population levels have increased by 1.2 to 1.4 million birds in the past 5 years. The North American population was estimated to be 6.6 to 6.9 million birds in 2004, and the total harvest increased by 24% in the last 5 years to over 900,000 birds. The number of turkey hunters increased during the same period by 6% to more than 2.8 million. In order to secure these population advances, a comprehensive North American wild turkey management plan is needed. Vance and his associates worked closely with state, federal and provincial wildlife agencies as well as NWTF regional field staff to identify future priorities and gaps in the long-term planning process for wild turkey management. Vance and his co-authors recommend that a comprehensive plan identifying collaborative goals, objectives and on-the-ground projects be formulated to take this process to the next level. The paper delineates a process that can be used to develop the North American Wild Turkey Management Plan.

Population Dynamics

This category of research is always a matter of interest, because productivity drives wild turkey populations. This is especially true for the western subspecies, as 5 of the 10 manuscripts in this category deal with Rio Grande wild turkeys. In Texas, Lusk and coworkers used neural-network modeling to determine that deviations from normal conditions best explained annual fluctuations in wild turkey productivity. Also in Texas, Petty and coworkers found increased poult production following intensive feral hog removal. The results from Schwertner and associates indicate that poult production is more influenced by cumulative weather effects over several months than by individual rain-fall events and suggest that precipitation-induced mortality does not substantially affect Rio Grande wild turkey production in Texas.

In south-central Pennsylvania, concerns for a declining population of wild turkeys prompted an investigation by Casalena and coworkers on the factors contributing to this decline. They found low poult survival and an unsustainable level of fall harvest, and recommended closing the fall turkey season until the population recovered.

New concerns about the possible effects of predation on wild turkey populations prompted a literature search on the subject by Hughes and coworkers. The literature showed that while predators were the most significant cause of wild turkey mortality, they seldom limited population growth. Additionally, predator control was not found to be effective as a broadscale management tool, but could be useful in short-term control of specific predators.

Most states use some method of determining or predicting wild turkey reproduction; many states use poult-hen counts as an index. Butler and his associates compared poult-hen counts to reproductive parameters derived from telemetry data in the Texas panhandle. They report that poult-hen counts can index reproduction and recruitment at the local level, but that these counts were unable to index either at an ecoregion level. They suggest larger and evenly distributed samples from standardized and randomized surveys for reliable region-wide predictions.

Accurate methods of population estimation for wild turkeys are lacking. Many methods have been tried, but the accuracy of most is unknown. In Florida, Nicholson and his colleagues used survey questionnaires with responses from over 600 individuals to map the distribution and relative abundance of wild turkeys in that state.

The results of several manuscripts in this category may provide important restoration and management information. In east Texas, Whiting and associates, investigating a supplementary stocking of eastern wild turkeys, found survival of the newly released turkeys increased when their home range overlapped with previously stocked turkeys familiar with the habitat. For Rio Grande wild turkeys in Texas, Phillips and his coworkers report that dispersal patterns of yearling females may play an important role in connecting relatively disjunct winter roost populations.

Warnke and Rolley investigated and summarized recent wild turkey population dynamics research. They identified several areas of needed research: compensatory mortality, acceptable harvest rates for females, and weather-related variation in recruitment. They suggest that a better understanding of factors that control and regulate population growth will be important as wild turkey management objectives evolve from population restoration to population control and sustained-yield harvesting.

Harvest Management

As wild turkey populations and numbers of turkey hunters continue to grow, management priorities have shifted from restoration to harvest strategies and hunter management. The 9 manuscripts in this category clearly illustrate this shift in priorities. For example, Backs, in Indiana, compared 4 years of half-day hunting to 2 years of all-day hunting. He found no differences in temporal distributions of harvest between the 2 season formats and very little difference in the percentage of adult gobblers in the harvest. Concerns about hunt quality also prompted a survey of spring turkey hunters by Dingman and her coworkers in Minnesota. They found that the most important factors defining a quality hunt were the number of turkeys shot at, number of turkeys seen in the field, and ease of access to land for hunting. A similar survey in Ohio, described by Swanson and colleagues, reported that a majority of turkey hunters ranked high gobbling activity as the primary factor contributing greatly to their enjoyment of the spring turkey hunting experience. The composite Ohio spring turkey hunter was male, 49 years old, had a rural background, and a total household income >$50,000.

There are growing concerns that gobbler harvest levels in some states may have surpassed sustainable levels. In fact, Wright and Vangilder found a human-caused mortality level of 60% for adult gobblers in a western Kentucky population, and they suggested this level of harvest could not be sustained unless recruitment remains high or hunting pressure declines. Hubbard and Vangilder found similar mortality rates for adult gobblers in Missouri and observed that spring turkey harvest on public land in the eastern Missouri Ozarks is approaching a level that may result in a decline in spring turkey hunting quality.

An unusual situation in Wyoming is described by Zornes and Lanka. There, isolated populations of Merriam's wild turkey declined, some to the point of local extirpation, with anecdotal evidence that the unusually high percentage of males in the populations were outcompeting the females for winter food. Increased harvest pressure on males resulted in a female-biased population after 2 years. The authors suggested that in situations where turkey habitat is limited, male harvest should be increased when flock surveys result in a male:female ratio ≥0.75:1.

Lehman and his associates, in the Black Hills region of South Dakota, studied gobbling of Merriam's turkeys in relation to nesting and hunting. They found 2 peaks of gobbling, one just after winter break-up of the flocks and the other just before or during peak incubation. In comparisons of hunted and non-hunted populations during the spring hunting season, gobbling behavior was reduced for the former.

Timing of spring seasons may have important management implications. Whitaker and coworkers, using data obtained from 34 states and provinces, found that 25 states opened spring hunting >2 weeks prior to the mean date of incubation initiation, and 18 of these also allowed fall either-sex hunting. This finding is important because fall hunting mortality combined with spring hunting during the pre-nesting period can lead to additive and unsustainable levels of female mortality.

Concerns about declining hunter numbers and lower hunter recruitment rates prompted the Missouri Department of Conservation to provide a 2-day youth turkey hunt prior to the opening of the regular season. Beringer and his colleagues investigated the effectiveness of the youth season at promoting recruitment and retention of hunters. They found that youth permit sales increased, apparently as a result of the youth season. Also, during the 4-year period of the youth season, recruitment rates almost doubled compared to the 4-year period immediately prior to the inception of the youth season.

Looking Ahead

As Bill Healy stated so succinctly in his paper in these proceedings, for the future of wild turkey management we are presented with changes, opportunities and challenges. In his essay, Healy provided a synopsis of forest dynamics, both past and present, as well as examinations of human demography, natural resource management, and the North American Model of Conservation.

I feel we have reached a crossroads in North America with wild turkey research and restoration. We have to weigh the value of research vs. common sense and the value of process vs. success. For example, in one state we've spent years studying the genetics of the turkey population to determine which subspecies in the state is the best to trap and transfer. Meanwhile that population has flourished, apparently with little regard by the turkeys for genetics issues. At the same time, wild turkeys continue to expand the northern boundaries of their range, even though we biologists for many years told hunters and the non-hunting public that turkeys couldn't live that far north. If we let them, the turkeys will show us where they can live. We have to be smart with our future research, learn from our mistakes, and look ahead.

In looking ahead, one of the first things I see is change in our profession itself. People like myself, Bill Healy and Bill Porter are retiring or may soon retire and the next generation of wildlife biologists will be very different than the ones that brought us to the dance. In the early days of our profession, every wildlife student was a hunter, but that is not the case these days, now most don't hunt, and non-hunters are sure to have a different perspective on wildlife management than we did. In my generation of wildlife biologists, population management was the focus, where now many biologists put more emphasis on the individual, and management strategies employed by these biologists will certainly be different as well. Native vs. non-native issues have become increasingly important to many, with little distinction between what is non-native and what is non-native and invasive. Population status and locations of wildlife species as it was in 1492 has become the politically correct standard for many in our profession, which means these biologists don't want wild turkeys in many places where they currently are located. State wildlife budgets are tight and will get tighter, and incoming biologists will have multi-species focus. In the future, I believe there will be few, if any biologists, who will have the luxury to dedicate their time solely to turkey management.

The 9 symposia have added greatly to our knowledge of the wild turkey. If there is to be a symposium in 2010, we now have to focus our efforts on areas that will be very different from past activities and not nearly as glamorous as tracking birds with radios or turning them out of a box. We must identify the barriers that may prevent us from managing turkeys in the decades ahead, and we have to do whatever it takes to maintain the public view of hunting as an acceptable endeavor.

We have to do more landscape research with emphasis on how to manage habitats and populations on a larger scale. We have more tools at our disposal than ever before to do a better job in this area. We can use GIS to overlay habitats, populations and opportunities as we plan management for multiple species and address major problems such as urban sprawl and development of energy resources. Advances in satellite technology now allow us to pinpoint locations of monitored animals using lightweight GPS transmitters. It is up to us to use the latest technology to meet future challenges.

We need to protect critical habitats not only for wild turkeys, but also for many other species that use the landscape. We need to research innovative approaches to integrate habitat protection with urban development. In addition, we need to maintain our hunting heritage in these urban settings. We must become more creative at selling our story to the non-hunting segment of the public. We must also become smarter with our research directions as we tie turkey management with management of non-game species such as neo-tropical migrant songbirds and red-cockaded woodpeckers.

We also need to look at ways to gather information like economic data to justify to decision-makers the importance of turkeys and turkey hunting to North America. Along with this is a need to measure human dimensions and to assess the opinions of the public on wild turkeys in order to convince them of their benefits. If we don't, we will lose the gains we have made with this magnificent bird over the last 5 decades because all the public will remember is that wild turkeys are a nuisance and a detriment to the environment.

We must be prepared for the possibility of catastrophic disease. As mycoplasma was a concern in the 1990s, we now are faced with the possibility of widespread effects from avian influenza, West Nile virus and exotic Newcastle's disease. While we have no evidence these have ever been a problem in wild turkeys, we must continue to use good science to assure the agricultural community and the public that they aren't a problem.

Last, but perhaps most importantly, we must develop a comprehensive management plan for wild turkeys. This plan will provide us with information to justify turkey management, protect critical habitat, accurately document population and harvest numbers and help us direct our financial resources to critical areas. As Vance stated in his presentation on the subject, there are many factors that support the need for state plans and a coordinated national plan. It is vital to the future of wild turkey management that state plans and a national plan be created now.

We are at a crossroads with wild turkey management and fortunately we have the tools, the people, the passion, and the history to carry us into the next decade. Let's go do it!

James Earl Kennamer is currently the senior vice president for conservation programs for the National Wild Turkey Federation. He holds a B.S. in game management from Auburn University, and M.S. and Ph.D. degrees in wildlife management from Mississippi State University.

Chapter I

Managing Wild Turkey Populations

Chapter 1

Managing Wildlife Populations

Wild Turkey Management:
Accomplishments, Strategies, and Opportunities
——— Grand Rapids, Michigan ———

WE'VE COME A LONG WAY. WHERE DO WE GO FROM HERE? THE NORTH AMERICAN WILD TURKEY MANAGEMENT PLAN

Anthony Scott Vance[1]
National Wild Turkey Federation,
770 Augusta Road,
Edgefield, SC 29824, USA

Mark Alan Hatfield
National Wild Turkey Federation,
770 Augusta Road,
Edgefield, SC 29824, USA

Al Stewart
Michigan Department of Natural Resources,
530 W. Allegan Street,
Lansing, MI 48909-7944, USA

Karen T. Cleveland
Michigan Department of Natural Resources,
530 W. Allegan Street,
Lansing, MI 48909-7944, USA

Abstract: Wild turkeys (*Meleagris gallopavo*) in North America made a significant recovery in the 20th century due to the dedicated efforts of federal, state and provincial wildlife agencies. The changing status of this species has resulted in a shifting of management needs. A survey of wild turkey biologists in 2004 yielded results indicating that a North American Wild Turkey Management Plan is needed to assist agencies in coordinating their efforts. This plan would act as a framework to allow jurisdictions to more readily share data, resources, and expertise. The North American Wild Turkey Management Plan structure, timeline to collect data and coordinate partners, and the planning and implementation process are delineated.

Proceedings of the National Wild Turkey Symposium 9:15–20

Key words: conservation, gamebird, habitat, North American, partnership, plan, population, research, trap and transplant, wild turkey.

Though no extensive censuses were undertaken during the early settlement of North America by Europeans, numerous first-hand reports mention seeing flocks of hundreds of wild turkeys (Wright 1914*a*). Many of these early reports describe the ease with which turkeys could be harvested to provide a vital source of sustenance for early European settlers and pioneers. Reports from the 18th and 19th centuries documented that the decimation of flocks on roosts may not have been uncommon while other reports discuss the utilization of traps to capture entire flocks. This led to the initial act of wild turkey conservation when these traps were prohibited in Canada in the mid-1800s (Wright 1914*b*).

By the early 1800s, observers in New England were starting to notice the absence of wild turkeys in areas where they once had been abundant (Wright 1915). This trend became more evident throughout the eastern United States during the mid-1800s (Wright 1915), and by the late 1800s the wild turkey was con-

sidered extirpated from Massachusetts, and possibly throughout New England (Slade 1888). In 1853 or 1854, the last wild turkeys in Iowa were thought to have been killed (Sherman 1913).

By the early 1900s, wild turkey populations were declining significantly throughout the United States (Mosby and Handley 1943). In the 1930s, the commitment to restore and manage wild turkey populations intensified. The Virginia Cooperative Wildlife Research Unit initiated a research effort on turkey propagation in 1935, and several other states started to develop wild turkey research projects in the late 1930s (Lewis 2001). The passage of the Federal Aid in Wildlife Restoration (Pittman-Robertson) Act in 1937 fueled this progression. Early restoration efforts were centered on raising and releasing pen–raised birds. These efforts were a disappointment since the pen-raised birds were deprived of normal parental influ-

[1] E-mail: svance@nwtf.net

ences and thus never developed wild social behaviors. The survival of these birds was very poor. The pen-raised approach hampered the wild turkey comeback for nearly two decades. It was not until the advent of the cannon net that agencies were able to trap large flocks of wild turkeys to relocate and populate new habitats. The cannon net was a major factor in the wild turkey restoration efforts, but research and management played an important role in identifying and creating suitable habitat (Kennamer et al. 1992).

The comeback of the wild turkey in North America is arguably the greatest conservation success story in history. In 2004, the population in the United States and Canada was estimated at over 6.6 million wild turkeys (Tapley et al. *this volume*). This increase is primarily due to the success of state and provincial restoration programs, improved habitat conditions, and increased conservation efforts that have focused primarily on population status assessment and harvest regulation promulgation. Due to these historic and ongoing efforts, and the adaptability of the wild turkey, the bulk of suitable habitat currently supports wild turkey populations. In 2004, an estimated 750 million acres of habitat had viable populations of wild turkeys while only 5 million acres (<1%) of suitable habitat remained uninhabited (Tapley et al. *this volume*). Currently, habitat once considered marginal across North America is being populated by the wild turkey.

These successes demonstrate the vital and challenging task of determining "where do we go from here?" Currently there is no formal strategy in place to coordinate efforts to ensure the perpetuation and evolution of our wild turkey legacy. The value of coordinated research efforts for wild turkey conservation was recognized a decade ago (Weinstein et al. 1996), including the need to develop standardized protocols and metrics for data collection. As management priorities for wild turkeys shift from the basic survival of the species, a more holistic, international, broad-based management strategy is needed to address evolving contemporary issues including but not limited to:

1. Identifying future factors that will inhibit growth and maintenance of wild turkey populations.
2. Identifying habitat projects and partnerships to complement the North American Bird Conservation Initiative (NABCI).
3. Identifying future research priorities across North America.
4. Spatially representing the status of wild turkey populations and potential habitat across North America.
5. Identifying strategies to increase hunter access, recruitment, and retention.

These and many other factors support the need for a coordinated plan to chart the future of turkey conservation into the 21st century. This brief introduction is the impetus for the historic planning endeavor to craft a North American Wild Turkey Management Plan.

CURRENT STATUS

During the summer of 2004, members of the National Wild Turkey Federation (NWTF) technical committee, composed of state and provincial biologists responsible for wild turkey programs in their respective areas, were asked to provide information regarding the status of wild turkeys and wild turkey management. While 55% of respondents indicated that a turkey management plan existed for their jurisdiction, less than half of those plans included habitat enhancement, habitat protection, or hunter recruitment sections. Technical representatives identified impediments to establishing, maintaining, and expanding wild turkey populations. Significant among these were the reduction of agency budgets, urbanization, and a reduction of forestry management. Traditionally, the conservation ethic of sportsmen drove the interest in and funding of restoration and management efforts. Recent declines in the numbers of sportsman-conservationists, evident in decreasing license sales to active hunters, imperil agencies' ability to continue or expand turkey management efforts. Respondents identified a number of factors which are eroding this base of support, including anti-hunting sentiment, privatization of hunting, lack of access and opportunity, and the inability to recruit young hunters.

Respondents described their state or provincial status regarding wild turkey range mapping and population estimation. The most popular estimation methods were harvest and hunter surveys. Very few states used direct census or observational indices to estimate populations. The most important wild turkey research needs identified included gobbler harvest and mortality estimation, improving survey and census methods, and research to measure the effect of specific habitat management practices on wild turkey populations. Other research topics included improved habitat assessment techniques, nuisance issues, winter habitat utilization, the effects of wild turkeys on sensitive species, general life science information in areas outside historic wild turkey range, and ways to improve hunter access and recruitment.

While many jurisdictions already participate with conservation groups, other government agencies, and tribal organizations in partnerships for wild turkey management, a lack of breadth and diversity in these efforts is noticeable in the survey results. Obvious gaps also exist where some respondents indicated that they lacked one or more type of partnering relationship; a majority of respondents do not have working relationships with Native American Reservations regarding wild turkey projects.

The Need for a Plan

The evolving challenges facing wild turkey managers, and the desires voiced by these same professionals to provide a high level of stewardship for this intrinsic North American resource, highlight the need for coordinated planning into the future and the inherent need for all interested groups to partner in assuring the health and viability of the species for generations yet to come. Today, almost half of the jurisdictions containing wild turkeys lack a turkey management plan. Less than half of existing turkey plans incorporate habitat management or land protection considerations though wild turkey biologists overwhelmingly agreed that conservation easements, land acquisition, and habitat improvement on federal and private lands would provide a vital benefit to wild turkeys in their respective areas.

Loss of habitat, inability to effectively identify habitat, privatization of hunting, and lack of management were all subjects that were identified as threats to wild turkey populations and hunting. These similarities of opinion and tactical planning deficiencies clearly indicate a need for a facilitated effort to identify regional and local strategies to confront these problems. By coordinating efforts across jurisdictional and organizational boundaries, habitat tools can be extended for range-wide use, and management agencies can gain access to both financial resources and the vital human capital which conservation organizations possess.

There is an obvious need for a standardized method of habitat analysis and the development of a quantitative method to identify focus areas. Additionally, most wild turkey programs do not have formal population estimation or mapping procedures in place. Development of guidance on these issues would bring a cohesive aspect to North American wild turkey management that currently does not exist.

A mid-scale Geographic Information System depicting wild turkey range, current and potential habitat, restoration priorities and critical habitat protection areas will be an integral component of the plan. The primary objective of this effort will be to provide a North American perspective on wild turkey habitat across political boundaries, depict baseline wild turkey data, and provide an intuitive tool to plan and compare habitat management and restoration efforts with important regional needs.

Across all boundaries, there is a lack of funding and a subsequent shortage of personnel for managing North America's wildlife resources. This makes it imperative to look for every potential source of support for wildlife programs and to identify long-term funding sources to ensure the continued success of this natural resource.

Several state and provincial programs are already in the process of incorporating non-governmental organization (NGO) volunteers to census and survey wild turkeys. With a majority of jurisdictions partnering with multiple groups on wild turkey projects, it is clear that many opportunities exist and are being capitalized upon. Agencies need to assess and fully utilize their ability to partner with conservation volunteers to aid in gathering needed data. While the potential and inherent problems with this type of data collection are well known, it may be vital to the initiation and maintenance of these important data collection procedures on a continental scale. A plan to identify partnering opportunities and maximize cooperation among groups is vital to this process.

Finally, a study in Washington (Duda et al. 2004) indicated that many hunters feel that access to private lands is poor and has gotten worse over the past 5 years. This is especially significant because a majority of these hunters hunted exclusively on private land and 86% hunted at least some time on private land. Improved private land access and habitat protection should be a primary consideration in conservation projects and programs.

The Role of the Plan

The North American Wild Turkey Management Plan will provide a framework to support long-term habitat improvement efforts, localized population restoration, conservation education, wild turkey research, conservation easements, and land acquisition projects. It must identify habitat protection and enhancement focus areas, recognize potential conservation partnerships, improve hunting opportunities, and formulate monitoring objectives. The completed plan will be utilized by wildlife professionals throughout North America to form habitat acquisition and management partnerships, gain support for wild turkey programs, direct wildlife research, and strategically plan landscape-based wildlife projects. The plan is a working document that will be updated as new information becomes available to better serve those who use it.

The plan will build on the model developed in existing, successful continental conservation efforts like the North American Waterfowl Management Plan (NAWMP) and the North American Bird Conservation Initiative (NABCI). The Turkey Plan will provide a defensible continental strategy with concrete goals and objectives that can be supported by potential partners and funding sources. The compilation of a fluid document containing all of the necessary information for the North American Wild Turkey Management Plan will require a unified effort among all interested parties. It is imperative that the goals, objectives and subject matter for the plan originate from a broad constituency to ensure consolidation and guarantee acceptance across all boundaries.

The Role of the NWTF

The NWTF recognizes the need for a North American Wild Turkey Management Plan and is willing to act as a coordinator to provide managers and researchers a framework and venue in which to complete this planning effort. Involvement and input from all interested parties is critical to the success and acceptance of the plan.

The federation is uniquely suited to this role as it has worked with many states and provinces over the past 20 years to assist with their wild turkey planning efforts. Most recently, several states have teamed with the NWTF to put together wild turkey habitat suitability maps to help complete trap and transplant efforts. Many states have also worked with the federation to target strategic habitat areas that benefit not only wild turkeys, but also native plants, threatened and endangered species, and neo-tropical migrant birds.

This document outlines the steps necessary to identify important aspects of the proposed North American Wild Turkey Management Plan. The challenging task of compiling the plan will require input from many sources. Fortunately, the NWTF Wild Turkey Technical Committee (wild turkey biologists from every state and province) already exists and can act as the core resource in the development of this plan. It is from their expert knowledge of the issues within their states and provinces that we hope to gain insight into what is important for wild turkeys both regionally and internationally.

The Role of Agencies

The planning process will require state, provincial and federal agency personnel to provide insight and recommendations for their respective agencies. This is critical to ensure agency needs and concerns are addressed in the plan. This process will require buy-in at all agency levels since its scope will cross jurisdictions, but its implementation and function will occur at the local level through existing and future partnerships. This input should reflect a compilation of state goals and needs that will make substantial contributions toward the conservation of not just wild turkeys, but all wildlife throughout North America.

NEXT STEPS

The following phases are necessary to ensure development of a unified, flexible, and dynamic plan for management and continued success of wild turkeys in North America:

1. Phase I will be completed by NWTF regional biologists in partnership with state and provincial Wild Turkey Technical Committee biologists. NWTF biologists will collect background information regarding the current status of wild turkey programs and future priorities for habitat management and protection on a state and provincial basis. This will be general information and will provide a foundation to build upon. This step will be achieved primarily through a comprehensive questionnaire and personal interviews. The NWTF staff will consolidate all pertinent information, goals, objectives, and timelines into a cohesive document. Phase I will then be disseminated to all interested and applicable parties. The projected completion date for Phase I is 1 August 2007.
2. Phase II will include the development of online tools to share technical expertise, research results, geographic data, and management experience with all committee members and turkey conservation partners. This system will allow individuals to utilize mapping tools and data to develop their own plans and map products.
3. Phase III will coordinate coalitions to implement and foster wildlife enhancement programs and projects with wild turkey components. Wild turkeys

will be integrated into other formal planning efforts at the state (e.g., Wildlife Action Plans), regional (e.g., Bird Conservation Regions, Joint Ventures), national, or international (e.g., NABCI) level.

CONCLUSION

There are tremendous challenges facing wildlife and wildlife managers across the continent. These challenges include habitat degradation and conversion, privatization of wildlife and hunting, locally over-abundant wildlife populations, expanding lists of species at risk, and the unending need for additional species monitoring data, to the loss of rural traditions that foster appreciation of wildlife. Our history of turkey management and restoration demonstrate that we are capable of rising to the challenges that we face in the future. Through coordinated efforts across jurisdictional boundaries, we can fully utilize our common resources to assure the continued success of wild turkey conservation. A plan can guide us in selecting population goals; it can assist us in prioritizing land acquisition and habitat management; it can enhance our ability to seek out and acquire funding and leverage existing funding across jurisdictional boundaries; and it can provide us with a framework to establish and maintain successful partnerships. It is for these reasons that a North American Wild Turkey Management Plan is of utmost importance.

We recognize and appreciate the tremendous efforts that have been made by thousands of individuals from state, provincial, and federal agencies and private conservation organizations. This dedication and commitment saved the wild turkey from the brink of extinction. An unrivaled effort of trap and transfer, regulatory enforcement, and land use changes has helped make the wild turkey an overwhelming conservation victory for North America.

Despite this success, it is our responsibility to look to the future and set the stage for new wildlife success stories. The North American Wild Turkey Management Plan will present wildlife managers across the continent with wild turkey management goals and the actions needed to achieve them.

LITERATURE CITED

Duda, M. D., P. E. De Michele, C. Zurawski, M. Jones, J. E. Yoder, W. Testerman, J. Marshall, A. Lanier, S. J. Bissell, P. Wang, and J. B. Herrick. 2004. Washington State's private lands hunting access programs. Washington Department of Fish and Wildlife, Olympia, Washington, USA.

Kennamer, J. E., M. Kennamer, and R. Brenneman. 1992. History. Pages 13–15 *in* James G. Dickson, editor. The wild turkey: biology and management. Stackpole Books, Harrisburg, Pennsylvania, USA.

Lewis, J. B. 2001. A success story revisited. Proceedings of the National Wild Turkey Symposium 8:7–13.

Mosby, H. S., and C. O. Handley. 1943. The wild turkey in Virginia: its status, life history and management. Virginia Division of Game, Commission of Game and Inland Fisheries, Federal Aid in Wildlife Restoration Project.

Sherman, A. R. 1913. The extermination of the wild turkey in Clayton County, Iowa. The Wilson Bulletin 25:87–90.

Slade, D. D. 1888. The wild turkey in Massachusetts. Auk 5: 204–205.

Tapley, J. L., R. K. Abernethy, and J. E. Kennamer. *This volume.* Status and distribution of the Wild Turkey in 2004. Proceedings of the National Wild Turkey Symposium 9: *This volume.*

Weinstein, M., D. A. Miller, L. M. Connor, B. D. Leopold, and G. A. Hurst. 1996. What affects turkeys? A conceptual model for future research. Proceedings of the National Wild Turkey Symposium 7:135–142.

Wright, A. H. 1914a. Early records of the wild turkey. Auk: 31: 334–358.

———. 1914b. Early records of the wild turkey. II. Auk: 31: 463–473.

———. 1915. Early records of the wild turkey. III. Auk: 32:61–81.

Scott Vance (left) is the Director of Partnership Programs with the National Wild Turkey Federation in Edgefield, South Carolina. He is responsible for identifying and managing conservation partnerships for the NWTF throughout North America. He is also tasked with overseeing all of the NWTF's regional habitat programs, GIS programs and the development of the North American Wild Turkey Management Plan. In addition, Vance serves as project manager on habitat grant projects and directs the NWTF's Energy for Wildlife stewardship program. He earned his Master's degree in Wildlife Toxicology from Clemson University, and his Bachelor's degree in Environmental Science from East Carolina University. He has an extensive knowledge of herbicides and their effects on wildlife and wildlife habitat, and is experienced in using selective herbicides to propagate native plants, improve wildlife habitat and compliment natural disturbances such as prescribed fire. Vance is a self-admitted hunting fanatic who also loves to fish, scuba dive, lift weights and train bird dogs. The photo is of Scott and his dad (Scott's best hunting buddy and his hero).

Mark Hatfield is a Wildlife Biologist for the National Wild Turkey Federation. He received his B.S. in Wildlife Biology and his M.S. degree in Biology from Murray State University. He was a research biologist for the Arizona Game and Fish Department from 2003 to 2005. He is been an active member in The Wildlife Society (TWS) since 1996 and serves as the Southeastern Section of TWS historian. His career interests focus on landscape wildlife management and conservation.

Al Stewart (pictured) is the Upland Game Bird Specialist for the Michigan Department of Natural Resources and is responsible for statewide conservation and management programs for ruffed grouse, American woodcock, sharp-tailed grouse, quail, pheasants, and wild turkey. He has worked on turkeys for more than 30 years. He has been actively involved with rocket-net safety training and wild turkey restoration in Michigan. He has participated in wild turkey capture activities beyond Michigan and has trapped the five subspecies of wild turkeys. He is currently serving as the Editor of the Ninth National Wild Turkey Symposium and Tenth American Woodcock Symposium. ***Karen Cleveland*** (not pictured) received a B.S. and M.S. in Fisheries & Wildlife and an M.S. in Computer Science from Michigan State University. She was the Data Manager for the Wildlife Division of the New Hampshire Fish & Game Department. She is currently the All-Bird Biologist with the Michigan Department of Natural Resources. She recently received the Special Conservation Award from the Michigan United Conservation Clubs for her role in the development of the Michigan Wildlife Action Plan.

9th National Wild Turkey Symposium

Wild Turkey Management:
Accomplishments, Strategies, and Opportunities
—— Grand Rapids, Michigan ——

STATUS AND DISTRIBUTION OF THE WILD TURKEY IN 2004

Jennifer L. Tapley
National Wild Turkey Federation,
770 Augusta Road,
Edgefield, SC 29824, USA

Robert K. Abernethy
National Wild Turkey Federation,
770 Augusta Road,
Edgefield, SC 29824, USA

James E. Kennamer
National Wild Turkey Federation,
770 Augusta Road,
Edgefield, SC 29824, USA

Abstract: Wild turkey (*Meleagris gallopavo*) populations in North America have increased steadily in the past 50 years since restoration began in earnest. This increase is the result of intensified restoration efforts, improved habitat conditions and increased protection. A North American survey of wild turkey populations was first published in the 1959 *Proceedings of the First Wild Turkey Symposium*. Similar surveys have been made every 5 years since 1970 and the results published in all but one of the subsequent wild turkey symposia. In 2004, we surveyed state and provincial wildlife agency biologists responsible for wild turkey programs to determine the status of the bird in their jurisdiction. Based on the survey, we describe the current distribution of wild turkeys in North America. We report population estimates by subspecies, compare current occupied range to that of 5 years ago, compare hunter numbers and harvest numbers with figures from 1999, and report on the status of each state's or province's restoration program. Wild turkey populations have increased between 1.2–1.4 million birds in the past 5 years, and in 2004 were estimated to be between 6.6–6.9 million birds. The total annual harvest increased by 24% to 920,012, which included 730,541 birds taken during the 2004 spring hunting season. The number of turkey hunters increased 6% in the past 5 years to more than 2.8 million.

Proceedings of the National Wild Turkey Symposium 9:21–31

Key words: distribution, harvest, hunters, *Meleagris gallopavo*, populations, range, restoration, wild turkey.

In 1941, there was serious doubt that the wild turkey would remain a game species in the United States because populations were on the decline throughout most of their range (Blakey 1941). Regional extirpation and severe population declines through habitat destruction and subsistence hunting caused some people to wonder if the species could survive at all (Davis 1949). As tenant farms and harvested forests of the

Table 1. Estimates of wild turkey populations by subspecies, 1999 and 2004.

Subspecies	1999[a]	2004
Eastern	4,213,862–4,231,862	5,131,384–5,389,384
Florida	80,000	80,000–100,000
Rio Grande	742,800	1,022,700–1,025,700
Merriam's	242,300–246,300	334,460–344,460
Gould's	350–500	650–800
Hybrid	181,100	116,600–117,800
Total	5,460,412–5,482,562	6,685,794–6,978,144

[a] Tapley et al. (2001*a*).

Table 2. States with largest wild turkey populations, 2004.

State	Population
Missouri	600,000–800,000
Texas	600,500
Alabama	450,000
Mississippi	395,784
Wisconsin	350,000+
Georgia	350,000
Pennsylvania	342,000
Tennessee	270,000–300,000
New York	250,000
California	244,000–246,000
Iowa	200,000
Kentucky	200,000
Michigan	180,000
Arkansas	175,000
Ohio	170,000
Virginia	145,000
Oklahoma	140,000
North Carolina	130,000
South Carolina	120,000
Illinois	120,000[a]

[a] Tapley et al. (2001*a*).

Table 3. Estimates of wild turkey populations by state and province, 1999 and 2004.

State/province	Subspecies	Population estimate 1999[a]	Population estimate 2004	Percent change
United States:				
Alabama	Eastern	350,000	450,000	+29
Arizona	Merriam's	20,000	20,000	0
	Gould's	150–300	500	N/A[b]
Arkansas	Eastern	153,000	175,000	+14
	Hybrid	2,000	N/A	N/A
California	Eastern	100	N/A	N/A
	Rio Grande	600	242,000[c]	+40,233
	Merriam's	400	2,000–4,000	N/A
	Hybrid	100,200	N/A	N/A
Colorado	Rio Grande	4,000	2,000–3,000	N/A
	Merriam's	18,000	20,000–22,000	N/A
Connecticut	Eastern	25,000–35,000	40,000	N/A
Delaware	Eastern	3,000	3,500	+17
Florida	Florida	80,000	80,000–100,000	N/A
	Eastern	20,000	20,000–25,000	N/A
Georgia	Eastern	400,000	350,000	−13
Hawaii	Rio Grande	33,000	33,000[a]	0
Idaho	Eastern	500	Unknown	N/A
	Rio Grande	3,000	500	−83
	Merriam's	21,000	30,000	+43
	Hybrid	5,500	Unknown	N/A
Illinois	Eastern	120,000	120,000[a]	0
Indiana	Eastern	70,000	90,000–100,000	N/A
Iowa	Eastern	130,000	200,000	+54
Kansas	Eastern	20,000	N/A	N/A
	Rio Grande	5,000	N/A	N/A
	Hybrid	40,000	N/A	N/A
Kentucky	Eastern	150,000	200,000	+33
Louisiana	Eastern	65,000	75,000	+15
Maine	Eastern	10,000	25,000+	+150
Maryland	Eastern	28,000–32,000	30,000–35,000	N/A
Massachusetts	Eastern	>15,000	25,000–28,000	N/A
Michigan	Eastern	135,000	180,000	+33
Minnesota	Eastern	35,000	60,000	+71
Mississippi	Eastern	300,000	395,784	+32
Missouri	Eastern	450,000	600,000–800,000	N/A
Montana	Eastern	<5,000	<5,000	0
	Merriam's	80,000	80,000	0
Nebraska	Eastern	50	N/A	N/A
	Rio Grande	<100	N/A	N/A
	Merriam's	10,000	20,000	+100
	Hybrid	25,000	60,000	+140
Nevada	Rio Grande	3,500	1,200	−66
	Merriam's	100	60	−40
New Hampshire	Eastern	15,000	28,000	+87
New Jersey	Eastern	18,000–22,000	23,000	N/A
New Mexico	Rio Grande	5,000	N/A	N/A
	Merriam's	25,000	25,000–30,000	N/A
	Gould's	200	150–300	N/A
	Hybrids	0	300–500	N/A
New York	Eastern	250,000	250,000	0
North Carolina	Eastern	100,000	130,000	+30
North Dakota	Eastern	10,000	10,000[a]	0
	Merriam's	1,200	1,200[a]	0
	Hybrid	800	800[a]	0
Ohio	Eastern	146,000	170,000	+16
Oklahoma	Eastern	15,000	30,000	+100
	Rio Grande	70,000	110,000	+57
Oregon	Rio Grande	25,000	25,000–27,000	N/A
	Merriam's	N/A	N/A	N/A
	Hybrid	2,000	2,000–3,000	N/A
Pennsylvania	Eastern	>300,000	342,000	+14
Rhode Island	Eastern	4,000	6,000	+50
South Carolina	Eastern	100,000	120,000	+20
South Dakota	Eastern	2,000	2,000	0
	Rio Grande	2,000	2,000[a]	0
	Merriam's	36,000	20,000	−44
	Hybrid	1,000	30,000	+2,900
Tennessee	Eastern	160,000	270,000–300,000	N/A

Table 3. Continued.

State/province	Subspecies	Population estimate		Percent change
		1999[a]	2004	
Texas	Eastern	5,012	15,000	+199
	Rio Grande	573,500	585,000	+2
	Merriam's	500	500	0
Utah	Rio Grande	5,500	15,000	+173
	Merriam's	2,500	3,500	+40
Vermont	Eastern	30,000	35,000–40,000	N/A
Virginia	Eastern	127,000	145,000	+14
Washington	Eastern	3,000	1,000	−67
	Rio Grande	12,000	5,000	−58
	Merriam's	15,000	40,000	+167
West Virginia	Eastern	120,000	105,000	−13
Wisconsin	Eastern	300,000+	350,000+	+17
Wyoming	Rio Grande	600	2,000	+233
	Merriam's	10,000–12,000	67,000	N/A
	Hybrid	1,000	16,500	+1,550
Canada:				
Alberta	Merriam's	600	1,200	+100
Brit. Columbia	Merriam's	2,000–4,000	4,000–5,000	N/A
Manitoba	Hybrid	3,500	7,000	+100
Nova Scotia	Eastern	<100[d]	0	0
Ontario	Eastern	24,000	55,000	+129
Quebec	Eastern	<100	100	0
Saskatchewan	Hybrid	<100	Unknown	N/A
Total		5,460,412–5,482,562	6,685,794–6,978,144	

[a] Tapley et al. (2001a).
[b] N/A = not available.
[c] California Department of Fish and Game stated as Rio Grande turkeys that may contain some hybrids.
[d] Pen-raised birds, from personal communication with Nova Scotia Department of Natural Resources 2003.

1930s began to revert back to suitable habitat, the stage was set for the comeback of the wild turkey (Kennamer et al. 1992). Mosby (1959) reported the first indication of positive change since the early 1940s at the First National Wild Turkey Symposium.

Wild turkey trap and transfer programs initiated by state wildlife agencies in the 1950s have increased populations and occupied range substantially in areas where wild turkeys had been extirpated, and they established huntable populations in several states and Canadian provinces (Mosby 1959, 1973, 1975; Bailey 1980; Kennamer 1986). During the past 50 years, state and provincial restoration programs have been largely responsible for the reestablishment and expansion of the species in North America. Wild turkeys now occur in all states, except Alaska. Six of 13 Canadian provinces also have wild turkey populations.

Here we describe the current distribution of birds in the United States and Canada. We report estimates of wild turkey populations of each subspecies and their current range, and compare these to that of 5 years ago. We also report hunter numbers and harvest numbers for the fall of 2003 and the spring of 2004, and document the status of each state or province's restoration program.

METHODS

Questionnaires were sent out during the fall of 2004 to members of the National Wild Turkey Federation (NWTF) Technical Committee, which is composed of state and provincial wildlife biologists responsible for the wild turkey programs in their respective states and provinces. A state map delineated with county lines was provided to Technical Committee members to outline wild turkey range and densities to the county level. Surveys also were sent to the wildlife agencies of the Canadian provinces and Central American countries not represented on the Technical Committee including Alberta, British Columbia, Manitoba, New Brunswick, Nova Scotia, Quebec, Saskatchewan, Belize, Guatemala, and Mexico. Some data were obtained from Alberta, British Columbia, Manitoba, Nova Scotia, Quebec, Saskatchewan, and Mexico (range map). However, data from New Brunswick was unavailable. We were unable to obtain consistent and accurate data on the Rio Grande (*M. g. intermedia*) and Gould's (*M. g. mexicana*) populations of wild turkeys in Mexico and the Ocellated turkey (*M. ocellata*) in Belize and Guatemala, so information from Central America is not included in the text or tables. However, an approximate range map for Central America is included.

Population and range estimates provided here were based on the most accurate information available at the time of the survey. Variation existed among states and provinces in the methods used to collect population data and identify range. Some of this variation was evident in inconsistencies in range estimates across state boundaries. However, we believe the population and range estimates are the best available given the technical limitations of estimating wild turkey densities and range.

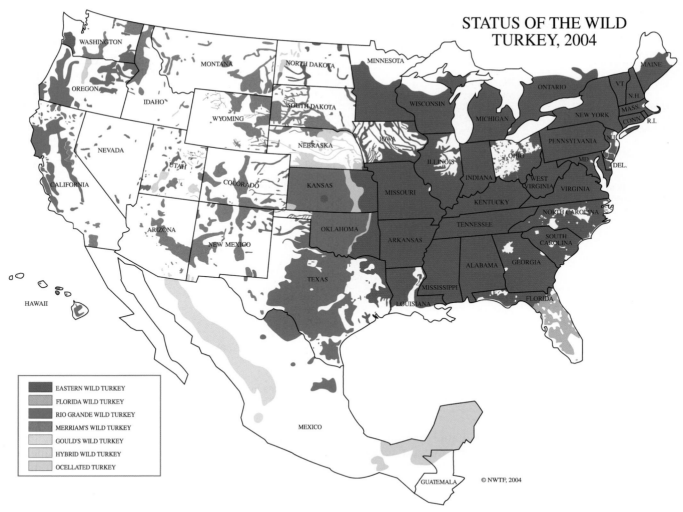

Fig. 1.   Distribution range of the wild turkey by subspecies.

RESULTS

Population Estimates by Subspecies

The eastern wild turkey subspecies (*M. g. silvestris*) is the most common and is estimated between 5.1–5.3 million, an increase of approximately 1 million birds from 1999 to 2004 (Table 1). The Rio Grande subspecies is estimated to number over 1 million birds, and the Merriam's (*M. g. merriami*) more than 334,000. The Florida subspecies (*M. g. osceola*) is estimated to number more than 80,000 birds, and the Gould's over 650. Some states delineated hybrid populations, and these are estimated at more than 116,000 birds.

Missouri had the largest wild turkey population with approximately 600,000 to 800,000 birds. Texas followed with a population of 600,500 birds, followed in descending order by Alabama, 450,000; Mississippi, 395,784; Wisconsin, 350,000+; Georgia, 350,000; and Pennsylvania, 342,000 (Table 2). Nevada (1,260) and Delaware (3,500) had the lowest population estimates in the United States (Table 3).

Distribution

Wild turkeys now range throughout much of North America (Figure 1). More than 3,041,009 km^2 of habitat was inhabited by wild turkeys (Table 4) in 2004 as compared to 2,349,764 km^2 in 1999 (Tapley et al. 2001a). About 20,195 km^2 of suitable habitat is currently being stocked. Ohio (7,770 km^2) contained the largest yet unoccupied habitat followed by Arizona, South Dakota, and Ontario all with (2,590 km^2).

Restoration

The status of 2004 restoration programs indicated that 5 states (Maine, Nevada, Oregon, South Dakota, and Wyoming) and Ontario finished in 2005, and 1 state (Minnesota) will finish within the next 5 years (Table 5). Alabama plans to do follow up stocking until 2010, and Arizona's Gould's restoration should be completed in 2010. Four states (Colorado, Hawaii, South Carolina, and Utah) listed completion dates as unknown.

Table 4. Estimated occupied range by wild turkeys, 1999 and 2004, and range remaining to be stocked.

State/province	1999[a] km²	1999[a] mi²	2004 km²	2004 mi²	Area to be stocked km²	Area to be stocked mi²
United States:						
Alabama	98,420	38,000	101,010	39,000	259	100
Arizona	21,238	11,624[b]	30,754	11,874[b]	2,590	1,000
Arkansas	113,313	43,750	89,031	34,375	0	0
California	19,425	7,500	75,545	29,168	N/A[c]	N/A
Colorado	45,714	17,650	49,210	19,000	N/A	N/A
Connecticut	9,466	3,655	9,420	3,637	0	0
Delaware	2,072	800	3,885	1,500	0	0
Florida	64,750	25,000	101,010	39,000	0	0
Georgia	93,240	36,000	102,587	39,609	0	0
Hawaii	4,271	1,649	4,271[a]	1,649[a]	0	0
Idaho	33,670	13,000	38,721	14,950	0	0
Illinois	20,202	7,800	N/A	N/A	N/A	N/A
Indiana	75,520	28,000	93,240	36,000	0	0
Iowa	8,904	3,438	9,992	3,858	0	0
Kansas	N/A	N/A	N/A	N/A	N/A	N/A
Kentucky	101,010	39,000	78,032	30,128	0	0
Louisiana	55,685	21,500	45,765	17,670	N/A	N/A
Maine	13,675	5,280	18,907	7,300	Unknown	Unknown
Maryland	9,065	3,500	14,245	5,500	0	0
Massachusetts	12,497	4,825	12,497	4,825	0	0
Michigan	110,171	42,537	115,359	44,540	0	0
Minnesota	113,960	44,000	113,960	44,000	N/A	N/A
Mississippi	75,110	29,000	112,898	43,590	0	0
Missouri	N/A	N/A	55,716	21,512	N/A	N/A
Montana	64,750	25,000	56,980	22,000	No estimate	No estimate
Nebraska	26	10	197,410	76,220	0	0
Nevada	427	165	2,598	1,003	648	250
New Hampshire	20,720	8,000	22,015	8,500	0	0
New Jersey	5,957	2,300	5,957	2,300	N/A	N/A
New Mexico	78,658	30,370	93,240	36,000	Unknown	Unknown
New York	N/A	N/A	124,320	48,000	N/A	N/A
North Carolina	93,240	36,000	80,290	31,000	130	<50
North Dakota	19,684	7,600	10,231	3,950	0	0
Ohio	50,647	19,555	58,275	22,500	7,770	3,000
Oklahoma	Unknown	Unknown	N/A	N/A	0	0
Oregon	61,124	23,600	89,233	34,453	N/A	N/A
Pennsylvania	67,962	26,240	117,332	45,302	0	0
Rhode Island	1,295	500	1,295	500	N/A	N/A
South Carolina	47,915	18,500	48,174	18,600	1,036	<400
South Dakota	27,713	10,700	54,779	21,150	2,590	1,000
Tennessee	98,420	38,000	103,600	40,000	0	0
Texas	337,995	130,500	385,825	148,967	0	0
Utah	Unknown	Unknown	N/A	N/A	N/A	N/A
Vermont	18,130	7,000	22,015	8,500	0	0
Virginia	62,160	24,000	64,623	24,951	0	0
Washington	Unknown	Unknown	N/A	N/A	N/A	N/A
West Virginia	59,283	22,889	62,937	24,300	0	0
Wisconsin	90,650	35,000	N/A	N/A	N/A	N/A
Wyoming	10,360	4,000	42,872	16,553	2,582	997
Canada:						
Alberta	1,900	734	1,813	700	N/A	N/A
Brit. Columbia	Unknown	Unknown	N/A	N/A	N/A	N/A
Manitoba	Unknown	Unknown	31,080	12,000	N/A	N/A
Nova Scotia	N/A	N/A	N/A	N/A	N/A	N/A
Ontario	29,340	11,328	88,060	34,000	2,590	1,000
Quebec	Unknown	Unknown	N/A	N/A	N/A	N/A
Saskatchewan	30	10	N/A	N/A	N/A	N/A
Total	2,349,764[d]	909,509[d]	3,041,009	1,174,134	20,195	7,797

[a] Tapley et al. (2001*a*).
[b] Includes White Mountain Apache Reservation.
[c] N/A = not available.
[d] Total occupied range corrected after publication of 8th National Wild Turkey Symposium.

Table 5. Status of wild turkey restoration programs by state and province, 2004.

State/province	Year begun	Year ended/ expected completion	No. release sites to date	No. birds moved to date	Source of birds
United States:					
Alabama	1943	follow ups until 2010	133	1,891	In state
Arizona	1939 Merriam's	1993[a]	N/A[b]	633	In state
	1983 Gould's	2010	25	310	In state and Mexico
Arkansas	1932				Game farm stock failed[a]
	1950[a]	2003	450	7,200	In state and Mississippi, Missouri, North Dakota, Texas
California	1928				Game farm stock failed[a]
	1959	2001	300	5,000[c]	In state and Idaho, Kansas, South Dakota, Washington, Wyoming
Colorado	1980	Unknown	55	2,700+	In state and Kansas, Oklahoma, Texas
Connecticut	1975	1992	14	356	In state and New York
Delaware	1984	1999	12	300	New Jersey, New York, Pennsylvania, South Carolina, Vermont, Virginia
Florida	1949	1969	3+	6,185	In state
Georgia	1973	1996	400+	4,845+	In state
Hawaii	Unknown	Unknown	2	50	In state
Idaho	1925	1946			Game farm stock failed[a]
	1961	2001–2002	205	5,074	In state and British Columbia, California, Colorado, Kansas, New Brunswick, New Mexico, Pennsylvania, Oklahoma, Oregon, South Dakota, Texas, Washington, Wyoming
Illinois	1958	2000	273	4,669	In state and Arkansas, Iowa, Mississippi, Missouri, New Jersey, West Virginia
Indiana	1956	1999	185	2,795	In state and Illinois, Iowa, Kentucky, Missouri
Iowa	1966	1990	260	3,583	In state and Missouri, North Dakota
Kansas	1962	1990[a]	105 (counties)	235	In state and Missouri, Oklahoma, Texas
Kentucky	1978	1997	433	6,785	In state and Arkansas, Florida, Illinois, Iowa, Mississippi, Missouri, Pennsylvania, South Carolina, Tennessee, Virginia, Wisconsin
Louisiana	1962	2002	230	3,814	In state and Alabama, Arkansas, Connecticut, Florida, Iowa, Mississippi, Missouri, South Carolina, Wisconsin
Maine	1977	2005	55	862	In state and Connecticut, Vermont
Maryland	1966	1997	71	1,306	In state and Florida, Pennsylvania, South Carolina, Virginia
Massachusetts	1972	1996	27	598	In state and New York
Michigan	1954	2000–2001	135	4,248[d]	In and out of state
Minnesota	1926				Game farm stock failed
	1976	2007	190	4,300	In state and Arkansas, Illinois, Missouri, New York, Oklahoma, Wisconsin
Mississippi	1934				Game farm stocked failed
	1940	2000	272	2,948	In state
Missouri	1954	1979	91	2,400	In state
Montana	1950s		91	2,686	In state
Nebraska	1959	Late 1980s	120	1,700	In state and South Dakota, Texas, Wyoming
Nevada	1962	1963			Arizona and South Dakota
	1986	2005	18+	1,531+	In state and California, Idaho, Texas
New Hampshire	1969	1970			West Virginia stock failed
	1975	1995	16	344	In state and New York, West Virginia
New Jersey	1977	2000	41+	1,600	Alabama, Arkansas, Georgia, New York, South Carolina, Vermont
New Mexico	late 1920s, early 1930s		82+	1,465+	In state and Oklahoma, Texas
New York	1960	1994	Unknown	1,400	In state
North Carolina	1970	2000	350	6,000	In state and Alabama, Arkansas, Connecticut, Iowa, Michigan, Pennsylvania, South Carolina, Virginia, West Virginia, Wisconsin
North Dakota					Birds are only trapped in problem areas and moved for nuisance control[a]

Table 5. Continued.

State/province	Year begun	Year ended/ expected completion	No. release sites to date	No. birds moved to date	Source of birds
Ohio	1956/2000[e]	1997	238	4,804	In state and Alabama, Arkansas, Florida, Kentucky, Missouri, Texas, West Virginia
Oklahoma	1956	1997	1,000	10,000	In state and Arkansas, Missouri, Texas
Oregon	1920s[a]	1930s[a]			Game farm stock failed[a]
	1961	2005	584	9,634	In state and Arizona, California, Colorado, Kansas, Montana, Nebraska, New Mexico, Oklahoma, Texas
Pennsylvania	1956	2003	47	3,573	In state
Rhode Island	1980	1998	7	137	New York, Pennsylvania, Vermont
South Carolina	1951	1958[a]	Unknown	328	In state
	1976	Unknown	205	3,562	In state
South Dakota	1948	1970sM[f]/ 60sRG[g]/ 2005E[h]	200	2,000	In state and Colorado, Iowa, Kentucky, Missouri, New Mexico, Oklahoma, Texas
Tennessee	1935	1949			Game farm stock failed
	1951	2000	682	31,220	In state and Florida, Missouri
Texas	1924	1996[c]	Unknown	Unknown	In state and Alabama, Connecticut, Florida, Georgia, Iowa, Louisiana, Mississippi, Missouri, Oklahoma, South Carolina, Wisconsin, West Virginia
	1979	1999[g]	319[g]	7,091[g]	
Utah	1925/1952[a]	Unknown			In state and out of state[a]
	1989	Unknown	52	N/A	In state and Colorado, Kansas, Oklahoma, South Dakota, Texas, Utah, Wyoming
Vermont	1969	1994	18	620	New York
Virginia	1929				Game farm stock failed
	1955	1993	25	925	In state
Washington	1960	1964	N/A	N/A	Arizona, Colorado, New Mexico
	1984	1990[a]	125–150	3,000	In state and Iowa, Missouri, Oklahoma, Pennsylvania, South Dakota, Texas
West Virginia	1950	1989	62	2,278	In state
Wisconsin	1976	1993[a]	80–100	4,364+	In state and Missouri
Wyoming	1935	2005	70	5,000	In state and New Mexico, Oklahoma, Texas
Canada:					
Ontario	1984	2005	275	4,400	In province and Iowa, Michigan, Missouri, New Jersey, New York, Tennessee, Vermont

[a] Kennamer and Kennamer (1996).
[b] N/A = not available.
[c] Since 1959.
[d] Since 1983.
[e] Reopened to fill in 10 western counties.
[f] Merriam's subspecies.
[g] Rio Grande subspecies.
[h] Eastern subspecies.

Harvest

The 2004 harvest was estimated to be more than 730,000 birds in the spring and over 189,000 in the fall (Table 6). The total harvest of 920,012 birds represented a 24% increase from 1999. During the spring, Missouri accounted for the largest harvest with 60,744 birds taken, followed by Alabama with 57,100. Alberta and Hawaii recorded the lowest harvest with 15 and 56 birds, respectively. Between 1999 and 2004, the spring harvest increased for 39 states and 2 provinces, and decreased for 8 states. Maine had the highest spring harvest increase (444%).

Forty-two states held a fall season in 2003. The largest fall harvests occurred in Texas with 36,000 birds and Pennsylvania with 31,100 birds taken. Mas-

sachusetts and Nevada recorded the smallest harvests with 111 and 31, respectively. Between 1999 and 2004, the fall harvest increased in 27 states and decreased in 9 states. Idaho had the largest increase (1,820%). Maine and North Carolina were the latest states to institute fall seasons between 1999 and 2004, leaving 7 states and 3 provinces that had spring seasons with no fall seasons.

Hunter Numbers

The total number of wild turkey hunters during the fall 2003 and spring 2004 hunting seasons were estimated to number 2.8 million compared to 2.6 million in 1999. This is a 6% increase (Table 7).

Spring 2004 hunters totaled 2,019,090 with Penn-

Table 6. Number of wild turkeys harvested in spring and fall hunting seasons by state and province, 1998–1999 and 2003–2004.

State/province	1998–1999[a]			2003–2004			Percent change		
	Fall (1998)	Spring (1999)	Total	Fall (2003)	Spring (2004)	Total	Fall	Spring	Total
United States:									
Alabama	5,100[b]	51,800[c]	56,900	5,500[d]	57,100[e]	62,600	+8	+10	+10
Arizona	516	760	1,276	893	811	1,704	+73	+7	+34
Arkansas	199	15,571	15,770	1,316	16,993	18,309	+561	+9	+16
California	5,165	5,798	10,963	5,823	19,125[e]	24,948	+13	+230	+128
Colorado	539	1,445	1,984	690	1,960[e]	2,650	+28	+36	+34
Connecticut	148	1,910	2,058	134	2,081	2,215	−9	+9	+8
Delaware	NS[f]	99	99	NS	108	108	NS	+9	+9
Florida	12,112[b]	23,419[c]	35,531	3,850[d]	15,500[e]	19,350	−68	−34	−46
Georgia	NS	29,168	29,168	NS	24,000	24,000	NS	−18	−18
Hawaii	156	317	473	N/A[g]	56	56	N/A	−82	−88
Idaho	100	5,500	5,600	1,920	4,310[e]	6,230	+1,820	−22	+11
Illinois	1,502	10,076	11,578	N/A	N/A	N/A	N/A	N/A	N/A
Indiana	NS	6,548	6,548	NS	10,765	10,765	NS	+64	+64
Iowa	3,468	18,290	21,758	8,559	25,504	34,063	+147	+39	+57
Kansas	1,755[b]	16,954[c]	18,709	5,468[d]	29,868[h]	35,336	+212	+76	+89
Kentucky	1,725	17,500[c]	19,225	2,781	26,963	29,744	+61	+54	+55
Louisiana	NS	4,000[c]	4,000	NS	9,000[e]	9,000	NS	+125	+125
Maine	NS	890	890	246	4,839	5,085	N/A	+444	+471
Maryland	300	2,650	2,950	163	2,760	2,923	−46	+4	−1
Massachusetts	270	2,363	2,633	111	2,068	2,179	−59	−12	−17
Michigan	6,427	24,973	31,400	5,000	37,580	42,580	−22	+50	+36
Minnesota	828	5,132	5,960	889	8,434	9,323	+7	+64	+56
Mississippi	791	32,017[c]	32,808	1,827[d]	40,125[e]	41,952	+131	+25	+28
Missouri	15,343	50,299	65,642	13,249	60,744	73,993	−14	+21	+13
Montana	1,350	1,100	2,450	N/A	N/A	N/A	N/A	N/A	N/A
Nebraska	3,020	6,200	9,220	3,300	12,860	16,160	+9	+107	+75
Nevada	25	120	145	31	93	124	+24	−23	−14
New Hampshire	200	1,500	1,700	270	2,700	2,970	+35	+80	+75
New Jersey	157	2,560	2,717	179	3,073	3,252	+14	+20	+20
New Mexico	157	1,216	1,373	149	663	812	−5	−45	−41
New York	15,000	25,000	40,000	15,800	26,300	42,100	+5	+5	+5
North Carolina	NS	5,340	5,340	181	8,846	9,027	N/A	+66	+69
North Dakota	2,114	1,173	3,287	4,410	2,532	6,942	+109	+116	+111
Ohio	1,250	14,419	15,669	2,060	16,927	18,987	+65	+17	+21
Oklahoma	4,800	20,000	24,800	7,000	40,000	47,000	+46	+100	+90
Oregon	113	2,621[c]	2,734	755	4,093[e]	4,848	+568	+56	+77
Pennsylvania	33,628	36,900	70,528	31,100	41,000	72,100	−8	+11	+2
Rhode Island	NS	147	147	NS	220	220	NS	+50	+50
South Carolina	NS	11,261	11,261	NS	12,950	12,950	NS	+15	+15
South Dakota	2,730	3,675	6,405	3,200	5,500	8,700	+17	+50	+36
Tennessee	450	16,511	16,961	2,393	33,560	35,953	+432	+103	+112
Texas	33,369	24,706	58,075	36,000	27,100	63,100	+8	+10	+9
Utah	NS	400	400	NS	703	703	NS	+76	+76
Vermont	538	3,126	3,664	1,049	3,925	4,974	+95	+26	+36
Virginia	8,802	12,762	21,564	6,556	14,338	20,894	−26	+12	−3
Washington	N/A	973	973	630	3,837	4,467	N/A	+294	+359
West Virginia	1,678	11,175	12,853	1,841	10,519	12,360	+10	−6	−4
Wisconsin	9,000	30,000	39,000	12,466	47,477	59,943	+39	+58	+54
Wyoming	720	1,420	2,140	1,682	2,370[e]	4,052	+134	+67	+89
Canada:									
Alberta	NS	9	9	NS	15[e]	15	NS	+67	+67
Brit. Columbia	NS	100	100	NS	N/A	N/A	NS	N/A	NS
Manitoba	50	250	300	N/A	N/A	N/A	N/A	N/A	N/A
Ontario	NS	1,934	1,934	NS	8,246	8,246	NS	+326	+326
Total	175,595	564,077	739,672	189,471	730,541	920,012	+8	+30	+24

[a] Tapley et al. (2001*b*).
[b] Fall of 1997.
[c] Spring of 1998.
[d] Fall of 2002.
[e] Spring of 2003.
[f] NS = no season.
[g] N/A = not available.
[h] Spring of 2002.

Table 7. Number of wild turkey hunters by state and province, 1998–1999 and 2003–2004.

State/province	1998–1999[a] Fall (1998)	Spring (1999)	Total[b]	2003–2004 Fall (2003)	Spring (2004)	Total[b]	Percent change Fall	Spring	Total[b]
United States:									
Alabama	5,100	51,800	56,900	5,500[c]	59,800[d]	65,300	+8	+15	+15
Arizona	4,225	4,700	8,925	4,750	5,300	10,050	+12	+13	+13
Arkansas	N/A[e]	65,000	65,000	N/A	75,000	75,000	N/A	+15	+15
California	7,637	11,270	18,907	11,892	24,949	36,841	+56	+121	+95
Colorado	2,025	6,550	8,575	1,150	10,300[d]	11,450	−43	+57	+34
Connecticut	3,750	6,700	10,450	3,300	7,600	10,900	−12	+13	+4
Delaware	NS[f]	1,125	1,125	NS	1,300	1,300	NS	+16	+16
Florida	25,276	29,316	54,592	N/A	23,600[d]	23,600	N/A	−19	−57
Georgia	NS	40,510	40,510	NS	36,800	36,800	NS	−9	−9
Hawaii	N/A	350	350	500	200	700	N/A	−43	+100
Idaho	450	13,000	13,450	4,584	18,232	22,816	+919	+40	+70
Illinois	17,850	40,600	58,450	N/A	N/A	N/A	N/A	N/A	N/A
Indiana	NS	25,581	25,581	NS	40,350	40,350	NS	+58	+58
Iowa	9,000	48,000	57,000	13,566	50,846	64,412	+51	+6	+13
Kansas	4,700	23,000	27,700	6,700	53,000	59,700	+43	+130	+116
Kentucky	8,050	55,000	63,050	22,375	87,614	109,989	+178	+59	+74
Louisiana	NS	13,140	13,140	NS	26,500	26,500	NS	+102	+102
Maine	NS	3,700	3,700	2,000	15,600	17,600	N/A	+322	+376
Maryland	5,000	17,000	22,000	3,660	13,300	16,960	−27	−22	−23
Massachusetts	12,787	13,712	26,499	14,230	13,912	28,142	+11	+1	+6
Michigan	28,925	66,790	95,715	20,100	111,000	131,100	−31	+66	+37
Minnesota	2,750	16,600	19,350	2,977	27,600	30,577	+8	+66	+58
Mississippi	2,500	46,000	48,500	3,778	46,640	50,418	+51	+1	+4
Missouri	32,593	109,663	142,256	30,500	140,000	170,500	−6	+28	+20
Montana	3,500	2,500	6,000	9,942	10,418	20,360	+184	+317	+239
Nebraska	5,370	14,000	19,370	7,500	24,000	31,500	+40	+71	+63
Nevada	50	210	260	116	308	424	+132	+47	+63
New Hampshire	3,300	10,900	14,200	6,700	17,755	24,455	+103	+63	+72
New Jersey	2,500	13,750	16,250	3,100	11,550	14,650	+24	−16	−10
New Mexico	752	6,957	7,709	1,200	12,000	13,200	+60	+72	+71
New York	96,000	105,000	201,000	80,000	100,000	180,000	−17	−5	−10
North Carolina	NS	N/A	N/A	N/A	42,000	42,000	N/A	N/A	N/A
North Dakota	3,141	1,835	4,976	6,886	4,497	11,383	+119	+145	+129
Ohio	9,000	55,000	64,000	26,484	68,975	95,459	+194	+25	+49
Oklahoma	16,500	48,000	64,500	28,000	78,000	106,000	+70	+63	+64
Oregon	366	10,263	10,629	2,675	14,700	17,375	+631	+43	+63
Pennsylvania	249,937	233,287	483,224	211,965	246,821[d]	458,786	−15	+6	−5
Rhode Island	NS	1,100	1,100	NS	1,600	1,600	NS	+45	+45
South Carolina	NS	37,000	37,000	NS	47,674	47,674	NS	+29	+29
South Dakota	3,550	9,100	12,650	4,200	12,200	16,400	+18	+34	+30
Tennessee	4,010	53,500	57,510	15,650	95,258	110,908	+290	+78	+93
Texas	83,171	121,840	205,011	94,118	64,391	158,509	+13	−47	−23
Utah	NS	3,830	3,830	NS	1,324	1,324	NS	−65	−65
Vermont	1,900	9,500	11,400	16,300	14,000	30,300	+758	+47	+166
Virginia	86,005	68,824	154,829	64,000	61,000	125,000	−26	−11	−19
Washington	150	7,500	7,650	2,000	15,800	17,800	+1,233	+111	+133
West Virginia	32,000	140,000	172,000	N/A	N/A	N/A	N/A	N/A	N/A
Wisconsin	80,300	132,000	212,300	76,630	158,600	235,230	−5	+20	+11
Wyoming	1,200	2,595	3,795	2,313	4,831[c]	7,144	+93	+86	+88
Canada:									
Alberta	NS	50	50	NS	45	45	NS	−10	−10
Brit. Columbia	NS	225	225	NS	N/A	N/A	NS	N/A	N/A
Manitoba	N/A	450	450	200	700[d]	900	N/A	+56	+100
Ontario	NS	7,925	7,925	NS	21,200	21,200	NS	+168	+168
Total	855,320	1,806,248	2,661,568	811,541	2,019,090	2,830,631	−5	+12	+6

[a] Tapley et al. (2001*b*).
[b] Total was sum of fall and spring hunters. This total overestimates number of hunters because hunters may participate in both seasons.
[c] Fall of 2002.
[d] Spring of 2003.
[e] N/A = not available.
[f] NS = no season.

sylvania (246,821) and Wisconsin (158,600) having the most hunters. Alberta (45) and Hawaii (200) reported the fewest hunters. Between 1999 and 2004, spring hunter numbers increased for 37 states and 2 provinces, and decreased for 9 states and 1 province. Maine had the largest increase (322%).

Fall turkey hunters numbered 811,541 for the fall 2003 hunting season. Pennsylvania and Texas reported the highest number of fall hunters, with 211,965 and 94,118, respectively. Nevada (116) and Manitoba (200) had the fewest fall hunters. Between 1999 and 2004, fall turkey hunter numbers increased in 26 states and decreased in 9 states. Washington had the largest increase of 1,233%.

DISCUSSION

Since restoration began, the wild turkey has made a remarkable comeback and has increased its numbers to a population estimated between 6.6–6.9 million birds. The 49 states with wild turkey populations all have a spring season and 42 states have a fall season. Maine and North Carolina instituted a fall season within the past 5 years. Four of the 6 Canadian provinces with wild turkeys also have a spring season and 1 has a fall season.

In comparing 1999 population data to 2004 population data, the increase of between 1.2–1.4 million (22–27%) wild turkeys in the past 5 years was similar to the increase recorded for the previous 5-year period between 1994 and 1999 (1.3 million). The overall occupied range increased 29% because of more wild turkeys being restored to unoccupied habitat, and existing populations expanding normally into adjacent unoccupied habitat. This large increase in occupied range also was the result of better data collection in several key states.

The total harvest also increased 24%, while the total number of hunters only increased 6%. This 6% increase in hunter numbers was considerably less than the increase recorded during the previous 5-year period (21%).

The turkey hunter of the 21st century is experiencing rapidly expanding turkey populations, additional occupied range, and increased overall harvest while the growth in overall hunter numbers has slowed. It is anticipated that these trends will continue for the foreseeable future as wild turkeys continue to fill unoccupied habitat and expand into marginal habitats.

ACKNOWLEDGMENTS

We sincerely thank the following members of the NWTF Technical Committee who provided the respective state/province information: R. Eakes and S. Barnett, Alabama; B. Wakeling, Arizona; B. McAnally and B. Carner, Arkansas; T. Blakenship and S. Gardner, California; E. Gorman, Colorado; H. Kilpatrick and M. Gregonis, Connecticut; K. Reynolds, Deleware; L. Perrin, Florida; B. Fletcher and H. Barnhill, Georgia; J. Polhemus, Hawaii; D. Kemner, Idaho; S. Backs and J. Olson, Indiana; T. Little and T. Gosselink, Iowa; R. Applegate and M. Mitchner, Kansas; J. Lane, Kentucky; F. Kimmel, Louisiana; P. Bozenhard and A. Weik, Maine; B. Long, Maryland; J. Cardoza, Massachusetts; A. Stewart and D. Luukkonen, Michigan; D. Kimmel and G. Nelson, Minnesota; R. Seiss and J. Austin, Mississippi; J. Beringer and E. Gallagher, Missouri; R. Northrup and D. Tribby, Montana; A. Harden and K. Hams, Nebraska; C. Mortimore, Nevada; M. Ellingwood and T. Walski, New Hampshire; T. McBride, New Jersey; L. Kamees, New Mexico; B. Sanford, New York; M. Seamster and S. Osborne, North Carolina; S. Kohn, North Dakota; D. Swanson, Ohio; R. Smith and J. Waymire, Oklahoma; D. Reid and M. Malhiot, Ontario, Canada; S. Denney and D. Budeau, Oregon; M. Casalena and B. Boyd, Pennsylvania; B. Tefft, Rhode Island; D. Baumann, South Carolina; T. Benzon, South Dakota; R. Huskey, Tennessee; S. DeMaso and T. W. Schwertner, Texas; D. Mitchell, Utah; D. Blodgett, Vermont; G. Norman, Virginia; M. Cope, Washington; J. Pack and C. Taylor, West Virginia; A. Mezera, Wisconsin; J. Emmerich and B. Lanka, Wyoming.

LITERATURE CITED

Bailey, R. W. 1980. The wild turkey status and outlook in 1979. Proceedings of the National Wild Turkey Symposium 4: 1–9.

Blakey, H. L. 1941. Status and management of the eastern wild turkey. American Wildlife 2:139–142.

Davis, H. E. 1949. The American wild turkey. Small-Arms Technical, Georgetown, South Carolina, USA.

Kennamer, J. E., editor. 1986. Guide to the American wild turkey. National Wild Turkey Federation, Edgefield, South Carolina, USA.

———, and M. C. Kennamer. 1996. Status and distribution of the wild turkey in 1994. Proceedings of the National Wild Turkey Symposium 7:203–211.

———, ———, and R. Brenneman. 1992. History. Pages 6–17 *in* J. G. Dickson, editor. The wild turkey: biology and management. Stackpole Books, Mechanicsburg, Pennsylvania, USA.

Mosby, H. S. 1959. General status of the wild turkey and its management in the United States. Proceedings of the National Wild Turkey Symposium 1:1–11.

———. 1973. The changed status of the wild turkey over the past three decades. Pages 71–76 *in* G. C. Sanderson and H. C. Schultz, editors. Wild turkey management: current problems and programs. The Missouri Chapter of the Wildlife Society and University of Missouri Press, Columbia, Missouri, USA.

———. 1975. The status of the wild turkey in 1974. Proceedings of the National Wild Turkey Symposium 3:22–26.

Tapley, J. L., R. K. Abernethy, and J. E. Kennamer. 2001a. Status and distribution of the wild turkey in 1999. Proceedings of the National Wild Turkey Symposium 8:15–22.

———, W. M. Healy, R. K. Abernethy, and J. E. Kennamer. 2001b. Status of wild turkey hunting in North America. Proceedings of the National Wild Turkey Symposium 8: 257–267.

Jennifer Tapley is currently a wildlife biologist for the National Wild Turkey Federation. She earned a B.S. in wildlife and fisheries ecology and a minor in journalism from Oklahoma State University. ***Robert Abernethey*** is currently the director for agency programs for the National Wild Turkey Federation. He earned his B.S. in wildlife biology from North Carolina State University and a M.S. in wetlands ecology from Louisiana State University.

James Earl Kennamer is currently the senior vice president for conservation programs for the National Wild Turkey Federation. He holds a B.S. in game management from Auburn University, and M.S. and Ph.D. degrees in wildlife management from Mississippi State University.

**Wild Turkey Management:
Accomplishments, Strategies, and Opportunities**
———— Grand Rapids, Michigan ————

THE USE OF MOLECULAR MARKERS IN WILD TURKEY MANAGEMENT

Emily K. Latch[1]
*Department of Forestry and Natural Resources,
715 W. State Street, Purdue University,
W. Lafayette, IN 47907, USA*

Karen E. Mock
*Department of Fisheries and Wildlife,
5230 Old Main Hill, Utah State University,
Logan, UT 84322, USA*

Olin E. Rhodes, Jr.
*Department of Forestry and Natural Resources,
195 Marstellar Street, Purdue University,
W. Lafayette, IN 47907, USA*

Abstract: A variety of genetic markers now are available for use in the management and conservation of wildlife species. In the wild turkey (*Meleagris gallopavo*), these markers have been used to address questions at levels ranging from the individual to the subspecies, and with issues ranging from species-wide evolution to forensics. Genetic studies involving translocated populations have provided managers with additional information to consider when designing optimal translocation strategies to maximize growth and long-term stability of such populations. In this paper, we discuss the molecular markers available for wild turkeys, and review their applications in wild turkey management, including subspecies identification, intraspecific hybridization, domestic introgression, genetic bottlenecks, population structure, gene flow, cryptic behavioral and social patterns, and forensics.

Proceedings of the National Wild Turkey Symposium 9:33–44
Key words: AFLP, allozyme, DNA sequencing, gene flow, genetic, hybridization, *Meleagris gallopavo*, microsatellite, mitochondrial, molecular marker, population, subspecies, translocation.

Genetic markers have become a standard tool in the management and conservation of wildlife species, enabling scientists to address wildlife management questions at levels of biological resolution that previously had been unattainable with traditional techniques. When integrated with information from disciplines such as ecology, morphology, or paleontology, genetic data allow us to better understand evolutionary and demographic phenomema such as population structure (Sarre 1995, Sinclair et al. 1996, Kyle et al. 2000), dispersal rates (Beheler 2001, Richardson et al. 2002, van Hooft et al. 2003, Zenger et al. 2003), population bottlenecks and range expansion (Rogers and Harpending 1992, Rogers 1995, Luikart et al. 1998), cryptic behavioral and social patterns (van Staaden et al. 1996, DeWoody et al. 1998, Piertney et al. 1999, Zenuto et al. 1999, Storz et al. 2001), parentage (DeWoody et al. 2000, Beheler et al. 2003, Carew et al. 2003, Sinclair et al. 2003, Stapley et al. 2003), hybridization (Adams et al. 2003), taxonomic status (Miththapala et al. 1996, Stephen et al. 2005a), and individual identity (Cronin 1991, Guglich et al. 1994, Boyd et al. 2001, Manel et al. 2002). It has become apparent that the tools of modern molecular biology hold great value for the field of wildlife management.

However, it also is clear that the selection of the most appropriate class of genetic markers, both in terms of inheritance patterns and rates of evolution, is important if these tools are to be applied successfully at varying scales of biological organization.

In the wild turkey, a number of different types of molecular markers have been developed. These tools have been used in a variety of different applications to address management-oriented concerns at scales ranging from the subspecies to the flock. Molecular markers also have been used to investigate evolutionary relationships among subspecies and populations. In this paper, we will provide a brief review of the molecular tools that are available for use in wild turkeys, and summarize the management-related research that has been or is being conducted using these tools.

MOLECULAR MARKERS AVAILABLE FOR WILD TURKEYS

Allozymes

Allozymes are alternate (allelic) forms of nuclear DNA-encoded enzymes. Mutations in the DNA se-

[1] E-mail: latche@purdue.edu

quence coding for an enzyme can induce changes in its protein structure. These differences in protein struc-ture are detectable by starch-gel electrophoresis, which separates the enzyme alleles based on size, shape, and electrical charge. Early studies of allozyme variation among populations, beginning with a series of papers in 1966, revealed a surprising amount of genetic variability in natural populations (Harris 1966, Hubby and Lewontin 1966, Johnson et al. 1966). Allozyme markers have proven to be useful for applications ranging from characterizing broad-scale variation across a species range to investigating local mating patterns (Rhodes et al. 1993, Pope 1998, Lode 2001, Gabor and Nice 2004). Analysis of allozyme markers is relatively inexpensive, and the markers are codominant, meaning that all variants at a locus can be visualized. However, the utility of allozyme markers is limited by low levels of polymorphism, resulting from the fact that allozyme analysis detects only a subset of the total variation (that which affects the migration of the enzyme through a gel). Most enzymes are not polymorphic (e.g., average of 23% polymorphism for 551 species of vertebrates), and polymorphic loci rarely have more than 3 alleles (Nevo et al. 1983). Thus, the relatively low expense and ease of data collection often are offset by the large number of allozyme loci typically needed to adequately assess genetic variability in a sample. Additionally, because allozymes are expressed genes, they are subject to selection, and patterns of population variation may not always reflect the neutral processes assumed to drive divergence and gene flow (Eanes 1999).

Twenty-eight allozyme loci have been optimized for surveys of genetic diversity in wild turkeys (Stangel et al. 1992). Although subsequent studies screened all 28 loci, they typically found only 4–5 loci that exhibited polymorphism among the groups of interest (Leberg 1991, Leberg et al. 1994, Rhodes et al. 1995, Boone and Rhodes 1996). Although turkeys exhibit slightly fewer polymorphic loci than the average for vertebrate species, they are well within the range of values described for bird species (Nevo et al. 1983). Despite reduced genetic variability in comparison to DNA-based markers, allozymes are still valuable tools for subspecies- and population-level applications in the wild turkey (Leberg 1991, Stangel et al. 1992, Leberg et al. 1994, Rhodes et al. 1995, Boone and Rhodes 1996).

DNA-based Markers

Nuclear DNA

In recent decades we have witnessed a shift from protein-based (allozyme) to DNA-based marker systems for estimation of genetic parameters in wildlife species. DNA-based markers not only reveal more genetic variation than their allozyme predecessors, but also allow investigators to choose among sets of loci with different patterns of inheritance (nuclear versus mitochondrial DNA) or evolutionary constraints (coding versus noncoding regions of the genome; Mitton

1994). Nuclear loci represent DNA inherited from both parents, and therefore can be useful for questions focused at almost any biological scale, from establishing relatedness among individuals to discernment of species (Sinclair et al. 2003, Verma and Singh 2003, Williams et al. 2003a). In particular, highly polymorphic nuclear markers, often associated with noncoding regions of the genome, are essential for studies in which individuals must be unambiguously identified (i.e., parentage studies or assignment of unknown individuals to a population of origin; Anderson et al. 2002, Manel et al. 2002, DeYoung et al. 2003). However, the abundant polymorphisms that make highly variable nuclear markers attractive for applications at the individual level can, in some cases, obscure patterns of differentiation at higher taxonomic levels (e.g., species; Hedrick 1999).

Microsatellites.—Nuclear microsatellites are short segments of noncoding DNA (typically 2–4 base pairs in length) which are tandemly repeated many times. Microsatellite loci tend to mutate by adding and subtracting these segments, so allelic variation is generally in the form of length, which is easily detectable using electrophoresis. Microsatellite length polymorphisms can be abundant within and among populations, and it is thought that slippage during DNA replication plays a major role in generating length variation among alleles (Levinson and Gutman 1987, Jeffreys et al. 1991, Schlötterer and Tautz 1992). Suites of highly polymorphic microsatellite loci can provide tremendous discriminatory power, allowing for the unique identification of individuals within populations and the exclusion of individuals as potential parents of offspring. The highly polymorphic nature of microsatellite loci also means that they can be prone to a phenomemon termed homoplasy, where convergent mutations in different lineages have led to the same allele. Thus, alleles that are alike may not represent common ancestry, resulting in inferred relationships among groups that may not accurately represent evolutionary histories. The potentially confounding effects of homoplasy often can be alleviated by analyzing many microsatellite loci.

Microsatellite markers are relatively inexpensive to analyze, and are available for countless species in virtually every major taxonomic group. Furthermore, microsatellites developed for one species often can be used in related taxa (Frankham et al. 2002), further reducing the time and expense of their development for newly studied species.

Currently, 24 microsatellite loci have been optimized for use in wild turkeys. Eighteen of these loci originally were developed for domestic turkeys (Donoghue et al. 1999, Huang et al. 1999, Reed et al. 2000), but proved to be polymorphic in wild turkeys with modifications (Shen 1999, Latch 2004). The remaining 6 loci were developed by screening microsatellite repeats found in wild and domestic turkey DNA sequences (Latch et al. 2002). Robust subsets of these 24 loci have been used for numerous studies of wild turkey ecology and taxonomy (Mock et al. 2001, 2002,

2004; Latch 2004; Krakauer 2005; Latch and Rhodes 2005, 2006; Latch et al. 2006*a,b*). Numerous additional microsatellite loci have been developed for domestic turkeys but have not been thoroughly screened for polymorphism in wild turkeys (e.g., Reed et al. 2000, 2002, 2003). Given the previous success of domestic turkey markers in their wild relatives (Shen 1999, Latch 2004, Krakauer 2005), this represents a potential reservoir of microsatellite loci for future applications. In the wild turkey, the utility of nuclear microsatellites has been shown for elucidating genetic structure among turkey populations and identifying individual animals (i.e., Latch and Rhodes 2005, Latch et al. 2006*b*).

Amplified Fragment Length Polymorphisms (AFLPs).—Amplified fragment length polymorphism (AFLP) is another type of nuclear DNA-based marker system available for rapid screening of genetic diversity among individuals (Vos et al. 1995, Mueller and Wolfenbarger 1999). AFLP polymorphisms result from differences in restriction fragment lengths caused by single base mutations, insertions, or deletions that create or destroy restriction enzyme recognition sites. AFLP methods involve the detection of these sites by polymerase chain reaction (PCR) amplification and electrophoresis. Because AFLP methods can generate hundreds of genome-wide polymorphic markers without any prior sequence knowledge, AFLPs can be a powerful, low-cost tool for use in systematics and population genetics, as well as for generating "DNA fingerprints" for individual identification and studies of kinship (Escaravage et al. 1998, Mueller and Wolfenbarger 1999, Whitehead et al. 2003). The primary limitation associated with AFLP markers is that they are a dominant marker system, requiring the assumption of Hardy-Weinberg equilibrium for the estimation of allele frequencies in populations. In addition, AFLP profiles can be sensitive to varying laboratory conditions, rendering them difficult to replicate over long periods of time in different laboratories.

AFLP protocols have been optimized in wild turkey, and these markers have been used effectively to resolve evolutionary relationships among subspecies and to determine the subspecies of origin of a given population (Mock et al. 2001, 2002). Because of the large number of polymorphic AFLP loci in wild turkey, this marker system may also prove to be informative for fine-scale questions at the population, flock, or individual level.

Mitochondrial DNA

In contrast to the nuclear genome, mitochondrial DNA (mtDNA) is cytoplasmically inherited, and thus is derived almost exclusively from maternal lineages. Although the mtDNA of any individual can be unique, the highly conserved nature of homologous functional genes across a wide variety of organisms allows for direct comparisons of mtDNA sequences at many different taxonomic scales. Thus, mitochondrial markers, particularly those representing coding regions of the genome, are particularly valuable for questions per-

taining to higher level systematics and phylogenetics (Saetre et al. 2001, Abbott and Double 2003). Because mitochondrial sequences are generally nonrecombining, molecular clocks can be used to estimate divergence times of various taxa. In addition, because of their mode of inheritance, mitochondrial markers associated with maternal lineages are also useful for questions focused on population establishment, social structure, and hybridization (Zink and Dittmann 1993, Pilgrim et al. 1998, Boyce et al. 1999, Adams et al. 2003). However, despite relatively high levels of polymorphism at certain hypervariable regions of the mitochondrial genome, mtDNA markers may not possess sufficient variability for individual identification. This low variability can be a major limitation for the use of mtDNA markers in population-level studies.

Control Region.—The most variable portions in the mitochondrial genome are within the control region (D-loop), a noncoding region. Control region sequences frequently are the mitochondrial marker of choice for assessing patterns of genetic differentiation below the species level. In many investigations, nuclear markers are combined with control region data to characterize differences in patterns of genetic differentiation between the sexes (Scribner et al. 2001, Johnson et al. 2003, Zenger et al. 2003) and to provide a temporal framework for phylogenetic reconstruction. Two sets of PCR primers have been developed to amplify the control region in wild turkeys. One set amplifies a product of approximately 1,300 base pairs (Mock et al. 2001, 2002), and the other set amplifies a smaller product of about 500 base pairs (Latch 2004, Latch et al. 2006*b*). In wild turkeys, control region sequences exhibit substantial variability at the subspecies and population levels. Questions concerning sex-specific processes, such as sex-biased dispersal and introgression, will benefit from the use of maternally inherited markers such as the control region (e.g., Latch et al. 2006*b*).

Cytochrome b.—The mitochondrial cytochrome b gene is a relatively large mitochondrial gene that codes for a protein that has been well studied with respect to structure and function (Howell and Gilbert 1988, Tron et al. 1991, Crozier and Crozier 1992). This gene as a whole evolves relatively slowly and therefore is fairly conserved across taxonomic groups, although the third codon positions within the gene can show higher levels of polymorphism than first or second positions. Because of the conserved nature of this gene, sequence polymorphisms at the DNA and amino acid level often provide information at higher levels of biological organization (e.g., species, subspecies) than might be achieved for more rapidly evolving markers such as microsatellites. Although cytochrome b has most often been used to describe genetic relationships between subspecies, species, or genera, it may sometimes be suitable for analyses at lower levels of biological organization (i.e., among populations; Wenink et al. 1993). Cytochrome b DNA amplification and sequencing methods have been developed in wild turkeys, yielding high-quality sequence data from a 500 base pair portion of the cytochrome b gene (Latch 2004, Latch et al. 2006*a*). Although there is not a substantial amount of diversity in this region, pilot studies suggest that cytochrome b sequences may be practical for comparisons among eastern (eastern [*M. g. silvestris*], Florida [*M. g. osceola*], and Rio Grande [*M. g. intermedia*]) and western (Merriam's [*M. g. merriami*] and Gould's [*M. g. mexicano*]) subspecies of the wild turkey (Latch 2004).

APPLICATIONS IN WILD TURKEY MANAGEMENT

Subspecies-level Applications

Subspecies Delineation in Naturally-occurring Populations

Subspecies are taxonomic units thought to represent evolutionary lineages below the species level. There is broad agreement among biologists that genetic variation below the species level could be important for the evolutionary flexibility of the species (Mitton and Grant 1984, Allendorf and Leary 1986). In the wild turkey, subspecies designations coincide with broad geographic/ecotypic regions and are presumed to represent units with some degree of common ancestry and local adaptation, which has been achieved over many thousands of years of evolutionary experience. Subspecies boundaries are an important management concept, because translocations of birds from one area to another may lead to the genetic "swamping" of locally adapted populations. Because translocation is one of the most widely used management practices for the wild turkey, understanding of historical relationships among subspecies is critical to the selection of appropriate source stock for translocations.

Mock et al. (2002) used a combination of DNA-based markers, both nuclear (AFLPs and microsatellites) and mitochondrial (control region DNA sequences), to characterize historical patterns of genetic diversity in relict wild turkey populations from each of the 5 recognized subspecies, and to assess the genetic validity of current subspecies designations (see range map available at http://www.nwtf.org/images/range_map_large.jpg or in Tapley et al. *this volume*). All 3 marker types showed less genetic diversity in the Gould's subspecies than in the other subspecies. Relationships among subspecies suggested by AFLP and control region data corroborated our understanding of historical habitat continuity. Microsatellite data suggested somewhat different evolutionary relationships among the subspecies. Mock et al. (2002) suggested that the relatively small number of microsatellite loci and the weak statistical support for the groupings may have led to the alternate pattern; however, adding 9 additional microsatellite loci and screening a subset of the samples used in Mock et al. (2002) did not change the inferred relationships among subspecies (Latch 2004). Differences in the evolutionary relationships among groups inferred by different marker systems are

not uncommon. Marker-related phenomena such as homoplasy can confound estimates of divergence times and relationships among groups, particularly at higher levels of biological organization. However, the inability of microsatellite markers to correctly resolve evolutionary relationships among wild turkey subspecies does not preclude their use at the subspecies level for classification purposes (see *Subspecies identification and hybridization in translocated populations* section below).

Latch (2004) performed a preliminary assessment of the utility of cytochrome b gene sequences for recreating the evolutionary relationships among wild turkey subspecies. These data indicate that although the differences between eastern (eastern, Florida, and Rio Grande) and western turkeys (Merriam's and Gould's) are substantial, the relatively slow rate of evolution within the cytochrome b gene has resulted in little or no structuring among subspecies within these broad regional groups.

Subspecies Identification and Hybridization in Translocated Populations

Although translocations have been a critical component of the successful restoration and expansion of wild turkey in North America (Kennamer and Kennamer 1996), the genetic implications of these translocations are poorly understood. Programs to reintroduce turkeys into previously occupied habitats, or to introduce them outside their historical range, often have not considered traditional species or subspecies ranges. Such programs threaten to disrupt historical patterns of genetic diversity and gene flow, which potentially could lead to irretrievable loss of genetic records of populations (Avise 2004), increased homogenization of subspecies and the loss of unique, locally adapted forms, not to mention forced extinctions of native populations (Avise 2004). Furthermore, some of these programs have led to situations in which multiple subspecies or variants now co-occur in regions where no such associations historically existed. Such situations have immediate implications for local hybridization between subspecies, and also mean that the best source stock for a translocation may no longer be that which is geographically closest. Before evolutionarily significant trajectories within the subspecies are completely eroded by human-mediated movements, it is important to understand their historical and contemporary distributions as well as the underlying genetic basis for differentiation among them.

DNA-based markers, including microsatellites, AFLPs, and mitochondrial control region sequences, can be used to determine the origin of an individual bird that has been translocated or that has migrated from one region to another (Paetkau et al. 1995, Rannala and Mountain 1997, Cornuet et al. 1999, Pritchard et al. 2000). Microsatellites are particularly promising for this application, because of their high level of polymorphism, their codominance, and the replicability of data within and among laboratories.

In southeastern Arizona, wild turkey managers

were concerned that efforts to reintroduce the Gould's subspecies into its historical range had been impeded by previous reintroductions of Merriam's turkeys into the area. Mock et al. (2001) used molecular markers to determine whether the turkeys currently inhabiting the Huachuca Mountains in southeastern Arizona were descended from the Gould's turkeys translocated there in the 1980s, or if interbreeding had occurred with descendents of Merriam's turkeys introduced to the area in 1950. Given the utility of these markers for distinguishing wild turkey subspecies (i.e., Mock et al. 2002), the authors used a combination of AFLPs, microsatellites, and control region sequences. They found that turkeys in the Huachuca Mountains consistently grouped with reference individuals from the Gould's subspecies (from Mexico) rather than with reference Merriam's turkeys from central Arizona (Mock et al. 2001). Thus, these data strongly indicated that the wild turkey population in the Huachuca Mountains was descended from the translocations of Gould's turkeys made in the 1980s, and showed no evidence of interbreeding with the Merriam's subspecies. Each of these 3 markers performed extremely well in this study, providing managers with several cost-efficient methods for distinguishing Merriam's and Gould's subspecies.

In Kansas, extensive translocation efforts have confounded subspecies distributions throughout the state. Today, 3 subspecies of wild turkey are believed to co-occur in Kansas—eastern, Rio Grande, and Merriam's. Given the likely disruption of historical subspecies structure within the state, and the inability of morphological methods to unambiguously resolve the subspecific status of turkeys, DNA-based methods were used to address these concerns. Microsatellites (Latch et al. 2006*a*) and control region and cytochrome b sequences (Latch 2004) were employed to characterize the genetic variability of wild turkey populations throughout Kansas, in an effort to clarify the current distribution of pure and mixed turkey subspecies. These molecular data were able to delineate subspecies boundaries and detect zones of hybridization between them. Furthermore, these data clearly indicated areas in which undocumented translocations significantly impacted the subspecific composition of turkeys in particular regions.

In the Davis Mountains of Texas and within nearby Rio Grande turkey populations, Latch et al. (2006*b*) assessed the subspecific status and degree of hybridization of individuals within an introduced population of Merriam's turkeys. Data from the Merriam's source population in New Mexico was used as a baseline reference for the genetic characteristics of the Merriam's subspecies. Nineteen years following the introduction event, microsatellite data indicated that the genetic integrity of the introduced population of Merriam's turkeys in the Davis Mountains Preserve has been eroded by both immigration from and hybridization with nearby Rio Grande populations. Data from the mitochondrial control region allowed for further characterization of parental contributions to hybrid individuals, and indicated that most hybrids were the result of immigrant Rio Grande males mating with resident Merriam's females.

Domestic Introgression

Early in the history of wild turkey translocation programs, managers considered the potential utility of game-farm or domestic turkeys as source stock for translocations into the wild. One concern was that the long history of artificial selection in non-wild stock had left these turkeys with insufficient genetic diversity for success in the wild. In 1985, Stangel et al. (1992) initiated a survey to characterize levels of genetic diversity in eastern wild turkeys, game-farm turkeys, and domestic turkeys. Using allozyme markers, the authors found significant differences in the distribution of allele frequencies among the 3 groups. Wild turkeys exhibited levels of genetic diversity comparable to that of other native game birds, whereas domestic turkeys possessed significantly less genetic diversity than wild or game farm turkeys. Game-farm turkeys exhibited a large range in genetic variability, likely due to the wide variety of different breeding strategies used by game farmers and the many different types of farms sampled for this study (Stangel et al. 1992). The authors did not find sufficient allozyme differentiation among wild, game-farm, and domestic turkeys to permit identification of domestic introgression in wild stock. However, a project is currently underway to screen a variety of DNA-based markers to assess their utility for the differentiation of wild turkeys from domestic breeds. A higher level of variability in DNA-based markers as compared to allozyme markers increases the probability of finding ways to detect domestic introgression into wild turkey stock.

Population-level Applications

Genetic Bottlenecks/Founder Effects

Genetic bottlenecks, resulting in a loss of genetic diversity, can occur as a result of genetic drift when a population is reduced in size for many generations (Nei et al. 1975). Founder effects, a related phenomenon, refer to the change in allelic composition when a small subset of one population is used to establish a new population, leading to allele frequencies that differ from those of the original population. In both phenomena, the effect is more pronounced when the bottlenecked or founding population is small (Baker and Moeed 1987, Merila et al. 1996, Mock et al. 2004). Populations established via translocation programs are at risk for diversity losses and changes in allelic composition as a result of both processes. A number of empirical studies have demonstrated significant reductions of genetic variability in translocated wildlife populations relative to their sources (Fitzsimmons et al. 1997, Williams et al. 2000, Williams et al. 2002, 2003*b*). Translocated populations also may exhibit shifts in allele frequency distributions relative to their source (Fitzsimmons et al. 1997, Luikart et al. 1998, Rowe et al. 1998, Williams et al. 2000), relative to other native populations (Baker and Moeed 1987, Perez et al. 1998, Stephen et al. 2005*b*), or relative to theoretical expectations (Scribner and Stuwe 1994, Fitzsimmons et al. 1997). Many, if not most, extant wild turkey populations have been established as a result of translocation, both within and beyond historical range boundaries. As a result the loss of genetic diversity in populations and shifts in allelic frequency distributions are potentially very serious issues in wild turkey management.

Leberg (1991) used allozyme markers to determine if populations of wild turkeys established as a result of translocations had higher levels of genetic differentiation among populations than turkeys that have not experienced founder events. Although the total amount of genetic differentiation he found was low, likely due to the time of sample collection (see *Social and Behavioral Dynamics* section below) and the low variability of allozymes, it nonetheless was evident that reintroduced wild turkey populations exhibited higher levels of genetic differentiation among populations (presumably due to genetic drift occurring independently among populations) than did relict populations that had not experienced severe reductions in size.

Ten years later, Mock et al. (2001) used microsatellite, control region, and AFLP data to detect reduced genetic diversity in a reintroduced population of Gould's turkeys in the Huachuca Mountains of southeastern Arizona compared to relict Gould's turkey populations in Mexico. Thus, Mock et al. (2001) recommended that although this population is stable, it may benefit from supplementation of turkeys from the more diverse relict populations.

Mock et al. (2004) assessed the genetic impact of 3 well-documented translocation events in the Merriam's subspecies, each occurring approximately 50 years ago. These translocations differed in the number of source individuals used, the number of trapping sites used to capture source individuals, and the size of the habitat into which founders were established. Microsatellite data indicated that all 3 translocations exhibited reduced genetic diversity relative to their founding populations, including 1 translocated population that is now very large and robust. Unfortunately, these results suggest that losses in genetic diversity are a common consequence of translocations, even under the best of circumstances. On the basis of their findings, Mock et al. (2004) recommended particular caution in the practice of "serial translocations", where translocated populations become the source for further translocation.

Gene Flow Among Local Populations

At a regional scale, if populations within a region exchange migrants (gene flow), the potential negative effects associated with genetic drift and low population sizes may be alleviated (Wright 1978, Allendorf 1983). Furthermore, the evolution of newly established populations is not limited by the genetic contribution of founders if gene flow among regional populations is possible. However, if dispersal among populations is low, genetic similarities between a reintroduced population and its source may persist.

Allozyme, microsatellite, and control region data have been used to characterize interactions among reintroduced populations and between reintroduced and native populations (Leberg et al. 1994, Latch and Rhodes 2005). Leberg et al. (1994) utilized allozymes to determine whether the genetic similarities among populations were more affected by geographic proximity or by shared reintroduction histories. The authors found that reintroduced populations from common sources were more similar than expected given their geographic proximity, even decades after the reintroduction events. Therefore, it seems that although dispersal likely has occurred, it has not resulted in a detectable relationship between genetic and geographic distance, as would be expected in naturally occurring populations. These results also suggested that while founders make genetic contributions to the populations into which they are released, they may have a minimal effect on nearby populations (although the reverse is not necessarily true; see *Subspecies identification and hybridization in translocated populations* section above).

Latch and Rhodes (2005*a*) also used microsatellite and control region sequences to demonstrate that the genetic relationships between reintroduced populations and their sources are not quickly eroded by dispersal from nearby populations, corroborating the findings of Leberg et al. (1994). Taking advantage of well-documented reintroduction histories of turkey populations in Indiana, the authors assessed the degree to which gene flow among reintroduced populations has obscured genetic signatures left by the founding events. Effects were measured in regions characterized by high habitat continuity and a high potential for dispersal among populations and as well as in regions where the opportunity for dispersal among populations was reduced due to the low density of turkey populations. The genetic signatures left by reintroduction events were strongly evident in most populations, even after several decades. Latch and Rhodes (2005*a*) further showed that the density of populations in a region did not significantly affect these relationships. For each of the reintroduced populations, the authors were able to identify the magnitude of the effect of dispersers, as well as their most likely population of origin. Despite a few cases in which the apparent presence of individuals from prior reintroductions significantly impacted the genetic structure of populations, the results of this study indicated an overall paucity of gene flow among reintroduced populations in Indiana, even where the opportunity for dispersal appeared high.

Social and Behavioral Dynamics

The underlying social organization of most wild species often can be difficult to resolve (Sugg et al. 1996). The social structure, mating tactics, and movement behaviors of a species ultimately sculpt the temporal and spatial patterns of genetic structure that it exhibits (Chesser 1991*a*, Chesser 1991*b*, Chesser et al. 1993). Therefore, examination of fine-scaled genetic structure in wild species can in turn lead to a clearer understanding of social and behavioral dynamics. In the wild turkey, interpreting patterns of genetic structure within localized regions may provide insight into the social organization of wintering flocks, interactions among flocks, and the mechanisms involved in the dissociation of flocks in the spring.

Leberg (1991) found that within regions, almost none of the allozyme variability he found in wild turkeys was accounted for by differences among sampling localities. However, the opposite result was found in Kansas, where allozymes revealed significant genetic variability among wintering flocks (Rhodes et al. 1995). Boone and Rhodes (1996) also found significant allozyme differentiation between two winter flocks in South Carolina. Latch and Rhodes (2005*b*) used microsatellites, control region sequences, and previously-collected allozyme data (Boone and Rhodes 1996) to investigate the reason for this dichotomy regarding genetic differentiation at a local scale. It appears that timing and method of sample collection are responsible for the discrepancy between estimates of local genetic structure. Leberg (1991) utilized samples from male turkeys collected during the spring, whereas Rhodes et al. (1995) and Boone and Rhodes (1996) used samples from both sexes of turkeys collected during winter trapping activities. In winter, samples are collected from discrete flocks, and thus genetic differentiation can be detected among them (Rhodes et al. 1995, Boone and Rhodes 1996, Latch and Rhodes 2005*b*). However, flocks dissociate in the spring; thus, spring-collected samples from a given geographic location contain turkeys from multiple flocks and do not exhibit local genetic structure (Leberg 1991, Latch and Rhodes 2005*b*). These results emphasize the need to interpret genetic data in light of the social organization of the species at the time of sample collection. These studies also have demonstrated the utility of molecular markers, both protein- and DNA-based, for investigating small scale genetic structure.

Very recently, microsatellite loci have been used to investigate kin selection and cooperative courtship in the wild turkey (Krakauer 2005). He used genetic data to estimate relatedness among individuals in a flock, and combined with data on reproductive success was able to demonstrate that the indirect fitness benefits obtained by non-breeding subordinate males offset the cost of helping. It is rare that a long-standing controversial theory such as kin selection can be confirmed, but this certainly is an example of where incredible progress can be made when the appropriate molecular tool is applied to a species in which the biology is well understood.

Individual-level Applications

Identification of individual animals has a multitude of potential applications for wildlife forensics: assignment of population or subspecies origin, studies of dis-

persal and migration, and detection of hybridization and introgression (Manel et al. 2002, Randi and Lucchini 2002, Cegelski et al. 2003, Haig et al. 2004, McLoughlin et al. 2004). Cases of poaching also could benefit from individual identification, where individual animals may be classified by location of harvest.

Additionally, mark-recapture studies based on individual molecular-based identification could be a valuable non-invasive method for estimating population sizes in managed populations (Mowat et al. 2002, Wilson et al. 2003). At a local scale, individual identification and measures of relatedness among individuals can be used to characterize family groups in wildlife studies, providing insight into behaviors such as paternity and mate choice (Okada and Tamate 2000, Kerth et al. 2002, Nievergelt et al. 2002).

Microsatellite loci are currently the marker of choice for identifying individual turkeys. High levels of polymorphism in microsatellites mean that this marker type is generally associated with lower probabilities of identity (the probability that two randomly chosen individuals will have the same multilocus genotype) than other marker types. Using 10 of the microsatellite loci most commonly used in turkeys, we can achieve an overall probability of identity of 3.5×10^{-14}, almost ensuring that species-wide, no two turkeys will share a multilocus genotype (Latch 2004). This attests to the tremendous power of multilocus microsatellite genotypes in individual identification. Highly variable microsatellites have been used successfully to assign individual turkeys to a population or subspecies (Latch and Rhodes 2005, Latch et al. 2006*b*) and to identify migrant individuals into a recently established population (Latch et al. 2006*b*). Assignment tests using the available set of microsatellite loci proved to be extremely useful for detecting and characterizing hybridization between wild turkey subspecies (Latch et al. 2006*a, b*). Ongoing research will determine the utility of these markers for detecting introgression of domestic genes into wild stock and for providing evidence in poaching cases.

CONCLUSIONS

A suite of molecular markers has been optimized for use in the wild turkey, representing an array of marker systems (protein- and DNA-based markers), inheritance patterns (biparental and maternal), and mutation rates. The body of existing research using molecular markers in the wild turkey illustrates their power for applications ranging from the subspecies-level to the individual-level, and for questions ranging from species evolution to forensics.

Highly variable markers such as nuclear microsatellites are particularly useful for elucidating genetic structure among turkey populations, and even for identifying individual birds. Maternally-inherited mitochondrial DNA markers such as cytochrome b and control region sequences exhibit less variability among individuals, but may be indispensable in questions regarding hybridization, sex-biased dispersal, and female lineage establishment. Low levels of genetic variability in allozymes have not precluded their use in the wild turkey; however, high levels of variability in DNA-based markers make them ideal candidates for studies of genetic variation in wild turkeys. Fortunately, several studies, including one in the wild turkey, have shown that allozyme data corroborates with data obtained from DNA-based markers (Spruell et al. 2003, Zhou et al. 2003, King and Eackles 2004, Latch 2004).

It has become apparent that the tools of modern molecular biology hold great value for wild turkey management. It also is clear that decisions pertaining to the selection of genetic markers, both in terms of inheritance patterns and rates of evolution, are important if these tools are to be applied successfully at varying scales of biological organization. In the wild turkey, appropriate utilization of molecular tools has led to a better understanding of the evolutionary history of turkeys, their behavior, and their population dynamics, which in turn can be used to manage populations to optimize growth and long-term stability. Similarly, genetic evaluations of previous translocations have advanced our understanding of founder events and post-translocation processes within and among populations.

The future of wild turkey management looks bright. The application of molecular tools will continue to advance our understanding of wild turkey biology and ecology, thereby improving our ability to effectively manage this species. Recent advances in our ability to determine the genetic composition (subspecies status) of individual animals, or even entire regions, have profound implications for the future of wild turkey management. We are now able to objectively determine what subspecies exist in what areas, and if turkeys in that area show evidence of hybridization with another subspecies. Another area of wild turkey management likely to show incredible growth is the prosecution of poaching cases. The ability of molecular tools to enable identification of individual animals and analysis methodology to assign individuals to a population of origin means that in many instances, poached animals can be objectively identified with confidence. Molecular tools may also advance our understanding of wild turkey biology, particularly at a local scale. We should be able to determine the genetic relationships among individuals within flocks, and such data could be combined with radio-telemetry data to better understand the movements and associations of turkeys within a flock throughout the year. It is an exciting time to be involved in wild turkey management, and we feel that molecular tools offer a unique perspective by which we can optimize wild turkey translocation strategies and management programs to ensure the future of this species.

LITERATURE CITED

Abbott, C. L., and M. C. Double. 2003. Genetic structure, conservation genetics and evidence of speciation by range expansion in shy and white-capped albatrosses. Molecular Ecology 12:2953–2962.

Adams, J. R., B. T. Kelly, L. P. Waits. 2003. Using faecal DNA sampling and GIS to monitor hybridization between red wolves (*Canis rufus*) and coyotes (*Canis latrans*). Molecular Ecology 12:2175–2186.

Allendorf, F. W. 1983. Isolation, gene flow, and genetic differentiation among populations. Pages 51–65 *in* C. M. Schonewald-Cox, S. M. Chambers, B. MacBryde, and L. Thomas, editors. Genetics and conservation: a reference for managing wild animal and plant populations. Benjamin/Cummings, Menlo Park, California, USA.

———, and R. F. Leary. 1986. Heterozygosity and fitness in natural populations of animals. Pages 57–56 *in* M. E. Soulé, editor. Conservation biology: the science of scarcity and diversity. Sinauer, Sunderland, Massachusetts, USA.

Anderson, J. D., R. L. Honeycutt, R. A. Gonzales, K. L. Gee, L. C. Skow, R. L. Gallagher, D. A. Honeycutt, and R. W. DeYoung. 2002. Development of microsatellite DNA markers for the automated genetic characterization of white-tailed deer populations. Journal of Wildlife Management 66:67–74.

Avise, J. C. 2004. Molecular Markers, Natural History, and Evolution, Second edition. Sinauer Associates, Sunderland, Massachusetts, USA.

Baker, A. J., and A. Moeed. 1987. Rapid genetic differentiation and founder effect in colonizing populations of common mynahs (*Acridotheres tristis*). Evolution 41:525–538.

Beheler, A. A. 2001. Characterization of dispersal and reproductive strategies in the eastern phoebe (*Sayornis phoebe*). Dissertation, Purdue University, West Lafayette, Indiana, USA.

———, and O. E. Rhodes, Jr. 2003. Within-season prevalence of extra pair young in broods of double-brooded and mate-faithful eastern phoebes (*Sayornis phoebe*) in Indiana. Auk 120:1054–1061.

Boone, M. D., and O. E. Rhodes, Jr. 1996. Genetic structure among subpopulations of the eastern wild turkey (*Meleagris gallopavo silvestris*). American Midland Naturalist 135:168–171.

Boyce, W. M., R. R. Ramey, T. C. Rodwell, E. S. Rubin, and R. S. Singer. 1999. Population subdivision among desert bighorn sheep (*Ovis canadensis*) ewes revealed by mitochondrial DNA analysis. Molecular Ecology 8:99–106.

Boyd, D. K., S. H. Forbes, D. H. Pletscher, and F. W. Allendorf. 2001. Identification of Rocky Mountain gray wolves. Wildlife Society Bulletin 29:78–85.

Carew, P. J., G. J. Adcock, and R. A. Mulder. 2003. Microsatellite loci for paternity assessment in the black swan (*Cygnus atratus*: Aves). Molecular Ecology Notes 3:1–3.

Cegelski, C. C., L. P. Waits, and N. J. Anderson. 2003. Assessing population structure and gene flow in Montana wolverines (*Gulo gulo*) using assignment-based approaches. Molecular Ecology 12:2907–2918.

Chesser, R. K. 1991a. Gene diversity and female philopatry. Genetics 127:437–447.

———. 1991b. Influence of gene flow and breeding tactics on gene diversity within populations. Genetics 129:573–583.

———, O. E. Rhodes, D. W. Sugg, and A. Schnabel. 1993. Effective sizes for subdivided populations. Genetics 135:1221–1232.

Cornuet, J. M., S. Piry, G. Luikart, A. Estoup, and M. Solignac. 1999. New methods employing multilocus genotypes to select or exclude populations as origins of individuals. Genetics 153:1989–2000.

Cronin, M. A. 1991. Mitochondrial DNA in wildlife forensic science: species identification of tissues. Wildlife Society Bulletin 19:94–105.

Crozier, R. H., and Y. C. Crozier. 1992. The cytochrome *b* and ATPase genes of honeybee mitochondrial DNA. Molecular Biology and Evolution 9:474–482.

DeWoody, J. A., D. E. Fletcher, M. MacKiewicz, S. D. Wilkins, and J. C. Avise. 2000. The genetic mating system of spotted sunfish (*Lepomis punctatus*): Mate numbers and the influence of male reproductive parasites. Molecular Ecology 9: 2119–2128.

———, ———, S. D. Wilkins, W. S. Nelson, and J. C. Avise. 1998. Molecular genetic dissection of spawning, parentage, and reproductive tactics in a population of redbreast sunfish, *Lepomis auritus.* Evolution 52:1802–1810.

DeYoung, R. W., S. Demarais, and R. L. Honeycutt, R. A. Gonzales, K. L. Gee, and J. D. Anderson. 2003. Evaluation of a DNA microsatellite panel useful for genetic exclusion studies in white-tailed deer. Wildlife Society Bulletin 31: 220–232.

Donoghue, A. M., T. S. Sonstegard, L. M. King, E. J. Smith, and D. W. Burt. 1999. Turkey sperm mobility influences paternity in the context of competitive fertilization. Biology of Reproduction 61:422–427.

Eanes, W. F. 1999. Analysis of section on enzyme polymorphisms. Annual Review of Ecology and Systematics 30: 301–326.

Escaravage, N., S. Questiau, A. Pornon, B. Doche, and P. Taberlet. 1998. Clonal diversity in a *Rhododendron ferrugineum L.* (Ericaceae) population inferred from AFLP markers. Molecular Ecology 7:975–982.

Fitzsimmons, N. N., S. W. Buskirk, and M. H. Smith. 1997. Genetic changes in reintroduced Rocky Mountain bighorn sheep populations. Journal of Wildlife Management 61: 863–872.

Frankham, R., J. D. Ballou, and D. A. Briscoe. 2002. Introduction to Conservation Genetics. Cambridge University Press, Cambridge, United Kingdom.

Gabor, C. R., and C. C. Nice. 2004. Genetic variation among populations of eastern newts, *Notophthalmus viridescens*: A preliminary analysis based on allozymes. Herpetologica 60: 373–386.

Guglich, E. A., P. J. Wilson, and B. N. White. 1994. Forensic application of repetitive DNA markers to the species identification of animal tissues. Journal of Forensic Sciences 39: 353–361.

Haig, S. M., T. D. Mullins, E. D. Forsman, P. W. Trail, and L. Wennerberg. 2004. Genetic identification of spotted owls, barred owls, and their hybrids: legal implications of hybrid identity. Conservation Biology 18:1347–1357.

Harris, H. 1966. Enzyme polymorphisms in man. Proceedings of the Royal Society of London, Series B 164:298–310.

Hedrick, P. W. 1999. Highly variable loci and their interpretation in evolution and conservation. Evolution 53:313–318.

Howell, N., and K. Gilbert. 1988. Mutational analysis of the mouse mitochondrial cytochrome *b* gene. Journal of Molecular Biology 203:607–618.

Huang, H.-B., Y.-Q. Song, M. Hsei, R. Zahorchak, J. Chiu, C. Teuscher, and E. J. Smith. 1999. Development and characterization of genetic mapping resources for the turkey (*Meleagris gallopavo*). Journal of Heredity 90:240–242.

Hubby, J. L., and R. C Lewontin. 1966. A molecular approach to studying genic variation in natural populations I. The number of alleles at different loci in *Drosophila pseudoobscura.* Genetics 54:577–594.

Jeffreys, A. J., N. J. Royle, I. Patel, J. A. L. Armour, A. MacLeod, A. Collick, I. C. Gray, R. Neumann, M. Gibbs, M. Crosier, M. Hill, E. Signer, and D. Monckton. 1991. Principles and recent advances in human DNA fingerprinting. Pages 1–19 *in* T. Burke, G. Dolf, A. J. Jeffreys, and R. Wolff, editors. DNA fingerprinting: approaches and applications. Birkhauser Verlag, Basel, Switzerland.

Johnson, F. M., C. G. Kanapi, R. H. Richardson, M. R. Wheeler, and W. S. Stone. 1966. An analysis of polymorphisms among isozyme loci in dark and light *Drosophila ananassae* strains from America and western Samoa. Proceedings of the National Academy of Sciences USA 56:119–125.

Johnson, J. A., J. E. Toepfer, and P. O. Dunn. 2003. Contrasting patterns of mitochondrial and microsatellite population structure in fragmented populations of greater prairie chickens. Molecular Ecology 12:3335–3347.

Kennamer, J. E., and M. C. Kennamer. 1996. Status and distribution of the wild turkey in 1994. Proceedings of the National Wild Turkey Symposium 7:203–211.

Kerth, G., K. Safi, and B. Konig. 2002. Mean colony relatedness is a poor predictor of colony structure and female philopatry in the communally breeding Bechstein's bat (*Myotis bechsteinii*). Behavioral Ecology and Sociobiology 52:203–210.

King, T. L., and M. S. Eackles. 2004. Microsatellite DNA markers for the study of horseshoe crab (*Limulus polyphemus*) population structure. Molecular Ecology Notes 4:394–396.

Krakauer, A. H. 2005. Kin selection and cooperative courtship in wild turkeys. Nature 434:69–72.

Kyle, C. J., C. S. Davis, and C. Strobeck. 2000. Microsatellite analysis of North American pine marten (*Martes martes*) populations from the Yukon and Northwest Territories. Canadian Journal of Zoology 78:1150–1157.

Latch, E. K. 2004. Population genetics of reintroduced wild turkeys: Insights into hybridization, gene flow, and social structure. Dissertation, Purdue University, West Lafayette, Indiana, USA.

———, and O. E. Rhodes. 2005. The effects of gene flow and population isolation on the genetic structure of reintroduced wild turkey populations: Are genetic signatures of source populations retained? Conservation Genetics 6:981–997.

———, and ———. 2006. Evidence for biases in estimates of genetic structure due to sampling scheme. Animal Conservation 9:308–315.

———, R. A. Applegate, and O. E. Rhodes, Jr. 2006*a*. Genetic composition of wild turkeys in Kansas following decades of translocations. Journal of Wildlife Management 70:in press.

———, L. A. Harveson, J. S. King, M. D. Hobson, and O. E. Rhodes, Jr. 2006*b*. Assessing hybridization in wildlife populations using molecular markers: A case study in wild turkeys. Journal of Wildlife Management 70:485–492.

———, E. J. Smith, and O. E. Rhodes. 2002. Isolation and characterization of microsatellite loci in wild and domestic turkeys (*Meleagris gallopavo*). Molecular Ecology Notes 2: 176–178.

Leberg, P. L. 1991. Influence of fragmentation and bottlenecks on genetic divergence of wild turkey populations. Conservation Biology 5:522–530.

———, P. W. Stangel, H. O. Hillestad, R. L. Marchinton, and M. H. Smith. 1994. Genetic structure of reintroduced wild turkey and white-tailed deer populations. Journal of Wildlife Management 58:698–711.

Levinson, G., and G. A. Gutman. 1987. Slipped-strand mispairing—a major mechanism for DNA sequence evolution. Molecular Biology and Evolution 4:203–221.

Lode, T. 2001. Mating system and genetic variance in a polygynous mustelid, the European polecat. Genes and Genetic Systems 76:221–227.

Luikart, G., W. B. Sherwin, B. M. Steele, and F. W. Allendorf. 1998. Usefulness of molecular markers for detecting population bottlenecks via monitoring genetic change. Molecular Ecology 7:963–974.

Manel, S., P. Bertier, and G. Luikart. 2002. Detecting wildlife poaching: identifying the origin of individuals with Bayesian assignment tests and multilocus genotypes. Conservation Biology 16:650–659.

McLoughlin, P. D., D. Paetkau, M. Duda, and S. Boutin. 2004. Genetic diversity and relatedness of boreal caribou populations in western Canada. Biological Conservation 118: 593–598.

Merila, J., M. Bjorklund, and A. Baker. 1996. The successful founder: genetics of introduced *Caruelis chloris* (greenfinch) populations in New Zealand. Heredity 77:410–422.

Miththapala, S., J. Seidensticker, and S. J. O'Brien. 1996. Phylogeographic subspecies recognition in leopards (*Panthera pardus*): molecular genetic variation. Conservation Biology 10:1115–1132.

Mitton, J. B. 1994. Molecular approaches to population biology. Annual Review of Ecology and Systematics 25:45–69.

———, and M. C. Grant. 1984. Associations among protein heterozygosity, growth rate, and developmental homeostasis. Annual Review of Ecology and Systematics 15:479–499.

Mock, K. E., E. K. Latch, and O. E. Rhodes. 2004. Assessing losses of genetic diversity due to translocations: long-term case histories in Merriam's turkey (*Meleagris gallopavo merriami*). Conservation Genetics 5:631–645.

———, T. C. Theimer, O. E. Rhodes, D. L. Greenberg, and P. Keim. 2002. Genetic variation across the historical range of the wild turkey (*Meleagris gallopavo*). Molecular Ecology 11:643–657.

———, ———, B. F. Wakeling, O. E. Rhodes, D. L. Greenberg, and P. Keim. 2001. Verifying the origins of a reintroduced population of Gould's wild turkey. Journal of Wildlife Management 65:871–879.

Mowat, G., and D. Paetkau. 2002. Estimation of marten *Martes americana* population size using hair capture and genetic tagging. Wildlife Biology 8:201–209.

Mueller, U. G., and L. L. Wolfenbarger. 1999. AFLP genotyping and fingerprinting. Trends in Ecology and Evolution 14:389–394.

Nei, M., T. Maruyama, and R. Chakraborty. 1975. The bottleneck effect and genetic variability in populations. Evolution 29:1–10.

Nevo, E., A. Beiles, and R. Ben-Shlomo. 1983. The evolutionary significance of genetic diversity: ecological, demographic, and life history correlates. Pages 172–206 *in* R. J. McIntyre, editor. Evolutionary dynamics of genetic diversity. Springer-Verlag, Heidelberg, Germany.

Nievergelt, C. M., T. Mutschler, A. T. C. Feistner, and D. S. Woodruff. 2002. Social system of alaotran gentle lemur (*Hapalemur griseus alaotrensis*): genetic characterization of group composition and mating system. Journal of Primatology 57:157–176.

Okada, A., and H. B. Tamate. 2000. Pedigree analysis of the Sika deer (*Cervus nippon*) using microsatellite markers. Zoological Science 17:335–340.

Paetkau, D., W. Calvert, I. Stirling, and C. Strobeck. 1995. Microsatellite analysis of population structure in Canadian polar bears. Molecular Ecology 4:347–354.

Perez, T., J. Albornoz, C. Nores, and A. Dominguez. 1998. Evaluation of genetic variability in introduced populations of red deer (*Cervus elaphus*) using DNA fingerprinting. Hereditas 129:85–89.

Piertney, S. B., A. D. C. MacColl, X. Lambin, R. Moss, and J. F. Dallas. 1999. Spatial distribution of genetic relatedness in a moorland population of red grouse (*Lagopus lagopus scoticus*). Biological Journal of the Linnean Society 68:317–331.

Pilgrim, K. L., D. K. Boyd, and S. H. Forbes. 1998. Testing for wolf-coyote hybridization in the Rocky Mountains using mitochondrial DNA. Journal of Wildlife Management 62:683–689.

Pope, T. R. 1998. Effects of demographic change on group kin structure and gene dynamics of populations of red howling monkeys. Journal of Mammalogy 79:692–712.

Pritchard, J. K., M. Stephens, and P. Donnelly. 2000. Inference of population structure using multilocus genotype data. Genetics 155:945–959.

Randi, E., and V. Lucchini. 2002. Detecting rare introgression of domestic dog genes into wild wolf (*Canis lupus*) populations by Bayesian admixture analysis of microsatellite variation. Conservation Genetics 3:31–45.

Rannala, B., and J. L. Mountain. 1997. Detecting immigration using multilocus genotypes. Proceedings of the National Academy of Sciences USA 94:9197–9201.

Reed, K. M., L. D. Chaves, M. K. Hall, T. P. Knutson, J. A. Rowe, and A. J. Torgerson. 2003. Microsatellite loci for genetic mapping in the turkey (*Meleagris gallopavo*). Animal Biotechnology 14:119–131.

———, ———, and J. A. Rowe. 2002. Twelve new turkey microsatellite loci. Poultry Science 81:1789–1791.

———, M. C. Roberts, J. Murtaugh, C. W. Beattie, and L. J. Alexander. 2000. Eight new dinucleotide microsatellite loci in turkey (*Meleagris gallopavo*). Animal Genetics 31:140–140.

Rhodes, O. E., D. J. Buford, M. S. Miller, and R. S. Lutz. 1995. Genetic structure of reintroduced Rio Grande wild turkeys in Kansas. Journal of Wildlife Management 59:771–775.

———, L. M. Smith, and R. K. Chesser. 1993. Temporal components of migrating and wintering American wigeon. Canadian Journal of Zoology 71:2229–2235.

Richardson, B. J., R. A. Hayes, S. H. Wheeler, and M. R. Yardin. 2002. Social structure, genetic structures, and dispersal strategies in Australian rabbit (*Oryctolagus cuniculus*) populations. Behavioral Ecology and Sociobiology 51:113–121.

Rogers, A. R. 1995. Genetic evidence for a Pleistocene population explosion. Evolution 49:608–615.

———, and H. Harpending. 1992. Population growth makes waves in the distribution of pairwise genetic differences. Molecular Biology and Evolution 9:552–569.

Rowe, G. T., J. C. Beebee, and T. Burke. 1998. Phylogeography of the natterjack toad *Bufo calamita* in Britain: genetic differentiation of native and translocated populations. Molecular Ecology 7:751–760.

Saetre, G. P., T. Borge, J. Lindell, T. Moum, C. R. Primmer, B. C. Sheldon, J. Haavie, A. Johnsen, and H. Ellegren. 2001. Speciation, introgressive hybridization and nonlinear rate of molecular evolution in flycatchers. Molecular Ecology 10:737–749.

Sarre, S. 1995. Mitochondrial DNA variation among populations of *Oedura reticulata* (Gekkkonidae) in remnant vegetation: implications for metapopulation structure and population decline. Molecular Ecology 4:395–405.

Schlötterer, C., and D. Tautz. 1992. Slippage synthesis of simple sequence DNA. Nucleic Acids Research 20:211–215.

Scribner, K. T., M. R. Petersen, R. L. Fields, S. L. Talbot, J. M. Pearce, and R. K. Chesser. 2001. Sex-biased gene flow in spectacled eiders (Anatidae): inferences from molecular markers with contrasting modes of inheritance. Evolution 55:2105–2115.

———, and M. Stuwe. 1994. Genetic relationships among alpine ibex *Capra ibex* populations re-established from a common ancestral source. Biological Conservation 69:137–143.

Shen, B. S. 1999. Development of DNA markers for cost effective surveys of genetic diversity in wild turkeys. Thesis, Purdue University, West Lafayette, Indiana, USA.

Sinclair, E. A., H. L. Black, and K. A Crandall. 2003. Population structure and paternity in an American black bear (*Ursus americanus*) population using microsatellite DNA. Western North American Naturalist 63:489–497.

———, N. J. Webb, A. D. Marchant, and C. R. Tidemann. 1996. Genetic variation in the little red flying fox *Pteropus scapulatus* (Chirpotera: Pteropodidae): implications for management. Biological Conservation 76:45–50.

Spruell, P., A. R. Hemmingsen, P. J. Howell, N. Kanda, and F. W. Allendorf. 2003. Conservation genetics of bull trout: geographic distribution of variation at microsatellite loci. Conservation Genetics 4:17–29.

Stangel, P. W., P. L. Leberg, and J. I. Smith. 1992. Systematics and population genetics. Pages 18–28 *in* J. G. Dickson, editor. The wild turkey: biology and management. Stackpole Books, Harrisburg, Pennsylvania, USA.

Stapley, J., C. M. Hayes, and J. S. Keogh. 2003. Population genetic differentiation and multiple paternity determined by novel microsatellite markers from the mountain log skink

(*Pseudemoia entrecasteauxii*). Molecular Ecology Notes 3: 291–293.

Stephen, C. L., J. C. deVos, T. L. Lee, J. W. Bickham, J. R. Heffelfinger, and O. E. Rhodes, Jr. 2005a. Genetic distinction of the sonoran pronghorn (*Antilocapra americana sonoriensis*). Journal of Mammalogy 86: 782–792.

———, D. G. Whittaker, D. Gillis, L. L. Cox, and O. E. Rhodes, Jr. 2005b. Genetic consequences of reintroductions: an example from Oregon pronghorn antelope. Journal of Wildlife Management 69:1463–1474.

Storz, J. F., H. R. Bhat, and T. H. Kunz. 2001. Genetic consequences of polygyny and social structure in an Indian fruit bat, *Cynopterus sphinx*. I. Inbreeding, outbreeding, and population subdivision. Evolution 55:1215–1223.

Sugg, D. W., R. K. Chesser, F. S. Dobson, and J. L. Hoogland. 1996. Population genetics meets behavioral ecology. Trends in Ecology and Evolution 11:338–342.

Tapley, J. L., R. K. Abernethy, and J. E. Kennamer. *This volume.* Status and distribution of the wild turkey in 2004. Proceedings of the National Wild Turkey Symposium 9:*This volume.*

Tron, T. M. Crimi, A.-M. Colson and M. Degli Esposti. 1991. Structure/function relationships in mitochondrial cytochrome *b* revealed by the kinetic and circular dichronic properties of two yeast inhibitor-resistant mutants. European Journal of Biochemistry 199:753–760.

van Hooft, W. F., A. F. Groen, and H. H. T. Prins. 2003. Genic structure of African buffalo herds based on variation at the mitochondrial D-loop and autosomal microsatellite loci: evidence for male-biased gene flow. Conservation Genetics 4: 467–477.

van Staaden, M. J., G. R. Michener, and R. K. Chesser. 1996. Spatial analysis of microgeographic genetic structure in Richardson's ground squirrels. Canadian Journal of Zoology 74:1187–1195.

Verma, S. K., and L. Singh. 2003. Novel universal established identity of an enormous number of animal species for forensic application. Molecular Ecology Notes 3:28–31.

Vos, P., R. Hogers, M. Bleeker, M. Reijans, T. Vandelee, M. Hornes, A. Frijters, J. Pot, J. Peleman, M. Kuiper, and M. Zabeau. 1995. AFLP—a new technique for DNA fingerprinting. Nucleic Acids Research 23:4407–4414.

Wenink, P. W., A. J. Baker, and M. G. J. Tilanus. 1993. Hyper-variable control-region sequences reveal global population structuring in a long-distance migrant shorebird, the dunlin (*Calidris alpina*). Proceedings of the National Academy of Sciences USA 90:94–98.

Whitehead, A., S. L. Anderson, K. M. Kuivila, J. L. Roach, and B. May. 2003. Genetic variation among interconnected populations of *Catostomus occidentalis*: implications for distinguishing impacts of contaminants from biogeographic structuring. Molecular Ecology 12:2817–2833.

Williams, C. L., K. Blejwas, J. J. Johnston, and M. M. Jaeger. 2003a. A coyote in sheep's clothing: predator identification from saliva. Wildlife Society Bulletin 31:926–932.

———, B. Lundrigan, and O. E. Rhodes, Jr. 2003b. Analysis of microsatellite variation in tule elk. Journal of Wildlife Management 68:109–119.

———, T. Serfass, R. Cogan, and O. E. Rhodes. 2002. Microsatellite variation in the reintroduced Pennsylvania elk herd. Molecular Ecology 11:1299–1310.

Williams, R. N., O. E. Rhodes, and T. L. Serfass. 2000. Assessment of genetic variance among source and reintroduced fisher populations. Journal of Mammalogy 81:895–907.

Wilson, G. J., A. C. Frantz, L. C. Pope, T. J. Roper, T. A. Burke, C. L. Cheeseman, and R. J. Delahay. 2003. Estimation of badger abundance in faecal DNA typing. Journal of Applied Ecology 40:658–666.

Wright, S. 1978. Evolution and the genetics of populations, Vol. 4: variability within and among natural populations. University of Chicago Press, Chicago, Illinois, USA.

Zenger, K. R., M. D. B. Eldridge, and D. W. Cooper. 2003. Intraspecific variation, sex-biased dispersal, and phylogeography of the eastern grey kangaroo (*Macropus giganteus*). Heredity 91:153–162.

Zenuto, R. R., E. A. Lacey, and C. Busch. 1999. DNA fingerprinting reveals polygyny in the subterranean rodent *Ctenomys talarum*. Molecular Ecology 8:1529–1532.

Zhou, H. F., Z. W. Xie, and S. Ge. 2003. Microsatellite analysis of genetic diversity and population genetic structure of a wild rice (*Oryza rufipogon Griff.*) in China. Theoretical and Applied Genetics 107:332–339.

Zink, R. M., and D. L. Dittmann. 1993. Gene flow, refugia, and evolution of geographic variation in the song sparrow (*Melospiza melodia*). Evolution 47:717–729.

Emily Latch is a post-doctoral research assistant under the supervision of Gene Rhodes in the Department of Forestry and Natural Resources at Purdue University. Her main research interests concern population and applied wildlife genetics. Her dissertation work on population genetics of reintroduced wild turkeys was completed in 2004 and included studies of gene flow, hybridization, and social structure. Currently, she is collaborating on a comprehensive phylogeographic study of mule deer throughout their range. Emily also has collaborated on projects using population genetic tools to address questions such as bighorn sheep colonization, fisher genetic structure and recolonization, and Louisiana water thrush migration patterns.

Karen Mock is an assistant professor in the Forest, Range, and Wildlife Sciences Department at Utah State University, where she has an active conservation/wildlife genetics laboratory. Her research interests are taxonomically broad, including not only wild turkeys but also grouse, a variety of western fish, pine beetles, and freshwater mussels.

Gene Rhodes is a full Professor at Purdue University in the Department of Forestry and Natural Resources. He has published 98 peer-reviewed articles and has trained over 20 graduate students and postdocs in the past 10 years. His research focus is in wildlife ecology and genetics, including studies of the genetic consequences of species reintroduction programs, the use of genetic markers in applied wildlife management and conservation programs, the use of genetic markers to elucidate mating systems, movement behavior, and population structure of wildlife species and sustainability of wildlife species in human-dominated landscapes with an emphasis on the resolution of human-wildlife conflicts.

9th National Wild Turkey Symposium

Wild Turkey Management:
Accomplishments, Strategies, and Opportunities
——— Grand Rapids, Michigan ———

USING REMOTE CAMERAS FOR POPULATION ESTIMATION OF GOULD'S TURKEYS IN SOUTHEASTERN ARIZONA

Shelli A. Dubay[1,2]
Research Branch,
Arizona Game and Fish Department,
2221 West Greenway Road,
Phoenix, AZ 85023, USA

Brian F. Wakeling
Game Branch,
Arizona Game and Fish Department,
2221 West Greenway Road,
Phoenix, AZ 85023, USA

Timothy D. Rogers
Research Branch,
Arizona Game and Fish Department,
2221 West Greenway Road,
Phoenix, AZ 85023, USA

Susan R. Boe
Research Branch,
Arizona Game and Fish Department,
2221 West Greenway Road,
Phoenix, AZ 85023, USA

Michael J. Rabe
Game Branch,
Arizona Game and Fish Department,
2221 West Greenway Road,
Phoenix, AZ 85023, USA

Abstract: We evaluated population estimation techniques for Gould's turkeys (*Meleagris gallopavo mexicana*) in southeastern Arizona. The Huachuca Mountain population of Gould's turkeys could be used as a source to further restoration efforts, but due to its unknown population size, we had concerns regarding overexploiting a limited population. Because these turkeys are limited in range within the United States and occupy isolated mountain ranges in Arizona (i.e., closed population), these Gould's turkeys provide a unique opportunity to compare and contrast techniques for estimating population size. Our study population in the Huachuca Mountains, Arizona, was reestablished following extirpation with the release of 9 and 12 turkeys in 1983 and 1987, respectively. We baited and trapped Gould's turkeys during winter 2000, 2001, and 2002 and affixed each bird with a radiotag and patagial wing markers. We used photographs taken with remotely activated cameras in 5 canyons in March and April 2002 as remarks. We used the joint hypergeometric maximum likelihood estimator from the NOREMARK computer program to estimate population size using number of known marked birds in the population and number of marked and unmarked birds photographed during each sampling period. We then extrapolated this estimate from 5 canyons to the entire mountain range and compared this estimate to that from a walking survey. Estimates included 84 (95% CI = 80–91) for the area within the 5 canyons sampled, 286 (range = 272–306) when the estimate was extrapolated to the entire mountain range, and 203 (range = 110–296) for the ground survey. The photographic technique yielded more precise estimates than the ground survey, but the photographic method required approximately twice as many hours to conduct. Decisions on methods selected for future surveys should be based on management requirements.

Proceedings of the National Wild Turkey Symposium 9:45–50
Key words: Arizona, Gould's turkey, mark-resight, *Meleagris gallopavo mexicana*, NOREMARK, population estimation, remotely activated cameras, surveys.

Estimating population size for turkeys is problematic, yet important in some locales. Gould's turkey restoration efforts are ongoing in Arizona. In the United States, Gould's turkeys currently inhabit the Animas and San Luis Mountains of New Mexico, the Peloncillo Mountains of New Mexico and Arizona, and the Huachuca and Chiricahua Mountains of Arizona. The Gould's turkey subspecies is classified as endangered by the State of New Mexico, but no such classification has been determined in Arizona. Nevertheless, decisions regarding when the appropriate time to use an individual Gould's turkey population as a source for transplants is an important consideration for agencies in Arizona, New Mexico, and Mexico. Population estimates of the source population play an important role in this decision.

In 1983 and 1987, the Arizona Game and Fish Department (AGFD) acquired Gould's turkeys from Chihuahua, Mexico and reintroduced the birds into the Fort Huachuca Army Garrison Base in the Huachuca Mountains in southeastern Arizona. Nine birds were released in 1983 and 12 were released in 1987 (Breland 1988). The population has increased dramatically since the 1980s, and limited hunting opportunities have been authorized by the Arizona Game and Fish Commission. The current goal is to reestablish Gould's turkeys into several mountain ranges in southeastern Arizona, potentially using the Huachuca Mountains population as a source (Heffelfinger et al. 2000). Currently, the number of Gould's turkeys in the Huachuca Mountains is unquantified and large-scale removal of birds as transplant stock may excessively exploit the turkey population without a reliable population estimate.

Accurate population estimates for turkeys are difficult to derive. A single, validated, widely acceptable survey method has not been developed (Welsh and Kimmel 1990, Cobb et al. 2000). Observation counts, call counts, roost surveys, and harvest information have been used as indices of population trends (Welsh and Kimmel 1990, York 1991, Cobb et al. 2000). However, Shaw (1973) found that some surveys had limited power to detect changes in populations. Buckland Jolly-Seber mark-recapture, mark-resight surveys, and bait station counts have been used to estimate turkey populations (Lint et al. 1995a, Cobb et al. 2000). Often, several methods are used in conjunction to determine overall population trends (York 1991, Zornes 1993). Cobb et al. (2000) evaluated several models to estimate Eastern turkey (*M. g. silvestris*) populations in Florida and recommended mark-resight techniques using remotely activated cameras for management level monitoring.

Objectives of our study were to (1) determine if a remotely-activated camera system is a feasible method to monitor Gould's turkey populations in southeastern Arizona, (2) compare the remote camera system to an existing annual walking survey system for population

estimation, and (3) calculate a population estimate for Gould's turkeys in the Huachuca Mountains.

STUDY AREA

We studied Gould's turkeys in the Huachuca Mountains (289 km^2), located primarily in the Coronado National Forest of southeastern Arizona (110°20′ W, 31°25′ N). A prominent sky island mountain range, the long axis of the Huachuca Mountains is oriented northwest to southeast and is adjacent to the northern border of Mexico. Rugged peaks and deep canyons with sloping foothills and wide bajadas characterize topography of the mountain range. Elevation varies from 1,400 m in the surrounding foothills to over 2,800 m at Miller and Carr peaks.

The Huachuca Mountains are among the most mesic mountain ranges in Arizona. Average annual precipitation was 46 cm with seasonal peaks in winter and late summer. At Canelo Hills adjacent to the Huachuca Mountains, average maximum temperature was 32.4°C in June and average minimum temperature was −3.3°C in January (Western Regional Climate Center records for Canelo, Arizona, USA). The geologic and hydrologic characteristics of the range supported many springs. Many canyons, including Huachuca, Garden, Ramsey, Miller, Scotia, and Sunnyside, contained yearlong water.

The Huachuca Mountains contained a complex array of vegetation associations. Warm season perennial grasses, including grama (*Bouteloua* spp.), and three-awn (*Aristida* spp.), interspersed with honey mesquite (*Prosopis juliflora*), occupied elevations up to 1,525 m. Madrean evergreen woodlands (Brown 1994), characterized by evergreen oaks (*Quercus emoryi, Q. oblongifolia, Q. arizonica, Q. toumeyi*), junipers (*Juniperus deppeana* and *J. monosperma*), and pinyon pine (*Pinus discolor*) occurred at moderate elevations of 1,525 m to 2,135 m. Montane riparian forests (Brown 1994) of Arizona sycamore (*Platanus wrightii*), Arizona ash (*Fraxinus velutina*), Fremont cottonwood (*Populus fremontii*), and willow (*Salix* sp.) predominated in canyon bottoms and along drainages. Madrean montane conifer forests (Brown 1994) with variable compositions of several pine species including Ponderosa pine (*P. ponderosa*), Apache pine (*P. engelmannii*), Chihuahua pine (*P. leiophylla*), and southwestern white pine (*P. strobiformis*) and Gambel oak (*Q. gambelii*), quaking aspen (*Populus tremuloides*), and Douglas fir (*Pseudotsuga menziesii*) occupied interior portions of the range above 2,135 m. Land ownership consisted of private, state trust, military (Fort Huachuca), and U. S. Forest Service (USFS) lands. Partial paved access to the range occurred at Huachuca, Garden, Ramsey, Carr, and Miller canyons. Other access was limited to primitive roads and an extensive network of foot trails.

METHODS

Turkey Capture

We captured Gould's turkeys during February 2000, and November–March of 2000–2001 and 2001–

---

[1] Present address: College of Natural Resources, University of Wisconsin-Stevens Point, Stevens Point, WI 54481, USA.

[2] E-mail: *sdubay@uwsp.edu*

Table 1. Number of Gould's turkeys captured and marked by canyon in the Huachuca Mountains, southeastern Arizona, 2000–2002.

Capture site	Patagial tag color	Total captured (years)		
		Male	Female	Total
Huachuca Canyon	Beige		7 (2001, 2002)	7
Ramsey Canyon	Green	5 (2002)		5
Sawmill Canyon	White	5 (2002)		9
	Red/White	4 (2002)		
Sunnyside Canyon	Red/White	5 (2001)	1 (2001)	6
Total		19	8	27

2002. During summer and fall of 2001, bait stations baited with cracked corn were placed at 10 sites in the Huachuca Mountains to attract Gould's turkeys at multiple sites for winter trapping. Baiting was initially accomplished manually, but we switched to a 115-L tripod game feeder (Moultrie Feeders, Alabaster, Alabama, USA). Use of feeders required less maintenance visits to bait sites, provided feed on a regular schedule, and attracted and held Gould's turkeys at bait sites.

Gould's turkeys were captured using rocket nets (Bailey et al. 1980), marked with patagial wing streamers, fitted with backpack style radiotags (Wakeling 1991), and released on site. We obtained aerial telemetry locations at least once per month from November 2000–March 2002 (Nelson and Fuller 1994), and 2 locations were obtained during the photographic period (20 Mar–17 Apr) in order to determine if deaths occurred during the sampling period. A Global Positioning System in the aircraft recorded locations once an individual was found (Carrel et al. 1997). Motion-sensing monitors within transmitters doubled the pulse rate after a period of inactivity of approximately 12 hours to indicate possible mortality. Color-coded, numbered, patagial wing streamers (5.1 cm × 20.3 cm) allowed visual field identification (Table 1).

Photography

We used remotely activated infrared-triggered camera systems (TrailMaster™ TM 1500 active infrared monitors with TM35-1 camera kits, Goodson and Associates, Lenexa, Kansas, USA) to photograph Gould's turkeys at 5 bait stations in different canyons of the Huachuca Mountains from 20 March–17 April 2002. We used photographic settings as described by Cobb et al. (1995). Receivers and cameras recorded time and date when each photograph was taken. Feeders were operating for several months prior to photographic data collection.

Infrared transmission boxes and receivers were mounted on blocks of wood approximately 33 cm above the ground. Cameras were mounted at varying heights on nearby trees to cover approximately 15 m on either side of each bait station in the field of view. A unique number was assigned to each bait station and these numbers were present in all photographs for identification. Camera delay between photographs (minimum time between pictures) was 10 minutes.

Color print film was replaced as needed, usually

every 3–4 days. Individual groups of Gould's turkeys visiting each bait station were easily distinguished using the date and time feature on photographs. Photographs showed that turkeys rarely moved among bait sites with cameras during short intervals. As a result, sampling events consisted of 2 consecutive days of photographs. The next sampling event began 24 hours after the first sampling event ended. We enumerated the number of marked and unmarked birds in each group during each sampling period. Because we had access to only 4 camera systems, 4 of 5 bait stations were photographed at any 1 time, and combined number of marked and unmarked birds photographed at all bait stations was used in the estimation process.

Walking Survey

A walking survey was conducted on 19–23 April 2002 (J. Millican, AGFD, unpublished data). This survey had been conducted for over 10 years and was used to determine population trends prior to the photographic survey method. Routes on USFS trails, maintained roads, and primitive roads within the mountain range were extensive. Routes were typically walked during calm weather at sunrise or prior to sunset, usually taking 2 hours to complete. Volunteers and AGFD employees walked routes while imitating female turkeys with slate, reed, or box calls. If a Gould's turkey responded to the call, all birds were located, counted, and sex, age, and color of the patagial streamers on marked birds were noted. We used a Lincoln-Peterson population estimate calculated from total number of Gould's turkeys observed and number of Gould's turkeys observed with patagial streamers on all routes (Lancia et al. 1994). We then compared approximate number of labor hours necessary to estimate population numbers via photographic and walking survey methods.

Population Estimates from Photographic Method

The NOREMARK computer program (White 1996) was used to estimate population size using mark-resight data recorded by cameras. We used the joint hypergeometric maximum likelihood estimator because the population was geographically closed within a sky island mountain range, number of marked birds in the population was known, and each animal had an equal chance of being sighted or photographed during sampling periods (White 1996). We did photograph 23 of 27 marked birds during 1 sampling event, so we felt that birds had an equal chance of being photographed during sampling.

Because radiotelemetry locations indicated that the turkeys we sampled photographically did not leave the 5 canyons during winter, we assumed that the population estimate was representative of turkeys that occupied that habitat. We assumed that plotting composite minimum convex polygons of January to April home ranges could approximate the habitat occupied by this population. After calculating a population estimate for this area, we expanded the estimate to the remainder of the mountain range using a habitat suit-

Table 2. Population estimates generated from photographing Gould's turkeys at 5 bait stations in the Huachuca Mountains, Arizona, from 20 March 2002 to 17 April 2002. The final estimate is derived from the 8 sampling occasion estimates.

Occasion	Total marked	Marked seen	Un-marked seen	Lincoln-Peterson Estimate	95% CI
1	27	19	20	55.0	45.9–64.1
2	27	6	23	119.0	55.9–182.1
3	27	18	31	72.7	58.3–87.1
4	27	9	21	85.8	52.0–119.6
5	27	23	52	87.7	76.8–98.5
6	27	8	23	98.6	55.5–141.6
7	27	8	10	58.1	36.2–80.0
8	27	15	30	79.5	59.3–99.7
Estimate				84	80.0–91.0

ability model derived from habitat use by previously radiotagged turkeys (Wakeling et al. 2001). This model correctly predicted 67% of Gould's turkey use locations in the Huachuca Mountains. We assumed that habitat quality correlated with turkey density, and therefore multiplied mean habitat quality by area to determine correction factors to expand the population estimate to the Huachuca Mountains.

RESULTS

During 2000–2001, Gould's turkeys were trapped at 3 sites, and during 2001–2002, birds were trapped at 4 sites. During the 2002 photographic sampling period, Gould's turkeys used stations at 5 canyons regularly, but anecdotal data showed that birds were present in at least 3 other canyons in the mountain range as well. At time of photographic sampling, 27 Gould's turkeys were marked, and birds remained in canyons where they were trapped.

Eight separate photographic sampling occasions were included in the mark-resight estimate (Table 2). The population estimate from the 5 photographed canyons was 84 birds (95% CI = 81–90), with as many as 23 of 27 marked birds being photographed in a sampling period.

The composite minimum convex polygon home-range area of marked birds in winter 2002 yielded 65.9 km² as occupied area. Mean habitat suitability within the minimum convex home range was 0.572 (scale of 0–1). The Huachuca Mountains encompassed 289 km² with a mean habitat suitability of 0.444. The expanded estimate of Gould's turkey in the area was 286 turkeys (range = 272–306).

For the walking survey, 72 Gould's turkeys were seen on 41 walking routes and 9 were marked. A simple Lincoln-Peterson calculation estimated 203 birds (95% CI = 110–296). The photographic method required approximately twice as many labor hours as the walking survey method (Table 3).

DISCUSSION

Cobb et al. (2000) recommended use of remote cameras for mark-recapture estimates of turkeys. We found that remotely activated cameras were able to detect marked and unmarked birds for a relatively closed population of Gould's turkeys. Furthermore, population estimates generated using the camera system and habitat model were precise. Because actual size of the population was unknown, we could not estimate bias.

Lint et al. (1995b) evaluated population indices for turkeys using a 9-year data set in Mississippi. They compared population estimates from a Buckland modified Jolly-Seber mark-recapture model to indices of spring gobbler harvest, spring harvest/hunter effort, and gobblers heard in call counts per day. Each index was compared to the population estimate using linear regression, and harvested gobbler numbers and harvest/effort were positively correlated with the population estimate, likely due to the fact that data from the harvest were used in the Buckland estimator. Population estimates that incorporated data from harvested gobblers via the Buckland model were precise (i.e., SE = 123 ± 22, SE = 98 ± 12), and were correlated with indices. Harvest numbers were integral in developing these correlations, but a hunt season was not initiated

Table 3. Costs (in hours) needed to calculate mark-recapture population estimate for Gould's turkeys using remote cameras when compared to the estimate using spring walking survey results.

Task	Time for survey	Survey hours	Time for cameras	Camera hours
Set up routes, sites	1 person, 10 hrs a week, 6 months	240	1 person, 1 week	40
Walk survey routes[a]	41 people, 2 hours	82	None	0
Pre-baiting for trapping	None	0	1 person, 2 days a week, 4 weeks	64
Trapping	3 people, 2 days per event, 8 events	364	3 people, 2 days per event, 8 events	364
Baiting between capture and photographs	None	0	1 person, 2 days a week, 4 months	256
Set up of cameras	None	0	1 person, 1 day per site	40
Trial run for cameras	None	0	1 person, 1 week	40
Change film	None	0	1 person, change film every 3 days	56
Project administration	1 person, 20 hrs a week, 3 weeks	60	1 person, 10 hrs per week, 1 year	520
Data management	1 person, 10 hrs a week, 1 week	10	1 person, 20 hrs a week, 3 weeks	60
Telemetry flights	2 people, 4 hrs per month, 12 months	96	2 people, 4 hrs per month, 12 months plus 3 flights	120
Total		852		1560

[a] Only includes actual time conducting surveys and does not include travel time to site.

until 2002 in the Huachuca Mountains, and only 2 permits were issued, so we could not compare our population estimates to harvest numbers.

We were able to compare our estimate of 286 turkeys (95% CI = 272–306) to an estimate from a ground survey of marked and unmarked birds on 19–23 April 2002 (203 birds, 95% CI = 110–296). The estimate from the ground survey was not nearly as precise as those generated from our expanded estimate, and the confidence interval encompassed our estimated number. The ground survey routes did not cover the entire mountain range, and birds have been seen in areas that routes did not cover. Therefore, we believe that using estimates from photographs applied to suitable habitat in the Huachuca Mountains was valid.

The remote camera method was approximately twice as costly in labor hours than the spring walking survey (Table 3). Time needed to develop and implement the habitat model was not included because not all projects would use this method of extrapolation. The number of hours needed to walk survey routes will also vary with travel time to the study site, numbers of volunteers used, and number of days needed to walk all routes. In addition, camera equipment and film cost in excess of $2,500, but this is a one-time cost. Both spring survey where turkeys are viewed and remote cameras seem to be viable options for population estimation of turkey populations, and the decision to use either method will depend upon time constraints, budget, and management needs in the area. Because Gould's turkeys are rare and difficult to obtain, we believe that the added cost needed to achieve precise estimates was justified in this reestablishment effort. Such costs may not be justified in other situations.

Precise population estimates were needed because Gould's turkeys from the Huachuca Mountains are a potential source population for future transplants. Obtaining a population estimate for Gould's turkeys in the Huachuca Mountains was identified as an objective in the Southeastern Arizona Turkey Management Plan (Heffelfinger et al. 2000). International transplant efforts are more complex than within state transplants; therefore, using Gould's turkeys from the Huachuca Mountains as a source population for transplants is ideal. Heffelfinger et al. (2000) outlined guidelines for source turkey populations. They recommend that source populations contain at least 50 individuals, the population should be increasing, no more than 10% of the hens and 30% of the gobblers in the population should be removed, and to use the most conservative estimate to determine total numbers of birds to be used in a transplant. Using these criteria, our estimates were valuable because they identified the Huachuca Mountain Gould's turkey population as sufficient to supply subsequent transplant activity.

The remote camera method may not be ideal for turkey populations that are not geographically closed, or in situations where turkeys are not attracted to bait sites so that large numbers of birds can be captured. However, calculating a mark-resight estimate with remote cameras on a subsample of sites and applying

that estimate to known turkey habitat could be feasible where habitat is contiguous. In addition, the Buckland Jolly-Seber method could be considered as a tool for population estimation of hunted populations of turkeys (Lint et al. 1995*b*). For a small Gould's turkey population, the remote camera method with extrapolation to the remaining habitat yielded precise population estimates.

ACKNOWLEDGMENTS

We are grateful to J. Millican (Arizona Game and Fish Department) for sharing his ground survey data from the Huachuca Mountains and his foresight in initiating them, to K. Bristow (Arizona Game and Fish Department) for help during initiation of the camera project, and S. Stone (Fort Huachuca Military Garrison) for his continued support and for helping with captures. R. Ockenfels and J. deVos reviewed the manuscript and provided administrative support. Funding was provided by State Trust Fund Grant Project W-78-R of the Arizona Game and Fish Department and by the National Wild Turkey Federation.

LITERATURE CITED

Bailey, W., D. Dennett, H. Gore, J. Pack, R. Simpson, and G. Wright. 1980. Basic considerations and general recommendations for trapping the wild turkey. Proceedings of the National Wild Turkey Symposium 4:10–23.

Breland, W. R. 1988. Reintroduction of the Gould's turkey in southeastern Arizona. Proceedings of the Western Wild Turkey Workshop 4:12–26.

Brown, D. E. 1994. Biotic communities: Southwestern United States and northwestern Mexico. University of Utah, Salt Lake City, Utah, USA.

Carrel, W. K., R. A. Ockenfels, J. A. Wennerlund, and J. C. deVos, Jr. 1997. Topographic mapping, Loran-C, and GPS accuracy for aerial telemetry locations. Journal of Wildlife Management 61:1406–1412.

Cobb, D. T., D. L. Francis, and R. W. Etters. 1995. Validating a wild turkey population survey using cameras and infrared sensors. Proceedings of the National Wild Turkey Symposium 7:213–218.

———, J. L. Kalso, and G. W. Tanner. 2000. Refining population estimation and survey techniques for wild turkeys. Proceedings of the National Wild Turkey Symposium 8:179–185.

Heffelfinger, J. H., B. F. Wakeling, J. Millican, S. Stone, T. Skinner, M. Fredlake, and M. Adkins. 2000. Southeastern Arizona turkey management plan. Arizona Game and Fish Department, Phoenix, Arizona, USA.

Lancia, R. A., J. D. Nichols, and K. H. Pollock. 1994. Estimating the number of animals in wildlife populations. Pages 215–253 *in* T. A. Bookhout, editor. Research and management techniques for wildlife and habitats. The Wildlife Society, Bethesda, Maryland, USA.

Lint, J. R., B. D. Leopold, and G. A. Hurst. 1995*a*. Comparison of abundance indexes and population estimates for wild turkey gobblers. Wildlife Society Bulletin 23:164–168.

———, ———, ———, and K. J. Gribben. 1995*b*. Population size and survival rates of wild turkey gobblers in central Mississippi. Proceedings of the National Wild Turkey Symposium 7:33–38.

Nelson, M. D., and M. R. Fuller. 1994. Wildlife radiotelemetry. Pages 370–418 *in* T. A. Bookhout, editor. Research and management techniques for wildlife and habitats. The Wildlife Society, Bethesda, Maryland, USA.

Shaw, H. 1973. The roadside survey for Merriam's turkeys in Arizona. Pages 285–293 *in* G. C. Sanderson and H. C. Schultz, editors. Wild turkey management: current problems and programs. University of Missouri Press, Columbia, Missouri, USA.

Wakeling, B. F. 1991. Population and nesting characteristics of Merriam's turkey along the Mogollon Rim. Arizona Game and Fish Department Technical Report 7.

———, S. R. Boe, M. M. Koloszar, and T. D. Rogers. 2001. Gould's turkey survival and habitat selection modeling in southeastern Arizona. Proceedings of the National Wild Turkey Symposium 8:101–108.

Welsh, R. J., and R. O. Kimmel. 1990. Turkey sightings by hunters of antlerless deer as an index to wild turkey abundance in Minnesota. Proceedings of the National Wild Turkey Symposium 6:126–132.

White, G. C. 1996. NOREMARK: Population estimation from mark-resighting surveys. Wildlife Society Bulletin 24:50–52.

York, D. L. 1991. Habitat use, diet, movements, and home range of Gould's turkey in the Peloncillo Mountains, New Mexico. Thesis, New Mexico State University, Las Cruces, New Mexico, USA.

Zornes, M. L. 1993. Ecology and habitat evaluation of Gould's wild turkeys in the Peloncillo Mountains, New Mexico. Thesis, New Mexico State University, Las Cruces, New Mexico, USA.

Shelli Dubay is currently an assistant professor of Wildlife at the University of Wisconsin-Stevens Point. She received an M.S. in Pathobiology and a Ph.D. in Zoology and Physiology from the University of Wyoming. After completing her doctorate, she served as a research biologist for the Arizona Game and Fish Department where she studied Gould's turkey population estimation, pronghorn antelope decline, and other wildlife health issues.

Brian F. Wakeling (left) received a B.S. in Wildlife Management and an M.S. in Environmental Resources from Arizona State University in 1985 and 1989, respectively. He served as a research biologist for the Arizona Game and Fish Department from 1988–2000, during which time he studied turkeys, mule deer, elk, and bighorn sheep. Currently, Brian is the big game management supervisor with the Arizona Game and Fish Department, a position he has held since 2000. Brian is a Certified Wildlife Biologist and a Past-President of the Arizona State Chapter of The Wildlife Society. Brian has served as a member of the National Wild Turkey Technical Committee since 1993. ***Timothy D. Rogers*** (not pictured) is an associate research biologist with the Arizona Game and Fish Department. Tim received a B.S. from Arizona State University in 1982. Tim has conducted research on Arizona's elk, white-tailed deer, pronghorn, and Merriam's and Gould's turkeys. ***Susan R. Boe*** (right) is a geographical information systems analyst with the Arizona Game and Fish Department. Sue received her undergraduate and graduate degrees from the University of Minnesota, Duluth campus. After obtaining her B.S. she volunteered with the USFWS to work on black footed ferret surveys in Wyoming, Colorado, Utah, and Chihuahua, Mexico. For her M.S., she compared bird species richness between wetlands based on habitat heterogeneity in central Minnesota. Sue moved to Arizona in 1992 and began working with the AGFD Research Branch where she works on a wide variety of projects, both terrestrial and aquatic. ***Michael (Mike) J. Rabe*** (center) is the statewide waterfowl biologist for Arizona Game and Fish Department. He previously worked in the Research Branch for Arizona Game and Fish. Mike received his B.S. in biology and an M.S. in forestry from Northern Arizona University. Although currently working on waterfowl and migratory bird issues, his past interests include bat roost selection, biometrics, wildlife habitat selection, and game survey techniques.

CURRENT AND HISTORICAL USE OF ALPHA-CHLORALOSE ON WILD TURKEYS

David L. Bergman[1]
US Department of Agriculture,
Animal and Plant Health Inspection Service,
Wildlife Services, 8836 N 23 Avenue, Suite 2,
Phoenix, AZ 85021, USA

Brian F. Wakeling
Arizona Game and Fish Department, Game Branch,
2221 West Greenway Road,
Phoenix, AZ 85023, USA

Timothy B. Veenendaal
US Department of Agriculture,
Animal and Plant Health Inspection Service,
Wildlife Services, 8836 N 23 Avenue, Suite 2,
Phoenix, AZ 85021, USA

John D. Eisemann
US Department of Agriculture,
Animal and Plant Health Inspection Service,
Wildlife Services, National Wildlife Research Center,
4101 LaPorte Avenue, Fort Collins, CO 80521, USA

Thomas W. Seamans
US Department of Agriculture, Animal and Plant Health Inspection Service,
Wildlife Services, National Wildlife Research Center,
℅ Plum Brook Station, 6100 Columbus Avenue,
Sandusky, OH 44870, USA

Abstract: Alpha-chloralose (AC) has been used as an anesthetic since 1897 to capture or sedate wildlife, including waterfowl, wood-pigeon (*Columba palumbus*), and black bear (*Ursus americana*). The first use of AC in the United States was for the capture of house sparrows (*Passer domesticus*), red-winged blackbirds (*Agelaius phoeniceus*), and wild turkeys (*Meleagris gallopavo*) in 1964. Prior to the 1990s, AC was not registered by the Food and Drug Administration (FDA) for use as an immobilizing agent in the United States for wild animals that might be used for human consumption. In 1992, the FDA granted the US Department of Agriculture (USDA), Animal and Plant Health Inspection Service (APHIS), Wildlife Services (WS) an Investigative New Animal Drug for AC to capture waterfowl, American coots (*Fulica americana*), and pigeons (rock doves, *Columba livia*). During the late 1990s, ravens (*Corvus corax*) were added the species list on which AC could be used. In 2004, the FDA authorized the addition of sandhill cranes (*Grus canadensis*) to the list. Knowing that AC had been used on turkeys, the Arizona Game and Fish Department requested WS assistance in reintroducing Gould's turkeys (*Meleagris gallopavo mexicana*) to southeastern Arizona. To reduce stress on the birds during handling and testing, we sedated turkeys at the rate of 2.04 g of AC per 1 cup of cracked corn for up to 3 turkeys. In 2003 and 2004, wild turkeys were sedated during quarantine trials, fully recovered from the sedation and were available for relocation. Based on these data and a review of the published literature, we recommend that AC should be considered for future sedations of wild turkeys and that wild turkeys be considered for inclusion on the current Investigative New Animal Drug (INAD) label for AC.

Proceedings of the National Wild Turkey Symposium 9:51–57
Key words: alpha-chloralose, anesthesia, Arizona, chloralose, drug, Gould's wild turkey, *Meleagris gallopavo mexicana,* narcosis, reintroduction, sedation.

Many techniques have been used to capture wild turkeys for management purposes during all stages of the life cycle. Oral drugs have been used successfully, yet clinical trials and FDA approval is lacking for some types. Alpha-chloralose ($C_8H_{11}Cl_3O_6$ is a chloral derivative of glucose, which depresses the cortical centers of the brain but does not affect the medulla (Borg 1955). Alpha-chloralose has been used in laboratory

[1] E-mail: David.L.Bergman@aphis.usda.gov

animals since 1897 (Balis and Monroe 1964), and has been used to capture free-ranging wildlife species since 1966 (Williams 1966).

From the 1960s through the mid-1990s, AC was used as a capture technique, but had not been approved for use as a capture agent in the United States by the FDA (Belant et al. 1999). The FDA, Center for Veterinary Medicine, Office of New Animal Drug Evaluation's website (http://www.fda.gov/cvm/aboutona.htm) states the following: "major responsibility is to review information submitted by drug sponsors who desire to obtain approval to manufacture and market animal drugs. A new animal drug is deemed unsafe unless there is an approved new animal drug application. Virtually all animal drugs are "new animal drugs" within the meaning of the term in the Federal Food, Drug, and Cosmetic Act" (21 U.S.C. 301). There are 2 main processes involved in regulating the interstate shipment of animal drug products. The first process, the INAD exemption, involves the interstate shipment of experimental drugs used for testing in animals. This testing may require drugs be given to animals that will later be used to produce human food products. The FDA must ensure that food products derived from these experimental animals will be safe for human consumption. The second process is the New Animal Drug Application (NADA) review. It includes the evaluation of data regarding an animal drug's safety to the target animal and to humans who might consume products from the treated animal; the review also evaluates effectiveness for the purposes claimed. To be legally marketed, a new animal drug product must be approved under a NADA.

In 1992, WS received approval from the FDA to use AC under an INAD (Woronecki et al. 1990, Woronecki et al. 1992). Currently, AC is approved for use on waterfowl, coots, pigeons, ravens, and sandhill cranes.

The stated objective of Arizona Game and Fish Department's (AGFD) Wildlife Management Strategic Plan was to maintain the range of all subspecies of turkey in Arizona by repopulating historical range through transplants, with emphasis on the reintroduction of Gould's turkey (Arizona Game and Fish Department 2001). Arizona Game and Fish Department and the National Wild Turkey Federation (NWTF) approached WS for assistance in the reestablishment of the Gould's turkey, because WS held the only INAD for AC in the United States, AC had been used successfully on wild turkeys in the past, and there was a critical need to minimize handling stress on the newly acquired birds.

Initial efforts to reestablish Gould's turkey occurred during 1983 and 1987 (Breland 1988). In 1983 and 1987, Gould's turkey were captured near Nuevas Casas Grandes, Chihuahua, Mexico, transported to the United States, and held in mandatory quarantine as stipulated by the USDA APHIS Veterinary Services (VS). Approximately 60% of both groups died while in the 30-day quarantine prior to the release in the Huachuca Mountains of Arizona (Breland 1988). During the winter of 1994 and 1997, Gould's turkeys were captured near Yecora, Sonora, Mexico, and free released (non quarantine) into the Galiuro Mountains of Arizona (Wakeling 1998). This effort failed due to poor habitat suitability, as well as poor reproductive performance, high predator density, poor climatic conditions, high initial mortality due to handling related stress (Wakeling et al. 2001), and possibly, capture myopathy. Capture myopathy, also known as exertional myopathy, is a non-infectious disease characterized by skeletal and cardiac muscle necrosis and severe metabolic disturbance following extreme exertion, struggle, or stress (Williams and Thorne 1996). Capture myopathy has not been extensively diagnosed in avian species, but it has been diagnosed previously in wild turkeys (Spraker et al. 1987).

Arizona Game and Fish Department, in cooperation with NWTF and the Republic of Mexico, imported Gould's turkeys from Mexico to be held in a quarantine facility prior to release during 2003 and 2004. Our objective was to use AC to reduce stress and minimize or eliminate losses of Gould's turkeys due to handling. Ultimately, the goal was to obtain adequate data, including a literature review, unpublished studies, and research data collected under an amendment to the INAD to petition FDA to add turkeys to the list of approved species specified under the INAD.

STUDY AREA

We studied the effects of AC on Gould's turkeys in a VS approved quarantine facility (Maddrey and Wakeling *this volume*) in the Chiricahua Mountains located in Cochise County, Arizona, USA. The USDA requires that all poultry entering the United States from a foreign country be shipped under a USDA import permit and be quarantined for a minimum of 30 days at a USDA Animal Import Center. The USDA defines wild turkeys as poultry; wild turkeys are consequently subject to the import requirements for poultry. Due to the quality of the new facility, Arizona was granted permission to transport the turkeys directly to the new facility instead of one of the import facilities in New York, Florida, or California.

METHODS

AC Use

A formal request had to be made to the FDA to use AC on Gould's turkeys because they were a species of wildlife that was not covered by the INAD. All use of AC occurred within the AGFD facility. Prior to anesthetizing Gould's turkeys, food and water were removed to ensure the birds would readily feed on the treated cracked corn, and to remove potential drowning sources while the turkeys were narcotized. Turkeys were anesthetized with either 2.04 g of AC per cup of cracked corn and 10 ml of corn oil or 2.04 g of AC per 648 g of cracked corn and 20 ml of corn oil, not to exceed 180-mg/kg body weight. Locally purchased cracked corn was sifted to remove dust and chaff. The

Table 1. Dose response data for Gould's wild turkeys treated with alpha-chloralose laced cracked corn during 2003 and 2004 in a quarantine facility in the Chiricahua Mountains, Arizona, USA.

Date	Amount of cracked corn	Amount of AC (g)	Amount of corn oil (mL)	Number of Gould's turkeys feeding	Time baits placed (hr)	Time of first feeding (hr)	Time of first capture (hr)	Number captured	Number recovered
4 Apr 2003	3240 g	8.77	100	22	1500	1512	NA	0	NA
4 Apr 2003	2592 g	7.14	80	18	1505	1518	NA	0	NA
5 Apr 2003	7 cups	14.28	70	22	0935	0937	1356	22	22
5 Apr 2003	5 cups	10.20	50	18	0901	0903	1252	18	18
30 Mar 2004	7 cups	14.28	70	20	0905	0921	1545	20	20
30 Mar 2004	8 cups	16.32	80	22	0905	0912	1500	22	22
20 Apr 2004	7 cups	14.28	70	20	Not required	Not required	Not required	20	20
20 Apr 2004	8 cups	16.32	80	24	Not required	Not required	Not required	24	24

required quantity of cleaned cracked corn was placed in a clear sealable storage bag. Pre-packaged AC in the amount of 2.04 g was added to the bag and shaken to distribute, followed by corn oil. The corn oil aided adherence of the AC to the corn. Each bag was used to sedate up to 3 turkeys. One bag of treated corn was used per bait pile, with piles spaced 1–3 m apart. Turkeys were monitored for signs of anesthesia based on symptoms as described by Williams et al. (1973*a*). While under anesthesia, turkeys were radio-collared, patagial tagged, and cloacal swabs were taken for Exotic Newcastle Disease and avian influenza. Turkeys were held in NWTF weatherproof cardboard boxes until recovery.

Literature Review

Literature searches were conducted on 11 databases to find published and unpublished reports of AC use on wild turkeys. Databases searched were AGRICOLA, Biological Sciences, CAB abstracts, CRIS, Google, Forest Service Research Publications, Proceedings of the National Wild Turkey Symposia, PubMed, Searchable Ornithological Research Archive, TEOMA, Wildlife Ecology and Studies Worldwide, and Zoological Record. Literature found was used to glean pertinent and potential registration data and build a bibliography to justify future use and registration submissions.

RESULTS

AC Use

The FDA required that the appropriate documentation of National Environmental Policy Act be completed prior to granting approval to use an INAD on a species for which it is not labeled (e.g., Gould's turkeys). WS used Categorical Exclusions to document relevant environmental effects. In addition, WS had to assure FDA that the turkeys would not be hunted for food for at least 30 days after treatment; this was accomplished because Gould's turkeys are a protected species in the Chiricahua Mountains. FDA granted approval to use AC on Gould's turkeys in Arizona on 13 March 2003.

Forty turkeys were treated with AC on 4 April 2003 (Table 1). At the previously stated dosing regimens, all turkeys received adequate doses to facilitate capture with minimal stress to the animal. A second capture operation occurred on 5 April 2003 using 2.04 g per cup of cracked corn (Table 1). For operational purposes, all birds were assumed to weigh approximately 4.0 kg. Forty birds were treated, captured, and all survived. Within 23 min of the first feeding of group 1 (22 turkeys), 4 turkeys were showing signs of heavy sedation or mild narcosis. After 93 min, 14 turkeys showed signs of moderate narcosis or shallow anesthesia, 4 showed signs of heavy sedation or mild narcosis, and 4 showed no signs or light sedation. After 4 hr and 10 min, turkeys were hand captured and placed in NWTF boxes. Two females had to be hand netted. In group 2 (18 turkeys), within 57 min, 8 turkeys showed signs of heavy sedation or mild narcosis, 4 showed signs of moderate narcosis or shallow anesthesia, and 6 showed no signs or light anesthesia. After 4 hr, 11 turkeys were captured and placed in boxes. After 5 hr and 19 min, 1 additional turkey was sedated and 6 females had to be hand netted.

On 30 March 2004, the second set of captured turkeys was baited using the same dosing regimen (Table 1). Group 1 was baited at 0905 hr, and the first female showed signs of light sedation after 40 min. The first female reached moderate narcosis within 65 min of feeding. After 3.5 hr, only 5 turkeys had reached narcosis. After 5 hr and 15 min, 10 turkeys had reached narcosis and 10 had to be captured with a net. In group 2, feeding on the bait began 25 min after placement in the room. One female showed signs of heavy sedation or mild narcosis after 30 min. One female showed signs of moderate narcosis 80 min after feeding. At 5.5 hr after feeding, captures were begun. Twenty-one turkeys were in moderate narcosis to anesthesia. Three birds were in mild narcosis and 2 never fed. At 0645 hr the next morning, 5 were still in anesthesia, 3 were in mild narcosis, and 44 were under light sedation or recovered.

During the third baiting, times of feeding and symptoms of recovery were not noted due to changes in forms and the required information needed for the FDA (Table 1). All 44 turkeys fully recovered, and none were lost due to drugging. Turkeys captured during baiting 1 and 2 were outfitted with radio-collars and patagial tags.

Table 2. Published reports of use of alpha-chloralose to anesthetize wild turkeys through 2004 as found through online searches.

Citation	Recommended AC dosage (g) per cup of cracked corn	Sample size	State of use	Mortality (%)	Post capture observation (hr)
Williams 1966	2	260	Florida	Not noted	24–120
Williams et al. 1966	2	592	Florida	8.9	Not noted
Williams et al. 1968a	2	35	Florida	Not noted	Not noted
Williams et al. 1968b	2	26	Florida	0	72
Speake et al. 1969	2	98	Alabama	0	Not noted
Barwick et al. 1970	2	Not noted	Florida	Not noted	Not noted
Gardner 1972	2	115 w/3 methods	Alabama	Not noted	Not noted
Austin et al. 1973	2	1712	Florida	9.0	Not noted
Barwick and Speake 1973	2	105	Alabama	Not noted	24–36
Hillestad 1973	2	15	Alabama	Not noted	Not noted
Williams et al. 1973a	2	1600	Florida	9.0	20–40
Williams et al. 1973b	2	56	Florida	Not noted	Not noted
Windham 1973	2	4	Texas	25	29
Speake et al. 1975	2	105 w/3 methods	Alabama, Kentucky	Not noted	Not noted
Donahue 1978; Donahue et al. 1982	2	25 (AL 2, GA/FL 21, PA 2)	Alabama, Georgia/Florida, Pennsylvania	0	Not noted
Everett et al. 1980	2	89 w/2 methods	Alabama	Not noted	Not noted
Hopkins et al. 1980	2	233 w/2 methods	Mississippi	Not noted	Not noted
Kennamer et al. 1980	2	32 w/2 methods	Alabama	Not noted	Not noted
Speake 1980	2	298 w/2 methods	Alabama	Not noted	Not noted
Exum et al. 1985	2	12	Alabama	Not noted	Not noted
Holbrook and Vaughan 1985	2	30 adult/sub adult, 26 poults	Virginia	5	50.4 adult, 26.4 poult
Metzler and Speake 1985	2	Not noted	Alabama	Not noted	Not noted
Speake et al. 1985	2	Not noted	Alabama	Not noted	Not noted
Anonymous 1988	Not noted	88	Georgia	Not noted	Not noted
McDougal et al. 1990	2	64 w/2 methods	Virginia	Not noted	Not noted
Seiss et al. 1990	2	38 w/2 methods	Mississippi	Not noted	Not noted
Sisson et al. 1990	2	37	Georgia	Not noted	Not noted
Sisson and Speake 1991	2	26	Georgia	Not noted	Not noted
Lint et al. 1995	Not noted	88	Mississippi	Not noted	Not noted
Peoples et al. 1995	2	67	Georgia/Florida	Not noted	Not noted
Miller et al. 1996	2	w/2 methods	Mississippi	Not noted	Not noted
Rumble and Anderson 1996	2	111 w/3 methods	South Dakota	Not noted	Not noted
Lovell et al. 1997	Not noted	Not noted	Mississippi	Not noted	Not noted
Hubbard et al. 2001	2	Not noted	Iowa	Not noted	Not noted

Turkeys fed according to pecking order. The largest males were first to feed followed by young males, females, and finally, subadult females. Each turkey reacted differently to the effects depending on the amount of bait consumed, movements and activities of other turkeys, and sounds external to the quarantine rooms. Some turkeys regressed from Stage II (mild narcosis) or III (moderate narcosis) back to Stage I (light sedation) after other turkeys or external sounds disturbed them.

During the study, 126 captures of 84 unique turkeys were made with AC over 3 capture events. We experienced no capture myopathy, morbidity, or mortality in our study.

Literature Review

Databases searched contained reports that dated back to the 15th century with the majority of records having been published since 1884. Search terms used were turkey, wild turkey, chloralose, and turkey plus chloralose.

We found 35 publications that referenced the use of AC on wild turkeys (Table 2) The first use of AC on wild turkeys was in Florida during 1966 (Williams 1966), which was also the state with the most publi-

cations on AC use in turkeys. Nine additional states (Alabama, Georgia, Iowa, Kentucky, Pennsylvania, Mississippi, South Dakota, Texas, and Virginia) were found to have used AC on wild turkeys. Subspecies of turkeys listed were Merriam's (*M. g. merriami*), Rio Grande (*M. g. intermidia*), Osceola (*M. g. Osceola*), and Eastern (*M. g. silvestris*). No mention was made of the use of AC on Gould's turkeys. The last cited use of AC on wild turkeys was in March 1995 in Iowa (Hubbard et al. 2001). The primary papers being referenced as providing direction on the use of AC in wild turkeys were Williams (1966), Williams et al. (1966), and Williams et al. (1973a).

DISCUSSION

For almost 30 years, AC was one of the most commonly used tools to capture wild turkeys in the United States (Table 2). Anecdotally, AC had been used annually by many states for capture, research, and management of wild turkeys (B. Maddrey, National Wild Turkey Federation, personal communication). Many of these states may have data within their historical files that could be used to further registration purposes.

Following the protocol initially set by Williams

(1966) and within the guidelines set by FDA, AC is a safe and effective tool for anesthetizing wild turkeys. Gould's turkeys fed according to pecking order on the piles of baits which had enough AC for up to 3 turkeys per bait pile. The largest males were first to feed followed by young males, adult females, and subadult females. We speculate that by feeding in this order, turkeys self regulated the AC dosage by the largest bird ingesting the largest share of treated bait and the smallest bird ingesting the least amount of treated bait (i.e., correlating bait intake to body size).

Our results agree with Williams (1966) in that dosages below 2 g AC per cup of cracked corn were ineffective in sedating Gould's turkeys. Turkeys should be maintained in a warm and dry condition during anesthesia. Williams et al. (1966) found that wild turkey body temperatures rise sharply to as high as 42°C and then gradually decline for several hours to as low as 34°C. If the air temperature drops below freezing, anesthetized turkeys can succumb to hypothermia. In addition, water sources should not be present to prevent drowning (Williams 1966). The majority of Gould's turkey reacted similarly to turkeys in Florida, which took 1.5 hours to reach narcosis and 2–3 hr to reach a state of anesthesia (Williams 1966). Our experience with AC in this study addressed many concerns regarding losses of Gould's turkeys due to handling identified by Breland (1988), Wakeling (1998), and Wakeling et al. (2001). We also hypothesize that the use of AC may actually alleviate stress in wild turkeys as suggested by Donahue et al. (1982).

MANAGEMENT IMPLICATIONS

Alpha chloralose continues to be a viable and important tool in the conservation and restoration of turkeys. Based on our study, limited published literature, and the potential for additional information in the archives of agencies and organizations, we recommend that WS continue to collect data on AC and petition FDA to add turkeys to the current INAD-6602.

ACKNOWLEDGMENTS

We would like to acknowledge M. Adkins, S. Baker, R. Day, G. Gonzales, J. McDivett, and D. Winterboer for assisting with the AC baiting and captures. We would like to thank the anonymous reviewers for their constructive critiques. We would also like to thank K. Fagerstone, J. Jones, C. Bausch, and their staffs in acquiring permission from the FDA to use the product on Gould's turkeys, and T. Hall and G. Littauer for their work to meet National Environmental Policy Act compliance.

LITERATURE CITED

Anonymous. 1988. Wild turkey Mycoplasma research Update. Southeastern Wildlife Disease Study 4:2.

Arizona Game and Fish Department. 2001. Wildlife 2006. Arizona Game and Fish Department, Phoenix, Arizona, USA.

Austin, D. H., T. E. Peoples, and L. E. Williams, Jr. 1973. Procedures for capturing and handling live wild turkeys. Proceedings of the Annual Conference of the Southeastern Association Game and Fish Commissions 26:222–236.

Balis, G. U., and R. R. Monroe. 1964. The pharmacology of chloralose. Psychopharmacologia 6:1–30.

Barwick, L. H., D. H. Austin, and L. E. Williams, Jr. 1970. Roosting of young turkey broods during summer in Florida. Proceedings of the Annual Conference of the Southeastern Association Game and Fish Commissions 24:231–243.

———, and D. W. Speake. 1973. Seasonal movements and activities of wild turkey gobblers in Alabama. Proceedings of the National Wild Turkey Symposium 2:125–133.

Belant, J. L., L. A. Tyson, and T. W. Seamans. 1999. Use of alpha-chloralose by the Wildlife Services program to capture nuisance birds. Wildlife Society Bulletin 27:938–942.

Borg, K. 1955. Chloralose and its use for catching crows, gulls, pigeons, etc. Viltrevy Jakbiologisk Tidskrift 1:88–121.

Breland, W. R. 1988. Reintroduction of the Gould's turkey in southeastern Arizona. Proceedings of the Western Wild Turkey Workshop 4:12–26.

Donahue, M. A. 1978. The effect of the capturing drug, alpha-chloralose, on several blood constituents in the eastern wild turkey (*Meleagris gallopavo silvestris*). Thesis, Auburn University, Auburn, Alabama, USA.

———, M. E. Lisano, and J. K. Kennamer. 1982. Effects of alpha-chloralose drugging on blood constituents in the eastern wild turkey. Journal of Wildlife Management 46:468–474.

Everett, D. D., D. W. Speake, W. K. Maddox. 1980. Natality and mortality of a north Alabama turkey population. Proceeding of the National Wildlife Turkey Symposium 4:117–126.

Exum, J. H., J. A. McGlincy, D. W. Speake, J. L. Buckner, and F. M. Stanley. 1985. Evidence against dependence upon surface water by turkey hens and poults in southern Alabama. Proceedings of the National Wild Turkey Symposium 5:83–89.

Gardner, D. T. 1972. Dynamics of a recently established wild turkey population in the Alabama piedmont. Dissertation, Auburn University, Auburn, Alabama, USA.

Hillestad, H. O. 1973. Movements, behavior, and nesting ecology of the wild turkey in eastern Alabama. Proceedings of the National Wild Turkey Symposium 2:109–123.

Holbrook, H. T., and M. R. Vaughan. 1985. Capturing adult and juvenile wild turkeys with adult dosages of alpha-chloralose. Wildlife Society Bulletin 13:160–163.

Hopkins, C. R., D. H. Arner, J. E. Kennamer, and R. D. Clanton. 1980. Movements of turkeys in a high density population in the Mississippi Delta. Proceedings of the National Wild Turkey Symposium 4:272–279.

Hubbard, M. W., D. L. Garner, and E. E. Klaas. 2001. Factors influencing wild turkey poult survival in southcentral Iowa. Proceedings of the National Wild Turkey Symposium 8:167–171.

Kennamer, J. E., J. R. Gwaltney, and K. R. Simms. 1980. Habitat preferences of eastern wild turkeys on an area intensively managed for pine in Alabama. Proceedings of the National Wild Turkey Symposium 4:240–245.

Lint, J. R., B. D. Leopold, G. A. Hurst, and K. J. Gribben. 1995. Population size and survival rates of wild turkey gobblers in central Mississippi. Proceedings of the National Wild Turkey Symposium 7:33–38.

Lovell, C. D., D. A. Miller, G. A. Hurst, and B. D. Leopold. 1997. Relationships between wild turkeys and raccoons in central Mississippi. Proceedings Eastern Wildlife Damage Conference 7:118–129.

Maddrey, R. C., and B. F. Wakeling. *This volume.* Crossing the border—the Arizona Gould's restoration experience. Proceedings of the National Wild Turkey Symposium 9:*This volume.*

McDougal, L. A., M. R. Vaughan, and P. T. Bromley. 1990. Wild turkey and road relationships on a Virginia National Forest.

Proceedings of the National Wild Turkey Symposium 6:96–106.

Metzler, R., and D. W. Speake. 1985. Wild turkey poult mortality rates and their relationship to brood habitat structure in northeast Alabama. Proceedings of the National Wild Turkey Symposium 5:103–111.

Miller, D. A., B. D. Leopold, and G. A. Hurst. 1996. Post-capture survival of wild turkeys: effects of age, sex and environment. Proceedings of the Annual Conference of the Southeastern Association of Fish and Wildlife Agencies 50: 442–449.

Peoples, J. C., D. C. Sisson, and D. W. Speake. 1995. Wild turkey brood habitat use and characteristics in coastal plain pine forests. Proceedings of the National Wild Turkey Symposium 7:89–96.

Rumble, M. A., and S. H. Anderson. 1996. Microhabitats of Merriam's turkeys in the Black Hills, South Dakota. Ecological Applications 6:326–334.

Seiss, R. S., P. S. Phalen, and G. A. Hurst. 1990. Wild turkey nesting habitat and success rate. Proceedings of the National Wild Turkey Symposium 6:18–24.

Sisson, D. C., and D. W. Speake. 1991. An incidence of second brood production by an eastern wild turkey. Wilson Bulletin 103:303–305.

———, ———, J. L. Landers, and J. L. Buckner. 1990. Effects of prescribed burning on wild turkey habitat preference and nest site selection in south Georgia. Proceedings of the National Wild Turkey Symposium 6:44–50.

Speake, D. W. 1980. Predation of wild turkeys in Alabama. Proceedings of the National Wild Turkey Symposium 4:86–101.

———, L. H. Barwick, H. O. Hillestad, and W. Stickney. 1969. Some characteristics of an expanding turkey population. Proceedings of the Annual Conference of the Southeastern Association Game and Fish Commissions 23:46–58.

———, T. E. Lynch, W. J. Fleming, G. A. Wright, and W. J. Hamrick. 1975. Habitat use and seasonal movements of wild turkeys in the southeast. Proceeding of the National Wild Turkey Symposium 3:122–130.

———, R. Metzler, and J. McGlincy. 1985. Mortality of wild turkey poults in northern Alabama. Journal of Wildlife Management 49:472–474.

Spraker, T. R., W. R. Adrian, and W. R. Lance. 1987. Capture myopathy in wild turkeys (*Meleagris gallopavo*) following trapping, handling, and transportation in Colorado. Journal of Wildlife Diseases 23:447–453.

Wakeling, B. F. 1998. Survival of Gould's turkey transplanted into the Galiuro Mountains of Arizona. Pages 227–234 *in* G. J. Gottfried, C. B. Edminster, and M. C. Dillon, compilers. Cross Border Waters: Fragile Treasures for the 21st Century; Ninth U.S./Mexico Border States Conference on Recreation, Parks, and Wildlife. U.S. Forest Service Proceedings RMRS-P-5.

———, S. R. Boe, M. A. Koloszar, and T. D. Rogers. 2001. Gould's turkey survival and habitat selection modeling in southeastern Arizona. Proceedings of the National Wild Turkey Symposium 8:101–108.

Williams, E. S., and E. T. Thorne. 1996. Exertional myopathy (capture myopathy). Pages 181–193 *in* A. Fairbrother, L. N. Locke, and G. L. Hoff, editors. Non-infections diseases of wildlife. Second edition. Iowa State University Press, Ames, Iowa, USA.

Williams, L. E., Jr. 1966. Capturing wild turkeys with alpha-chloralose. Journal of Wildlife Management 30:50–56.

———, D. H. Austin, N. F. Eichholz, and T. E. Peoples. 1968a. A study of nesting turkeys in southern Florida. Florida Game and Fresh Water Fish Commission, Project Number Florida W-041-R.

———, ———, ———, ———, and R. W. Phillips. 1968b. Study of nesting turkeys in southern Florida. Proceedings of the Annual Conference of the Southeastern Association Game and Fish Commissioners 22:16–30.

———, ———, and J. Peoples. 1966. Progress in capturing turkeys with drugs applied to baits. Proceedings of the Annual Conference of the Southeastern Association Game and Fish Commissions 20:219–226.

———, T. E. Peoples, and R. W. Phillips. 1973a. Capturing turkeys with oral drugs. Proceedings of the National Wild Turkey Symposium 2:219–227.

———, ———, ———, and ———. 1973b. Observations on movement, behavior, and development of turkey broods. Proceedings of the National Wild Turkey Symposium 2:79–99.

Windham, J. D. 1973. Specific characteristics pertaining to home range and territory selection and the test of oral anesthetics for trapping the Rio Grande turkey (*Meleagris gallopavo intermedia*) in southwestern Callahan County, Texas. Thesis, Abilene Christian University, Abilene, Texas, USA.

Woronecki, P. P., R. A. Dolbeer, and T. W. Seamans. 1990. Use of alpha-chloralose to remove waterfowl from nuisance and damage situations. Proceedings of the Vertebrate Pest Conference 14:343–349.

———, ———, and W. R. Lance. 1992. Alpha-chloralose efficacy in capturing nuisance waterfowl and pigeons and current status of FDA regulation. Proceedings of the Vertebrate Pest Conference 15:72–78.

David L. Bergman (left) is the State Director for the United States Department of Agriculture, Animal and Plant Health Inspection Service, Wildlife Services' Arizona Program. He earned his B.S. in wildlife biology from the University of Nebraska–Kearney. He served as a research technician, wildlife biologist and staff wildlife biologist for Wildlife Services from 1989–2001 which included overseeing drug registration issues and research for drug and pesticide registration.. Currently, David oversees a diverse program that includes wildlife damage management for airports, agriculture, property and natural resources. David is a Certified Wildlife Biologist. ***Brian F. Wakeling*** (middle) received a B.S. in Wildlife Management and an M.S. in Environmental Resources from Arizona State University in 1985 and 1989, respectively. He served as a research biologist for the Arizona Game and Fish Department from 1988–2000, during which time he studied turkeys, mule deer, elk, and bighorn sheep. Currently, Brian is the big game management supervisor with the Arizona Game and Fish Department, a position he has held since 2000. Brian is a Certified Wildlife Biologist and a Past-President of the Arizona State Chapter of The Wildlife Society. Brian has served as a member of the National Wild Turkey Technical Committee since 1993. ***Timothy B. Veenendaal*** (right) is currently working as a supervisory wildlife biologist for the Wildlife Services Arizona program. Prior to this position he worked with Wildlife Services in Washington and NWRC-Olympia Field Station. He received his B.S. in Fisheries and Wildlife from Utah State University in 1995. ***John D. Eisemann*** (not pictured) has been working in the field of Wildlife Biology for nearly 25 years. He studied Wildlife Biology as an undergraduate at Colorado State University. He went on to obtain a Masters'

in Environmental Science at the University of Maryland emphasizing contaminants in urban runoff and their impact on birds. During his years pursuing a career as a Wildlife Biologist, he worked for the U. S. Fish and Wildlife Service refuge system and in the contaminants lab at the Patuxent Wildlife Research Center. While at Patuxent, he became interested in the effects of industrial contaminants and pesticides on wildlife and was subsequently hired by the U.S. Environmental Protection Agency in the mid-1990's to conduct ecological risk assessments of pesticides. After two and a half years with the EPA, the USDA National Wildlife Research Center (NWRC) brought him on to manage their vertebrate pesticide and wildlife drug registrations. He has been with NWRC for 8 years. **Thomas W. Seamans** (not pictured) is a Certified Wildlife Biologist for the Wildlife Services/National Wildlife Research Center field station in Sandusky, Ohio. Tom has spent the last 18 years conducting research focused on finding biologically sound solutions to conflicts between people and wildlife. He received a B.S. degree in wildlife science from Cornell University and an M.S. in wildlife management from the Ohio State University.

CROP DEPREDATION BY WILDLIFE IN NORTHCENTRAL INDIANA

Lee A. Humberg[1,2]
Department of Forestry and Natural Resources,
195 Marsteller Street, Purdue University,
West Lafayette, IN 47907, USA

Travis L. DeVault
Department of Forestry and Natural Resources,
195 Marsteller Street, Purdue University,
West Lafayette, IN 47907, USA

Brian J. MacGowan
Department of Forestry and Natural Resources,
Purdue University,
1250 North Franklin Avenue, P.O. Box 265,
Brookville, IN 47012, USA

James C. Beasley
Department of Forestry and Natural Resources,
195 Marsteller Street,
Purdue University,
West Lafayette, IN 47907, USA

Olin E. Rhodes, Jr.
Department of Forestry and Natural Resources,
195 Marsteller Street,
Purdue University,
West Lafayette, IN 47907, USA

Abstract: Perceptions of agricultural producers concerning crop depredation may influence wildlife management decisions. We quantified the amount, type, and temporal pattern of damage to corn (*Zea maize*) and soybeans (*Glycine max*) by wild turkey (*Meleagris gallopavo*), white-tailed deer (*Odocoileus virginianus*), raccoons (*Procyon lotor*), and other vertebrates in the agricultural region of northcentral Indiana. Using stratified random sampling, we conducted depredation surveys of 160 fields (100 corn and 60 soybean) ranging in size from 1 to 125 ha from May through October in 2003 and 2004. We recorded 582,515 depredation events (73,100 to corn and 509,415 to soybeans). We defined a "depredation event" as any damage to a single plant caused by wildlife. Raccoons and white-tailed deer were responsible for >97% of the damage to corn (87% and 10%, respectively), whereas white-tailed deer (61%) and groundhogs (*Marmota monax*; 38%) were responsible for nearly all damage to soybean plants. Small rodents, birds, canids, and all other vertebrates had very little effect on corn and soybean production in our study area. Although turkeys were relatively common on the study area and turkey sign was evident in several fields, no depredation events were attributed to wild turkey. We assessed landowner perceptions concerning crop depredation by wildlife with mail and telephone surveys. Seventy-eight percent of landowners reported having ≥1 crop type damaged by wildlife within the previous 12 months; however, their perceptions regarding the species responsible for monetary losses to corn and soybeans did not correspond closely with our field survey data.

Proceedings of the National Wild Turkey Symposium 9:59–65

Key words: corn, crop, damage, depredation, Indiana, perceptions, raccoon, soybeans, white-tailed deer, wild turkey.

Agricultural damage by wildlife species in the U.S. is substantial, widespread, and is a serious concern to many agricultural producers. Conover (2002) estimated wildlife-related, economic losses to agricultural producers (farmers and ranchers) currently exceed 4.5 billion dollars annually in the U.S. Results of nationwide surveys conducted in 1993 and 1994 indicated 80% of farmers and ranchers suffered wildlife

[1] E-mail: lee.humberg@us.army.mil
[2] Present address: Department of the Army, 110 E Headquarters Road, Fort McCoy, WI 54656

damage in the prior year, and 53% suffered damage exceeding their tolerance (Conover 1998).

Data from agriculture and wildlife professionals indicate wildlife damage to field crops has increased significantly in recent years. Based on producer estimates, wildlife-caused losses to field crops increased from $237 million in 1989 to $316 million in 1994 (Wywialowski 1994, 1997). From 1957 to 1987, the percentage of wildlife agencies reporting damage to crops by deer increased from 83% to 100% and raccoon damage increased from 10% to 94% (McDowell and Pillsbury 1959, Conover and Decker 1991).

Crop damage by deer and raccoons is probably the most recognized and widespread (Conover and Decker 1991; Craven and Hygnstrom 1994; Wywialowski 1994, 1997; Conover 1998, 2002). While no estimates exist of nationwide annual crop losses due to deer, information is available for some states. Estimates of crop damage in a non-hunted setting (Gettysburg National Military Park and the Eisenhower National Historic Site) in Pennsylvania from 1986 and 1987 indicated white-tailed deer reduced yields of field corn an average of 20% (19 bushels/ha) (Vecellio et al. 1994). In the 10 top corn-producing states, deer-specific losses averaged 0.87 bushels/ha, representing 0.23% of the 10-state harvest of corn for grain in 1993 (Wywialowski 1996). Crop damage by raccoons also has become a serious concern of agricultural producers, with 25% of producers reporting raccoon damage (second only to deer) (Conover 1998, 2002).

Several other wildlife species are commonly responsible or perceived to be responsible for substantial damage to field crops. Groundhogs often damage soybean plants around their burrows (Loven 2000). In some parts of North America, blackbirds (Icteridae) cause extensive damage to agricultural crops, especially sunflowers (*Helianthus* spp.) (Conover 2002). Although generally rare, cases of crop depredation by wild turkeys also have been reported (Gabrey et al. 1993, Paisley et al. 1995, Payer and Craven 1995, Swanson et al. 2001).

The restoration of wild turkeys in North America is generally considered one of the greatest wildlife management successes. Agricultural landscapes once thought to contain insufficient habitat for wild turkey have proven productive (Dickson 1992). However, with the increased presence of wild turkey in agricultural regions, the number of perceived conflicts between wild turkey and agricultural producers over crop damage has increased (Payer and Craven 1995). Although wild turkey may potentially damage agricultural crops, research has shown most cases of turkey depredation result in minimal damage or are actually caused by other wildlife species (Gabrey et al. 1993, Paisley et al. 1996, Swanson et al. 2001, Tefft et al. 2005). The misidentification of crop damage by wild turkey most likely stems from their diurnal nature and coincidental presence in fields already damaged.

While most landowners hold a generally favorable view of wildlife on agricultural lands (Pomeratz et al. 1986, Siemer and Decker 1991), many agricultural producers complain of excessive and intolerable wildlife damage to their crops (Brown et al. 1978, Brown and Decker 1979). Agriculture and wildlife professionals in the U.S. also view wildlife damage as a widespread problem (Conover and Decker 1991). Because of the potential economic losses to agricultural producers, the priorities of wildlife agencies in agricultural regions often are influenced by the perceptions of agricultural producers toward crop damage. An improved understanding of factors underlying crop depredation and the development of strategies to reduce crop losses by wildlife would not only decrease negative agricultural impacts, but also improve public perceptions about wildlife.

In August 2002 we began a study to quantify the amount and type of crop damage caused by vertebrate wildlife species in crop fields (corn and soybean) in northcentral Indiana. Our long term objective is to develop spatially explicit models to predict probabilities of species-specific crop depredation in corn and soybean fields with respect to landscape features. In this paper, we document the amount of crop damage, the species responsible, timing of depredation, and preliminary results of a survey to evaluate attitudes of producers regarding wildlife depredation to corn and soybeans.

STUDY AREA

We selected a 1165-km² study area within the Upper Wabash River Basin (UWB) of northcentral Indiana encompassing portions of Grant, Huntington, Miami, and Wabash counties. Agriculture was the dominant land use type (88%), primarily row crops of corn and soybeans interspersed with small fields of hay and small grains. Agricultural field size averaged 17 ha (range = 1–130 ha) and >75% of fields were 24 ha or less in size. Woodlands occurred primarily as interspersed woodlots (mostly <16 ha) or as forested corridors along the rivers. Elevation averaged 243 m above sea level and topography was flat with gently rolling river drainages.

METHODS

Field Sampling

We constructed a Geographic Information System to categorize land use and classify individual agricultural fields by size and crop type. We assigned a sample of fields representing the distribution of field sizes in the study area to 1 of 3 categories: <12 ha, 12–24 ha, or >24 ha. We surveyed 82 fields (n = 53 corn fields; n = 29 bean fields) in 2003 and 78 fields (n = 47 corn fields; n = 31 bean fields) in 2004 for evidence of wildlife crop depredation.

After plant emergence, we established edge and interior transects in each field using hand-held Global Positioning Satellite (GPS) receivers and survey flags. All transects ran parallel with the fields' row plantings and transects continued through the end cross rows to the ends of the fields. We established 2-edge transects within 15 m of the edges of each field; transects followed curvatures of field edges. We spaced interior field transects (2 for <12 ha, 4 for 12–24 ha, and 6 for >24 ha fields) equidistantly within the remainder of the fields. Most fields had 4 definable edges, of which we surveyed only the 2 edges that ran parallel to the entire field row planting orientation (e.g., north-south orientation, east-west orientation). Some irregularly shaped fields had more than 4 edges. For fields with >4 edges, we surveyed the 2 major edges that ran parallel to entire field planting orientation and any other edge of the same orientation that was greater than one-quarter the length of the field in the direction being surveyed. Wildlife biologists (Indiana Department of Natural Resources and Purdue University Wildlife Extension), experienced in assessing various types of crop damage, trained our technicians on techniques to determine wildlife species responsible for damage and the age of corn and soybean plants.

Technicians walked field transects and surveyed each field approximately once per month from plant emergence until harvest. Survey crews of 2 technicians walked in tandem along transects and documented all plants that exhibited any sign of wildlife-caused damaged visible from transects (i.e., variable-width transects). At each plant damage location, crews recorded the number of plants damaged, wildlife species responsible, amount of leaf area damaged, amount of seed damage, height of damage, growth stage of plant at the time of damage, and remaining yield. At locations where ≤20 plants were damaged we collected data for each damaged plant, and in areas where >20 plants were damaged we collected data on 20 randomly-selected damaged plants. All documented damage was marked clearly with paint to avoid recounting during subsequent surveys. In addition to collecting plant damage characteristics, we recorded UTM coordinates using hand-held GPS units at the epicenter of each location where we collected damage information. We defined a "depredation event" as any previously unrecorded damage to a single plant caused by wildlife.

Crop Producer Surveys

In December 2003 we mailed a survey to producers who grew a total of 20–320 ha of corn and soybeans according to Indiana National Agricultural Statistics Service records. We mailed surveys to all producers meeting this criteria ($n = 848$) in 4 counties within our study area (Grant, Huntington, Miami, Wabash) and a random sample ($n = 625$) of producers meeting the criteria in the remaining 7 counties located entirely within the UWB (Carroll, Cass, Fulton, Howard, Tippecanoe, Wells, Whitley). The survey included questions regarding the severity of crop depredation on the landowner's property, the wildlife species perceived to be responsible, the landowner's annual economic losses from wildlife crop depredation, and the landowner's general attitudes towards wildlife. We separated responses pertaining to corn and soybean for statistical analyses. To check for non-respondent bias, we conducted a telephone survey of a random sample of non-respondents ($n = 154$) from 13–26 January 2004. We used a chi-square goodness of fit test to test

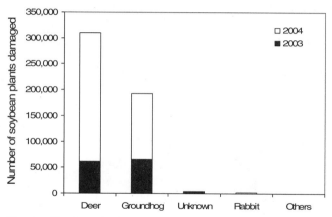

Fig. 1. Number of soybean plants damaged by wildlife species in northcentral Indiana during the 2003 and 2004 growing seasons. We surveyed 29 fields in 2003 and 31 fields in 2004 between May and September of each year.

for differences in responses between mail and telephone surveys (Zar 1996). We weighted responses that differed ($P < 0.05$) between the groups based on the sample size (i.e., $n = 388$ for mail and $n = 1,091$ for telephone).

RESULTS

Field Sampling

We documented a total of 582,515 depredation events in 149 of 160 fields surveyed over the 2 growing seasons. We recorded no wildlife damage in 5 corn fields and 6 soybean fields. Overall, soybean plants were damaged more often than corn plants (509,415 and 73,100, respectively), despite a greater sampling effort in corn ($n = 100$) than in soybean fields ($n = 60$).

Our surveys in soybean fields yielded 131,556 depredation events in 2003 and 377,859 depredation events in 2004. The average number of soybean plants damaged per field was 8,490 (SD = 23,708) and the maximum number of plants damaged in a single field was 162,453. White-tailed deer (61%) and groundhogs (38%) were most often responsible for damage to soybean plants. Eastern cottontails (*Sylvilagus floridana*), raccoons, small rodents (e.g., fox squirrel [*Sciurus niger*], thirteen-lined ground squirrel [*Spermophilus tridecemlineatus*], Eastern chipmunk [*Tamias striatus*]), and unidentified species combined were responsible for less than 2% of the total damage to soybean plants (Figure 1). We detected no wild turkey damage to soybeans.

Our surveys in corn fields yielded 24,623 depredation events in 2003 and 48,477 depredation events in 2004. The average number of corn plants damaged per field was 731 (SD = 1,440) and the maximum number of plants damaged in a single field was 8,357. Raccoons and white-tailed deer were responsible for >97% of the damage to corn (87% and 10%, respectively). Small mammals (e.g., eastern cottontail, fox squirrel, thirteen-lined ground squirrel, chipmunk), beaver (*Castor canadensis*), birds, and other wildlife had little effect on field corn in our study area (Figure 2). We detected no wild turkey damage to corn.

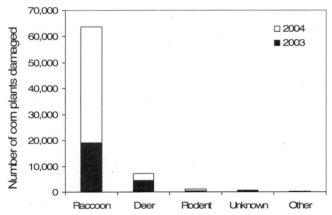

Fig. 2.   Number of corn plants damaged by wildlife species in northcentral Indiana during the 2003 and 2004 growing seasons. We surveyed 53 fields in 2003 and 47 fields in 2004 between May and October of each year.

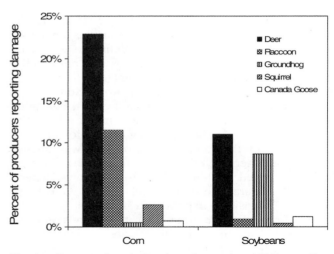

Fig. 4.   Percent of agricultural producers (*n* = 529) reporting corn and soybean damage by wildlife in northcentral Indiana in 2003. The top 5 species for each crop type reported are shown.

Our 2 years of crop depredation surveys revealed strikingly different temporal patterns of corn depredation by white-tailed deer and raccoons (Figure 3). Deer damaged corn steadily from plant emergence (May) through harvest (Oct). Conversely, raccoons damaged corn only rarely until the beginning of the reproductive stage (early to mid-Jun), but subsequently exhibited substantial depredation through harvest (Oct).

Crop Producer Surveys

Of the 1,500 mail surveys sent to crop producers, 396 (26%) were returned; of these, 388 were usable. For the call-back surveys, 141 of 154 were usable. Seventy-eight percent of producers reported having ≥1 crop type damaged by wildlife within the previous 12 months. Eleven percent reported deer damage to soybeans within the previous 12 months, and less than 2% of producers reported damage to soybeans by raccoons, squirrels, or Canada geese (*Branta canadensis*). Twenty-three percent of producers surveyed reported deer damage to corn, and 12% reported raccoon dam-

age to corn. Less than 3% of producers reported damage to corn by groundhogs, squirrels, or Canada geese (Figure 4).

Average reported damage by wildlife ranged from $105-$585 and $39-$479 to corn and soybeans, respectively (Figure 5). Respondents indicated crop value losses in corn of 2.1% for deer and 2.2% for raccoon. In soybeans, crop value losses to deer and groundhogs were 2.8% and 1.7%, respectively. Total reported losses by respondents were highest for deer and raccoon in corn, and deer and groundhog in soybeans (Figure 6).

Regarding crop producers' general attitudes towards wildlife, groundhogs were most disliked and considered a nuisance species by 85% of those surveyed. Raccoons had the second highest nuisance rating at 54%, and deer were considered a nuisance species by 21% of producers surveyed. Wild turkey were considered a nuisance by only 2% of the respondents although a relatively large percentage (16%) were unsure about their feelings towards wild turkey; less than

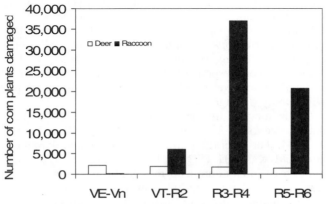

Fig. 3.   Number of corn plants in 100 fields surveyed in northcentral Indiana in 2003 and 2004 damaged by wildlife relative to corn plant development. Vegetative stages (VE, V1, V2, . . . , Vn); tassel stage (VT); reproductive stages: silking (R1), blister (R2), milk (R3), dough (R4), dent (R5), and maturity (R6) (Ritchie et al. 1997).

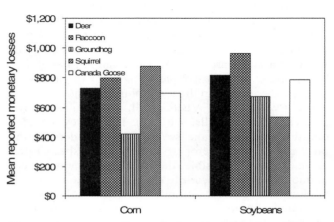

Fig. 5.   Mean reported monetary losses attributed to wildlife reported by agricultural producers (*n* = 529) to corn and soybean by wildlife in northcentral Indiana in 2003. The top 5 species for each crop type reported are shown.

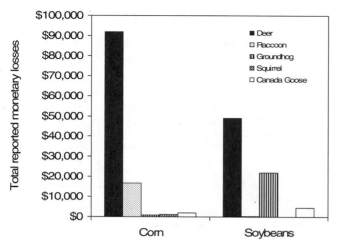

Fig. 6. Total reported monetary losses attributed to wildlife by agricultural producers (*n* = 529) in northcentral Indiana in 2003. The top 5 species for each crop type reported are shown.

2% of respondents indicated the same for deer, raccoon, or groundhog.

DISCUSSION

Crop depredation by wildlife is a substantial concern to most agricultural producers in northcentral Indiana. Although our field surveys indicated most fields incurred only light to moderate damage, the fields exhibited a high variance in levels of depredation. For example, we found no wildlife damage in 11 of 160 surveyed fields; conversely, we recorded a maximum of 162,453 damaged plants in 1 soybean field and 8,357 damaged plants in 1 corn field. The potential for severe wildlife damage to field crops varies greatly and potentially depends on factors such as animal densities across habitat mosaics and landscape-level habitat features.

Of the 160 crop fields we surveyed, 149 (93%) incurred some degree of wildlife depredation, which corresponded reasonably with landowner perceptions; our survey indicated 78% of agricultural producers reported having ≥1 crop type damaged by wildlife within the previous 12 months. Likewise, Conover (1998) reported 80% of farmers and ranchers nation-wide suffered wildlife damage during the year prior to 1993 or 1994.

Soybeans were damaged most often by deer (61%) and groundhogs (38%). Although most soybean damage by deer was only light browsing (which rarely affects yield adversely; Garrison and Lewis 1987), groundhog damage was more extensive and concentrated (i.e., near the burrow), resulting in reduced plant height or reduced bean production. The potential for groundhog damage to limit soybean harvest yields in the UWB may be substantial, depending on field size and the number of groundhogs present.

Perceptions of crop producers regarding species-specific damage to soybeans were similar to our findings. However, crop producers cited deer as the species most often responsible for damage to corn, when in reality, deer depredation to corn in our study area was minimal compared to raccoon depredation. Raccoon depredation may be more problematic to producers who grow corn in the UWB than in corn-producing regions of the U.S. in general. For example, Kelley et al. (1982) described raccoon depredation to corn fields in Ohio as negligible on a state-wide basis, and in Pennsylvania, Tzilkowski et al. (2002) reported that deer were responsible for most damage to corn.

Throughout the Midwest, raccoon populations have increased over the past 100 years (Lehman 1977), and are currently at or near record population levels in Indiana (Plowman 2003). Increases in raccoon abundance are due primarily to the conversion of native forest and prairie to agriculture (Page et al. 2001) and decreases in fur prices (Gehrt et al. 2002). Differences in depredation levels by raccoons between our study and previous studies (e.g., Kelley et al. 1982, Garrison and Lewis 1987) may be caused by regional differences in raccoon population sizes or the misidentification of raccoon damage as deer damage in previous studies. Annual fluctuations in raccoon population numbers or distributions as well as the availability of alternative food sources may have accounted for the differences observed in damage levels to corn between years in our study area (19,031 plants in 2003; 44,774 plants in 2004).

Crop producers' perceptions regarding monetary losses did not correspond closely to our field data. For example, producers reported deer were responsible for an average of $585 damage within the previous 12 months in all corn fields on their property; whereas only $283 was attributed to raccoon. These reported figures were unlikely to approach reality, given the proportionally high amount of damage our data attributed to raccoon compared to deer. When expressed as a percentage of total damage in corn fields, respondents attributed 82% of damage to deer and 15% to raccoon, which again was contradictory to our field data. However, when asked to describe the damage to corn in terms of percent value of crop lost, the same group attributed a 7.7% loss to raccoon and a 2.3% loss to deer, which was more in line with our field data that indicated more raccoon damage than deer damage in corn fields. Thus, producers we surveyed seem much more adept at expressing damage as a function of percent crop damaged as opposed to actual dollar amounts.

Our surveys of 160 agricultural fields yielded no cases of crop depredation by wild turkey. Turkey sign was evident in several fields and turkeys often were observed in fields we surveyed. Because of their relative conspicuousness, the wild turkey is commonly perceived as a species that damages crops (Payer and Craven 1995, Swanson et al. 2001). Studies of crop use by wild turkey in several midwestern states (Gabrey et al. 1993, Paisley et al. 1995, Payer and Craven 1995, Swanson et al. 2001) documented only trivial damage by wild turkeys to agricultural crops. Our study supports previous research and suggests that the occurrence of crop depredation by wild turkey is very low, even though they often occupy agricultural lands throughout the year. Future work in the area of crop depredation should consider the beneficial aspects of wild turkey in agricultural landscapes.

Proper identification of species responsible for damage is vitally important so landowners and producers can implement the correct management strategies. Determining the amount and cause of species-specific damage to field crops can be difficult, especially for untrained individuals. Our study demonstrates the need to improve education and training in identifying wildlife damage to agricultural crops. Accurate assessment of wildlife damage by producers is important because those experiencing damage may be less likely to encourage wildlife use of their properties (Conover 1998).

ACKNOWLEDGMENTS

This study would not have been possible without the cooperation of numerous landowners who allowed us access to their land, M. Retamosa for her work in constructing our GIS, all of our field technicians for their assistance in sampling fields, S. Backs and numerous state biologists and conservation officers for their assistance in trapping and with public relations, and L. Lawson and the USDA National Agricultural Statistics Service for assistance in conducting the mail and telephone surveys. Funding was provided by the Indiana Department of Natural Resources, the National Wild Turkey Federation, the Indiana Chapter of the National Wild Turkey Federation, and Purdue University.

LITERATURE CITED

Brown, T. L., and D. J. Decker. 1979. Incorporating farmers' attitudes into management of white-tailed deer in New York. Journal of Wildlife Management 43:236–239.

———, ———, and C. P. Dawson. 1978. Willingness of New York farmers to incur white-tailed deer in New York. Wildlife Society Bulletin 6:235–239.

Conover, M. R. 1998. Perceptions of American agricultural producers about wildlife on their farms and ranches. Wildlife Society Bulletin 26:597–604.

——— 2002. Resolving human-wildlife conflicts: the science of wildlife damage management. Lewis Publishers, Boca Raton, Florida, USA.

———, and D. J. Decker. 1991. Wildlife damage to crops: perceptions of agricultural and wildlife professionals in 1957 and 1987. Wildlife Society Bulletin 19:46–52.

Craven, S. R., and S. E. Hygnstrom. 1994. Deer. Pages D25-D40 in S.E. Hyngstrom, R. M. Timm, and G. E. Larson, editors. Prevention and control of wildlife damage. University of Nebraska Cooperative Extension, Lincoln, Nebraska, USA.

Dickson, J. G., editor. 1992. The wild turkey: biology and management. Stackpole Books. Harrrisburg, Pennsylvania, USA.

Gabrey, S. W., P. A. Vohs, and D. H. Jackson. 1993. Perceived and real crop damage by wild turkeys in northwestern Iowa. Wildlife Society Bulletin 21:39–45.

Garrison, R. L., and J. C. Lewis. 1987. Effects of browsing by white-tailed deer on yields of soybeans. Wildlife Society Bulletin 15:555–559.

Gehrt, S. D., G. F. Hubert, Jr., and J. A. Ellis. 2002. Long-term population trends of raccoons in Illinois. Wildlife Society Bulletin 30:457–463.

Kelley, S. T., D. A. Andrews, and D. T. Palmer. 1982. Bird and mammal damage to field corn in Ohio, 1977–1979. Ohio Journal of Science 82:133–136.

Lehman, L. E. 1977. Population ecology of the raccoon on the Jasper-Pulaski wildlife study area. Indiana Department of Natural Resources Publication. Pittman-Robertson Bulletin 9.

Loven, J. 2000. Woodchucks. Purdue University Cooperative Extension Service Publication, ADM-16, Department of Entomology, Purdue University, West Lafayette, Indiana, USA.

McDowell, R.D., and H. W. Pillsbury. 1959. Wildlife damage to crops in the United States. Journal of Wildlife Management 23:240–241.

Page, K. L., R. K. Swihart, and K. R. Kazacos. 2001. Changes in transmission of *Baylisascaris procyonis* to intermediate hosts as a function of spatial scale. Oikos 93:213–220.

Paisley, R. N., R. G. Wright, and J. F. Kubisiak. 1996. Use of agricultural habitats and foods by wild turkeys in southwestern Wisconsin. Proceedings of the National Wild Turkey Symposium 7:69–73.

Payer, D. C., and S. R. Craven. 1995. Wild turkeys: a problem for Wisconsin farmers? Wisconsin Department of Natural Resources Report G3623.

Plowman, B. W. 2003. March 2003 raccoon road-kill survey. Indiana Department of Natural Resources Research Report 841.

Pomerantz, G. A., C. Ng, and D. J. Decker. 1986. Summary of research on human tolerance of wildlife damage. Resource and Extension Series No. 25. Department of Natural Resources, New York State College of Agriculture and Life Sciences, Cornell University, Ithaca, New York, USA.

Ritchie, S. W., J. J. Hanway, and G. O. Benson. 1997. How a corn plant develops. Special Report No. 48. Iowa State University Cooperative Extension Service, Ames, Iowa, USA.

Siemer, W. F., and D. J. Decker. 1991. Human tolerance of wildlife damage: synthesis of research and management implications. Human Dimensions Research Unit Publication 91–7. Cornell University, Ithaca, New York, USA.

Swanson, D. A., G. E. Meyer, and R. J. Stoll, Jr. 2001. Crop damage by wild turkey in Ohio. Proceedings of the National Wild Turkey Symposium 8:139–140.

Tefft, B. C., M. A. Gregonis, and R. E. Eriksen. 2005 Assessment of crop depredation by wild turkey *Meleagris gallopavo* in the United States and Ontario, Canada. Wildlife Society Bulletin 33:590–595.

Tzilkowski, W. M., M. C. Brittingham, and M. J. Lovallo. 2002. Wildlife damage to corn in Pennsylvania: farmer and on-the-ground estimates. Journal of Wildlife Management 66:678–682.

Vecellio, G. M., R. H. Yahner, and G. L. Storm. 1994. Crop damage by deer at Gettysburg Park. Wildlife Society Bulletin 22:89–93.

Wywialowski, A. P. 1994. Agricultural producers' perceptions of wildlife-caused losses. Wildlife Society Bulletin 22:370–382.

———. 1996. Wildlife damage to field corn in 1993. Wildlife Society Bulletin 24:264–271.

———. 1997. Wildlife-caused losses of agricultural commodities in 1994 with emphasis on the Great Plains. Pages 171–172 in C. D. Lee and S. E. Hygnstrom, editors. Proceedings of the Thirteenth Great Plains Wildlife Damage Control Workshop. Kansas State University Agricultural Experiment Station and Cooperative Extension Service, Manhattan, Kansas, USA.

Zar, J. H. 1996. Biostatistical Analysis. Third edition. Prentice-Hall, Upper Saddle River, New Jersey, USA.

Lee Humberg (far left) is currently working as a biological science technician for the U.S. Department of the Army at Fort McCoy, Wisconsin. He received his B.S. in Wildlife and M.S. in Wildlife Ecology from Purdue University. Before returning to graduate school to investigate crop depredation and wild turkey ecology, Lee worked for the Pennsylvania Game Commission researching wild turkey ecology and Auburn University assisting in northern bobwhite quail research in longleaf pine ecosystems. His future professional interests include game bird ecology and management, human-wildlife conflicts, and predator-prey interactions. *Travis L. DeVault* (far right) is a Research Wildlife Biologist with the National Wildlife Research Center-USDA Wildlife Services in Brewerton, New York. He received a B.A. and M.A. in Biology from Indiana State University and a Ph.D. in Wildlife Science from Purdue University. He then served as a postdoctoral research associate and instructor at Purdue University. His current research interests include ecology and conservation of birds, management of human/wildlife conflicts, and scavenging behaviors of terrestrial vertebrates. *Brian MacGowan* (second from right) has been an Extension Wildlife Specialist with the Department of Forestry & Natural Resources, Purdue University since 1999. He earned a B.S. in Natural Resources from Ohio State University and a M.S. in Wildlife Science from Purdue University. His current educational programs and research include forest wildlife management, human-wildlife conflicts, warm season grass management, and the natural history and ecology of native fauna. Brian is a Certified Wildlife Biologist and a member of The Wildlife Society and Association of Natural Resources Extension Professionals. *James Beasley* (center) is currently pursuing a Ph.D. in Wildlife Ecology at Purdue University. He received his A.A.S. in Forestry from Paul Smith's College, a B.S. in Wildlife Management from the State University of New York College of Environmental Science and Forestry, and a M.S. in Wildlife Ecology from Purdue University. He is currently studying the effects of forest fragmentation on raccoon populations. His professional interests include carnivore and ungulate ecology, population dynamics, and wildlife management. *Gene Rhodes* (second from left) is a full Professor at Purdue University in the Department of Forestry and Natural Resources. He has published 98 peer-reviewed articles and has trained over 20 graduate students and postdocs in the past 10 years. His research focus is in wildlife ecology and genetics, including studies of the genetic consequences of species reintroduction programs, the use of genetic markers in applied wildlife management and conservation programs, the use of genetic markers to elucidate mating systems, movement behavior, and population structure of wildlife species and sustainability of wildlife species in human-dominated landscapes with an emphasis on the resolution of human-wildlife conflicts.

9th National Wild Turkey Symposium

**Wild Turkey Management:
Accomplishments, Strategies, and Opportunities**
—— Grand Rapids, Michigan ——

FALL ILLEGAL KILL OF FEMALE WILD TURKEYS IN VIRGINIA AND WEST VIRGINIA

Gary W. Norman[1]
*Virginia Department of Game and Inland Fisheries,
P.O. Box 996,
Verona, VA 24482, USA*

James C. Pack
*West Virginia Division of Natural Resources,
P.O. Box 67,
Elkins, WV 26241, USA*

David E. Steffen
*Virginia Department of Game and Inland Fisheries,
6701 Parkway Drive,
Roanoke, VA 24018, USA*

Curtis I. Taylor
*West Virginia Division of Natural Resources,
Capital Complex, Building 3,
Charleston, WV 25305, USA*

Abstract: State wildlife agencies recognize illegal kill of eastern wild turkeys (*Meleagris gallopavo silvestris*) occurs but the extent of losses are often unknown. As part of a 5-year cooperative study of population dynamics of female wild turkeys in our region, we radio-tagged 1,032 females from 3 separate areas to determine survival and sources of mortality including known illegal and potential illegal deaths. Fall turkey seasons and other big and small game seasons varied between our states and we sought to identify potential patterns of illegal kill related to different fall turkey hunting seasons. Annual and fall-winter mortality rates from known illegal deaths were not significantly different among our study areas. Known illegal mortality rate in the fall-winter period, averaged for the 3 study sites over 5 years, was 0.05. Patterns of illegal mortality during the fall hunting seasons were similar among our study sites. We used a model selection procedure to determine that mast abundance influenced illegal mortality rates during the fall hunting seasons. Law enforcement agencies may improve effectiveness in apprehension of turkey poachers by timing enforcement efforts to coincide with patterns of illegal kills, particularly during years of mast failures. We recommend several changes in outreach to hunters, which may reduce illegal killing of hens.

Proceedings of the National Wild Turkey Symposium 9:67–73
Key words: acorns, female illegal mortality, female wild turkey, law enforcement, *Meleagris gallopavo silvestris*, Virginia, West Virginia.

Poaching of wild turkeys has been recognized as a potential factor that could impact population dynamics (Wright and Speake 1975, Fleming and Speake 1976, Williams and Austin 1988, Little et al. 1990, Vangilder and Kurzejeski 1995, Davis et al. 1995, Miller et al. 1997, Alpizara-Jara et al. 2001). Illegal mortality rates are difficult to determine and monitor so state wildlife agencies are often left to assume poaching levels are not significant and do not limit wild turkey population levels.

As part of a 5-year cooperative population dyanamics study in Virginia and West Virginia, we investigated illegal mortality rates to assess potential impacts on populations. We also examined several variables that we thought might influence poaching including the extent of fall turkey hunting seasons and the availability of mast (acorn) crops. The availability of acorns has been found to influence fall harvests (Norman and Steffen 2003, Ryan et al. 2004) and legal hunting mortality rates (Steffen et al. 2002), thus the same effect could be expected with poaching.

STUDY AREA

The study was conducted in 3 geographic regions of western Virginia and West Virginia from September 1989 to August 1994 (Figure 1). Study area names were adopted from Pack et al. (1999) to be consistent. The Virginia region (Area 1–2; 21,709 km²) was in

[1] E-mail: gnorman@dgif.state.va.us

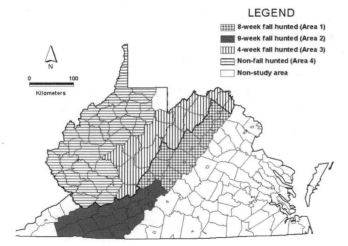

LEGEND

▦ 8-week fall hunted (Area 1)
■ 9-week fall hunted (Area 2)
▥ 4-week fall hunted (Area 3)
▱ Non-fall hunted (Area 4)
☐ Non-study area

Fig. 1. Virginia and West Virginia study areas in female wild turkey survival study from 1989–1994.

the Allegheny Mountain Range of the Ridge and Valley Province and had 8- or 9-week fall either-sex hunting seasons. Fourteen counties (16,837 km²) in eastern West Virginia's Potomac Plateau and Ridge and Valley Regions had a 4-week fall either-sex hunting season (Area 3). The remaining area of western West Virginia (Area 4; 30,386 km²) had no fall hunting. Regions were mostly forested (Area 1–2: 66%, Area 3: 77%, Area 4: 77%). Spring gobbler seasons were 4 weeks long in West Virginia and 5 weeks long in Virginia (Norman et al. 2001). Primary forest types included oak (*Quercus* spp.), oak-hickory (*Carya* spp.), oak-pine (*Pinus* spp.), yellow poplar (*Liriodendron tulipifera*), and northern hardwood (beech, *Fagus grandifolia*; cherry, *Prunus* spp.; and maple, *Acer* spp.).

METHODS

We captured wild turkeys throughout each region at 47 different trapping areas during fall (Sep–Nov) and winter (Jan–Apr) 1989–1994. We captured the birds at baited sites with rocket- or mortar-propelled nets. We weighed females and fitted them with transmitters, and released them at the capture location (Norman et al. 1997, Pack et al. 1999). We used transmitters (Advanced Telemetry Systems, Isanti, Minnesota, USA; Telonics, Mesa, Arizona, USA) that were equipped with an 8-hr mercury switch to indicate inactivity or potential mortality. We determined the birds' sex and age by examining their leg length, primary molt pattern (Healy and Nenno 1980), and feather coloration (Pelham and Dickson 1992).

We located the transmitter-equipped hens by triangulation 1–3 times per week throughout the year. We used airplanes to search for transmitters that could not be located during ground searches. Carcasses were recovered when mortality signals were detected to determine causes of mortality. We closely examined the carcass, harness, transmitter, and recovery site to determine cause of mortality. We radiographed carcasses when necessary to evaluate the potential effects of shot from illegal or crippling losses.

To minimize the potential effects of trapping on survival we used a 14-day conditioning period before entering hens in the study. If our radio-marked hens lived longer than 1 year during the study they were readmitted the following year (Pack et al. 1999).

We used the Kaplan–Meier product limit estimator modified for staggered entry (Pollock et al. 1989) to estimate survival and the generalized Trent-Rongstad analyses (Heisey and Fuller 1985) to identify cause-specific mortality agents. Trent-Rongstad survival estimates were based on spatial replicates of ≥4 wild turkeys per study area, based on forest cover type (Pack et al. 1999). We censored birds from analyses that we could not locate (Vangilder and Sheriff 1990). All mortalities except known illegal deaths were censored to estimate known illegal mortality rates. We combined independent tests using Fisher's meta-analysis procedure to examine the effect of illegal kill on survival (Hedges and Olkin 1985).

Because we observed a significant number of lost signals at suspicious times, we conducted a separate analysis of our data and considered some lost signals as potential illegal deaths. Potential illegal mortality rate was calculated by including both known illegal deaths and potential illegal deaths. All mortalities except potential illegal deaths were censored to estimate potential illegal mortality rates. Examples of potential illegal deaths included the disappearance of the transmitter signal on the opening weekend of squirrel, deer, or spring gobbler season.

Fall-winter season was defined as 1 September through 4 January. Differences in survival distribution between the states in the fall-winter period with illegal kills as deaths were tested using log-rank analyses (Pollock et al. 1989).

A priori we developed a series of linear models to explain variability in illegal mortality rates. These models incorporated explanatory variables that might impact poaching including days of fall turkey hunting seasons, acorn abundance, and the interaction of fall turkey hunting season length and acorns. The global model incorporated all potential parameters and was used to initially assess model potential. Model 1 was included to assess the importance of the presence of different fall hunting seasons (0, 24, and ≥48 days) as a potential factor influencing poaching rates. The abundance of acorns has been shown to influence legal hunting harvest rates (Norman and Steffen 2003, Steffen et al. 2002); therefore, Model 2 included an index of acorn abundance.

Acorns were counted along 16 survey routes in Virginia (Norman et al. 2005) while a qualitative measure of mast availability was made throughout West Virginia (Igo and Pack 1994). Because these indices were of different measures of mast we standardized the data using the following equation:

WV Correction factor =

(highest annual VA acorn index/WV acorn index

for that year) + (lowest VA acorn index/WV

acorn index for that year)/2.

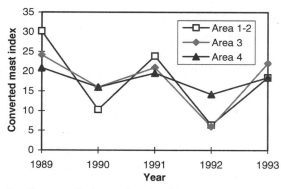

Fig. 2. Converted mast indices for Study Areas 1–2 (Virginia), Study Area 3 (eastern West Virginia), and Study Area 4 (western West Virginia).

The correction factor for the WV index was 0.68. To evaluate the accuracy of the correction factor we compared red and white oak indices between the states over 28 years (T. Fearer, Virginia Tech, unpublished data). We found no difference in red oak conversions between states but noticed white oak indices for West Virginia tended to be higher than Virginia indices. For both species groups we noticed greater variability in Virginia's acorn indices, due to the nature of the range in values for the West Virginia data. This implies that while converted indices may reflect the same trends in production, the converted West Virginia indices may underestimate the magnitude of fluctuations in production (T. Fearer, Virginia Tech, unpublished data). Alternately, Area 4 may have less variation in mast conditions due to lower elevations and milder climate in western West Virginia (Figure 2). We assumed this potential bias would not affect our investigations of a relationship between illegal harvest and mast. Finally, we considered the interaction between acorn abundance and fall season length in Model 3.

We evaluated models and ranked them using information-theoretic model selection techniques (Burnham and Anderson 2002). We used F statistics, P values, and R-square values to assess global model fit using $P \leq 0.10$. We evaluated candidate models within the set based on Akaike's Information Criterion adjusted for sample size (AIC_c), AIC_c differences (Δ_i),

Table 1. Sample sizes of known illegal deaths, potential illegal deaths, and radio-marked female wild turkeys in Virginia (Area 1–2) and West Virginia (Area 3, 4) during fall (1 Sep–4 Jan), 1989–1994.

	Area 1–2			Area 3			Area 4		
Year	Known illegal	Pot. illegal[a]	Radi-oed total	Known illegal	Pot. illegal	Radi-oed total	Known illegal	Pot. illegal	Radi-oed total
1989	0	0	34	3	3	24	0	3	21
1990	7	8	105	2	9	74	2	9	56
1991	2	4	80	0	0	54	3	5	63
1992	12	18	129	6	11	88	3	15	62
1993	7	11	104	1	7	62	3	11	80
Total	28	41	452	12	30	302	11	43	282

[a] Potential illegal deaths include known illegal deaths and lost signals that were suspicious due to the timing of the disappearance.

Table 2. Annual mortality rates of known illegal deaths of radio-marked female wild turkeys in Virginia (Area 1–2) and West Virginia (Area 3, 4) during 1989–1994.

	Area 1–2		Area 3		Area 4	
Year	Illegal rate	SE	Illegal rate	SE	Illegal rate	SE
1989	0.11	0.04	0.16	0.05	0.12	0.05
1990	0.18	0.05	0.08	0.05	0.09	0.05
1991	0.09	0.04	0.05	0.03	0.09	0.04
1992	0.21	0.05	0.12	0.05	0.07	0.03
1993	0.12	0.04	0.01	0.02	0.07	0.04
Average	0.14	0.12	0.08	0.02	0.09	0.02

explanatory power (R^2_{adj}), and Akaike weights (ω_i) (Burnham and Anderson 2002). We considered models with AIC values ≤ 4 as competing models. Akaike weight (ω_i) estimates the probability that a particular model is the best model in the candidate set (Burnham and Anderson 2002).

RESULTS

We radio-tagged 1,032 female wild turkeys between 1989 and 1994. Females that lived more than 1 year were reentered in the study the following year. The total sample size including new captures and reentered birds was 1,543 females (Table 1).

During the 5-year study we found 633 mortalities and determined 100 (15.8%) were known illegal deaths. Annual mortality from known illegal deaths averaged over the 5-year study ranged from 0.08 in Area 3 to 0.14 in Area 1–2 (Table 2). Annual known illegal mortality rate, averaged for the 3 study sites over 5 years, was 0.11.

Known illegal mortality during the 17-week fall-winter (1 Sep–4 Jan) period totaled 51 birds, representing 8% of mortalities. Fall-winter known illegal mortality rates ranged from 0.04 (Area 4) to 0.07 (Area 1–2; Table 3). We found no significant difference ($P > 0.05$) in known illegal mortality rates between states and study areas based on fall turkey season structure except in 1 comparison in 1993–1994 (Table 4). Additionally, weekly patterns of known illegal kill suggest poaching patterns were not significantly different between the states ($P > 0.05$) based on log-rank analyses for each year of the 5-year study (Pollock et al. 1989). Known illegal mortality rate in the fall-winter

Table 3. Fall–winter mortality rates from known illegal deaths of radio-marked female wild turkeys in Virginia (Area 1–2) and West Virginia (Area 3, 4) during 1989–1994.

	Area 1–2		Area 3		Area 4	
Year	Illegal rate	SE	Illegal rate	SE	Illegal rate	SE
1989	0.00	0.00	0.14	0.08	0.00	0.00
1990	0.09	0.04	0.03	0.02	0.04	0.03
1991	0.03	0.02	0.00	0.00	0.05	0.03
1992	0.14	0.04	0.08	0.03	0.05	0.03
1993	0.08	0.03	0.01	0.01	0.04	0.02
Average	0.07	0.02	0.05	0.03	0.04	0.01

Table 4. Meta-analysis of Trent-Rongstad estimates of fall–winter mortality rates from known illegal deaths in Virginia (Area 1–2) and West Virginia (Area 3, 4), 1989–1994.

	1–2 vs. 3, 4		3 vs. 4		1–2, 3 vs. 4		1–2 vs. 3		1–2 vs. 4	
	X	P	X	P	X	P	X	P	X	P
Annual[a]										
1989–90	12.25	0.14	8.48	0.39	9.65	0.29	10.45	0.23	8.11	0.42
1990–91	8.05	0.43	2.42	0.96	4.71	0.79	6.91	0.55	6.66	0.57
1991–92	3.09	0.93	6.26	0.62	5.66	0.69	4.13	0.84	4.30	0.83
1992–93	4.01	0.86	3.96	0.86	6.16	0.63	4.35	0.82	9.73	0.28
1993–94	19.63	0.01	4.26	0.83	11.60	0.17	12.71	0.12	10.10	0.26
Overall[b]	47.03	0.21	25.39	0.96	37.79	0.57	38.56	0.54	38.91	0.52
Fall–winter[c]	15.66	0.11	9.09	0.52	9.92	0.45	15.18	0.13	8.65	0.57

[a] Years combined over seasons.
[b] Combined over seasons and years.
[c] Fall–winter season combined over years.

period, averaged for the 3 study sites over 5 years, was 0.05.

Potential illegal mortalities totaled 114 birds in the fall-winter period (Table 1). Areas with fall hunting (Area 1–2 and 3) had comparable potential illegal mortality rates (0.10 and 0.11, respectively; Table 5). Potential illegal mortality rate in the area without fall hunting (Area 4) was 0.07 (Table 5). Potential illegal mortality rate in the fall-winter period, averaged for the 3 study sites over 5 years, was 0.09.

Our global model provided an acceptable fit ($F_{3,14}$ = 2.78, P = 0.091, R^2 = 0.43). Model 3, which incorporated mast as an explanatory factor, was clearly the best fit model given the suite of models we examined (Table 6). The model weight indicated the mast model had a 71% probability of being the best fit model. The mast model accounted for 23% of the variation in illegal mortalities we observed (R^2_{adj} = 0.23). The equation for the linear regression model was known illegal mortality rate = 0.117 − 0.0036 (mast index).

DISCUSSION

We found no difference in illegal mortality rates and patterns of illegal mortality between our states and study areas during the fall and early winter period. We assumed some difference in illegal mortality might be expected due to different histories of fall turkey hunting seasons and the timing of different fall hunting seasons. Area 4 in western West Virginia had no fall

Table 5. Fall–winter mortality rates from potential illegal deaths of radio-marked female wild turkeys in Virginia (Area 1–2) and West Virginia (Ara 3, 4), 1989–1994. Potential illegal deaths included known illegal deaths and lost signals that were suspicious due to the timing of the disappearance.

	Area 1–2		Area 3		Area 4	
Year	Potential illegal	SE	Potential illegal	SE	Potential illegal	SE
1989	0.00	0.00	0.14	0.08	0.00	0.00
1990	0.11	0.04	0.14	0.05	0.11	0.05
1991	0.05	0.03	0.00	0.00	0.09	0.04
1992	0.19	0.04	0.14	0.04	0.09	0.04
1993	0.13	0.04	0.11	0.04	0.07	0.03
Average	0.10	0.03	0.11	0.04	0.07	0.02

hunting seasons and the turkey population was more recently established whereas Areas 1–2 and 3 had long traditions of fall hunting with long established populations. We found significant differences in illegal mortality rates in spring between our states, but the higher illegal mortality rate in Virginia was attributed to earlier opening date of the spring gobbler season (Norman et al. 2001). Overall, we found no significant difference in know illegal mortality rates on an annual basis among our study areas.

Poaching rates higher than we observed have been reported in studies in Kentucky (63% in 1974; Wright and Speake 1975), Florida (63%; Williams and Austin 1988:200), and South Carolina (18%; Davis et al. 1995). Poaching levels in New York (13% Roberts et al. 1995) and Mississippi's Tallahala Wildlife Management Areas (9% Miller et al. 1997) were slightly lower than we observed. Poaching was much less of a mortality factor in Missouri (5% in spring; Vangilder and Kurzejeski 1995), Mississippi's Kemper County (3%; Palmer et al. 1993), and Wisconsin (2%; Wright et al. 1996).

Poaching in our study took place throughout the fall and early winter season but some periods of time appeared to have greater losses. Higher illegal losses tended to take place immediately before or after the fall turkey season (Figures 3 and 4). Some losses were noted before and during early squirrel seasons, but these losses were typically not as severe as losses later in the fall (Figures 3 and 4). Kurzejeski et al. (1987) noted significant poaching of wild turkey hens in Missouri's early squirrel seasons. Poaching levels generally declined during the fall turkey season in our study, but some instances were found and may have been related to exceeding the daily/seasonal bag limit, trespass, or not having a license. We observed some poaching during firearms deer seasons, particularly in West Virginia, and those results are similar to findings in Alabama (Fleming and Speake 1976, Everett et al. 1978). Miller et al. (1997) suggested hunter densities likely governed illegal mortality rates.

Illegal harvest rates were generally lower than legal harvest rates in our study. Legal harvest of wild turkey hens averaged 0.16 in Virginia (Area 1–2) while the illegal mortality rate averaged 0.07 (Pack et

Table 6. Results of information-theoretic model selection to evaluate competing models explaining illegal mortality rates in wild turkeys in Virginia and West Virginia, 1989–1994.

Model	n	SSE[a]	K[b]	AIC[c]	Δ_i[d]	R^2	R^2_{adj}[e]	ω_i[f]
Model 2: Illegal = mast (acorn indices) + ε	15	0.021	3	—90.2	0.0	0.28	0.23	0.71
Model 1: Illegal = fall hunting days + ε	15	0.027	3	—86.6	3.6	0.09	0.02	0.12
Model 3: Illegal = fall hunting days × mast + ε	15	0.029	3	—85.4	4.7	0.01	0.00	0.7
Global: Illegal = fall hunting days + mast + (fall days × mast) + ε	15	0.017	5	—85.2	5.0	0.43	0.28	0.06

[a] Sum of squares error.
[b] Number of estimable parameters in an approximating model.
[c] Akaike's Information Criterion adjusted for small sample size.
[d] Akaike's Information Criterion differences, relative to the smallest AIC value in model set.
[e] R^2_{adj} = Adjusted R square or explanatory power.
[f] Akaike weight. Weights may be interpeted as the probability that the model is the best supported by the data, given a set of alternative models.

al. 1999). This relationship was similar in West Virginia's fall hunted region with legal mortality rates averaging 0.08 (Pack et al. 1999) and illegal rates 0.05. However, if potential illegal rates actually reflect real poaching losses, then the differences between legal and illegal kills becomes smaller (Tables 3 and 5).

Seasonal survival rates were lowest in the fall-winter period due to the combination of legal, illegal, and natural mortality influences (Pack et al. 1999). We found no significant difference in illegal and natural mortality among our study sites and concluded legal hunting mortality was additive because annual survival rates varied with legal hunting mortality rates (Pack et al. 1999). Results of our modeling work suggest that fall survival rates have the greatest influence on turkey population growth rates (Alpizar-Jara et al. 2001) in our region and our management measures should concentrate on the fall season.

Our model selection approach identified acorn crops as an important explanatory factor that influenced poaching rates. The availability of acorns had a negative relationship on poaching rates. A similar relationship has been found with acorn abundance and fall harvests (Ryan et al. 2004, Norman and Steffen 2003, Steffen et al. 2002). Wild turkeys may be more vulnerable to legal and illegal hunting mortality in mast failure years as they expand their range into fields and clearings (Steffen et al. 2002). Conversely, during years of mast abundance, wild turkeys spend more time in forested areas and have smaller home ranges making them less vulnerable to legal or illegal hunting.

MANAGEMENT IMPLICATIONS

Poaching of wild turkeys is a significant problem in our study areas. Potential solutions to address this problem will not be easy, but by addressing the problem we may increase wild turkey populations in the region if these losses are an additive form of mortality. Given that fall hunting mortality is an additive form of mortality (Pack et al. 1999) and fall survival rates have the potential to impact populations and harvests (Alpizar-Jara et al. 2001), we assume fall mortality from illegal deaths have the potential to likewise impact populations. Programs to reward individuals that report wild turkey violations were in place during our study. While these programs offer potential help to address poaching, we feel these programs need more advertising and perhaps greater cash rewards to improve deterrence and assist law enforcement efforts. Greater

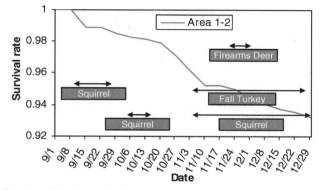

Fig. 3. Fall-winter (1 Sep–4 Jan) weekly survival rates of female wild turkeys in Study Area 1–2 (Virginia) averaged over 1989–1994. Times of hunting seasons are approximate as dates varied by year.

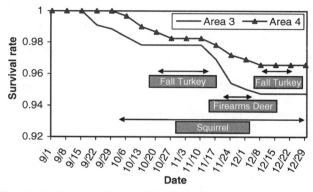

Fig. 4. Fall-winter (1 Sep–4 Jan) weekly survival rates of female wild turkeys in Study Areas 3 and 4 (West Virginia) averaged over 1989–1994. Times of hunting seasons are approximate as dates varied by year.

awareness of poaching and its impacts could be stressed to young hunters in hunter education programs and other programs such as the National Wild Turkey Federation JAKES events. Finally, law enforcement efforts to apprehend poachers may be more efficient if activities are focused during periods of peak illegal activity, particularly during years of mast failures.

ACKNOWLEDGMENTS

R. W. Duncan and R. W. Ellis, Virginia Department of Game and Inland Fisheries, and P. R. Johansen of the West Virginia Division of Natural Resources provided administrative support for this project. This project was primarily funded by Virginia's WE99R and West Virginia's W48R Federal Aid in Wildlife Restoration Programs. Financial support for telemetry and other equipment was provided by the National Wild Turkey Federation (NWTF) and their local chapters in Virginia and West Virginia. We thank J. E. Kennamer, the NWTF Technical Committee, and the Virginia State and West Virginia State Chapters NWTF for their support. Additional funding was provided by the Region V Northeast Administrative Funds through the USFWS Federal Aid in Wildlife Restoration Program, which was initiated and coordinated by J. F. Organ and supported by the Northeast Wild Turkey Technical Committee.

LITERATURE CITED

Alpizar-Jara, R., E. N. Brooks, K. H. Pollock, D. E. Steffen, J. C. Pack, and G. W. Norman. 2001. Eastern wild turkey population dynamics model for Virginia and West Virginia. Journal of Wildlife Management 65:415–424.

Burnham, K. P., and D. R. Anderson. 2002. Model selection and multimodel inference. A practical information-theoretic approach. Springer-Verlag, New York, New York, USA.

Davis, J. R., H. R. Barnhill, D. C. Guynn, Jr., R. E. Larkin, and W. M. Baughman. 1995. Wild turkey nesting ecology in the Lower Coastal Plain of South Carolina. Proceedings of the Annual Conference of the Southeastern Association of Fish and Wildlife Agencies 49:454–465.

Everett, D. D., D. W. Speake, and D. R. Hillestad, and D. N. Nelson. 1978. Impact of managed public hunting on wild turkeys in Alabama. Proceedings of the Annual Conference of the Southeastern Association of Fish and Wildlife Agencies 32:116–125.

Fleming, W. J., and D. W. Speake. 1976. Losses of the eastern wild turkey from a stable Alabama population. Proceedings of the Southeastern Association of Game and Fish Commissioners 30:377–385.

Healy, W. M., and E. S. Nenno. 1980. Growth parameters and sex and age criteria for juvenile eastern wild turkeys. Proceedings of the National Wild Turkey Symposium 4:168–185.

Hedges, L. V., and I. Olkin. 1985. Statistical methods for meta-analysis. Academic Press, San Diego, California, USA.

Heisey, D. D., and T. K. Fuller. 1985. Evaluation of survival and cause specific mortality rates using telemetry data. Journal of Wildlife Management 49:668–674.

Igo, W. K., and J. C. Pack. 1994. Mast survey and West Virginia hunting outlook. West Virginia Division of Natural Resources, Charleston, West Virginia, USA.

Kurzejeski, E. W., L. D. Vangilder, and J. B. Lewis. 1987. Survival of wild turkey hens in north Missouri. Journal of Wildlife Management 51:188–193.

Little, T. W., J. M. Kienzler, and G. A. Hanson. 1990. Effects of fall either-sex hunting on survival in an Iowa wild turkey population. Proceedings of the National Wild Turkey Symposium 6:119–125.

Miller, D. A., G. A. Hurst, B. D. Leopold. 1997. Chronology of wild turkey nesting, gobbling, and hunting in Mississippi. Journal of Wildlife Management 61:840–845.

Norman, G. W., T. M. Fearer, and P. K. Devers. 2005. Factors affecting wild turkey recruitment in western Virginia. Proceedings of the Southeast Association of Game and Fish Commissioners. 48:248–262.

———, J. C. Pack, and G. A. Hurst. 1997. Transmitter selection and attachment technique for wild turkey research. National Wild Turkey Federation Research Bulletin 4.

———, and D. E. Steffen. 2003. Effects of recruitment, oak mast, and fall-season format on wild turkey harvest rates in Virginia. Wildlife Society Bulletin 31:553–559.

———, ———, C. I. Taylor, J. C. Pack, K. H. Pollock, and K. Tsai. 2001. Reproductive chronology, spring hunting, and illegal kill of female wild turkeys. Proceedings of the National Wild Turkey Symposium 8:269–280.

Pack, J. C., G. W. Norman, C. I. Taylor, D. E. Steffen, D. A. Swanson, K. H. Pollock, and R. Alpizar-Jara. 1999. Effects of fall hunting on wild turkey populations in Virginia and West Virginia. Journal of Wildlife Management 63:964–975.

Palmer, W. E., S. R. Priest, R. S. Seiss, P. S. Phalen, and G. A. Hurst. 1993. Reproductive effort and success in a declining wild turkey population. Proceedings of the Annual Conference of the Southeastern Association of Fish and Wildlife Agencies 47:138–147.

Pelham, P. H., and J. G. Dickson. 1992. Physical characteristics. Pages 32–45 *in* J. G. Dickson, editor. The wild turkey: biology and management. Stackpole Books, Harrisburg, Pennsylvania, USA.

Pollock, K. H., S. R. Winterstein, C. M. Bunck, and P. D. Curtis. 1989. Survival analysis in telemetry studies: the staggered entry design. Journal of Wildlife Management 53:7–15.

Roberts, S. D., J. M. Coffey, and W. F. Porter. 1995. Survival and reproduction of female wild turkeys in New York. Journal of Wildlife Management 59:437–447.

Ryan, C. W., J. C. Pack, W. K. Igo, J. C. Riffenberger, and A. B. Billings. 2004. Relationship of mast production to big-game harvest in West Virginia. Wildlife Society Bulletin 32:786–794.

Steffen, D. E., N. L. Lafon, and G. W. Norman. 2002. Turkeys, acorns, and oaks. Pages 241–255 *in* W. J. McShea and W. M. Healy, editors. Oak forest ecosystems: ecology and management for wildlife. Johns Hopkins University Press, Baltimore, Maryland, USA.

Vangilder, L. V., and E. W. Kurzejeski. 1995. Population ecology of the eastern wild turkey in northern Missouri. Wildlife Monographs 130.

———, and S. L. Sheriff. 1990. Survival estimation when fates of some animals are unknown. Transactions of the Missouri Academy of Science 24:56–68.

Williams, L. E., Jr., and D. H. Austin. 1988. Studies of the wild turkey in Florida. Florida Game and Fresh Water Fish Commission Technical Bulletin 10.

Wright, G. A., and D. W. Speake. 1975. Compatibility of eastern wild turkey with recreational activities at Land Between the Lakes, Kentucky. Proceedings of the Annual Conference of the Southeastern Association of Fish and Wildlife Agencies 29:578–584.

Wright, R. G., R. N. Paisley, and J. F. Kubisiak. 1996. Survival of wild turkey hens in southwestern Wisconsin. Journal of Wildlife Management 60:313–320.

Gary W. Norman received a B.S. Degree from West Virginia University and M.S. from Virginia Tech. He worked for the West Virginia Department of Natural Resources (WVDNR) for 7 years and has been employed with the Virginia Department of Game and Inland Fisheries since 1987. Gary currently serves as Forest Game Bird Project Leader and is responsible for statewide research, conservation, and management programs for ruffed grouse and wild turkey. Gary's research efforts have centered on population dynamics studies of wild turkey and ruffed grouse. He coordinated a 5-year wild turkey hen project with the WVDNR and served as coordinator for the 8-state Appalachian Cooperative Grouse Research Project. He is currently working on a cooperative study of wild turkey gobblers and gobbling with the WVDNR.

David E. Steffen is the forest wildlife program manager for the Virginia Department of Game and Inland Fisheries. Previously he was a biologist with the Mississippi Department of Fisheries, Wildlife, & Parks. Dave earned B.S. and M.S. degrees from Virginia Tech and a Master of Applied Statistics from Louisiana State University. He is a Certified Wildlife Biologist and past-president of the Virginia Chapter of The Wildlife Society. His interests include population dynamics with an emphasis on turkey, deer, and bear management applications.

James C. Pack received his B.S. in Forestry from West Virginia University and M. S. in Wildlife Science from Virginia Tech (Virginia Polytechnic Institute and State University). Former Positions: Forestry Aid, Summer 1961, DNR; Research Assistant, 1963–64 West Virginia University, Division of Forestry; District Game Biologist, Virginia Department of Game and Inland Fisheries, 1966–67; Forest Habitat Research Leader and Co-leader National Forest Development, DNR, 1967–1970; Supervisor Game Management Services Unit, 2000–2001; Turkey Project Leader, Game Management Services Unit, Wildlife Resources Section, Elkins, West Virginia, 1971–2005. Has been involved with the management or research of the wild turkey for 37 years. Present Position: Retired. Has authored or co-authored over 140 published articles dealing primarily with research and management of forest game wildlife species. His main professional interest is forest ecology and management for wildlife and wild turkey harvest management research. Currently he is enjoying his first grandson and retirement with Ramona, his wife of over 42 years.

Curtis I. Taylor is currently Chief of the Wildlife Resources Section for the West Virginia Division of Natural Resources. He served as co-project leader on the Wild Turkey Populations Dynamics Study and has worked on various turkey research projects during his 25 years with the agency. He also directed the first radio telemetry study of ocellated turkeys in Guatemala. He received a B.S. in Wildlife from West Virginia University and his M.S. from the University of Tennessee. Curtis received the highly coveted Henry S. Mosby Award from the National Wild Turkey Federation in February, 2005.

PATTERNS OF CAPTURE-RELATED MORTALITY IN RIO GRANDE WILD TURKEYS

John H. Brunjes IV[1,2]
*Department of Natural Resources Management,
Mail Stop 42125, Texas Tech University,
Lubbock, TX 79409, USA*

Mark C. Wallace
*Department of Natural Resources Management,
Mail Stop 42125, Texas Tech University,
Lubbock, TX 79409, USA*

Derrick P. Holdstock[3]
*Department of Natural Resources Management,
Mail Stop 42125, Texas Tech University,
Lubbock, TX 79409, USA*

Matthew J. Butler
*Department of Natural Resources Management,
Mail Stop 42125, Texas Tech University,
Lubbock, TX 79409, USA*

Nancy E. McIntyre
*Department of Biological Sciences,
Texas Tech University, Mail Stop 43131,
Lubbock, TX 79409, USA*

Roger Applegate[5]
*Kansas Department of Wildlife and Parks,
1830 Merchant, Box 1525,
Emporia, KS 66801, USA*

Warren B. Ballard
*Department of Natural Resources Management,
Mail Stop 42125, Texas Tech University,
Lubbock, TX 79409, USA*

Richard S. Phillips
*Department of Natural Resources Management,
Mail Stop 42125, Texas Tech University,
Lubbock, TX 79409, USA*

Brian L. Spears[4]
*Department of Natural Resources Management,
Mail Stop 42125, Texas Tech University,
Lubbock, TX 79409, USA*

Michael S. Miller
*Texas Parks and Wildlife Department,
Tarleton State University,
Stephenville, TX 76402, USA*

Stephen J. DeMaso
*Texas Parks and Wildlife Department,
4200 Smith School Road,
Austin, TX 78744, USA*

Philip S. Gipson
*Kansas Cooperative Fish and Wildlife Research Unit,
205 Leasure Hall, Kansas State University,
Manhattan, KS 66506, USA*

Abstract: Researchers investigating survival of wild turkeys (*Meleagris gallopavo*) traditionally have assumed mortalities within the first 14 days may be capture-related, and have excluded those data from analyses. Few have explored ways to reduce mortality during this period. In 2000, we initiated a long-term radiotelemetry study of the ecology of Rio Grande wild turkeys (*M. g. intermedia*) in the southern Great Plains. During 2000–2002, we captured and outfitted 667 turkeys with backpack-style radio transmitters. We recaptured 123 previously trans-mittered birds for 790 14-day survival periods. Sixty-seven birds (8.5%) died ≤14 days post capture and were considered capture-related mortalities. Male mortality (13.4%) was greater than female (5.8%) mortality (*P* = 0.001). Birds captured in the afternoon had higher (*P* = 0.035) mortality rates (11.6%) versus morning (8.0%) or mid-day (7.1%) captures. We found no differences in mortality among study sites (*P* = 0.14), years (*P* = 0.27), age class for males (*P* = 0.38) or females (*P* = 0.99), or capture method (*P* = 0.64). We found no relationship between weather conditions and 14-day postcapture survival of turkeys with the exception of precipitation 48 hours post capture ($P = 0.01$). We recommend minimizing handling of males and avoiding afternoon captures to reduce capture-related mortalities.

Proceedings of the National Wild Turkey Symposium 9:75–81

Key words: capture-related mortality, Great Plains, Kansas, *Meleagris gallopavo intermedia*, Rio Grande wild turkey, survival, Texas.

Trent and Rongstad (1974) recognized the value of radio transmitters in survival analyses. They used telemetry to study survival in eastern cottontail rabbits (*Sylvilagus floridanus*) and since that time, radio transmitters have proven to be a valuable tool in studying survival and mortality of wild animals (White and Garrott 1990, Millspaugh and Marzluff 2001). Stress resulting from capture and handling needed to attach radio transmitters may cause increased mortality post-capture in turkeys (McMahon and Johnson 1980, Spraker et al. 1987, Miller 1996, and Nicholson et al. 2000). Therefore, researchers generally exclude from analyses birds that die ≤14 days post-capture as capture-related mortalities (Hennen and Lutz 2001, Hohensee and Wallace 2001, Wakling et al. 2001, Wright and Vangilder 2001, Nguyen et al. 2003). Capture-related mortalities in wild turkeys have been documented (McMahon and Johnson 1980, Clark 1985, Spraker et al. 1987, and Nicholson et al. 2000) at both capture and relocation sites; however only Miller et al. (1996) addressed capture-related mortalities in turkeys (*M. g. silvestris*) released immediately at original capture sites. No studies have investigated capture-related mortalities in the Rio Grande subspecies.

In 1999, prompted by apparent widespread population declines and a lack of basic life-history information, we initiated a long-term study of the ecology of Rio Grande turkeys in the southern Great Plains. As part of this study, one of our objectives was to investigate factors that might contribute to capture-related mortality and determine methods that may reduce mortality following capture events in the future.

STUDY AREAS

We captured Rio Grande wild turkeys at 3 sites in the Texas Panhandle and one in southwestern Kansas. The Texas sites occurred along the intersection of the Rolling Plains and High Plains physiogeographic regions. Cattle production was the primary landuse. The southernmost site was centered on the Matador Wildlife Management Area near Paducah, Texas (Matador). The Pease River flowed west to east through the center of the study area. Dominant vegetation types included mesquite (*Proposis glandulosa*), grassland, prickly pear cactus (*Opuntia* sp.), and juniper (*Juniperis* sp.) shrubland in the uplands and western cottonwood (*Populus fremontii*) in the riparian areas, with mesquite covering the largest area. Elevations ranged from 488 to 610 m above sea level.

The Salt Fork site was composed of private ranches along the Salt Fork of the Red River northeast of Clarendon, Texas. The Salt Fork of the Red River flowed west to east through the center of the study area. Dominant vegetation types included mesquite, grassland, shinnery oak (*Quercus havardii*), and sandsage (*Artemisia filifolia*) in the uplands, and western cottonwood in the riparian areas. Mesquite covered the largest area. Elevations ranged from 632 to 995 m above sea level.

The northernmost Texas site was centered on the Gene Howe Wildlife Management Area east of Canadian, Texas (Gene Howe). The Canadian River flowed west to east through the center of the study area. Dominant vegetation types included sandsage, grassland, and mesquite in the upland areas, and salt cedar (*Tamarisk gallica*) and western cottonwoods in the riparian areas. Sandsage habitats covered the largest area.

The Kansas-Colorado site was located in the southwestern corner of Kansas and the southeastern corner of Colorado, and was centered on the Cimmaron National Grassland (Kansas). The Cimmaron River flowed west to east through the center of the study area. Cattle production and oil-gas production were the only land uses on the grassland, but privately owned portions of the study area included dry cropland and irrigated cropland. Dominant vegetation types were western cottonwood woodland dominating the riparian areas and sandsage dominating the uplands.

METHODS

Capture

We captured Rio Grande wild turkeys at the 3 Texas sites during January–March, 2000–2002, and at the Kansas site during January–March, 2000–2001. We captured birds using drop nets (Davis and DelMonte 1986), rocket nets (Bailey et al. 1980, Wunz 1984) and walk-in traps (Davis 1994). Once captured, we removed birds from the nets and placed them in transport boxes (76.2 × 35.6 × 61.0 cm) provided by the National Wild Turkey Federation (Edgefield, South Carolina, USA) until processing. Boxes were placed together a short distance away from where the birds

[1] Present Address: Kentucky Department of Fish and Wildlife Resources, #1 Sportsman's Lane, Frankfort, KY 40601, USA.

[2] E-mail: john.brunjes@ky.gov

[3] Present Address: Texas Parks and Wildlife Department, 15412 FM 2266, Canadian, TX 79014, USA.

[4] Present Address: U.S. Fish and Wildlife Service, 11103 E. Montgomery Drive, Spokane, WA 99206, USA.

[5] Present Address: Tennessee Wildlife Resources Agency, P.O. Box 40747, Nashville, TN 37204, USA.

were processed to minimize disturbance. Once removed from the box for processing, birds were hooded and restrained. Handling time once the bird was removed from the box averaged approximately 5 minutes per bird. We classified turkeys as male or female and adult (≥1.5 years old) or sub-adult (approx. 0.5 years old; Williams and Austin 1988), then fitted each turkey with a 110-g backpack transmitter equipped with an 8-hour mortality switch (Model A1155, Advanced Telemetry Systems, Insanti, Minnesota, USA). We measured body temperature using digital thermometers inserted in the cloaca. Thermometers were cleaned between each use using rubbing alcohol. We collected a 10 ml blood sample from the brachial vein of the wing. All captured birds were weighed and received a uniquely numbered aluminum leg band. The general condition of the bird was recorded immediately prior to release. Condition was classified as "poor" if the bird had lost most or all tail feathers and a significant portion of contour feathers leaving bare patches, "fair" if some tail feathers and a small amount of contour feathers were lost, or "good" if the bird had almost no feather loss. Time of release was recorded to calculate total handling time (from capture to release). We released previously transmittered turkeys that we captured immediately after assessment, with no temperature or blood samples taken. We obtained the following weather data from the nearest weather station to each site: high and low ambient temperature for day of capture, low ambient temperature the night after capture, and precipitation 24 and 48 hours post-capture (National Oceanic and Atmospheric Administration 2000a, 2000b, 2001a, 2001b, 2002). Capture periods were grouped into 3 categories based on time of capture: morning (dawn through 1059 hours), midday (1100 through 1359 hours), and evening (1400 hours through dusk).

We attempted to maintain 75 transmittered turkeys at each site: 35–45 adult females, 15 adult males, and 15–25 sub-adults (both male and female). Birds that died before the end of the trapping season were replaced in the final capture at each site. Most turkeys that died within the 14-day period were killed by predators or scavenged immediately after death. Of the mortalities, only 1 turkey was found intact, thus eliminating the possibility of doing necropsies.

Survival Analyses

We monitored captured turkeys at least every other day during the 14-day post-capture period using either a truck-mounted omni-directional whip antenna or null-peak system. We chose a 14-day period because this is the point where most previous authors considered capture-related mortalities to occur, and our data seemed to support this (Figure 1) as mortality rates after 14 days were similar to winter mortality (Holdstock 2003, Phillips 2004). If a mortality signal was detected, we located the bird as soon as possible to determine if the bird died or had lost its transmitter.

We calculated survival rates using the Kaplan-Meier staggered entry design (Pollock et al. 1989).

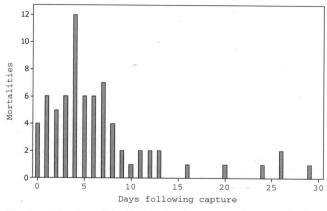

Fig. 1. Number of deaths occurring, by day, following the capture of 790 Rio Grande wild turkeys at 3 study sites in the Texas panhandle and 1 study site in southwest Kansas, 2000–2002.

Turkeys killed at the trap site by a rocket or falling pole ($n = 3$), birds that lost transmitters ($n = 8$), or birds captured in a walk-in trap ($n = 5$) were excluded from analyses. We used a log-linear model (Fienberg 1977) to examine differences and interactions among the variables. Because none of the models were significant, we conducted a series of univariable analyses of each variable (Hosmer and Lemeshow 2000) to determine which variables might impact survival. While using a series of univariable analyses increases the potential for Type I error, we feel this is the conservative approach as we are trying to identify factors that might influence capture related mortality, and committing Type I error is more conservative than committing Type II errors. We used a likelihood ratio chi-square test with k-1 degrees of freedom for nominal and ordinal data (Hosmer and Lemeshow 2000). Continuous data were tested using a univariable logistic regression model for significance of the coefficient (Hosmer and Lemeshow 2000).

RESULTS

During 2000–2003, we captured and outfitted 667 turkeys with backpack radio transmitters. Previously captured birds were recaptured 123 times. Of these recaptures, 97 birds were captured twice, 23 were captured 3 times, and 4 were captured 4 times. Total captures ($n = 790$) included 319 adult females, 194 sub-adult females, 136 adult males, and 141 sub-adult males. We had 42 capture events: 28 rocket net captures, 13 drop net captures, and 1 walk-in trap capture. Drop nets were used to capture 384 turkeys (mean group size = 43.9, range = 5–87), rocket nets were used to capture 403 turkeys (mean group size = 24.9, range = 2–74), a walk-in trap was used to capture 5 turkeys. Most captures were conducted in the morning ($n = 25$), followed by afternoon ($n = 10$), and midday ($n = 7$).

Total handling time of turkeys after removal from drop net or rocket net until release (including time-in-box and processing) ranged from 13 min to 315 min. Low ambient temperatures the night prior to capture averaged −3°C (range = −12°C to 9°C). High ambient temperatures the day of capture averaged 13°C (range = −7°C to 27°C). Low ambient temperatures the night after capture averaged −2°C (range = −12°C to 9°C). Precipitation occurred within 24 hours following capture events 8 times and occurred within 48 hours following capture events 15 times.

Of 790 individual turkey captures, 67 (8.5%) died within 14 days of capture and were classified as capture-related mortalities. The mean number of days survived by those birds was 5.6 days. The Kaplan-Meyer survival rate for all birds was 92.4%.

The proportion of males dying from capture-related stress (37 of 277; 13.4%) was higher (χ^2 = 12.4, df = 1, P < 0.001) than female turkeys (19 of 319; 5.8%). The proportion of sub-adult and adult females (χ^2 = 0.00, df = 1, P = 0.997) and males (χ^2 = 0.78, df = 1, P = 0.378) dying from capture-related stress did not differ; therefore, we pooled data from both age classes for both sexes in further analyses.

When considering each capture method, the proportion of turkeys dying did not differ (χ^2 = 0.22, df = 1, P = 0.637) between rocket nets (7.94%) and drop nets (7.85%). The probability of capture-related mortality was not different among study sites (χ^2 = 2.2, df = 1, P = 0.137), nor among years (χ^2 = 1.2, df = 1, P = 0.266). Differences did occur between capture periods (χ^2 = 6.4, df = 1, P = 0.035). The afternoon period (11.6%) had a higher probability of mortality than did mid-day (7.1%) and morning (8.1%) captures. A difference did not occur when comparing the survival probability to the number of recaptures a bird had experienced (χ^2 = 3.0, df = 1, P = 0.081). The condition of the bird at release did impact survival (χ^2 = 5.8, df = 1, P = 0.016). Turkeys released in Poor condition had a higher percentage of mortalities (28.6%, n = 14) than those in fair (11.9%, n = 67) or good (9.2%, n = 578) conditions.

There was no relationship between body temperature and the probability of mortality (χ^2 = 0.05, df = 1, P = 0.818) in turkeys. Mean body temperature for turkeys at release was similar (t = 0.356, df = 1, P = 0.63) in males ($\bar{x}$ = 41.2°C) and females ($\bar{x}$ = 41.12°C), and body temperature did not impact survival within the 14-day period (χ^2 = 0.50, df = 1, P = 0.478). Body mass influenced the probability of survival in turkeys (χ^2 = 15.3, df = 1, P < 0.001) as a whole. Body mass did impact the probability of mortality for male (χ^2 = 28.5, df = 1, P < 0.001) turkeys but did not inpact the probability of survival of female (χ^2 = 1.1, df = 1, P = 0.300) turkeys. Handling time had no relationship with probability of mortality (χ^2 = 0.37, df = 1, P = 0.543). Low ambient temperature the morning of capture (χ^2 = 0.02, df = 1, P = 0.888), high ambient temperature the day of capture (χ^2 = 0.05, df = 1, P = 0.819), low ambient temperature the night after capture (χ^2 = 0.69, df = 1, P = 0.407), rainfall 24 hours after capture (χ^2 = 2.7, df = 1, P = 0.102), handling time (χ^2 = 0.37, df = 1, P = 0.406) and number of birds captured (χ^2 = 2.9, df = 1, P = 0.543) all did not show relationships with probability of mortality. Only rain 48 hours following capture (χ^2 = 10.27, df = 1, P = 0.001) had a positive relationship with probability of mortality.

DISCUSSION

The use of radio transmitters is invaluable to wildlife research; capture stress and associated mortality is an unfortunate side effect of these captures (Spraker et al. 1987, Miller et al 1996, Nicholson et al. 2000). Our results suggested that several factors initially suspected of increasing mortality risk were not associated with greater mortality. However, sex, capture period, and precipitation post-capture were associated with increased risk.

Our observation of increased capture-related mortality in male Rio Grande wild turkeys is different from the findings of Spraker et al. (1986) who found no differences in capture myopathy between male and female eastern wild turkeys. In Mississippi, Miller et al. (1996) observed that females were less likely to survive the 14-day post-capture period. They hypothesized that the greater body mass of males allowed them to better tolerate the physical stress of capture and handling. However, we found no relationship between body mass and mortality for either sex during the post-capture period. Although we found no relationship between handling time and mortality, male turkeys were captured in small groups, which reduced handling time. The body temperature at release was not higher in males than females. Nor did body temperature at release differ in males that died within the 14-day period compared to those that survived. We believe a behavioral issue may be responsible for these differences, rather than body mass. The smaller winter flock size of male (approx. 4–15 birds; personal observation), compared to female Rio Grande wild turkeys (approx. 25–250 birds; personal observation) in this region, may increase susceptibility to predators. Male mule deer (*Odocoileus hemionus*) that tended to remain solitary much of the year suffered higher mortality from mountain lions (*Puma concolor*) than females in groups (Geist 1981). Our survival data also indicated male Rio Grande wild turkeys had lower winter survival rates (77.8%) than females (94.6%), with most identifiable deaths (33.7%) of males being attributed to coyotes (*Canis latrans*) and bobcats (*Lynx rufus*) (J. Brunjes, Texas Tech University, unpublished report).

Previous studies found juvenile or sub-adult turkeys were more susceptible to capture-related mortality than adults (Spraker et al. 1887, Miller et al. 1996). In Mississippi, 21% of sub-adult female eastern wild turkeys and 7% of adult females died ≤14 days post-capture (Miller et al. 1996). Sub-adult and adult eastern wild turkeys in Oklahoma survived the post-capture period at similar rates (21% and 14%, respectively; Nicholson et al. 2000). We found no differences between the probability of mortality of adult (6.0%) and sub-adult (5.7%) female turkeys or between adult (14.7%) and sub-adult (12.1%) male Rio Grande wild turkeys.

Although others have suggested ambient temperatures may impact survival of birds post-capture, there is scant data to support this supposition. Bailey et al. (1980) recommended that turkeys not be trapped in temperatures >21.6°C; however, they did not confirm increased mortality when captures were conducted in warmer conditions. Miller et al. (1996) also recommended not trapping during periods of high temperature, but did not specify an upper limit. They further recommended only trapping in temperatures >15°C. This recommendation could have been influenced by the fact they were using alpha-chloralose, which reduces the thermoregulatory ability of birds, in some of their capture events. In contrast, Nicholson et al. (2000) found that mortality in the post-capture period decreased with decreasing temperatures. They recommended not trapping in conditions where temperatures exceeded 10°C. Temperature did not impact post-capture survival in our birds, with temperature ranging from −12°C to 18°C. We did not observe any adverse effects from low temperatures. In our coldest capture (−12°C), 31 of 31 (100%) birds survived ≥14 days. We do not believe low temperatures, as experienced in this region, negatively impact mortality rates in the post-capture period. The lowest temperatures we recorded the night after capture did not impact survival, but extreme low temperatures combined with wet conditions immediately following capture may increase post-capture mortality.

The effect of precipitation on wild turkeys following capture events has not been previously investigated. We found a significant effect of rainfall within 48 hours post-capture while rainfall 24 hours post-capture did not impact survival within the post-capture period. We believe this observation was due likely to a 9.1-cm freezing rain event which followed 1 capture event in which 4 of 8 birds captured (50%) died ≤14-days post capture. We, therefore, recommend avoiding captures when heavy or freezing rain is forecasted within 48 hours following the capture event. When this event was removed from analyses, light rain and snowfall 48 hours post capture did not appear to impact survival. Bailey (1980) recommended wet or snow-covered nets not be fired because the net could malfunction and injure birds during capture, not because of concern that precipitation immediately before or during capture might decrease survival after release.

The increased mortality rates associated with afternoon captures versus morning (8.1%) or mid-day (7.1%) captures has not been reported previously. Other studies have reported post-capture related mortalities (Spraker et al. 1987, Nicholson et al. 2000). Birds in those studies, however, were being relocated and thus were held for extended periods before release, which likely impacted survival differently than immediate on-site release. Miller et al. (1996) suggested trapping early in the morning in the summer months to avoid heat, but did not report capture times or associated mortality rates. Because we observed no relationship between temperature and mortality, the reason for increased mortality in birds captured after 1400 hours is unclear. Many birds, after being outfitted with transmitters and losing tail feathers during capture, had difficulty flying after release. Possibly, turkeys require a time to adjust to the transmitter or sudden feather loss to become comfortable flying. Birds released late in the day may have had difficulty flying into the roost or otherwise avoiding predators.

Potential differences between birds captured with rocket nets versus drop nets have not been investigated. Miller et al. (1996) found no differences in survival when comparing alpha-chloralose and cannon nets. We found similar capture-related mortality rates for drop nets (7.8%) and rocket nets (7.9%). Although low sample size precluded comparison with nets, all 5 turkeys captured in walk-in traps survived ≥14 days. We used rocket nets on 28 capture events and drop nets for 13 events. We used the rocket nets more frequently because they were simpler to set up, required less acclimation time for the birds, the number of birds captured per event was smaller, and fewer personnel were required. During our first season we perceived that drop nets had increased mortality; however, data did not confirm this. One drop net that had been dipped in a rubber coating to protect it from the elements caused unacceptably high amounts of feather loss in most of the captured turkeys and thus was used only once. We recommend avoiding using nets that have been weather-coated.

Eastern wild turkeys subjected to handling time ≥180 min suffered mortality rates of nearly 50% (Nicholson et al. 2000). In our study, 56 turkeys with handling times between 180 and 315 minutes had a post-capture mortality rate of 7.1%, which was similar to the overall mortality rate of 8.5%.

No previous studies have addressed the impact of recaptures on survival. The post-capture mortality of recaptured birds in this study (4.1%) was lower ($P = 0.003$) than that of birds captured only once (10.1%). This suggested that capture-related stress was temporary.

MANAGEMENT IMPLICATIONS

Our data suggested that male Rio Grande wild turkeys were more susceptible to capture-related mortalities than females. We suggest processing and releasing male turkeys first when both sexes are captured to reduce possible stress. We also recommend using experienced and additional personnel when males are the goal of capture efforts. Based on our data, we feel trapping in late afternoon should be avoided. Although we found no relationship between temperature and survival, we also recommend avoiding captures when temperatures exceed 10°C, as we observed that turkeys captured on warmer days overheated in the boxes awaiting processing (J. Brunjes, Texas Tech University, personal observation). At 1 capture event, birds appeared so heat stressed (i.e., rapid panting, decreased alertness) that we released the remaining birds ($n = 4$) without workup or transmitters in an effort to decrease post-capture mortality. We also recommend avoiding captures in which heavy or freezing rains are predicted within 48 hours post-capture. Drop nets and rocket nets did not differ in their capture-related deaths; however, larger potential captures may occur with drop nets, thus we suggest more personnel be present during drop net captures. We found that a minimum of 5 experienced personnel were required for rocket net captures, and suggest a minimum of 7 people when using a drop net.

ACKNOWLEDGMENTS

We thank T. Brunjes, D. Lucia, B. Simpson, J. Hughes, and S. Sudkamp for logistical support, M. Butler for guidance and help with the statistical analyses and G. Hall, R. Houchin, R. Huffman, and B. Bullock for field assistance. We deeply appreciate the access to private land provided by landowners. Funding and support was provided by Texas Parks and Wildlife Department, the National Wild Turkey Federation, the Texas state superfund of the National Wild Turkey Federation, Kansas Department of Wildlife and Parks, Texas Tech University, and Kansas State University. All field protocols were approved by the Texas Tech University Animal Care and Use Committee (protocol numbers 99917 and 01173B). This is Texas Tech University College of Agricultural Sciences and Natural Resources technical publication T-901122.

LITERATURE CITED

Bailey, W., D. Dennett, H. Gore, J. Pack, R. Simpson, and G. Wright. 1980. Basic considerations and general recommendations for trapping the wild turkey. Proceedings of the National Wild Turkey Symposium 4:10–23.

Clark, L. G. 1985. Adjustment by transplanting wild turkeys to an Ohio farmland area. Proceedings of the National Wild Turkey Symposium 5:33–47.

Davis, B. D. 1994. A funnel trap for Rio Grande turkey. Proceedings of the Annual Conference of the Southeastern Association of Fish and Wildlife Agencies 48:109–116.

———, and B. E. DelMonte. 1986. A non-electric method for releasing a drop net. Proceedings of the Annual Conference of the Southeastern Association of Fish and Wildlife Agencies 40:334–337.

Fienberg, S. E. 1977. The analysis of cross-classified data. Massachusetts Institute of Technology Press, Cambridge, Massachusetts, USA.

Geist, V. 1981. Behavior: adaptive strategies. Pages 157–224 in O. C. Wallmo, editor. Mule and black-tailed deer of North America. University of Nebraska Press, Lincoln, Nebraska, USA.

Hennen, R. S., and S. Lutz. 2001. Rio Grande turkey female survival in south-central Kansas. Proceedings of the National Wild Turkey Symposium 8:117–122.

Hohensee, S. D., and M. C. Wallace 2001. Nesting and survival of Rio Grande turkeys in north-central Texas. Proceedings of the National Wild Turkey Symposium 8:85–91.

Holdstock, D. P. 2003. Survival, movement, and habitat selection of male Rio Grande wild turkeys in the Texas Panhandle and southwestern Kansas. Thesis, Texas Tech University, Lubbock, Texas, USA.

Hosmer, D. W. and S. Lemeshow. 2000. Applied Logistic Regression. Second edition. John Wiley & Sons, New York, New York, USA.

McMahon, G. L., and R. N. Johnson. 1980. Introduction of the wild turkey into the Carlos Avery Wildlife Management Area. Proceedings of the National Wild Turkey Symposium 4:32–44.

Miller, D. A., B. D. Leopold, and G. A. Hurst. 1996. Post-capture survival of wild turkeys: effect of age, sex and environment. Proceedings of the Annual Conference of the Southeastern Association of Fish and Wildlife Agencies 50:442–449.

Millspaugh, J. J., and J. M. Marzluff. 2001. Radio tracking and animal populations. Academic Press, San Diego, California, USA.

National Oceanic and Atmospheric Administration. 2000a. Climatological data annual summary; Texas. Volume 105, Number 13. National Climatic Data Center, Ashville, NC, USA.

———. 2000b. Climatological data annual summary; Kansas. Volume 114, Number 13. National Climatic Data Center, Ashville, North Carolina, USA.

———. 2001a. Climatological data annual summary; Texas. Volume 106, Number 13. National Climatic Data Center, Ashville, North Carolina, USA.

———. 2001b. Climatological data annual summary; Kansas. Volume 115, Number 13. National Climatic Data Center, Ashville, North Carolina, USA.

———. 2002. Climatological data annual summary; Texas. Volume 107, Number 13. National Climatic Data Center, Ashville, North Carolina, USA.

Nicholson, D. S., R. L. Lochmiller, M. D. Stewart, R. E. Masters, and D. M. Leslie. 2000. Risk factors associated with capture-related death in eastern wild turkey hens. Journal of Wildlife Diseases 36:308–315.

Nguyen, L. P., J. Hamr, and G. H. Parker. 2003. Survival and reproduction of wild turkey hens in central Ontario. Wilson Bulletin 115:131–139.

Phillips, R. S. 2004. Movement, survival and reproduction of Rio Grande wild turkeys in the Texas Panhandle. Thesis, Texas Tech University, Lubbock, Texas, USA.

Pollock, K. H., S. R. Winterstein, C. M. Buncy, and P. D. Curtis. 1989. Survival analysis in telemetry studies: the staggered entry design. Journal of Wildlife Management 53:137–142.

Spraker, T. R., W. J. Adrian, and W. R. Lance. 1987. Capture myopathy in wild turkeys (*Meleagris gallopavo*) following trapping, handling and transportation in Colorado. Journal of Wildlife Diseases 23:447–453.

Trent, T. T., and O. J. Rongstad. 1974. Home range and survival of cottontail rabbits in southwestern Wisconsin. Journal of Wildlife Management 47:716–728.

White, G. C., and R. A. Garrott. 1990. Analysis of wildlife radio-tracking data. Academic Press, San Diego, California, USA.

Williams, L. E., and D. H. Austin. 1988. Studies of the wild turkey in Florida. Florida Game and Fresh Water Fish Commission Technical Bulletin 10.

Wright, G. A., and L. D. Vangilder. 2001. Survival of eastern wild turkey males in Kentucky. Proceedings of the National Wild Turkey Symposium 8:187–194.

Wunz, G. A. 1984. Rocket-net innovations for capturing wild turkeys and waterfowl. Pennsylvania Game Commission, Pittman-Robertson Federal Aid Progress Report, Project W-46-R-21.

John H. Brunjes, IV (pictured) is a wildlife biologist in the Migratory Bird Program with the Kentucky Department of Fish and Wildlife Resources where he works with Webless migratory birds. He received his Bachelor of Science degree in Biology from the University of North Carolina at Wilmington in and his Master of Science degree in Wildlife Ecology and Management from the University of Georgia. He recently completed his Doctor of Philosophy in Wildlife Science in the Department of Range and Wildlife Management at Texas Tech University. His doctoral research focused on the landscape ecology and population dynamics or Rio Grande wild turkeys. ***Warren B. Ballard*** is professor of wildlife sciences in the Department of Range, Wildlife, and Fisheries Management at Texas Tech University. He received his B.S. in fish and wildlife management at New Mexico State University, his M.Sc. in environmental biology from Kansas State University, and his Ph.D. in wildlife science from the University of Arizona. His professional interests include predator-prey relationships and population dynamics of carnivores and ungulates. ***Mark Wallace*** is an Associate Professor in the Department of Range, Wildlife and Fisheries Management at Texas Tech University. He has a B.S. in forestry—wildlife science from the University of Washington, and an M.S. in wildlife ecology, and Ph.D. in wildlife and fisheries sciences from the University of Arizona. Mark's interests include integrating traditional and landscape scale habitat research, modeling plant-animal interactions and community responses to habitat changes. In particular, he is intent on finding new ways to involve our increasingly urban students into the profession and the problems facing wildlife management in the coming century. ***Richard S. Phillips*** is a doctoral candidate in Wildlife Science at Texas Tech University. His work is focused on the impacts of dispersal on population structure of Rio Grande wild turkeys in the Texas Panhandle. Richard received his bachelors degree in Biology and Human and Natural Ecology from Emory University and his masters degree from in Wildlife Science from Texas Tech. ***Derrick P. Holdstock*** received his Bachelor of Science degree in Environmental and Forest Biology from the State University of New York, College of Environmental Science and Forestry from Syracuse, a Master of Science degree in Secondary Science Education at Syracuse University, and a Master of Science degree in Wildlife Science from Texas Tech University. His research focused on the survival, movements, and habitat use of Rio Grande wild turkeys in the Texas Panhandle and southwestern Kansas. He currently works for Texas Parks and Wildlife

Department where he recently served as the Black-tailed Prairie Dog Program Coordinator and currently serves as the Assistant Project Leader for the Panhandle Wildlife Management Areas. ***Brian Spears*** received his bachelors degree from the University of Arizona in Ecology and Evolutionary Biology and masters degree from Texas Tech University in Wildlife Science. Brian is a Resource Contaminants Specialist for the US Fish and Wildlife Service working on technical issues and research regarding wildlife toxicology in the Coeur d'Alene Basin, Idaho, as well as developing wetland restoration partnerships between federal agencies, the Coeur d'Alene Indian Tribe, and private land owners. He currently lives with his wife and daughter in Coeur d'Alene, Idaho. ***Matthew J. Butler*** is currently a doctoral student in wildlife science at Texas Tech University in Lubbock. His dissertation research is focused on evaluating population estimation techniques for Rio Grande wild turkeys in the Texas Panhandle and southwestern Kansas. He received a M.S. in forest resources from the University of Arkansas at Monticello in 2001 where he studied the foraging requirements of red-cockaded woodpeckers. In 1999, he received a B.S. in fisheries and wildlife biology from Arkansas Tech University in Russellville. Also, Matt has worked for the U.S. Forest Service as a wildlife biologist and as a forestry technician on the Ouachita National Forest. ***Michael Miller*** is a wildlife diversity biologist in Region 2 at Texas Parks and Wildlife Department. He received his B.S. and M.S. degrees in Wildlife Management from Texas Tech University. Mike provides technical guidance to private landowners and works on projects that benefit rare and declining resources in north-central Texas. ***Nancy E. McIntyre*** is an Associate Professor of Biological Sciences at Texas Tech University and Curator of Birds at the Natural Science Research Laboratory of TTU. She earned her B.S. and M.S. degrees in Zoology from the University of Georgia, completed her Ph.D. in Ecology at Colorado State University, and did postdoctoral work on urban ecology at Arizona State University. Her research program focuses on habitat selection and community structure in heterogeneous and dynamic landscapes, with a focus on arthropods and birds. ***Steve DeMaso*** is the Upland Game Bird Program Leader for the Texas Parks and Wildlife Department in Austin, Texas. Prior to moving to Texas, he worked for the Oklahoma Department of Wildlife Conservation and served as the lead researcher on the nationally recognized Packsaddle Quail Research Project. Currently, Steve serves as Chairman of the Southeast Quail Study Group and a member of the National Wild Turkey Federation's Technical Committee. Steve is a member of the National and Texas Chapters of The Wildlife Society. Steve also served as the Program Chairman and Editor for the Proceedings of the Fifth National Quail Symposium. Steve was raised in southern Michigan and received his B.S. from Michigan State University, M.S. from Texas A&I University, and is currently pursuing a Ph.D. in the Wildlife and Fisheries Sciences Joint Program between Texas A&M University and Texas A&M–Kingsville. ***Roger D. Applegate*** is the Small Game and Wildlife Disease Coordinator for Tennessee Wildlife Resources Agency. He formerly was the Small Game Coordinator for Kansas Department of Wildlife and Parks. He has a B.S. from Western Illinois University and an M.S. from the University of Illinois. ***Philip S. (Phil) Gipson*** is leader of the Kansas Cooperative Fish and Wildlife Research Unit at Kansas State University. His principal duties include research with mammalian predators and responses of ecological systems to military training, advising graduate students, and teaching wildlife management courses. Phil received his M.S. and Ph.D. in zoology at the University of Arkansas, where he studied the dynamics of wildlife populations and predator ecology.

Wild Turkey Management:
Accomplishments, Strategies, and Opportunities
——— Grand Rapids, Michigan ———

CROSSSING THE BORDER—THE ARIZONA GOULD'S RESTORATION EXPERIENCE

Robert C. Maddrey
National Wild Turkey Federation,
770 Augusta Road,
Edgefield, SC 29824, USA

Brian F. Wakeling
Arizona Game and Fish Department, Game Branch,
2221 West Greenway Road,
Phoenix, AZ 85023, USA

Abstract: Gould's wild turkeys (*Meleagris gallopavo mexicana*) were imported from Mexico into the United States during March 2003 and 2004. Ninety-nine Gould's wild turkeys were trapped in Sonora, Mexico, and released in isolated mountain ranges of southeastern Arizona to establish new turkey populations, following a 30-day quarantine required by U.S. Department of Agriculture (USDA) regulations. A state of the art quarantine facility was constructed in the Chiricahua Mountains of southeastern Arizona to reduce mortality associated with quarantine holding. In 2003, 2 birds died in transit from Mexico and 47 birds were placed into the quarantine. After a 35-day period, 39 birds (83%) were released. In 2004, a single bird died in transit and 49 birds were placed in quarantine; 43 birds (88%) were later released.

Proceedings of the National Wild Turkey Symposium 9:83–87

Key words: disease, Gould's wild turkey, quarantine, restoration, transplant, trapping.

Wild turkeys have been successfully restored to native habitat throughout the United States. Restoration efforts for Gould's wild turkeys are less complete than those of other subspecies for 2 primary reasons: (1) less is known about the biology of this subspecies and (2) primary source stock resides within a country outside of the United States requiring substantial international coordination.

Gould's wild turkeys once occurred in southern Arizona and New Mexico and throughout the Sierra Madre Occidental in Mexico (Leopold 1948, Schorger 1966). Many populations were extirpated due to habitat destruction and subsistence hunting, but populations have survived to the present day in the mountains of Chihuahua, Sonora, Durango, Zacatecas, and other states in the region. Within Mexico, populations are currently being restored in Sonora, Aguascalientes, and Jalisco (Lafon and Schemnitz 1995, R. Maddrey, National Wild Turkey Federation, unpublished data).

Gould's wild turkey historic range in the United States is limited to southeastern Arizona and southwestern New Mexico (Rea 1980). The montane oak (*Quercus spp.*)-pine (*Pinus spp.*) habitat in southeastern Arizona and southwestern New Mexico is similar to habitat in the northern Sierra Madres. Early settler accounts listed wild turkeys in all southern Arizona mountain ranges (Hodge 1877, Bailey 1923). These populations were extirpated by 1920 (Davis 1982). Small populations persisted in the Peloncillo Mountains on the Arizona–New Mexico border, but the population did not expand due to unsuitable habitat between islands of good habitat (Schemnitz and Zeedyk 1992).

The first attempt to restore Gould's wild turkeys in Arizona occurred in 1983 when 17 birds were captured using drop nets near Nuevas Casas Grandes, Chihuahua, Mexico, by U.S. Army biologists from Fort Huachuca. These birds were transported by truck to Fort Huachuca Army Base in Sierra Vista, Arizona, where they were quarantined for 39 days. Nine surviving birds were released on the base on 9 May 1983. In 1987, 29 birds were captured in Chihuahua by Mexican biologists and transferred at the border to Fort Huachuca biologists. Twelve survived a >30 day quarantine and were released in late April and May (Breland 1988).

The Arizona Game and Fish Department (AGFD) obtained a waiver of quarantine from USDA in December 1993 to bring birds from Mexico. In February 1994, 21 turkeys were captured by AGFD biologists

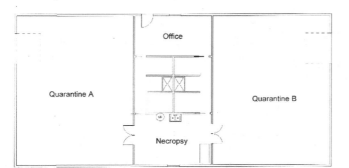

Gould's Wild Turkey Quarantine Facility

Fig. 1.   Schematic of the Gould's wild turkey quarantine facility built in the Chiricahua Mountains, Arizona.

in Sonora, Mexico, and released into the Galiuro Mountains. Two-thirds of the turkeys died within 2 months of the release. An additional 46 birds were captured in Sonora in 1997 and released with similar results in the Galiuro Mountains (Wakeling 1998). This release was supplemented in 1999 and 2001 with birds from the Huachuca Mountains. A small but viable population remains in the Galiuro Mountains.

The Gould's restoration project resumed in 2002. Wingshooter's Lodge in Yecora, Sonora, agreed to assist in another restoration attempt by permitting the capture of 50 birds from their leased property. The National Wild Turkey Federation (NWTF) took the lead in this capture effort which initially centered on restoration in the Chiricahua Mountains. A list of other release sites was drawn up based on a habitat model of mountain ranges in southeastern Arizona (Wakeling et al. 2001).

The USDA required a 30-day quarantine period for live turkeys to enter from Mexico. Permission was obtained from USDA to establish a quarantine facility in Arizona. A landowner in the Chiricahua Mountains agreed to build the quarantine facility to USDA specifications on his ranch (Figure 1).

Customs brokers on both sides of the border were employed to facilitate completion of all paperwork and ensure timely crossings for each shipment. A customs broker was also employed to assist in bringing the nets and capture equipment into Mexico. The list of permits and authorizations to conduct an international trap and transplant activity was lengthy (Appendix A).

METHODS

Trapping operations were initiated by NWTF and AGFD personnel near Yecora, Sonora, during March 2003 and 2004. Turkeys were prebaited with corn by participating landowners in the Yecora area for a month prior to the trapping period. Wingshooter's Lodge personnel supplied the landowners with bait and assisted in choosing and clearing bait sites. An effort was made to bring rocket nets into Mexico for the project, but the permit was never granted by the Mexican military. Turkeys were trapped using drop nets with a pull string release.

Captured turkeys were transported in waxed cardboard boxes by truck to the trapping headquarters in Yecora, and stored overnight in a cool room. Birds were transported by aircraft the following morning to Hermosillo, Sonora, to clear Mexican customs. Project personnel accompanied all shipments to Hermosillo. In Hermosillo, the birds were transferred to a shady area until customs documents were completed; temperatures in Hermosillo were 25°C by mid-morning. Turkeys were placed back on the aircraft immediately prior to departure. The birds were flown to Douglas, Arizona, to clear U.S. customs and for transfer by trailer to the quarantine facility. Upon release in the quarantine facility, fecal samples were taken from each transport box by USDA personnel for Exotic Newcastle Disease (END) testing.

Quarantined turkeys were fed a 2:1 ratio of Purina's Mazuri Exotic Gamebird Breeder feed-cracked corn and supplied with grit, using 3 plastic wading pools (2 m diameter, 0.3 m high) as feed troughs. Each bird was supplied with 200 g of feed/day. Fresh water was provided on a continuous basis through the quarantine's watering system. Initially, we fed birds during nighttime hours, but feeding was switched to daylight hours because turkeys were less disturbed during periods when personnel were visible.

Turkeys that died during the quarantine period were placed in large plastic bags and frozen until they could be necropsied by USDA veterinarians to determine cause of death. After 20 days in quarantine, live birds were recaptured for testing. Alpha-chloralose (AC) was applied to cracked corn and small piles of this mixture were placed in each quarantine area for consumption by the turkeys following procedures described by Williams (1966) and Bergman et al. (*this volume*). Birds not adequately sedated were captured with hand nets. The turkeys were cloacally swabbed for END testing, leg-banded, patagial-tagged, and fitted with telemetry transmitters. Disease samples were sent to the USDA Veterinary Diagnostics Lab in Ames, Iowa. When disease-free status was declared, the birds were either released by opening the large door in each quarantine to allow birds to escape into the surrounding woodlands or by re-drugging the birds with AC, placing the birds within transport boxes, waiting 24 hrs for recovery, and transporting them to release sites.

RESULTS

One hundred four turkeys were trapped during 2003–2004 by biologists from the NWTF, AGFD, Sonoran Outfitters Association, and Secretaria de Medio Ambiente y Recursos Naturales (SEMARNAT) (Table 1). In 2003, 49 turkeys were shipped via air charter to Arizona. One female was released at Yecora due to extreme loss of back feathers. In 2004, 50 birds were shipped and 2 males and 2 females were released at the trap site. Losses during transportation were minimal because air travel was much quicker and much less stressful than truck transportation. In 2003, 2 fe-

Table 1. Number, age, and sex of Gould's wild turkeys captured in 2003 and 2004 near Yecora, Sonora, Mexico, and held in quarantine in Arizona.

Year	Adult males	Subadult males	Adult females	Subadult females
2003	13	1	34	2
2004	4	10	27	13

males died en route, and in 2004, 1 male died en route. Heat stress was suspected in the 2003 deaths, while capture myopathy was the likely cause in the 2004 death.

Once at the quarantine site, birds reacted wildly when first released out of the boxes. In 2003, 8 birds died after entering the quarantine (4 within 2 days of placement in quarantine from capture myopathy, 4 from injuries sustained in capture, handling, or self-induced trauma within the quarantine). Thirty-nine birds (12 gobblers, 27 hens) survived the quarantine and were released in good health on 16 April 2003 into the Chiricahua Mountains.

In 2004, interior tarps were hung from ceiling to ground inside the quarantine facilities to minimize injuries turkeys sustained from flying into the walls. Four turkeys died of capture myopathy within the first 4 days following placement within quarantine facility, but only 2 turkeys died of injuries sustained in capture, handling, or self-induced trauma while in quarantine. Forty-three birds survived the quarantine and were released on 22 April 2004 in the Pinaleno, Huachuca, and Chiricahua Mountains (Figure 2).

DISCUSSION

An international project of this magnitude is wrought with challenges. The initial challenge was the construction of the quarantine facility, which had to be completed in about 4 months, with a team of NWTF staff and volunteers acting as general contractors. Because the building was built on a private ranch in a remote location, logistics were a constant challenge.

The overall trapping operation was successful, although the importation of trapping equipment was challenging. We discovered after arrival that the Mexican military would not grant approval to import rocket nets.

The trapping operation in Yecora went smoothly. Prebaited sites were located and baited by the landowners for a month, and the Wingshooter's Lodge personnel knew the number and sex ratios of birds coming to bait sites. Several net sizes were used, because some sites were in small forest clearings while others were in agricultural fields. All captures were made under nets set up 1 day prior to capture. Turkeys were caught under 4 of 5 net sets.

The air transportation from Yecora to Douglas kept bird stress to a minimum and few people were needed to run the trapping operation. Previous Gould's turkey restoration projects used long distance truck transportation which tended to be stressful on the birds and required additional human resources for truck

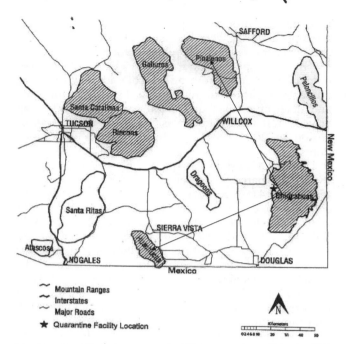

Fig. 2. Gould's turkeys were held in quarantine within the Chiricahua Mountains and released in 3 mountain ranges following a mandatory 30-day quarantine in 2003 and 2004. Arrows indicate the release sites for Gould's turkeys.

drivers and escorts. Clearing Mexican and United States customs took about 2 hours and 1 hour, respectively. Smaller hen boxes were developed for 2004 to fit more birds onto each flight.

We overcame several additional challenges during the quarantine period. First, birds flew into walls in an effort to escape during initial release into the quarantine area. In 2004 we installed an interior tarp screen to cushion impacts and covered external light sources to minimize flight toward natural light. Second, in 2003 the temperature in the quarantine holding area rose to about 28°C on the second day of the quarantine period. We purchased and installed 2 portable evaporative coolers to keep the temperature below 22°C and installed permanent evaporative coolers before the 2004 quarantine period. Also in 2003, an abrupt change from light to dark due to lighting on timers resulted in disruption of roosting behavior. We installed new lighting in 2004 to darken the quarantine areas over 30 minutes to give the birds time to find roost spaces. Daily feeding also produced stress in turkeys. We found that providing enough food for several days reduced stress caused by human contact with birds. Finally, confined wild turkeys were territorial on the roost, vying for prime positions in each holding area. We suggest that birds captured together be housed together and abundant tall-roosting areas be provided to limit new dominance fighting and competition for prime roosting sites.

In previous quarantines, a large number of birds were lost during the disease-testing recapture event to stress-related capture myopathy (Breland 1988). Alpha-chloralose was used to eliminate capture stress related mortalities. No birds were lost from the recapture and handling process. In the 1983 and 1987 quarantine attempts, 5 birds were lost each year during the quarantine recapture phase (Breland 1988).

In 2003, personnel from NWTF, AGFD, or volunteers were on-site during part of each day the entire quarantine period to monitor turkeys, provide feed, and determine that equipment was functioning properly. A full time intern was hired for the quarantine period in 2004 to standardize protocols and procedures.

Survival during the quarantine period was high (86%) compared to earlier attempts in 1983 and 1987 (53% and 41%, respectively). Wild turkeys are susceptible to capture myopathy (Spraker et al. 1987) even without the further stress of quarantine. With 80% in 1993 and 86% in 2004 surviving the quarantine period, losses were not dramatically different than normal translocation releases. Losses were exacerbated by injuries sustained from birds flying into walls, especially in 2003. Continually adding new safety features to the quarantine facility kept additional mortality to a minimum.

This project demonstrated that Gould's wild turkeys can be successfully quarantined with minimal mortality for international restoration purposes.

ACKNOWLEDGMENTS

This project was a direct outcome of the concerted efforts of a great many people. M. Adkins, S. Vance, S. Baker, J. "Catfish" McDivitt, S. Hopkins, G. Gonzalez, J. Heffelfinger, D. Bergman, and T. Veenendahl assisted with quarantine construction and logistics. Without their Herculean efforts, the project would not have been successful. This project was funded by private landowners, the National Wild Turkey Federation, and State Trust Fund Grant W-53-M.

LITERATURE CITED

Bailey, F. M. 1923. Birds recorded from the Santa Rita Mountains in southern Arizona. Cooper Ornithological Club, Berkeley, California, USA.

Bergman, D. L., B. F. Wakeling, T. B. Veenendaal, J. D. Eisemann, and T. W. Seamans. *This volume.* Current and historical use of alpha-chloralose on wild turkeys. Proceedings of the National Wild Turkey Symposium 9:*This volume.*

Breland, W. R. 1988. Reintroduction of the Gould's turkey in southeastern Arizona. Proceedings of the Western Wild Turkey Workshop 4:12–26.

Davis, G. P., Jr. 1982. Man and wildlife in Arizona: the American exploration period 1824–1865. N. B. Carmony and D. E. Brown, editors. Arizona Game and Fish Department, Phoenix, Arizona, and the Arizona Cooperative Wildlife Research Unit, Tucson, Arizona, USA.

Hodge, H. C. 1877. Arizona as it is; or, the coming country. Hurd and Houghton, New York, New York, USA.

Lafon, A., and S. D. Schemnitz. 1996. Distribution, habitat use, and limiting factors of Gould's turkey in Chihuahua, Mexico. Proceedings of the National Wild Turkey Symposium 7:185–191.

Leopold, A. S. 1948. The wild turkeys of Mexico. Transactions of the North American Wildlife Conference 13:393–401.

Rea, A. M. 1980. Late Pleistocene and Holocene turkeys in the Southwest. Contributions of the Scientific Nature Museum, Los Angeles County 330:209–224.

Schemnitz, S. D., and W. D. Zeedyk. 1992. Gould's turkey. Pages 350–360 *in* J. G. Dickson, editor. The wild turkey: biology and management. Stackpole Books, Harrisburg, Pennsylvania, USA.

Schorger, A. W. 1966. The wild turkey: its history and domestication. University of Oklahoma Press, Norman, Oklahoma, USA.

Spraker, T. R., W. J. Adrian, and W. R. Lance. 1987. Capture myopathy in wild turkeys (*Meleagris gallopavo*) following trapping, handling and transportation in Colorado. Journal of Wildlife Diseases 23:447–453.

Wakeling, B. F. 1998. Survival of Gould's turkey transplanted into the Galiuro Mountains, Arizona. Pages 227–234 *in* G. J. Gottfried, C. B. Edminster, and M. C. Dillon, compilers. Cross border waters: fragile treasures for the 21st century: ninth U.S./Mexico Border States conference on recreation, parks, and wildlife. U.S. Forest Service Rocky Mountain Research Station RMRS-P-5.

———, S. R. Boe, M. M. Koloszar, and T. D. Rogers. 2001. Gould's turkey survival and habitat selection modeling in southeastern Arizona. Proceedings of the National Wild Turkey Symposium 8:101–108.

Williams, L. E. 1966. Capturing wild turkeys with alpha chloralose. Journal of Wildlife Management 30:50–56.

APPENDIX A

Permits and Authorizations Required for Gould's Wild Turkey Transport from Mexico and Quarantine in the United States during 2003–2004

- Trapping Permit from SEMARNAT (Mexican Wildlife Agency)
- Export permit from SEMARNAT
- Quarantine Facility permit from USDA
- Rocket net import permit from Mexican Military
- Authorization from Arizona Game and Fish Department to import nets into Mexico
- USDA-Animal and Plant Health Inspection Service (APHIS) Import permit
- Declaration from USDA declaring turkeys did not need veterinary permit from Mexico
- USFWS designated port exception permit
- USFWS declaration for importation or exportation of fish or wildlife
- US Customs Service Inward Cargo Manifest
- Mexican Customs Manifiesto de Carga

Robert C. Maddrey is currently the Division Wildlife Biologist for Georgia Pacific Corporation. He began his career with the USFWS at Pea Island NWR, worked 14 years with the North Carolina Wildlife Resources Commission and 9 years with the National Wild Turkey Federation where he administered the Gould's Restoration Program and other Mexican projects. He holds a B.S. in Wildlife Biology from North Carolina State University and a M.S. in Wildlife and Fisheries Science from the University of Tennessee, Knoxville.

Brian F. Wakeling received a B.S. in Wildlife Management and an M.S. in Environmental Resources from Arizona State University in 1985 and 1989, respectively. He served as a research biologist for the Arizona Game and Fish Department from 1988–2000, during which time he studied turkeys, mule deer, elk, and bighorn sheep. Currently, Brian is the big game management supervisor with the Arizona Game and Fish Department, a position he has held since 2000. Brian is a Certified Wildlife Biologist and a Past-President of the Arizona State Chapter of The Wildlife Society. Brian has served as a member of the National Wild Turkey Technical Committee since 1993.

Chapter II

Population Dynamics

LESSONS FROM WILD TURKEY POPULATION DYNAMICS STUDIES

D. Keith Warnke[1]
*Wisconsin Department of Natural Resources, Bureau
of Wildlife Management—WM/6, PO Box 7921,
Madison, WI 53707, USA*

Robert E. Rolley
*Wisconsin Department of Natural Resources, Bureau
of Integrated Science Services, 1350 Femrite Dr.,
Monona, WI 53716, USA*

Abstract: Case studies of wild turkey (*Meleagris gallopavo*) population dynamics abound, providing estimates of the range of variation in demographic variables under current management strategies (spring and/or fall hunting). However, the ultimate mechanisms regulating wild turkey populations are poorly understood. Our objectives are to synthesize recent population dynamic research, identify important population processes, discuss the implications of these for harvest management strategies, and recommend approaches for future research. Wild turkey population growth appears to be primarily a function of recruitment and female survival. Recent research has demonstrated that recruitment can be highly variable and is primarily affected by nest predation. Many studies have reported weather-related variation in recruitment, but the mechanisms remain unclear. Female survival is affected largely by predation, legal harvest, poaching, and in some situations, starvation and disease. Relatively little is known about possible compensatory interactions among these factors. Most population models developed have assumed that fall harvest of females is additive to other causes of mortality. Appropriate harvest rates for females depend on the management objective and will be affected by regional and temporal variation in rates of recruitment and natural mortality. Monitoring of recruitment is important to guard against overharvest during periods of poor recruitment. Social considerations and management objectives, more than biological factors, govern appropriate harvest rates of males. A better understanding of factors that control and regulate population growth will be important as wild turkey management objectives evolve from population restoration to population control and sustained yield harvesting.

Proceedings of the National Wild Turkey Symposium 9:91–99

Key words: harvest, management, *Meleagris gallopavo*, mortality, predation, recruitment, survival, wild turkey.

Wild turkeys were abundant throughout the United States at the time of European settlement. However, unregulated market hunting, disease and habitat destruction caused widespread population declines to a low point at the end of the nineteenth century (Dickson 1992). Restoration efforts intensified following World War II and the strategies behind reintroduction and the successful result are well known stories (Dickson 1992).

Turkey populations have continued to increase in abundance and expand their range in recent years. In many cases, turkeys have expanded into habitat that was previously considered unsuitable. The focus of turkey management programs is shifting from restoration to population maintenance (and control in some cases) and sustained yield harvesting. A thorough understanding of turkey population dynamics, including carrying capacity, interactions of population parameters, and effects of harvest management strategies is critical to successful turkey management. The ability to adaptively manage harvest and population levels to the satisfaction of a wide variety of publics will become the measure of success.

Our objectives are to synthesize recent population dynamics research, identify important population processes, discuss implications of these for harvest management strategies, and recommend approaches for future research.

POPULATION DYNAMICS

Numerous studies of the dynamics of wild turkey populations have generated many estimates of demographic parameters, such as reproduction, sex and age-specific survival, and rates of population growth (see Vangilder 1992, Vangilder and Kurzejeski 1995, and Healy and Powell 1999 for summaries). Estimates of recruitment (reproduction and poult survival) are high-

[1] E-mail: keith.warnke@dnr.state.wi.us

ly variable, particularly over the northern half of the range while estimates of survival are somewhat less variable (Vangilder 1992, Porter et al. 1990a, Roberts et al. 1995, Rolley et al. 1998). The consequence of annual variability in recruitment and survival is moderate annual fluctuation in population level (Healy and Powell 1999). For example, in New York, Porter et al. (1990a) reported a dynamic population that did not maintain high numbers for prolonged periods.

Several investigators have combined estimates of individual population parameters (e.g., reproduction and survival) into models describing dynamics of turkey populations on local study areas (see Suchy et al. 1983, Vangilder and Kurzejeski 1995, Roberts et al. 1995, Rolley et al. 1998). Fewer have had the resources to develop more statewide models (Brooks et al. llenp2
1999, Alpizar-Jara et al. 2001). Brooks et al. (2002) built a widely applicable model with stochastic and deterministic phases and made it available on the Internet. Generally, these models were stochastic using random fluctuations in the range of measured population parameters, assumed hunting related mortality was additive, and did not include density dependent effects. Objectives for developing these models have included (1) estimating the finite rate of increase of a population from estimates of reproduction and survival, (2) assessing potential impacts of various spring and fall harvest strategies on population size and age structure, (3) assessing how variation in reproduction alters effect of harvest strategies, and (4) determining relative importance of demographic parameters to annual changes in abundance. Models can forecast plausible outcomes to alternative management scenarios, assisting managers in selecting among the alternatives but must be used as aids to decision making rather than complete representations of reality.

Male Survival

Estimates of annual survival for male wild turkeys have varied from 24%–26% in Virginia (Norman et al. 2004) and Kentucky (Wright and Vangilder 2001), to 36% in Georgia (Ielmini et al. 1992), to 44% for sub-adult and 36% for adult males in the Missouri Ozarks (Vangilder 1996), to 46% for sub-adult and adult males in Mississippi (Godwin et al. 1991), to 51% in Wisconsin (Paisley et al. 1996), to 71% for recently restocked males in Texas (Campo et al. 1984). Most studies of harvested populations reported that legal harvest was responsible for the majority of male deaths (Godwin et al. 1991, Paisley et al.1996, Wright and Vangilder 2001); however, predation caused the majority of male deaths in southern Missouri (Vangilder 1996). Wright and Vangilder (2001) concluded that adults were more vulnerable to harvest than sub-adults. Illegal kill was responsible for 9% of male deaths in Kentucky (Wright and Vangilder 2001) and for 13% and 18% of deaths on 2 study areas in Missouri (Vangilder 1996). Illegal kill was not a major source of mortality in Wisconsin (Paisley et al. 1996).

Simulation modeling indicates that increasing the harvest rate of males has relatively little effect on population growth (Vangilder 1992). However, harvesting males can reduce the density of males and can substantially alter the age structure of males in the population (Vangilder and Kurzejeski 1995). Additionally, population modeling in Virginia and West Virginia (Alpizar-Jara et al. 2001) concluded that fall harvest of males had the greatest impact on future male harvest. This result was contradicted by a conclusion that fall hunting mortality was not additive in those states (Norman et al. 2004).

Female Survival

Female survival varies significantly year to year (Vangilder and Kurzejeski 1995, Pack et al. 1999). Survival of adult and sub-adult females is variable among seasons, and is frequently lowest during the reproductive period (Roberts et al. 1995, Wright et al. 1996, Miller et al. 1998a, Hubbard et al. 1999). However, Pack et al. (1999) found in West Virginia and Virginia that survival was lowest during the hunting season and was higher in an unhunted population. Nguyen et al. (2003) reported lowest female survival in Central Ontario was during the summer period. In Wisconsin, Rolley et al. (1998) identified female survival as one factor that influenced population growth and Pack et al. (1999) agreed that female survival was important in terms of long term population growth.

Winter female survival in agricultural situations was not considered a primary limiting factor in Massachusetts (Vander Haegen et al. 1988). In fact, recent work has identified winter as a period of high survival (Wright et al. 1996, Hubbard et al. 1999). Other studies have concluded that severe winter weather substantially reduced over-winter survival in northern populations that did not have ready access to agricultural crops (Austin and DeGraff 1975, Wunz and Hayden 1975, Porter et al. 1983).

Additive versus Compensatory Mortality

An understanding of relations among harvest and nonharvest mortality is important for the management of any harvested species. Theoretical models of this relationship have been characterized as additive, or compensatory (Nichols et al. 1984, Roseberry and Klimstra 1984). Under the additive model, annual survival rate declines linearly as hunting mortality rate increases. Under the compensatory mortality model, the nonharvest mortality rate decreases as the hunting mortality rate increases so that annual survival rate does not change. Because nonharvest mortality rate can only decline to a minimum of 0, there is a limit to the amount compensation possible. Hunting mortality rates above some threshold will decrease annual survival rates. Variations of the compensatory mortality model have raised the lower limit of nonhunting mortality and consequently lowered the threshold above which hunting mortality rates become additive. The additive and compensatory mortality models should be viewed as 2 ends of a continuum of possible relationships between harvest and nonharvest mortality. The true relationship for any one species will likely lie somewhere between these 2 extremes. The ability to compensate for harvest mortality likely depends on the species' life-history strategy; higher for short-lived species with high natural mortality rates than for long-lived species with low natural mortality rates (Anderson and Burnham 1976).

The relationship of harvest and nonharvest mortality for turkeys has received considerable speculation. Vangilder (1992) assumed in his population model that both spring male hunting and fall either-sex hunting were additive. Similarly, Rolley et al. (1998) assumed that fall harvest was additive to natural mortality. Suchy et al. (1983) concluded that the assumption of additive harvest mortality was conservative and most reasonable. The inverse relationship between fall harvest rates and the growth rate in spring harvests observed in Virginia was suggestive of additive mortality but the authors cautioned specific population studies were needed to confirm the mechanism causing this relationship (Steffen and Norman 1996).

Although most authors have assumed that harvest mortality was largely additive for wild turkeys, we are aware of 3 studies that were designed to assess the relationship between harvest and nonharvest mortality. Little et al. (1990) estimated annual survival rates of wild turkeys on a state forest before and after the advent of fall hunting on the area. After fall hunting was initiated, annual survival rates declined 21–23% for adult male, juvenile male, and juvenile females, and 6% for adult females. Recently, Pack et al. (1999) compared survival rates of radio-tagged females among areas closed to fall hunting, open to 4 weeks of fall hunting, and open to 8–9 weeks of fall hunting. Mean annual survival rates were higher in areas closed to fall hunting than in areas where fall hunting occurred. They found no difference in nonharvest mortality rates among the 3 regions. Population growth rate, as indexed by harvest over a 10-year period, was highest for areas with no fall hunting. Pack et al. (1999) concluded that their study supported the additive mortality model for fall hunting of females. Norman et al. (2003) somewhat contradict these conclusions reporting that fall survival was higher than the winter-summer period and that fall hunting mortality did not appear to be additive for males.

Recruitment

Recruitment in wild turkey populations has shown even more annual and regional variability than survival and was influenced by variation in a number of parameters including nesting rate, nest success, female success, clutch size and poult survival. Nest success and female success can vary considerably from year to year (Roberts et al. 1995, Vangilder and Kurzejeski 1995, Miller et al. 1998b, Godfrey and Norman 2001). Predation is implicated as an important factor influencing recruitment by many investigators (see Vander Haegen et al. 1988, Little et al. 1990, Palmer et al. 1993, Vangilder and Kurzejeski 1995, Paisley et al. 1998), but Norman et al (2001) concluded that production was limited by nesting rate rather than poult

survival. In addition, 2 recent studies have suggested that poor habitat quality may be associated with poor nutritional condition and low rates of nest initiation and smaller clutch sizes (Miller et al. 1995, Thogmartin and Johnson 1999).

Weather Effects on Recruitment

Many investigators have reported weather-related effects on reproduction and poult survival. In Missouri, colder March temperatures appeared to be associated with delayed onset of incubation and lower female success. Vangilder and Kurzejeski (1995) hypothesized that delays in spring green-up may postpone the accumulation of sufficient nutrient reserves needed to initiate nesting and be successful. In Wisconsin, cold-wet weather during March and April was related to lower indices of recruitment (Rolley et al. 1998). Beasom and Pattee (1980) documented a strong association between poult:hen ratios and rainfall the previous fall. They proposed that rainfall stimulated plant growth which improved the nutritional condition of females. Porter et al. (1983) also found that females in poor condition, following severe winter weather, had low nesting rates and hatching success. Rainfall during incubation has been associated with predation on nests and incubating females, possibly due to moisture improving scenting conditions for predators (Palmer et al. 1993, Roberts et al. 1995, Roberts and Porter 1998a). Nesting success was related to the number of rainfall events and rainfall totals and nest predation was correlated with number of days since rainfall and rainfall amount on the day of predation (Lowery et al. 2001) suggesting that precipitation patterns and timing influence recruitment. Amount of precipitation was a indicator of recruitment in New York (Roberts and Porter 2001). Godfrey and Norman (2001) concluded that lower nest success may have been attributable to colder wetter conditions in western Virginia.

Healy (1992) summarized several studies that associated poult mortality with prolonged periods of rain and/or localized flooding. Vangilder and Kurzejeski (1995) found that poult survival was correlated with the number of days in June with rainfall exceeding 2.54 cm. Roberts and Porter (1998b) reported a weak negative association between poult survival and both cold temperatures during the first week after hatch and departure from normal rainfall during the second week post hatch.

Predicting effect of weather on nest success and poult survival is complicated by annual variation in the timing of nesting and hatching and is likely confounded by the extensive latitudinal range of wild turkeys. However, Roberts and Porter (2001) concluded that weather based indices can be viable alternatives to brood surveys.

Importance of Recruitment Versus Survival

Recent studies have debated the relative importance of recruitment versus female survival on population growth. Simulations by Suchy et al. (1983)

showed that a 4.8% decrease in female survival had the same effect on population growth as a 13.9% decrease in fecundity. Vangilder and Kurzejeski's (1995) modeling showed that increasing nest success or poult survival had large positive effects on population growth in Missouri. They also found that changes in female survival, especially illegal kill during the spring nesting season, had significant impacts on population growth. Based on the range of parameter estimates reported in the literature, Roberts et al. (1995) assumed greater variation in nest success than in annual survival and concluded that nest success had a greater impact on changes in abundance than poult or adult survival. In a later paper, Roberts and Porter (1996) used somewhat different relative variations of survival and reproduction and found that importance of nest success and annual survival were nearly identical. Further population dynamics work (Roberts and Porter 2001) concluded that nest success has the greatest influence on annual changes in New York wild turkey populations. Modeling by Rolley et al. (1998) indicated that both reproduction and survival are important in controlling population growth. A proportional sensitivity analysis performed by Brooks et al. (1999) took into account that survival and fecundity are measured on different scales and concluded that rates of population change were most sensitive to changes in fall-winter survival. Specifically, change in fall hunting survival was identified as the primary factor in follow-up analysis (Alpizar-Jara et al. 2001). Hubbard et al. (1999) compared estimates of nest success and survival from 2 time periods on the same study area in southcentral Iowa. They felt that the population decline on the study area was more likely due to a decrease in reproduction than changes in female survival. In addition, Miller et al. (1998*b*) attributed a population decline in Mississippi to an extended period of poor reproduction. Clearly both recruitment and female survival impact the growth of wild turkey populations and both must be monitored. However, managers have the greatest ability to control female survival through education and hunting regulation.

Predation

Predation has often been identified as a primary cause of mortality for turkey eggs, poults, and adults. Recent reviews by Miller and Leopold (1992) and Hurst et al. (1996) documented the significant effects of predation on nest success and survival of poults and females. Although Hurst et al. (1996) discounted importance of predators as a cause of mortality for adult males, Paisley et al. (1996) and Vangilder (1996) identified predation as an important source of adult male mortality. Female mortality during incubation and brood rearing was primarily due to predation (Vander Haegen et al. 1988, Wright et al. 1996). Nearly all nest loss was due to mammalian predation in Wisconsin (Paisley et al. 1998), and poult mortality also was negatively influenced by predators (Vander Haegen et al. 1988, Roberts et al. 1995, Vangilder and Kurzejeski 1995). Lowery et al. (2001) documented a significant

relationship between predation and rainfall in Mississippi.

While many studies have estimated predation rates, the relationship of predator and prey is complex and still poorly understood. This relationship is affected by many interacting factors, some of which include the intrinsic rate of increase of prey species, the functional and numerical responses of predators to changing prey density, the species composition of the predator community, habitat quality and landscape pattern, availability of alternative prey, the nutritional condition of the prey, and human harvests of both predator and prey. The increase in predator populations following the decline in pelt prices and harvest's in the 1980s has heightened concerns over the impact of predators on turkey populations (Hurst et al. 1996, Lovell et al. 1998, Hubbard et al. 1999). Leopold and Hurst (1994) discuss the importance of long-term, multi-species, replicated, experiments for improving our understanding of the role of predation in the control and regulation of turkey populations.

Density Dependence

Density-dependent changes in reproduction and/or survival are fundamental components underlying the sustained yield harvest model (Holt and Talbot 1978, Caughley 1985, Robertson and Rosenberg 1988). This model proposes that harvest reduces population size and intraspecific competition, increasing availability of resources (food, water, space, etc.) for survivors, resulting in increased fecundity and survival. The increased fecundity and survival creates a potential rate of increase that would be realized if harvesting was discontinued.

Although density dependent changes in reproduction have been extensively documented in ungulates (e.g., McCullough 1979, Fowler 1987) and some game birds (Roseberry and Klimstra 1984:96–97), there is little documentation of density dependent population effects in wild turkeys (Healy and Powell 1999). Vangilder et al. (1987) in Missouri and Miller et al. (1998*b*) in Mississippi interpreted relatively low reproductive success of an established population as support for the hypothesis that recruitment decreases as turkey populations stabilize. Vander Haegen et al. (1988) concluded that predation was having a substantial effect on productivity and speculated that the population was near carrying capacity. However, we are not aware of any study that has documented a negative relationship between population size and reproductive success.

Steffen and Norman (1996) found that population growth rates, estimated from trends in spring harvest, were higher in Virginia counties with low initial spring harvests than in counties with higher harvests. They believed this was suggestive of density dependence. In later work, they suggested that recruitment in Virginia is density dependent based on 30 years of data (Norman and Steffen 2004). Porter et al. (1990*a*) observed an inverse relationship between turkey abundance and subsequent growth rate and interpreted this as suggestive of density dependence. However, Johnson (1994) warned that correlating rate of change and population size from a series of counts could give spurious results.

Reliable knowledge regarding density dependence is important for sound harvest management decisions (Romesburg 1981). However, documenting existence of density-dependent effects in turkey populations will likely be difficult. Carrying capacity in forested landscapes varies greatly with variable mast crops (Healy and Powell 1999). In some regions, density-independent weather effects may suppress turkey abundance well below levels where density-dependence becomes apparent (Porter et al. 1990*b*). Although density-dependent responses can be masked by variation in the environment, McCullough (1990) and White and Bartmann (1997) warned managers not to be misled in thinking that density dependence does not operate.

Movements

Changes in the size of wild turkey populations are caused not only by births and deaths, but also by movements (ingress and egress). Recent studies on turkey population dynamics have focused on the birth and death processes and all of the published models on turkey population dynamics have assumed geographically closed populations with no net ingress or egress.

Dispersal is clearly important in the spread of newly established populations from release sites and several studies have estimated rates of spread during the first 2–3 years following stocking (Little and Varland 1981, Hopkins et al. 1982, Miller et al. 1985). However, the role of movements on the dynamics of established populations is poorly understood. A number of studies have estimated dispersal distances following the breakup of winter flocks (Kulowiec and Haufler 1985, Kurzejeski and Lewis 1990, Lint et al. 1992), typically in the range of 1–10 km. However, little is known about the spatial patterns of such movements. For example, Godwin et al. (1990) found that on average 34% of the male turkeys radio-tagged on a wildlife management area in Mississippi were off the area during the spring hunting season, but they had no information about birds that may have moved onto the area from surrounding areas. The relative importance of movements on changes in turkey populations likely varies depending on the geographic scale at which populations are defined and the variability in reproduction and survival among adjacent populations. Ingress could be very important for maintaining populations on heavily hunted public properties. In contrast, movements may be of little concern to the manager making harvest decisions for county-sized areas.

ACCEPTABLE RATES OF HARVEST

Females

Although available information on the relation of harvest and nonharvest mortality is limited, it suggests that harvest mortality of females is largely additive. Therefore, control of female harvest (legal and illegal) is important to successful population management. Most legal female harvest occurs in the fall and fall turkey numbers are variable depending upon recruitment (Healy and Powell 1999). Fall hunting seasons vary widely in structure and length. Reported sustainable harvest rates vary with recruitment and nonharvest mortality and range from 12% in Virginia (Pack et al. 1999) to <10% in Missouri (Vangilder and Kurzejeski 1995) and Iowa (Suchy et al. 1983) to <7% in Wisconsin (Rolley et al. 1998). These reported rates are guidelines applicable to average conditions. The acceptable rate of harvest is ultimately determined by the programmatic objective in concert with availability and reliability of recruitment parameter estimates.

Illegal female kill (poaching) must be considered in developing a fall hunting strategy. In some instances, poaching has been shown to be a substantial portion of total female mortality. Pack et al. (1999) reported that illegal female kill had a substantial impact on population dynamics in Virginia and West Virginia and at times, exceeded legal harvest. Illegal harvest of females in Missouri accounted for over 20% of all female mortality (Vangilder and Kurzejeski 1995). To the contrary, illegal female kill in Wisconsin made up only 2% of female mortality (Wright et al. 1996). Little et al. (1990) and Hubbard et al. (1999) did not consider poaching a problem in Iowa, and Miller et al. (1998*a*) found that illegal harvest was very low in Mississippi. The regional variance in levels of illegal female harvest illustrates that local information is necessary for effective sustained yield management.

Males

Annual harvest of males ranges from 15–62% of the population (Vangilder 1992:156, Wright and Vangilder 2001). Managers may want to consider the effect of harvest on the age structure of males in the population when formulating harvest management strategies because hunter's perception of the quality of the hunt can be affected by the proportion of older males in the population (Vangilder and Kurzejeski 1995).

The age structure of males is a function of recruitment and age-specific survival. For a given level of recruitment, an increase in the harvest rate of males will reduce the proportion of adult males in the population in subsequent years. Simulation modeling by Vangilder and Kurzejeski (1995) suggested that a spring harvest of 25% of the males would yield a harvest composed of 72% adult males, while a harvest of 50% of the male population would reduce the percentage of adults in the harvest to 56%. This relationship would be affected by differences in harvest vulnerability between subadults and adults. Based on band recovery data, Vangilder and Kurzejeski (1995) assumed that adults were twice as vulnerable as subadults to spring harvest. They hypothesized that breeding behavior by sub-adults may be suppressed by the presence of dominant adults thereby reducing their vulnerability to spring harvest. In Kentucky, the annual rate of human-caused mortality (legal harvest, illegal kill, and crippling) for adults was twice as great as for sub-adults (Wright and Vangilder 2001). In contrast, Godwin et al. (1991) and Paisley et al. (1996) were unable to document age-related differences in harvest rate.

The acceptable rate of male harvest is primarily determined by the programmatic objective be it hunter opportunity, hunter satisfaction, trophy management, or a high male population. Programmatic objectives based on user attitudes vary regionally and temporally making periodic hunter attitude surveys important to male harvest management. Hunters in Missouri indicated that they would oppose a longer season if proportion of adult males available would decline (Vangilder et al. 1990). However, in Arkansas, hunters were unwilling to accept a reduction in spring permits to increase the proportion of adult males in the population (Cartwright and Smith 1990).

Minnesota regulates participation in the spring season to limit the harvest rate of males to 30%, in part to maintain the quality of the hunt (Kimmel 2001). Alternatively, Mississippi recently implemented a minimum 6-inch beard length regulation to protect sub-adults from harvest in a effort to increase the number of adults available for harvest (G. Hurst, Mississippi State University, personal communication).

SUMMARY AND CONCLUSIONS

Wild turkey restoration in North America is fast approaching a successful conclusion and a period in which management objectives will shift to population maintenance, optimizing hunter opportunity and, in some cases, population control. Along with this success comes uncertainty. Biologists have been effective to this point in identifying and utilizing available knowledge. Our understanding of turkey population dynamics has grown dramatically in the past decade. We have a greater appreciation for the spatial and temporal variation in rates of reproduction and survival. Most studies indicate that turkey population growth is sensitive to changes in female survival and recruitment. It is important for managers to consider not only effect on population growth of changes in recruitment and survival, but also their ability to alter these parameters. The potential to alter female survival rates through harvest regulations (Pack et al. 1999) is widely utilized, but managers have no direct control over reproduction and poult survival (Vangilder and Kurzejeski 1995). Habitat management to improve reproduction may be feasible, but the effectiveness of such practices for altering recruitment is largely unknown.

An understanding of the density-dependent and density-independent processes that control the growth of wild turkey populations and how these processes can be influenced by management actions are important gaps in our knowledge. We lack basic information on environmental carrying capacity relative to habitat composition. Replicated, random, and controlled experiments will be needed to advance our understanding of population regulation in wild turkeys (Macnab

1983, Caughley 1985, Weinstein et al. 1996). In addition, better techniques for estimating turkey population size are needed to improve our understanding of the effect of density on population processes (Vangilder 1992).

Because we do not understand the relation of harvest and non-harvest mortality for most harvested species, Caughley (1985) concluded that we lack the knowledge to manage harvest scientifically. The recent studies by Little et al. (1990), Pack et al. (1999), and Norman et al. (2004) are important steps toward improving our understanding of this relationship for wild turkeys. Additional research on population response to various female harvest rates is needed to build upon these initial findings. In addition, an understanding of effects of specific harvest regulations (season length, bag limits, number of permits issued) on harvest rates is needed to improve population and harvest management. Burger et al. (1994) concluded that careful manipulation of harvest regulations provides an opportunity to rigorously test hypotheses regarding the nature of harvest mortality. Large-scale, long-term management experiments that adhere to the rules of experimental design (controls, replication, etc.) will be needed. Treatments must include varying levels of turkey density (Leopold and Hurst 1994) as well as varying levels of harvest (off-take) for at least 2 generations (see Caughley 1985). An active adaptive harvest management strategy, similar to that proposed for waterfowl harvesting (Johnson et al. 1993), may be the most effective approach to reducing the uncertainty about the dynamics of wild turkey populations. Implementing such studies will require extensive cooperation among management agencies, universities, organizations like the National Wild Turkey Federation, turkey hunters, and landowners.

Management Implications

Given our current understanding of wild turkey population dynamics, adjusting harvest rates of females appears to be the most direct means to regulate the size of turkey populations, however conflicting information does exist (Alpizar-Jara et al. 2001). Based on recent research and modeling, managers have attempted to set fall harvest rates that could be sustained without the population declining. The emphasis has been on maintaining current population levels. Although this strategy is conservative, it may not result in optimal harvest levels. Sustained yield harvesting theory suggests that there are many possible sustainable harvesting rates depending on the size of the population relative to environmental carrying capacity. Relatively low levels of harvest are sustainable when populations are low or near carrying capacity. Higher levels of harvest can be sustained at intermediate population levels. However, until we have a better understanding of effect of density on rates of recruitment and natural mortality it will be difficult for managers to determine optimum harvest rates.

Further complicating harvest management decisions is an increasing appreciation for the temporal variability in recruitment rates. Caughley (1977) described 2 strategies for harvesting in a variable environment, the "mean" and "tracking" strategies. Under the mean strategy, the variability in the population is ignored and a constant harvesting rate is set. In contrast, the tracking strategy varies the harvesting rate, increasing it when the population is growing and decreasing it when the population is declining. Caughley felt that the mean strategy required considerable information to implement properly and the tracking strategy was safer in the face of uncertainty about the magnitude of population and environmental fluctuation. Successful implementation of a tracking strategy requires monitoring of trends in population size and/or recruitment and the ability to respond to changes in population status with changes in harvest regulations.

In Wisconsin, we have been using a tracking strategy. Hunter success rate (harvest/permit) in spring, determined from mandatory registration stations, is our primary index of population change. We monitor recruitment through surveys of rural landowner observations of poults and hens, and the proportion of juvenile males in the spring harvest. Together, these indices appear to be reliable and relatively inexpensive means of monitoring recruitment and population change. Our variable permit system allows us to adjust fall harvest management strategies to respond to population fluctuation. This tracking strategy appears to have been effective in protecting against overharvest of females during prolonged periods of low recruitment while allowing for expanded harvests during periods of high recruitment. Future research will provide us with increased information from which to draw inferences when regulating turkey hunting and refine our techniques to meet the goals of turkey management in Wisconsin.

ACKNOWLEDGMENTS

We thank P. D. Beringer, D. A Miller, T. J. Schwartz, and L. D. Vangilder for reviewing this manuscript. The Wisconsin Department of Natural Resources Bureaus of Wildlife Management and Integrated Science Services provided support for the authors.

LITERATURE CITED

Alpizar-Jara, R., E. N. Brooks, K. H. Pollock, D. E Steffen, J. C. Pack, and G. W. Norman. 2001. An eastern wild turkey population dynamics model for Virginia and West Virginia. Journal of Wildlife Management 65:415–424.

Anderson, D. R., and K. P. Burnham. 1976. Population ecology of the mallard: VI. The effect of exploitation on survival. United States Department of Interior, Fish and Wildlife Service Resource Publication 128.

Austin, D. E., and L. W. DeGraff. 1975. Winter survival of wild turkeys in the southern Adirondacks. Proceedings of the National Wild Turkey Symposium 3:55–60.

Beasom, S. L., and O. H. Pattee. 1980. The effect of selected climatic variables on wild turkey productivity. Proceedings of the National Wild Turkey Symposium 4:127–135.

Brooks, E. N., R. Alpizar-Jara, and K. H. Pollock. 1999. Final report on the eastern wild turkey population dynamic model for the Virginias. North Carolina State University, Raleigh, North Carolina, USA.

———, ———, ———, D. E. Steffen, J. C. Pack, and G. W. Norman. 2002. An online wild turkey population dynamics model. Wildlife Society Bulletin 30:41–45.

Burger, L. W., Jr., Kurzejeski, E. W., L. D. Vangilder, T. V. Daily, and J. M. Schulz. 1994. Effects of harvest on population dynamics of upland game birds: are bobwhite the model? Transactions of the North American Wildlife and Natural Resources Conference 50:466–476.

Campo, J. J., C. R. Hopkins, and W. G. Swank. 1984. Mortality and reproduction of stocked eastern turkeys in east Texas. Proceedings of the Annual Conference Southeast Association of Fish and Wildlife Agencies 38:78–86.

Cartwright, M. E., and R. A. Smith. 1990. Attitudes, opinions, and characteristics of a select group of Arkansas spring turkey hunters. Proceedings of the National Wild Turkey Symposium 6:177–187.

Caughley, G. 1977. Analysis of vertebrate populations. John Wiley & Sons, New York, New York, USA.

———. 1985. Harvesting of wildlife: past, present and future. Pages 3–14 in S. L. Beasom and S. F. Roberson, editors. Game harvest management. Caesar Kleberg Wildlife Research Institute, Kingsville, Texas, USA.

Dickson, J. G., editor. 1992. The wild turkey. Biology and management. Stackpole, Harrisburg, Pennsylvania, USA.

Fowler, C. W. 1987. A review of density dependence in populations of large mammals. Pages 401–441 in H. H. Genoways, editor. Current Mammalogy Volume 1. Plenum Press, New York, New York, USA.

Godfrey, C. L., and G. W. Norman. 2001. Reproductive ecology and nesting habitat of eastern wild turkeys in western Virginia. Proceedings of the National Wild Turkey Symposium 8:203–210.

Godwin, K. D., G. A. Hurst, and R. L. Kelley. 1991. Survival rates of radio-equipped wild turkey gobblers in east-central Mississippi. Proceedings of the Annual Conference Southeast Association of Fish and Wildlife Agencies 45:218–226.

———, W. E. Palmer, G. A. Hurst, and R. L. Kelly. 1990. Relationship of wild turkey gobbler movements and harvest rates to management area boundaries. Proceedings of the Annual Conference Southeast Association of Fish and Wildlife Agencies 44:260–267.

Healy, W. M. 1992. Population influences: environment. Pages 129–143 in J. G. Dickson, editor. The wild turkey: biology and management. Stackpole, Harrisburg, Pennsylvania, USA.

———, and S. M. Powell. 1999. Wild turkey harvest management: biology, strategies, and techniques. A report of the Northeast Wild Turkey Technical Committee to the Northeast Wildlife Administrators Association.

Holt, S. J., and L. M. Talbot. 1978. New principles for the conservation of wild living resources. Wildlife Monographs No. 59.

Hopkins, C. R., J. J. Campo, W. G. Swank, and D. J. Martin. 1982. Dispersal of restocked eastern wild turkeys in east Texas. Proceedings of the Annual Conference Southeast Association of Fish and Wildlife Agencies 36:578–585.

Hubbard, M. W., D. L. Garner, and E. E. Klaas. 1999. Factors influencing wild turkey hen survival in southcentral Iowa. Journal of Wildlife Management 63:731–738.

Hurst, G. A., L. W. Burger, and B. D. Leopold. 1996. Predation and Galliforme recruitment: an old issue revisited. Transactions of the North American Wildlife and Natural Resources Conference 61:62–76.

Ielmini, M. R., A. S. Johnson, and P. E. Hale. 1992. Habitat and mortality relationships of wild turkey gobblers in the Georgia Piedmont. Proceedings of the Annual Conference Southeast Association of Fish and Wildlife Agencies 46:128–137.

Johnson, D. H. 1994. Population analysis. Pages 419–444 in T.

A. Bookhout, editor. Research and management techniques for wildlife and habitats. Fifth edition. The Wildlife Society, Bethesda, Maryland, USA.

Johnson, F. A., B. K. Williams, J. D. Nichols, J. E. Hines, W. L. Kendall, G. W. Smith, and D. F. Caithamer. 1993. Developing an adaptive management strategy for harvesting waterfowl in North America. Transactions of the North American Wildlife and Natural Resources Conference 58:565–583.

Kimmel, R. O. 2001. Regulating spring wild turkey hunting based on population and hunting quality. Proceedings of the National Wild Turkey Symposium 8:243–250.

Kulowiec, T. G., and J. B. Haufler. 1985. Winter and dispersal movements of wild turkeys in Michigan's northern Lower Peninsula. Proceedings of the National Wild Turkey Symposium 5:145–153.

Kurzejeski, E. W., and J. B. Lewis. 1990. Home ranges, movements, and habitat use of wild turkey hens in northern Missouri. Proceedings of the National Wild Turkey Symposium 6:67–71.

———, L. D. Vangilder, and J. B. Lewis. 1987. Survival of wild turkey hens in North Missouri. Journal of Wildlife Management 51:188–193.

Leopold, B. D., and G. A. Hurst. 1994. Experimental designs for assessing impacts of predators on gamebird populations. Transactions of the North American Wildlife and Natural Resources Conference 59:477–487.

Lint, J. R., B. D. Leopold, G. A. Hurst, W. J. Hamrick. 1992. Determining effective study area size from marked and harvested wild turkey gobblers. Journal of Wildlife Management 56:556–562.

Little, T. W., J. M. Kienzler, and G. A. Hanson. 1990. Effects of either-sex hunting on survival in an Iowa wild turkey population. Proceedings of the National Wild Turkey Symposium 6:119–125.

———, and K. L. Varland. 1981. Reproduction and dispersal of transplanted wild turkeys in Iowa. Journal of Wildlife Management 45:419–427.

Lowery, D. K., G. A. Hurst, S. R. Priest, and B. S. Weemy. 2001. Influences of selected weather variables on predation of wild turkey females and nest success. Proceedings of the National Wild Turkey Symposium 8:173–178.

Lovell, C. D., B. D. Leopold, and C. C. Shropshire. 1998. Trends in Mississippi predator populations, 1980–1995. Wildlife Society Bulletin 26:552–556.

Macnab, J. 1983. Wildlife management as scientific experimentation. Wildlife Society Bulletin 11:397–401.

McCullough, D. R. 1979. The George Reserve deer herd: population ecology of a K-selected species. University of Michigan Press, Ann Arbor, Michigan, USA.

———. 1990. Detecting density dependence: filtering the baby from the bathwater. Transactions of the North American Wildlife and Natural Resources Conference 55:534–543.

Miller, B. K., P. D. Major, and S. E. Backs. 1985. Movements and productivity of transplanted eastern wild turkeys in west-central Indiana farmland. Proceedings of the National Wild Turkey Symposium 5:233–244.

Miller, D. A., L. W. Burger, B. D. Leopold, and G. A. Hurst. 1998a. Survival and cause-specific mortality of wild turkey hens in central Mississippi. Journal of Wildlife Management 62:306–313.

———, B. D. Leopold, and G. A. Hurst. 1998b. Reproductive characteristics of a wild turkey population in central Mississippi. Journal of Wildlife Management 62:903–910.

———, M. Weinstein, S. R. Priest, B. D. Leopold, and G. A. Hurst. 1995. Wild turkey reproductive parameters from two different forest ecosystems in central Mississippi. Proceedings of the Annual Conference Southeast Association of Fish and Wildlife Agencies 49:466–475.

Miller, J. E., and B. D. Leopold. 1992. Population influences: predators. Pages 119–128 in J. D. Dickson, editor. The wild turkey: biology and management. Stackpole, Harrisburg, Pennsylvania, USA.

Nguyen, L. P., J. Hamr, and G. H. Parker. 2003. Survival and reproduction of wild turkey hens in central Ontario. Wilson Bulletin 115:131–139.

Nichols, J. D., M. J. Conroy, D. R. Anderson, and K. P. Burnham. 1984. Compensatory mortality in waterfowl populations: a review of the evidence and implications for research and management. Transactions of the North American Wildlife and Natural Resources Conference 49:535–554.

Norman, G. W., M. M. Conner, J. C. Pack, and G. C. White. 2004. Effects of fall hunting on survival of male wild turkeys in Virginia and West Virginia. Journal of Wildlife Management 68:393–404.

———, J. C. Pack, C. I. Taylor, D. E. Steffen, and K. H. Pollock. 2001. Reproduction of eastern wild turkeys in Virginia and West Virginia. Journal of Wildlife Management 65:1–9.

———, and D. E. Steffen. 2003. Effects of recruitment, oak mast, and fall-season format on wild turkey harvest rates in Virginia. Wildlife Society Bulletin 31:553–559.

Pack, J. C., G. W. Norman, C. I. Taylor, D. E. Steffen, D. A. Swanson, C. H. Pollock, and R. Alpizar-Jara. 1999. Effects of fall hunting on wild turkey populations in Virginia and West Virginia. Journal of Wildlife Management 63:964–975.

Paisley, R. N., R. G. Wright, and J. F. Kubisiak. 1996. Survival of wild turkey gobblers in southwestern Wisconsin. Proceedings of the National Wild Turkey Symposium 7:39–44.

———, ———, ———, and R. E. Rolley. 1998. Reproductive ecology of eastern wild turkeys in southwestern Wisconsin. Journal of Wildlife Management 62:911–916.

Palmer, W. E., G. A. Hurst, J. E. Stys, D. R. Smith, and J. D. Burk. 1993. Survival rates of wild turkey hens in loblolly pine plantations in Mississippi. Journal of Wildlife Management 57:783–789.

Porter, W. F., G. C. Nelson, and K. Mattson. 1983. Effects of winter conditions on reproduction in a northern wild turkey population. Journal of Wildlife Management 47:281–290.

———, D. J. Gefell, and H. B. Underwood. 1990a. Influence of hunter harvest on the population dynamics of wild turkeys in New York. Proceedings of the National Wild Turkey Symposium 6:188–195.

———, H. B. Underwood, and D. J. Gefell. 1990b. Application of population modeling techniques to wild turkey management. Proceedings of the National Wild Turkey Symposium 6:107–118.

Roberts, S. D., J. M. Coffey, and W. F. Porter. 1995. Survival and reproduction of female wild turkeys in New York. Journal of Wildlife Management 59:437–447.

———, and W. F. Porter. 1996 Importance of demographic parameters to annual changes in wild turkey abundance. Proceedings of the National Wild Turkey Symposium 7:15–20

———, and W. F. Porter. 1998a. Relation between weather and survival of wild turkeys. Journal of Wildlife Management 62:1492–1498.

———, and ———. 1998b. Influence of temperature and precipitation on survival of wild turkey poults. Journal of Wildlife Management 62:1499–1505.

———, and ———. 2001. Annual changes in May rainfall as an index to wild turkey harvest. Proceedings of the National Wild Turkey Symposium 8:43–51.

Robertson, P. A., and A. A. Rosenberg. 1988. Harvesting gamebirds. Pages 177–201 in P. J. Hudson and M. R. W. Rands, editors. Ecology and management of gamebirds. BSP Professional, Oxford, United Kingdom.

Romesburg, H. C. 1981. Wildlife science: gaining reliable knowledge. Journal of Wildlife Management 45:293–313.

Rolley, R. E., J. F. Kubisiak, R. N. Paisley, and R. G. Wright. 1998. Wild turkey population dynamics in southwestern Wisconsin. Journal of Wildlife Management 62:917–924.

Roseberry, J. L., and W. D. Klimstra. 1984. Population ecology of the bobwhite. Southern Illinois University, Carbondale, Illinois, USA.

Steffen, D. E., and G. W. Norman. 1996. Dynamics between spring and fall harvest of wild turkeys in Virginia. Proceedings of the National Wild Turkey Symposium 7:231–237.

Suchy, W. J., G. A. Hanson, and T. W. Little. 1983. Evaluation of a population model as a management tool in Iowa. Proceedings of the National Wild Turkey Symposium 6:196–204.

Thogmartin, W. E., and J. E. Johnson. 1999. Reproduction in a declining population of wild turkeys in Arkansas. Journal of Wildlife Management 63:1281–1290.

Vander Haegen, W. M., W. E. Dodge, and M. W. Sayre. 1988. Factors affecting productivity in a northern wild turkey population. Journal of Wildlife Management 52:127–133.

Vangilder, L. D. 1992. Population dynamics. Pages 144–164 *in* J. G. Dickson, editor. The wild turkey: biology and management. Stackpole, Harrisburg, Pennsylvania, USA.

———. 1996. Survival and cause-specific mortality of wild turkeys in the Missouri Ozarks. Proceedings of the National Wild Turkey Symposium 7:21–32.

———, and E. W. Kurzejeski. 1995. Population ecology of the eastern wild turkey in northern Missouri. Wildlife Monographs 130.

———, ———, V. L. Kimmel-Truitt, and J. B. Lewis. 1987. Reproductive parameters of wild turkey hens in north Missouri. Journal of Wildlife Management 51:535–540.

———, S. L. Sheriff, and G. S. Olson. 1990. Spring turkey hunters. Proceedings of the National Wild Turkey Symposium 6:167–176.

Weinstein, M., D. A. Miller, L. M. Connor, B. D. Leopold, and G. A. Hurst. 1996. What affects turkeys? A conceptual model for future research. Proceedings of the National Wild Turkey Symposium 7:135–142.

White, G. C., and R. M. Bartmann. 1997. Density dependence in deer populations. Pages 120–135 *in* W. J. McShea, H. B. Underwood, and J. H. Rappole, editors. The science of overabundance: deer ecology and population management. Smithsonian Institution Press, Washington District of Columbia, USA.

Wright, G. A., and L. D. Vangilder. 2001. Survival of eastern wild turkey males in western Kentucky. Proceedings of the National Wild Turkey Symposium 8:187–194.

Wright, R. G., R. N. Paisley, and J. F. Kubisiak. 1996. Survival of wild turkey hens in southwestern Wisconsin. Journal of Wildlife Management 60:313–320.

Wunz, G. A., and A. H. Hayden. 1975. Winter mortality and supplemental feeding of turkeys in Pennsylvania. Proceedings of the National Wild Turkey Symposium 3:61–69.

Keith Warnke received a B.S in Wildlife Ecology from the University of Wisconsin, Madison, and an M.S. in Wildlife Conservation from the University of Minnesota. He served as the Upland Wildlife Ecologist and Turkey Specialist for WI DNR from 1997–2004. He is currently the WI DNR Big Game Ecologist stationed in Madison, WI. He enjoys many outdoor activities with his family including hunting and fishing.

Robert E. Rolley serves as a Wildlife Population Ecologist for the Wisconsin Department of Natural Resources. He is responsible for monitoring wildlife population trends, modeling population response to management strategies, and advising on harvest management strategies for wild turkeys, white-tailed deer, black bear, and furbearer species. Robert received a B.S. from the University of California, a M.S. from the University of Wisconsin and a Ph.D. from Oklahoma State University.

THE DISTRIBUTION AND RELATIVE ABUNDANCE OF WILD TURKEYS IN FLORIDA

David S. Nicholson[1]
Florida Fish and Wildlife Conservation Commission,
663 Plantation Road, Perry, FL 32347, USA

Larry S. Perrin
Florida Fish and Wildlife Conservation Commission,
5300 High Bridge Road, Quincy, FL 32351, USA

Cory Morea
Florida Fish and Wildlife Conservation Commission,
5300 High Bridge Road, Quincy, FL 32351, USA

Roger Shields
Florida Fish and Wildlife Conservation Commission,
3900 Drane Field Road, Lakeland, FL 33811, USA

Abstract: Updated information concerning the distribution and relative abundance of wild turkeys (*Meleagris gallopavo*) is important for prioritizing future management efforts, especially in light of the rapid human population growth and subsequent habitat loss that has occurred in Florida during the last 3 decades. Survey questionnaires were mailed to 2,220 natural resource personnel and others having potential knowledge of wild turkey populations in Florida. Valid responses were received from 604 individuals who provided 1,174 county maps depicting turkey distribution and relative abundance (i.e., absent, low number of turkeys, or moderate to high number of turkeys). Associated maps were digitized into a geographic information system (GIS) and ordinal responses (i.e., categorical abundance scores) were averaged for each 30-m × 30-m pixel. The number of responses received per pixel averaged 3.3 (range 1–16). Standard errors for areas of the state receiving >1 response averaged 0.1798 and ranged from 0.00–1.41. Wild turkey relative abundance index values resulted in moderate to high abundance indices for 61,200 km², low abundance indices for 39,500 km², and rare or absent designations for 41,100 km². This information will be used in conjunction with habitat suitability models, landownership, and other available data to prioritize future wild turkey management efforts in Florida.

Proceedings of the National Wild Turkey Symposium 9:101–106
Key words: abundance, distribution, Florida, *Meleagris gallopavo*, population, wild turkey.

Florida had a sizable turkey population during the early 1900s (Wright 1915) even as turkeys were disappearing from most of the eastern United States. Florida's low human population during this period, and refugia provided by large expanses of habitat inhospitable to humans, are factors that probably allowed turkey populations in Florida to remain high relative to the eastern U.S. as a whole. However, increasing numbers of settlers and unregulated commercial and subsistence hunting began to have a negative effect on Florida's turkey population. By 1948, the number of turkeys in Florida had reached its lowest level with an estimated population of 26,000 (Newman and Griffin 1950). In 1949, the Florida Game and Fresh Water Fish Commission (GFC; presently the Florida Fish and Wildlife Conservation Commission [FWC]) identified areas of good turkey habitat that were devoid of turkeys and initiated a restoration program (Powell 1965). The restoration program was completed by 1970, at which time the fall turkey population was estimated to

be approximately 100,000 birds (Williams and Austin 1988).

The GFC conducted wild turkey population assessments in 1973 and 1977 to document statewide distribution during that period. Survey maps were distributed to biologists, game managers, and GFC law enforcement officers throughout the state. Survey participants were asked to identify areas where turkeys were known to occur (i.e., presence versus absence). Because the results from 1973 and 1977 were similar, the data was combined to create a composite map of turkey distributions for the state. The results of this assessment indicated that wild turkeys were present in all Florida counties (Williams 1978).

Since completion of the 1973 and 1977 turkey surveys, Florida's human population has increased by over 64% (from 9.7 million in 1980 to 16.0 million in 2000; U.S. Bureau of Census 2001). In addition, the

---

[1] E-mail: David.Nicholson@MyFWC.com

tourism industry in Florida continues to attract an increasing number of tourists (estimated 75.6 million visitors during 2003, Florida Commission on Tourism). New development and infrastructure needed to support these increases may have resulted in the loss of substantial amounts of suitable turkey habitat. In light of these changes, the FWC initiated a project to determine the present distribution and relative abundance of wild turkeys in Florida to compare with past turkey distribution data and for use in prioritizing future turkey management efforts.

METHODS

An initial survey questionnaire was sent to designated survey groups that included FWC wildlife biologists and law enforcement officers, Florida Chapter of The Wildlife Society members, antlerless deer program enrollees, natural resource professionals (e.g., Water Management District land managers, Department of Defense biologists, etc.), and others with potential knowledge of turkey populations in Florida (e.g., Florida Chapter of the National Wild Turkey Federation members, etc.). This questionnaire asked participants to indicate counties with which they were knowledgeable of wild turkey populations on tracts of land at least 405 ha (1,000 acres) in size during the previous 3 years (i.e., 1999–2001). Respondents to the initial survey were then sent maps for those counties with which they indicated knowledge of 405 ha or more, instructions for completing the map(s), 3 colored china markers, a short questionnaire, and a return envelope. County maps were GIS derived 27.9-cm × 43.2-cm maps including roads, city limits, water bodies, and conservation lands (e.g., public wildlife management areas, state and federal parks, Nature Conservancy lands, etc). Participants were asked to shade the portions of the map(s) they were familiar with and indicate the relative abundance of turkeys for these areas using red, green, or blue shading.

Relative abundance values were defined as (1) absent, (2) low, (3) moderate to high based on observations during the previous 3 years. We defined absent values as areas where turkeys or their sign had not been observed and no turkeys had been harvested. We defined the low value as areas where turkeys and/or sign were seen no more than once or twice for every 10 site visits and wild turkeys were observed in low numbers (flocks with less than 5 birds), or where few turkeys were harvested relative to the number of hunters. We defined a moderate to high value as areas where turkeys and/or fresh sign were routinely located (observations made 3 or more times for every 10 trips) and where moderate to high numbers of wild turkeys (flocks with 5 or more birds) were observed, or turkeys were regularly harvested relative to the number of hunters. Participants were asked to leave blank portions of county maps for which they did not have knowledge during the previous 3 years.

Completed maps were digitized into ArcView (Version 3.2, Environmental Systems Research Insti-

tute, Redlands, CA, USA) by county. For each digitized polygon, the associated attribute table included the relative abundance value (absent = 1, low = 2, moderate to high = 3), the respondent's name and contact information, an assigned identification number, the survey group they were assigned to (see Table 1), the county, the date the polygon was digitized, and comments. The digitized files were converted to grids with a cell size of 30 m × 30 m for use with Spatial Analyst extension (Version 1.1, Environmental Systems Research Institute, Redlands, CA, USA). Responses for individual cells were averaged to determine a relative abundance index, and the number of responses per cell was computed. Areas where no responses were received were then isolated. Abundance estimates in null areas less than 405 ha were calculated by averaging the neighboring 15 × 15 pixels (i.e., 450-m × 450-m area). Null areas 405 ha or larger were compared to land-use data (Northwest Florida, St. Johns River, Suwannee River, Southwest Florida, and South Florida Water Management Districts 1995), and those areas designated as unsuitable turkey habitat (i.e., moderate to high density residential areas, commercial and service-oriented business activities, industrial, and transportation) were assigned an absent designation, while those areas designated as potentially suitable habitat were isolated and selected for further review. Maps of null areas for further review were sent to each FWC Regional Biologist ($n = 5$) to determine persons who may have information concerning these areas. Identified individuals were then contacted to assist with filling the gaps in the statewide assessment. Updated information was digitized and merged into the statewide coverage as it was received. As updated information was digitized, null areas were again examined and null areas less than 405 ha in size were populated by averaging the neighboring 15 × 15 pixels (i.e., 450-m × 450-m area). These steps were repeated until the entire state was completed. Relative abundance index grids were then converted from floating point (i.e., decimal) grids to integer grids using standard rounding conventions (i.e., 1.0–1.49 = 1 [rare or absent], 1.50–2.49 = 2 [low], 2.49–3.00 = 3 [moderate to high]).

To compare the updated distribution with the 1970s composite map (Williams 1978), the 1970s distribution was also hand-digitized into ArcView and converted to a grid. The 2 coverages were then merged and areas of concordance (i.e., turkeys absent in the 1970s distribution and rare or absent in the updated distribution or present in the 1970s and still present at low, or moderate to high densities in 2001) and discordance (i.e., turkeys absent before but now present at low or moderate to high densities, or turkeys were present before and are now rare or absent) were computed.

RESULTS

Initial survey questionnaires were mailed to 2,220 individuals. Responses were received from 690 individuals (Table 1). These individuals were mailed a fi-

Table 1. Number of initial surveys sent and returned, the number of individuals responding to the final Florida statewide turkey distribution survey, and overall response rate (i.e., percent) by designated survey group, 2001.

Group	Number of initial surveys sent	Number of initial returns	Individuals returning final survey	Overall response rate[a]
FWC—Wildlife	195	80	72	36.9
FWC—Law Enforcement	699	150	127	18.2
FLTWS	256	46	40	15.6
Antlerless Deer Program Members	1,033	377	333	32.2
Other[b]	37	37	32	86.5
Total	2,220	690	604	27.2

[a] Calculated based on the number of initial surveys sent and the number of final surveys returned. These values should be considered minimums since in some instances multiple individuals submitted their responses on the same map(s).
[b] Includes Florida Chapter of National Wild Turkey Federation members, land managers with other governmental agencies or private corporations, and others who were deemed to have knowledge of wild turkey populations.

nal survey, including 1,403 county maps. Final surveys were received from 604 individuals (Table 1), which provided 1,174 individual county maps. After digitizing these maps, about 3% of the state (4,268 km^2) remained unaccounted for, of which, 77 areas were ≥405 ha (range 406–107,678 ha). Additional responses were then solicited and subsequently received from 23 individuals, resulting in complete coverage of the state.

Statewide, moderate to high relative abundance index values totaled 61,200 km^2, low index values totaled 39,500 km^2, and rare or absent indices totaled 41,100 km^2 (Figure 1). The number of survey responses received per pixel averaged 3.3 (SE = 2.0; range 1–16; Figure 2). Standard errors for areas of the state receiving >1 response (19,637 km^2 only had 1 response thus standard errors could not be computed) averaged 0.1798 and ranged from 0.00–1.41 (Figure 3).

The updated distribution again documented the presence of wild turkeys in all 67 Florida counties. Areas of concordance between the 1970s and the updated distributions occurred in 74.3% of the pixels (105,222 km^2) whereas discordance occurred in 25.7% of the cells (36,371 km^2) (Figure 4, Table 2). Where discordance occurred, decreases in the distribution of turkeys accounted for 8,518 km^2 as compared to the 1970s data, whereas increases in the distribution of turkeys accounted for 27,853 km^2 as compared to the 1970s data.

DISCUSSION

The intent of this project was to develop a map of statewide wild turkey distributions to facilitate management or regulatory measures at a landscape scale. Although <⅓ of the individuals initially contacted actually completed the final survey across all survey groups, more than 80% of the respondents who said they would complete a survey did so. The 604 participants who completed surveys were sufficient enough to allow for multiple responses over most areas of the state. In general, survey responses were in sufficient agreement to lend confidence to the results. This is further supported by the fact that average spring turkey harvest records for 2000 through 2002 (Florida Fish and Wildlife Conservation Commission, unpublished

data), as determined by an annual mail survey, also corresponded well with the wild turkey distribution assessment such that counties with relatively high turkey harvest per square kilometer of land area estimates were predominately classified as having a moderate to high turkey population (Spearman rank order correlation; $r_s = 0.77$, $P < 0.01$). Conversely, counties with estimated low or absent wild turkey distribution values tended to have relatively low turkey harvest per square kilometer of land area estimates. This level of confidence should be suitable to identify potential "focus" areas (i.e., areas of significant size [e.g., 4,000 ha or more] with suitable turkey habitat but low or absent turkey populations).

Additionally, wild turkey monitoring efforts (radio-telemetry and bait-station surveys) from an ongoing countywide turkey restoration project in Holmes County further indicate the relative accuracy of the statewide wild turkey distribution project. In this regard, the distribution of wild turkeys throughout Holmes County ascertained from population monitoring data from 2001 matched closely with the information obtained for this county from the statewide turkey distribution assessment. Moreover, it should be noted that principle investigators for the Holmes County turkey restoration project did not provide input for this county as part of the statewide turkey distribution assessment.

Although no specific reference was used in determining the 405 ha minimum criteria for responses, we believe this was a good compromise area to prevent receiving a large number of "small" area responses for digitizing, but at the same time, this amount of area would allow information to be collected at a fine enough scale for management related purposes. The criteria is also comparable to overall average daily ranges that have been reported for wild turkeys (Williams 1991). The overall results of the study would likely not have changed substantially if a different minimum area was utilized, but would have likely influenced the amount of digitizing to be completed.

The 1995 land-use data was the most current data we had available for assessing unsuitable habitats when trying to "fill" null areas after the initial survey. We recognize that changes in land-use had taken place within the six-year period between the compilation of land-use data and the completion of the turkey assess-

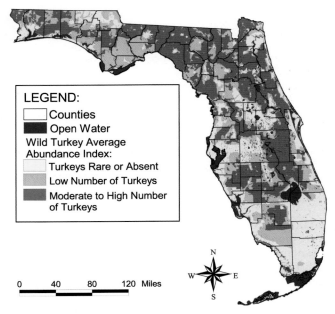

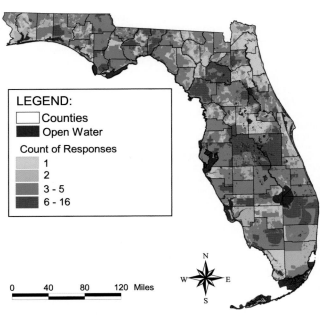

Fig. 1.   Relative abundance index values depicting areas of Florida having rare or absent turkey populations, a low number of turkeys, or a moderate to high number of turkeys according to a survey of natural resource professionals and others in 2001.

Fig. 2.   Number of responses received per pixel for a statewide wild turkey distribution and relative abundance survey, 2001.

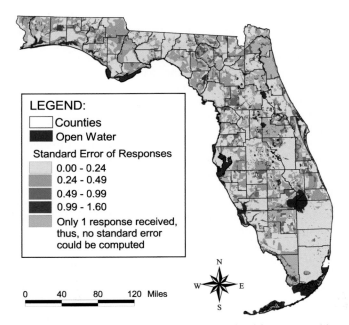

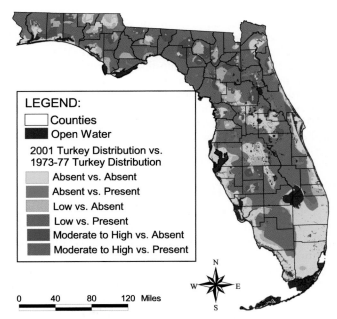

Fig. 3.   Standard errors of responses received for a statewide wild turkey distribution and relative abundance survey, 2001.

Fig. 4.   Spatial comparison between a turkey distribution and relative abundance survey conducted in 2001 and a similar turkey distribution survey completed during 1973 and 1977 (Williams 1978) in Florida.

Table 2. Comparison between a turkey distribution and relative abundance survey conducted in 2001 (FWC [2001]) and a similar turkey distribution survey completed during 1973 and 1977 (GFC [1973–77]; Williams 1978) in Florida. Results are presented as area (km²) for which the various combinations of results of the 2 surveys occurred.

FWC (2001)	GFC (1973–77)	km²
Turkeys Rare or Absent	Absent	32,424
Turkeys Rare or Absent	Present	8,518
Low Number of Turkeys	Absent	14,285
Low Number of Turkeys	Present	25,213
Moderate to High Number of Turkeys	Absent	13,568
Moderate to High Number of Turkeys	Present	47,585

ment survey, especially with respect to development. However, those lands converting from potentially suitable to unsuitable (e.g., development) during this timeframe would not have affected our results as these areas were likely denoted as absent of turkeys when contact was made with individuals knowledgeable of the area. If areas reverted from unsuitable to suitable turkey habitat, then potential problems would have been possible with our methods, but it is highly unlikely that this reversion occurred.

Based on survey results, the greatest abundance and widest distribution of turkeys occurs in north-central and northeast Florida and a wide swath extending north of Lake Okeechobee and east of the Kissimmee River system in central Florida. Relatively abundant populations also occur on the large ranches of southwest Florida where turkeys utilize a patchwork of agriculture and limited forested areas. However, densities reported in these southwest Florida areas may be somewhat inflated since turkeys are typically concentrated in the areas of available habitat, but individuals completing the surveys did not record in detail where turkeys did and did not occur across individual ranches. Additionally, the more open habitats of southwest Florida tend to increase the visibility of turkeys which may have also contributed to inflated densities. Relatively lower than expected abundance indices were observed in the panhandle west of Leon County (Tallahassee), even though these areas appear to offer similar amounts of forest as compared to the rest of northern Florida.

Despite the dramatic increases in the human population and land development during the past 3 decades, the distribution of wild turkeys in Florida appears to have expanded somewhat since the 1970s. Visual inspection of the results indicates that losses to the occupied range primarily occurred around urban centers, where habitat alteration and loss associated with the growing human population and urban sprawl has been most pronounced. Increases in the distribution of turkeys occurred chiefly through the filling of "gaps" in the 1970s distribution within the panhandle and interior northern peninsular portions of the state. These areas are largely forest plantation and agricultural based communities that have not experienced the same level of human population growth as occurred in south Florida and along the coasts. The observed increases to these regions were likely a result of further expansion of the turkey populations introduced during the intensive restoration program of the 1950s and 1960s. Other potential reasons for the observed increase in distributions include conversions of habitats (Brown and Thompson 1988, Brown 1999) to conditions more favorable for turkeys, the tendency of private lands to be more protected, especially commercial timberland, as a result of leasing hunting rights and the increased protection this has afforded (i.e., gated roads, posted boundaries, etc.), and increased law enforcement presence.

To facilitate the identification of "focus" areas (i.e., areas where turkey abundance does not correspond with habitat potential), the most recent statewide turkey distribution map should ideally be compared with an updated model of available turkey habitat. From a management perspective, the primary interest should be in identifying substantial areas of suitable turkey habitat that are indicated as having an absent or low turkey population. In this regard, the FWC is presently "fine-tuning" a wild turkey habitat model (Cox et al. 1994) using 2003 land-cover classifications (Stys et al. 2004) to identify areas of suitable turkey habitat in Florida. The resultant habitat map will be compared to the statewide turkey distribution map, and areas of the state with suitable turkey habitat and low or absent turkey populations will be isolated for further evaluation. These evaluations will be useful for planning future management efforts which could include regulatory measures, population restoration, public land management, and/or private land initiatives.

ACKNOWLEDGMENTS

This project was funded with wild turkey permit funds by the Florida Fish and Wildlife Conservation Commission through its Wild Turkey Management Section. We would like to thank N. E. Wilson, R. M. Monaghan, and M. Wilson for their assistance in digitizing returned maps, and P. S. Kubilis for assistance with developing ArcView scripts and data analysis. We would also like to thank T. E. O'Meara and P. A. Schulz for planning assistance throughout the project, and T. E. O'Meara, M. J. Allen, and 3 anonymous reviewers for valuable comments provided on the manuscript.

LITERATURE CITED

Brown, M. 1999. Florida's forests, 1995. Resource Bulletin SRS-48. U.S. Department of Agriculture, Forest Service, Southern Research Station, Ashville, North Carolina, USA.

———, and M. Thompson. 1988. Forest statistics for Florida, 1987. Resource Bulletin SE-101. U.S. Department of Agriculture, Forest Service, Southeastern Forest Experiment Station, Ashville, North Carolina, USA.

Cox, J., R. Kautz, M. MacLaughlin, and T. Gilbert. 1994. Closing the gaps in Florida's wildlife habitat conservation system. Florida Game and Fresh Water Fish Commission, Tallahassee, Florida, USA.

Newman, C. C, and E. Griffin. 1950. Deer and turkey habitats and populations of Florida. Florida Game and Fresh Water Fish Commission. Technical Bulletin No. 1.

Powell, J. A. 1965. The Florida wild turkey. Florida Game and Fresh Water Fish Commission. Technical Bulletin No. 8.

Stys, B., R. Kautz, D. Reed, M. Kertis, R. Kawula, C. Keller, and A. Davis. 2004. Florida vegetation and land cover – 2003. Florida Fish and Wildlife Conservation Commission. Tallahassee, Florida, USA.

United States Bureau of Census. 2001. Florida Quick Facts. http://quickfacts.census.gov/qfd/states/12000.html

Williams, L. E. 1978. Distribution of the turkey in Florida—1973–1977. Florida Field Naturalist 6:33–35.

———. 1991. Managing wild turkeys in Florida. Real Turkey Publishers, Gainesville, Florida, USA.

———, and D. H. Austin. 1988. Studies of the wild turkey in Florida. University Presses of Florida, Gainesville, Florida, USA.

Wright, A. H. 1915. Early records of the wild turkey. IV. Auk 32:207–224.

David Nicholson (center) is currently a District Biologist with the Florida Fish and Wildlife Conservation Commission's (FWC) Terrestrial Habitat Conservation and Restoration Section. He received his B.S. (1994) and M.S. (2000) in Wildlife and Fisheries Ecology and a minor in Agronomy (1994) from Oklahoma State University. David began his employment with the FWC in 1998, where he served as a wildlife biologist with the Wild Turkey Management Section and continues to serve as a member of the wild turkey standing team. In his spare time, he enjoys hunting, fishing, and spending time with his family. *Larry Perrin* (right) has been serving as the program coordinator for the Florida Fish and Wildlife Conservation Commission's (FWC) Wild Turkey Management Program since 1994. He received a degree in Wildlife Ecology from the University of Florida. Larry began his career with the FWC (previously the Florida Game and Fresh Water Fish Commission) in 1978. He enjoys hunting, fishing, and windsurfing. *Cory R. Morea* (not pictured) is currently the Northwest Public Hunting Areas Coordinator with the Florida Fish and Wildlife Conservation Commission's (FWC) Division of Hunting and Game Management. He received his B.S. (1996) and M.S. (1999) in Wildlife Ecology and Conservation with a minor in Forestry (1996) from the University of Florida. Cory began his employment with the FWC in 1999. He enjoys hunting, fishing and camping. *Roger Shields* (left) is currently a wildlife biologist with the Florida Fish and Wildlife Conservation Commission. He received a B.S. in Range and Wildlife Resources from Brigham Young University (1997) and an M.S. in Wildlife and Fisheries Sciences from South Dakota State University (2001). He joined the FWC in 2001, where his work has focused on wild turkey management and research, first as a member of the Wild Turkey Management Section and now as a member of the Fish and Wildlife Research Institute's Avian Research Program. His professional interests focus on ecology and management of wild turkeys and other upland gamebirds.

FACTORS SUPPRESSING A WILD TURKEY POPULATION IN SOUTHCENTRAL PENNSYLVANIA

Mary Jo Casalena[1]
Pennsylvania Game Commission,
2001 Elmerton Avenue,
Harrisburg, PA 17110-9797, USA

Mark A. Lowles
Pennsylvania Cooperative Fish and Wildlife Research
Unit, Pennsylvania State University,
419 Forest Resources Building,
University Park, PA 16802, USA

Duane R. Diefenbach
U.S. Geological Survey,
Pennsylvania Cooperative Fish and Wildlife Research Unit,
Pennsylvania State University, 419 Forest Resources Building,
University Park, PA 16802, USA

Abstract: Eastern wild turkey (*Meleagris gallopavo silvestris*) population indices in a portion of south-central Pennsylvania (PA) indicated a decreasing population trend since the late 1980s. In 1995, the fall turkey-hunting season was reduced from 2 weeks to 1 week to attempt to reduce hunting mortality and increase population size. Although the population has not exhibited a further decline, it has remained low. To investigate factors responsible for continued population suppression, we conducted a 2.5-year study (1999–2001) monitoring cause-specific mortality, reproductive rates, and population demographics of 163 radiotagged hens. We used these data in a stochastic population model to investigate factors having the greatest influence on population dynamics. Annual survival of subadult hens (13.3% in 2000, 27.7% in 2001) was less than similar studies (39–57%). Adult hen annual survival (47.8% in 2000, 64.4% in 2001) was lower than similar studies (57–75%) during year 1, but similar to these studies during year 2. Predation rates were normal (48.1%). However, average fall hen harvest mortality (12.3%, range = 6.2–28.6%) was greater than the harvest rate (10% for both males and females) at which population declines are generally expected. Additionally, 5.1% of marked hens died from legal use of rodenticides in fruit orchards. Relative to other studies, nest incubation rates were low (69%) during 2000 but nest success was average (72%), and in 2001 nest incubation rates were similar to other studies (88%), but nest success was below average (42%). Poult survival in both years (11.8% and 23.3%, respectively) was less than other studies (24–60%). Sensitivity analyses of the stochastic model indicated that subadult and poult mortality rates had the greatest influence on the population decline. Consequently, to attempt to reduce subadult mortality, fall turkey hunting in this area was closed indefinitely beginning in 2003. Also, a cooperative project was started with local orchard owners to reduce accidental rodenticide poisoning. In an attempt to improve poult survival, herbaceous openings of 0.2–1.0 ha are being maintained and rehabilitated throughout the study area in an accompanying study to determine the importance of these openings to poult survival.

Proceedings of the National Wild Turkey Symposium 9:107–116
Key words: harvest, *Meleagris gallopavo silvestris,* mortality, Pennsylvania, population dynamics, population model, reproduction, sensitivity analysis, survival, wild turkey.

Eastern wild turkeys were restored to south-central Pennsylvania through wild trap-and-transfers during the late 1970s. In the mid 1980s, trends in spring turkey harvest densities (harvest/km^2 of forest) and summer turkey sighting indices indicated that the turkey population was declining in a portion of southcentral

[1] Email: mcasalena@state.pa.us

PA, managed as Turkey Management Area (TMA) 7B (Bureau of Wildlife Management 1994). The same indices indicated that other TMAs had stationary or increasing population trends. By 1994, spring and fall harvest densities in TMA 7B were the lowest in Pennsylvania, indicating a precipitous decline in population size.

Harvest densities of turkeys in Pennsylvania are manipulated by setting the fall turkey season length from 0–3 weeks, for each of the 12 TMAs, rather than setting harvest quotas (all purchasers of a hunting license are permitted to harvest 1 turkey in any open TMA during the fall season). In an attempt to increase the turkey population via reduced harvest densities in TMA 7B, the Pennsylvania Game Commission (PGC) shortened the fall either-sex turkey-hunting season from 2 weeks to 1 week in 1995. Conversely, due to increasing population trends in TMA 7A, which is west of TMA 7B within the same Ridge and Valley geographic province as TMA 7B, the fall season was extended from 2 to 3 weeks that same year. As of 2003, population indices in TMA 7B had not increased, whereas similar management actions from 1997–1999 reversed declining trends in TMA 7A (Pennsylvania Game Commission, unpublished data).

Low nesting rates, nest success, and poult recruitment were suspected as possible reasons for the declining population. Roberts et al. (1995) found that nest success and poult survival were the primary factors contributing to annual population change in the mixed agricultural and forested habitat of southcentral New York.

Predation, harvest, weather, and other environmental factors also can affect turkey population recovery. Lowrey et al. (2000) found total number of rainfall events during the spring was negatively correlated to nest success in Mississippi. Predation is a major factor in mortality of wild turkey hens (Rolley et al. 1998), and harvest (legal and illegal) can limit turkey population growth (Pack et al. 1999, Healy and Powell 1999, Wright et al. 1996). Pack et al. (1999) reported predation, poaching, and fall hunting had the greatest negative effects on turkey populations in Virginia and West Virginia with 0–9 weeks of fall hunting. Researchers have suggested that harvesting >10% of the turkey population during the fall season can cause turkey population declines (Little et al. 1990, Suchy et al. 1983, Vangilder and Kruzejeski 1995). Also, there were anecdotal reports of turkey mortality from legal, fall rodenticide applications in fruit orchards on the study area to control meadow voles (*Microtus pennsylvanicus*).

We studied survival and reproductive rates of hen wild turkeys during 2.5 years, which encompassed 3 years of fall hunting season mortality, 1999–2001, and 2 years of reproductive data, 2000–2001. The objective of this study was to obtain empirical estimates of population parameters for hen wild turkeys (hunting mortality, seasonal survival rates, nesting rates, nest success rates, and poult survival rates) and use these estimates in a population model to identify the most likely causes of population suppression.

STUDY AREA

The study area, encompassing the Michaux State Forest (MSF) in southcentral PA, was located on South Mountain, 48 km south of Harrisburg, PA, and 19 km west of Gettysburg, PA, in the center of TMA 7B. The MSF was approximately 35,000 ha and contained most of the forested habitat in TMA 7B (46% of the 76,262 ha) and South Mountain contained most of the turkey population in TMA 7B. Sixty percent of the land area surrounding South Mountain was agricultural and residential and supported comparatively fewer turkeys except in areas adjacent to the large forested blocks. In this TMA, wild turkeys were not reintroduced into the valleys surrounding South Mountain because of the large area of intensive agriculture, and, therefore, turkey populations in these valleys were very low density.

The MSF was predominately upland oak (*Quercus* spp.) vegetation on xeric sites. Chestnut oak (*Q. prinus*) was the dominant mast producing tree, but scarlet oak (*Q. coccinea*), black oak (*Q. velutina*), and white oak (*Q. alba*) also were common. Sustained production of these oaks was the main objective of timber management on both private and public forestland. Other common tree species included red maple (*Acer rubrum*), black birch (*Betula lenta*), and Virginia pine (*Pinus virginiana*). The understory was dominated by blueberries (*Vaccinium* spp.), mountain laurel (*Kalmia latifolia*), and greenbriar (*Smilax* spp.).

The MSF and much of the private forestland was a patchwork of different successional stages resultant from a primarily even-aged management system. In addition to the temporary openings created by timber harvesting operations, 40 Special Wildlife Management Areas (SWMA) of 0.2–1.0 ha, were created and dispersed throughout the MSF. These herbaceous openings were intended to provide wildlife foraging areas especially for wild turkey hens with broods. They were maintained in a grass and legume mix with fruit and nut-producing trees and shrubs planted in clumps or along the edges. Most Pennsylvania State Forests in other TMAs also contain SWMAs. The MSF and South Mountain appeared to contain adequate habitat for wild turkeys, but population densities were low. For a more detailed study area description, see Lowles (2002).

METHODS

Data Collection

We used electronic command-detonated rocket nets to capture hen turkeys during mid-August to mid-September and mid-January to mid-March each year. Upon capture, we held turkeys individually in wax-coated cardboard boxes (67 cm length × 53 cm width × 30 cm depth) specifically designed for holding turkeys. We fitted hens with motion sensing, backpack-style radiotransmitters (Telonics, Mesa, Arizona, USA) using a thin elastic shock cord. Radiotransmitters were 76 g for subadults (i.e., young-of-the-year birds) and 110 g for adult hens. We determined age by tail fan pattern and tip structure of primary wing feathers and determined sex based on presence of a beard and spurs, and color pattern of breast feathers (Pelham and Dickson 1992). In the fall, we determined sex of captured subadults using molt pattern of the ninth and tenth primary feathers coupled with leg length (Healy and Nenno 1980, Larson and Tabor 1980). We fitted all captured turkeys with a uniquely numbered aluminum butt-end leg-band stamped with a telephone number to call the PGC and report if the bird were harvested or found dead.

Any radiotransmittered turkey that died within 14 days of capture was excluded from analyses to reduce the influence of capture-related stress or movements on survival estimates. We monitored hens throughout the year, which we divided into 5 biological seasons: fall (1 Sep–31 Dec), winter (1 Jan–14 Mar), dispersal (15 Mar–14 Apr), nesting (15 Apr–14 Jul), and brooding (15 Jul–31 Aug). We located each hen from ground-based telemetry ≥3 days per week during fall and winter, and daily during the remainder of the year.

Following the dispersal period, we presumed a hen to be incubating a nest after 2 successive days of an inactive, but non-mortality signal from the same location. We also used the motion sensing function of the radiotransmitter as an indicator of probable nesting, because incubating hens would often remain motionless for >8 hours.

We determined nest locations by approaching the radiotransmitter signal and locating its position with a hand-held telemetry receiver and antenna. We monitored nesting hens daily from the same location to detect if the hen had left the nest, indicating hatching or failure. When a hen was located >0.5 km away from the nest, we investigated the nest site for signs of disturbance or hatching. We determined clutch size of nests by counting eggshell membranes and examining eggshells for presence of membranes to determine how many eggs successfully hatched (i.e., hatching success). We defined nest success as a nest with ≥1 eggs of a clutch that hatched.

We located all hens whose transmitter signal was in mortality mode via a hand-held telemetry receiver and antenna to determine hen fate, including cause of death, if possible (Campa et al. 1987). If we did not recover a carcass, the mortality was recorded as an unknown cause, except in cases determined likely to be poaching.

We obtained counts of the number of poults alive at 4 weeks of age by locating radio-marked hens and playing a tape-recorded lost poult call. This call was intended to bring the hen and her brood within visual range so observers could count the brood. If this failed, observers attempted to flush the hen and count the poults.

Data Analysis

We used all hens alive at the beginning of nesting season (15 Apr) for nesting season analyses (32 adults, 16 subadults in 2000; 52 adults, 12 subadults in 2001). We used nest incubation rather than nest initiation as a measure of nesting effort because we believe nesting incubation is less prone to observer error and more readily confirmed because nests are usually hidden while a hen is away from the nest during nest initiation. However, this estimate may be positively biased because hens that initiate nests but do not reach incubation stage (i.e., nest disturbed/depredated prior to incubation, etc.) are not counted as failed nest attempts. We defined nest incubation rate as the percent of hens that began to incubate a clutch. We defined renest incubation rate as percent of hens that failed in a previous nesting attempt, and began to incubate a second clutch. All average annual reproductive rates used in the population model were calculated by averaging the point estimates weighted by sample size.

We used the Kaplan-Meier estimator (Kaplan and Meier 1958, Pollock et al. 1989) to estimate nest success rate. We analyzed data as if all nests started on the same date and a successful nest hatched ≥1 live poult. We estimated nesting and renesting success separately for adults and subadults in 2000 and 2001. Also, we calculated separate estimates of nesting and renesting success in 2000 and 2001. We estimated poult survival as number of poults from each nest alive at 4 weeks post-hatch divided by number of poults known to have hatched from the same nest.

We estimated survival rates and hunting season mortality rates via the staggered entry design of the Kaplan-Meier estimator (Pollock et al. 1989) for adults and subadults separately for each year. We estimated annual survival rates for the period 1 September–31 August because the initial sample of turkeys was captured in September. Also, we estimated survival rates for the 5 separate biological seasons defined earlier. So that we could compare survival rates among seasons, we calculated weekly survival estimates from seasonal survival estimates as $S_{week} = (S_{season})^{1/w}$, where w = the length of the biological season of interest in weeks, and calculated a Taylor series approximation of the standard error (SE) of weekly survival (Seber 1982). We calculated annual and seasonal average survival rate estimates as the mean value weighted by sample size. Hens alive at the end of each year were included in survival analyses for the next year.

We used program VORTEX (Conservation Breeding Specialist Group, Apple Valley, Minnesota, USA) to create stochastic models of population growth rates (the stochastic model incorporates process variation in the parameters and resulting population viability measures). This program used an individual-based modeling approach. We made several assumptions in the construction of the models: sex ratio was 50:50, all turkeys died by 5 years of age, all turkeys were capable of breeding at 1 year of age, and all hens were available to nest. We used the observed clutch sizes from monitored nests ($\bar{x}$ = 10.6, SD = 3.15, n = 62, range = 1–19). The mating system was polygamous, reproduction was not correlated with survival (i.e., reproduction was not density dependent), and no environmental catastrophes were incorporated in the simulation. The subadult age class was from hatching to the fall hunting season. If a juvenile survived to the

Table 1. Incubation rates, hen success (percent of hens alive at the beginning of the nesting season that hatched ≥1 eggs) of all nests (first attempts + renests), mean clutch sizes, mean number of poults hatched per hen, mean incubation dates, and mean hatching dates of turkey hens nesting in Turkey Management Area 7B, in southcentral Pennsylvania, 2000–2001.

Age and Year	Incubation rate %	n	Hen Success %	n	Clutch size $\bar{x}$	SD	Poults/hen $\bar{x}$	SD	Incubation date $\bar{x}$	SD	Hatching date $\bar{x}$	SD
Adults												
2000	75.0	32	46.9	25	11.5	2.098	10.1	4.562	10 May	7.8 days	6 June	8.3 days
2001	92.3	53	30.8	64	11.4	3.765	10.9	3.711	5 May	9.3 days	2 June	9.0 days
Subadults												
2000	56.3	16	31.3	9	10.0	1.902	9.6	2.059	19 May	7.2 days	17 June	5.1 days
2001	66.7	12	33.3	9	9.6	1.506	8.8	1.378	11 May	9.1 days	10 June	7.5 days

fall hunting season, we considered it to then have the same population parameters as adults.

Values used in the scenarios were based on estimates obtained from this study. We incorporated hunter harvest into the model by increasing adult mortality rate rather than specifying number of animals to be harvested. We set the model to simulate population trajectories for a 10-year time interval, and conducted 1,000 simulations of each scenario. Three variables used in the model were evaluated via sensitivity analysis: nest success, adult mortality, and subadult mortality. We grouped variables in the model into 27 scenarios, which were different combinations of nest success, adult survival and subadult survival. Nest success varied in increments of 10%, and ranged from 40–60% of all nesting hens producing a successful nest. The adult mortality rate varied from 40–60% in 10% increments, and subadult mortality varied from 70–90% in 10% increments.

We used r, the intrinsic rate of population growth, from the program output to calculate λ, the finite population growth rate, as $\lambda = e^r$. For each scenario, we used the standard deviation (SD) calculated from the point estimates of annual survival for nesting success, adult and subadult survival. We used the SD of each annual estimated parameter to provide a measure of annual variation in sampling rates, although this measure of demographic variability did include sampling error (White and Burnham 1999).

RESULTS

Estimated Population Parameters

We captured and monitored 163 hens during the study. Mean date of incubation and hatching was approximately 1 week later in 2000 than in 2001 (Table 1). Nest incubation rates for adults were 75.0% in 2000 and 92.3% in 2001, whereas nest success rates

were 66.9% and 36.1%, respectively (Tables 1 and 2). Subadult nest incubation rates were 56.3% in 2000 and 66.7% in 2001, with nest success rates of 50.0% and 55.6%, respectively (Tables 1 and 2).

Adult annual survival for the first year (Sep 1999–Aug 2000) was 47.8% (SE = 6.90, 95% CI = 36.0–63.3), and for the second year (Sep 2000–Aug 2001) was 64.4% (SE = 6.40, 95% CI = 53.0–78.2). Subadult annual survival for the first year was 13.3% (SE = 3.43, 95% CI = 8.1–21.9), and for the second year was 27.7% (SE = 7.45, 95% CI = 16.5–46.5). We used the average survival for both years for adults ($\bar{x}$ = 56.1%, SD = 11.74) and subadults ($\bar{x}$ = 20.5%, SD = 10.18) in the population model. Mean estimate of poult survival was 11.8% (SE = 4.9) in 2000 and 23.3% (SE = 3.7) in 2001.

Seasonal and weekly survival rates of adults (Tables 3 and 4) and subadults (Tables 5 and 6) lacked precision to detect differences among seasons or between age classes. However, the general pattern of greater survival estimates during dispersal and brood-rearing periods was consistent between adults and subadults. Weekly survival rates for adult hens showed a general pattern of being lowest in the nesting season (Table 4).

Mortality Causes

The greatest source of known mortality was caused by predation, followed by legal harvest. Fates of 18 hens were unknown because of radiotransmitter failure, and these hens were not used to calculate the following percentages from each type of mortality. Nineteen hens (24.1%) were killed by unknown causes, 38 (48.1%) died from predation, 12 (15.2%) were legally harvested during the fall hunting seasons, 1 (1.3%) was legally harvested during the spring 2000 hunting season (bearded hen), 4 (5.1%) were illegally harvested during the fall season, 4 (5.1%) died from

Table 2. Nesting success (hens that hatched ≥1 eggs of a clutch) of turkey hens in Turkey Management Area 7B, in southcentral Pennsylvania, 2000–2001.

Nesting attempt	Adult 2000 n	Ŝ	95% CI	2001 n	Ŝ	95% CI	Subadult 2000 n	Ŝ	95% CI	2000 n	Ŝ	95% CI
First	24	0.655	0.492–0.872	49	0.392	0.283–0.541	9	0.500	0.273–0.916	8	0.500	0.273–0.916
All	25	0.669	0.510–0.916	64	0.361	0.266–0.490	9	0.500	0.273–0.916	9	0.556	0.329–0.938

Table 3.   Seasonal survival rates (fall, 1 Sep–31 Dec; winter, 1 Jan–14 Mar; dispersal, 15 Mar–14 Apr; nesting, 15 Apr–14 Jul; and brooding, 15 Jul–31 Aug) of adult turkey hens in Turkey Management Area 7B, in southcentral Pennsylvania, 1999–2001.

Season	1999 Ŝ	1999 95% CI	2000 Ŝ	2000 95% CI	2001 Ŝ	2001 95% CI	Mean Ŝ	Mean 95% CI
Fall	0.766	0.549–1.068	0.926	0.850–1.010	0.795	0.700–0.904	0.850	0.749–0.957
Winter			0.936	0.862–1.015	0.871	0.789–0.961	0.898	0.818–0.930
Dispersal			0.944	0.874–1.020	1.000	1.000–1.000	0.977	0.950–1.018
Nesting			0.706	0.571–0.873	0.820	0.718–0.936	0.777	0.662–0.913
Brooding			1.000	1.000–1.000	0.974	0.923–1.027	0.982	0.982–1.018

rodenticide poisoning, and 1 (1.3%) died from a vitamin A deficiency. Legal fall harvest mortality ranged from 6.2–28.6% and averaged 12.3% over 3 years of 1-week fall seasons.

Population Models

Population simulation scenarios with 70% subadult mortality resulted in 8 scenarios with $\lambda > 1$ and 1 scenario with $\lambda < 1$ (Table 7). Extinction probabilities were low within this group (range = 0.00–0.02). The 80% subadult mortality simulation scenarios resulted in 1 scenario with $\lambda > 1$ and 8 scenarios with $\lambda < 1$, and extinction probabilities ranged from 0.00–0.27. All scenarios with 90% subadult mortality resulted in $\lambda < 1$, and population extinction probabilities were greatest in this group (range = 0.26–0.88). In general, changes in adult mortality rates and nest success had relatively minor effects on population persistence, whereas changes in subadult mortality rates greatly affected population persistence (Table 7).

DISCUSSION

The population model indicated a stable population when we used empirical estimates of population parameters from this study, which agrees with indices of abundance for this management area (Casalena and Swimley 2001). Furthermore, our sensitivity analyses indicated that subadult survival, which included poult survival, had the greatest effect on extinction rates. Decreasing or increasing subadult survival by 10% resulted in decreasing or increasing population trends. Similarly, Vangilder and Kurzejeski (1995) modeled a Missouri turkey population and observed that decreases in poult mortality of 10 and 20% resulted in substantial increases in average simulated population size.

In program VORTEX, subadult survival cannot be subdivided into biologically distinct intervals (e.g.,

poult survival and fall survival). However, our empirical estimates of these parameters indicated that poult survival and fall survival of subadults were below average. The mean annual subadult survival rate for this study (20.5%) was less than similar studies (39.4–56.8%, Vangilder 1992). Adult annual survival in the first year (47.8%) was less than that in other studies (57–75%, Vangilder 1992). Hen survival rates are typically lowest during nesting (Vangilder and Kurzejeski 1995, Miller et al. 1998, Vangilder 1992) and fall (Pack et al. 1999) and in this study survival estimates exhibited a similar pattern. Nesting season mortality was entirely caused by predation, whereas the causes of fall mortality were predation, hunter harvest, and rodenticide poisoning.

Poult survival in our study was consistently low. At 4 weeks post-hatch, our poult survival was less than similar studies (Figure 1; Vangilder 1992). Roberts et al. (1995) in south-central New York, reported that annual nest success and poult survival influenced annual population fluctuations more than annual survival rates, and Everett et al. (1980) in Alabama found that poult survival was the major factor controlling population density.

The cause of the high poult mortality was not investigated, but we hypothesize that cool, wet weather during peak of hatching coupled with predation were the leading causes. Sightings of broods throughout the study area during weekly turkey sighting surveys, and during fieldwork, suggested that poult survival was greater in years of milder, drier spring weather after the conclusion of the study. Other researchers have shown that weather conditions are partly responsible for annual variations in poult survival (Healy and Nenno 1985, Healy 1992, Rolley et al. 1998). Predators have been reported to cause a significant reduction in midwestern ringneck pheasant (*Phasianus colchicus*) populations in harsh weather (Riley and Schulz 2001). We believe weather and predation accounted for most poult deaths.

Table 4.   Weekly survival rates of adult turkey hens by season (fall, 1 Sep–31 Dec; winter, 1 Jan–14 Mar; dispersal, 15 Mar–14 Apr; nesting, 15 Apr–14 Jul; and brooding, 15 Jul-31 Aug) in Turkey Management Area 7B, in southcentral Pennsylvania, 1999–2001.

Season	1999 Ŝ	1999 95% CI	2000 Ŝ	2000 95% CI	2001 Ŝ	2001 95% CI
Fall	0.985	0.977–0.992	0.996	0.993–0.998	0.987	0.984–0.990
Winter			0.994	0.989–0.998	0.987	0.982–0.992
Dispersal			0.987	0.977–0.998	1.000	1.000–1.000
Nesting			0.974	0.968–0.979	0.985	0.980–0.989
Brooding			1.000	1.000–1.000	0.996	0.991–1.000

Table 5. Seasonal survival rates (fall, 1 Sep–31 Dec; winter, 1 Jan–14 Mar; dispersal, 15 Mar–14 Apr; nesting, 15 Apr–14 Jul; and brooding, 15 Jul–31 Aug) of subadult turkey hens in Turkey Management Area 7B, in southcentral Pennsylvania, 1999–2001.

Season	1999		2000		2001		Mean	
	$\hat{S}$	95% CI	$\hat{S}$	95% CI	$\hat{S}$	95% CI	$\hat{S}$	95% CI
Fall	0.332	0.184–0.600	0.400	0.173–0.924	0.663	0.511–0.860	0.564	0.408–0.805
Winter			0.633	0.486–0.825	1.000	1.000–1.000	0.787	0.706–0.896
Dispersal			0.944	0.847–1.053	1.000	1.000–1.000	0.965	0.913–1.029
Nesting			0.667	0.488–0.911	0.692	0.492–0.974	0.679	0.490–0.936
Brooding			1.000	1.000–1.000	1.000	1.000–1.000	1.000	1.000–1.000

Means of increasing poult survival were not studied, but habitat management actions that improve quality of habitat for brooding hens have been suggested for improving poult survival (Metzler and Speake 1985, Wunz and Pack 1992, Peoples et al. 1996, Harper et al. 2001, Hubbard et al. 2001), and are being explored in the study area. Means of increasing subadult survival are removal of the human-caused mortality factors from fall mortality, such as fall turkey-hunting season closure and elimination of rodenticide poisoning. These actions are being taken on the study area.

The observed reproductive attempts and success of our radiotagged hens varied among years and age classes, although some estimates were similar to other published studies (Vangilder 1992, Vangilder and Kurzejeski 1995, Godfrey and Norman 2001). Nest incubation rates for adults (75.0% in 2000; 92.3% in 2001) were slightly lower than those of similar studies, which average 96.7% and vary between 75–100% (Vangilder 1992). Subadult nest incubation rates (56.3% in 2000; 66.7% in 2001), which often are lower than adult incubation rates, also were slightly lower than those of similar studies, which vary between 55.5–100% (Vangilder 1992). However, most of the studies cited by Vangilder (1992) defined nesting as a pattern of localized hen movements over a period of several days indicating nest initiation, which may result in greater estimates of nesting rates than the methods we used.

Adult nest success was slightly less than similar studies but subadult nest success was within the range of several other studies (Vangilder 1992). It is typical for nest success to vary and influence populations on an annual basis (Vangilder 1992, Godfrey and Norman 2001); thus, nest success did not seem to be an important factor producing the long-term population suppression during this study. However, the below-average incubation rates may have contributed somewhat to population suppression, especially when combined with greater than average poult and subadult fall mortality.

Pack et al. (1999) reported predation, poaching, and legal fall harvest were the major causes (71.7%) of hen mortality in Virginia and West Virginia. The fall hunting mortality we observed was average compared to other studies (Table 8), but substantial given the short 1-week hunting season. In addition, fall hunter density was greater than all other studies, although less than the statewide average for Pennsylvania (23.1 hunters/km² of forest). Also, harvest density on the study area was low (Table 8), especially compared to the statewide average (4.2 turkeys/km² of forest). The low average harvest density we observed compared to high hunter density suggests that harvest could have been one factor contributing to the suppressed turkey population.

Additionally, several wild turkey population models predict that sustained fall harvests >10% (both males and females) forecast future population declines (Healy and Powell 1999). Although our population models predicted a stable wild turkey population using our empirical estimates of population parameters, we speculate that the 12.3% average hen hunting mortality rate may have been an important reason why the population failed to increase.

Poaching during the fall accounted for 5.1% of all known causes of mortality, but the effect of poaching on population trends is difficult to detect with small samples. Pack et al. (1999) had a sample of 1,543 hens over a 6-year period, which provided more precise estimates of poaching than was possible with our 2.5-year sample of 163 hens. However, poaching in this study did not exceed legal average fall harvest as it did during some years in Virginia and West Virginia. In Missouri, in only 1 of 7 years did the mortality rate from illegal hen kill in the fall exceed legal fall harvest, which varied from 0.0–0.11 (Vangilder and Kurzejeski 1995). Additionally, we recorded only 1 known illegal hen mortality during 2

Table 6. Weekly survival rates of subadult turkey hens by season (fall, 1 Sep–31 Dec; winter, 1 Jan–14 Mar; dispersal, 15 Mar–14 Apr; nesting, 15 Apr–14 Jul; and brooding, 15 Jul–31 Aug) in Turkey Management Area 7B, in southcentral Pennsylvania, 1999–2001.

Season	1999		2000		2001	
	$\hat{S}$	95% CI	$\hat{S}$	95% CI	$\hat{S}$	95% CI
Fall	0.939	0.936–0.941	0.949	0.943–0.954	0.977	0.972–0.981
Winter			0.957	0.951–0.965	1.000	1.000–1.000
Dispersal			0.987	0.973–1.000	1.000	1.000–1.000
Nesting			0.969	0.962–0.977	0.972	0.934–0.981
Brooding			1.000	1.000–1.000	1.000	1.000–1.000

Table 7. Stochastic population model (1,000 replications) for wild turkey hens with subadult mortality of 70%, 80%, and 90%, based on observed mortality and nesting rates in Turkey Management Area 7B, in southcentral Pennsylvania, 1999–2001.

Nesting success (%)	Adult mortality (%)	70% subadult mortality			80% subadult mortality			90% subadult mortality		
		$\bar{\lambda}$	SD (λ)	Probability of extinction[a]	$\bar{\lambda}$	SD (λ)	Probability of extinction[a]	$\bar{\lambda}$	SD (λ)	Probability of extinction[a]
40	40	1.144	0.4108	0.000	0.904	0.3804	0.016	0.636	0.3285	0.446
	50	1.039	0.4172	0.004	0.805	0.3819	0.066	0.544	0.3143	0.720
	60	0.933	0.4288	0.018	0.699	0.4094	0.267	0.475	0.3104	0.884
50	40	1.298	0.4704	0.001	0.999	0.4443	0.004	0.670	0.3716	0.382
	50	1.197	0.4820	0.000	0.907	0.4481	0.029	0.591	0.3633	0.582
	60	1.086	0.4869	0.002	0.806	0.4597	0.107	0.502	0.3518	0.816
60	40	—[b]			1.109	0.4971	0.002	0.729	0.4099	0.259
	50	1.349	0.5350	0.000	0.994	0.5089	0.010	0.627	0.3958	0.498
	60	—[b]			0.889	0.5315	0.074	0.540	0.3962	0.726

[a] Proportion of 1,000 simulations in which the turkey population went extinct within 10 years.
[b] Model output exceeded program Vortex capacity because of extreme population levels ($\bar{\lambda} > 1$).

spring gobbler seasons. Consequently, we do not believe illegal harvest (spring or fall) was an important limiting factor in this study.

Accidental poisoning from ingestion of rodenticides that were broadcast (in pellet form) in nearby orchards also accounted for 5.1% of the total mortality. However, this human-caused mortality is avoidable. Placing rodenticides inside enclosed bait stations, rather than broadcasting them throughout the orchards, may reduce mortality of non-target species, such as wild turkeys (Poppenga et al. 2005).

Numerous studies have documented that predation is a major cause of hen mortality (e.g., Miller et al. 1998). In this study, predators were the greatest known cause of hen mortality (48.1%). When the wild turkey population was restored in TMA 7B in the late 1970s and early 1980s, density of meso-predators was likely at a low point for two reasons: (1) furbearer harvests were large because prices were at an all-time high and (2) the Pennsylvania rabies epizootic of the early 1980s was greatest in TMA 7B (Brown et al. 1990,

Moore 1999). These conditions may have suppressed mammalian predator populations to a level such that turkey populations could increase, possibly to greater than normal densities. By the mid-1980s the price of fur dropped drastically, resulting in fewer harvested furbearers, and the incidence of rabid animals also declined. Control of predators, besides traditional harvest management, is often a controversial matter. Although it is commonly perceived that predators limit turkey populations (Miller et al. 2000), a more productive management strategy for increasing poult survival may be brood habitat improvement. The current habitat on the MSF is highly fragmented with 210 km of maintained roads, 436 km of gated roads and 518 km of established trails. The MSF receives the most human use of all Pennsylvania State Forests. Additionally, timber harvests have created forest patches of many different age classes. These habitat conditions may be indirectly detrimental to turkeys by providing predators access and travel corridors (Jimenez and Conover 2001).

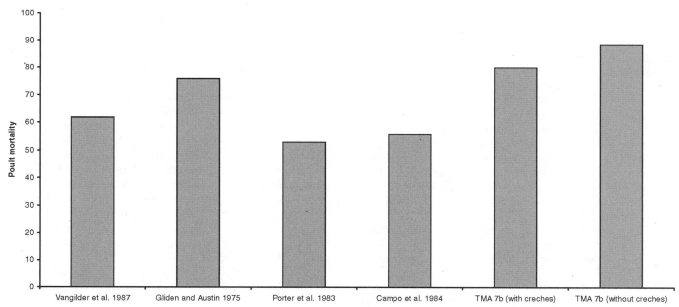

Fig. 1. Wild turkey poult mortality rates from 4 studies and poult mortality in Turkey Management Area 7B, in southcentral Pennsylvania, 2000–2001.

Table 8. Reported fall turkey-hunting mortality and fall hunting characteristics reported in the literature and on Turkey Management Area 7B, in southcentral Pennsylvania, 1999–2001.

Age	Hunting mortality rate (%)	Length of season	Hunters/km²	Harvest/ km² forest	State	Publication
Adult	19	8–9 weeks			VA, WV	Pack et al. 1999
Adult	12	4 weeks			VA, WV	Pack et al. 1999
Adult	8	15 days	14.1	4.3	IA	Little et al. 1990
Both	4	2 weeks	≤4.6	<4	MO	Vangilder and Kurzejeski 1995
Both	12	1 week	19.9	1.5	PA	This study
Subadult	14	8–9 weeks			VA, WV	Pack et al. 1999
Subadult	4	4 weeks			VA, WV	Pack et al. 1999
Subadult	24	15 days	14.1	4.3	IA	Little et al. 1990

The variability in annual survival and nest success among individual hens was considerable in this study and variability among individuals is proportional to misestimation of demographic parameters (Fox and Kendall 2002). Therefore, the risk of extinction is overstated in most population viability analyses, and hence may have been over estimated in our model simulations. However, the fact that we observed poult and subadult survival to be less than most other populations, and the fact that our model results were most sensitive to these parameters indicated these parameters are most likely the reasons the population has not increased.

MANAGEMENT IMPLICATIONS

Our use of short-term (2.5-year) data to predict long-term trends is a shortcoming of this study (Leopold et al. 1996, Miller et al. 2000), but we believe the comparison of our results to similar studies makes these findings relevant. The long-term management goal for the wild turkey population on TMA 7B is to obtain a sustainable harvest rate comparable to other management areas in Pennsylvania. The 2 most likely areas where we can effect change in the reproductive and survival rates of hen turkeys are decreasing human-caused mortality and habitat management, especially habitat activities designed to improve poult survival.

Before 1995, the fall hunting season was ≥2 weeks long, possibly resulting in additive mortality, and the 1995 reduction in fall season length to 1 week may have been too small of a change to have a effect. Closing the fall turkey-hunting season on the study area may aid in population growth if hen survival increases as a result. Increasing hen survival increases the adult hen breeding population, and adult hens have greater nest incubation rates and poult survival rates than subadults (Healy and Powell 1999, Vangilder 1992, Vangilder and Kurzejeski 1995).

The second factor in decreasing human-induced mortality is eliminating accidental rodenticide poisoning. Even though rodenticide poisoning accounted for only 5.1% of the hen mortality, this factor can be reduced readily. The local chapters of the National Wild Turkey Federation, together with the Pennsylvania Game Commission, are working with local orchard owners to place rodenticides in enclosed bait stations rather than broadcasting them in the orchards. This should reduce poisoning of nontarget species, including wild turkeys (Poppenga et al. 2005). Although we have documented rodenticide poisoning in other TMAs within Pennsylvania, our emphasis for reducing this mortality factor in TMA 7B is based on the assumption that minimizing human-caused mortalities may increase annual survival of this population.

Third, improvements in habitat management activities can be used to increase recruitment (Jimenez and Conover 2001). Herbaceous openings (SWMAs) of 0.2–1.0 ha are being maintained and rehabilitated throughout the MSF in an attempt to increase poult survival, although the effect of these openings on poult survival is unknown. Proponents of herbaceous openings claim they enhance brood survival and are generally beneficial to wildlife (Metzler and Speake 1985, Wunz and Pack 1992, Peoples et al. 1996, Harper et al. 2001). No empirical data exists for these claims in the MSF, but the importance of these SWMAs to poult survival is being assessed in an accompanying study.

ACKNOWLEDGMENTS

The Pennsylvania Chapter National Wild Turkey Federation (PANWTF) and the Safari Club International, Sables of the Valley Chapter provided partial funding for this project. The Pennsylvania Department of Conservation, Bureau of Forestry provided tremendous assistance from their personnel and loaning/storing equipment. Many thanks go to the technicians who conducted fieldwork and data input; D. Little, M. Niebauer, L. Humberg, P. Bowen and C. B. Swope. Thanks also to Wildlife Conservation Officers R. Karper, L. Haynes, B. Leonard, K. Mountz, and E. Steffan and their deputies. Numerous volunteers assisted with fieldwork and trapping turkeys, including S. Miller, R. Miller, and G. Zinn, and many members of the local NWTF chapters. Thanks also to the countless landowners who graciously permitted us to trap and monitor turkeys on their property. Special thanks are extended to members of the TMA 7B Wild Turkey Task Force, especially chairman D. Heckman, whose efforts and comments helped initiate and shape the study. We are grateful to R. C. Boyd and J. K. Vreeland for reviewing earlier drafts of the manuscript.

LITERATURE CITED

Bureau of Wildlife Management. 1994. Fall turkey season recommendations for turkey management areas 7 and 8. Pennsylvania Game Commission, Harrisburg, Pennsylvania, USA.

Brown, C. L., C. E. Rupprecht, and W. M. Tzilkowski. 1990. Adult raccoon survival in an enzootic rabies area of Pennsylvania. Journal of Wildlife Diseases 26:346–350.

Campa, H., III, M. L. Rabe, P. I. Padding, E. J. Flegler, Jr., G. Y. Belyea, and H. H. Prince. 1987. An evaluation of the release of Sichuan pheasants in Livingston County Michigan, 1987. Michigan Department of Natural Resources, Federal Aid for Wildlife Restoration Project W-127-R.

Campo, J. J., C. R. Hopkins, and W. G. Swank, 1984. Mortality and reproduction of stocked eastern turkeys in east Texas. Proceedings of the Annual Conference of the Southeastern Association of Fish and Wildlife Agencies 38:78–86.

Casalena, M. J., and T. Swimley. 2001. Wild turkey productivity and spring harvest trends. Annual Report, Project No.06270, Job No. 27001. Pennsylvania Game Commission, Harrisburg, Pennsylvania, USA.

Everett, D. D., D. W. Speake, and W. K. Maddox. 1980. Natality and mortality of a north Alabama wild turkey population. Proceedings of the National Wild Turkey Symposium 4: 117–126.

Fox, G. A., and B. E. Kendall. 2002. Demographic stochasticity and the variance reduction effect. Ecology 83:1928–1934.

Glidden, J. W., and D. E. Austin. 1975. Natality and mortality of wild turkey poults in southwestern New York. Proceedings of the National Wild Turkey Symposium 3:48–54.

Godfrey, C. L., and G. W. Norman. 2001. Reproductive ecology and nesting habitat of eastern wild turkeys in western Virginia. Proceedings of the National Wild Turkey Symposium 8:203–210.

Harper, C. A., J. K. Knox, D. C. Guynn, Jr., and J. R. Davis. 2001. Invertebrate availability for wild turkey poults in the southern Appalachians. Proceedings of the National Wild Turkey Symposium 8:145–156.

Healy, W. M. 1992. Population Influences: environment. Pages 129–143 *in* J. G. Dickson, editor. The wild turkey: biology and management. Stackpole Books. Mechanicsburg, Pennsylvania, USA.

———, and E. S. Nenno. 1980. Growth parameters and sex and age criteria for juvenile eastern wild turkeys. Proceedings of the National Wild Turkey Symposium 4:168–185.

———, and ———. 1985. Effects of weather on wild turkey poult survival. Proceedings of the National Wild Turkey Symposium 5:91–101.

———, and S. M. Powell. 1999. Wild turkey harvest management: biology, strategies, and techniques. U.S. Fish and Wildlife Service, Biological Technical Publication R5001.

Hubbard, M. W., D. L. Garner, and E. E. Klass. 2001. Factors influencing wild turkey poult survival in southcentral Iowa. Proceedings of the National Wild Turkey Symposium 8: 167–171.

Jimenez, J. E., and M. R. Conover. 2001. Ecological approaches to reduce predation on ground-nesting gamebirds and their nests. Wildlife Society Bulletin 29:62–69.

Kaplan, E. L., and P. Meier. 1958. Nonparametric estimation from incomplete observations. Journal of the American Statistical Association 53:457–481.

Larson, J. S., and R. D. Taber. 1980. Criteria of sex and age. Pages 143–202. *in* D. S. Shemnitz, editor. Research and management techniques for wildlife and habitats. The Wildlife Society, Washington D.C., USA.

Leopold, B. D., G. A. Hurst, and D. A. Miller. 1996. Long-versus short-term research and effective management: a case study using the wild turkey. North American Wildlife and Natural Resources Conference 61:477–487.

Little, T. W., J. M. Kienzler, and G. A. Hansen. 1990. Effects of fall either-sex hunting on survival in an Iowa wild turkey

population. Proceedings of the National Wild Turkey Symposium 6:119–125.

Lowles, M. A. 2002. Reproduction and survival of eastern wild turkey hens in south-central Pennsylvania, 1999–2001. Thesis, The Pennsylvania State University, University Park, Pennsylvania, USA.

Lowrey, D. K., G. A. Hurst, S. R. Priest, and B. S. Weemy. 2000. Influences of selected weather variables on predation of wild turkey females and nest success. Proceedings of the National Wild Turkey Symposium 8:167–178.

Metzler, R., and D. W. Speake. 1985. Wild turkey poult mortality rates and their relationship to brood habitat structure in northeast Alabama. Proceedings of the National Wild Turkey Symposium 5:103–111.

Miller, D. A., L. W. Burger, B. D. Leopold, and G. A. Hurst. 1998. Survival rates and cause-specific mortality of eastern wild turkey hens in central Mississippi. Journal of Wildlife Management 62:306–313.

———, M. J. Chamberlain, B. D. Leopold, and G. A. Hurst. 2000. Lessons from Tallahala: what have we learned for turkey management into the 21st century? Proceedings of the National Wild Turkey Symposium 8:23–34.

Moore, D. A. 1999. Spatial diffusion of raccoon rabies in Pennsylvania, USA. Preventive Veterinary Medicine 40:19–32.

Pack, J. C., G. W. Norman, C. I. Taylor, D. E. Steffen, D. A. Swanson, K. H. Pollock, and R. Alpizar-Jara. 1999. Effects of fall hunting on wild turkey populations in Virginia and West Virginia. Journal of Wildlife Management 63:964–975.

Pelham, P. H, and J. G. Dickson. 1992. Physical characteristics. Pages 33–45 *in* J. G. Dickson, editor. The wild turkey: biology and management. Stackpole Books. Mechanicsburg, Pennsylvania, USA.

Peoples, J. C., D. C. Sisson, and D. W. Speake. 1996. Wild turkey brood habitat use and characteristics in coastal plain pine forests. Proceedings of the National Wild Turkey Symposium 7:89–96.

Pollock, K. H., S. R. Winterstein, C. M. Bunck, and P. D. Curtis. 1989. Survival analysis in telemetry studies: the staggered entry design. Journal of Wildlife Management 53:7–15.

Poppenga, R. H., A. F. Ziegler, P. L. Habecker, D. L. Singletary, M. K. Walter, and P. G. Miller. 2005. Zinc phosphide intoxication of wild turkeys. Journal of Wildlife Diseases 41: 218–223.

Porter, W. F., G. C. Nelson, and K. Mattson. 1983. Effects of winter conditions on reproduction in a northern wild turkey population. Journal of Wildlife Management 47:281–290.

Riley, T. Z., and J. H. Schulz. 2001. Predation and ring-necked pheasant population dynamics. Wildlife Society Bulletin 29: 33–38.

Roberts S. D., J. M. Coffey, and W. F. Porter. 1995. Survival and reproduction of female wild turkeys in New York. Journal of Wildlife Management 59:437–447.

Rolley, R. E., J. F. Kubisiak, R. N. Paisley, and R. G. Wright. 1998. Wild turkey population dynamics in southwestern Wisconsin. Journal of Wildlife Management 62:917–914.

Seber, G. A. F. 1982. The estimation of animal abundance and related parameters. Second edition. C. Griffin, London, U.K.

Suchy, W. J., W. R. Clark, and T. W. Little. 1983. Influence of simulated harvest on Iowa wild turkey populations. Proceedings of the Iowa Academy of Sciences 90:98–102.

Vangilder, L. D. 1992. Population dynamics. Pages 144–164 *in* J. G. Dickson, editor. The wild turkey: biology and management. Stackpole Books. Mechanicsburg, Pennsylvania, USA.

———, and E. W. Kurzejeski. 1995. Population ecology of the eastern wild turkey in northern Missouri. Wildlife Monographs 130:1–50.

———, ———, V. L. Kimmel-Truitt, and J. B. Lewis. 1987. Reproductive parameters of wild turkey hens in north Missouri. Journal of Wildlife Management 51:535–540.

White, G. C., and K. P. Burnham. 1999. Program MARK: survival estimation from populations of marked animals. Bird Study 46 (Supplement):120–138.

Wright, R. G., R. N. Paisley, and J. F. Kubisiak. 1996. Survival of wild turkey hens in southwestern Wisconsin. Journal of Wildlife Management 60:313–320.

Wunz, G. A., and J. C. Pack. 1992. Eastern wild turkey in eastern oak-hickory and northern hardwood forests. Pages 232–264 *in* J. G. Dickson, editor. The wild turkey: biology and management. Stackpole Books. Mechanicsburg, Pennsylvania, USA.

Mary Jo Casalena (pictured) is a certified Wildlife Biologist with the Pennsylvania Game Commission's Bureau of Wildlife Management. Her responsibilities as state wild turkey biologist include wild turkey research, harvest, population, and habitat management, and technical committee advisor to the National Wild Turkey Federation. Mary Jo received her M.S. in Wildlife and Fisheries Science from The Pennsylvania State University, with a concentration in Wetlands Ecology, and her B.S. in Wildlife and Fisheries Science from the University of Massachusetts. ***Mark A. Lowles*** received his B.S. in forestry and wildlife science, with a minor in Entomology, from Virginia Polytechnic Institute and State University in 1999. He completed his M.S. degree in Wildlife and Fisheries Science at The Pennsylvania State University in 2002, where he studied population demographics and habitat characteristics related to the nest success of wild turkeys in south-central Pennsylvania. ***Duane R. Diefenbach*** is Assistant Unit Leader of the Pennsylvania Cooperative Fish and Wildlife Research Unit and adjunct associate professor of wildlife ecology in the School of Forest Resources at The Pennsylvania State University. His research addresses developing and empirically testing methods of estimating population parameters. Current research involves black bear, white-tailed deer, and grassland songbirds.

9th National Wild Turkey Symposium

Wild Turkey Management:
Accomplishments, Strategies, and Opportunities
———— Grand Rapids, Michigan ————

THE IMPACTS OF PREDATION ON WILD TURKEYS

Thomas W. Hughes[1]
National Wild Turkey Federation, 770 Augusta Road,
Edgefield, SC 29824, USA

Jennifer L. Tapley
National Wild Turkey Federation, 770 Augusta Road,
Edgefield, SC 29824, USA

James E. Kennamer
National Wild Turkey Federation, 770 Augusta Road,
Edgefield, SC 29824, USA

Chad P. Lehman[2]
National Wild Turkey Federation, RR 2, Box 244B,
Custer, SD 57730, USA

Abstract: Concerns that greater predator populations and accelerating habitat fragmentation may exacerbate impacts of predation on wild turkey (*Meleagris spp.*) populations prompted our examination of the literature on this subject. We found several major themes throughout this search. Variability in nest and renest initiation may account for low production in some populations and may be confused with effects of nest predation. For most wild turkey populations, nesting success was low, with predation responsible for the loss of most unsuccessful nests. Raccoons (*Procyon lotor*) were the most commonly reported nest predator. Poult survival was low, with predation the major cause of mortality. Predation also was the major cause of mortality among yearling and adult wild turkey hens and yearling gobblers. Hunting was the major cause of mortality for adult gobblers. Predator control was successful in increasing wild turkey productivity in short-term specific instances where a small cadre of identified nest and poult predators was targeted, but numerous factors impact the success of control programs. Control of wild turkey predators is cost ineffective as a broad management strategy and is not accepted by the public.

Proceedings of the National Wild Turkey Symposium 9:117–126

Key words: fragmentation, habitat, *Meleagris spp.*, nest, predation, predator, predator control, predator management, wild turkey.

The wild turkey has made a remarkable comeback in North America from what many considered the road to extinction. Due to restoration efforts by state game agencies and many other entities, wild turkeys now number over 5.4 million (Tapley et al. 2001). Viable populations exist in every state, except Alaska, and in Mexico and several Canadian provinces. The ocellated turkey (*M. ocellata*) exists in viable populations in Mexico, Guatemala, and Belize.

In most areas, wild turkey numbers are stable or continue to increase, but some local-level populations are declining. These declines have prompted concern among biologists and the public that predation may cause these declines. Anecdotal reports of the devastating effects of predation on wild turkeys abound, and include everything from nest destruction to decimation of adults by a variety of predators. In the past, recommendations to lessen predation rates have been generally indirect and habitat based rather than centering on direct predator control. Recently, however, concerns have been raised among the biological community that changing habitats and increasing predator populations may call for more direct methods.

With development and expansion of urban areas and other changing land uses, habitat fragmentation is increasing (Flather et al. 1989). Areas of high-quality wild turkey habitat are lost resulting in smaller segments left for foraging, nesting, and brood rearing. With the declining fur market, populations of mammalian predators are increasing (Sargeant et al. 1993, Woolf and Hubert 1998) and regulatory protection and curtailed use of certain pesticides has allowed a similar increase in many avian predators (Sauer et al. 2004).

Therefore, our objectives were to (1) examine the literature on effects of predation on wild turkeys at each stage of the life cycle, (2) determine if predators are limiting turkey populations, and if so, (3) evaluate

[1] E-mail: thughes@nwtf.net
[2] Present address: 13329 US HWY 16A, Custer, SD 57730, USA.

if predator management is an effective tool to increase turkey populations.

RESULTS

Nesting

Nest Initiation

To fully understand effects that predation has during the nesting phase of the wild turkey's life cycle, it is necessary to examine the dynamics and variability of nest initiation. High production may confound detection of predation losses, and low production may appear to be related to high predation rates when it may simply result from a low rate of nest initiation.

Different turkey populations exhibit wide ranges of nest initiation rates, often with varying rates for adult and yearling hens. Roberts et al. (1995) for eastern hens (*M. g. silvestris*) in New York, found higher nesting rates for adult hens than for yearlings. In Alabama, Hillestad (1973) noted that of 5 hens radiotracked in 1968, only one was known to nest. However, on the same site in 1969, nest initiation was 100% (5 of 5) for adults and 60% (3 of 5) for yearlings. On a different Alabama site, Everett et al. (1980) found an initial nesting rate of 88% (29 of 33) for adult hens, whereas 85% (11 of 13) of the yearlings attempted to nest. Lower rates were reported in Mississippi, where overall initial nest initiation rates during 1984–1995 averaged 72% (Miller et al. 1998*b*).

Nesting rates may differ among subspecies. Typically, the eastern subspecies shows high nest initiation rates, even for yearlings. In Wisconsin, Paisley et al. (1998) found nesting rates for adults to range from 95% to 100% compared to 67% to 100% for yearlings. Even where they have been translocated from Iowa and Missouri to South Dakota, nest initiation rates remain high for eastern turkeys, ranging from 81 to 94% (Lehman et al. 2001, Leif 2001).

Nest initiation rates for the Merriam's subspecies (*M. g. merriami*) are often reported as low, especially for yearlings. Wakeling (1991), in Arizona, found a high of 62% nest initiation for adults in 1988 and a low of 33% in 1989. Similar results were reported for a South Dakota population where Wertz and Flake (1988) found an average adult nesting rate of 42% during 1984–1985 and no nest initiation by yearlings, while Flake and Day (1996) found nesting rates of 77% (36 of 47) and 17% (1 of 6) for adult and yearling hens, respectively. However, in the central Black Hills of South Dakota, Rumble and Hodorff (1993) reported a nest initiation rate of 97% for adults and 73% for yearlings. An Oregon population of Merriam's turkeys exhibited similarly high nest initiation for adults (100%), but a much lesser rate for yearlings (31%) (Lutz and Crawford 1987). Rumble et al. (2003) suggested a correlation between adult and yearling nesting rates for Merriam's turkeys in which yearling nesting rates are low or nonexistent until adult nesting rates exceed 60%.

Two studies of the Rio Grande subspecies (*M. g. intermedia*) reproductive behavior show an interesting contrast. The first, in ancestral Rio Grande turkey range on the Edwards Plateau in central Texas, recorded nesting behavior for only 38 of 53 hens for a nest initiation rate of 72% (Reagan and Morgan 1980). The second study, on a translocated Rio Grande turkey population in Oregon, showed a much greater nest initiation rate of 99% (67 of 68) for adults and 94% (31 of 33) for yearlings (Keegan and Crawford 1993). This may suggest that habitat quality may be more important than subspecies or other factors in influencing nest initiation.

In a south Florida study, the Osceola subspecies (*M. g. osceola*) exhibited a relatively low rate of nest initiation, with nests discovered for only 59% (202 of 345) of monitored hens (Williams and Austin 1988). Greater nest initiation rates were seen for ocellated turkeys in Guatemala, where 89% (8 of 9) instrumented hens attempted to nest (Gonzalez et al. 1996). For the Gould's turkey (*M. g. mexicana*), Schemnitz et al. (1990) reported that 1 of 2 radio-transmittered hens attempted to nest.

Renest Initiation

An important factor in the overall examination of nesting, renesting can contribute significantly to the overall productivity of a population. The rates at which hens attempt to renest after loss of a clutch or brood, also may be an indicator of population viability.

In an Oregon Rio Grande population, Keegan and Crawford (1993) found renesting to be very important to overall nesting success. Renesting rates for adult and yearling hens that lost clutches were 74% (39 of 53) and 25% (4 of 16), respectively. Total renesting accounted for 30% (43 of 141) of all nests, 19% (12 of 63) of successful nests, and 17% (98 of 568) of poults hatched during the study period. Renesting after brood loss accounted for 30% (13 of 43) of all renesting attempts and 33% (4 of 13) of all successful renesting attempts. None of the 16 yearling hens that lost broods renested.

Renesting may be of varied importance in other populations. For the Osceola subspecies, Williams and Austin (1988) found a relatively low renest initiation rate of only 28% (26 of 93). Similar results were found for eastern wild turkeys in Alabama, where only 22% (3 of 13) adults and 0.0% (0 of 4) yearlings attempted to renest (Everett et al. 1980) and in Mississippi (Miller et al. 1998*b*) where renest initiation rates averaged only 34%. However, in Wisconsin, Paisley et al. (1998) found renesting to average 55% for that eastern population and also found that 13% of adult hens attempted a third nest, but no yearlings did so. For 27 eastern hens in South Dakota that lost their first nest, 26% (7 of 27) attempted to renest (Leif 2001). Renesting was an important reproductive parameter for eastern and Rio Grande turkeys in northeastern South Dakota, ranging from 50 to 100% during 3 years of study (Lehman et al. 2001). Renesting may be important for the ocellated turkey in Guatemala, because Gonzalez et al. (1996) found a renesting rate of 40% (2 of 5). Renesting was much more common in Merriam's turkeys in South Dakota (Rumble and Hodorff 1993) than in Arizona (Wakeling et al. 1998).

When combined with variable first nest initiation rates, the considerable variability of renest initiation serves to illustrate the complexity of attempting to analyze the factors influencing wild turkey productivity, particularly when nest success is added to the mix.

Nesting Success

Even when wild turkey hens initiate nests, the successful hatching of eggs is far from certain. Nests are lost from a variety of causes, including human disturbance, flooding, inclement weather, fire, and predation. Nest success may be the primary factor affecting annual population change. Roberts et al. (1995) considered the variability of annual nesting success to be the most important factor in determining annual population fluctuation in New York.

There appears to be little difference in nesting success due to the hen age. Keegan and Crawford (1999) found nesting success for a Rio Grande population in Oregon to range from 50 to 70% among years, but found no difference between adults and yearlings. Roberts et al. (1995) also reported no difference in nesting success due to age of the hen in New York. Adult hens, though, may fare better in some areas, as they are more likely than yearlings to choose nesting sites in core habitat as opposed to edges (Thogmartin 1999). In the Arkansas Ozarks, Badyaev et al. (1996) found smaller breeding season (spring) home ranges for adult hens than for yearlings, possibly causing differences in vulnerability to predation between adult and yearling hens,

Wild turkey research has consistently documented relatively low nesting success. In Alabama, Speake (1980) found that over 44% of 119 eastern wild turkey nests were lost to predation. Vander Haegan et al. (1988), in Massachusetts, found even lower nesting success, with over 55% of wild turkey nests failing to produce young. Of the nests lost (21 of 38), 12 were lost to predation (7 to egg predation and 5 to predation of the hen). On the Waterhorn Unit of the Francis Marion National Forest in South Carolina, from 1982–1984 radiomarked adult hens produced a total of 27 nests. Only 11 (55%) of these were successful, 7 (26%) were abandoned due to human disturbance, 6 (30%) were destroyed by predators, 2 (10%) were flooded, and 1 (5%) was abandoned for unknown reasons (Still and Baumann 1990).

Western subspecies also show relatively low nesting success. Flake and Day (1996), for a Merriam's turkey population in South Dakota, found a nesting success rate of 44% (17 of 39), with predation accounting for the failure of 19 of 22 unsuccessful nests. In northern Texas, Hohensee and Wallace (2001) found that 6 of 19 Rio Grande turkey nests were successful, with nest depredation by mammals accounting for 53% of the nest loss. Ransom et al. (1987) found that of 10 nests by Rio Grande hens monitored in south Texas, all were destroyed by nest predators.

Nest studies in which artificial nests are made us-

ing chicken or domestic turkey eggs typically show high rates of predation. In Alabama, Davis (1959) found that of 107 artificial nests, only 16 remained undisturbed. In one set of 78 artificial nests in Texas, 77 were destroyed by predators (Baker 1979).

In a declining population of eastern wild turkeys in the Ouachita Mountains in Arkansas, Thogmartin (1998) found that 87% of wild turkey nests failed, primarily due to predation. Lowery et al. (2001) states that predation is thought to be a more important factor in nest success than weather conditions. Certainly, predation is the most consistently reported cause of nest failure for adults and yearling hens and by subspecies.

Nest Predators

The raccoon is the primary nest predator over most of the wild turkey's range (Davis 1959, Speake 1980, Ransom et al. 1987, Williams and Austin 1988). In an early poisoned egg study, Davis (1959) found that almost one-third of 107 artificial nests were destroyed by raccoons.

Raccoons have demonstrated learned behavior associated with predation of wild turkey nests. In a test of their ability to learn, Johnson (1970) provided chicken eggs to captive raccoons. Those raccoons captured from areas with good turkey populations immediately ate the eggs, whereas raccoons from areas with no turkeys did not open the eggs and did not seem to know that they contained food. Raccoons may increase their home range size during turkey nesting season, possibly in search of nests. Priest et al. (1995) observed an increase in home range and a shift from bottomland hardwoods to upland pine areas for raccoons during the spring in Mississippi. At the same time, most of the wild turkey hens on this area also left their winter range in the bottomland areas and initiated nests in the upland pine habitat (Seiss 1989).

Other significant mammalian nest predators include the opossum (*Didelphis virginiana),* spotted and striped skunks (*Spilogale putorius* and *Mephitis mephitis*), gray foxes (*Urocyon cinereoargenteus*), red foxes (*Vulpes vulpes*), and coyotes (*Canis latrans*) (Davis 1959, Baker 1979, Williams et al. 1980, Williams and Austin 1988, Paisley et al. 1998, Hohensee and Wallace 2001). Feral or free-ranging dogs (*Canis familiaris*) also may be significant nest predators (Speake 1980).

The most significant avian nest predator is the crow (*Corvus* spp.), and they are widely reported as responsible for wild turkey nest predation (Davis 1959, Speake 1980, Williams et al. 1980, Vander Haegan et al. 1988, Rumble and Hodorff 1993). In Montana, nest predation is also attributed to ravens (*Corvus corax*) and black-billed magpies (*Pica pica*) (Thompson 1993).

A variety of other species have been reported to prey on turkey nests, but usually not at significant levels. However, in Texas, Reagan and Morgan (1980) attributed nearly 50% of the nest predation they observed to snakes, including rat snakes (*Elaphe obosoleta*) and bull snakes (*Pituophis melanoleucus*). In this same study, a rock squirrel (*Spermophilus variegatus*) was observed destroying a nest.

Other species that are popularly suspected as nest predators include the feral hog (*Sus scrofa*) and the armadillo (*Dasypus novemcinctus*), but most evidence suggests that they are not significant turkey nest predators. Feral hogs have occasionally been implicated for wild turkey nest disturbance (Davis 1959, Hohensee and Wallace 2001), but even at high population levels they normally do little damage (Williams et al. 1980). Kennamer and Lunceford (1973), using artificial nests, observed some nest disturbance by armadillos, but no evidence that they ate any eggs. In Florida, Williams et al. (1980) also found no evidence of egg predation by armadillos.

Poult Predation

Mortality

Low poult survival is very well documented for the eastern subspecies of wild turkeys, with most losses occurring during the first 2 weeks after hatching. Overall poult mortality is usually reported to range from 60 to 80% (Glidden and Austin 1975, Everett et al. 1980, Speake 1980, Speake et al. 1985, Vangilder et al. 1987, Vander Haegan et al. 1988, Hubbard et al. 1999a). Even greater rates have been reported, however. In south Georgia and north Florida, Peoples et al. (1995), found a 6-year average poult mortality >90%, with 96% of the total mortality occurring within 14 days of hatching.

Less information is available for other wild turkey subspecies, but low poult survival rates are documented in 2 studies on Merriam's turkeys. In South Dakota, Flake and Day (1996) found a mortality rate of 57% during the first 2 weeks post-hatch, but no further poult loss was documented through mid-August. In Wyoming, Hengel (1990) found a poult mortality rate of 64%. Reported Gould's turkey poult mortality of about 60% is consistent with the other subspecies, with all or most mortality occurring during the first 2 weeks after hatching (Schemnitz et al. 1990). Little research has been conducted on poult mortality among ocellated turkeys, but Gonzalez et al. (1996) observed a very high mortality rate of 87%, with only 4 of 31 poults surviving the summer.

Cause for poult mortality is difficult to determine because poults at their most vulnerable age are small and hard to observe. However, predation is obviously an important factor. Speake et al. (1985) determined the cause of death for 49% of poults that died during their study. Among the group of poults where cause of death could be determined, predation accounted for 82% of losses. Mammal, avian, and reptile predators accounted for 42, 16, and 7% of losses, respectively. Unknown predators caused 17% of the losses. An even greater predation rate of 88% of poult losses was reported by Peoples et al. (1995).

Predators

Mammalian predators may be particularly efficient at finding poults. In Alabama, Speake et al. (1985) found that free-ranging dogs and raccoons accounted for 57 and 24% of the identifiable mammalian predation, respectively. Gray foxes and bobcats (*Lynx rufus*) accounted for the rest of the mammal predation. Mammals accounted for about 93% of the poult predation in an Iowa population, with red foxes, weasels (*Mustela* spp.), mink (*Mustela vison*), and coyotes identified and listed in declining order of importance (Hubbard et al. 1999a). In Florida and south Georgia, Peoples et al. (1995) attributed 71% of total poult predation to mammals, primarily raccoons, bobcats, and gray foxes.

Some avian predators also are implicated regularly in poult losses. In Alabama, broad-winged hawks (*Buteo platypterus*) and red-tailed hawks (*Buteo jamaicensis*) accounted for 92% of the identifiable avian predation. The remaining avian predation was attributed to an eastern screech-owl (*Otus asio*) (Speake et al. 1985). In an Iowa study, red-tailed hawks were the only avian predator documented to take poults. Cooper's hawks (*Accipiter cooperii*), great horned owls (*Bubo virginianus*), and barred owls (*Strix varia*) also were present on the study area but were never observed attacking or killing poults (Hubbard et al. 1999a). Peoples et al. (1995) documented poult losses from red-tailed hawks, Cooper's hawks, and barred owls, but found red-shouldered hawks (*Buteo lineatus*) responsible for the greatest avian predation. In South Dakota, Merriam's turkey poults in the southern Black Hills were attacked by golden eagles (*Aquila chrysaetos*) and goshawks (*Accipiter gentilis*) (Lehman 2003, Lehman and Thompson 2004).

Reptiles are seldom documented as poult predators, but Speake et. al. (1985) reported poult losses from gray rat snakes. Alligators (*Alligator mississippiensis*) and corn snakes (*Elaphe guttata*) also have been documented to take poults (Peoples et al. 1995).

Yearling-Adult Predation

Hen Mortality

Most research shows no difference in mortality rates between yearling and adult hens (Miller et al. 1995, Roberts et al. 1995, Vangilder 1996, Wright et al. 1996) but some studies have determined lesser survival for yearlings than adult hens (Vander Haegan et al 1988, Miller et al. 1998a, Hubbard et al. 1999b).

Overall, annual eastern wild turkey hen survival averages from 50 to 65% (Vander Haegan et al. 1988, Roberts et al. 1995, Vangilder 1996, Hubbard et al. 1999b). Little difference is reported in survival of Merriam's turkey hens (Wertz and Flake 1988) and Rio Grande turkey hens (Hohensee and Wallace 2001). Arizona Merriam's turkey yearling hens had lower survival rates than adult hens during the winter which may be attributed to inexperience, but higher survival rates during the summer that may be influenced by the fact that yearling hens were not accompanied by broods (Wakeling 1991). According to Gonzalez et al. (1996), ocellated turkey hens have survival rates of 60%.

Mortality may be attributed to many causes, but predation is well documented as the main cause of death. For eastern wild turkey hens in Massachusetts, Vander Haegan et al. (1988) determined predation to be the cause of 75% (12 of 16) documented deaths. Hubbard et al. (1999b), in Iowa, found predators to be the cause of death for 79% (42 of 53) of the hens that died in that study. Roberts et al. (1995) and Wright et al. (1996) determined that predators caused 74% and 71%, respectively, of documented hen deaths. For Rio Grande hens in Oregon, Keegan and Crawford (1999) attributed 73% of known mortality to predators.

Hens are most at risk during the nesting season and the greatest percentage of hen mortality occurs during that period (Kurzejeski et al. 1987, Vander Haegan et al. 1988, Miller et al. 1995, Roberts et al. 1995, Miller et al. 1998a).

Hen Predators

Mammals are by far the most common predators of wild turkey hens (Miller et al. 1995, Roberts et al. 1995, Chamberlain et al. 1996, Hubbard et al. 1999b, Hennen and Lutz 2001). Among mammals, canids, especially coyotes, but also including red and gray foxes and domestic dogs, are often listed as predators of hens (Everett et al. 1980, Speake 1980, Palmer et al. 1993a, Wright et al. 1996). However, the most commonly reported predator of turkey hens is the bobcat (Everett et al. 1980, Speake 1980, Vander Haegan et al. 1988, Still and Baumann 1990, Vangilder 1996). Other mammalian predators include the raccoon (Palmer et al. 1993a, Roberts et al. 1995, Miller et al. 1998a, Hennen and Lutz 2001) and according to Hennen and Lutz (2001) the badger (*Taxidea taxus*).

The great horned owl is the only avian predator of wild turkey hens regularly reported (Palmer et al. 1993a, Roberts et al. 1995, Wright et al. 1996, Hubbard et al. 1999b, Hennen and Lutz 2001) and is even recorded as the major predator in a Mississippi study (Miller et al. 1998a). The golden eagle is listed as an occasional hen predator (Speake 1980) and a northern goshawk may have been responsible for the death of a hen in New York (Roberts et al. 1995). Golden eagles were witnessed to have attacked Merriam's turkeys several times in the Black Hills; however, only one kill on an adult female was confirmed (Lehman and Thompson 2004; C. Lehman, National Wild Turkey Federation, unpublished data).

Gobbler Mortality

Gobblers are generally reported to be less vulnerable to predation than hens, and yearling gobblers are reported to be more susceptible to predators than adults (Everett et al. 1980, Speake 1980). Two factors are probably responsible for these differences: healthy gobblers seldom or never spend the night on the ground as do nesting or brood-rearing hens, and adult gobblers are so large as to make them difficult prey for all but the largest and most capable predators. However, adult gobblers are more vulnerable to human-caused mortality than are yearlings (Paisley et al. 1996, Wright and Vangilder 2001). Other factors also affect predation on gobblers. Paisley et al. (1996), found predation on gobblers to be greatest in the breeding season in Iowa. Possibly, gobblers become focused on breeding activities and may lose some degree of caution. The approach of predators also may be obscured by the fanned tail while gobblers strut during their mating display.

Gobbler Predators

As previously mentioned, gobblers, especially adults, are large enough to make them difficult prey for many predators. Bobcats, however, are quite capable of killing gobblers and are the most commonly reported gobbler predator (Everett et al. 1980, Speake 1980, Vangilder 1996, Wright and Vangilder 2001). Great horned owls are regularly reported to prey on gobblers (Vangilder 1996, Wright and Vangilder 2001). Coyotes are often implicated as gobbler predators, and predation has been documented (Paisley et al. 1996, Vangilder 1996), but some gobbler kills attributed to coyotes are probably from coyotes scavenging kills made by other predators (Wright and Vangilder 2001). Other predators reported to take gobblers include the golden eagle and the gray fox (Speake 1980).

Mitigating Predation

Predator Control

It is clear from the studies on wild turkeys that except for adult gobblers, predation is the major source of mortality for wild turkeys at every stage of their life. The major predators are well documented, and while the raptors are completely protected by law, most of the mammalian predators can be either hunted or trapped. In simple terms, a method by which to increase turkey numbers or prevent declining populations is to implement predator control.

From a nationwide survey on the public's attitudes toward predator control among a random sample of United States households, most respondents would support predator control to enhance avian recruitment, but only in specific circumstances (Messmer et al. 1999). Respondents supported control of specific mammalian predators when control was recommended to reverse declines of desirable avian species, but did not support predator control as a landscape-level management strategy applied without appropriate focus. Control of raptors was not supported under any circumstances described in the survey.

Nesting success and poult production can be improved following intensive predator control. Speake (1980) found a 5-year average of 3.5 poults/hen on an Alabama study area under intensive predator removal. An adjacent area with no control averaged only 1.1 poults/hen over the same period. Beasom (1974a), after intensive predator control efforts in a south Texas area, found that turkeys and white-tailed deer (*Odocoileus virginianus*) exhibited large increases in reproductive success and potential increases in density. In this study, control was most effective when carried out just prior to and during the breeding season. Control efforts had more impact during dry years when there was little vegetative cover. In years of good rainfall, the differences between treated on untreated areas were less evident.

Intensive predator control is expensive and time consuming. In Alabama, Speake (1980) calculated a total cost of $3,270 at 1975 prices for predator control on the 2,024 ha study area, and this figure does not include cost of traps or trapping labor. Beasom (1974*b*), to achieve mammalian predator control on a 2,185 ha south Texas study area, used a variety of methods for 5 months per year for 2 years. This intensive effort used 135 M-44 cyanide sets, 250 man-hours of hunting, 8,000 strychnine baits, and 27,446 steel trap days (1 trap for 1 day = 1 trap day) and removed 183 coyotes, 117 bobcats, 34 raccoons and 48 striped skunks, as well as other, less significant predators. Effort was made in this study to avoid killing or capturing non-target species, but deer, turkeys, songbirds, and several raptor species were captured or killed, as well as the targeted predators.

Speake (1980) noted that even with no predator control, the turkey population either maintained or increased abundance. He concluded that intensive predator control is expensive and seldom justified, but that trapping should be encouraged and that control of feral or free-ranging dogs is probably desirable. Even when predators are successfully removed, intensive predator control efforts are likely to have only short-term benefits. Beasom (1974*a*) noted that predators repopulated a south Texas study area each year when removal efforts ceased.

In addition to calculations on expense and labor involved in predator control, there are other considerations. Coyote populations were lowered on a Texas study site, but with a 9-month lag time, and only after intense and expensive effort. Mesopredator populations, including bobcat, badger and gray fox, increased on the treatment areas (Henke and Bryant 1999). Rodent density and black-tailed jackrabbit (*Lepus californicus*) density increased as well.

Weather

Other abiotic factors may confound efforts to mitigate the effects of predation on turkeys. In Mississippi, Palmer et al. (1993*b*) found predation on incubating hens and nests to be related directly to the last rainfall event. They hypothesized that rainfall increases efficiency of nest predators by increasing the detection of scent from nesting hens. Lowrey et al. (2001) suggested that although predation may be a more important factor in nesting success than weather, relationships between the 2 factors are important to hen survival and productivity. Roberts and Porter (1998) found daily nest survival was negatively correlated with increased rainfall. High predator populations dur-

ing dry springs may actually have less impact on nesting turkeys than lesser predator populations under wet conditions.

Habitat Management

Management and manipulation of the juxtaposition and interspersion of habitats may reduce the efficiency and impacts of predation on wild turkeys. As opposed to short-term effects from predator control (Beasom 1974*b*, Speake 1980, Henke and Bryant 1999), habitat management may have longer-term effects in increasing turkey population abundance or preventing declines.

According to Roberts and Porter (1996), nest success is one of the most important parameters affecting annual wild turkey population change. For the hen, one of the most crucial factors influencing the success of her nest is her choice of nesting sites. In Mississippi, Seiss et al. (1990) found that hens selected nest sites in forest stands <4-years-old. Additionally, nests in forested areas were more successful than nests in non-forested areas, possibly due to greater predator populations in non-forested habitat. Similarly, Thogmartin (1999) found that hens in Arkansas generally nested in large patches of pine and avoided patches containing oak, apparently preferring the thicker, grassy understory found in the pine stands.

Traditionally, land managers have encouraged creating or promoting the amount of "edge" or transition zones between different habitat types. Diversity and interspersion of habitat types has become commonplace because this arrangement of plant foods and cover types may provide the optimum habitat for a wide variety of wildlife. Seiss et al. (1990) found that successful wild turkey nests in forested areas were generally located <10 m from more than 1 man-made edge and speculated that proximity of edges may have provided hens with travel lanes to and from the nest. These travel lanes may provide the hen with better access to resources such as food and water, limit time off the nest, and reduce scent trails from the nest. However, spatial arrangement and interspersion of habitat types affects the efficiency of many turkey predators, especially during the nesting season. Fragmentation of habitat and increase in edge favors many predators of ground nesting birds. Thogmartin (1999) states that the 2 most common nest predators in the Ouachita Mountains in Arkansas are black rat snakes and raccoons, both of which favor forest edges for hunting (Durner and Gates 1993, Pedlar et al. 1997). Management activities that promote increased edge may enhance efficiency of these nest predators.

Certain factors mitigate effectiveness of nest predators. Baker (1979) found significant differences in nest predation rates due to effects of different grazing regimes and due to differences in plant communities where the nest occurs. Typically, nests with greater cover suffered lower rates of predation. In some areas, proximity to deer feeders may increase predation rates. Cooper and Ginnet (2000), in an artificial nest study in Texas, found higher nest predation rates at sites near feeders than at nest sites farther away.

Habitat type and spatial arrangement also affect predation on turkeys beyond the nesting season. After assessing 80 mortalities of radiomarked turkeys over a 5-year period, Thogmartin and Schaeffer (2000) found that mortality occurred nearly twice as often in edge as in core habitat, especially during summer and fall when vegetation density was greatest. Interestingly, canid predation was most pronounced within edge habitat where 7 of 8 kills occurred. Bobcat predation was nearly equally distributed between edge and core habitats. There were species differences in predation by season, as bobcat predation occurred in winter and spring, whereas canid predation occurred throughout all seasons equally.

DISCUSSION

For all wild turkeys except adult gobblers, predation is the major cause of mortality. This is well documented for all habitats, all subspecies, and at all stages of life. For most wild turkey populations, predation is not a regulating factor. Most populations continue to grow and in many places wild turkeys are expanding their range (Tapley et al. 2000). However, some local and regional populations are declining (Thogmartin 1998, Miller et al. 1998b), and in these declining populations, high rates of predation and low productivity are common threads. For the land manager attempting to reverse these declines, there are two options: reduce the number of predators or increase the productivity of the hens.

In the absence of other factors, variations in nest initiation rates alone may account for great differences in the productivity of different populations. Where nest initiation rates are low, or nonexistent as in the case of yearlings in some populations, population growth may be slow or limited even without the effects of other factors such as predation. When low rates of nest initiation are combined with the effects of predation or inclement weather, the combined effects on population growth are more severe. In such instances predation may be additive; however, little information exists on the effects of predation on populations with lowered reproductive potential. Typically, wild turkeys are thought to be under a compensatory biological system, and predation has little effect in annual survival.

Reducing predator numbers on a broad scale is expensive, time-consuming, and is not universally supported by the public as a management tool. The benefits are often confined to a brief time period during and immediately after control efforts. However, for certain local wild turkey populations, there may be a benefit to short-term, intensive predator control where this control is designed to allow population recovery and targets a specific predator species or guild. This targeted, "surgical" approach is acceptable to the public as a method to enhance avian recruitment (Messmer et al. 1999). Stochastic modeling on the effects of intensive coyote removal on pronghorn (*Antilocapra*

americana) populations in Oregon showed relatively long-term pronghorn population stability (to about 10 years after initiating control) after only 3 years of intensive coyote control (Phillips and White 2003). In this case, coyotes had been identified as the species responsible for regulating that population. It is possible that some turkey populations may show a similar response to predator control. Great care must be taken to remove only the predators impacting turkey abundance, because removal of some predators may result in increased abundance of other predators that may prey on turkeys.

Habitat management that addresses habitat deficiencies or factors that promote predator efficiency is much more likely to provide long-term increases in wild turkey population abundance than is predator control. Urban development, land management decisions that influence recreational use, and silvicultural treatment of public and private lands are creating habitat fragmentation that may improve habitat suitability for predators. Techniques that reduce fragmentation, providing larger, more homogeneous blocks of nesting habitat increase nesting success (Seiss et al. 1990, Thogmartin 1999). Large block forest management may reduce efficiency of many nest predators. Grazing regimes that allow time for vegetative cover to mature, especially in larger pastures, increase nest and brood success (Baker 1979). Improving habitat quality for turkeys by large-scale methods such as prescribed fire and thinning of over-stocked stands may promote the growth of seed producing grasses and legumes, which are desirable for seed and insect production. There is evidence that increasing the hen's nutritional plane increases productivity, perhaps increasing nest and renest initiation rates, with the potential for correspondingly greater poult production (Pattee and Beasom 1979). More research is underway on this topic (W. Kuvlesky, Texas A&M University, Kingsville, personal communication) with the potential to add nutritional considerations to management objectives.

Turkeys have evolved with a host of predators. The literature indicates that predation has not been a regulating factor for most turkey populations, nor has predator control been shown to have long-term benefits. Predator control may be justified in site-specific instances. Widespread use of predator control to benefit turkey abundance is probably not a prudent expenditure of management dollars.

ACKNOWLEDGMENTS

We thank all the members of the NWTF technical committee who have provided assistance and advice on this complex subject, NWTF support staff who have assisted with compiling and editing source material, especially K. Deloach. We thank R. Abernethy for review of the manuscript and advice on the topic, and all of the dedicated volunteers of the NWTF, without whom none of this would have been possible. We also thank the anonymous reviewers of the manuscript for the many valuable comments and suggestions they provided.

LITERATURE CITED

Badyaev, A. V., W. J. Etges, and T. E. Martin. 1996. Ecological and behavioral correlates of variation in seasonal home ranges of wild turkeys. Journal of Wildlife Management 60: 154–164.

Baker, B. W. 1979. Habitat use, productivity, and nest predation of Rio Grande turkeys. Dissertation, Texas A&M University, College Station, Texas, USA.

Beasom, S. L. 1974a. Intensive short-term predator removal as a game management tool. Transactions of the North American Wildlife and Natural Resources Conference 39:230–240.

———. 1974b. Selectivity of predator control techniques in south Texas. Journal of Wildlife Management 38:837–844.

Chamberlain, M. J., D. A. Miller, B. D. Leopold, and G. A. Hurst. 1996. Predation rates on wild turkey hens in a hardwood bottomland forest and a mixed forest in Mississippi. Proceedings of the Annual Conference of the Southeastern Association of Fish and Wildlife Agencies 50:428–435.

Cooper, S. M., and T. F. Ginnett. 2000. Potential effects of supplemental feeding of deer on nest predation. Wildlife Society Bulletin 28:660–666.

Davis, J. R. 1959. A preliminary progress report on nest predation as a limiting factor in wild turkey populations. Proceedings of the National Wild Turkey Symposium 1:138–145.

Durner, G. M., and J. E. Gates. 1993. Spatial ecology of black rat snakes on Remington Farms, Maryland. Journal of Wildlife Management 57:812–826.

Everett, D. D., D. W. Speake, and W. K. Maddox. 1980. Natality and mortality of a north Alabama wild turkey population. Proceedings of the National Wild Turkey Symposium 4: 117–126.

Flake, L. D., and K. S. Day. 1996. Wild turkey reproduction in a prairie-woodland complex in South Dakota. Proceedings of the National Wild Turkey Symposium 7:153–158.

Flather, C. H., T. W. Hoekstra, D. E. Chalk, N. D. Cost, and V. A. Rudis. 1989. Recent historical and projected regional trends of white-tailed deer and wild turkey in the southern United States. U.S. Forest Service General Technical Report RM-172.

Glidden, J. W., and D. E. Austin. 1975. Natality and mortality of wild turkey poults in southwestern New York. Proceedings of the National Wild Turkey Symposium 3:48–54.

Gonzalez, M. J., C. I. Taylor, and H. B. Quigley. 1996. Habitat use, reproductive behavior, and survival of ocellated turkeys in Tikal National Park, Guatemala. Proceedings of the National Wild Turkey Symposium 7:193–199.

Hengel, D. A. 1990. Habitat use, diet and reproduction of Merriam's turkeys near Laramie Peak, Wyoming. Thesis, University of Wyoming, Laramie, Wyoming, USA.

Henke, S. E., and F. C. Bryant. 1999. Effect of coyote removal on the faunal community in western Texas. Journal of Wildlife Management 63:1066–1081.

Hennen, R. S., and R. S. Lutz. 2001. Rio Grande turkeys female survival in southcentral Kansas. Proceedings of the National Wild Turkey Symposium 8:117–122.

Hillestad, H. O. 1973. Movements, behavior, and nesting ecology of the wild turkey in eastern Alabama. Pages 109–123 in G. C. Sanderson and H. C. Schultz, editors. Wild turkey management: current problems and programs. University of Missouri Press, Columbia, Missouri, USA.

Hohensee, S. D., and M. C. Wallace. 2001. Nesting and survival of Rio Grande Turkeys in northcentral Texas. Proceedings of the National Wild Turkey Symposium 8:85–91.

Hubbard, M. W., D. L. Garner, and E. E. Klaas. 1999a. Wild turkey poult survival in southcentral Iowa. Journal of Wildlife Management 63:199–203.

———, ———, and ———. 1999b. Factors influencing wild turkey hen survival in southcentral Iowa. Journal of Wildlife Management 63:731–738.

Johnson, A. S. 1970. Biology of the raccoon (*Procyon lotor various,* Nelson and Goldman) in Alabama. Auburn University, Agricultural Experiment Station Bulletin 402.

Keegan, T. W., and J. A. Crawford. 1993. Renesting by Rio Grande wild turkeys after brood loss. Journal of Wildlife Management 57:801–804.

———, and ———. 1999. Reproduction and survival of Rio Grande turkeys in Oregon. Journal of Wildlife Management 63:204–210.

Kennamer, J. E., and W. H. Lunceford, Jr. 1973. Armadillos tested as potential egg predators of wild turkey in the Mississippi Delta. Pages 175–177 in G. C. Sanderson and H. C. Schultz, editors. Wild turkey management: current problems and programs. University of Missouri Press, Columbia, Missouri, USA.

Kurzejeski, E. W., L. D. Vangilder, and J. B. Lewis. 1987. Survival of wild turkey hens in north Missouri. Journal of Wildlife Management 51:188–193.

Leif, A. P. 2001. Survival, reproduction, and home ranges of translocated wild turkeys in South Dakota. Proceedings of the National Wild Turkey Symposium 8:211–220.

Lehman, C. P. 2003. Poult protection by Merriam's turkey females towards a northern goshawk. The Prairie Naturalist 35(1):47–48.

———, L. D. Flake, A. P. Leif, R. D. Shields. 2001. Comparative survival and reproduction of sympatric eastern and Rio Grande wild turkey females in northeastern South Dakota. Proceedings of the National Wild Turkey Symposium 8:123–135.

———, and D. J. Thompson. 2004. Golden eagle (*Aquila chrysaetos*) predation attempts on Merriam's turkeys (*Meleagris gallopavo merriami*) in the southern Black Hills, South Dakota. Journal of Raptor Research 38:192.

Lowrey, D. K., G. A. Hurst, and S. R. Priest. 2001. Influences of selected weather variables on predation of wild turkey females and nest success. Proceedings of the National Wild Turkey Symposium 8:173–178.

Lutz, R. S., and J. A. Crawford. 1987. Reproductive success and nesting habitat of Merriam's wild turkeys in Oregon. Journal of Wildlife Management 51:783–787.

Messmer, T. A., M. W. Brunson, D. Reiter, and D. G. Hewitt. 1999. United States public attitudes regarding predators and their management to enhance avian recruitment. Wildlife Society Bulletin 27:75–85.

Miller, D. A., L. W. Burger, B. D. Leopold, and G. A. Hurst. 1998a. Survival and cause-specific mortality of wild turkey hens in Central Mississippi. Journal of Wildlife Management 62:306–313.

———, B. D. Leopold, and G. A. Hurst. 1998b. Reproductive characteristics of a wild turkey population in central Mississippi. Journal of Wildlife Management 62:903–910.

Miller, M. S., D. J. Buford, and R. S. Lutz. 1995. Survival of female Rio Grande turkeys during the reproductive season. Journal of Wildlife Management 59:766–771.

Paisley, R. N., J. F. Kubisiak, and R. G. Wright. 1996. Survival of wild turkey gobblers in southwestern Wisconsin. Proceedings of the National Wild Turkey Symposium 7:39–44.

———, R. G. Wright, J. F. Kubisiak, and R. E. Rolley. 1998. Reproduction ecology of eastern turkeys in southwestern Wisconsin. Journal of Wildlife Management 62:911–916.

Palmer, W. E., G. A. Hurst, J. E. Stys, D. R. Smith, and J. D. Burk. 1993a. Survival rates of wild turkey hens in loblolly pine plantations in Mississippi. Journal of Wildlife Management 57:783–789.

———, S. R. Priest, R. S. Seiss, P. S. Phalen, and G. A. Hurst. 1993b. Reproductive effort and success in a declining wild turkey population. Proceedings of the Annual Conference of the Southeastern Association of Fish and Wildlife Agencies 47:138–147.

Pattee, O. H., and S. L. Beasom. 1979. Supplemental feeding to increase wild turkey productivity. Journal of Wildlife Management 43:512–516.

Pedlar, J. H., L. Fahrig, and H. G. Merriam. 1997. Raccoon habitat use at 2 spatial scales. Journal of Wildlife Management 61:102–112.

Peoples, J. C., D. C. Sisson, and D. W. Speake. 1995. Mortality of wild turkey poults in coastal plain pine forests. Proceedings of the Annual Conference of the Southeastern Association of Fish and Wildlife Agencies 49:448–453.

Philips, G. E., and G. C. White. 2003. Pronghorn population response to coyote control: modeling and management. Wildlife Society Bulletin 31:1162–1175.

Priest, S. L., M. Conner, G. A. Hurst, and B. D. Leopold. 1995. Raccoon home range size and habitat use during the wild turkey reproductive period in Mississippi. Proceedings of the International Symposium on Biolotelemetry 13:264–269.

Ransom, D., Jr., O. J. Rongstad, and D. H. Rusch. 1987. Nesting ecology of Rio Grande turkeys. Journal of Wildlife Management 51:435–439.

Reagan, J. M., and K. D. Morgan. 1980. Reproductive potential of Rio Grande turkey hens in the Edwards Plateau of Texas. Proceedings of the National Wild Turkey Symposium 4:136–144.

Roberts, S. D., J. M. Coffey, and W. F. Porter. 1995. Survival and reproduction of female wild turkeys in New York. Journal of Wildlife Management 59:437–447.

———, and W. F. Porter. 1996. Importance of demographic parameters to annual changes in wild turkey abundance. Proceedings of the National Wild Turkey Symposium. 7:15–20.

———, and ———. 1998. Relation between weather and survival of wild turkey nests. Journal of Wildlife Management 62:1492–1498.

Rumble, M. A., and R. A. Hodorff. 1993. Nesting ecology of Merriam's turkey in the Black Hills, South Dakota. Journal of Wildlife Management 57:789–801.

———, B. F. Wakeling, and L. D. Flake. 2003. Factors affecting survival and recruitment in female Merriam's turkeys. Intermountain Journal of Sciences 9:26–37.

Sargeant, A. B., R. J. Greenwood, M. A. Sovada, and T. L. Shaffer. 1993. Distribution and abundance of predators that affect duck production—Prairie Pothole Region. U.S. Fish and Wildlife Service Resource Publication 194.

Sauer, J. R., J. E. Hines, and J. Fallon. 2004. The North American Breeding Bird Survey, Results and Analysis 1966–2003. Version 2004.1. U.S. Geological Service, Patuxent Wildlife Research Center, Laurel, Maryland, USA.

Schemnitz, S. D., D. E. Figert, and R. C. Willing. 1990. Ecology and management of Gould's turkeys in southwestern New Mexico. Proceedings of the National Wild Turkey Symposium 6:2–83.

Seiss, R. S. 1989. Reproductive parameters and survival rates for wild turkey hens in east-central Mississippi. Thesis, Mississippi State University, Mississippi State, Mississippi, USA.

———, P. S. Phalen, and G. A. Hurst. 1990. Wild turkey nesting habitat and success rates. Proceedings of the National Wild Turkey Symposium 6:18–24.

Speake, D. W. 1980. Predation on wild turkeys in Alabama. Proceedings of the National Wild Turkey Symposium 4:86–101.

———, R. Metzler, and J. McGlincy. 1985. Mortality of wild turkey poults in northern Alabama. Journal of Wildlife Management 49:472–474.

Still, H. R., Jr., and D. P. Baumann, Jr. 1990. Wild turkey nesting ecology on the Francis Marion National Forest. Proceedings of the National Wild Turkey Symposium 6:13–17.

Tapley, J. L., R. K. Abernethy, and J. E. Kennamer. 2000. Status and distribution of the wild turkey in 1999. Proceedings of the National Wild Turkey Symposium 8:15–22.

Thogmartin, W. E. 1998. Factors influencing the decline of an eastern wild turkey (*Meleagris gallopavo silvestris*) population in the Ouachita Mountains of Arkansas. Thesis, University of Arkansas, Fayetteville, Arkansas, USA.

———. 1999. Landscape attributes and nest-site selection in wild turkeys. Auk 116:912–23.

———, and B. A. Schaeffer. 2000. Landscape attributes associated with mortality events of wild turkeys in Arkansas. Wildlife Society Bulletin 28:865–874.

Thompson, W. L. 1993. Ecology of Merriam's turkeys in relation to burned and logged areas in southeastern Montana. Dissertation, Montana State University, Bozeman, Montana, USA.

Vander Haegan, W. M., W. E. Dodge, and M. W. Sayre. 1988. Factors affecting productivity in a northern wild turkey population. Journal of Wildlife Management 52:127–133.

Vangilder, L. D. 1996. Survival and cause-specific mortality of wild turkeys in the Missouri Ozarks. Proceedings of the National Wild Turkey Symposium 7:21–31.

———, E. W. Kurzejeski, V. L. Kimmel-Truitt, and J. B. Lewis. 1987. Reproductive parameters of wild turkey hens in north Missouri. Journal of Wildlife Management 51:535–540.

Wakeling, B. F. 1991. Population and nesting characteristics of Merriam's turkey along the Mogollon Rim, Arizona. Arizona Game and Fish Department Research Branch Technical Report 7.

———, H. G. Shaw, and S. S. Rosenstock. 1998. Forest stand characteristics of successful and unsuccessful Merriam's turkey nest sites in north-central Arizona. Southwestern Naturalist 43:242–248.

Wertz, T. L., and L. D. Flake. 1988. Wild Turkey nesting ecology in south central South Dakota. Prairie Naturalist 20(1):29–37.

Williams, L. E., Jr., and D. H. Austin. 1988. Studies of the wild turkey in Florida. Florida Game and Freshwater Fish Commission Technical Bulletin 10.

———, ———, and T. E. Peoples. 1980. Turkey nesting success on a Florida area. Proceedings of the National Wild Turkey Symposium 4:102–107.

Woolf, A., and G. F. Hubert, Jr. 1998. Status and management of bobcats in the United States over three decades: 1970s–1990s. Wildlife Society Bulletin 26:287–293.

Wright, G. A., and L. D. Vangilder. 2001. Survival of Eastern wild turkey males in Western Kentucky. Proceedings of the National Wild Turkey Symposium 8:187–194.

Wright, R. G., R. N. Paisley, and J. F. Kubisiak. 1996. Survival of wild turkey hens in southwestern Wisconsin. Journal of Wildlife Management 60:313–320.

Tom Hughes (right) received a B.S. in Biology from Georgia Southern University (1974) and an M.S. in Wildlife Biology from Clemson University (1985). Tom worked in private game management for years and is now a senior wildlife biologist with the National Wild Turkey Federation where he directs their research grant program. Tom and his wife Nanette love to hunt (especially turkeys) and fish, and spend as much time outdoors as possible. ***Jennifer Tapley*** (left) is currently a wildlife biologist for the National Wild Turkey Federation. She earned a B.S. in wildlife and fisheries ecology and a minor in journalism from Oklahoma State University.

James Earl Kennamer is currently the senior vice president for conservation programs for the National Wild Turkey Federation. He holds a B.S. in game management from Auburn University, and M.S. and Ph.D. degrees in wildlife management from Mississippi State University.

Chad P. Lehman received a B.S. in Biological Science from the University of Minnesota–Duluth (1994) and M.S. in Wildlife Science from South Dakota State University (1998). He received a Ph.D. in Biological Science from South Dakota State University (2005) and his research focused on Merriam's turkey ecology, particularly the influence of weather and habitat selection/availability on survival and reproduction. As a wildlife biologist for Custer State Park, Chad conducts research and manages habitats for game and nongame wildlife species. For hobbies, Chad enjoys hiking with his wife Michelle and son Drew, and hunting birds with his yellow Labrador Retrievers.

EFFECT OF PRECIPITATION ON RIO GRANDE WILD TURKEY POULT PRODUCTION IN TEXAS

T. Wayne Schwertner[1]
Texas Parks and Wildlife Department, P.O. Box 1583,
Mason, TX 76856, USA

Markus J. Peterson
Department of Wildlife and Fisheries Sciences,
Texas A&M University,
College Station, TX 78743, USA

Nova J. Silvy
Department of Wildlife and Fisheries Sciences,
Texas A&M University,
College Station, TX 78743, USA

Abstract: Precipitation can strongly influence the population dynamics of gallinaceous birds in semiarid regions. Little is known, however, about the interaction of precipitation and Rio Grande wild turkey (*Meleagris gallopavo intermedia*; RGWT) production in Texas, particularly across broad spatial and temporal scales. We compared RGWT production data with precipitation and drought data across 5 ecological regions of Texas for 1976–2000. Poult production was positively correlated with both the June Modified Palmer Drought Severity Index (PMDI) and September–June raw precipitation in all ecological regions. We found weaker correlations with June raw precipitation in all ecological regions except the Post Oak Savannah, and with cumulative September–June PMDI in the Edwards Plateau, Cross Timbers and Prairies, and South Texas Plains. Our results indicate that poult production is more influenced by cumulative weather effects over several months than by individual rainfall events, suggesting that direct precipitation-induced mortality does not substantially affect RGWT production in Texas. Further, precipitation data provides managers with an inexpensive, effective indicator of RGWT production in Texas.

Proceedings of the National Wild Turkey Symposium 9:127–132
Key words: *Meleagris gallopavo intermedia*, poult production, precipitation, Rio Grande wild turkey, Texas.

Precipitation is one of the most important factors influencing the distribution and abundance of terrestrial organisms (Krebs 1994). It is known to affect avian populations directly by killing individuals (Welty and Baptist 1988), destroying nests, and regulating the timing of breeding (Marshall 1959), and indirectly through its effects on vegetation and other environmental factors (Welty and Baptista 1988). Precipitation affects the abundance or production of several species of gallinaceous birds, including black grouse (*Tetrao tetrix*; Baines 1991), capercaillie (*Tetrao urogallus*; Moss 1986), gray partridge (*Perdix perdix*; Panek 1992), northern bobwhites (*Colinus virginianus*; Bridges et al. 2001, Lusk et al. 2002), and scaled quail (*Callipepla squamata*; Campbell et al. 1973, Bridges et al. 2001).

The influence of precipitation also extends to wild turkeys. Precipitation can directly affect turkey pro-

duction by flooding nests or drowning poults (De-Arment 1969, Kennamer et al. 1975, Zwank et al. 1988, Healy 1992), and causing hypothermia-induced mortality among poults (Markley 1967, Healy and Nenno 1985, Roberts and Porter 1998*a*). It also might indirectly influence turkey production by facilitating predation (Palmer et al. 1993, Roberts et al. 1995, Roberts and Porter 1998*b*) or altering intermediate environmental variables believed to be correlated with turkey production. These include the structure of vegetative cover (Beasom 1973, Cable 1975), as well as the abundance of forbs (Beasom 1973) and arthropods (Johnson and Worobec 1988, Belovsky and Slade 1995, Frampton et al. 2000), which are important food items for turkey poults (Hurst 1992).

Most research regarding the influence of precipi-

---

[1] E-mail: schwertner@verizon.net

A. Ecological regions   **B. Climate divisions**

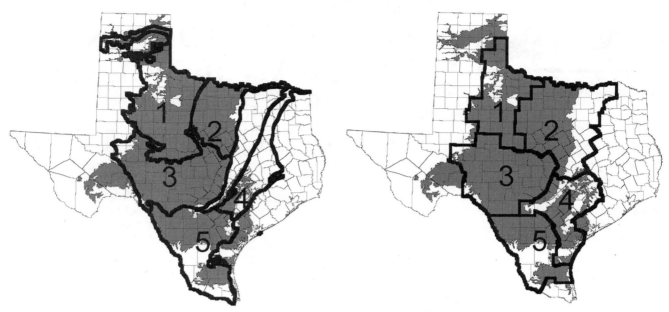

Fig. 1.   (**A**) Ecological regions (Gould 1975) and (**B**) climate divisions (National Climate Data Center) of Texas containing significant populations of Rio Grande wild turkey. Names of ecological regions (and climate divisions, where different) are 1 = Rolling Plains (Low Rolling Plains), 2 = Cross Timbers and Prairies (North Central), 3 = Edwards Plateau, 4 = Post Oak Savannah (South Central), and 5 = South Texas Plains (Southern). Gray area indicates approximate range of the Rio Grande wild turkey in Texas, adapted from Texas Parks and Wildlife Department (1997).

tation on wild turkey populations has been conducted in the eastern and northern United States, where the climate is relatively wet and/or cool. In New York, Roberts and Porter (1998*a,b*) found that nest survival of eastern wild turkeys (*M. g. sylvestris*) was negatively correlated with precipitation during incubation, and poult survival was negatively correlated with precipitation during the second week following hatching. Precipitation also was negatively correlated with eastern wild turkey production in West Virginia (Healy and Nenno 1985), and wild turkey recruitment declined in Mississippi following droughts (Palmer et al. 1993).

Studies addressing how precipitation affects RGWT are uncommon. DeArment (1969:31) maintained that RGWT hen:poult ratios on 3 study areas in the Texas panhandle "closely paralleled" rainfall during 1954–1958. On 2 study areas in south Texas, Beasom and Pattee (1980) found a strong correlation between previous year's rainfall and poult production. However, both studies investigated localized effects of precipitation over relatively short (≤10 years) periods. To our knowledge, no one has examined the relationship between weather and RGWT production at broad spatial scales over long time-periods (>20 years).

We tested 2 precipitation-related hypotheses: (1) precipitation strongly influences RGWT production in Texas, and (2) RGWT production in Texas responds indirectly to cumulative effects of precipitation (e.g., effects on vegetation structure or food availability), rather than directly to episodic events such as flooding, exposure, or enhanced predation. If our first hypothesis

is supported by data, then RGWT production and precipitation should be strongly correlated. If this correlation is strongest with cumulative precipitation over several months, rather than individual monthly precipitation, it would lend support to our second hypothesis. Also, positive correlations would suggest that precipitation influences turkey production by affecting factors that respond positively to soil moisture, such as vegetation structure or food availability; negative correlations would suggest precipitation directly increases mortality by increasing risk to drowning, nest inundation, and hypothermia. Finally, we performed exploratory analyses to determine whether a moisture index that incorporated a number of weather variables would be a better predictor of turkey production than raw precipitation alone, in order to suggest to managers a suitable weather-based index to RGWT production in Texas.

STUDY AREA

We evaluated the effects of precipitation on RGWT production in the Edwards Plateau, Rolling Plains, Cross Timbers and Prairies, Post Oak Savannah, and South Texas Plains ecological regions of Texas (Gould 1975; Figure 1A). These regions encompassed the majority of RGWT range in Texas (Figure 1A). Mean annual precipitation was 584–864 mm, and generally decreased from east to west. Rio Grande wild turkey also were present in the High Plains, Trans-Pecos, and Gulf Prairies and Marshes ecological

Table 1. Raw Rio Grande wild turkey poult production by Texas ecological region (Gould 1975), 1976–2000.

Year	Region				
	EP	RP	CT&P	POS	STP
1976	0.33		0.66		
1977	0.78	0.62	0.77	0.73	0.57
1978	0.51	0.47	0.72	0.16	0.29
1979	0.79	0.80	0.83	0.64	
1980	0.39	0.64	0.74	0.46	0.11
1981	0.84	0.80	0.81	0.71	0.57
1982	0.44	0.67	0.71	0.58	0.40
1983	0.60	0.58	0.66	0.46	0.51
1984	0.21	0.29	0.58	0.23	0.24
1985	0.78	0.74	0.71	0.61	0.68
1986	0.66	0.64	0.67	0.57	0.30
1987	0.77	0.73	0.74	0.57	0.66
1988	0.27	0.18	0.40	0.41	0.12
1989	0.47	0.63	0.61	0.26	0.16
1990	0.66	0.55	0.55	0.72	0.73
1991	0.63	0.77	0.65	0.53	0.62
1992	0.70	0.75	0.59	0.72	0.80
1993	0.39	0.55	0.64	0.52	0.53
1994	0.41	0.40	0.39	0.33	0.56
1995	0.71	0.68	0.53	0.26	0.24
1996	0.17	0.44	0.39	0.23	0.05
1997	0.78	0.84	0.70	0.64	0.67
1998	0.31	0.38	0.49	0.53	0.29
1999	0.60	0.70	0.50	0.41	0.50
2000	0.11	0.24	0.46	0.25	0.22

regions (Gould 1975). However, populations tended to be confined to small portions of these regions, thus limiting their region-wide abundance. TPWD historical data for these regions were relatively limited, thus precluding analysis.

METHODS

Production Data

Texas Parks and Wildlife Department (TPWD) biologists conducted annual RGWT brood counts during 1976–2000 across the subspecies' range in Texas. Biologists recorded all RGWT observed in the course of routine daily activities during 1 June–15 August. Although these counts were not conducted along standardized routes, observers were encouraged to observe ≥10–25 hens per county during each 2-week period of the count. Observations were recorded by county and latitude-longitude coordinates (Graham and George, 2002). Retrospective power analysis of

TPWD brood-count data revealed that it had sufficient power $(1 - \beta \geq 0.80, \alpha = 0.05)$ to detect a 40% annual change at the ecological-region scale during most years (Schwertner et al. 2003).

We grouped each year's data according to ecological region prior to analysis. Data from the Edwards Plateau and Cross Timbers and Prairies were available for 1976–2000, data from the Rolling Plains and Post Oak Savannah were available for 1977–2000, and data from the South Texas Plains were available for 1977–1978 and 1980–2000. We calculated the total number of hens and poults observed per year during the counts in each ecological region. We then calculated an index of RGWT poult production as $n_p/(n_p + n_h)$, where n_p = the number of poults, and n_h = the number of hens observed per year (Table 1).

Climate Data

We selected *a priori* 4 precipitation indices, based on either PMDI or raw precipitation, for analysis: June PMDI, September–June PMDI, June raw precipitation, and September–June raw precipitation. We used precipitation indices for June or periods ending in June because this coincided with peak RGWT hatching across Texas (Beasom 1973, Ransom et al. 1987, Hohensee and Wallace 2001). Therefore, precipitation-induced alterations in RGWT production should have been most pronounced during this period. Also, because precipitation across most RGWT range in Texas exhibits a bimodal pattern, with peaks in early autumn and late spring (Carr 1967), and rainfall prior to the growing season plays an important role in plant growth (Cable 1975), we chose precipitation and drought indices for the previous September–June to access cumulative weather effects.

We obtained PMDI and raw precipitation data for the Edwards Plateau, Low Rolling Plains, North Central, South Central, and Southern Texas climate divisions (http://lwf.ncdc.noaa.gov/oa/climate/onlineprod/drought/xmgrg3.html). The boundaries of these climate divisions matched closely, but not exactly, those of the Edwards Plateau, Rolling Plains, Cross Timbers and Prairies, Post Oak Savannah, and South Texas Plains ecological regions, respectively (Figure 1).

The PMDI is a meteorological drought index that uses deviations from long-term average precipitation and temperature, and the duration of the current dry

Table 2. Correlations between monthly and 9-month sums of raw precipitation (Precip) and the Modified Palmer Drought Severity Index (PMDI) and Rio Grande Wild Turkey poult production by Texas ecological region (Gould 1975), 1976–2000 (EP = Edwards Plateau, RP = Rolling Plains, CT&P = Cross Timbers and Prairies, POS = Post Oak Savannah, and STP = South Texas Plains). All data were detrended over years.

Region	June				September–June			
	PMDI		Precip		PMDI		Precip	
	r_s	P	r_s	P	r_s	P	r_s	P
EP	0.84	<0.001	0.60	0.002	0.66	<0.001	0.86	<0.001
RP	0.83	<0.001	0.53	0.009	0.27	0.216	0.81	<0.001
CT&P	0.76	<0.001	0.64	0.001	0.48	0.020	0.69	<0.001
POS	0.54	0.008	0.10	0.651	0.43	0.039	0.65	0.001
STP	0.74	<0.001	0.48	0.021	0.31	0.143	0.74	<0.001

or wet period, to estimate the severity of a dry or wet period (Heddinghaus and Sabol 1991). Usual PMDI values range between −4.0 and 4.0, although more extreme values occasionally occur. Negative values indicate dry periods, positive values indicate wet periods, and values near 0 indicate near normal conditions. Bridges et al. (2001) determined that 12-month cumulative and monthly PMDI were more correlated with quail abundance than were a number of other precipitation indices, including raw precipitation. We chose June PMDI to represent cumulative weather effects for the months during and immediately preceding the Rio Grande turkey nesting season. September–June PMDI (calculated by summing the PMDI values of each Sep–Jun period) represented cumulative weather effects beginning with the onset of the autumn wet-season prior to breeding.

Unfortunately, PMDI data are readily available only at the spatial scale of the climate division (Figure 1B). Calculation of this index for geographic areas that do not closely approximate the size or geographic extent of these divisions requires weather data and specialized knowledge that may not readily be available to wildlife managers. For this reason, we examined total raw precipitation as well. We chose total June precipitation as an index of monthly precipitation at the peak of hatching, and total September–June precipitation as an index of cumulative precipitation prior to and during the breeding season.

Analysis

Because both climate and production data could be serially correlated, we detrended these data using the first differences method to determine year-to-year change in precipitation and production indices (Ott and Longnecker 2001). Because the detrended poult production data from some climate divisions were nonnormally distributed (Ryan and Joiner 1976), we used Spearman rank correlation (Zar 1999) to evaluate how poult production varied with values for each index of precipitation. Correlations were considered significant if $P \leq 0.05$. We compared the correlation coefficients (r_S) of June PMDI, September–June PMDI, September–June total rainfall, and June total rainfall for each climate division to determine which variable was most correlated with RGWT production.

RESULTS

June PMDI and September–June raw precipitation were similarly correlated with poult production in all ecological regions (Table 2). June precipitation was correlated with poult production in all ecological regions except the Post Oak Savannah, although the relationship typically was weaker than for June PMDI or September–June raw precipitation (Table 2). September–June PMDI was correlated with poult production in the Edwards Plateau, Cross Timbers and Prairies, and Post Oak Savannah, but not in the Rolling Plains or South Texas Plains (Table 2).

DISCUSSION

Rio Grande wild turkey poult production showed a positive correlation with precipitation in Texas during 1976–2000. This correlation was stronger with indices that included multi-month cumulative weather data than with June raw precipitation alone. This lends support to the hypothesis that precipitation influences RGWT production in Texas, and this influence arises from the cumulative effects of precipitation over several months rather than individual rainfall events.

Our findings differed from those of Healy and Nenno (1985) and Roberts and Porter (1998a), who found that poult survival was negatively correlated with spring rainfall in West Virginia and New York, respectively. They attributed their results to exposure-related mortality among poults. Climatic differences could explain this discrepancy, as poult mortality due to wetting and hypothermia probably was of greater significance in these comparatively cool and wet eastern wild turkey habitats than in Texas.

Quail in Texas also have been found to be influenced by weather, including precipitation. Lusk et al. (2002) found that previous autumn rainfall was the most important variable influencing broad-scale northern bobwhite abundance in Texas. In south Texas, northern bobwhite production was found to be sensitive to both precipitation and temperature, and this relationship was most pronounced with spring weather variables (Guthery et al. 2002). Bridges et al. (2001) used 12-month cumulative PMDI, monthly PMDI, and raw precipitation indices to predict changes in northern bobwhite and scaled quail abundance among years in the Edwards Plateau, Rolling Plains, Cross Timbers and Prairies, South Texas Plains, Gulf Prairies and Marshes, and Trans-Pecos ecological regions of Texas. They found that 12-month cumulative PMDI was highly correlated with northern bobwhite and scaled quail abundance in the Rolling Plains and South Texas Plains ecological regions, but not in the Edwards Plateau, Cross Timbers and Prairies, or Gulf Prairies and Marshes. Only in the South Texas Plains was there a correlation between quail abundance and 12-month (Sep–Aug) raw precipitation, and this correlation was weaker than with 12-month PMDI. Northern bobwhite abundance also was correlated with June PMDI, but not June precipitation, in the Rolling Plains and South Texas Plains ecological regions. Scaled quail abundance was correlated with June PMDI in the Edwards Plateau and South Texas Plains, but with June raw precipitation in the Edwards Plateau only.

We failed to find evidence that PMDI was a better predictor of RGWT production than precipitation alone. Whereas Bridges et al. (2001) concluded that both 12-month cumulative and monthly PMDI measures were much better predictors of quail abundance than precipitation alone, we found that September–June precipitation and June PMDI did a comparable job of predicting changes in poult production among years, and were superior to both June precipitation and September–June cumulative PMDI. This was despite Palmer's (1965) assertion that PMDI was better at capturing moisture-induced variability in vegetation dynamics.

Because raw precipitation data are more readily available for user-defined geographic areas, wildlife managers probably would find these data more useful for predicting RGWT production in Texas. Further, because PMDI was superior to raw precipitation for quantifying weather effects on vegetation (Palmer 1965), yet no better at predicting RGWT production, it is possible that turkey population dynamics in Texas were not related to vegetation in the same way as were northern bobwhite and scaled quail populations. Thus, the mechanism by which precipitation influences turkey production (e.g., vegetation change) merits further study.

MANAGEMENT IMPLICATIONS

Although managers cannot control the weather, understanding how such exogenous variables influence turkey population dynamics is important to understanding the context in which management actions operate. Our results suggest that managers can anticipate RGWT production based on weather variables, and adjust management recommendations accordingly. Moreover, managers can use their knowledge of existing weather conditions, along with an understanding of how precipitation influences factors thought to limit abundance to judge, a priori, the potential efficiency and effectiveness of management practices directed at these limiting factors.

Brood counts typically require intensive manpower in order to collect sufficient data to provide meaningful results. As the demands on conservation agencies increase, rarely with concomitant increases in agency budgets, managers must seek less-expensive alternatives to traditional practices. Further, brood counts typically are conducted during mid- to late-summer, generally after harvest regulations have been made. The close correlation between precipitation and poult production provides managers with a cost effective alternative to brood counts for determining RGWT breeding success in Texas, insofar as brood counts are indicative of RGWT production.

ACKNOWLEDGMENTS

Texas A&M University, TPWD, the Texas Turkey Stamp fund, the Texas Chapter of The Wildlife Society, the Lower Colorado River Authority, and the Texas Agricultural Experiment Station, Texas A&M University provided support for this project. We thank the numerous TPWD biologists who collected RGWT production data during 1976–2000. We thank M. C. Frisbie for providing TPWD production data. Data collection and analysis was supported by Federal Aid in Wildlife Restoration through TPWD. We thank the National Climate Data Center for providing climate data used in our analysis.

LITERATURE CITED

Baines, D. 1991. Factors contributing to local and regional variation in black grouse breeding success in northern Britain. Ornis Scandinavica 22:264–269.

Beasom, S. L. 1973. Ecological factors affecting wild turkey reproductive success in south Texas. Dissertation, Texas A&M University, College Station, Texas, USA.

———, and O. H. Pattee. 1980. The effect of selected climatic variables on wild turkey productivity. Proceedings of the National Wild Turkey Symposium 4:127–135.

Belovsky, G. E., and J. B. Slade. 1995. Dynamics of two Montana grasshopper populations: relationships among weather, food abundance, and intraspecific competition. Oecologia 101:383–396.

Bridges, A. S., M. J. Peterson, N. J. Silvy, F. E. Smeins, and X. B. Wu. 2001. Differential influence of weather on regional quail abundance in Texas. Journal of Wildlife Management 65:10–18.

Cable, D. R. 1975. Influence of precipitation on perennial grass production in the semidesert southwest. Ecology 56:981–986.

Campbell, H., D. K. Martin, P. E. Ferkovich, and B. K. Harris. 1973. Effects of hunting and some other environmental factors on scaled quail in New Mexico. Wildlife Monographs 34:1–49.

Carr, J. T. 1967. The climate and physiography of Texas. Texas Water Resources Board Report 53.

DeArment, R. 1969. Turkey hen:poult ratios as an index to reproductive trends. Proceedings of the National Wild Turkey Symposium 1:27–31.

Frampton, G. K., P. J. Van Den Brink, and P. J. L. Gould. 2000. Effects of spring drought and irrigation on farmland arthropods in Britain. Journal of Applied Ecology 37:865–883.

Gould, F. W. 1975. Texas plants: a checklist and ecological summary. Texas A&M University, Agricultural Experiment Station, College Station, Texas, USA.

Graham, G. L., and R. R. George. 2002. Operational plan: fiscal year 2003. Texas Parks Wildlife Department, Austin, Texas, USA.

Guthery, F. S., J. L. Lusk, D. R. Synatzske, J. Gallagher, S. J. DeMaso, R. R. George, and M. J. Peterson. 2002. Weather and age ratios of northern bobwhites in south Texas. Proceedings of the National Quail Symposium 5:99–105.

Healy, W. M. 1992. Population influences: environment. Pages 129–143 in J. D. Dickson, editor. The wild turkey: biology and management. Stackpole Books, Harrisburg, Pennsylvania, USA.

———, and E. S. Nenno. 1985. Effect of weather on wild turkey poult survival. Proceedings of the National Wild Turkey Symposium 5:91–101.

Heddinghaus, T. R., and P. Sabol. 1991. A review of the Palmer Drought Severity Index and where do we go from here? Proceedings of the Conference on Applied Climatology 7:242–246.

Hohensee, S. D., and M. C. Wallace. 2001. Nesting and survival of Rio Grande turkeys in northcentral Texas. Proceedings of the National Wild Turkey Symposium 8:85–91.

Hurst, G. A. 1992. Foods and feeding. Pages 66–83 in J. D. Dickson, editor. The wild turkey: biology and management. Stackpole Books, Harrisburg, Pennsylvania, USA.

Johnson, D. L., and A. Worobec. 1988. Spatial and temporal computer analysis of insects and weather: grasshoppers and rainfall in Alberta. Memoirs of the Entomological Society of Canada 146:33–48.

Kennamer, J. E., D. H. Arner, C. R. Hopkins, and R. C. Clanton. 1975. Productivity of the eastern wild turkey in the Mississippi Delta. Proceedings of the National Wild Turkey Symposium 3:41–47.

Krebs, C. J. 1994. Ecology: the experimental analysis of distribution and abundance. Fourth edition. Harper Collins, New York, New York, USA.

Lusk, J. J., F. S. Guthery, R. R. George, M. J. Peterson, and S. J. DeMaso. 2002. Relative abundance of bobwhites in relation to weather and land use. Journal of Wildlife Management 66:1040–1051.

Markley, M. H. 1967. Limiting factors. Pages 199–244 *in* O. H. Hewitt, editor. The wild turkey and its management. The Wildlife Society, Washington, D.C., USA.

Marshall, A. J. 1959. Internal and environmental control of breeding. Ibis 101:456–478.

Moss, R. 1986. Rain, breeding success and distribution of capercaillie (*Tetrao urogallus*) and black grouse (*Tetrao tetrix*) in Scotland. Ibis 128:65–72.

Ott, R. L., and M. Longnecker. 2001. An introduction to statistical methods and data analysis. Fifth edition. Duxbury, Pacific Grove, California, USA.

Palmer, W. C. 1965. Meteorological drought. United States Department of Commerce Weather Bureau Research Paper Number 45.

Palmer, W. E., S. R. Priest, R. S. Seiss, P. S. Phalen, and G. A. Hurst. 1993. Reproductive effort and success in a declining wild turkey population. Proceedings of the Annual Conference of the Southeastern Association of Fish and Wildlife Agencies 47:138–147.

Panek, M. 1992. The effect of environmental factors on survival of grey partridge (*Perdix perdix*) chicks in Poland during 1987–89. Journal of Applied Ecology 29:745–750.

Ransom, D., Jr., O. J. Rongstad, and D. H. Rusch. 1987. Nesting ecology of Rio Grande turkeys. Journal of Wildlife Management 51:435–439.

Roberts, S. D., J. M. Coffey, and W. F. Porter. 1995. Survival and reproduction of female wild turkey in New York. Journal of Wildlife Management 59:437–447.

———, and W. F. Porter, 1998a. Influence of temperature and precipitation on survival of wild turkey poults. Journal of Wildlife Management 62:1499–1505.

———, and ———. 1998b. Relation between weather and survival of wild turkey nests. Journal of Wildlife Management 62:1492–1498.

Ryan, T. A., Jr., and B. L. Joiner. 1976. Normal probability plots and tests for normality. Technical Report, Department of Statistics, Pennsylvania State University, State College, Pennsylvania, USA.

Schwertner, T. W., M. J. Peterson, N. J. Silvy, and F. E. Smeins. 2003. Brood-survey power and estimates of Rio Grande turkey production in Texas. Proceedings of the Annual Conference of the Southeastern Association of Fish and Wildlife Agencies 57:in press.

Texas Parks and Wildlife Department. 1997. Wild turkey distribution in Texas. Texas Parks and Wildlife Department Leaflet PWD LF W7000–038 (11/97).

Welty, J. C., and L. Baptista. 1988. The life of birds. Fourth edition. Saunders College, New York, New York, USA.

Zar, J. H. 1999. Biostatistical analysis. Fourth edition. Prentice-Hall, Upper Saddle River, New Jersey, USA.

Zwank, P. J., T. H. White, Jr., and F. G. Kimmel. 1988. Female turkey habitat use in Mississippi River batture. Journal of Wildlife Management 52:253–560.

T. Wayne Schwertner (pictured) is an Upland Gamebird Specialist and the White-winged Dove Program Leader to the Texas Parks and Wildlife Department. He received his B.S and Ph.D. in from Texas A&M University, and his M.S. from Texas State University. His research interests include gamebird ecology, ecological modeling, and invasive species. *Markus J. Peterson* is an Associate Professor in the Department of Wildlife and Fisheries Sciences at Texas A&M University. He received his B.S. from University of Idaho, D.V.M. from Washington State University, and M.S. and Ph.D. from Texas A&M University. His research interests include the ecology and management of terrestrial vertebrate populations with an emphasis on factors influencing animal abundance, such as wildlife disease, predation, weather, habitat conditions, and human exploitation. He also has a keen interest in environmental policy formation and implementation. *Nova J. Silvy* is a Regents Professor with the Department of Wildlife and Fisheries Sciences at Texas A&M University. He received his B.S. and M.S. from Kansas State University and his Ph.D. from Southern Illinois University–Carbondale. Nova served as President of The Wildlife Society in 2000–2001 and received the Aldo Leopold Award in 2003. His research focus is upland game ecology.

Wild Turkey Management:
Accomplishments, Strategies, and Opportunities
———— Grand Rapids, Michigan ————

CLIMATE-BASED NEURAL MODELS OF RIO GRANDE TURKEY PRODUCTIVITY IN TEXAS

Jeffrey J. Lusk[1,2]
Department of Forestry, Oklahoma State University,
Stillwater, OK 74074, USA

Stephen J. DeMaso
Texas Parks and Wildlife Department,
4200 Smith School Road, Austin, TX 78744, USA

Fred S. Guthery
Department of Forestry, Oklahoma State University,
Stillwater, OK 74074, USA

Abstract: We used neural-network modeling to assess the effects of weather and climate variables in predicting production (poults:hen ratios) of Rio Grande turkeys (*Meleagris gallopavo intermedia*) in Texas. We used poult: hen data from Texas Parks and Wildlife (TPWD) surveys collected by TPWD biologists during 1977 through 2003. Datasets contained seasonal rainfall and temperature data, deviations from long-term mean rainfall and temperature, or Modified Palmer Drought Severity indices for winter (Dec–Feb), spring (Mar–May), summer (Jun–Aug), and fall (Sep–Nov). We used the adjusted sum-of-squares for model selection. The model with the best performance included deviations from long-term mean conditions as predictor variables. The selected model accounted for 28% of the variation in the training data. Wetter than normal years, and particularly springs, resulted in declines in poults:hen ratios. Warmer than normal winters and falls resulted in increases in poults:hen ratios. Based on ecoregion-level means, climate conditions in the Edwards Plateau are best for turkey production; the model predicted 1.71 poults/hen for the Edwards Plateau compared with 1.43 based on statewide climate conditions. Our analysis provisionally supported the hypothesis that deviations from normal conditions best explain annual fluctuations in production. However, we were not able to rule out the possibility that weather catastrophes play a significant role.

Proceedings of the National Wild Turkey Symposium 9:133–141
Key words: climate, ecoregion-level analysis, *Meleagris gallopavo intermedia,* neural network model, Rio Grande wild turkey, Texas, weather.

A detailed understanding of the factors influencing the population dynamics of the Rio Grande turkey is essential for successful management. Although precipitation is 1 factor thought to influence the population dynamics of eastern wild turkeys (*M. g. silvestris*; Healy 1992, Hohensee and Wallace 2001) relatively little is known about the factors influencing Rio Grande turkeys. Miller et al. (1995) hypothesized that spring and early summer rainfall influence the vegetation community in which Rio Grande turkeys nest, resulting in the higher survival rate of hens incubating second and third nests

they observed in Kansas. For the eastern subspecies, little or no production occurs during drought years (Healy 1992) and nest success in Mississippi was negatively related to the number of rainfall events and cumulative rainfall (Lowrey et al. 2001).

Healy (1992:137) noted, "Extreme local variation

[1] Present address: Wildlife Division, Nebraska Game and Parks Commission, 2200 N. 33rd Street, Lincoln, NE 68503, USA.
[2] E-mail: jeff.lusk@ngpc.ne.gov

in effects of weather seems to be a general phenomenon in turkey populations." Such variation makes broad-scale analyses of the effects of weather ineffectual. Therefore, an ecoregional analysis of the effects of climate and weather on poult:hen ratios in Texas was undertaken. Our objectives were to provide descriptive data on the effects of climate on production and to better understand the relative effects of weather and climate on Rio Grande turkey poult:hen ratios using neural network models. The knowledge gleaned from such models should allow managers to more effectively manage populations within a particular climate or weather context. Our analysis also allowed us to test the hypothesis that departures from normal conditions better explain annual variability in turkey production than yearly weather conditions (Bailey and Rinell 1968).

METHODS

Our analysis was based on data collected in Texas. Texas counties were grouped into 10 ecoregions: Pineywoods, Gulf Prairies and Marshes, Post Oak Savannah, Blackland Prairies, Cross Timbers, South Texas Plains, Edwards Plateau, Rolling Plains, High Plains, and Trans-Pecos Mountains and Basins (Gould 1975). Poult:hen data for Rio Grande turkeys were available for 8 of those 10 ecoregions (all except Pineywoods and High Plains), so we focused on those 8 ecoregions.

Annual rainfall in Texas ranges from <200 mm in the Trans-Pecos to 1,400 mm in the Gulf Prairies and Marshes on the Louisiana border. The annual frost-free period ranges from 179 days in the northwest Texas Panhandle to 330 days in the lower Rio Grande Valley (Gould 1975).

Wild Turkey Data

We obtained poult:hen data from TPWD summer turkey surveys. These surveys were conducted in the Trans-Pecos, Rolling Plains, South Texas Plains, Edwards Plateau, Post Oak Savannah, and Cross Timbers ecoregions during 1 June–15 August, 1977 through 2003. Counts were conducted incidentally to the normal duties of TPWD biologists and were recorded on prepared forms to show county, date, number of turkeys observed, and number of adults and poults. Observers were asked to observe 10–25 hens/county during the survey period. We modeled poult:hen ratios as poults per total hens observed using the raw count data from those surveys.

Weather and Climate Data

We differentiated weather, the short-term rainfall and temperature regimes in a given locale within years, from climate, the long-term patterns in precipitation and temperature across years. We obtained climate and weather data from the National Climate Data Center, compiled by EarthInfo (Boulder, Colorado, USA). We selected weather stations with records ≥95% complete

over the period of interest from 5 counties in each ecoregion. We used this method of weather station selection because surveys were not systematic, but occurred incidentally during the normal duties of TPWD biologists and, therefore, there were no set survey routes or points to which weather stations could be assigned based on proximity.

Weather data were extracted from NCDC records and summarized to obtain total monthly precipitation and mean maximum daily temperature for each month. These values were then averaged within ecoregions to obtain a single ecoregion mean. We used these data to estimate mean total seasonal precipitation and mean seasonal maximum daily temperature. Season classes were winter (Dec–Feb), spring (Mar–May), summer (Jun–Aug), and fall (Sep–Nov). Climate data were obtained by averaging the weather records over the entire period of record (range: 30–100 years) and subtracting the yearly weather values. Therefore, the climate data represented the deviation of annual weather conditions from the long-term mean conditions of the ecoregion. We also summarized the Palmer Drought Severity Index (PDSI) from NCDC records to obtain seasonal estimates. Because surveys were conducted during June–August each year and because some research suggested that, at least of eastern wild turkeys, previous fall rainfall affected turkey production (Healy 1992:136), we used previous fall rainfall and temperature as predictors in our models.

We created 4 datasets from the extracted data. The first dataset contained weather data. As defined previously, these data represented the mean annual rainfall and temperature observed at weather stations during the year of record. The second dataset contained the climate data. It quantified the magnitude of difference between annual conditions and the long-term climate means. We used those first 2 datasets to determine whether climate or weather patterns were the predominant factor influencing Rio Grande turkey production. The third dataset contained seasonal and annual estimates of the PDSI. We included this dataset because some research has indicated the PDSI better represents the effects of weather than simple temperature and precipitation in models of population abundance of some species (e.g., Northern Bobwhites *Colinus virginianus*; Bridges et al. 2001). Finally, the fourth dataset was a compilation of the important variables identified during the analysis of the other 3 datasets.

Modeling and Analysis

We used a neural network model (Smith 1996, Fielding 1999) to determine the relationship between poult:hen ratios and weather, climate, and the PDSI. Neural networks were implemented using Statistica Neural Networks (StatSoft, Tulsa, Oklahoma, USA). We used a 3-layer perceptron architecture and a hyperbolic transfer function. We allowed the program to determine model complexity (number of neurons) automatically based on relative performance of each model trained. We systematically partitioned the data into training and testing datasets by ordering the data by the dependent variable and selecting every fifth case. Using this process we set aside 20% of the overall data for assessing the model performances. Testing data were used to assess performance, but were not used for training the neural models. Performance was gauged by comparing the correlations between predicted and observed poult:hen ratios. We wanted models with strong, positive correlations between training and testing datasets. This ensured that the selected model accurately encapsulated the underlying relationships among variables and that the model could generalize to new data. We compared climate, weather and PDSI models using the adjusted sum-of-squares (Hilborn and Mangel 1997).

We created a series of datasets in which the independent variable of interest was allowed to vary between the minimum and maximum observed values while all other independent variables were held constant at their mean value. These datasets were then processed by the trained neural model and the predicted poult:hen ratio was plotted against the range of the variable of interest. These results were then used to interpret the model output.

The relative contribution of each variable to model predictions was determined by calculating a relevance score of each variable (Goodman 1996, Özesmi and Özesmi 1999). A relevance score is a measure of relative influence of each variable over the final prediction and is calculated as the sum of squared connection weights of the variable of interest (where connection weights link each variable to each neuron) divided by the sum of squared connection weights of all variables. If all of the independent variables had no effect on the dependent variable, we would expect them to have similar relevance scores. That is, each variable would have the same influence over the model's predictions because none of the predictors would be related to the response. We report simulations for only the variables which had greater than expected relevance scores.

To investigate ecoregion variation in the response of poult:hen ratios to climate, weather, and drought severity, we estimated the ecoregion means for each independent variable and presented these means to the trained neural model (cf. Lusk et al. 2002). The technique we employed shows regional responses based on the general statewide model.

RESULTS

Neural model performance varied among datasets. For Rio Grande turkeys, models for weather and PDSI datasets performed poorly. The best performing weather model contained 3 neurons and accounted for 23.2% of the variation in the training data, but only 6.5% of the variation in the testing data. Similarly, the best performing model based on the PDSI contained 3 neurons and accounted for 25% of the variation in the training data, but only 1.3% of the variation in the testing data. The neural model based on climate data performed better; the best model contained 2 neurons

Table 1. Relevance scores (%) for independent variables used to predict Rio Grande turkey production (poults/hen) in Texas, 1977–2003. The relevance of a variable is a measure of the relative influence of the variable on model predictions. The expected relevance assuming all variables to have an equal influence on model outcome was 11.1%.

Variable	Relevance (%)
Deviation from mean total annual precipitation	15.0
Deviation from mean total winter precipitation	12.1
Deviation from mean total spring precipitation	17.8
Deviation from mean total summer precipitation	5.9
Deviation from mean total fall precipitation	4.7
Deviation from mean maximum winter temperature	14.9
Deviation from mean maximum spring temperature	5.0
Deviation from mean maximum summer temperature	4.4
Deviation from mean maximum fall temperature	20.2

and accounted for 28% of the variation in the training data and 22% of the variation in the testing data.

Using the relevance score, we selected variables from each of the 3 datasets and created a fourth dataset. There were 4 variables included in this model: summer PDSI, mean total spring rainfall, deviation of spring rainfall from normal, and deviation of fall temperature from normal. The best performing neural model containing these variables contained 3 neurons and accounted for 20.5% of the variation in the training data and 19.7% of the variation in the testing data. The climate model had a lower adjusted sum-of-squares (1.94) than the relevant-variable model (2.2), so we used the climate model for simulations and ecoregion analyses.

The expected relevance of each variable given no relationship was 11.1% for the climate model. Using this as a cutoff threshold, we found that 4 variables had a greater influence on model outcome than expected and 1 variable was within 1% of the threshold (Table 1). Deviation from long-term mean maximum fall temperature had the greatest influence on model outcome and deviation from long-term summer temperature had the least influence (Table 1).

As total annual precipitation increased above normal, poults:hen ratios declined (Figure 1). The same pattern held for spring precipitation, poults:hen ratio was highest (2.5 poults/hen) when precipitation was approximately 80 mm less than the long-term average (Figure 2). When mean winter temperature was above normal the poult:hen ratio increased and when below normal the poult:hen ratio decreased (Figure 3). Similarly, poult:hen ratios increased with increases in mean fall temperature above normal and declined with decreases in mean fall temperature below normal (Figure 4).

Using the mean climate data for each ecoregion as inputs into the neural model resulted in poult:hen ratios that would be expected given the general climate in each ecoregion. We contrasted the predictions for each ecoregion with that produced from statewide means. Given statewide climate averages, the neural model predicted that production would equal 1.44 poults/hen. The Edwards Plateau region had the highest predicted poult:hen ratio based on average climate

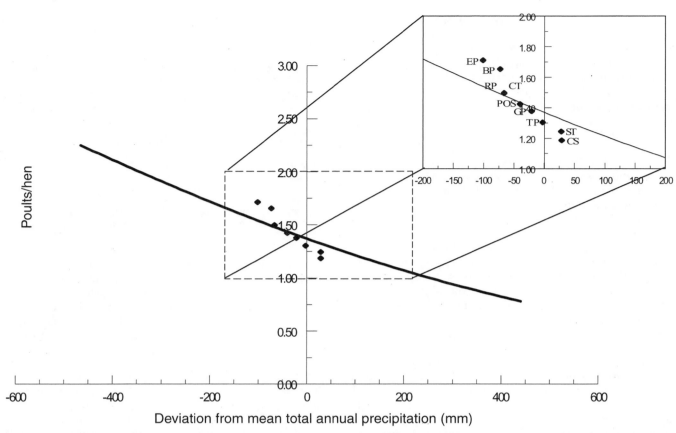

Fig. 1. Rio Grande turkey production (poults/hen) in Texas as a function of the deviation of total annual precipitation from the long-term mean. Inset shows the predicted poult:hen ratios for each ecoregion based on the long-term ecoregion means. Ecoregion abbreviations are as in Table 2.

conditions in the ecoregion (1.71 poults/hen; Table 2). Predicted poult:hen ratios were smallest for the South Texas Plains (1.24; Table 2). Overall, 4 ecoregions had predicted poult:hen ratios that were greater and 4 ecoregions had predicted poult:hen ratios that were smaller than that predicted from statewide climate (Table 2).

Of the 4 variables that were influential in the neural model, only deviation from mean total annual precipitation seemed to be related to the variation in predicted poult:hen ratios among ecoregions (Figures 1–4 inset). The Edwards Plateau had the largest negative deviation in mean total annual precipitation and had the largest poult:hen ratio (Table 2, Figure 1 inset). Each subsequent ecoregion had a smaller negative deviation and a smaller resulting poult:hen ratio (Figure 1 inset). The South Texas Plains, which had a positive deviation in mean total annual precipitation, had the smallest predicted poult:hen ratio, smaller than the predicted ratio based on statewide climate (Figure 1 inset). A similar pattern was apparent for spring precipitation (Figure 2 inset), except that the Blackland Prairies had a mean positive deviation from long-term conditions that was greater than that for the South Texas Plains, yet the predicted poult:hen ratio for the Blackland Prairies was the second highest of all ecoregions (Figure 2 inset).

MODELING CAVEATS

The nature of the data and of the analyses requires that we address some caveats to the interpretation of results. First, there is a lack of information on the accuracy of convenience sampling used to obtain the hen:poult data. Such data are commonly used by state management agencies for tracking turkey abundance (Kurzejeski and Vangilder 1992). Wunz and Shope (1980) found that survey data for eastern turkeys were well correlated with fall harvest in Pennsylvania. DeArment (1969) reported that poult:hen ratios were effective for monitoring production of Rio Grande turkeys in the Texas Panhandle. A power analysis of the Texas data indicated that it had sufficient power to detect a 30% change in poult production given the annual sample sizes of the data (range: 65–306; Schwertner et al. 2003). Second, data were collected in an ad hoc manner during the normal duties of TPWD biologists. Therefore, each observation in each year comes from a potentially different location within each specific ecoregion. As a result, the same populations were not surveyed each year. The data-collection scheme also prevented us from assigning the closest weather station to the survey location. We selected weather stations from around each ecoregion and estimated average conditions in order to capture the cli-

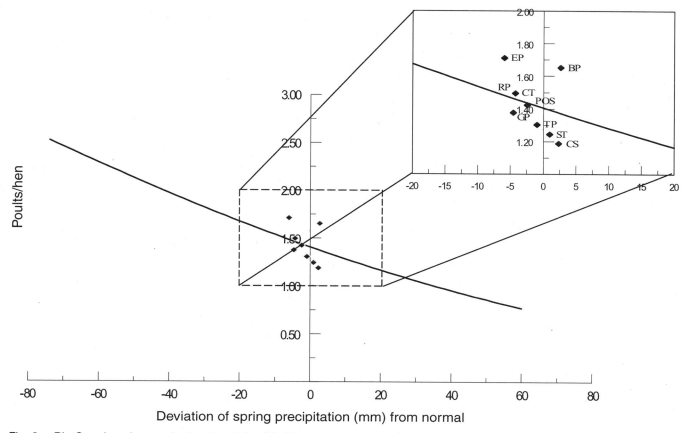

Fig. 2.   Rio Grande turkey production (poults/hen) in Texas as a function of the deviation of spring precipitation from the long-term mean. Insets show the predicted poult:hen ratios for each ecoregion based on the long-term ecoregion means. Ecoregion abbreviations are as in Table 2.

mate over the entire ecoregion. This method, however, ignored within-ecoregion climate gradients and dampened weather and climate variation. This could be the reason for the weak performance of the neural models we developed; ecoregion averages were only weakly associated with the poult:hen ratios gathered therein. However, it is not possible for us to definitively say whether given ideal data our models would have explained a higher proportion of the variation in production or if other unmeasured factors exerted stronger control.

DISCUSSION

Our analyses provided preliminary support for the hypothesis that departures from normal conditions help explain annual variation in wild turkey production (Bailey and Rinell 1968); the climate model had the best performance of the models tested. Further research should investigate this conclusion in more detail and test other hypotheses to explain variability in productivity. Similar results have been reported for northern bobwhites in Oklahoma (Lusk et al. 2001) and might indicate that local populations are adapted to local conditions within the genotypic range of the species. Healy (1992:138) concurred with this opinion: "Turkey populations are adapted to the average weath-

er conditions of their region. Weather must deviate substantially from the average—and do so for some time—before it affects populations."

Four variables contributed more than expected to the neural model's predictions. Those variables were the deviation from mean maximum fall temperature, deviation from mean total spring precipitation, deviation from total annual precipitation, and deviation from mean maximum winter temperature. Production declined with annual and spring precipitation above the long-term means. Rain exceeding 380 mm were sufficient to kill poults 12–15 days old, but only at temperatures <8°C over an 18-hour period (Healy and Nenno 1985). Rainfall could be positively related to the ability of nest predators to find and destroy turkey nests (Palmer et al. 1993, Roberts et al. 1995, Roberts and Porter 1998). Predation accounted for 94% of all Rio Grande hen mortalities in Kansas (Hennen and Lutz 2001).

Healy (1992) reported that August through September rainfall was the most important weather-related factor determining wild turkey production, with breeding season rainfall of secondary importance. Our results showed that deviations from spring (breeding season) rainfall had more influence on production than previous fall rainfall (Table 1). Higher Rio Grande turkey productivity in south Texas was thought to be re-

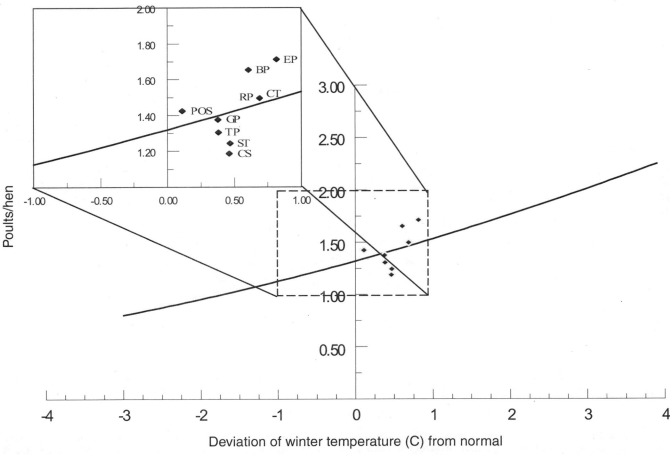

Fig. 3. Rio Grande turkey production (poults/hen) in Texas as a function of the deviation of winter temperature from the long-term mean. Insets show the predicted poult:hen ratios for each ecoregion based on the long-term ecoregion means. Ecoregion abbreviations are as in Table 2.

lated to heavy late summer and early fall rainfall the previous year acting indirectly through vegetation (Baker et al. 1980). Hennen and Lutz (2001) found that low female survival during brood rearing and recruitment seemed to be related to above-average rainfall during the same period. Beasom and Pattee (1980) found that variability in annual Rio Grande turkey productivity was best explained by fall (Sept-Oct) and spring (Mar) rainfall. Although causal mechanisms probably differ among subspecies, breeding season rainfall seems to influence eastern wild turkey production, as well. For example, successful eastern wild turkey nests experienced less cumulative rainfall and fewer rainfall events than did their unsuccessful counterparts (Lowrey et al. 2001).

Temperature has been considered of secondary importance to wild turkey survival and production (Healy 1992). However, our results showed that deviations from long-term mean fall and winter temperatures together had a relevance of 35.1%. Further, the results showed that above-average temperatures in the fall and winter resulted in higher poult:hen ratios the following year. Although Healy (1992) stated that most winter losses were due to starvation rather than the direct effects of temperature, this is not likely the case in Texas where resources are rarely buried under snow cover.

However, warmer than average fall and winter temperatures could reduce the energetic demands of overwintering and allow resources to be available for reproduction in the spring. Further, an unusually dry fall could reduce the availability of food resources in the spring exacerbating the effects of a cold winter.

At the ecoregion level in Texas, climate conditions within the Edwards Plateau were best for Rio Grande turkey production. It is, therefore, not surprising that the Edwards Plateau is at the center of the Rio Grande's range in Texas (Beasom and Wilson 1992). Predicted poult:hen ratios were greatest in the Edwards Plateau based on the climate within that region, and production exceeded that predicted from average statewide climate. Ecoregions appeared to fall out along a rainfall gradient, with production declining in increasingly wetter ecoregions (Figure 1, inset), even though in drought years approximately 40% of hens do not lay. The western boundary of the Rio Grande turkey's range occurs where rainfall is insufficient to support trees needed for roosting (Healy 1992).

Future analyses should include catastrophic weather events. A weather catastrophe could be considered to have occurred if ≥1 day within the specified time frame exhibited rainfall events of >380 mm or temperatures <8°C (Healy and Nenno 1985). Such an

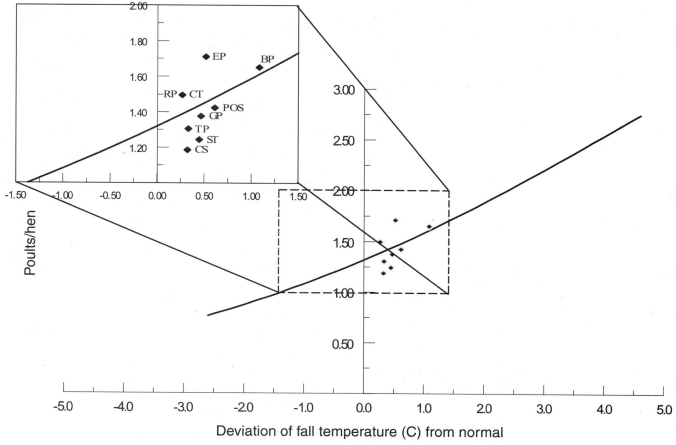

Fig. 4. Rio Grande turkey production (poults/hen) in Texas as a function of the deviation of fall temperature from the long-term mean. Insets show the predicted poult:hen ratios for each ecoregion based on the long-term ecoregion means. Ecoregion abbreviations are as in Table 2.

analysis will allow researchers to test the hypothesis that weather catastrophes predict annual fluctuations in turkey production as suggested by Healy (1992).

MANAGEMENT IMPLICATIONS

Climate and weather are outside the realm of management activities. However, the results presented above provide the environmental context within which management activities must be implemented. As such, it is necessary for managers to understand this environmental context so that more effective management options can be implemented with the aim of maintaining or increasing Rio Grande turkey abundance. The existing repertory of management techniques is still available to managers. However, the implementation of these techniques should consider the overarching climate influences. For example, Beasom and Wilson

Table 2. Predicted poult:hen ratios for Rio Grande turkeys for each ecoregion in Texas based on the average climate conditions of that ecoregion. The average climate conditions ($\pm$SE) for the 4 variables that had more than expected influence on the neural model are also provided to aid interpretation of the predicted age ratios. Statewide climate averages predicted 1.43 poults/hen for Texas.

		Deviations from mean . . .			
Ecoregion[a]	Poults/hen	Total annual precipitation (mm)	Total spring precipitation (mm)	Maximum winter temperature (°C)	Maximum fall temperature (°C)
GP	1.38	−21.1 (50.3)	−4.6 (8.1)	0.38 (0.27)	0.47 (0.22)
POS	1.42	−40.1 (48.1)	−2.4 (6.0)	0.11 (0.35)	0.62 (0.24)
BP	1.65	−72.5 (34.2)	2.7 (7.5)	0.61 (0.22)	1.08 (0.18)
CT	1.50	−66.3 (23.7)	−4.3 (3.7)	0.69 (0.33)	0.27 (0.29)
ST	1.24	28.5 (24.8)	1.0 (4.6)	0.47 (0.33)	0.45 (0.20)
EP	1.71	−101.1 (34.5)	−6.0 (4.4)	0.82 (0.29)	0.52 (0.23)
RP	1.50	−66.3 (23.7)	−4.3 (3.7)	0.69 (0.33)	0.27 (0.29)
TP	1.30	−2.6 (25.7)	−0.9 (2.7)	0.38 (0.28)	0.33 (0.21)

[a] Ecoregion codes: GP = Gulf Prairie and Marshes; POS = Post Oak Savannah; BP = Blackland Prairie; CT = Cross Timbers and Prairies; ST = South Texas Plains; EP = Edwards Plateau; RP = Rolling Plains; TP = Trans-Pecos.

(1992) reported that production could be enhanced up to 300% during low-rainfall years using food supplementation. Beasom (1973) reported that in years of higher than normal rainfall, the abundant cover that resulted increased reproductive success up to 700 times compared to dry years when little cover was available. Therefore, if precipitation is expected to be below average, managers might consider steps to improve screening cover for nests as a method of mitigating reduced nest success.

The results reported above also demonstrated the importance of local climate to Rio Grande turkey production. We found that deviations from long-term conditions (i.e., climate) were more important in determining poult:hen ratios than were observed weather patterns, which supports the hypothesis of Bailey and Rinell (1968). Results from our model would seem to imply that Rio Grande turkeys have adapted to local conditions and that production will be increasingly affected as the magnitude of the deviation from normal increases. As a result, managers should consider the local climate conditions when implementing translocations in order to increase the chances of successful establishment.

Climate conditions in the Edwards Plateau were most favorable for Rio Grande turkey production. However, grazing in this ecoregion leads to reductions in nesting cover (Beasom and Wilson 1992) and food availability, especially of important mast species (Blakey 1944). Increased research attention to the effects of grazing on Rio Grande turkeys, therefore, seems warranted.

ACKNOWLEDGMENTS

Support for this project was provided by the Texas Parks and Wildlife Department, the Department of Forestry at Oklahoma State University, the Bollenbach endowment, the Game Bird Research Fund, and the Oklahoma Agricultural Experiment Station. We thank 3 anonymous reviewers for helpful suggestions for improving the content and clarity of this manuscript. This paper was approved for publication by the Oklahoma Agricultural Experiment Station.

LITERATURE CITED

Bailey, R. W., and K. T. Rinell. 1968. History and management of the wild turkey in West Virginia. West Virginia Department of Natural Resources Bulletin 6.

Baker, B. W., S. L. Beasom, and N. J. Silvy. 1980. Turkey productivity and habitat use on South Texas rangelands. Proceedings of the National Wild Turkey Symposium 4:145–158.

Beasom, S. L. 1973. Ecological factors affecting wild turkey reproductive success in south Texas. Dissertation, Texas A&M University, College Station, USA.

———, and O. H. Pattee. 1980. The effect of selected climatic variables on wild turkey productivity. Proceedings of the National Wild Turkey Symposium 4:127–135.

———, and D. Wilson. 1992. Rio Grande turkey. Pages 306–330 in J. G. Dickson, editor. The wild turkey: biology and management. Stackpole Books, Harrisburg, Pennsylvania, USA.

Blakey, H. L. 1944. Welfare of the wild turkey closely associated with range management. Agricultural Experiment Station Progress Report 894, College Station, Texas, USA.

Bridges, A. S., M. J. Peterson, N. J. Silvy, F. E. Smeins, and X. B. Wu. 2001. Differential influence of weather on regional quail abundance in Texas. Journal of Wildlife Management 65:10–18.

DeArment, R. 1969. Turkey hen-poult ratios as an index to reproductive trends. Proceedings of the National Wild Turkey Symposium 1:27–31.

Fielding, A. H. 1999. An introduction to machine learning methods. Pages 1–35 in A. H. Fielding, editor. Machine learning methods for ecological application. Kluwer Academic Publishers, Boston, Massachusetts, USA.

Goodman, P. H. 1996. NevProp software. Version 3. University of Nevada, Reno, Nevada, USA.

Gould, F. W. 1975. Texas plants: a checklist and ecological summary. Texas Agricultural Experiment Station, MP-585/Revised, College Station, Texas, USA.

Healy, W. M. 1992. Population influences: environment. Pages 129–143 in J. G. Dickson, editor. The wild turkey: biology and management. Stackpole Books, Harrisburg, Pennsylvania, USA.

———, and E. S. Nenno. 1985. Effects of weather on wild turkey poult survival. Proceedings of the National Wild Turkey Symposium 5:91–101.

Hennen, R. S., and S. Lutz. 2001. Rio Grande turkey female survival in southcentral Kansas. Proceedings of the National Wild Turkey Symposium 8:117–122.

Hilborn, R., and M. Mangel. 1997. The ecological detective. Princeton University Press, Princeton, New Jersey, USA.

Hohensee, S. D., and M. C. Wallace. 2001. Nesting and survival of Rio Grande turkeys in northcentral Texas. Proceedings of the National Wild Turkey Symposium 8:85–91.

Kurzejeski, E. W., and L. D. Vangilder. 1992. Population management. Pages 165–184 in J. G. Dickson, editor. The wild turkey: biology and management. Stackpole Books, Harrisburg, Pennsylvania, USA.

Lowrey, D. K., S. R. Priest, G. A. Hurst, and B. S. Weemy. 2001. Influences of selected weather variables on predation of wild turkey females and nest success. Proceedings of the National Wild Turkey Symposium 8:173–178.

Lusk, J. J., F. S. Guthery, and S. J. DeMaso. 2001. Northern bobwhite (Colinus virginianus) abundance in relation to yearly weather and long-term climate patterns. Ecological Modelling 146:3–13.

———, ———, R. R. George, M. J. Peterson, and S. J. DeMaso. 2002. Relative abundance of bobwhites in relation to weather and land use. Journal of Wildlife Management 66:1040–1051.

Miller, M. S., D. J. Buford, and R. S. Lutz. 1995. Survival of female Rio Grande turkeys during the reproductive season. Journal of Wildlife Management 59:766–771.

Özesmi, S. L., and U. Özesmi. 1999. An artificial neural network approach to spatial habitat modelling with interspecific interaction. Ecological Modelling 116:15–31.

Palmer, S. R., S. R. Priest, R. S. Seiss, P. S. Phalen, and G. A. Hurst. 1993. Reproductive effort and success in a declining wild turkey population. Proceedings of the Annual Conference of the Southeastern Association of Fish and Wildlife Agencies 47:138–147.

Roberts, S. D., J. M. Coffey, and W. F. Porter. 1995. Survival and reproduction of wild turkeys in New York. Journal of Wildlife Management 59:437–447.

———, and W. F. Porter. 1998. Relation between weather and survival of wild turkey nests. Journal of Wildlife Management 62:1492–1498.

Schwertner, T. W., M. J. Peterson, N. J. Silvy, and F. E. Smeins. 2003. Brood-count power estimates of Rio Grande turkey production in Texas. Proceedings of the Annual Conference of the Southeastern Association of Fish and Wildlife Agencies 57:213–221.

Smith, M. 1996. Neural networks for statistical modeling. International Thompson Computer Press, London, United Kingdom.

Wunz, G. A., and W. K. Shope. 1980. Turkey brood survey in Pennsylvania as it relates to harvest. Proceedings of the National Wild Turkey Symposium 4:69–75.

Jeffrey J. Lusk is currently the Upland Game Program Manager for Nebraska Game and Parks Commission in Lincoln, Nebraska. He recently completed a postdoctoral research position in the Department of Forestry and Natural Resources at Purdue University in West Lafayette, Indiana, where he was a member of the Purdue Climate Change Research Center. He is a member of the Wildlife Society, the Ecological Society of America, and the American Ornithologists' Union. He received his Ph.D. from Oklahoma State University in July 2004 and his MS from Southern Illinois University's Cooperative Wildlife Research Laboratory in 1998. *Steve J. DeMaso* is the Upland Game Bird Program Leader for the Texas Parks and Wildlife Department in Austin, Texas. Prior to moving to Texas, he worked for the Oklahoma Department of Wildlife Conservation and served as the lead researcher on the nationally recognized Packsaddle Quail Research Project. Currently, Steve serves as Chairman of the Southeast Quail Study Group and a member of the National Wild Turkey Federation's Technical Committee. Steve is a member of the National and Texas Chapters of The Wildlife Society. Steve also served as the Program Chairman and Editor for the Proceedings of the Fifth National Quail Symposium. Steve was raised in southern Michigan and received his B.S. from Michigan State University, M.S. from Texas A&I University, and is currently pursuing a Ph.D. in the Wildlife and Fisheries Sciences Joint Program between Texas A&M University and Texas A&M–Kingsville. *Fred S. Guthery* is the Bollenbach Chair in Wildlife Ecology at Oklahoma State University, where he studies upland game birds. He received his MS and Ph.D. degrees from Texas A&M University, and has worked at the Caesar Kleberg Wildlife Research Institute.

SURVIVAL OF SUPPLEMENTALLY STOCKED EASTERN WILD TURKEYS IN EAST TEXAS

R. Montague Whiting, Jr.
Arthur Temple College of Forestry,
Stephen F. Austin State University,
Nacogdoches, TX 75962, USA

Jimmy D. Kelly[1]
Arthur Temple College of Forestry,
Stephen F. Austin State University,
Nacogdoches, TX 75962, USA

Brian P. Oswald
Arthur Temple College of Forestry,
Stephen F. Austin State University,
Nacogdoches, TX 75962, USA

Michael S. Fountain
Arthur Temple College of Forestry,
Stephen F. Austin State University,
Nacogdoches, TX 75962, USA

Abstract: We evaluated survival of supplementally stocked eastern wild turkeys (*Meleagris gallopavo silvestris*) as impacted by home range overlap with previously stocked eastern wild turkeys. In early 1994, 60 wild-trapped eastern wild turkeys were radio-tagged and released in the Pineywoods Region of east Texas. In early 1997, 80 additional turkeys were released at the same sites. In both years, equal numbers of birds were from the midwestern and southeastern United States. In 1994 and 1997, male:female sex ratios were 1:4 and 1:3, respectively. Surviving turkeys were regularly radio-located from 1 March 1997 to 30 June 1999. We used CALHOME to construct size and shape of each turkey's home range during 1 March–30 June 1997 (spring), 1 July–31 October 1997 (summer), and 1 November 1997–28 February 1998 (winter). We used ArcView (Environmental Systems Research Institute, Redlands, California, USA) to overlay home ranges of 1997 turkeys with those of 1994 birds and static territorial interaction to measure percent overlap. For 1997 turkeys, we regressed percent home range overlap with survival in days for spring, summer, winter, and the entire study period. Regardless of broodstock source, home range overlap and survival were positively correlated ($P \leq 0.05$) for both sexes during spring and for females during winter and the entire study period; there were no correlations ($P > 0.05$) between variables during summer. These results suggest survival of recently released turkeys increases as home range overlap with birds familiar with the habitat increases.

Proceedings of the National Wild Turkey Symposium 9:143–148
Key words: East Texas, eastern wild turkeys, *Meleagris gallopavo silvestris*, supplemental stocking, survival.

Wild turkeys populations in the United States began to decline prior to 1900 and reached their lowest levels in the 1930s (Mosby 1975). Eastern wild turkeys were naturally occurring in east Texas, and their decline paralleled that of the birds nationwide (Newman 1945). Since the 1940s, strict game laws, reforestation, and re-introduction programs have been instrumental in increasing turkey populations throughout much of the nation. However, early restoration attempts in east Texas resulted in limited success or complete failure. Pen-raised eastern wild turkeys lacked parental influence and suffered a high intolerance to disease (Bailey and Putman 1979, Schorr et al.

1988). The Rio Grande (*M. g. intermedia*) and Florida (*M. g. osceola*) subspecies did not adapt well to the east Texas environment (Boyd and Oglesby 1975). Research in the late 1970s demonstrated that it was necessary to use wild-trapped eastern wild turkeys for successful restoration (Hopkins 1981, Campo 1983).

As a result of this research, the Texas Parks and Wildlife Department (TPWD) began using wild-trapped eastern wild turkeys in its restoration program. Between 1987 and 2000, over 7,200 turkeys were re-

[1] Present address: U.S. Army Corps of Engineers, P.O. Box 17300, Fort Worth, TX 76102, USA.

leased in east Texas (J. D. Burk, TPWD, unpublished data). In 1994, TPWD initiated a program to evaluate survival and reproduction of introduced eastern wild turkeys. In the Pineywoods Region, turkeys were monitored at 4 release sites in Tyler County near Woodville, Texas; these sites were classified as marginal turkey habitat (J. D. Burk, TPWD, personal communication). Fifteen wild-trapped eastern wild turkeys equipped with backpack style radio transmitters were released at each site during January and February of 1994. Turkeys from the Midwest (primarily Iowa) and the Southeast (primarily Georgia) were released in approximately equal numbers at each site while maintaining a sex ratio of 4 females to 1 male. Radio-telemetry was used to monitor movement, survival, and reproduction of the turkeys after their release in February of 1994 (George 1997).

In 1997, TPWD began the second phase of the restoration program. This phase included supplementally stocking release sites on which the original restocking efforts were classified as unsuccessful. All 4 Tyler County sites were so classified. Therefore, TPWD released turkeys at the same sites used in the 1994 release.

Backs and Eisfelder (1990) questioned the value of supplementally stocking wild turkeys in marginal habitats. However, Bailey (1967) stated that turkeys exhibit imitative behavior and that the flock is a well-coordinated group that functions as an individual. If this is true, the assumption can be made that newly released turkeys which share home ranges and probably associate with turkeys already established in an area survive better than those that do not. The objectives of this study was to determine if turkeys released in 1997 shared home ranges with surviving 1994 birds and if there were differences in seasonal and long-term survival of 1997 turkeys that shared home ranges and those that did not. We also compared survival values of southeastern turkeys released in 1997 to those of midwestern birds released in 1997 and between turkeys released in 1994 and turkeys released in 1997.

STUDY AREA

The Pineywoods Ecological Region of Texas is bordered on the south by the Gulf Prairies and Marshes, on the west by the Post-oak Savanna Region, and on the east and north by Arkansas, Louisiana, and Oklahoma (Gould 1962). The land is gently rolling to flat with acidic to highly acidic, sandy and sandy loam soils. Loblolly (*Pinus taeda*), longleaf (*P. palustris),* and shortleaf pines (*P. echinata*), oaks (*Quercus* spp.), magnolias (*Magnolia* spp.), elms (*Ulmus* spp.), hickories (*Carya* spp.), maples (*Acer* spp.), and sweetgum (*Liquidambar styraciflua*) were common overstory and midstory tree species (Simpson 1988). Tyler County received approximately 125 cm of rainfall annually and is 33 to 135 m above sea level. The major industry was forest products; other industries involved livestock and chickens (Kingston 1992).

METHODS

Data Collection

In January and February of 1997, TPWD released at least 20 turkeys at each site used in the 1994 stocking. Approximately equal numbers of southeastern and midwestern turkeys were released on each site while maintaining a sex ratio of 15 females to 5 males. Releases were completed by 25 February 1997. At that time, 21 of the 60 turkeys from the 1994 release were being radio-located: 12 from southeastern broodstock (9 females and 3 males) and 9 females from midwestern broodstock.

Prior to release, the gender and age of each turkey was determined. Each turkey was then fitted with a leg band and a radio transmitter. Transmitters were equipped with a mortality switch (12-hour timed activation) and attached with a backpack style harness (Williams et al. 1968). Radio-locating of the birds began immediately after release. Turkeys that died of stress-related causes during the first 2 weeks after release were removed from the databases.

Each turkey was radio-located a minimum of 2 times per week in the spring and early summer and once a week during the remainder of the year. Radio-locating was accomplished using a truck-mounted Yagi antenna, hand-held receivers, and a network of predetermined listening stations established for the 1994 study. Additional stations were added as needed. The compass reading in the direction of peak transmitter signal strength from a station was assumed to be the correct azimuth to the transmitter's location. If possible, a minimum of 2 azimuths were recorded for each bird every day that is was radio-located. Two or more daily azimuths documented a particular bird's location whereas a single daily azimuth documented survival only. If a bird was not radio-located for 3 weeks, it was classified as missing. Missing birds were searched for on a continuous basis, and periodic aerial searches were conducted in an attempt to locate them. If a mortality signal was received, the transmitter was recovered. Surviving turkeys were radio-located through 30 June 1999.

Telemetry Error

To evaluate telemetry accuracy, radio transmitters were placed at known locations around the study sites. Error testing was conducted in the springs of 1998 and 1999. Field technicians rotated duties as transmitter hiders and transmitter trackers in an attempt to make the process blind. True azimuths from a known station to the known location of the transmitter were compared to recorded azimuths and a mean error was calculated.

Home Ranges

We used the computer program CALHOME (U.S. Forest Service Pacific Southwest Research Station, Fresno, California, USA) to construct home ranges of 1994 and 1997 turkeys. Three parts of the CALHOME program were used: LOCATE (established locations), SELECT (created a file for an individual turkey from a file that contained data for multiple birds), and CAL-HOME, which constructed the home range shape (95% minimum convex polygon) and size (ha ± SE) for each turkey. If there were less than 5 locations for an individual bird during a given time period, that bird was removed from analyses for that time period. Like-wise, if there were less than 20 locations, CALHOME did not exclude any locations, but obvious outliers were manually removed (e.g., Kelly 2001:22). We used *t*-tests to compare home range sizes of turkeys released in 1997 by origin and sex.

The SELECT and CALHOME files were down-loaded as ArcInfo (Environmental Systems Research Institute, Redlands, California, USA) GIS databases where each file was converted with a "generate" and "build" command. After generating and building the files, each could be viewed in ArcView as a theme. The SELECT files were viewed as points, each point representing the radio-location of an individual turkey on a tracking day. The CALHOME files were viewed as a polygon representing the home range of the turkey during the selected time period. Themes in ArcView could be viewed independently or simultaneously, dis-playing the points and polygons for individual birds or overlaying themes for multiple birds at the same time.

Using the ArcInfo GIS database, the seasonal home ranges of 1997 birds were overlain on those of 1994 birds. Then an "intersect themes" command was used to calculate the area (ha) of each bird's home range and of the overlapped portion of the home rang-es. Static territorial interaction (White and Garrott 1990) was used to determine the percentage of over-lap. If the home range of a specific turkey overlapped the home range of more than 1 other bird, we used the highest percent overlap. We assumed that if the sur-vival of a 1997 turkey was affected by sharing its home range with that of a 1994 turkey, the affect would be evident during the first year after release. Therefore, we examined the impact of home range overlap during the first spring (1 Mar–30 Jun 1997), summer (1 Jul–31 Oct 1997), and winter (1 Nov 1997–28 Feb 1998) of the study.

Survival

We summed the number of days each turkey sur-vived each season and for the entire study period. A turkey that did not survive an entire season was de-leted from the files for the following seasons. For each season, we regressed percent home range overlap with survival in days. We also regressed seasonal home range overlap with survival in days during the entire study period. We performed regressions using home range overlap of 1997 turkeys with 1994 birds as well as overlap of 1997 turkeys with each other.

We calculated survival rates for turkeys released in 1997 using the Kaplan-Meier product-limit method (Kaplan and Meier 1958, Sall and Lehman 1996), the same method used in the 1994 study (George 1997). We compared seasonal (i.e., spring, summer, and win-

ter 1997–1998 and 1998–1999 and spring 1999) and cumulative survival rates (i.e., for duration of the 28-month study) between broodstock sources of supple-mentally stocked turkeys using chi-square log-rank tests. Finally, we compared cumulative survival rates of the 1994 turkeys to those of 1997 turkeys using the computer program CONTRAST, a chi-square analysis with multiple comparisons (Hines and Sauer 1989). CONTRAST was used because survival rates and var-iances of the 1994 turkeys were taken from George's 1997 study, not calculated in Kaplan-Meier, and CON-TRAST provides a non-biased chi-square analysis.

RESULTS

The mean error for telemetry in this study was $0.00 \pm 2.97°$ ($n = 18$) with a range of $-25°$ to $+22°$. A mean of $0.00°$ indicates that the recorded azimuths were not biased, but the wide range of errors indicates relatively poor precision. Because this study focused mainly on comparisons of radio-telemetry data and the error was distributed evenly throughout the data, the precision of the telemetry locations was considered ac-ceptable.

Survival

Regressions of Survival with Percent Home Range Overlap

Regardless of broodstock source or sex, survival in days of 1997 turkeys was positively related to per-cent overlap of their home ranges with those of 1994 turkeys during the first spring after release (Table 1). Likewise, home range overlap during spring was re-lated to survival during the entire study period for fe-males with broodstock sources pooled and for mid-western females. Conversely, during summer, there was no relationship between percent home range over-lap and survival regardless of broodstock source or sex. Winter home range overlap was related to survival of females as a group during the winter season and for the entire study period (Table 1).

When home ranges of 1997 turkeys were overlain with each other, the relationships were similar with the following exceptions: spring home range overlap was not related to survival in days of southeastern females during spring or midwestern females during the entire study period. Also, home range overlap did not in-crease survival of females as a group during winter or the entire study period (Table 2).

Survival of Supplementally Stocked Turkeys

For the 28-month study period, survival probabil-ities of females and males released in 1997 were 0.754 and 0.350, respectively (Kelly 2001:36). By season, survival probabilities of females were 18 to 66% high-er than those of males (Kelly 2001:37). However, due to the difference in numbers of females and males, survival probabilities were not statistically compared between sexes. No differences in survival probabilities

Table 1.   The relationship of percent overlap of home ranges of restocked and supplementally stocked eastern wild turkeys on survival (in days) of the supplementally stocked turkeys in east Texas. Home range overlap was calculated by season (spring: 1 Mar–30 Jun 1997; summer: 1 Jul–31 Oct 1997; winter: 1 Nov 1997–28 Feb 1998). Survival was computed for the same seasons and the entire study period (1 Mar 1997–30 Jun 1999). For the 1994 restocking and 1997 supplemental stocking, equal numbers of turkeys were relocated from southeastern and midwestern states.

Population	N	Season Home range	Survival	R^2	P
All females	57	Spring	Spring	0.2005	<0.001
		Spring	Study period	0.1280	0.005
	45	Summer	Summer	0.0004	0.897
		Summer	Study period	0.0001	0.952
	42	Winter	Winter	0.1127	0.030
		Winter	Study period	0.0905	0.028
All males[a]	19	Spring	Spring	0.2428	0.032
		Spring	Study period	0.0155	0.612
	13	Summer	Summer	0.0960	0.303
		Summer	Study period	0.0271	0.591
		Winter	Winter	0.3403	0.099
		Winter	Study period	0.2651	0.156
Southeastern females	29	Spring	Spring	0.1970	0.016
		Spring	Study period	0.0673	0.174
	22	Summer	Summer	0.0341	0.399
		Summer	Study period	0.0344	0.408
	20	Winter	Winter	0.0843	0.214
		Winter	Study period	0.1753	0.066
Midwestern females	28	Spring	Spring	0.2217	0.011
		Spring	Study period	0.2472	0.007
	23	Summer	Summer	0.0730	0.213
		Summer	Study period	0.0341	0.399
	22	Winter	Winter	0.0350	0.404
		Winter	Study period	0.0607	0.269

[a] Southeastern and midwestern males not separately evaluated due to small sample sizes.

Table 2.   The relationship of percent overlap of home range of supplementally stocked eastern wild turkeys on survival (in days) in east Texas. Home range overlap was calculated by season (spring: 1 Mar–30 Jun 1997; summer: 1 Jul–31 Oct 1997; winter: 1 Nov 1997–28 Feb 1998). Survival was computed for the same seasons and the entire study period (1 Mar 1997–30 June 1999). Approximately equal numbers of turkeys were relocated from southeastern and midwestern states.

Population	N	Season Home range	Survival	R^2	P
All females	57	Spring	Spring	0.1486	0.003
		Spring	Study period	0.0815	0.031
	45	Summer	Summer	0.0240	0.310
		Summer	Study period	0.0006	0.874
	42	Winter	Winter	0.0099	0.530
		Winter	Study period	0.0296	0.277
All males[a]	19	Spring	Spring	0.3950	0.005
		Spring	Study period	0.0324	0.226
	13	Summer	Summer	0.2540	0.086
		Summer	Study period	0.0690	0.386
	9	Winter	Winter	0.0446	0.586
		Winter	Study period	0.0330	0.640
Southeastern females	29	Spring	Spring	0.1281	0.057
		Spring	Study period	0.0458	0.265
	22	Summer	Summer	0.0314	0.430
		Summer	Study period	0.0100	0.658
	20	Winter	Winter	0.1287	0.120
		Winter	Study period	0.1434	0.093
Midwestern females	28	Spring	Spring	0.1691	0.030
		Spring	Study period	0.1263	0.064
	23	Summer	Summer	0.0314	0.571
		Summer	Study period	0.0437	0.781
	22	Winter	Winter	0.0580	0.280
		Winter	Study period	0.0001	0.960

[a] Southeastern and midwestern males were not separately evaluated due to small sample sizes.

were detected between broodstock origins or between southeastern and midwestern males or females for any season (Kelly 2001:38) or for the entire study period (Kelly 2001:39). Although there was no difference in survival of adult southeastern and midwestern turkeys for the entire study period, midwestern juveniles had higher survival than did southeastern juveniles (Kelly 2001:39). Finally, there was no difference between survival probabilities of turkeys released as adults (0.352 ± 0.065, $n = 54$) and those released as juveniles (0.483 ± 0.093, $n = 29$, $\chi^2 = 1.333$, df $= 1$, $P = 0.248$).

Comparisons of Restocked and Supplementally Stocked Turkeys

There was no difference in cumulative 28-month survival of southeastern 1994 and 1997 broodstock ($\chi^2 = 2.803$, df $= 1$, $P = 0.094$), or 1994 and 1997 midwestern broodstock ($\chi^2 = 0.510$, df $= 1$, $P = 0.475$). Likewise, cumulative survival did not differ between 1994 and 1997 southeastern females ($\chi^2 = 0.328$, df $= 1$, $P = 0.567$) or between 1994 and 1997 midwestern females ($\chi^2 = 0.335$, df $= 1$, $P = 0.563$); however, 1994 southeastern males had a higher survival rate (0.833 ± 0.152) than that of 1997 southeastern males (0.200 ± 0.127) ($\chi^2 = 10.213$, df $= 1$, $P = 0.001$). No 1994 midwestern males survived until the end of George's (1997) study; survival of midwestern males released in 1997 was 0.200 ± 0.127 ($\chi^2 = 5.050$, df $= 1$, $P = 0.025$).

DISCUSSION

There was a general trend of increased survival of 1997 turkeys as overlap of their home ranges with those of 1994 turkeys increased. However, the impact of that relationship was most important during the first season (spring) after release. Newly released turkeys lacked familiarity with the habitat and contact with birds that had lived in the area for several years probably aided the 1997 birds in predator avoidance, food gathering, and roost site selection.

Our data indicate that increased overlap was more important to female survival than male survival, and most important to survival of midwestern females. Midwestern turkeys were not only unfamiliar with the habitat, but also with the habitat type. George (1997) documented long distance movements by several midwestern turkeys shortly after release and hypothesized that they were searching for familiar habitat. Also, a 1994 midwestern male was legally taken by a hunter about 80 km north of where it was released 5 years earlier. None of the 1997 midwestern turkeys made such movements, which suggests that contact with 1994 birds reduced wandering. Although 5 southeastern and 8 midwestern turkeys were missing when the study ended, we recorded no long distance movements similar to those documented by George (1997).

Lack of a relationship between home range overlap and survival during the first summer was most likely due to breeding behavior. Behavior of female turkeys changes drastically when they begin searching for nest sites. They disperse from the winter range and avoid other females (Healy 1992), and males range widely, seeking females. We found no evidence that 32 of the 56 females released in 1997 attempted to nest the first spring/summer. However, some of these females probably were physiologically in the nesting mode, thus avoiding other females.

By winter 1997, most surviving 1997 turkeys were in small flocks. Home range overlap during winter did increase survival of females, but not when the birds were separated by broodstock source, likely because of reduced sample sizes. Regardless, our results indicate that home ranges shared by supplementally stocked and previously stocked turkeys benefits survival of the supplementally stocked birds and that turkeys unfamiliar with the habitat type gain greater benefits than those familiar with it.

Kelly (2001) used home range overlap as a measure of association. If the home range of a 1997 turkey overlapped that of a 1994 turkey by at least 68%, he classified the 1997 turkey as associating with the 1994 bird. Although he found no differences in survival of associating and non-associating turkeys, the number and percentage of 1997 females that associated with 1994 birds increased each of the first 3 seasons. During the first spring, 4 of 7 adult males were classified as associating whereas none of the 12 juveniles were so classified. He hypothesized that dominant males remained in the vicinity of females whereas subdominant males, primarily juveniles, dispersed into habitats with few or no radio-tagged females (Kelly 2001).

Although home range sizes of 1997 females did not differ by origin in any season, sizes did decline each season after release. Over the first 3 seasons after release, average home range sizes of southeastern and midwestern females declined from 957 to 668 ha (30%) and 1251 to 563 ha (55%), respectively. These results parallel those of George (1997) and demonstrate that released turkeys settle into smaller home ranges as they become familiar with the habitat. George (1997) also found that resident females had smaller home ranges than restocked females. In this study, average home range sizes of 1994 females were at least 25% smaller than those of 1997 females each season (Kelly 2001).

As with George's (1997) study, cumulative survival values of southeastern (0.452 ± 0.089) and midwestern (0.469 ± 0.088) 1997 females were similar; these values are similar to those of his study. However, George (1997) recorded better survival of southeastern males and poorer survival of midwestern males than found in our study. In both studies, male sample sizes were relatively small, thus comparisons must be viewed with caution. Regardless, survival rates of females in both studies were similar to those recorded in other studies (Hopkins 1981, Campo 1983) and are considered acceptable (George 1997).

In restocking efforts, survival is critical, but so is reproduction. In this study, the supplementally stocked females had very poor reproductive success. During the 3-year study, 128 females entered a nesting season.

They produced 95 known or assumed nests of which 90 were abandoned or depredated. Two females were depredated as their eggs hatched, thus only 3 clutches were successful and only 2 poults definitely fledged. These findings suggest that due to poor reproduction, Backs and Eisfelder's (1990) reservations about supplementally stocking wild turkeys in marginal habitats are correct.

ACKNOWLEDGMENTS

This study was funded by TPWD and the Arthur Temple College of Forestry. We thank International Paper Company, Louisiana Pacific Corporation, Temple-Inland Forest Products Corporation, and numerous individuals for granting access to their lands. We are especially grateful to Temple-Inland for providing overnight lodging and to R. Woods for his regular assistance. H. Bragg, J. Hoffman, J. Laing, and R. Mangham aided in data collection. R. Bates, B. Bishop, and P. Siska provided GIS assistance, and L. Whiting typed the manuscript.

LITERATURE CITED

Backs, S. E., and C. H. Eisfelder. 1990. Criteria and guidelines for wild turkey release priorities in Indiana. Proceedings of the National Wild Turkey Symposium 6:134–143.

Bailey, R. W. 1967. Behavior. Pages 93–112 in O. H. Hewitt, editor. The wild turkey and its management. The Wildlife Society, Washington, D. C., USA.

———, and D. J. Putnam. 1979. The 1979 turkey restoration survey. Turkey Call 6:28–30.

Boyd, C. E., and R. D. Oglesby. 1975. Status of wild turkey restoration in east Texas. Proceedings of the National Wild Turkey Symposium 3:14–21.

Campo, J. J. 1983. Brood habitat use, reproduction, and movement of recently restocked eastern wild turkeys in east Texas. Dissertation, Texas A&M University, College Station, Texas, USA.

George, J. R. 1997. Survival, reproduction, and movements of supplementally stocked eastern wild turkeys in the Pineywoods Region of Texas. Thesis, Stephen F. Austin State University, Nacogdoches, Texas, USA.

Gould, F. W. 1962. Texas plants—a checklist and ecological summary.
Texas Agricultural Experiment Station, College Station, Texas, USA.

Healy, W. M. 1992. Behavior. Pages 46–65 in J. G. Dickson, editor. The wild turkey: biology and management. Stackpole Books, Harrisburg, Pennsylvania, USA.

Hines, J. E., and J. R. Sauer. 1989. Program CONTRAST—a general program of the analysis of several survival or recovery rate estimates. U.S. Fish and Wildlife Service Technical Report 24.

Hopkins, C. R. 1981. Dispersal, reproduction, mortality, and habitat utilization of restocked eastern turkeys in east Texas. Dissertation, Texas A&M University, College Station, Texas, USA.

Kaplan, E. L., and P. Meier. 1958. Nonparametric estimation from incomplete observations. Journal of the American Statistical Association 53:457–481.

Kelly, J. D. 2001. The effects of supplemental stocking of eastern wild turkeys in the Pineywoods Ecological Region of east Texas. Thesis, Stephen F. Austin State University, Nacogdoches, Texas, USA.

Kingston, M. 1992. Texas almanac and state industrial guide. The Dallas Morning News, Dallas, Texas, USA.

Mosby, H. S. 1975. The status of the wild turkey in 1974. Proceedings of the National Wild Turkey Symposium 3:22–26.

Newman, C. C. 1945. Turkey restocking efforts in east Texas. Journal of Wildlife Management 9:279–289.

Sall, J., and A. Lehman. 1996. JMP start statistics. Duxbury Press, Belmont, California, USA.

Schorr, L. F., W. R. Davidson, V. F. Nettles, J. E. Kennamer, P. Villegas, and H. W. Yoder. 1988. A survey of parasites and diseases of pen-reared wild turkeys. Proceedings of the Annual Conference of the Southeastern Association of Fish and Wildlife Agencies 42:315–328.

Simpson, B. J. 1988. A field guide to Texas trees. Gulf Publishing, Houston, Texas, USA.

White, G. C., and R. A. Garrott. 1990. Analysis of wildlife radio-tracking data. Academic Press, San Diego, California, USA.

Williams, L. E., Jr., D. H. Austin, N. F. Eichholz, T. E. Peoples, and R. W. Phillips. 1968. A study of nesting turkeys in southern Florida. Proceedings of the Southeastern Association of Game and Fish Commissioners 22:16–30.

R. Montague Whiting, Jr. (center) earned a BS in forestry from Auburn University, a MS in watershed management from the University of Arizona, and the Ph.D. in Forest Science on the cooperative Texas A&M—Stephen F. Austin State University program. He joined the faculty of the College of Forestry at SFASU in 1972 and retired as Professor Emeritus in 2002. At SFASU, he taught a variety of forestry and wildlife courses and conducted research on game and nongame birds. ***Jimmy D. Kelly (not pictured)*** earned a bachelor and master of science in forest wildlife from SFASU in 1997 and 2001, respectively. This paper is based on his MS thesis. Jimmy is currently a wildlife biologist with the NRCS in central Texas. ***Brian P. Oswald (left)*** is Professor of Forestry in the Arthur Temple College of Forestry and Agriculture, SFASU. Winner of the SAF's 2002 Carl A. Schenck award for outstanding forestry education, he obtained his degrees from the University of Idaho (Ph.D.), Northern Arizona University (MS) and Michigan State University (BS). Brian is a board member of the Association for Fire Ecology. ***Michael S. Fountain (right)*** is the Associate Dean and the Laurence C. Walker Distinguished Professor in the Arthur Temple College of Forestry and Agriculture, SFASU. He obtained a bachelor and master of science in forestry from SFASU and Ph.D. in silviculture/ecology from West Virginia Unviersity. Current research/teaching fields are silviculture and dendrology.

MOVEMENT, FIDELITY AND DISPERSAL OF RIO GRANDE WILD TURKEYS IN THE TEXAS PANHANDLE

Richard S. Phillips[1]
Department of Range, Wildlife and Fisheries
Management, Mail Stop 2125,
Texas Tech University,
Lubbock, TX 79413, USA

Warren B. Ballard
Department of Range, Wildlife and Fisheries
Management, Mail Stop 2125,
Texas Tech University,
Lubbock, TX 79413, USA

Mark C. Wallace
Department of Range, Wildlife and Fisheries
Management, Mail Stop 2125,
Texas Tech University,
Lubbock, TX 79413, USA

Derrick P. Holdstock
Texas Parks and Wildlife Department,
Gene Howe Wildlife Management Area,
Canadian, TX 79014, USA

Brian L. Spears[2]
Department of Range, Wildlife and Fisheries
Management, Mail Stop 2125,
Texas Tech University,
Lubbock, TX 79413, USA

Michael S. Miller
Texas Parks and Wildlife Department,
Tarleton State University,
Stephenville, TX 76402, USA

John H. Brunjes
Department of Range, Wildlife and Fisheries
Management, Mail Stop 2125,
Texas Tech University,
Lubbock, TX 79413, USA

Stephen J. DeMaso
Texas Parks and Wildlife Department,
4200 Smith School Road,
Austin, TX 78744, USA

Abstract: Wild turkey (*Meleagris gallopavo*) studies have traditionally focused on factors associated with population change from within the population. Consequently, movement into and out of turkey populations is poorly understood. From 2000–2002, we monitored 554 Rio Grande wild turkeys (*M. g. intermedia*) at 3 sites in the Texas Panhandle to determine the pattern, prevalence, composition and importance of movements among winter roosts. The majority (85.6%) of all monitored birds exhibited winter range fidelity. Differences among age and sex classes existed. Adult females exhibited the highest winter range fidelity (96.7%), while yearling females exhibited the lowest (62.5%). Further, yearling females were responsible for the majority of permanent movements away from winter roosts (dispersal). For both residents and dispersers, winter was the season of least movement, while dispersers exhibited the greatest movement during spring. We found no evidence of decreased survival or productivity between yearling dispersers and yearling residents. Our findings suggest yearling females may play an important role in connecting relatively disjunct winter roost populations.

Proceedings of the National Wild Turkey Symposium 9:149–157

Key words: dispersal, emigration, *Meleagris gallopavo intermedia*, movement, nesting, Rio Grande wild turkey, Rolling Plains, survival, yearling.

Leopold suggested some local game populations are dependent upon immigrants from other populations for their continued existence as well as for expansion of species distributions (Leopold 1933). Recent ecological paradigms (e.g., island biogeography and meta-population dynamics) emphasize the importance of movement among populations and have found their primary application in conservation biology (Hanski 1997). Dispersal of individuals has rarely been examined in North American game species even though dispersal among populations may influence sustainable harvest rates at larger scales (McCullough 1996). Although genetics data on wild turkey suggests little interchange among flocks even at the local level (Boone and Rhodes 1996), little work has addressed the role of movements of individuals between winter roosts of wild turkeys.

Studies on wild turkeys have generally focused on localized movements (Brown 1980) and documented larger home ranges for yearling females than adult females (Schmutz and Braun 1989, Hoffman 1991, Badyaev et al. 1996). Several studies on Rio Grande turkeys have documented longer straight-line distances traveled from winter to summer ranges by juvenile (yearling) females compared with adults (Schmutz and Braun 1989, Stevens 1989, Miller et al. 1995). Such distances may represent migration (a roundtrip movement with return to the origin) or dispersal (a one-way movement without return). Classifying these movements as migration or dispersal is contingent upon defining some aspect of range fidelity (White and Garrott 1990).

While studies have assessed wild turkey fidelity to nesting ranges (Everett et al. 1979, Badyaev and Faust 1996), few studies have addressed winter range fidelity. Early studies documented high winter roost fidelity (Thomas et al. 1966, Smith 1975) with migratory movements from winter to summer ranges (Thomas et al. 1973). However, several studies suggested that yearling females may play a key role in movement among winter roost sites and population expansion (Thomas et al. 1966, Logan 1970, Brown 1980, Healy 1992).

In the majority of bird species, females disperse more frequently than males (Greenwood 1980). From the population perspective, however, dispersal is significant only if dispersers effectively contribute to subsequent generations. Studies suggest decreased survival (Murray 1967) and/or decreased reproductive output (Danchin and Cam 2002) may be costs associated with dispersal. Such dispersal costs may explain some of the extreme variation in both survival and reproductive rates in yearling wild turkey females (see Vangilder 1992). Further, such costs may explain low rates of genetic interchange among local flocks (Boone and Rhodes 1996).

We are unaware of any studies empirically ex-

ploring movement among winter roosts, dispersal patterns or subsequent costs or benefits to wild turkeys that disperse. Given the patchy distribution of Rio Grande wild turkeys over western portions of their native range, an understanding of these types of movements could influence the scale at which management occurs. The presence or absence of dispersers in Rio Grande wild turkey populations may (1) reveal disjunct populations of turkeys connected by long-distance movements by relatively few individuals, (2) provide information on the expansion of populations through winter roost colonization, and (3) explain some of the variation associated with survival and nesting rates in the yearling cohort of Rio Grande wild turkeys.

Objectives of our study were to (1) assess age and sex-specific movement patterns for Rio Grande wild turkey and (2) examine the influence of these movement patterns on survival and reproduction. We predicted yearling females would move greater straight-line distances and constitute the majority of dispersers. Further, we predicted yearling females that dispersed would experience decreased survival and decreased reproductive success. To test these predictions, we evaluated (1) straight-line distances from winter roost to subsequent roosts both within and among years, (2) proportion of birds exhibiting winter site fidelity, (3) proportion of dispersers, and (4) survival and nesting rates of residents versus dispersers.

STUDY AREA

We collected data at 3 study sites along riparian corridors in the Texas Panhandle near the western edge of Rio Grande wild turkey distribution in Texas (Beasom and Wilson 1992). All 3 study sites were located in the Rolling Plains of Texas and were characterized by narrow, wooded riparian corridors surrounded by mixed grass prairie. Predominant land use was cattle production with varied amounts of both irrigated and non-irrigated agriculture. Riparian species along main waterways and tributaries consisted primarily of hackberry (*Celtis* spp.), black locust (*Robinia pseudo-acacia*), honey locust (*Gleditsia triacanthos*), western soapberry (*Sapindus drummondi*) and cottonwoods (*Populus deltoides*). Both Russian olive (*Eleagnus angustifolia*) and honey mesquite (*Prosopis glandulosa*) trees were also common. Spears et al. (2002) provide detailed descriptions of vegetation types at each study site.

Gene Howe Wildlife Management Area (GHWMA), along the Canadian River near Canadian, Texas, served as the northernmost site (35°57′00″N, 100°17′45″W), while Matador Wildlife Management Area (MWMA), the southern-most site, was located north of Paducah, Texas, along the Pease River (34°07′30″N, 100°02′45″W). The third site was located on private lands along the Salt Fork of the Red River (Salt Fork) between Clarendon and Hedley, Texas (35°02′00″N, 100°37′30″W).

¹ E-mail: Richard.Phillips@ttu.edu
² Present address: U.S. Fish and Wildlife Service, 11103 E. Montgomery Drive, National Wildlife Refuge, Spokane, WA 99206, USA.

METHODS

Capture

We captured Rio Grande wild turkeys using drop nets, rocket nets, and walk-in funnel traps baited with milo or corn (Glazner 1964, Bailey 1980) during winters 2000–2002. We determined sex and age (adult vs. yearling) of all captured birds using methods described by Williams (1961). We attached 95-g backpack-style radio transmitters with 8-hour mortality switches (Model # A1155 Advanced Telemetry Systems, Isanti, Minnesota, USA) to birds using 6-mm nylon over-braid rubber harness cord. Each year, between January and March, we captured Rio Grande wild turkeys at each of the 3 study sites to maintain approximately 15 yearling females, 10 yearling males, 35 adult females and 15 adult males for a total of 75 telemetered birds per site. We reclassified yearlings as adults during January of their second winter.

Monitoring

Each year, we located marked birds ≥2 times per week between capture date and August and once weekly from August to December. We used vehicle-mounted 4-element null-peak Yagi antenna systems to triangulate turkey locations. To estimate system biases for vehicle-mounted null peak systems, we triangulated test transmitters in known locations to determine errors (7.5° to 10.6°) associated with location estimates.

We also recorded all visual observations and, using handheld 3-element Yagi antennas, employed homing techniques (White and Garrott 1990) to locate nests and to make direct observations of turkeys. All visual locations were recorded using handheld Global Positioning System receivers.

Movement Terminology

Three general types of movements are often addressed in wildlife studies: (1) localized movements, (2) migration, and (3) dispersal (White and Garrott 1990, Kernohan et al. 2001). Localized movements refer to movements within home ranges or core use areas (Laundré et al. 1987). Migration is defined as a two-way movement from one established range to another with subsequent return and is often associated with seasons (Arguedas and Parker 2000). Dispersal is defined as a one-way movement from an established area to another area without return and with no predetermined direction (Schroeder and Boag 1988, Schwartz and Franzmann 1992). For our study, residents were birds that exhibited winter range fidelity. Dispersers were birds that did not exhibit winter range fidelity for consecutive years.

Analyses

To determine winter range fidelity and consequently resident or disperser status, we used both autumn and winter locations to calculate 100% minimum convex polygons (MCP) using ArcView (Version 3.3, Environmental Systems Research Institute, Redlands, California, USA) and the Animal Movement program extension (Hooge et al. 1999). We considered any degree of overlap between winter MCP range in $year_x$ and range in $year_{x+i}$ winter range fidelity. We categorized birds exhibiting permanent winter range shifts as dispersers, while those that did not were classified as residents.

Wild turkeys that did not survive the entire year (or long enough to calculate 2 winter ranges) were classified as residents or dispersers based upon movement criteria established from those with known fates. We calculated 2 types of straight-line distances between individual turkey roost locations to assess movement: consecutive and displacement. Average consecutive distances represented the average distance moved among all locations for a given bird during a given season. These distances were used to estimate the season of greatest movement. Displacement distances represented maximum distance from the first to the last known roost location for each individual turkey within 1 year. These distances were used to assess range shifts.

Survival Analyses

We included turkeys relocated ≥1 time/week in survival analyses between movement classifications. Using the SAS function PROC PHREG (SAS Institute 1999), we calculated annual survival curves using the Cox proportional-hazards model with 95% confidence intervals using movement classification (resident vs. disperser) as the single variable. We right-censored individual turkeys once they reached the adult classification (1 Jan of subsequent year).

Nesting Analyses

We used locations during the nesting season to determine possible nesting hens. We confirmed nesting attempts by visual observation of incubating hens or evidence of eggs upon investigation of mortalities. We considered a nest successful if ≥1 egg in a clutch hatched (Badyaev 1995). Yearling nests were classified as dispersers only for those attempted during the year of actual dispersal.

All statistical analyses were conducted using the computer program SAS (SAS Institute 1999). Parametric tests were conducted using PROC ANOVA. Kruskal-Wallis nonparametric tests were performed using PROC NONPAR procedure (Conover 1999, SAS Institute 1999). Friedman's tests were conducted by ranking variables by group (PROC RANK) and then performing analysis of variance (PROC ANOVA) on the ranked values (Conover 1999, SAS Institute 1999). *F*-values produced by SAS approximated those values produced by Friedman's test (SAS Institute 1999). Chi-square tests for independence were used to assess proportional differences between and among groups (Zar 1999). Significance was assessed at the α = 0.05 level for all tests. In cases where main effects justified further analysis, mean or median separation was conducted using Tukey's test at the α = 0.05 level.

Table 1. Mean consecutive distances traveled (m) during periods and annual displacement distances for known residents and dispersers in Rio Grande wild turkey populations studied in the Texas Panhandle, 2000–2002. Means (between periods) with the same letters are not different ($P > 0.05$).

Classification	Periods[a]				
	Spring	Summer	Autumn	Winter	Annual[b]
Resident	1,244[A]	1,398[A]	1,318[A]	751[B]	2,012
Disperser	3,597[A]	1,820[B]	1,554[B]	1,042[C]	12,030

[a] Spring: 15 Mar–14 Apr; Summer: 15 Apr–14 Aug; Autumn: 15 Aug–14 Nov; Winter: 15 Nov–14 Mar.
[b] Annual distances were significantly different ($\alpha = 0.05$, Tukeys test) between residents and dispersers.

RESULTS

We captured 554 Rio Grande wild turkeys at 3 study sites during winters 2000–2002. Of these, 34 died within 2 weeks of capture and were censored from analyses. An additional 14 yearling females were censored due to lost signals or transmitter failure. We obtained a total of 20,969 locations using the Maximum Likelihood Estimator in the computer program LOAS (Ecological Software Solutions 2002). Location error varied among sites but averaged ≤216,160 m² for all sites.

We identified winter, spring, summer and autumn periods based on hen behavior observed across study sites. The dates of 16 November to 15 March represented the winter roost period, with most hens localized in large numbers (typical range = 75–350 birds) at traditional winter roosts. Spring period was based on winter flock breakup and the beginning of nesting was from 16 March (mean earliest nest initiation date [range = 9–20 Mar]) to 15 April. The summer period ranged from 16 April to 15 August when most hens were in various stages of nesting and brood rearing. The autumn period, 16 August to 15 November, was characterized by the end of nesting and the beginning of movement back to winter roost sites.

Movement Analyses

Winter Home Range

Winter home range overlap was compared for turkeys ($n = 181$) with sufficient locations ($n \geq 3$ per winter) to generate MCP$_{100}$ ranges in year$_x$ and year$_{x+1}$. Rio Grande wild turkeys had high (85.6%) annual winter range fidelity. Adult females had the highest winter fidelity (96.7%), whereas yearling females had the lowest (62.5%). No turkey that moved >3.1 km between MCP$_{100}$ winter range peripheries in consecutive years returned to a previously used winter range. Turkeys with identified winter ranges that overlapped or with peripheries that were ≤3.1 km apart were classified as known residents. Turkeys with winter range peripheries >3.1 km apart were classified as dispersers.

Percentage of known dispersers ranged from 5.7% at GHWMA to 18.9% at Salt Fork but did not differ ($\chi^2 = 4.46$, df = 2, $P = 0.108$) among sites. A greater

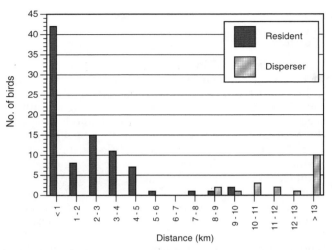

Fig. 1. Displacement distances (km) traveled by known residents and known dispersers of Rio Grande wild turkeys in the Texas Panhandle, 2000–2002.

proportion of yearling females ($n = 18$, 37.5%) dispersed and established new winter home ranges ($\chi^2 = 29.74$, df = 3, $P < 0.001$) than did yearling males ($n = 4$, 11.8%), adult males ($n = 2$, 5.4%) or adult females ($n = 2$, 3.2%) among all sites.

Straight-line Analyses

Consecutive seasonal distances ($n = 686$) were calculated for all seasons for all known fate birds. Among all sites, turkeys moved less ($F = 19.65$, df = 3, $P < 0.001$) during winter than in other seasons (Table 1). Known residents had smaller ($F \geq 11.90$, df = 2, $P < 0.001$) consecutive movement distances than dispersers in each season. Within movement classifications, known residents moved similar distances ($F = 18.54$, df = 2, $P \leq 0.001$) during summer, autumn, and spring seasons. However, known dispersers moved greater ($F = 5.52$, df = 3, $P = 0.002$) distances during spring than during summer, indicating spring was the period of greatest disperser movement.

Annual displacement distances ($n = 294$) were greater ($F = 38.10$, df = 2, $P < 0.001$) for known dispersers ($N = 25$, $\bar{x} = 12.03 \pm 4.20$ km) than for known residents ($N = 257$, $\bar{x} = 2.03 \pm 2.30$ km). We used 6.63 km, which represented >95% of all displacement distances moved by all known residents (Figure 1) to classify (resident vs. disperser) turkeys ($n = 241$) whose range use was undetermined in year$_{x+1}$. Annual displacement distances for turkeys classified as dispersers did not differ ($F = 1.57$, df = 3, $P = 0.214$) among age and sex classifications.

Yearling females dispersed with greater frequency than any other age and sex classification ($\chi^2 \leq 5.7161$, df = 1, $P \leq 0.016$). Proportions of residents and dispersers determined by distances calculated did not differ ($\chi^2 \leq 3.0088$, df = 1, $P \geq 0.083$) from proportions of known dispersers and residents for any age or sex class. Both known and calculated movement categories were combined for subsequent analyses (Table 2).

Table 2.   Numbers and percentages of Rio Grande wild turkeys by movement category in the Texas Panhandle, 2000–2002.

Age	Sex	Resident (%)[a]	Dispersers (%)[b]	Total
Adult	Female	138 (94.5)	8 (5.5)	146
Yearling	Female	76 (65.0)	41 (35.0)	117
Adult	Male	80 (88.9)	10 (11.1)	90
Yearling	Male	60 (89.6)	7 (10.4)	67
Adult	All	220 (92.4)	18 (7.6)	238
Yearling	All	136 (73.9)	48 (26.1)	184
All	Female	214 (81.4)	49 (18.6)	263
All	Male	142 (89.3)	17 (10.7)	159
Total		367 (84.4)	66 (15.6)	422

[a] Total percentage of a cohort classified as residents.
[b] Total percentage of a cohort classified as dispersers.

Survival Analyses

From 2000–2002, 116 yearling females were monitored for 27,972 radiodays to compare survival between yearling residents and dispersers. No differences were detected (Figure 2).

Nesting Analyses

From 2000–2002, yearling females attempted 42 nests (Table 3) representing 29.17% to 33.33% of the cohort. Nesting attempts were detected for only 13 dispersing yearlings. No differences were detected between movement classes for proportions of nests attempted (χ^2 = 2.7253, df = 1, P = 0.099) or the percentage of successful attempts (χ^2 = 0.3415, df = 1, P = 0.559). At MWMA, yearling females that dispersed never successfully nested despite 3 attempts. Whereas at both GHWMA and Salt Fork 3 of 5 yearling dispersers that attempted nests were successful.

DISCUSSION

Rio Grande wild turkeys in the Texas Panhandle exhibit migratory movements during the spring and autumn resulting in disjunct summer and winter ranges. In contrast to migratory movement, some wild turkeys exhibit dispersal, permanently leaving winter roosts. Yearling females are the wild turkey cohort primarily responsible for linking winter roost populations in the Texas Panhandle via dispersal. Yearling females routinely (1 out of 3) left natal winter roosts and never returned. Similar patterns occur in other bird species (Greenwood 1980). Anecdotal evidence (*see* Healy 1992) suggested that eastern (Ellis and Lewis 1967, Fleming and Speake 1976) and Rio Grande turkeys in eastern Colorado (Schmutz and Braun 1989) also exhibit this pattern.

While our results support our hypothesis that yearling females dispersed more than other age classes, our results do not support our other hypotheses addressing inherent risks traditionally identified with dispersal movements: decreased survival (Murray 1967) and decreased reproductive performance (Danchin and Cam 2002). Few studies (e.g., Forsman et al. 2002) have addressed dispersal utilizing radio telemetry; most have used unknown fate mark-recapture (Turchin 1998). Radio telemetry allows analysis of post-dis-

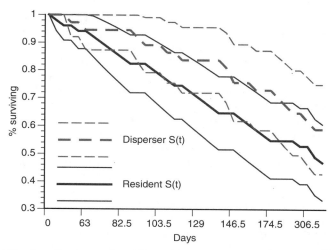

Fig. 2.   Cox proportional hazards output with 95% CI for yearling female Rio Grande wild turkey survival by movement category in the Texas Panhandle, 2000–2002.

persal data and consequently may be better able to assess biological costs of dispersal to the individual (McShea and Madison 1992). Our data do not support the costs typically associated with dispersal.

In telemetry studies on other Galliformes, there was no consensus on individual costs of dispersal. Beaudette and Keppie (1992) found no differences in survival between resident and dispersing spruce grouse (*Dendragapus canadensis*). In ruffed grouse (*Bonasa umbellus*), Small et al. (1993) found decreased survival by dispersers but suggested such a decrease may not be solely attributed to dispersal, while in blue grouse (*Dendragapus obscurus*), similar reproductive and survival rates for residents and dispersers were reported (Hines 1986). Studies on white-tailed ptarmigan (*Lagopus leucurus*) found dispersers almost exclusively responsible for recruitment in Colorado (Martin et al. 2000).

To our knowledge, no studies on wild turkeys have addressed survival or reproduction by movement category. Interpretation of our survival analyses are hindered by small sample sizes associated with dispersal. Biases may also be associated with our survival and nesting analyses: (1) the longer a disperser lived the

Table 3.   Number of yearling female nesting attempts and successes by year, site and movement class for Rio Grande wild turkeys in the Texas Panhandle, 2000–2002. (No. of possible nesting birds:No. of attempts:No. of successes)

Site[a]	Movement	2000	2001	2002	Total
GHWMA	Resident	12:4:1	6:2:0	7:2:0	25:8:1
GHWMA	Disperser	2:2:2	2:2:0	4:5:3	8:9:5
MWMA	Resident	11:3:1	9:3:2	12:5:1	31:11:4
MWMA	Disperser	6:1:0	0:0:0	4:2:0	10:3:0
Salt Fork	Resident	9:4:4	1:2:0	6:5:2	16:11:6
Salt Fork	Disperser	1:0:0	6:2:1	14:3:2	21:5:3
All	Resident	32:11:6	16:7:2	25:12:3	73:30:11
All	Disperser	9:3:2	8:4:1	22:6:3	39:13:6

[a] GHWMA = Gene Howe Wildlife Management Area; MWMA = Matador Wildlife Management Area; Salt Fork = Salt Fork of the Red River.

greater the probability it would be found; (2) conversely, residents were logistically easier to monitor and may have been more quickly documented as nesters thus decreasing nesting success rates, or (3) fewer numbers of dispersers attempted nests and this could have increased their chances of survival. Further, assessing dispersal across 3 sites and years may confound interpretation. Despite these commonly encountered problems with the study of dispersal, our observations merit further discussion.

Dispersal has traditionally been associated with density (McCullough 1996). Long-term studies on the eastern subspecies suggest almost no nesting by juvenile females and that density-dependent factors may be limiting populations in Mississippi (Miller et al. 2001). High nesting rates by yearling females have been documented in recently introduced populations of wild turkey (Schmutz and Braun 1989; Keegan and Crawford 1999). Such findings suggest density-dependence may influence yearling nesting rates. Yearling females may also be expected to disperse at greater frequency from areas of high density than from areas with low densities (Sutherland et al. 2002). Fleming and Speake (1976) suggested emigration played a substantial role in the loss of turkeys from a stable population on their study site in Alabama.

Populations at our 3 sites were thought to be exhibiting different dynamics: MWMA's population was thought to be decreasing, while GHWMA and Salt Fork were thought to be stable or increasing (Ballard et al. 2001). The Salt Fork had more successful yearling nests ($n = 9$) than the MWMA ($n = 4$) and GHWMA ($n = 4$) combined. Further, at the Salt Fork, a greater proportion (56.7%; 21 of 37) of telemetered yearling females dispersed than at GHWMA (31.0%; 10 of 32) or MWMA (32.0%; 8 of 25). Unfortunately, 9 of 14 censored yearling females were from the GHWMA. Our findings at the Salt Fork and MWMA lend support to the idea of density-related dispersal. Further, in our study, the site with the greatest annual variation in yearling survival rate (Salt Fork: range = 21–58%) also produced the greatest number of dispersers.

Interpretation of our findings in relation to published literature on wild turkeys is often confounded by terminology. Dispersal in the majority of published wild turkey studies has referred to breeding dispersal, a measure of distance from some estimate of winter range to nesting or breeding range, or natal dispersal, referring to a distance moved from place of birth to the place of first breeding. Neither of these address whether such movements represent two-way movement (e.g., with return to winter roost area) or a permanent movement away from an area. As a result they do not allow assessment of egress in wild turkey populations. Future studies may benefit from explicitly stating directionality (or lack thereof) of movement (as in Schumutz and Braun 1989).

The role of these movements in determining population structure remains relatively unknown. In the eastern subspecies, Leberg (1991) suggests there is "nothing inherent in the population structure of turkeys leading to large genetic differences among populations (1991:527)." However, behavioral observations of lekking behavior in Rio Grande wild turkey (Watts and Stokes 1971) were recently verified genetically in California (Kraukauer 2005) and may decrease genetic diversity in subsequent generations (Chesser 1991). Large-scale studies generally found poor relationships between genetic and geographic distances (Leberg et al. 1994, Mock et al. 2002). At smaller scales, findings on the Rio Grande subspecies suggest genetic structure may occur at scales as small as local flocks (Boone and Rhodes 1996) or among winter roosts at small (<30 km) scales (Rhodes et al. 1996).

While the role of yearling female dispersal in wild turkey populations is poorly understood, our findings suggest movement into and out of turkey populations may play an important role in population dynamics. Relationships among population density and yearling female dispersal, reproductive, and survival rates merit further investigation as do habitat variables associated with dispersal movement (e.g., connectivity of riparian areas). The role of yearling dispersal and its influence on genetic population structure should also be investigated. An understanding of yearling female dispersal may allow management appropriate to the scale at which population structure occurs.

ACKNOWLEDGMENTS

We thank numerous field personnel that assisted with data collection on this project. We would also like to thank numerous landowners who allowed access to their property and 3 anonymous reviewers for comments that greatly improved this manuscript. This project was generously funded by Texas Parks and Wildlife, The Texas Chapter of the National Wild Turkey Federation, the National Wild Turkey Federation and Texas Tech University. This is Texas Tech University, College of Agricultural Sciences and Natural Resources manuscript #T-9-1067.

LITERATURE CITED

Arguedas, N., and P. G. Parker. 2000. Seasonal migration and genetic population structure in house wrens. The Condor 102:517–528.

Badyaev, A. V. 1995. Nesting habitat and nesting success of eastern wild turkey in the Arkansas Ozark Highlands. The Condor 97:221–232.

———, W. J. Etges, and T. E. Martin. 1996. Ecological and behavioral correlates of variation in seasonal home range of wild turkeys. Journal of Wildlife Management 60:154–164.

———, and J. D. Faust. 1996. Nest site fidelity in female wild turkey: potential causes and reproductive consequences. The Condor 98:589–594.

Bailey, R. W., D. Dennett, Jr., H. G. Gore, J. C. Pack, R. Simpson, and G. Wright. 1980. Basic considerations and general recommendations for trapping the wild turkey. Proceedings of the National Wild Turkey Symposium 4:10–23.

Ballard, W. B., M. C. Wallace, J. H. Brunjes, T. Barnett, D. Holdstock, R. Phillips, B. Spears, M. S. Miller, B. Simpson,

S. Sudkamp, R. D. Applegate, and P. Gipson. 2001. Changes in land use patterns and their effects on Rio Grande wild turkeys in the Rolling Plains of Texas. Texas Tech University, Lubbock, Texas, USA.

Beasom, S. L., and D. Wilson. 1992. Rio Grande wild turkey. Pages 306–330 *in* J. G. Dickson, editor. The wild turkey: biology and management. Stackpole Books, Mechanicsburg, Pennsylvania, USA.

Boone, M. D., and O. E. Rhodes, Jr. 1996. Genetic structure among subpopulations of the Eastern wild turkey (*Meleagris gallopavo silvestris*). American Midland Naturalist 135:168–171.

Brown, E. K. 1980. Home range and movements of wild turkeys—a review. Proceedings of the National Wild Turkey Symposium 4:251–261.

Chesser, R. K. 1991. Influence of gene flow and breeding tactics on gene diversity within populations. Genetics 129:573–583.

Conover, W. J. 1999. Practical nonparametric statistics. John Wiley & Sons, New York, New York, USA.

Danchin, E., and E. Cam. 2002. Can non-breeding be a cost of breeding dispersal? Behavioral Ecology and Sociobiology 51:153–163.

Ellis, J. E., and J. B. Lewis. 1967. Mobility and annual range of wild turkeys in Missouri. Journal of Wildlife Management 31:568–581.

Ecological Software Solutions. 2002. LOAS—Location of a signal. Version 2.08. Ecological Software Solutions, Sacramento, California, USA.

Everett, D. D., D. W. Speake, and W. K. Maddox. 1979. Wild turkey ranges in Alabama mountain habitat. Proceedings of the Southeast Association of Game and Fish Agencies 33:233–238.

Fleming, W. J., and D. W. Speake. 1976. Losses of the eastern wild turkey from a stable Alabama population. Proceedings of the Southeast Association of Game and Fish Agencies 30:377–385.

Forsman, E. D., R. G. Anthony, J. A. Reid, P. J. Loschl, S. G. Sovern, M. Taylor, B. L. Biswell, A. Ellingson, E. C. Meslow, G. S. Miller, K. A. Swindle, J. A. Thrailkill, F. F. Wagner, and D. E. Seaman. 2002. Natal and breeding dispersal of northern spotted owls. Wildlife Monographs 149.

Glazner, W. C., A. S. Jackson, and M. L. Cox. 1964. The Texas drop-net turkey trap. Journal of Wildlife Management 28:280–287.

Greenwood, P. J. 1980. Mating systems, philopatry and dispersal in birds and mammals. Animal Behaviour 28:1162.

Hanski, I., and D. Simberloff. 1997. The metapopulation approach, its history, conceptual domain, and application to conservation. Pages 5–26 *in* I. Hanski and M. E. Gilpin, editors. Metapopulation biology: ecology, genetics and evolution. Academic Press, San Diego, California, USA.

Healy, W. M. 1992. Behavior. Pages 46–65 *in* J. G. Dickson, editor. The wild turkey: biology and management. Stackpole Books, Mechanicsburg, Pennsylvania, USA.

Hines, J. E. 1986. Survival and reproduction of dispersing blue grouse. The Condor 88:43–49.

Hoffman, R. W. 1991. Spring movements, roosting activities and home-range characteristics of male Merriam's wild turkey. The Southwestern Naturalist 36:332–337.

Hooge, P. N., W. Eichenlaub, and E. Solomon. 1999. The animal movement program. Version 2.0. Alaska Biological Science Center, U. S. Geological Survey, Anchorage, Alaska, USA.

Keegan, T. W., and J. A. Crawford. 1999. Reproduction and survival of Rio Grande turkeys in Oregon. Journal of Wildlife Management 63:204–210.

Kernohan, B. J., R. A. Gitzen, and J. J. Millspaugh. 2001. Analysis of animal space use and movements. Pages 125–166 *in* J. J. Millspaugh and J. M. Marzluff, editors. Radio tracking and animal populations. Academic Press, San Diego, California, USA.

Krakauer, A. H. 2005. Kin selection and cooperative courtship in wild turkeys. Nature 434:69–72.

Laundré, J. W., T. D. Reynolds, S. T. Knick, and I. J. Ball. 1987. Accuracy of daily point relocations in assessing real movement of radio-marked animals. Journal of Wildlife Management 51:937–940.

Leberg, P. L. 1991. Influence of fragmentation and bottlenecks on genetic divergence of wild turkey populations. Conservation Biology 5:522–530.

————, P. W. Stangel, H. O. Hillestad, R. L. Marchinton, and M. H. Smith. 1994. Genetic structure of reintroduced wild turkey and white-tailed deer populations. Journal of Wildlife Management 58:698–711.

Leopold, A. 1933. Game management. University of Wisconsin Press, Madison, Wisconsin, USA.

Logan, T. H. 1970. A study of Rio Grande wild turkey by radio telemetry. Oklahoma Department of Wildlife Conservation, Federal Aid in Wildlife Restoration Project W-86-R.

Martin, K., P. B. Stacey, and C. E. Braun. 2000. Recruitment, dispersal and demographic rescue in spatially-structured white-tailed ptarmigan populations. The Condor 102:503–516.

McCullough, D. R. 1996. Spatially structured populations and harvest theory. Journal of Wildlife Management 60:1–9.

McShea, W. J., and D. M. Madison 1992. Alternative approaches to the study of small mammal dispersal: insights from radiotelemetry. Pages 319–322 *in* N. C. Stenseth and W. Z. Lidicker, Jr., editors. Animal dispersal: small mammals as a model. Chapman & Hall, London, United Kingdom.

Miller, D. A., M. J. Chamberlain, B. D. Leopold, and G. A. Hurst. 2001. Lessons from Tallahala: what have we learned for turkey management into the 21st century? Proceedings of the National Wild Turkey Symposium 8:23–33.

Miller, M. S., D. J. Buford, and R. S. Lutz. 1995. Survival of female Rio Grande turkeys during the reproductive season. Journal of Wildlife Management 59:766–771.

Mock, K. E., T. C. Theimer, O. E. Rhodes, Jr., D. L. Greenberg, and P. Keim. 2002. Genetic variation across the historical range of the wild turkeys (*Meleagris gallopavo*). Molecular Ecology 11:643–657.

Murray, B. G., Jr. 1967. Dispersal in vertebrates. Ecology 48:975–978.

Rhodes, O. E., Jr., D. J. Buford, M. S. Miller, and R. S. Lutz. 1996. Genetic structure of reintroduced Rio Grande wild turkeys in Kansas. Journal of Wildlife Management 59:771–775.

SAS Institute. 1999. SAS/STAT user's guide. Version 8.2. SAS Institute, Cary, North Carolina, USA.

Schmutz, J. A., and C. E. Braun. 1989. Reproductive performance of Rio Grande wild turkeys. The Condor 91:675–680.

Schroeder, M. A., and D. A. Boag. 1988. Dispersal in spruce grouse. Animal Behaviour 36:305–307.

Schwartz, C. C., and A. W. Franzmann. 1992. Dispersal and survival of subadult black bears from the Kenai Peninsula, Alaska. Journal of Wildlife Management 56:426–431.

Small, R. J., J. C. Holzwart, and D. H. Rusch. 1993. Are ruffed grouse more vulnerable to mortality during dispersal? Ecology 74:2020–2026.

Smith, D. M. 1975. Behavioral factors influencing variability of roost counts for Rio Grande turkeys. Proceedings of the National Wild Turkey Symposium 3:170–175.

Spears, B. L., W. B. Ballard, M. C. Wallace, R. S. Phillips, D. P. Holdstock, J. H. Brunjes, R. Applegate, P. S. Gipson, M. S. Miller, and T. Barnett. 2002. Retention times of miniature radiotransmitters glued to wild turkey poults. Wildlife Society Bulletin 30:861–867

Stevens, R. L. 1989. Spring dispersal and summer habitat selection of Rio Grande turkeys (*Meleagris gallopavo intermedia*) in west-central Texas. Thesis, Angelo State University, San Angelo, Texas, USA.

Sutherland, W. J., J. A. Gill, and K. Norris. 2002. Density-dependent dispersal in animals: concepts, evidence, mechanisms and consequences. Pages 134–148 *in* J. C. Bullock, R. E. Kenward, and R. S. Hails, editors. Dispersal ecology: the 42nd symposium of the British Ecological Society, Blackwell Publishing, Malden, Massachusetts, USA.

Thomas, J. W., C. V. Hoozer, and R. G. Marburger. 1966. Wintering concentrations and seasonal shifts in range in the Rio Grande turkey. Journal of Wildlife Management 30:34–49.

———, R. G. Marburger, and C. Van Hoozer. 1973. Rio Grande turkey migrations as related to harvest regulation in Texas. Pages 301–308 *in* G. C. Sanderson and H. C. Schultz, editors. Wild turkey management: current problems and programs. University of Missouri, Columbia, Missouri, USA.

Turchin, P. 1998. Quantitative analysis of movement. Sinauer Associates, Sunderland, Massachusetts, USA.

Vangilder, L. D. 1992. Population Dynamics. Pages 144–164 *in* J. G. Dickson, editor. The wild turkey: biology and management. Stackpole Book, Harrisburg, Pennsylvania, USA.

Watts, C. R., and A. W. Stokes. 1971. The social order of turkeys. Scientific American 224:112–118.

White, G. C., and R. A. Garrott. 1990. Analysis of wildlife radio-tracking data. Academic Press, San Diego, California, USA.

Williams, L. E., Jr. 1961. Notes on wing molt in the yearling wild turkey. Journal of Wildlife Management 25:439–440.

Zar, J. H. 1999. Biostatistical analysis. Prentice Hall, Upper Saddle River, New Jersey, USA.

Richard S. Phillips (pictured) is a doctoral candidate in Wildlife Science at Texas Tech University. His work is focused on the impacts of dispersal on population structure of Rio Grande wild turkeys in the Texas Panhandle. Richard received his bachelors degree in Biology and Human and Natural Ecology from Emory University and his masters degree in Wildlife Science from Texas Tech. ***Warren B. Ballard*** is professor of wildlife sciences in the Department of Range, Wildlife, and Fisheries Management at Texas Tech University. He received his B.S. in fish and wildlife management at New Mexico State University, his M.Sc. in environmental biology from Kansas State University, and his Ph.D. in wildlife science from the University of Arizona. His professional interests include predator-prey relationships and population dynamics of carnivores and ungulates. ***Mark C. Wallace*** received a B.S. degree in forestry-wildlife sciences from the University of Washington in 1981, and M.S. in wildlife ecology from the University of Arizona in 1984, and a Ph.D. from the University of Arizona in 1992. Since 1996 he as been on the faculty in the Department of Range, Wildlife, and Fisheries Management at Texas Tech University, where his research interests have been focused on wildlife-habitat relationships.

Derrick P. Holdstock (pictured) received his Bachelor of Science degree in Environmental and Forest Biology from the State University of New York, College of Environmental Science and Forestry from Syracuse, a Master of Science degree in Secondary Science Education at Syracuse University, and a Master of Science degree in Wildlife Science from Texas Tech University. His research focused on the survival, movements, and habitat use of Rio Grande wild turkeys in the Texas Panhandle and southwestern Kansas. He currently works for Texas Parks and Wildlife Department where he recently served as the Black-tailed Prairie Dog Program Coordinator and currently serves as the Assistant Project Leader for the Panhandle Wildlife Management Areas. ***Brian Spears*** received his bachelors degree from the University of Arizona in Ecology and Evolutionary Biology and masters degree from Texas Tech University in Wildlife Science. Brian is a Resource Protection Specialist for the US Fish and Wildlife Service working on technical issues and research regarding wildlife toxicology in the Coeur d'Alene Basin, Idaho, as well as developing wetland restoration partnerships between federal agencies, the Coeur d'Alene Indian Tribe, and private land owners. He currently lives with his wife and daughter in Coeur d'Alene, Idaho.

Mike Miller (pictured) is a wildlife diversity biologist in Region 2 at Texas Parks and Wildlife Department. He received his B.S. and M.S. degrees in Wildlife Management from Texas Tech University. Mike provides technical guidance to private landowners and works on projects that benefit rare and declining resources in north-central Texas. ***John H. Brunjes, IV*** received his Bachelor of Science degree in Biology from the University of North Carolina at Wilmington in and his Master of Science degree in Wildlife Ecology and Management from the University of Georgia. He recently completed his Doctor of Philosophy in Wildlife Science in the Department of Range and Wildlife Management at Texas Tech University. His doctoral research focused on the landscape ecology and population dynamics of Rio Grande wild turkeys. ***Steve DeMaso*** is the Upland Game Bird Program Leader for the Texas Parks and Wildlife Department in Austin, Texas. Prior to moving to Texas, he worked for the Oklahoma Department of Wildlife Conservation and served as the lead researcher on the nationally recognized Packsaddle Quail Research Project. Currently, Steve serves as Chairman of the Southeast Quail Study Group and a member of the National Wild Turkey Federation's Technical Committee. Steve is a member of the National and Texas Chapters of The Wildlife Society. Steve also served as the Program Chairman and Editor for the Proceedings of the Fifth National Quail Symposium. Steve was raised in southern Michigan and received his B.S. from Michigan State University, M.S. from Texas A&I University, and is currently pursuing a Ph.D. in the Wildlife and Fisheries Sciences Joint Program between Texas A&M University and Texas A&M–Kingsville.

UTILITY OF POULT-HEN COUNTS TO INDEX PRODUCTIVITY OF RIO GRANDE WILD TURKEYS

Matthew J. Butler[1]
Department of Natural Resources Management,
Texas Tech University, Lubbock, TX 79409, USA

Mark C. Wallace
Department of Natural Resources Management,
Texas Tech University, Lubbock, TX 79409, USA

Richard S. Phillips
Department of Natural Resources Management,
Texas Tech University, Lubbock, TX 79409, USA

Ross T. Huffman
Department of Natural Resources Management,
Texas Tech University, Lubbock, TX 79409, USA

James C. Bullock
Department of Natural Resources Management,
Texas Tech University, Lubbock, TX 79409, USA

Roger D. Applegate
Kansas Department of Wildlife and Parks,
Emporia, KS 66801, USA

Galon I. Hall
Department of Natural Resources Management,
Texas Tech University, Lubbock, TX 79409, USA

Warren B. Ballard
Department of Natural Resources Management,
Texas Tech University, Lubbock, TX 79409, USA

John H. Brunjes IV
Department of Natural Resources Management,
Texas Tech University, Lubbock, TX 79409, USA

Rachael L. Houchin
Department of Natural Resources Management,
Texas Tech University, Lubbock, TX 79409, USA

Stephen J. DeMaso
Texas Parks and Wildlife Department,
Austin, TX 78744, USA

Michael C. Frisbie
Texas Parks and Wildlife Department,
San Marcos, TX 78666, USA

Abstract: Many states use poult-hen counts to index wild turkey (*Meleagris gallopavo*) population parameters such as reproduction, recruitment, and density. Texas Parks and Wildlife Department (TPWD) personnel have conducted poult-hen counts of Rio Grande wild turkeys (*M. g. intermedia*) since 1978. In 2000, we began estimating recruitment and reproductive parameters at 3 study sites in the Texas Panhandle and 1 site in southwestern Kansas. During 2000–2004, we estimated reproductive parameters by intensively monitoring 374 radio-tagged wild turkey hens. From annual January–March trapping efforts during 2000–2005, we used the percent of all captured wild turkeys that were juveniles (percent juveniles captured) to index recruitment for 1999–2004. We used the TPWD poult-hen count data from 1999–2004 to estimate poults/hen for counties that contained our study sites. In 2002, we began conducting our own poult-hen counts at the study sites in order to estimate poults/hen at a localized scale. Nesting success rate, mean number of eggs laid per hen, mean number of eggs hatched per hen, percent of juvenile females captured, and percent of juveniles captured were correlated ($r^2 > 0.349$, $9 \leq n \leq 10$, $P < 0.05$) to our poults/hen estimates. However, none of the reproductive or recruitment parameters were correlated to TPWD poults/hen estimates ($r^2 < 0.143$, $13 \leq n \leq 16$, $P > 0.10$). Our analyses suggested poult-hen counts could index reproduction and recruitment at localized scales. However, on an ecoregion scale, TPWD poults/hen estimates were unable to index reproduction or recruitment ($r^2 < 0.299$, $5 \leq n \leq 6$, $P > 0.15$). The inability of the TPWD poults/hen estimates to index reproduction or recruitment at local or ecoregion scales may have resulted from small sample sizes used to calculate TPWD estimates and uneven and inadequate coverage of samples across the ecoregion. If TPWD poults/hen estimates are to be valuable indices at local or ecoregion scales, larger and evenly distributed samples from standardized and randomized surveys must be obtained.

Proceedings of the National Wild Turkey Symposium 9:159–168

Key words: density, Kansas, *Meleagris galopovo intermedia,* poult-hen count, poults/hen index, recruitment, reproduction, Rio Grande wild turkey, Texas.

Poult-hen counts have been used to index population densities, reproduction, and recruitment of upland game birds such as eastern wild turkey (*M. g. silvestris*; Bartush et al. 1985), Rio Grande wild turkey (DeArment 1959, Schwertner et al. 2003), Merriam's wild turkey (*M. g. merriami*; Hoffman 1962, Shaw 1973), ring-necked pheasant (*Phasianus colchicus*; Riley and Riley 1999), and gray partridge (*Pardix pardix*; Suchy et al. 1991). Wild turkey poult-hen counts have been used by many state natural resource agencies (Kurzejeski and Vangilder 1992) and many researchers have examined aspects of poult-hen counts. For example, the effects of environmental conditions and time of day on poult-hen counts were examined for pheasants (McClure 1945, Kozicky 1952, Klonglan 1955) and wild turkeys (Shaw 1973, Bartush et al. 1985). The power to detect trends in poult-hen counts was examined for pheasants (Rice 2003) and wild turkeys (Schultz and McDowell 1957, Schwertner et al. 2003). In addition, the relationship between harvest and poult-hen counts was examined for wild turkeys (Kennamer et al. 1975, Wunz and Shope 1980, Wunz and Ross 1990) and pheasants (Rice 2003). Many of these studies reported a positive relationship between poults/hen estimates and wild turkey harvest in the fall (e.g., Menzel 1975, Wunz and Shope 1980). These relationships were used to infer that poults/hen is a valid index of recruitment and density even though there is limited information regarding such a relationship.

In Texas, TPWD personnel have been conducting poult-hen counts as an index of recruitment in Rio Grande wild turkey populations since 1978 (TPWD, unpublished data). However, the validity of poults/hen estimates as an index of population parameters was questioned by Caughley (1974). The assumption was that poult-hen counts were a surrogate for population abundance or density (e.g., Bartush et al. 1985, Roberts and Porter 1996, Healy and Powell 1999). However, no studies examined the validity of using poult-hen count data to index recruitment, reproduction, or density though some conducted power analyses for trend detection (e.g., Schultz and McDowell 1957, Schwertner et al. 2003). Thus, our objective was to evaluate poult-hen counts as an index of reproduction and recruitment. Specifically, we were interested in determining if a positive linear relationship between poults/hen estimates and measures

of reproduction and recruitment existed at local and ecoregion scales.

STUDY AREA

The ecoregion-scale study area was a 29-county area located in the Texas Panhandle (hereafter, referred to as the Panhandle Rolling Plains ecoregion) (Figure 1). The local-scale research was conducted at 3 study sites in the Texas Panhandle and 1 site in southwestern Kansas (Figure 1). The Texas Panhandle study sites were centered on (1) the Matador Wildlife Management Area (WMA), located in northwestern Cottle County along the confluence of the Middle and South Pease rivers; (2) the Gene Howe WMA, located in northern Hemphill County along the Canadian River; and (3) private ranches surrounding the Salt Fork of the Red River, located in western Collinsworth and eastern Donley counties. The southwestern Kansas study site was centered on the Cimarron National Grasslands in southwestern Stevens and southern Mor-

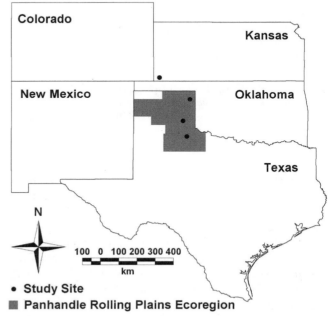

● Study Site

■ Panhandle Rolling Plains Ecoregion

Fig. 1. Locations of the Rio Grande wild turkey study sites used in local-scale correlation analyses (from north to south: Cimarron National Grasslands, Gene Howe Wildlife Management Area [WMA], private ranches surrounding the Salt Fork of the Red River, and Matador WMA) and the boundary of the 29-county, Texas Panhandle Rolling Plains ecoregion used in the broad-scale ecoregion analyses.

---

[1] E-mail: matthew.j.butler@ttu.edu

Table 1. Texas Parks and Wildlife Department (TPWD) poults/hen estimates[a] for Rio Grande wild turkeys in the Texas Panhandle, 1999–2004.

Study site[b]	Year											
	1999		2000		2001		2002		2003		2004	
	$\bar{x}$	n	$\bar{x}$	n	$\bar{x}$	n	$\bar{x}$	n	$\bar{x}$	n	$\bar{x}$	n
Gene Howe WMA[c]	3.3	4			5.7	14	2.5	8	2.6	7		
Salt Fork[c]	7.3	3	3.0	2	1.3	2	6.5	2	5.3	3	1.4	6
Matador WMA[c]	4.6	3	3.2	1	5.2	8	5.0	5	1.8	38	4.3	3
Ecoregion[d]	3.3	22	3.1	8	4.7	31	3.4	27	2.3	62	3.0	35

[a] The TPWD poults/hen estimates were derived from opportunistic observations made by TPWD personnel (see Schwertner et al. 2003).
[b] Research was conducted at the Gene Howe Wildlife Management Area (WMA), private ranches surrounding the Salt Fork of the Red River and Matador WMA.
[c] The TPWD poults/hen estimates for the study sites were derived from poult-hen counts conducted by TPWD personnel in counties that contained our study sites.
[d] Pooled TPWD data from the 29-county, Texas Panhandle Rolling Plains ecoregion were used in the broad-scale ecoregion analyses.

ton counties, Kansas, and southeastern Baca County, Colorado, along the Cimarron River.

Little information was available concerning wild turkey population densities at the study sites or across the ecoregion though it was suspected that wild turkey populations were stable or increasing (Brunjes 2005). Also, we selected the study sites because they represented the range of environmental and anthropogenic influences in the ecoregion. Wild turkey populations at our study sites were primarily tied to roosting habitat associated with riparian communities. Study sites were primarily dominated by agriculture (2–21%), brushland (6–40%), grassland (35–89%), and riparian and upland trees (2–4%) (Brunjes 2005). Detailed descriptions of the vegetative communities of the study sites are available in Spears et al. (2002), Butler et al. (2005), Hall (2005), Butler et al. (2006), and Huffman et al. (2006). Primary land uses at the study sites were cattle ranching interspersed with center-pivot agriculture and oil and gas development.

METHODS

Though logistic constraints and other problems often limited sampling, sampling protocols were designed to set numerical goals for observers. The TPWD poult-hen survey protocol was an opportunistic

Table 2. Texas Tech University (TTU) poults/hen estimates[a] for Rio Grande wild turkeys in the Texas Panhandle and southwestern Kansas, 2002–2004.

Study site[b]	Year					
	2002		2003		2004	
	$\bar{x}$	n	$\bar{x}$	n	$\bar{x}$	n
Cimarron NG			1.4	56	0.3	65
Gene Howe WMA			0.9	53	0.7	56
Salt Fork	2.7	35	1.7	57	1.5	68
Matador WMA	0.2	8	1.4	29	0.7	40

[a] The TTU poults/hen estimates were derived from opportunistic observations made by TTU personnel.
[b] Research was conducted in southwestern Kansas at the Cimarron National Grasslands (NG) and in the Texas Panhandle at the Gene Howe Wildlife Management Area (WMA), private ranches surrounding the Salt Fork of the Red River, and Matador WMA.

sampling scheme which encouraged TPWD personnel to record (during their daily activities) ≥25 observations of wild turkey hens for each 2-week period from 1 July–15 August each year (e.g., Schwertner et al. 2003). Because of concerns regarding inadequate sample sizes (number of flocks observed) in the TPWD counts (Schwertner et al. 2003), we began conducting poult-hen counts (hereafter, referred to as TTU counts) in 2002 at our study sites. The TTU survey protocol also was an opportunistic sampling scheme which encouraged TTU personnel to record (during their daily activities) ≥30 observations of wild turkey flocks for each 2-week period from 1 July–15 August each year. Primarily, each protocol differed in sampling goals; the TPWD protocol focused on hens but the TTU protocol focused on flocks. Flocks, the sample units, were independent groups of wild turkeys; a flock could be 1 or more wild turkeys. Regardless of survey protocol, the sampling units were wild turkey flocks and observers recorded the sex, age, and number of wild turkeys seen in each flock. However, because the TPWD protocol was focused on hens, 1 flock of 25 hens fulfilled the TPWD quota but was considered only 1 sample under the TTU protocol.

We used both the TTU and TPWD poult-hen counts to calculate poults/hen estimates for each year (TTU 2002–2004; TPWD 1999–2004). We used the TPWD poult-hen count data from counties that contained our study sites to estimate the annual TPWD poults/hen estimates for each of our study sites. No TPWD data was available for the Cimarron National Grassland study site. We also used TPWD poult-hen count data from the Panhandle Rolling Plains ecoregion to calculate TPWD poults/hen estimates for the ecoregion.

As part of a larger study (e.g., Spears 2002, Holdstock 2003, Phillips 2004, Hall 2005, Huffman 2005), we captured Rio Grande wild turkeys using drop-nets (Glazener et al. 1964), rocket nets (Bailey et al. 1980), and walk-in-traps (Davis 1994). We attached a 95-g backpack-style radio-transmitter with an 8-hour mortality switch (Model #A1155, Advanced Telemetry Systems, Isanti, Minnesota, USA) to Rio Grande wild turkeys using 6-mm nylon over-braid rubber harness

Table 3. Rio Grande wild turkey nesting success rate[a] in the Texas Panhandle and southwestern Kansas, 2000–2004.

Study site[b]	Year									
	2000		2001		2002		2003		2004	
	$\bar{x}$	n	$\bar{x}$	n	$\bar{x}$	n	$\bar{x}$	n	$\bar{x}$	n
Cimarron NG	43.8	16	40.6	32			35.3	17	27.8	18
Gene Howe WMA	39.1	23	27.3	33	26.3	19	46.3	13	14.3	21
Salt Fork	55.6	9	27.3	22	41.4	29	50.0	12	50.0	14
Matador WMA	42.9	21	33.3	21	15.0	20	31.8	22	25.0	12
Ecoregion[c]	43.4	53	28.9	76	29.4	68	40.4	47	27.7	47

[a] Nests were considered successful if ≥1 poult per clutch hatched. We determined annual success rate by calculating the percentage of successful hens at each study site.
[b] Research was conducted in southwestern Kansas at the Cimarron National Grasslands (NG) and in the Texas Panhandle at the Gene Howe Wildlife Management Area (WMA), private ranches surrounding the Salt Fork of the Red River, and Matador WMA.
[c] Data from the Texas Panhandle study sites were pooled and used in the broad-scale, Texas Panhandle Rolling Plains ecoregion analyses.

cord using the methods of Holdstock (2003) and Phillips (2004). We considered wild turkeys <1 year of age as juveniles; we determined age based on characteristics of the ninth and tenth primaries and rectrice length (Petrides 1942). From annual January–March trapping efforts during 2000–2005, we used the percent of all captured wild turkeys that were juveniles (percent juveniles captured) to index recruitment for 1999–2004. Specifically, we used the percent of juvenile female, juvenile male, and all juvenile wild turkeys captured as indices of recruitment at each study site.

During 2000–2004, we estimated reproductive parameters by monitoring 374 radio-tagged wild turkey hens; we monitored 19.7 ± 1.5 hens ($\bar{x} \pm$ SE) at each study site per year (ranged from 9 to 33 hens at each study site per year). All radio-tagged hens were located via triangulation or visual observation ≥2 times per week during the nesting period to determine the onset of nesting and incubation by activation and deactivation of mortality signals and continuous location at a specific point (e.g., Miller et al. 1998, Keegan and Crawford 1999). Once we suspected incubation, we determined nest locations by close proximity (within 50 m) triangulation of the hens (Spears 2002, Huffman 2005). Fourteen days after the beginning of incubation, we approached nests, and counted and floated eggs in order to estimate hatch date (Westerskov 1950). Though concerns about observer induced abandonment exist, only 6.6% of nests were abandoned and in many of those cases the hen was

accidentally flushed early (Huffman 2005). After hatching, we examined the nests and made visual observations of the hens in order to estimate the number of eggs hatched. We considered nests successful if ≥1 poult per clutch hatched. We determined annual success rate by calculating the percentage of successful hens at each study site.

We conducted analyses at 2 scales: local (study site) and ecoregion (Figure 1). At the local scale, we compared the TTU and TPWD poults/hen estimates using a paired t-test (Zar 1999). In order to validate poult-hen counts as indices of recruitment and reproduction, we conducted one-tailed correlation analyses. We used Pearson's correlation coefficient (Zar 1999) to determine the linear relationship between the TPWD and TTU poults/hen estimates. We also calculated correlation coefficients between each poults/hen estimate and nesting success rate, mean number of eggs laid per hen, mean number of eggs hatched per hen, percent juvenile females captured, percent juvenile males captured, and percent juveniles captured. We used data from the Cimarron National Grasslands, Kansas, for the correlation analyses between all of the above measures except the TPWD poults/hen estimates. At the ecoregion scale, we pooled data for the Texas study sites for each year and we combined TPWD poult-hen count data for the Panhandle Rolling Plains ecoregion (Figure 1) in order to conduct correlation analyses. We considered correlations significant when $P < 0.05$ and $r^2 > 0.30$.

Table 4. Mean number of eggs laid per hen for Rio Grande wild turkeys in the Texas Panhandle and southwestern Kansas, 2000–2004.

Study site[a]	Year									
	2000		2001		2002		2003		2004	
	$\bar{x}$	n	$\bar{x}$	n	$\bar{x}$	n	$\bar{x}$	n	$\bar{x}$	n
Cimarron NG	7.7	11	7.9	32			10.1	17	9.0	18
Gene Howe WMA	9.3	23	10.3	32	9.0	19	8.3	12	10.0	21
Salt Fork	8.4	8	8.5	22	11.1	25	10.3	12	7.9	13
Matador WMA	10.5	21	9.5	20	5.2	20	8.1	22	9.3	10
Ecoregion[b]	9.5	52	9.5	74	8.6	64	8.7	49	9.2	44

[a] Research was conducted in southwestern Kansas at the Cimarron National Grasslands (NG) and in the Texas Panhandle at the Gene Howe Wildlife Management Area (WMA), private ranches surrounding the Salt Fork of the Red River, and Matador WMA.
[b] Data from the Texas Panhandle study sites were pooled and used in the broad-scale, Texas Panhandle Rolling Plains ecoregion analyses.

Table 5. Mean number of eggs hatched per hen for Rio Grande wild turkeys in the Texas Panhandle and southwestern Kansas, 2000–2004.

Study site[a]	Year									
	2000		2001		2002		2003		2004	
	$\bar{x}$	n	$\bar{x}$	n	$\bar{x}$	n	$\bar{x}$	n	$\bar{x}$	n
Cimarron NG	1.3	11	3.7	32			3.2	17	2.3	18
Gene Howe WMA	3.0	23	2.4	32	2.1	19	4.3	12	1.3	21
Salt Fork	4.4	7	2.3	22	3.3	25	4.8	12	3.7	14
Matador WMA	3.5	20	3.4	20	0.7	20	2.9	22	1.9	10
Ecoregion[b]	3.4	50	2.6	74	2.1	64	3.7	46	2.2	45

[a] Research was conducted in southwestern Kansas at the Cimarron National Grasslands (NG) and in the Texas Panhandle at the Gene Howe Wildlife Management Area (WMA), private ranches surrounding the Salt Fork of the Red River, and Matador WMA.
[b] Data from the Texas Panhandle study sites were pooled and used in the broad-scale, Texas Panhandle Rolling Plains ecoregion analyses.

RESULTS

At the local (study site) scale, the TPWD poults/hen estimates were 2.5 ± 0.7 poults/hen ($\bar{x}$ ± SE) larger than the TTU poults/hen estimates ($t = 3.557$, df = 6, $P = 0.012$). In addition, a linear relationship was not evident between the TTU and TWPD poults/hen estimates ($r^2 = 0.064$, $n = 7$, $P = 0.292$). Among study sites and years, the TPWD poults/hen estimate ranged from 1.3–7.3 poults/hen (Table 1) and the TTU poults/hen estimate ranged from 0.2–2.7 poults/hen (Table 2). Variation existed among study sites and years for nesting success rate (14.3–55.6%; Table 3), mean number of eggs laid per hen (5.2–11.1; Table 4), mean number of eggs hatched per hen (0.7–4.8; Table 5), percent juvenile females captured (0.0–73.1%; Table 6), percent juvenile males captured (8.3–89.5%; Table 7), and percent juveniles captured (3.1–71.6%; Table 8).

However, at the Panhandle Rolling Plains ecoregion scale, there was reduced variation among years. The TPWD poults/hen estimates for the ecoregion ranged from 2.3–4.7 poults/hen (Table 1). For the reproductive measures, nesting success rate ranged from 27.7–43.4% (Table 3), mean number of eggs laid per hen ranged from 8.6–9.5 (Table 4), and mean number of eggs hatched per hen ranged from 2.1–3.7 (Table 5). For the recruitment indices, percent juvenile females captured ranged from 23.0–55.9% (Table 6), percent juvenile males captured ranged from 17.9–

66.3% (Table 7), and percent juveniles captured ranged from 38.3–60.1% (Table 8).

At the local scale, nesting success rate, mean number of eggs laid per hen, mean number of eggs hatched per hen, the percent of juvenile females captured, and the percent of juveniles captured were correlated ($r^2 > 0.349$, $9 \leq n \leq 10$, $P < 0.05$) to the TTU poults/hen estimates (Figure 2). However, none of the reproductive or recruitment parameters were correlated with the TPWD poults/hen estimates ($r^2 < 0.143$, $13 \leq n \leq 16$, $P > 0.10$; Figure 3). On the ecoregion scale, we observed no linear relationship between the TPWD poults/hen estimates and the reproduction or recruitment parameters ($r^2 < 0.299$, $5 \leq n \leq 6$, $P > 0.15$; Figure 4).

DISCUSSION

These analyses suggested poults/hen estimates indexed reproduction and recruitment at localized scales, such as our study sites, but the efforts of TPWD were not adequate at local or ecoregion scales. Though the TTU and TPWD survey protocols were similar in most aspects except effort, the difference between the poults/hen estimates and the lack of concordance between them reveals how effort can influence the poults/hen index. Inadequate sample size was a problem for the TPWD poults/hen estimate. For the local scale, sample size averaged 6.8 ± 2.2 ($\bar{x}$ ± SE) flocks

Table 6. Percent juvenile female[a] Rio Grande wild turkeys captured during annual January–March trapping efforts in the Texas Panhandle and southwestern Kansas, 1999–2004.

Study site[b]	Year											
	1999		2000		2001		2002		2003		2004	
	$\bar{x}$	n	$\bar{x}$	n	$\bar{x}$	n	$\bar{x}$	n	$\bar{x}$	n	$\bar{x}$	n
Cimarron NG	11.3	53	19.4	36			0.0	20	51.2	82		
Gene Howe WMA	21.3	61	45.3	53	48.6	37	71.7	46	25.6	43	5.2	7
Salt Fork	54.2	68	50.6	87	29.6	81	73.1	26	41.3	75	30.3	37
Matador WMA	32.4	68	37.7	53	47.4	57	30.4	46	50.0	38	34.1	46
Ecoregion[c]	40.6	250	45.6	229	39.4	175	55.9	138	39.1	238	23.0	90

[a] We used the percent of juvenile females captured during annual January–March trapping efforts to index annual female recruitment at each study site.
[b] Research was conducted in southwestern Kansas at the Cimarron National Grasslands (NG) and in the Texas Panhandle at the Gene Howe Wildlife Management Area (WMA), private ranches surrounding the Salt Fork of the Red River, and Matador WMA.
[c] Data from the Texas Panhandle study sites were pooled and used in the broad-scale, Texas Panhandle Rolling Plains ecoregion analyses.

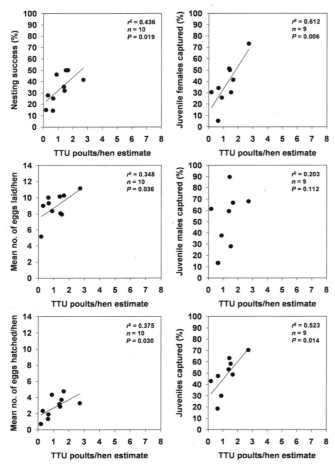

Fig. 2. Local scale, linear relationships among the Texas Tech University (TTU) poults/hen estimates for Rio Grande wild turkeys and measures of reproduction and recruitment in the Texas Panhandle and southwestern Kansas, 2002–2004. Each point represents 1 year at 1 study site.

Schwertner et al. (2003) suggested conducting >200 poult-hen counts per ecoregion per year was necessary to detect (80% power) an inter-annual change of 10–20%.

Additionally, uneven and inadequate coverage of samples across the Panhandle Rolling Plains ecoregion may have contributed to the inability of the TPWD poults/hen estimates to predict reproduction or recruitment on our study sites or the ecoregion. During the period of study, TPWD personnel conducted 1.1 ± 0.3 poult-hen counts in each county of the ecoregion per year. Typically, TPWD personnel conducted poult-hen counts in 8.3 ± 1.1 counties of the Panhandle Rolling Plains ecoregion and in only 3 of those counties were poult-hen counts conducted every year. The uneven distribution and inconsistencies in the TPWD poult-hen counting effort may have contributed to the lack of concordance with reproduction and recruitment.

The TTU poults/hen estimate exhibited a linear relationship with many measures of reproduction and recruitment at the local scale. This indicated poult-hen counts can be used as a surrogate for reproduction and recruitment at local scales. However, only about 35–45% of the variation in measures of reproduction was explained by the poults/hen estimates (Figure 2). The ability to explain this amount of variation in reproduction is important in wild turkey populations that are influenced by many ecological forces. However, from a management perspective, this may lack value as an informational tool. Though measures of recruitment were indices, about 52–62% of variation in the recruitment indices was explained by poults/hen estimates (Figure 2). This could be valuable information for wildlife managers. However, without density estimates, an index of recruitment may be of little value to managers (e.g., McDonald 1964). Also, Caughley (1974) suggested age-ratio trends can appear identical for 2 populations, one irrupting and the other crashing.

Thus, we suggest establishment of survey routes with a strict survey protocol that provides for randomization and controls effort. Though randomization and wild turkey behavioral issues arise in road surveys (e.g., Butler et al. 2005), unpublished data

per study site per year. On the ecoregion scale, sample size averaged 30.8 ± 7.3 flocks per year. Thus, more effort must be applied if the TPWD poults/hen estimate is to be valuable at local or ecoregion scales. For example, the TTU sample size averaged 46.7 ± 5.9 flocks per study site per year. Also, the results of

Table 7. Percent juvenile male[a] Rio Grande wild turkeys captured during annual January–March trapping efforts in the Texas Panhandle and southwestern Kansas, 1999–2004.

	Year											
	1999		2000		2001		2002		2003		2004	
Study site[b]	$\bar{x}$	n	$\bar{x}$	n	$\bar{x}$	n	$\bar{x}$	n	$\bar{x}$	n	$\bar{x}$	n
Cimarron NG	36.4	44	75.0	4			8.3	12	59.3	27		
Gene Howe WMA	45.3	24	58.3	36	31.6	19	71.4	21	37.5	24	13.3	18
Salt Fork	41.9	31	55.3	38	29.6	27	67.9	28	66.7	30	27.9	34
Matador WMA	70.0	50	48.6	35	42.2	45	61.3	31	89.5	19	13.3	18
Ecoregion[c]	50.4	113	54.1	109	36.3	91	66.3	80	63.0	73	17.9	70

[a] We used the percent of juvenile males captured during annual January–March trapping efforts to index annual male recruitment at each study site.
[b] Research was conducted in southwestern Kansas at the Cimarron National Grasslands (NG) and in the Texas Panhandle at the Gene Howe Wildlife Management Area (WMA), private ranches surrounding the Salt Fork of the Red River, and Matador WMA.
[c] Data from the Texas Panhandle study sites were pooled and used in the broad-scale, Texas Panhandle Rolling Plains ecoregion analyses.

Table 8. Percent juvenile[a] Rio Grande wild turkeys captured during annual January–March trapping efforts in the Texas Panhandle and southwestern Kansas, 1999–2004.

	Year											
	1999		2000		2001		2002		2003		2004	
Study site[b]	$\bar{x}$	n	$\bar{x}$	n	$\bar{x}$	n	$\bar{x}$	n	$\bar{x}$	n	$\bar{x}$	n
Cimarron NG	22.7	97	25.0	40			3.1	32	53.2	109		
Gene Howe WMA	23.7	85	50.6	89	42.9	56	71.6	67	29.9	67	18.5	25
Salt Fork	51.9	99	52.0	125	29.6	108	70.4	54	48.6	105	58.2	71
Matador WMA	48.3	118	42.0	88	45.1	102	42.9	77	63.2	57	47.4	64
Ecoregion[c]	43.6	399	48.7	342	38.3	226	60.1	230	46.7	338	40.8	160

[a] We used the percent of juveniles captured during annual January–March trapping efforts to index annual recruitment at each study site.
[b] Research was conducted in southwestern Kansas at the Cimarron National Grasslands (NG) and in the Texas Panhandle at the Gene Howe Wildlife Management Area (WMA), private ranches surrounding the Salt Fork of the Red River, and Matador WMA.
[c] Data from the Texas Panhandle study sites were pooled and used in the broad-scale, Texas Panhandle Rolling Plains ecoregion analyses.

(M. J. Butler, Texas Tech University) suggested sample sizes greater than those collected previously by TPWD can be obtained from surveying at least 400 km of roads in wild turkey habitat. This would transform the TPWD poult-hen count into an estimator of the adult population while providing reproduction and recruitment information, the valuable components of

population dynamics necessary in species management.

Application at ecoregion scales may continue to be elusive because of potential asynchronous productivity and recruitment between local wild turkey populations (T. W. Schwertner, TPWD, personal communication). As our results suggested, pooling across the

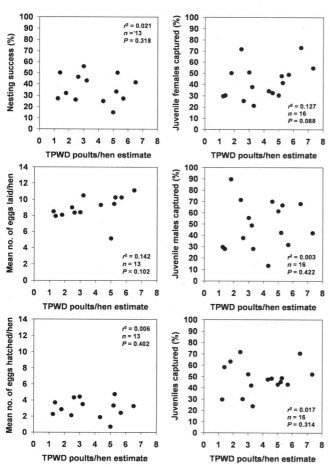

Fig. 3. Local scale, linear relationships among the Texas Parks and Wildlife Department (TPWD) poults/hen estimates for Rio Grande wild turkeys and measures of reproduction and recruitment in the Texas Panhandle, 1999–2004. Each point represents 1 year at 1 study site.

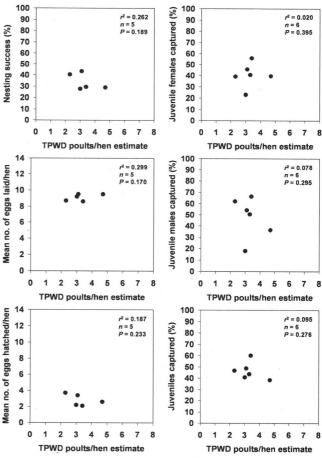

Fig. 4. Ecoregion scale, linear relationships among the Texas Parks and Wildlife Department (TPWD) poults/hen estimates for Rio Grande wild turkeys and measures of reproduction and recruitment in the Texas Panhandle Rolling Plains ecoregion, 1999–2004. Each point represents data pooled across the Texas Panhandle Rolling Plains ecoregion for 1 year.

large, Panhandle Rolling Plains ecoregion will result in a loss of the local variation associated with asynchronous productivity and recruitment across the ecoregion (Tables 3–8). This potential asynchrony may require state natural resource agencies to evaluate trends at smaller scales. Moreover, if sample sizes are improved, efforts distributed evenly, and survey techniques standardized and randomized, then the TPWD poult-hen count may prove valuable.

ACKNOWLEDGMENTS

The study was funded by Texas Parks and Wildlife Department, National Wild Turkey Federation, Texas Chapter (Superfund) of the National Wild Turkey Federation, Kansas Department of Wildlife and Parks, and Kansas Federal Aid Grant W-54-R. We thank numerous field technicians who aided in data collection and many private landowners who allowed access to their land. We gratefully acknowledge D. P. Holdstock, B. L. Spears, T. L. Barnett, J. Vacca, B. R. Bedford, and B. R. Buckley for their diligence in the field. Also, H. A. Whitlaw, T. W. Schwertner, D. P. Holdstock, N. J. Silvy, M. W. Hubbard, and 2 anonymous reviewers provided valuable comments and suggestions on earlier drafts of the manuscript. This is Texas Tech University, College of Agricultural Science and Natural Resources technical publication T-9-1055.

LITERATURE CITED

Bailey, W., D. Dennett, Jr., H. Gore, J. Pack, R. Simpson, and G. Wright. 1980. Basic considerations and general recommendations for trapping the wild turkey. Proceedings of the National Wild Turkey Symposium 4:10–23.

Bartush, L. H., M. S. Sasser, and D. L. Francis. 1985. A standardized turkey brood survey method for northwest Florida. Proceedings of the National Wild Turkey Symposium 5: 173–181.

Brunjes, J. H., IV. 2005. The population biology and landscape ecology of Rio Grande wild turkeys in the rolling plains of Texas and Kansas. Dissertation, Texas Tech University, Lubbock, Texas, USA.

Butler, M. J., W. B. Ballard, M. C. Wallace, S. J. DeMaso, and R. D. Applegate. 2006. Comparing techniques for counting Rio Grande wild turkeys at winter roosts. Pages 112–117 *in* J. W. Cain III and P. R. Krausman, editors. Managing wildlife in the southwest: new challenges for the 21st century. The Southwest Section of The Wildlife Society, 9–11 August 2005, Alpine, Texas, USA.

———, M. C. Wallace, W. B. Ballard, S. J. DeMaso, and R. D. Applegate. 2005. From the field: the relationship of Rio Grande wild turkey distributions to roads. Wildlife Society Bulletin 33:745–748.

Caughley, G. 1974. Interpretation of age ratios. Journal of Wildlife Management 38:557–562.

Davis, B. D. 1994. A funnel trap for Rio Grande turkey. Proceedings of the Annual Conference of the Southeastern Association of Fish and Wildlife Agencies 48:109–116.

DeArment, R. 1959. Turkey hen-poult ratios as an index to reproductive trends. Proceedings of the National Wild Turkey Symposium 1:27–31.

Glazener, W. C., A. S. Jackson, and M. L. Cox. 1964. The Texas drop-net turkey trap. Journal of Wildlife Management 28: 280–287.

Hall, G. I. 2005. Relationships between cattle grazing and Rio

Grande wild turkeys in the Southern Great Plains. Thesis, Texas Tech University, Lubbock, Texas, USA.

Healy, W. M., and S. M. Powell. 1999. Wild turkey harvest management: biology, strategies, and techniques. U.S. Fish and Wildlife Service Biological Technical Publication BTP-R5001-1999.

Hoffman, D. M. 1962. The wild turkey in eastern Colorado. Colorado Department of Game and Fish Technical Publication 12.

Holdstock, D. P. 2003. Survival, movement, and habitat selection of male Rio Grande wild turkeys in the Texas Panhandle and southwestern Kansas. Thesis, Texas Tech University, Lubbock, Texas, USA.

Huffman, R. T. 2005. The effect of precipitation and cover on Rio Grande wild turkey nesting ecology in the Texas Panhandle and southwestern Kansas. Thesis, Texas Tech University, Lubbock, Texas, USA.

———, M. C. Wallace, W. B. Ballard, G. Hall, R. Houchin, R. Applegate, S. J. DeMaso, and P. S. Gipson. 2006. Nesting habitat of Rio Grande wild turkeys. Pages 103–111 *in* J. W. Cain III and P. R. Krausman, editors. Managing wildlife in the southwest: new challenges for the 21st century. The Southwest Section of The Wildlife Society, 9–11 August 2005, Alpine, Texas, USA.

Keegan, T. W., and J. A. Crawford. 1999. Reproduction and survival of Rio Grande turkeys in Oregon. Journal of Wildlife Management 63:204–210.

Kennamer, J. E., D. H. Arner, C. R. Hopkins, and R. C. Clanton. 1975. Productivity of the eastern wild turkey in the Mississippi Delta. Proceedings of the National Wild Turkey Symposium 3:41–47.

Klonglan, E. D. 1955. Factors influencing the fall roadside pheasant census in Iowa. Journal of Wildlife Management 19:254–262.

Kozicky, E. L. 1952. Variations in two spring indices of male ring-necked pheasant populations. Journal of Wildlife Management 16:429–437.

Kurzejeski, E. W., and L. D. Vangilder. 1992. Population management. Pages 165–184 *in* J. D. Dickson, editor. The wild turkey: biology and management. Stackpole Books, Mechanicsburg, Pennsylvania, USA.

MacDonald, D. 1964. Turkey hen:poult ratios—are they an accurate index of production? Proceedings of Annual Conference of Western Association of State Game and Fish Commissioners 44:206–210.

McClure, H. E. 1945. Comparison of census methods for pheasants in Nebraska. Journal of Wildlife Management 9:38–45.

Menzel, K. E. 1975. Population and harvest data for Merriam's turkeys in Nebraska. Proceedings of the National Wild Turkey Symposium 3:184–188.

Miller, D. A., L. W. Burger, B. D. Leopold, and G. A. Hurst. 1998. Survival and cause specific mortality of wild turkey hens in central Mississippi. Journal of Wildlife Management 62:306–313.

Petrides, G. A. 1942. Age determination in American gallinaceous game birds. Transactions of the North American Wildlife and Natural Resources Conference 7:308–328.

Phillips, R. S. 2004. Movements, survival, and reproduction of Rio Grande wild turkeys in the Texas Panhandle. Thesis, Texas Tech University, Lubbock, Texas, USA.

Rice, C. G. 2003. Utility of pheasant call counts and brood counts for monitoring population density and predicting harvest. Western North American Naturalist 63:178–188.

Riley, T. Z., and S. P. Riley. 1999. Temporal comparison of pheasant brood sizes in the Midwest. Wildlife Society Bulletin 27:366–373.

Roberts, S. D., and W. F. Porter. 1996. Importance of demographic parameters to annual changes in wild turkey abundance. Proceedings of the National Wild Turkey Symposium 7:15–20.

Schultz, V., and R. D. McDowell. 1957. Some comments on a

wild turkey brood study. Journal of Wildlife Management 21:85–89.

Schwertner, T. W., M. J. Peterson, N. J. Silvy, and F. E. Smeins. 2003. Brood-count power estimates of Rio Grande turkey production in Texas. Proceedings of the Annual Conference of the Southeastern Association of Fish and Wildlife Agencies 57:213–221.

Shaw, H. G. 1973. The roadside survey for Merriam's turkeys in Arizona. Proceedings of the National Wild Turkey Symposium 2:285–293.

Spears, B. L. 2002. Wild turkey pre-flight poult habitat characteristics and survival. Thesis, Texas Tech University, Lubbock, Texas, USA.

———, W. B. Ballard, M. C. Wallace, R. S. Phillips, D. P. Holdstock, J. H. Brunjes, R. Applegate, P. S. Gipson, M. S. Miller, and T. Barnett. 2002. Retention times of miniature radiotransmitters glued to wild turkey poults. Wildlife Society Bulletin 30:861–867.

Suchy, W. J., R. J. Munkel, and J. M. Kienzler. 1991. Results of the August roadside survey for upland wildlife in Iowa: 1963–1988. Journal of Iowa Academy of Science 98:82–90.

Westerskov, K. 1950. Methods for determining the age of game bird eggs. Journal of Wildlife Management 14:56–67.

Wunz, G. A., and A. S. Ross. 1990. Wild turkey production, fall and spring harvest interactions and responses to harvest management in Pennsylvania. Proceedings of the National Wild Turkey Symposium 6:205–207.

———, and W. K. Shope. 1980. Turkey brood survey in Pennsylvania as it relates to harvest. Proceedings of the National Wild Turkey Symposium 4:69–75.

Zar, J. H. 1999. Biostatistical analysis. Prentice Hall, Upper Saddle River, New Jersey, USA.

Matthew [Matt] J. Butler (center) is currently a post doctoral research associate in the Department of Natural Resources Management at Texas Tech University in Lubbock. He earned his Ph.D. in wildlife sciences in 2006 from Texas Tech University. His dissertation research was focused on evaluating survey techniques for Rio Grande wild turkeys in the Southern Great Plains. He received a M.S. in forest resources from the University of Arkansas at Monticello in 2001 where he studied the foraging requirements of red-cockaded woodpeckers. In 1999, he received a B.S. in fisheries and wildlife biology from Arkansas Tech University in Russellville. Also, Matt has worked for the U.S. Forest Service as a wildlife biologist and as a forestry technician on the Ouachita National Forest. ***Mark C. Wallace*** (left) received a B.S. degree in forestry-wildlife sciences from the University of Washington in 1981, and a M.S. in wildlife ecology from the University of Arizona in 1984, and a Ph.D. from the University of Arizona in 1992. Since 1996, he as been a faculty member in the Department of Natural Resources Management at Texas Tech University. His research interests are focused on wildlife-habitat relationships. ***Warren B. Ballard*** (right) is the Bricker Chair in wildlife management at Texas Tech University. He received his B.S. in fish and wildlife management at New Mexico State University, his M.Sc. in environmental biology from Kansas State University, and his Ph.D. in wildlife science from the University of Arizona. His professional interests include predator-prey relationships and population dynamics of carnivores and ungulates.

Gallon I. Hall (pictured) was born and raised in Pensacola, Florida. He completed his B.S. in Biology at the University of South Alabama in 2002. At the time of this research, he was a graduate research assistant at Texas Tech University where he earned his M.S. in wildlife science in the spring of 2005. Currently, Galon is a district wildlife biologist for the Virginia Department of Game and Inland Fisheries. ***Richard S. Phillips*** is a doctoral student in wildlife science at Texas Tech University in Lubbock. His dissertation research is focused on the role of dispersal in population dynamics of Rio Grande wild turkeys. He received a B.A. in biology from Emory University in Atlanta and a M.S. in wildlife science at Texas Tech University. His M.S. research was focused on dispersal in yearling female Rio Grande wild turkeys. ***John H. Brunjes, IV*** received his B.S. in biology from the University of North Carolina at Wilmington and his M.S. in wildlife ecology and management from the University of Georgia. He recently completed his Ph.D. in wildlife science at Texas Tech University in Lubbock. His doctoral research focused on the landscape ecology and population dynamics of Rio Grande wild turkeys. John is currently the in the migratory bird program leader for the Kentucky Department of Fish and Wildlife Resources. ***Ross T. Huffman*** is currently employed as the Wyoming Stewardship Department manager for Conservation Seeding and Restoration, Inc. He received his M.S. in wildlife science at Texas Tech University in Lubbock in 2005 and his B.S. in wildlife management with a minor in range management at Washington State University in 1999. He has worked for the U.S. Forest Service and the Idaho Department of Fish and Game as a wildlife technician, and for the USGS and the Army Corp of

Engineers as a fisheries technician. He enjoys working with wildlife habitat and wildlife habitat restoration. **Rachael L. Houchin** recently completed her M.S. in wildlife science at Texas Tech University in Lubbock. In 2002, she received her B.S. in wildlife and fisheries science with a minor in forestry at The University of Tennessee in Knoxville. In August 2005, Rachael began working as the Renewable Resources Extension Act (RREA) coordinator and wildlife biologist for Oklahoma State University Extension. **James C. Bullock** completed his B.S. in wildlife and fisheries management at Texas Tech University in Lubbock in 2002. For several years, he has served as a wildlife technician at Texas Tech University. **Stephen [Steve] J. DeMaso** is the upland game bird program leader for the Texas Parks and Wildlife Department in Austin, Texas. Prior to moving to Texas, he worked for the Oklahoma Department of Wildlife Conservation and served as the lead researcher on the nationally recognized Packsaddle quail research project. Currently, he serves as Chairman of the Southeast Quail Study Group and a member of the National Wild Turkey Federation's Technical Committee. He is a member of the National and Texas Chapters of The Wildlife Society. He also served as the Program Chairman and Editor for the Proceedings of the Fifth National Quail Symposium. Steve was raised in southern Michigan and received his B.S. from Michigan State University, M.S. from Texas A&I University, and is currently pursuing a Ph.D. in the Wildlife and Fisheries Sciences Joint Program between Texas A&M University and Texas A&M–Kingsville. **Roger D. Applegate** is the small game coordinator for Tennessee Wildlife Resources Agency in Nashville since August 2005. Prior to that, he was the small game coordinator for Kansas Department of Wildlife and Parks. **Michael [Mike] C. Frisbie** is the database systems analyst for the migratory, upland, and small game program for Texas Parks and Wildlife Department in San Marcos, Texas. Since 1992, he has worked for the Department developing and analyzing current and historical digital datasets for a variety of Department field surveys and coordinates the use of these datasets with various researchers. A life-long Texan, Mike was raised in Lubbock and Austin, Texas, and studied wildlife biology and geographic information systems at Southwest Texas State University (now Texas State University–San Marcos).

**Wild Turkey Management:
Accomplishments, Strategies, and Opportunities**
———— Grand Rapids, Michigan ————

EFFECTS OF FERAL HOG CONTROL ON NEST FATE OF EASTERN WILD TURKEY IN THE POST OAK SAVANNAH OF TEXAS

Blake D. Petty
Department of Wildlife and Fisheries Sciences,
Texas A&M University,
College Station, TX 77843, USA

Roel R. Lopez
Department of Wildlife and Fisheries Sciences,
Texas A&M University,
College Station, TX 77843, USA

James C. Cathey[1]
Gus Engeling Wildlife Management Area,
Texas Parks and Wildlife Department,
Athens, TX 75751, USA

Shawn L. Locke
Department of Wildlife and Fisheries Sciences,
Texas A&M University,
College Station, TX 77843, USA

Markus J. Peterson
Department of Wildlife and Fisheries Sciences,
Texas A&M University,
College Station, TX 77843, USA

Nova J. Silvy
Department of Wildlife and Fisheries Sciences,
Texas A&M University,
College Station, TX 77843, USA

Abstract: Feral hogs (*Sus scrofa*) have been implicated as a major cause of depredation on nests of reintroduced eastern wild turkeys (*Meleagris gallopavo silvestris*) in Texas. To evaluate this assertion, we compared reproduction of radio-marked turkeys on an area prior to (1998) and after (1999) intensive feral hog control on the Gus Engeling Wildlife Management Area (WMA) in northeast Texas. In 1998, 69 feral hogs were removed (49 by trapping and 19 by hunters), whereas during 1999, 314 feral hogs were removed (313 by trapping and 1 by hunters). None of 28 nests hatched during 1998 when feral hog control was minimal. During 1999, 2 of 8 nests hatched and 3 poults were still alive at 2 weeks of age. Our results suggest that intensive feral hog control may have increased nest success and poult survival of relocated eastern wild turkeys on the Gus Engeling WMA.

Proceedings of the National Wild Turkey Symposium 9:169–172

Key words: control, eastern wild turkey, feral hog, *Meleagris gallopavo silvestris,* nest fate, poult survival, predation, *Sus scrofa,* Texas.

Eastern wild turkeys were once common to most of eastern Texas, but by 1942 populations were limited to 5 isolated flocks and numbered <100 birds (Newman 1945). Modern efforts to restore declining numbers in eastern Texas began in 1979–1980, when wild-trapped eastern turkeys from Louisiana and Mississippi were released on 2 eastern Texas sites (Campo 1983). From 1979 through 1999, 7,200 eastern wild turkeys were released into eastern Texas with variable success (Lopez et al. 1999).

Earlier studies of eastern wild turkeys relocated into eastern Texas were restricted to the Pineywoods ecoregion (Walker and Springs 1952, Hopkins 1981,

[1] Present address: Department of Wildlife and Fisheries Sciences, Texas A&M University, College Station, TX 77843, USA.

Campo 1983, Martin 1984). In 1987, the Gus Engeling WMA, located within the northern Post Oak Savannah, was identified by Texas Parks and Wildlife Department (TPWD) as a suitable release site. This area has served as a release and research area for eastern wild turkeys since 1988. An evaluation of restoration efforts at Gus Engeling WMA showed that poor reproductive success resulting from high nest depredation was limiting population expansion (Burk et al. 1998). Further evaluation indicated that 40% of nest destruction was caused by feral hogs (Burk et al. 1998). Our objective was to assess the influence of an intensive feral hog control program on nest fate of relocated eastern wild turkeys on Gus Engeling WMA. Specifically, our hypothesis was that intensive feral hog control would increase nest success of reintroduced wild turkeys.

STUDY AREA

This study was conducted at Gus Engeling WMA (4,400 ha) in Anderson County, Texas, approximately 34 km northwest of Palestine in the Post Oak Savannah ecological region of Texas (Gould 1975). Topography of the region was gently rolling to hilly. Annual precipitation was 89–114 cm, with the highest rainfall month being May. Upland soils consisted of sandy loams or sands over clay pans. Bottomland soils are sandy loams to clays.

The overstory in the Post Oak Savannah was primarily post oak (*Quercus stellata*) and blackjack oak (*Q. marilandica*) (Gould 1975). Most of this region was pastureland dominated by improved pastures (Petty 2000). Improved pastures were commonly seeded to bermudagrass (*Cynodon dactylon*), dallisgrass (*Paspalum dilatatum*), vaseygrass (*P. urvillei*), carpetgrass (*Axonopus*), and clovers (*Trifolium*). Climax grasses included little bluestem (*Schizachyrium scoparium*), Indiangrass (*Sorghastrum nutans*), switchgrass (*Panicum virgatum*), purpletop (*Tridens flavus*), and silver bluestem (*Bothriochloa saccaroides*). Some invasive plants included yaupon (*Ilex vomitoria*), broomsedge bluestem (*Andropogon virginicus*), bullnettle (*Cnidoscolus texanus*), and red lovegrass (*Eragrostis oxylepis*). Grazing did not occur on the GEWMA and feral hog density was unknown.

METHODS

Trapping and Radiotelemetry

From 1996 through 1999, eastern wild turkeys were live trapped at sites in Iowa, Missouri, and South Carolina, and transported in boxes via airplane to the Gus Engeling WMA within 1–4 days of capture. Prior to release, turkeys were fitted with mortality-sensitive, battery-powered, radio transmitters (150–152 MHz; 79–115 g; Advanced Telemetry Systems [ATS], Isanti, Minnesota, USA). Transmitters were attached using elastic "shock" cord (Williams et al. 1968), and birds were aged, sexed (Pelham and Dickson 1992), and released at least 1 hour prior to sunset. Birds surviving

Table 1. Numbers of eastern wild turkeys radio-tagged and released into the Gus Engeling Wildlife Management Area by year, broodstock, age (A = adult, J = juvenile), and sex (M = male, F = female).

Year	Broodstock	Age/sex				Row total
		AM	JM	AF	JF	
1996	Iowa	4	0	6	0	10
1997	Missouri	3	0	12	0	15
1999	South Carolina	0	7	10	8	25
Column total		7	7	28	8	50

<8 days post-release were excluded from analyses to minimize capture-related biases (Nenno and Healy 1979).

Radio-marked birds were relocated at least twice weekly via homing (White and Garrott 1990) for the entire study. During the nesting season (1 Apr–15 Jul), birds were located 4–5 times weekly so that nesting activity could be monitored. If hens were found in the same location on 2 successive tracking days, they were considered to be nesting. Within 10 days of initial nesting behavior, the approximate location of the nest was determined using methods described by Lopez (1996). Poult survival was determined 2 weeks post-hatch by locating roosting hens suspected of hatching a clutch.

Feral Hog Control

During 1999, TPWD biologists conducted an intensive feral hog control program to coincide with the turkey reintroduction. Using corral and box traps located in approximately 15 sites and baited with corn, feral hogs were trapped and removed from the study site throughout the year.

Data Analysis

Reproductive parameters examined in this study (nest success, and poult success) were described by Vangilder et al. (1987). We defined nest success as the percentage of incubating females that were successful (≥1 egg hatched). We defined poult success as the percentage of hatched nests that produced ≥1 poult surviving 2 weeks post-hatch. Adult turkey hens that nested off-site were excluded from the analyses. Because juvenile hens were released only in 1999, they also were excluded from all analyses. Because this is a case study and sample sizes were small, no statistical analyses were conducted.

RESULTS

From 1996 through 1999, 50 wild turkeys (14 M, 36 F) were radio-marked and released on Gus Engeling WMA (Table 1). Fifteen turkeys were obtained from Missouri, 10 from Iowa, and 25 from South Carolina. However, during the 1998 reproductive season, only 32 radio-marked adult hens (4 of which were released in March 1998) were still alive or had functional transmitters. By the 1999 reproductive season, only 17 adult hens (10 of which were released in March 1999) were still alive or had functional transmitters.

In 1998, prior to intensive feral hog control, 68 feral hogs were removed from Gus Engeling WMA through trapping (49) and hunter harvest (19). During intensive trapping efforts in 1999, 313 feral hogs were removed and 1 additional feral hog taken during the hunting season.

Prior to feral hogs being intensely controlled (1998), 32 hens produced 28 nests and none were successful. During 1999, when feral hogs were intensely controlled, 17 hens produced 8 nests and 2 were successful. Each successful hen produced 1 and 2 poults, respectively, that survived past 2 weeks. During 1999, no nest depredation was attributed to feral hogs.

DISCUSSION

We documented the removal of >4.6 times the number of hogs from the Gus Engling WMA during 1999 as opposed to 1998. Observational evidence of areas disturbed by rooting (Petty 2000) also indicated the feral hog population in the study site had been greatly reduced. In addition, hunters only harvested 1 feral hog during 1999, down from 19 during 1998. Further, feral hogs affected no wild turkey nests on the WMA during 1999. For these reasons, we assumed that feral hog numbers on the Gus Engeling WMA had been substantially reduced during 1999.

Nest success appeared to improve from 1998 (0%) to 1999 (25%) in response to limited and intensive feral hog control, respectively. Success rates recorded in 1999 were comparable to those observed during other studies conducted in the Post Oak Savannah (Lopez 1996, Feuerbacher 1997, Gainey 1997, Thorne 1999). However, success rates found in the Post Oak Savannah were low compared to those reported in other studies of eastern wild turkeys (30–68%) (Glidden and Austin 1975, Everett et al. 1980, Porter et al. 1983, Campo et al. 1984, Vangilder et al. 1987, Vander Haegen et al. 1988, Vangilder and Kurzejeski 1995). This suggests suitable nesting habitat may be limited in the Post Oak Savannah.

In this study, only 2 of 36 (5.5%) nests produced poults (3 total) to 2 weeks of age. Surprisingly, poult survival during the period of intensive feral hog control was higher than reported during other studies conducted in the Post Oak Savannah, where no poults survived to 2 weeks of age from 113 nests (Lopez 1996, Feuerbacher 1997, Gainey 1997, Lopez et al. 1998, Thorne 1999). Poult survival rates 2-weeks post-hatch ranged from 27–43% for restocked and established eastern wild turkey populations elsewhere (Gidden and Austin 1975, Everett et al. 1980, Porter et al. 1983, Campo et al. 1984, Vangilder et al. 1987, Vander Haegen et al.1988, Vangilder and Kurzejeski 1995).

Results from our study suggested that feral hog control may have led to increased nest success at Gus Engeling WMA. It is possible that during a 6-year period when 171 eastern wild turkey hens were released into other parts of the Post Oak Savannah of Texas and no poults survived (Petty 2000), that some of the loss was due to feral hogs. However, some of the release areas did not have feral hog problems. In these areas, brood range was probably the limiting factor (Petty 2000) because the habitat was inadequate to raise poults. Moreover, 10 of the 17 adult hens available for nesting were newly reintroduced hens, which Lopez et al. (1999) indicated were less likely to nest. We recognize that a number of factors other than feral hog depredation probably contributed to reduced nest and poult success on Gus Engeling WMA and elsewhere in the Post Oak Savannah of Texas (Lopez et al. 1999). However, our data suggest that feral hog depredation on nests might be one key contributor to reproductive failure in this region.

MANAGEMENT IMPLICATIONS

Evidence from our study indicates that intensive feral hog control can lead to increased wild turkey nest success and poult survival. Managers should consider these options if evidence suggests feral hogs are destroying turkey nests, particularly during reintroduction efforts. We controlled hogs throughout the year, but it is possible that feral hog control just prior to and during the reproductive season could be sufficient to reduce feral hog impact on nesting wild turkeys.

ACKNOWLEDGMENTS

Funding for the project was provided by TPWD (Turkey Stamp) and Texas A&M University System. Special thanks to Iowa Department of Natural Resources, Missouri Department of Conservation, South Carolina Department of Natural Resources, and the National Wild Turkey Federation for providing birds for this study. We are grateful to J. D. Burk of TPWD for contributing information on the eastern wild turkey in the Post Oak Savannah in Texas and J. K. Thorne for his contributions to this project.

LITERATURE CITED

Burk, J. D., S. Willis, J. C. Cathey, and D. Prochaska. 1998. An assessment of eastern wild turkey restoration efforts at Gus Engeling Wildlife Management Area. Texas Parks and Wildlife Department, Austin, Texas, USA.

Campo, J. J. 1983. Brood habitat use, reproduction, and movement of recently restocked eastern wild turkeys in east Texas. Dissertation, Texas A&M University, College Station, Texas, USA.

———, C. R. Hopkins, and W. G. Swank. 1984. Mortality and reproduction of stocked eastern wild turkeys in east Texas. Proceedings of the Annual Conference of the Southeastern Association of Fish and Wildlife Agencies 38:78–86.

Everett, D. D., D. W. Speake, and W. K. Maddox. 1980. Natality and mortality of a north Alabama wild turkey population. Proceedings of the National Wild Turkey Symposium 4: 117–126.

Feuerbacher, C. K. 1997. Effects of supplemental stocking on eastern wild turkey restoration in the post oak savannah of Texas. Thesis, Texas A&M University, College Station, Texas, USA.

Gainey, J. W. 1997. A comparison of Texas and Iowa brood-stocks for eastern wild turkey restoration in the post oak savannah of Texas. Thesis, Texas A&M University, College Station, Texas, USA.

Glidden, J. W., and D. E. Austin. 1975. Natality and mortality of wild turkey poults in southwestern New York. Proceedings of the National Wild Turkey Symposium 3:48–54.

Gould, F. W. 1975. Texas plants—a checklist and ecological summary. Texas Agricultural Experiment Station, Publication 585, College Station, Texas, USA.

Hopkins, C. R. 1981. Dispersal, reproduction, mortality, and habitat utilization of restocked eastern turkeys in east Texas. Dissertation, Texas A&M University, College Station, Texas, USA.

Lopez, R. R. 1996. Population dynamics of eastern wild turkeys relocated into the post oak savannah of Texas. Thesis, Texas A&M University, College Station, Texas, USA.

———, C. K. Feuerbacher, M. A. Sternberg, N. J. Silvy, and J. D. Burk. 1998. Survival and reproduction of eastern wild turkeys relocated into the Post Oak Savannah of Texas. Proceedings of the Annual Conference of Southeastern Association of Fish and Wildlife Agencies 52:384–396.

———, J. H. Yantis, M. J. Peterson, C. K. Feuerbacher, and N. J. Silvy. 1999. Evaluating 2 potential limiting factors for relocated turkeys in Texas. Proceedings of the Annual Conference of the Southeastern Association of Fish and Wildlife Agencies 53:305–312.

Martin, D. J. 1984. The influence of selected timber management practices on habitat use by wild turkeys in east Texas. Thesis, Texas A&M University, College Station, Texas, USA.

Nenno, E. S., and W. M. Healy. 1979. Effects of radio packages on behavior of wild turkey hens. Journal of Wildlife Management 43:760–765.

Newman, C. C. 1945. Turkey restocking efforts in east Texas. Journal of Wildlife Management 9:279–289.

Pelham, P. H., and J. G. Dickson. 1992. Physical characteristics. Pages 32–45 *in* J. G. Dickson, editor. The wild turkey: biology and management. Stackpole Books, Harrisburg, Pennsylvania, USA.

Petty, B. D. 2000. An evaluation of efforts to reestablish eastern wild turkeys into the Post Oak savannah of Texas. Thesis, Texas A&M University, College Station, Texas, USA.

Porter, W. F., G. C. Nelson, and K. Mattson. 1983. Effects of winter conditions on reproduction in a northern wild turkey population. Journal of Wildlife Management 47:281–290.

Thorne, J. K. 1999. Differential survival and reproduction of mid-western and southeastern wild turkey broodstock reintroduced into the post oak savannah of Texas. Thesis, Texas A&M University, College Station, Texas, USA.

Vander Haegen, W. M., W. E. Dodge, and W. M. Sayre. 1988. Factors effecting productivity in northern turkey populations. Journal of Wildlife Management 52:127–133.

Vangilder, L. D., and E. W. Kurzejeski. 1995. Population ecology of the eastern wild turkey in northern Missouri. Wildlife Monographs 130.

———, ———, V. L. Kimmel-Truitt, and J. B. Lewis. 1987. Reproductive parameters of wild turkey hens in north Missouri. Journal of Wildlife Management 51:535–540.

Walker, E. A., and A. J. Springs. 1952. Factors concerned with the success and failure of turkey transplants in Texas. Texas Game, Fish, and Oyster Commission 23:46–58.

White, G. C., and R. A. Garrott. 1990. Analysis of wildlife radio-tracking data. Academic Press, San Diego, California, USA.

Williams, L. E., Jr., D. H. Austin, N. F. Eichholz, T. E. Peoples, and R. W. Phillips. 1968. A study of nesting turkeys in southern Florida. Proceedings of the Annual Conference of the Southeastern Association of Fish and Wildlife Agencies 22:16–30.

Blake D. Petty (pictured with son Jackson) holds a BS and MS in Wildlife & Fisheries Sciences from Texas A&M University. His masters' research was a study of the restoration of eastern wild turkeys into the Post Oak Savannah of Texas. Blake currently works in the Technology Commercialization Center for the Texas A&M University System, where he coordinates commercialization efforts for agricultural and life science innovations from the University. ***Shawn L. Locke*** is a doctoral student at Texas A&M University studying methods for estimating Rio Grande wild turkey abundance. He received a B.S. in forestry from Stephen F. Austin State University and a M.S. in range and wildlife management from Sul Ross State University. His research interests include ecology and management of ungulates and upland game birds. ***Markus J. Peterson*** is an Associate Professor in the Department of Wildlife and Fisheries Sciences at Texas A&M University and at the Center for Public Leadership Studies at the George Bush School of Government and Public Service. He received his B.S. from University of Idaho, D.V.M. from Washington State University, and M.S. and Ph.D. from Texas A&M University. Markus has a wide array of research interests ranging from ecology and management of terrestrial wildlife populations to the formation and implementation of environmental policy. ***Roel R. Lopez*** is an Assistant Professor with the Department of Wildlife and Fisheries Sciences at Texas A&M University. His previous employment was with U.S. Fish and Wildlife Service, National Key Deer Refuge. He received his B.S. in Forestry from Stephen F. Austin State University and his M.S. and Ph.D. from Texas A&M University. His research focus is urban wildlife ecology, deer ecology, wildlife population dynamics, and habitat management. ***James C. Cathey*** is an Assistant Professor and Extension Wildlife Specialist in the Department of Wildlife and Fisheries Sciences stationed at the Texas Agricultural Research and Extension Center in Uvalde, Texas. Previously, he served as Natural Resource Specialist for Texas Parks and Wildlife where he coordinated the research at the Gus Engeling and Richland Creek Wildlife Management areas. He earned his B.S. and M.S. from Texas A&M University and his Ph.D. from Texas Tech University. His research background includes the use of genetic techniques to better manage wildlife populations, assessing the effects of land management practices on wildlife, and more recently the interactions of livestock and wildlife for the purpose of combating disease transmission. ***Nova J. Silvy*** is a Regents Professor with the Department of Wildlife and Fisheries Sciences at Texas A&M University. He received his B.S. and M.S. from Kansas State University and his Ph.D. from Southern Illinois University-Carbondale. Nova served as President of The Wildlife Society in 2000–2001 and received the Aldo Leopold Award in 2003. His research focus is upland-game ecology.

Chapter III

Habitat Ecology of Wild Turkeys

Wild Turkey Management:
Accomplishments, Strategies, and Opportunities
——— Grand Rapids, Michigan ———

EFFECT OF LANDSCAPE FEATURES AND FRAGMENTATION ON WILD TURKEY DISPERSAL

Kathleen K. Fleming[1,2]
Faculty of Environmental and Forest Biology,
State University of New York,
College of Environmental Science and Forestry,
1 Forestry Drive, Syracuse, NY 13210, USA

William F. Porter
Faculty of Environmental and Forest Biology,
State University of New York,
College of Environmental Science and Forestry,
1 Forestry Drive, Syracuse, NY 13210, USA

Abstract: Wild turkeys (*Meleagris gallopavo silvestris*) are now found in almost every county of New York State. Population recovery has probably been facilitated by the ability of individuals to disperse into unoccupied habitat. We investigated the effect of landscape patterns and barriers to movement on wild turkey dispersal in New York to determine if these landscape characteristics may have affected the statewide pattern of wild turkey population recovery. First, we simulated the effect of landscape features and landscape fragmentation (measured by edge/area) on dispersal patterns in a wild turkey population in New York State using land-cover data derived from satellite imagery. We used cost–distance analysis in ArcView, a method that involves calculating least costly dispersal paths through a landscape, to determine the average least cost incurred by wild turkeys dispersing through landscapes along a gradient of fragmentation. We compared this cost to the edge density in each landscape. Average cost incurred was negatively correlated with edge/area ($r = -0.80$, $P < 0.001$). Second, we simulated the expansion of the wild turkey population in New York from wild birds released at sites throughout the state and birds crossing northward from Pennsylvania, and compared it visually to the spatial pattern of expansion of the fall wild turkey harvest in New York from 1982 to 2000. The analysis predicted a similar visual pattern of population expansion as the fall harvest. As managers seek to fill remaining vacant habitat, they should be aware of the extent to which landscape features may inhibit or facilitate dispersal of individuals from release sites.

Proceedings of the National Wild Turkey Symposium 9:175–183

Key words: agriculture, dispersal, edge, fragmentation, habitat, landscape, *Meleagris gallopavo silvestris*, movement, New York, population, wild turkey.

Wild turkey populations have been restored to almost all states in the U.S. (Tapley et al. 2001). The success of population recovery efforts in most cases has been attained through trap and transfer of wild birds into unoccupied habitat. This success has been facilitated by the natural dispersal behavior of juvenile wild turkeys as well as seasonal movements of adult birds from winter to spring range (Eaton et al. 1976). In many translocation programs, population restoration has been dependent upon a relatively small number of released birds being able to colonize and reproduce in large expanses of new habitat. Adverse genetic effects may occur in the restored population if connectivity with other populations is not maintained, especially if the founder birds originate from the same flock (Backs

and Eisfelder 1990). Because turkeys disperse by walking, rather than flying, connectivity can be influenced by features of the landscape that act to facilitate or hinder movement (Backs and Eisfelder 1990, Gustafson et al. 1994). Several studies have documented preferential use of edge habitats during dispersal or other seasonal movements, especially forest/field edges (Raybourne 1968, Eichholz and Marchinton 1975, Porter 1978). Connectivity of these preferred habitat types is needed for dispersal (Eaton 1992, Gustafson

[1] E-mail: Kathy_Fleming@fws.gov
[2] US Fish and Wildlife Service, Division of Migratory Bird Management, 11510 American Holly Drive, Laurel, MD 20708, USA.

et al. 1994, Peoples et al. 1996). Most of these features are a by-product of landscape fragmentation.

Fragmented landscapes contain abundant edge habitat which should facilitate movement of turkeys. However, wild turkeys tend to avoid roads, developed areas, and the centers of large fields, presumably due to the perceived cost or risk of traversing or foraging in these habitats (Eichholz and Marchinton 1975, McDougal et al. 1990). Landscapes dominated by extensive agriculture, roads, and high-intensity development might hinder dispersal or be avoided altogether.

We used a spatially explicit cost-distance analysis to predict how landscape features associated with fragmentation, such as roads, edges, and the spatial arrangement of land-cover types, might influence broad-scale dispersal patterns of wild turkeys across New York. Wildlife researchers have utilized cost-distance analysis to identify wildlife movement corridors and to investigate effects of habitat fragmentation (e.g., Verbeylen et al. 2003, Wikramanayake et al. 2004). This method is suitable for use in analyzing costs associated with movement paths across a landscape represented by a raster land-cover data set (i.e., pixel rather than polygon data). Using cost-distance analysis, we addressed the following objectives: (1) determine the relationship between landscape fragmentation and cost of dispersal, (2) predict the broad-scale pattern of population expansion in New York following releases and movement of birds from northern Pennsylvania, based on known habitat use and avoidance behavior, (3) compare the predicted pattern of population expansion with the history of population growth in the state, indexed by wild turkey fall harvest data.

STUDY AREA

The study area was the state of New York: 126,000 km² partitioned into 11 major ecozones. The Appalachian plateau in southwest New York (43,430 km²) is characterized by broad hills (elevation approximately 600 m) and steep valleys, with agriculture (primarily dairy farms, vineyards) concentrated in lowland areas (Dickinson 1983). The Great Lakes Plain in northwest New York (15,930 km²) is a low-elevation (mostly <250 m), low-relief plain created by glaciation, with extensive agriculture (vegetables, grains, and fruits). The ecozones of eastern New York are defined primarily by mountains (Adirondacks, Catskills) or valleys (Mohawk River, Hudson River, and Lake Champlain), and vary widely with respect to environment and land use. River valleys were predominantly agricultural, while both Adirondacks and Catskills regions were primarily forested. Widespread upland forest communities included Appalachian oak–hickory forest (*Quercus* spp., *Carya* spp.), which ranged throughout New York south of the Adirondacks and north of Long Island; beech–maple mesic forest (*Fagus grandifolia, Acer* spp.), throughout New York; and mixed northern hardwood forest, with hemlock (*Tsuga canadensis),* white pine (*Pinus strobus*), or spruce (*Picea* spp.) associations, located at higher elevations or

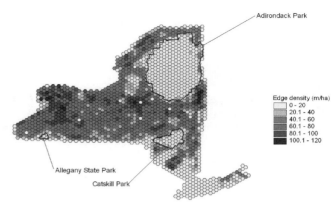

Fig. 1. Edge density (m/ha) within 7,850-ha hexagon landscapes measured from the National Land Cover Data Set (EPA/MRLC) for New York State, 1992.

latitudes (Reschke 1990). Approximately 62% of New York State was forested (Alerich and Drake 1995). Nonforested areas were primarily active or abandoned agriculture, or else 1 of 21 natural nonforested upland communities (Reschke 1990).

METHODS

We used the land-cover map of New York State produced as part of the National Land Cover Data Set (NLCD) by the Environmental Protection Agency (EPA)/Multi-Resolution Land Characteristics Consortium (MRLC). The NLCD was derived from satellite imagery acquired in 1988–1993 and has 30-m resolution and 15 cover classes: water, low- and high-intensity residential, commercial/industrial/transportation, hay/pasture, row crops, urban/recreational grasses (e.g., golf courses, airports, soccer fields), conifer forest, mixed conifer/deciduous forest, deciduous forest, forested wetland, nonforested wetland, quarry/strip mine, sand beach, and barren or transitional (i.e., clearcuts, plowed soil). To reduce processing time, we reduced the resolution of the original NLCD from 30-m to 90-m pixel size using a nearest-neighbor resampling technique in ArcView. Although resampling tends to remove small (i.e., <90 m wide) habitat patches in the land-cover data, in some cases it may also increase the accuracy of the land-cover data when these small patches are an artifact of the classification process (Fleming et al. 2004).

Effect of Landscape Fragmentation on Dispersal Cost

All analyses using the NLCD were conducted in ArcView (Version 3.2, Environmental Systems Research Institute [ESRI], Redlands, California, USA). We subdivided the state into experimental landscape units by overlaying a hexagonal grid created using the Patch Analyst extension for ArcView (Rempel and Carr 2003) on the NLCD, with area of each hexagon 7,850 ha (roughly equivalent to a circle with radius 5 km; Figure 1). This size resulted in relatively homo-

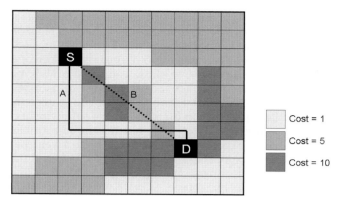

Fig. 2. Example of cost paths calculated using cost-distance analysis. A and B represent 2 possible paths from a source pixel (S) to a destination pixel (D) in a landscape where pixels are assigned costs ranging from 1 (low cost) to 10 (high cost). The accumulated cost–distance of moving along each path is calculated as the summation, over all pixels in the path, of the cost of each pixel multiplied by the distance moved through the pixel (90 m for a horizontal or vertical movement, 127.2 m for diagonal movement). Thus, for Path A, the accumulated cost–distance is (1 × 90) + (1 × 90) + (1 × 90) + (1 × 90) + (1 × 90) + (1 × 90) + (1 × 90) + (1 × 90) + (5 × 90) + (1 × 90) = 1170; and for Path B, the accumulated cost–distance is (10 × 127.2) + (10 × 127.2) + (5 × 127.2) + (5 × 127.2) = 3816. The analysis calculates accumulated cost–distance for all possible paths from S to D, and assigns the lowest accumulated cost–distance of all these paths to the pixel D. This process is repeated for all non-source pixels in the landscape, which results in the creation of a cost–distance grid.

geneous configuration (i.e., degree of fragmentation) within landscapes.

We measured 2 characteristics of each hexagonal landscape. First, we measured edge density by tabulating the total number of edge pixels (pixels that were adjacent to at least one different pixel type) and dividing by the total land area in the landscape (not including area of the landscape covered by water). Although many other types of edges were present, we were primarily interested in edges within wild turkey habitat, so we did not include edges of developed land, water, or barren/transitional land. However, if developed land was adjacent to turkey habitat (e.g., forest, agriculture), those habitat pixels at the forest or agriculture edge would be included as edge pixels. We calculated the amount of linear edge by multiplying the number of edge pixels within each hexagon by their width (90 m).

Second, we measured the average dispersal cost in each hexagonal landscape using a cost-distance analysis (Cost-distance Grid Tools extension for Spatial Analyst 1.1, ESRI, Redlands, California, USA). This type of spatial analysis measures the accumulated cost-distance of moving along a path within a landscape from a source pixel to a destination pixel, taking into account both the distance traveled and the relative cost incurred in each cover type traversed along the path (Figure 2). The analysis uses an iterative process to evaluate the path with the least accumulated cost-distance, cd_l:

$$cd_l = \min \sum_{i=j} c_i d_i$$

where c_i is the cost of pixel i, d_i is the distance traveled through pixel i (90 m for horizontal and vertical movements, 127.2 m for diagonal movements), and j is the total number of pixels in the path going from the source to that point in the landscape. For each destination pixel, the accumulated cost-distance along every possible path of travel through the landscape is calculated, starting from the source pixel and ending at the destination pixel (Figure 2). After this iterative process is completed for all possible paths, the path with the lowest accumulated cost-distance value is chosen, and this value is assigned to the destination pixel.

We used a 2-step process to evaluate average cost–distance for each hexagon. First, we created a cost landscape where we identified barriers to movement and costs associated with each land-cover type. Second, using Spatial Analyst in ArcView we analyzed the accumulated least cost-distance of moving through this landscape.

We created the cost landscape based on information on wild turkey habitat use and dispersal behavior reported in the literature. We labeled each land-cover type as a barrier to movement (was not crossed), or as low (cost = 1), moderate (cost = 5), or high cost (cost = 10). For wild turkeys, the cost of traveling through a specific habitat type can be broken down into 2 components: the risk of predation and the benefit provided by food resources. Some habitats are avoided completely: wild turkeys are reluctant to cross agricultural fields 150–200 m wide (Eichholz and Marchinton 1975), large clearcuts (Raybourne 1968), and busy roads, especially when flanked by open areas (McDougal et al. 1990). These features may act as barriers to dispersal. Female turkeys prefer streamside zones for travel (Palmer and Hurst 1995), smaller rather than larger forest patches (Wigley et al. 1985), and forested areas with open understories located near escape cover (Sisson et al. 1990).

Dispersing turkeys may avoid human development and intensively farmed areas (Backs and Eisfelder 1990). We labeled areas without sufficient cover (bare rock, quarries, and transitional areas such as plowed fields), high-intensity residential areas, and conifer forest interior as high cost. We labeled low-intensity residential, urban/recreational grasses, woody wetlands, and deciduous and mixed forest interiors (>120 m from edge) as moderate cost, and all forest and agriculture edges (land cover <120 m from edge) as low cost. Based on the common perception that wild turkeys disperse by walking rather than flying, we assumed that turkeys would walk around water or emergent herbaceous wetlands, and would avoid crossing the interior of agricultural fields (Eichholz and Marchinton 1975) or busy roads (McDougal et al. 1990). Therefore, we labeled these cover types (major highways were included in the commercial/industrial/transportation class) as barriers.

To calculate average least accumulated cost-distance in each hexagon, we arbitrarily designated the

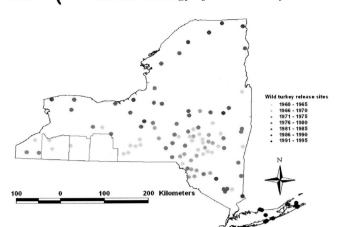

Fig. 3. Locations and years when wild turkeys were released in New York from 1960 to 2000. Points represent geographic centroids of townships or state wildlife management areas where releases occurred, not the actual location of the releases. For the cost-distance analysis we assumed that the present population of wild turkeys in New York descended from birds released at these sites and wild birds dispersing northward from Pennsylvania in (from left to right, outlines shown in blue) Cattaraugus, Allegany, and Steuben counties.

center pixel of each hexagon as the source, and evaluated least accumulated cost–distance from the source to all other pixels in the landscape. We took the average of all pixels' values in the hexagon to represent the cost associated with dispersal in that landscape.

We used PROC CORR in SAS (SAS Institute 1990) to estimate correlation between edge density and average accumulated dispersal cost in each hexagonal landscape with the Pearson product–moment correlation coefficient (Zar 1984).

Simulation of Population Expansion

We used a similar cost-distance analysis to simulate the pattern of population expansion following wild turkey releases and the spread of wild birds northward from northern Pennsylvania into New York. For this analysis, we used information on trap and transfer locations where wild turkeys were released in New York from 1960 to 1994 (R. Sanford, New York State Department of Environmental Conservation, unpublished data). We conducted 7 successive cost-distance analyses representing population expansion during each 5-year period from 1960 to 1995. For the first analysis (1960–1965) we assumed all sites where turkeys were released within this time period, as well as the New York–Pennsylvania state line in Steuben, Allegany, and Cattaraugus counties in western New York, to be source locations for dispersing turkeys (Figure 3). Because information on release locations was limited to town name or wildlife management area, we used the geographic centroids of these areas as the location of the sources. The accumulated least cost was calculated from sources to all other pixels in the state using the cost landscape created by the process described previously.

For each analysis we used a threshold of cost-dis-

tance to represent the limit of expansion during that 5-year period. We assumed that range expansion would occur at a rate similar to that estimated for populations in Pennsylvania, approximately 8 km/year (Healy 1992). However, to allow comparison with the pattern of abundance indexed by harvest effort data, we added a 5-year time lag to that estimate to account for population growth to huntable levels following expansion into new habitat. This resulted in an estimate of population expansion of 8 km for each 5-year period. For each successive 5-year analysis, we used the area of expansion predicted by the previous cost-distance analysis as the source, as well as any sites where releases had occurred in that 5-year period.

Comparison of Predicted Population Expansion with Harvest Index

We considered 2 characteristics of the fall harvest data which could be used to reflect the expansion of the wild turkey population in New York: the pattern of increase in the number of townships in the state with a fall harvest, and the average effort expended in those townships during the fall harvest season. As population expansion occurred in a township, we assumed that, first, a perceived threshold in population density was reached when a fall harvest season was added, and second, as the population density continued to increase the average effort expended by hunters to find a turkey would decrease. We created maps showing the pattern of increase in fall harvest seasons by township and an abundance index based on hunter effort (time-to-first-kill) derived from fall harvest data collected by the New York Department of Environmental Conservation from 1982 to 2001 (Porter and Gefell 1996, Glennon and Porter 1999). This index was calculated as the reciprocal of the average number of days taken by hunters in each township to find and kill a wild turkey during the fall season (in townships with a 2-bird bag limit we used only the first kill effort to avoid incorporating errors by hunters incorrectly reporting total effort for the second kill). We calculated 5-year averages of the abundance index (except for the first, 3-year interval from 1982 to 1995) for the following intervals: 1986–1990, 1990–1995, and 1995–2000. During this overall time period, the number of townships in the state with a fall harvest greatly increased; therefore, most townships in the state were not represented in the earlier year intervals. We assumed that turkey population densities were lower in these townships than any township with a fall harvest. We displayed average index values on maps to visually compare with the pattern of expansion predicted by our cost-distance analyses.

Lastly, to test the assumption that the pattern predicted by the cost-distance analysis reflected turkey use and avoidance of landscape features such as edge density, rather than just the limited distance turkeys can travel, we ran the same cost-distance analyses using a neutral landscape where all pixels regardless of their land cover type were assigned cost = 1. This analysis took only distance into account when determining the limit to population expansion. We visually

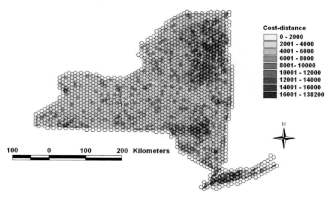

Fig. 4. Dispersal cost-distance within 7,850-ha hexagon landscapes calculated using a cost-distance analysis in ArcView from the National Land Cover Data Set (EPA/MRLC) for New York State, 1992.

compared the predicted pattern of expansion using the neutral landscape to that predicted using the cost landscape, and also to the pattern of the harvest index in townships with a fall turkey harvest.

RESULTS

Effect of Landscape Fragmentation on Dispersal Cost

Average edge density was 42 m/ha (range 0–119 m/ha) within hexagonal landscapes (Figure 1). Highest edge density was found south of Lake Ontario and the region east of Buffalo, in the state's most intensively farmed landscapes. Lowest edge density occurred in the Adirondack, Catskill, and Allegany Parks, and in the Tug Hill region west of the Adirondack Park (Figure 1).

Cost was distributed unevenly across the land-cover data (Figure 4). Highest cost pixels were concentrated in areas with relatively large tracts of conifer and deciduous forest (Adirondack and Catskill Mountains) and metropolitan areas. Most (41%) of the pixels were classified as low cost; 27% were moderate cost, 3% were high cost, and 29% were classified as barriers. Average accumulated cost–distance of all pixels in each landscape ranged from 720 m to 48,176 m, with average of all landscapes 6,890 m (Figure 4). Average cost–distance was highly negatively correlated with edge density in hexagons ($r = -0.80$, $P < 0.001$).

Predicted Dispersal Pattern

The pattern of dispersal predicted by our cost-distance analysis showed some regions of the state without established populations up to the year 2000 (Figure 5). These areas included most of the Adirondack Park, the agricultural area north of the Adirondack Park and south of the U.S.–Canadian border, the central region of the Catskills, the intensively farmed area in the Finger Lakes region between Cayuga and Seneca lakes, and areas surrounding the major urban centers (e.g., Buffalo, Rochester, Syracuse, Binghamton, and Utica). These areas contain many barriers to movement

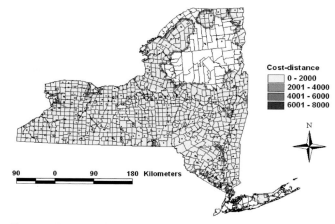

Fig. 5. Predicted expansion of wild turkey population in New York from 1960 to 2000 based on cost-distance analyses. Source locations for wild turkeys were sites where wild birds were released and the Pennsylvania–New York state line in Cattaraugus, Allegany, and Steuben counties (see Fig. 3).

(roads, urban land, large agricultural fields, water) or high-cost land-cover types (e.g., high-intensity residential land).

Comparison with Harvest Abundance Index

The number of townships in New York with a fall wild turkey season increased from 362 to 759 in 1982–2000. Townships without a fall harvest season in 2000 were located primarily in the western Great Lakes Plain, southern and eastern Adirondacks, central Catskills, between Seneca and Cayuga Lakes in the Finger Lakes region, Long Island, and the New York City metropolitan area. The pattern of increase in fall harvest seasons was similar to the pattern of population expansion predicted by the cost-distance analysis, which showed high cost or a lack of expansion into most of these areas (Figure 6). However, some differences did exist. Most of the townships at the northwestern edge of the Adirondack Park had a fall season by 2000 although the cost-distance analysis predicted limited expansion into most of these townships. We did not detect a strong spatial pattern in the average harvest index although average harvest effort tended to be lower in townships along the edge of the expanding population (those that had more recently added a fall harvest) than those where presumably the turkey population had already become established.

The result of the cost-distance analysis using the neutral landscape was a pattern similar to that using the cost landscape, with some notable exceptions (Figure 7). The original cost-distance analysis predicted that the area in the Finger Lakes region between Seneca and Cayuga lakes would not have an established wild turkey population by 2000, but this area was easily reached by dispersers when water and large agricultural fields were assigned equal cost as other landscape features. Also, the neutral cost-distance analysis did not predict any hindrance to population expansion into suburban and urban areas in western New York, unlike the original cost-distance analysis.

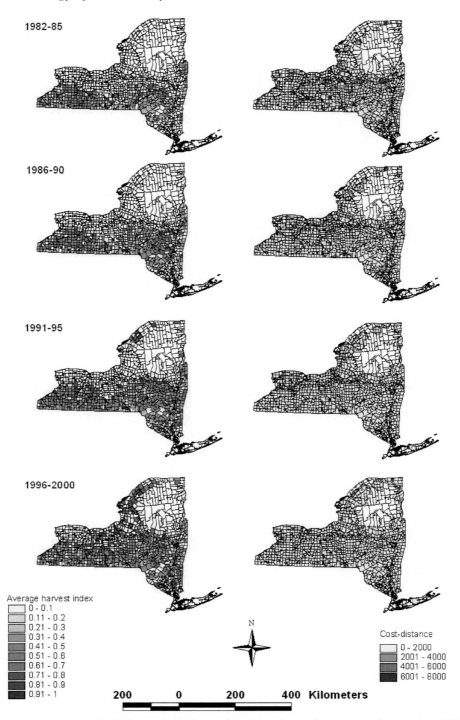

Fig. 6. Comparison of average time-to-first-kill harvest index and increase in number of townships with a fall harvest in New York (on left) to pattern of wild turkey population expansion predicted by cost-distance analyses (on right), 1980–2000. Filled townships on left represent those with a fall harvest; color of township represents value of average harvest index for that township (see legend on left). Cost-distance values represent the expansion of the wild turkey population away from release sites in New York during each 3-year (1982–1985) or 5-year time interval when releases took place.

DISCUSSION

Our cost-distance analysis predicted that fragmented landscapes facilitate dispersal of wild turkeys in New York, despite the presence of roads and other barriers. The negative correlation between dispersal cost and edge density resulted from the preference by turkeys for edge habitat during dispersal. Edge density represents the increasing interspersion of agriculture into forested areas. Even areas of intensive agriculture in New York, such as the Great Lakes Plain south of Lake Ontario or the Finger Lakes region in central

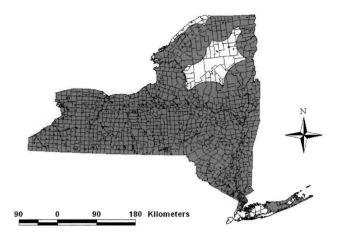

Population expansion from 1960 to 2000 predicted using neutral landscape analysis

Fig. 7. Result of cost-distance analysis to predict wild turkey population expansion in New York using a neutral cost landscape (all land-cover types assigned cost = 1) from 1960 to 2000. Area shown in red represents the expansion of the population following wild turkey releases that occurred from 1960–1995.

New York, probably contain enough forest edge to provide travel routes for dispersing turkeys. This is in contrast to the agricultural Midwest where large field size and small forest patches with low connectivity can inhibit movement of wild turkeys (Gustafson et al. 1994). The difference may lie in the broad-scale interspersion of farmland and public land in New York. Unlike the Midwest, even intensively farmed areas of New York tend to have smaller fields and larger forest patches due to the more rugged topography of the region. Although barriers and high-cost habitat types exist, any hindrance to dispersal they represent may only be on a local scale. In our model, dispersal would be substantially inhibited at a landscape scale only if a much larger proportion of the landscape consisted of barriers (e.g., interiors of large cropfields).

The landscapes of the Adirondacks and Catskills are potentially costly for dispersing turkeys. Forest is a necessary component of habitat for turkeys, especially during dispersal. However, as forest patches become larger and more aggregated, it is likely that the interior of these areas will be avoided by turkeys if they are a greater distance from edge habitat than a turkey could travel before the onset of breeding season. Wild turkeys undoubtedly do move through these landscapes, but are probably restricted to less costly paths (e.g., bottomland edges, near openings). Their population distribution in these landscapes may be patchy, owing to low proximity of suitable reproductive habitat and limited paths of dispersal within it.

Dispersal, and thus population expansion, may not only be affected by the local landscape, but also the larger spatial arrangement of these landscapes. In New York, the forests of the Adirondack Park may hinder population expansion at a regional scale, much the same as the large expanse of mature hemlock and white pine forest was thought to limit historic wild turkey distributions in northern Pennsylvania (Hayden and Wunz 1975). Although the northern hardwood forests of the Adirondacks may contain sufficient mast-producing species to support turkey populations, deep snow in most winters probably limits the extent to which turkeys can make use of this winter food resource (Porter 1978).

Comparison of Simulated Expansion with Harvest Data

Although the predicted pattern of population expansion in New York closely followed the pattern of increase in fall harvest seasons, the average effort index did not show the pattern we anticipated, that of lower hunting effort in townships with an established turkey population. Instead, we observed a tendency for hunting effort to increase in townships after populations became established, with lowest effort observed in townships that had recently added a fall season. This might be due to the higher productivity observed for turkeys in newly occupied habitat. In New York, the highest poult:hen ratios observed during the summer brood surveys have consistently been found in some parts of the state with the lowest turkey densities, such as the Adirondacks (R. Sanford, New York State Department of Environmental Conservation, unpublished data). Alternatively, the relationship between harvest index and population density could be confounded by differences in hunter skill and knowledge of the area hunted, which might be substantial among townships with different histories of fall harvest. Although this would not affect the pattern of expansion we predicted, it could limit our ability to compare wild turkey densities among townships.

Differences between the pattern of expansion predicted using the cost landscape with that predicted using the neutral landscape were most conspicuous in 2 regions: the intensively farmed area within Seneca County in the Finger Lakes region of central New York, and urban areas surrounding Buffalo and Rochester in western New York (Figures 4 and 6). The slow expansion into the Finger Lakes region is supported by fall harvest data; Seneca County lagged behind the rest of central New York in terms of when the fall harvest was added (1996) and average harvest index (Figure 6). Wild turkeys are currently found in suburban Buffalo and Rochester; however, they are not commonly associated with the intensively developed or industrial sites of these urban centers. While these differences do suggest that turkey avoidance or preference for certain habitats during dispersal does play a role in determining patterns of expansion, there are more similarities between the 2 expansion models than differences. Both models showed a lack of population expansion into the Adirondacks, the northern boundary of New York, and New York City, due only to their distance from release sites. Limited dispersal ability in wild turkeys is probably the primary factor determining the pattern of population expansion following release; avoidance or selection of specific habitats may only play a substantial role when these habitats are aggregated across a large region (such as Adirondack forests or the intensively farmed landscapes of western New York).

One of the challenges of modeling spatial patterns of habitat over time is the lack of long-term land-cover datasets. We used land-cover data from the late 1980s–early 1990s. Substantial change in the landscapes of New York occurred during the period in which wild turkeys were released, including a loss of agricultural land and subsequent gain in forest and developed land. While these changes undoubtedly influenced the dispersal of wild turkeys from release sites, it is difficult to quantify this effect without a comparable source of early land-cover data.

Incorporating information on wild turkey use and avoidance of certain habitat types into a cost-distance analysis provides insight into how landscape features might influence the spread of a wild turkey population following reintroduction. However, many other factors such as breeding habitat, weather, or predator densities also affect population expansion. For example, in northern New York, snow depth and duration of winter severely limit turkeys' ability to exploit natural food sources in the northern hardwood forest (Porter 1977, Porter et al. 1980). Wild turkeys have been found in the central Adirondacks for several years but they are closely associated with human development and the little agriculture that is found there. Although our cost-distance model predicted that wild turkey populations would become established in the Great Lakes Plain by 2000, townships in this intensively farmed region were among the last in western New York to be open for a fall hunting season due to perceived low turkey densities. Our recent research in this region suggests that its abundant edge habitat, which should act to facilitate wild turkey dispersal, may also promote high predator densities (Fleming 2003). Ultimately many of the habitat factors that influence dispersal probably play a role in other aspects of the wild turkey's life history that also affect population expansion.

One important caveat to the use of resampled land-cover data in this analysis is that small openings in the forest canopy, as well as small forest patches, may not be well represented, especially if they are <90 m across. These openings may be very important to wild turkeys dispersing through large contiguous forested tracts or agricultural lands, by providing food and cover resources that attract birds from the surrounding landscape. Similarly, the lack of information in the land-cover data on vegetation characteristics underneath the forest canopy may also limit its usefulness in predicting dispersal patterns of wild turkeys. A landscape-level analysis may be valuable for identifying large-scale landscape features that affect wild turkey dispersal, but many other small-scale factors that we did not consider (e.g., small forest openings, characteristics of ground cover and shrub layer) may also be important in shaping dispersal patterns for this species.

MANAGEMENT IMPLICATIONS

Although wild turkey population recovery in New York is considered complete, in many other areas of the U.S. wildlife managers are still actively working to restore wild turkeys or supplement existing populations within and outside their historic range. The results of our cost-distance analysis of wild turkey population expansion in New York suggest that landscape features such as habitat edges and barriers to movement can influence large-scale patterns of dispersal. Managers may want to consider how landscape features and habitat types surrounding the release site act to inhibit or facilitate dispersal prior to choosing sites for release. The selection of reintroduction sites in high-quality habitat is important for ensuring the survival and reproduction of released birds; however, selecting sites in landscapes with high connectivity is also important to ensure the persistence and expansion of that population. Abundant literature on habitat use and avoidance by wild turkeys, as well as easily obtained high-resolution land-cover data, can be utilized to predict how (and if) population expansion will occur following the release of wild birds. In the western U.S., where genetic effects of population isolation are a concern, cost-distance analysis can be used to identify habitat corridors that facilitate dispersal and interaction with other existing populations.

ACKNOWLEDGMENTS

This study was generously funded by the New York Chapter of the National Wild Turkey Federation and the Wilford A. Dence Fellowship Program at SUNY College of Environmental Science and Forestry. We thank R. Sanford (NYSDEC) for providing data on turkey releases in New York, M. Hall and J. Gibbs for helpful suggestions on the manuscript, and B. Miranda and the Quantitative Studies Lab at SUNY College of Environmental Studies and Forestry for technical support and use of computer facilities.

LITERATURE CITED

Alerich, C. L., and D. A. Drake. 1995. Forest statistics for New York: 1980 and 1993. U.S. Forest Service Resource Bulletin NE-132.

Backs, S. E., and C. H. Eisfelder. 1990. Criteria and guidelines for wild turkey release priorities in Indiana. Proceedings of the National Wild Turkey Symposium 6:134–143.

Dickinson, N. R. 1983. Physiographic zones of southern and western New York State. New York State Department of Environmental Conservation, Wildlife Resources Center, Delmar, New York, USA.

Eaton, S. W. 1992. Wild turkey. The Birds of North America 22:1–28.

———, F. M. Evans, J. W. Glidden, and B. D. Penrod. 1976. Annual range of wild turkeys in southwestern New York. New York Fish and Game Journal 23:21–33.

Eichholz, N. F., and R. L. Marchinton. 1975. Dispersal and adjustment to habitat of restocked wild turkeys in Georgia. Southeastern Association of Game and Fish Commissioners, Proceedings of Annual Conference 29:373–378.

Fleming, K. K. 2003. Scale-explicit spatial determinants of population structure in wild turkeys (*Meleagris gallopavo silvestris*). Dissertation, State University of New York College of Environmental Science and Forestry, Syracuse, New York, USA.

———, K. A. Didier, B. R. Miranda, and W. F. Porter. 2004. Sensitivity of a white-tailed deer habitat-suitability index model to error in satellite land-cover data: implications for wildlife habitat-suitability studies. Wildlife Society Bulletin 32:158–168.

Glennon, M. J., and W. F. Porter. 1999. Use of Landsat imagery in habitat analysis for wild turkey. Wildlife Society Bulletin 27:646–653.

Gustafson, E. J., G. R. Parker, and S. E. Backs. 1994. Evaluating spatial pattern of wildlife habitat: a case study of the wild turkey (*Meleagris gallopavo*). American Midland Naturalist 131:24–33.

Hayden, A. H., and G. A. Wunz. 1975. Wild turkey population characteristics in northern Pennsylvania. Proceedings of the National Wild Turkey Symposium 3:131–140.

Healy, W. M. 1992. Behavior. Pages 46–65 *in* J. G. Dickson, editor. 1992. The wild turkey: biology and management. Stackpole Books, Harrisburg, Pennsylvania, USA.

McDougal, L. A., M. R. Vaughan, and P. T. Bromley. 1990. Wild turkey and road relationships on a Virginia national forest. Proceedings of the National Wild Turkey Symposium 6:96–106.

Palmer, W. E., and G. A. Hurst. 1995. Drainage systems as minimum habitat management units for wild turkey hens. Proceedings of the National Wild Turkey Symposium 7:97–101.

Peoples, J. C., D. C. Sisson, and D. W. Speake. 1996. Wild turkey brood habitat use and characteristics in coastal plain pine forests. Proceedings of the National Wild Turkey Symposium 7:89–96.

Porter, W. F. 1977. Home range dynamics of wild turkeys in southeastern Minnesota. Journal of Wildlife Management 41:434–437.

———. 1978. The ecology and behavior of the wild turkey (*Meleagris gallopavo*) in southeastern Minnesota. Dissertation, University of Minnesota, Minneapolis, Minnesota, USA.

———, and D. J. Gefell. 1996. Influences of weather and land use on wild turkey populations in New York. Proceedings of the National Wild Turkey Symposium 7:75–80.

———, R. D. Tangen, G. C. Nelson, and D. A. Hamilton. 1980. Effects of corn food plots on wild turkeys in the upper Mississippi Valley. Journal of Wildlife Management 44:456–462.

Raybourne, J. Q. 1968. Telemetry of turkey movements. Southeastern Association of Game and Fish Commissioners, Proceedings of Annual Conference 22:47–54.

Rempel, R. S., and A. P. Carr. 2003. Patch Analyst extension for ArcView: version 3. <http://flash.lakeheadu.ca/~rrempel/patch/index.html> Accessed 24 Apr 2006.

Reschke, C. 1990. Ecological communities of New York State. New York Natural Heritage Program, New York State Department of Environmental Conservation, Latham, New York, USA.

SAS Institute. 1990. SAS/STAT users guide. Version 6. Fourth edition. SAS Institute Inc., Gary, North Carolina, USA.

Sisson, D. C., D. W. Speake, J. L. Landers, and J. L. Buckner. 1990. Effects of prescribed burning on wild turkey habitat preference and nest site selection in South Georgia. Proceedings of the National Wild Turkey Symposium 6:44–50.

Tapley, J. L., R. K. Abernathy, and J. E. Kennamer. 2001. Status and distribution of the wild turkey in 1999. Proceedings of the National Wild Turkey Symposium 8:15–22.

Verbeylen, G., L. De Bruyn, F. Adriaensen, and E. Matthysen. 2003. Does matrix resistance influence red squirrel (*Sciurus vulgaris* L. 1758) distribution in an urban landscape? Landscape Ecology 18:791–805.

Wigley, T. B., J. M. Sweeney, M. E. Garner, and M. A. Melchiors. 1985. Forest habitat use by wild turkeys in the Ouachita Mountains. Proceedings of the National Wild Turkey Symposium 5:183–197.

Wikramanayake, E., M. McKnight, E. Dinerstein, A. Joshi, B. Gurung, and D. Smith. 2004. Designing a conservation landscape for tigers in human-dominated environments. Conservation Biology 18:839–844.

Zar, J. H. 1984. Biostatistical analysis. Second edition. Prentice–Hall, Englewood Cliffs, New Jersey, USA.

Kathy Fleming received her MS in wildlife biology from California University of Pennsylvania and her PhD in wildlife ecology from SUNY College of Environmental Science and Forestry. Her research interests include avian habitat modeling, scale issues in habitat analysis, and the effect of landscape patterns on wildlife populations. She also has a strong interest in private lands habitat conservation and management, and currently works as an ecologist in the Maryland DNR Wildlife and Heritage Service's Landowner Incentive Program.

William Porter is Professor of Wildlife Science at the State University of New York College of Environmental Science and Forestry in Syracuse. His research interests include habitat-population relationships at the landscape scale. He has been studying the wild turkey for more than 30 years.

Wild Turkey Management:
Accomplishments, Strategies, and Opportunities
—— Grand Rapids, Michigan ——

LANDSCAPE-LEVEL HABITAT USE BY MERRIAM'S TURKEY IN NORTH-CENTRAL ARIZONA

Brian F. Wakeling[1]

Arizona Game and Fish Department, Game Branch,
2221 West Greenway Road, Phoenix, AZ 85023, USA

Abstract: I studied Merriam's turkeys (*Meleagris gallopavo merriami*) on the Mogollon Rim, Arizona, from 1988–1997 to learn what influence land management practices had on landscape-level habitat use. During this period, I radiotagged 252 Merriam's turkeys (213 female, 39 male) and visually located them >2 times monthly. Each location was topographically mapped and Universal Transverse Mercator (UTM) coordinates recorded. I obtained maps of livestock allotments, stocking levels, and silvicultural treatment boundaries from the United States Department of Agriculture (USDA) Forest Service. I used Digital Elevation Models to obtain slope and elevation. United States Geological Survey (USGS) Digital Line Graphs were used to delineate roads, drainages, and water sources. Roosting sites were located by following radiotagged turkeys. Vegetation associations were based on Terrestrial Ecosystem Surveys. I used forward stepwise logistic regression to develop models describing roosting, nesting, winter, and summer habitat use in a Geographic Information System (GIS). These models described winter habitat use with greater accuracy (81.3% overall classification) than summer habitat use (72.2%). Roosting site location influenced both winter and summer habitat use most. Roosting site selection was influenced primarily by slope. Roost proximity and vegetation association influenced nesting site selection. Models had a higher overall classification rate for roosting sites (77.2%) than for nesting sites (71.5%). Topography and vegetation association influenced habitat use more than silvicultural or livestock management in my study.

Proceedings of the National Wild Turkey Symposium 9:185–188

Key words: habitat selection, habitat use, landscape model, logistic regression, Merriam's turkey, *Meleagris gallopavo merriami*.

Substantial research has been dedicated to the identification of site-specific characteristics of nesting (Rumble and Hodorff 1993, Wakeling et al. 1998), brood rearing (Mollohan et al. 1995), loafing (Wakeling et al. 1997), and seasonal roosting and feeding habitat (Rumble 1992, Mollohan et al. 1995, Wakeling and Rogers 1996) of Merriam's turkeys. This research has been valuable to identify habitat selection needs of these birds, yet has been somewhat difficult to implement during landscape planning for land management. Land management planning, such as that provided in U. S. Forest Service Land Management Plans, identifies the proximity, juxtaposition, and interspersion of a variety of activities, including silvicultural (timber) management, livestock use, wildlife use, and recreational activities. Small-scale descriptions of habitats (i.e., descriptions requiring site specific characterization through field sampling) selected by turkeys may be difficult to factor into these broad plans without site-specific, detailed knowledge of the entire landscape (Fleming and Porter 2001). Even then, the knowledge of impacts that a variety of activities will have on the suitability of that habitat is difficult to discern without specific scientific treatments that have yet to be conducted.

My objective in this study was to develop landscape-level habitat models based on locations where site-specific data had been collected during previous studies. This landscape analysis would provide broadscale evaluation of the importance of the site-specific data previously collected. For instance, roosting sites of Merriam's turkeys are well known to be large, overmature trees with broad spreading horizontal branches (Hoffman et al. 1993). However, the effective distribution of trees with these characteristics across the landscape is not well understood or studied. Similarly the factors that influence the distribution of roosting sites are not well documented.

[1] E-mail: bwakeling@gf.state.az.us

STUDY AREA

The 860-km² Chevelon study area (CSA) was located on the Mogollon Rim, about 65 km south of Winslow, Arizona, on the Apache-Sitgreaves National Forests. Home ranges of turkeys seldom exceeded 40 km² and radiotagged turkeys rarely left the CSA (Wakeling 1991). Elevations ranged from 1,700 m in the northern portion to 2,430 m in the southern portion. Annual precipitation averaged 47.2 cm, with 2 concentrations: the first during winter storms in January through March, and the second during summer storms in July through early September (National Oceanic and Atmospheric Administration 1998).

Five cover types were present on the CSA based on U.S. Forest Service Terrestrial Ecosystem Surveys (Laing et al. 1989): (1) mixed-conifer (20.1% of area), (2) ponderosa pine (*Pinus ponderosa*)-Gambel oak (*Quercus gambelii*) (34.9%), (3) pinyon pine (*Pinus edulis*)-juniper (*Juniperus* spp.) (44.4%), (4) aspen (*Populus tremuloides*) (0.4%), and (5) grassland meadow (0.2%). The mixed-conifer cover type was dominant above 2,340 m and extended downward along east-facing slopes and drainages. This habitat included Douglas-fir (*Pseudotsuga menziesii*), white fir (*Abies concolor*), limber pine (*Pinus flexilis*), and Rocky Mountain maple (*Acer glabrum*). Ponderosa pine dominated west-facing slopes between 2,340 and 1,850 m. At elevations below 2,150 m, pinyon pine and alligator juniper (*Juniperus deppeana*) increased. Below 1,850 m, the pinyon-juniper cover type was dominant, with ponderosa pine present along drainages. Gambel oak occurred as a widespread codominant tree with ponderosa pine, and in pockets in the mixed-conifer and pinyon-juniper associations.

Timber harvesting and livestock grazing were major land uses on the CSA. Logging began in the late 1930s, and initial harvests were group or individual tree selections. Even-aged management was prevalent in the 1980s, but has been limited since 1990. Within individual stands, timber harvests generally occurred every 20 years, although some stands received subsequent silvicultural treatment within as few as 5 years of previous harvests. Most ponderosa pine stands on level terrain have been logged at least once; little logging has occurred on steeper slopes in larger canyons. Cutting of fuel wood, particularly in the pinyon-juniper cover type, has increased over the past 2 decades. Until the 1960s, sheep were the primary livestock on the CSA. The predominant livestock use on the CSA since that time was by cattle during summer.

METHODS

I radiotagged 252 turkeys (213 female, 39 male) during 1988–1997. These turkeys were relocated >2 times monthly and visual locations were topographically mapped and UTM coordinates recorded. I used 691 locations, of which 155 were during winter (Nov–Mar) and 366 were during summer (May–Sep) time intervals. Additionally 67 nesting sites and 103 roosting sites (located yearlong) were observed during the study.

Habitat maps for comparing habitat use and availability were derived from Terrestrial Ecosystem Survey (TES) (Laing et al. 1989). I classified these habitats into mixed conifer, ponderosa pine, pinyon-juniper, aspen, and meadow grassland vegetation associations. I obtained slope, distance-from-water sources (springs and impoundments), elevation, and distance-from-road data using GIS calculations for each turkey location. Slope, distance-from-water, and elevation data were derived from USGS digital elevation maps (90 m resolution), and distance-from-road data were derived from USGS digital line graphs (1:100,000 scale). I obtained digital maps of livestock allotments, stocking levels, and silvicultural treatment boundaries from the USDA Forest Service.

I used forward stepwise logistic regression to model habitat use (Hosmer and Lemeshow 1989). As predictors, I used vegetation association, distance (m) to point water sources and impoundments, slope (%), elevation (m), distance (m) to open and closed system roads, distance (m) to polygons silviculturally treated, and distance (m) to occupied cattle allotment. For nesting, summer, and winter habitat models, I also included proximity (m) to known roosting sites. I used 0.5 as the classification cutpoint (the predictor value at which sites were separated into used or random classifications) in this modeling effort. I modeled habitat use for roosting, nesting, summer, and winter. I used a jackknife resampling procedure to evaluate the classification bias of the final models (Verbyla and Litvaitis 1989).

RESULTS

The roosting habitat model had an overall correct classification rate of 77.2%. Factors that influenced roosting included greater slope, closer proximity to closed and open system roads, closer proximity to point water sources, and greater distance from water impoundments (Table 1). The nesting habitat model had an overall correct classification rate of 71.5% and included closer proximity to roost site. Ponderosa pine and mixed conifer vegetation associations positively influenced nesting habitat selection, whereas grassland meadow, aspen, and pinyon-juniper vegetation associations negatively influenced nesting selection (Table 1). Classification bias for both roosting and nesting habitat models was <0.8%.

The seasonal habitat selection models included a larger number of variables than did either roosting or habitat selection models. The summer habitat selection model had an overall classification accuracy of 76.1%, whereas the winter habitat selection model had an 81.4% overall classification accuracy. The summer model was positively influenced by ponderosa pine and mixed conifer vegetation associations, proximity to roosting sites and point water sources, timber harvests that had occurred 1 or 2 years prior, and closer proximity to open system roads. Proximity to closed system roads and water impoundments, timber harvests <1 year in age, and aspen, pinyon-juniper, and grassland meadow vegetation associations negatively influenced the selection model. Ponderosa pine and

Table 1. Logistic regression models (logit scale) of observed Merriam's turkey habitat use for roosting, nesting, summer, and winter on the Mogollon Rim, Arizona, 1988–1997.

Activity	n Use	Random	χ^2	P	Logistic regression equations[a]	Predictions (%) correct Use	Random	Overall
Roosting	103	103	110.868	<0.001	Y = 1.20 + 3.77S + 0.11CR + 0.09OR + 0.03WS − 1.12WB	85.3	69.4	77.2
Nesting	67	67	87.323	<0.001	Y = 3.34 + 5.23DR + 2.10MC + 1.16PP − 0.05PJ − 2.21AS	84.9	58.5	71.5
Summer	366	359	323.223	<0.001	Y = −13.21 + 8.16PP + 1.91MC + 0.02DR + 0.02WS + 0.01PC1 + 0.01PC2 + 0.01OR − 0.01CR − 0.01WB − 0.01PC − 2.20AS − 7.22PJ	81.4	70.8	76.1
Winter	155	152	165.012	<0.001	Y = −13.08 + 1.44PP + 1.07PJ + 0.02DR + 0.01PC2 + 0.01WS − 0.01PL2 − 0.01E − 1.73MC − 1.84AS	84.5	78.3	81.4

[a] Variables in the logistic regression equations include: DR = Distance (m) to roosting site, MC = mixed conifer vegetation association, PP = ponderosa pine vegetation association, PJ = pinyon-juniper vegetation association, AS = aspen vegetation association, S = slope (%), CR = distance (m) to closed system road, OR = distance (m) to open system road, WS = distance (m) to point water source, WB = distance (m) to water body, PC = distance (m) to current timber harvest polygon, PC1 = distance (m) to timber harvest polygon that occurred last year, PC2 = distance (m) to timber harvest polygon that occurred 2 years ago, PL2 = distance (m) to allotment stocked with cattle 2 years ago, and E = elevation (m).

pinyon-juniper vegetation associations, proximity to roosting sites and point water sources, and proximity to timber harvests that had occurred 2 years prior positively influenced the winter habitat selection model. The winter selection model was negatively influenced by mixed conifer, aspen, and meadow grassland vegetation associations, proximity to active livestock allotments occupied 2 years prior, and elevation (Table 1). Classification bias for winter and summer habitat models was <1.0%.

DISCUSSION

Logistic regression models are useful in understanding landscape features that influence habitat selection. A great deal of research has been conducted on characteristics at specific use sites to identify features important to turkeys, but managing landscapes for site-specific characteristics can be difficult for land management agencies.

The importance of large trees with wide spreading horizontal branches for Merriam's turkey roosting sites has been described extensively in the literature (Rumble 1992, Mollohan et al. 1995). Past research indicated that greater slope was important, and seemed like a logical indicator for habitat suitability. The model developed in my study further indicates that slopes are important to roosting site selection and may be used from a landscape perspective to identify potential roosting areas.

Roads have been identified as detriments to roosting habitat due to potential disturbance (Hoffman et al. 1993). The relationship to roads in my study is probably a result of historic road construction in proximity to roosting habitat. In other words, roads were built to facilitate historic timber harvest. Burbridge and Neff (1975) noted that vehicles moving rapidly on roads were less disturbing than vehicles moving slowly, although less often, on lower quality roads. Rogers et al. (1999) found that turkeys avoided the first 200 m around roads, and habitats beyond that distance were used as available. From a landscape perspective, roads do not seem to have an overriding influence on roosting habitat use.

From a landscape perspective, nesting habitat is best described by proximity to roosting sites and vegetation association. On the CSA, nesting sites were most frequently located on slopes (Mollohan et al. 1995, Wakeling et al. 1998) that are characterized by distinct mesic vegetation associations, like mixed conifer. These same areas are also similar to those selected for roosting site location. The models from my study will be useful for identifying landscapes where roosting and nesting may occur, but then the site-specific descriptions (Rumble 1992, Hoffman et al. 1993, Rumble and Hodorff 1993, Mollohan et al. 1995, Wakeling and Rogers 1998, Wakeling et al. 1998) will best assist in defining suitable habitat within the identified landscapes. Previously, site-specific descriptions would need to be compared with the entire landscape; with this approach, site-specific descriptions need only be compared within smaller portions of the landscape identified by these models.

Winter and summer habitat selection models developed in my study are probably of most value in identifying important seasonal ranges. Both roosting sites and vegetation association influenced turkey use of habitat in both winter and summer, as had been reported previously (Wakeling 1997).

The most interesting aspect of the seasonal selection modeling was the influence of timber treatments on habitat use, especially during summer. Site-specific habitat characteristic studies in Arizona have cautioned land managers regarding the potential for long-term impacts to habitat suitability following timber treatments (Mollohan et al. 1995). My study indicates that timber treatments, while aversive for the first year, may become a positive influence during the next 2 years for both winter and summer habitat selection. I urge caution in implementing the results of this research. Timber harvests should not be planned indiscriminately; care should be used to plan harvests to achieve desired future conditions described for Merriam's turkeys (Rumble 1992, Hoffman et al. 1993, Rumble and Hodorff 1993, Mollohan et al. 1995, Wakeling and

Rogers 1998, Wakeling et al. 1998) when planning harvests to favor turkey habitat.

Landscape level habitat selection modeling has proven useful for management purposes with other subspecies of turkey (Porter and Fleming 2001, Wakeling et al. 2001). The models developed during my study should prove useful for land management planning considerations for Merriam's turkeys. Although predicted patterns of suitability remain to be validated, these models should be useful tools for Arizona land management planning.

ACKNOWLEDGMENTS

This research was funded through the State Trust Fund Grant W-78-R of the Arizona Game and Fish Department. I am grateful to the many field biologists that assisted in data collection for the various studies undertaken during the years of study, including C. H. Lewis, T. D. Rogers, C. Staab, M. A. Koloszar, and W. Rosenberg. I am also grateful to Susan R. Boe for her assistance with the GIS analysis. This manuscript has benefited from the reviews of 3 anonymous reviewers.

LITERATURE CITED

Burbridge, W. R., and D. J. Neff. 1975. Coconino National Forest-Arizona Game and Fish Department cooperative roads-wildlife study. Pages 44–57 *in* Proceedings of the Elk-Logging-Roads Symposium. University of Idaho, Moscow, Idaho, USA.

Fleming, K. K., and W. F. Porter. 2001. A habitat suitability approach to evaluating landscape patterns for eastern wild turkeys. Proceedings of the National Wild Turkey Symposium 8:157–166.

Hoffman, R. W., H. G. Shaw, M. A. Rumble, B. F. Wakeling, C. M. Mollohan, S. D. Schemnitz, R. Engel-Wilson, and D. A. Hengel. 1993. Management guidelines for Merriam's wild turkeys. Colorado Division of Wildlife Report 18.

Hosmer, D. W., Jr., and S. Lemeshow. 1989. Applied logistic regression. John Wiley and Sons, New York, New York, USA.

Laing, L., N. Ambos, T. Subirge, C. McDonald, C. Nelson, and W. Robbie. 1989. Terrestrial ecosystem survey of the Apache-Sitgreaves National Forests. USDA Forest Service, Albuquerque, New Mexico, USA.

Mollohan, C. M., D. R. Patton, and B. F. Wakeling. 1995. Habitat selection and use by Merriam's turkey in north-central Arizona. Arizona Game and Fish Department Technical Report 9.

National Oceanic and Atmospheric Administration. 1998. Arizona climatological data. Volume 101. National Climatic Data Center, Phoenix, Arizona, USA.

Rogers, T. D., B. F. Wakeling, and S. R. Boe. 1999. Merriam's turkey distribution in relation to the U. S. Forest Service Recreational Opportunity Spectrum forest classification and road proximity in northern Arizona. Biennial Conference of Research on the Colorado Plateau 4:133–142.

Rumble, M. A. 1992. Roosting habitat of Merriam's turkeys in the Black Hills, South Dakota. Journal of Wildlife Management 56:750–759.

———, and R. A. Hodorff. 1993. Nesting ecology of Merriam's turkey in the Black Hills, South Dakota. Journal of Wildlife Management 59:437–447.

Verbyla, D. L., and J. A. Litvaitis. 1989. Resampling methods for evaluating classification accuracy of wildlife habitat models. Environmental Management 13:783–787.

Wakeling, B. F. 1991. Population and nesting characteristics of Merriam's turkeys along the Mogollon Rim, Arizona. Arizona Game and Fish Department Technical Report 7.

———. 1997. Winter movement patterns of Merriam's turkeys in north-central Arizona. Biennial Conference of Research on the Colorado Plateau 3:93–100.

———, S. R. Boe, M. M. Koloszar, and T. D. Rogers. 2001. Gould's turkey survival and habitat selection modeling in southeastern Arizona. Proceedings of the National Wild Turkey Symposium 8:101–108.

———, C. H. Mehling, and C. M. Mollohan. 1997. Characteristics of Merriam's turkey loafing habitat reused following silvicultural treatment. Biennial Conference of Research on the Colorado Plateau 3:85–91.

———, and T. D. Rogers. 1996. Winter diet and habitat selection by Merriam's turkeys in north-central Arizona. Proceedings of the National Wild Turkey Symposium 7:175–184.

———, and ———. 1998. Summer resource selection and year-long survival of male Merriam's turkeys in north-central Arizona, with associated implications from demographic modeling. Arizona Game and Fish Department Technical Report 28.

———, S. S. Rosenstock, and H. G. Shaw. 1998. Forest stand characteristics of successful and unsuccessful Merriam's turkey nest sites in north-central Arizona. Southwestern Naturalist 43:242–248.

Brian F. Wakeling received a B.S. in Wildlife Management and an M.S. in Environmental Resources from Arizona State University in 1985 and 1989, respectively. He served as a research biologist for the Arizona Game and Fish Department from 1988–2000, during which time he studied turkeys, mule deer, elk, and bighorn sheep. Currently, Brian is the big game management supervisor with the Arizona Game and Fish Department, a position he has held since 2000. Brian is a Certified Wildlife Biologist and a Past-President of the Arizona State Chapter of The Wildlife Society. Brian has served as a member of the National Wild Turkey Technical Committee since 1993.

Wild Turkey Management:
Accomplishments, Strategies, and Opportunities
————— Grand Rapids, Michigan —————

STATEWIDE ASSESSMENT OF WILD TURKEY HABITAT USING SATELLITE IMAGERY IN ARKANSAS

Sharon L. Goetz[1,2]
Department of Environmental and Forest Biology,
State University of New York,
College of Environmental Science and Forestry,
1 Forestry Drive,
Syracuse, NY 13210, USA

William F. Porter
Faculty of Environmental and Forest Biology,
State University of New York,
College of Environmental Science and Forestry,
1 Forestry Drive,
Syracuse, NY 13210, USA

Abstract: We explored the potential provided by classified digital land cover maps derived from remotely sensed satellite imagery for assessing statewide habitat suitability for eastern wild turkeys (*Meleagris gallopavo silvestris*) in Arkansas. We adapted habitat variables used for ground-based habitat evaluation to classified land cover and assessed quality of the landscape for turkeys by using 2 approaches: a habitat suitability index (HSI) model and logistic regression model. We acquired digital land cover data derived from satellite imagery from the Multi-Resolution Land Characteristics (MRLC) consortium, and computed composition and configuration variables with FRAGSTATS (ArcView Patch Analyst). The HSI model incorporated food and cover variables into a geographic information system (GIS; ArcView Spatial Analyst) and evaluated habitat at a pixel resolution of 30 m. We summarized HSI scores at the county level and regressed against harvest records for wild turkeys. HSI values for the statewide model ranged from 0.52 to 0.79 and explained 32% of the variation in harvest ($r^2 = 0.32$, $n = 68$, $P < 0.05$). Models tailored to each of 4 regions showed habitat suitability ranged from 0.07 to 0.92 and accounted for nearly 70% of the variation in harvest (Ouachita region; adjusted $r^2 = 0.68$, $n = 13$, $P < 0.05$). We used logistic regression to derive a habitat model by comparing land cover characteristics and harvest. We identified 2 variables as most often associated with low harvest of wild turkeys statewide: percentage of land in Row Crops ($\chi^2 = 10.08$, df $= 1$, $P < 0.002$) and percentage of land in Commercial-Industrial-Transportation ($\chi^2 = 8.96$, df $= 1$, $P = 0.028$). Our findings suggest that NLCD satellite imagery and GIS tools can be used to identify habitat characteristics that allow assessment of the potential of landscapes to support wild turkey harvest. If harvest statistics provide a reasonable surrogate for relative population abundance for wild turkeys, then these models are good indicators of habitat suitability.

Proceedings of the National Wild Turkey Symposium 9:189–198

Key words: Arkansas, geographic information system, habitat assessment, habitat suitability, habitat suitability index, harvest, landscape, *Meleagris gallopavo silvestris,* satellite imagery, wild turkey.

Habitat inventory at the statewide scale is costly in time and personnel (Johnson 2003). However, recent advances in satellite image analysis and geographic information systems may allow high quality habitat inventories to be conducted at a much-reduced cost. Our intent was to explore the potential of using digital land cover maps derived from remotely sensed imagery for assessing statewide habitat suitability for wild turkeys.

Most existing habitat models for wild turkeys are designed for application at a local level (Miller et al. 2000). The U.S. Fish and Wildlife Service identified several ground-based variables (e.g., average height of

[1] Present address: Minnesota Department of Natural Resources, 500 Lafayette Road, Saint Paul, MN 55155, USA.
[2] E-mail: sharon.goetz@dnr.state.mn.us

herbaceous canopy and percent tree canopy cover) for the summer food/brood, fall/winter/spring food, and cover components of their HSI model for the eastern wild turkey (Schroeder 1985). However, ground-based evaluations are difficult to implement statewide because of their labor-intensive nature.

Satellite imagery could allow wildlife managers the opportunity to apply habitat evaluation procedures statewide using GIS. Effectiveness of HSI models is dependent on their ability to capture habitat requirements so that GIS-based variables adequately represent the life requisites (Donovan et al. 1987). The wild turkey is a potentially good candidate for landscape-level models because habitat quality for turkey populations has a spatial component related to arrangement of habitat elements across large geographic areas (Gustafson et al. 1994). Research in New York demonstrated that transforming traditional variables into landscape-level variables that are applicable to satellite imagery can create models for habitat evaluation of wild turkeys (Glennon and Porter 1999, Fleming and Porter 2001). However, these previous studies were limited to smaller regions within a state.

In this study our objectives were to examine potential for logistic regression models developed from satellite imagery to distinguish between high-quality and low-quality habitat for wild turkeys, and compare regional and statewide assessments of habitat suitability indices for wild turkeys.

STUDY AREA

This study was conducted in the state of Arkansas. Arkansas is composed of 4 principal physiographic regions: the Ozark Mountains, Ouachita Mountains, the Gulf Coastal Plain, and the Mississippi River Alluvial Plain or Delta (Hanson and Moneyhon 1989; Figure 1). Elevation throughout the state ranges from 17 m in the Delta region to 839 m in northwestern Arkansas.

The Ozark Mountain region in northern Arkansas contains highlands characterized by flat-topped mountains and narrow ridges with steep-sided valleys (Smith 1989). This region consisted of upland hardwood forests with some conifers and contained most of the 485,000 ha Ozark National Forest. Dominant species included oak (*Quercus* spp.), hickory (*Carya* spp.), maple (*Acer* spp.), cedar (*Juniperus virginiana*), and pine (*Pinus* spp.).

The Ouachita Mountain region extends across the west-central portion of Arkansas and contains the Arkansas River Valley. East-west trending ridges and valleys are characteristic. Pine-hardwood forests were found throughout the Ouachita region and the 666,046 ha Ouachita National Forest was within this region. These forests were predominantly loblolly pine (*P. taeda*) and shortleaf pine (*P. echinata*) with scattered hardwoods (Hanson and Moneyhon 1989) and were managed for timber production.

The Gulf Costal Plain has flat to rolling topography. This region covers the portion of Arkansas south of the Ouachita Mountains. Commercial forestry operations were the dominant economic land-use in this region (Hanson and Moneyhon 1989). Pine-hardwood forests of similar composition to the Ouachita Region were found in the Gulf Coastal Plain.

The Delta region of Arkansas covers the eastern portion of the state. Topography is flat and contains rich though poorly drained soil. Land use in this area was predominantly agriculture: rice, soybean, and wheat were the primary crops (Hanson and Moneyhon 1989). Bottomland hardwood forests persisted along major river valleys in the Delta region. Bald cypress (*Taxodium distichum*) and tupelo (*Nyssa* spp.) were found in wetland areas. Drier riverbanks supported black willow (*Salix nigra*), water hickory (*Carya aquatica*), river birch (*Betula nigra*), and cottonwood (*Populus deltoides*). The northern portion of this region was covered with upland hardwood forests of oak and hickory (Hanson and Moneyhon 1989).

METHODS

To evaluate the potential of habitat assessment using satellite imagery, we sought variables that could be measured from classified land cover using GIS and assessed their ability to characterize habitat suitability. We used 2 approaches to identify variables. First, we designed an HSI model to evaluate the quality of the landscape based on variables that could be measured from classified land cover. Second, we employed logistic regression to select habitat variables empirically from among those variables measurable with classified land cover. We used harvest data, an index of relative abundance, as an independent index of habitat quality for validation of HSI models and as the dependent variable in logistic regression. We created statewide and regional models for both HSI and logistic regression analysis for comparison. We used Statistical Analysis System (SAS) software version 8.1 (SAS Institute 1990) for assessing the models.

Satellite Imagery

National Land Cover Database (NLCD) satellite imagery classified by the MRLC consortium was used because data was readily available nationwide and the classification identified land-cover classes appropriate for wild turkey habitat (Figure 1). The imagery consisted of leaf-off Landsat 5 Thematic Mapper (TM) satellite data, nominal-1992 (1988–1993) acquisitions (U.S. Geological Survey 2000). There were 18 land-cover classes included in the Arkansas MRLC modified Anderson level II classification, and the imagery had a resolution of 30 m. At the time of project completion imagery accuracy was unknown; accuracy assessment has since been completed. The pixel-level accuracy for the South-central United States (Region 6) classified land cover was 44% (U.S. Geological Survey 2004).

Population Index

We used wild turkey harvest data both as a direct measure and as a means of estimating relative abun-

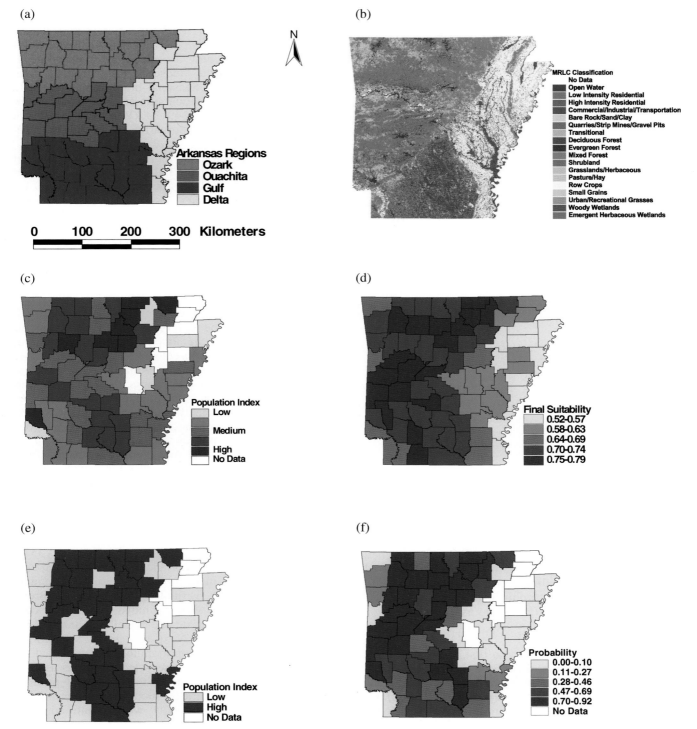

Fig. 1. Habitat assessment for wild turkeys in Arkansas based on 1992 satellite imagery and summarized to county-level resolution. (a) Arkansas counties stratified into the 4 physiographic regions. (b) National Land Cover Dataset satellite imagery for Arkansas. (c) Wild turkey population index used for validation of habitat suitability index (HSI) models for each county. (d) Statewide HSI values summarized at the county level. (e) Logistic regression classification of high or low turkey population index. (f) Logistic regression probability of a county having a high turkey population index.

dance. Lint (1990) demonstrated that harvest data provides a reasonable index of relative abundance. We standardized the index by dividing total harvest by the area of each county. To reduce effects of annual variation in turkey harvest, we used a 6-year (1992–1997)

average. We chose the years 1992–1997 because they approximate the time of satellite image collection (1988–1993 vintage). Because many counties were closed to hunting before 1992, using 1992–1997 data allowed for the retention of more counties. The years

Table 1. Habitat suitability index (HSI) values for wild turkey food and cover assigned to the 18 Anderson level-II land-cover classes depicted in 1992 satellite imagery of Arkansas.

Land-cover class	HSI value	
	Food	Cover
Open water	0	0
Low intensity residential	0.5	0.5
High intensity residential	0	0
Com-ind-trans[a]	0	0
Bare rock-sand-clay	0	0
Quarries-strip mines-gravel pits	0	0
Transitional	0.7	0.4
Deciduous forest	1	0.6
Evergreen forest	0.6	1
Mixed forest	0.8	1
Shrubland	1	1
Grasslands-herbaceous	1	0.6
Pasture-hay	1	0.5
Row crops	1	0.5
Small grains	1	0.5
Urban-recreational grasses	0.6	0
Woody wetlands	0.8	0.8
Emergent herbaceous wetlands	0.8	0.8

[a] Com-ind-trans = Commercial-Industrial-Transportation.

1994–1997 extend past the data used for the imagery; however, change in land use was assumed small during this period. Seven counties were closed to hunting at least 1 year from 1992 to 1997 and were excluded from analysis, leaving 68 counties. Harvest data were square-root transformed to approximate a normal distribution (Zar 1999).

Habitat Suitability Index

We developed an HSI model for habitat characteristics measurable with classified land cover based on a review of literature and existing habitat evaluation models for wild turkey (Schroeder 1985, Wigley et al. 1985, Donovan et al. 1987, Hurst and Dickson 1992, Gustafson et al. 1994, Thogmartin 1999). We assigned each land-cover class a value from 0.0–1.0 for food and cover based on quality of that cover class for wild turkeys (Table 1). We combined the food and cover values to yield the final HSI value as:

$$HSI = (Cover\ HSI \times Food\ HSI)^{1/2}.$$

We used the geometric mean so that a zero value for either food or cover would confer a final HSI value of zero. The imagery was then reclassified (each land-cover class assigned its corresponding HSI value) according to final HSI values using the reclassify function in Spatial Analyst extension of ArcView (Environmental Systems Research Institute 1999). We calculated mean HSI values by county. We assessed the quality of our initial HSI values by fitting HSI versus harvest in a simple linear regression model.

Next, the model was adjusted to tailor fit the HSI values to statewide and regional landscapes. We individually changed the food and cover HSI values (at 0.1 increments) while holding all other model variables constant and fit a new regression model to harvest data. The values producing the best fit were retained for the statewide and 4 regional models. This process was intended to explore the values of the explanatory variables derived from remotely sensed data.

We also summarized HSI values for 1,000 ha polygons to determine how a scale more appropriate to wild turkey use of the landscape influenced the final range of suitabilities. Seasonal home ranges for wild turkeys in the Ozark Mountains and Ouachita Mountains range from 71–1,149 ha (Wigley et al. 1986, Badyaev et al. 1996, Thogmartin 2001).

Logistic Regression Model

We developed logistic regression models (Hosmer and Lemeshow 2000) for wild turkey habitat quality based on the LOGISTIC procedure in SAS (SAS Institute 1990). The binary response (dependent) variable was a high or low population index of turkeys (i.e., high or low harvest of turkeys; Figure 1c). The median value of the population index was used to distinguish between high and low densities.

For independent variables in our logistic regression models, we computed composition (amount of a land-cover class) and configuration (arrangement of land-cover classes) landscape metrics from the classified land cover at the county level (the same scale as harvest data) using the Patch Analyst extension of ArcView. This extension calculates landscape metrics using FRAGSTATS functions within the ArcView environment (McGarigal and Marks 1995). Other composition variables computed included human population density, road density and land in public ownership. We obtained human population density and road density (km/ha) from U.S. Bureau of Census data for 1990. We acquired land ownership information from the Gap Analysis Program (Center for Advanced Spatial Technology 1998, Smith et al. 1998).

Variables were selected for the models through a process described by Hosmer and Lemeshow (2000). Univariate analysis was performed on 76 variables; each variable was independently regressed on the dependent variable (Y). Those with P-values <0.25 or those with biological importance were considered candidates for model inclusion. To eliminate redundant FRAGSTAT metrics, variables with Pearson correlation coefficients >0.8 were excluded from further consideration. After univariate and correlation analysis, 20 variables were retained. Next, an *a priori* selection of variables thought to be important to wild turkey habitat and finally forward stepwise selection were used to further reduce the number of variables and produce parsimonious and significant models (Hosmer and Lemeshow 2000). Ten models were identified from which the final state and the 4 regional models were selected. Regional models were explored due to the degree of heterogeneity found among the regions.

We evaluated significance of individual variables and interaction terms through likelihood ratio chi-square tests using the −2 Log Likelihood (−2 Log L) value, a goodness-of-fit statistic describing fit of the explanatory variables in the model (SAS Institute 1990). We judged overall model significance with the likelihood ratio chi-square test (Hosmer and Lemeshow 2000). We used Akaike's Information Criterion (AIC) for comparing different models for the

Table 2. Food (F) and cover (C) values for statewide and regional habitat suitability index models used to assess habitat quality for wild turkeys in Arkansas from 1992 satellite imagery.

Land-cover class	Statewide F	Statewide C	Ozark F	Ozark C	Ouachita F	Ouachita C	Gulf F	Gulf C	Delta F	Delta C
Open water	0.1	0.0	0.1	0.0	1.0	0.0	0.1	0.0	0.0	0.0
Low intensity residential	0.0	0.5	0.0	0.5	0.0	0.5	0.5	0.5	0.5	0.5
High intensity residential	0.0	0.0	0.0	0.0	0.0	0.0	0.0	0.0	0.0	1.0
Com-ind-trans[a]	0.0	0.0	0.0	0.0	0.0	0.0	0.0	0.0	0.0	1.0
Bare rock-sand-clay	1.0	0.0	0.0	0.0	0.0	0.0	1.0	0.0	0.0	0.0
Quarry-strip mine-gravel pit	0.0	0.0	0.0	0.0	0.0	0.0	0.0	0.0	0.0	0.0
Transitional	0.0	0.4	1.0	0.4	0.0	0.4	1.0	0.4	0.7	0.0
Deciduous forest	1.0	0.6	1.0	0.6	0.7	0.6	0.6	0.6	1.0	0.4
Evergreen forest	0.5	1.0	0.9	1.0	0.8	1.0	1.0	1.0	0.6	1.0
Mixed forest	0.9	1.0	1.0	1.0	0.6	1.0	1.0	1.0	0.8	0.2
Shrubland	1.0	1.0	0.0	1.0	1.0	1.0	1.0	1.0	1.0	1.0
Grasslands-herbaceous	1.0	0.6	1.0	0.6	1.0	0.6	1.0	0.6	1.0	0.6
Pasture-hay	1.0	0.5	0.2	0.5	1.0	0.5	1.0	0.5	1.0	0.6
Row crops	0.6	0.5	1.0	0.5	1.0	0.5	0.7	0.5	1.0	0.0
Small grains	0.4	0.5	0.3	0.5	0.3	0.5	1.0	0.5	1.0	0.0
Urban-recreational grasses	0.6	0.0	0.0	0.0	0.0	0.0	0.9	0.0	0.6	0.0
Woody wetlands	0.6	0.8	1.0	0.8	0.2	0.8	1.0	0.8	0.8	0.7
Emergent herbaceous wetlands	0.6	0.8	1.0	0.8	0.2	0.8	0.8	0.8	0.8	0.8

[a] Com-ind-trans = Commercial-Industrial-Transportation.

same data (Burnham and Anderson 1992). The models with the lowest AIC values were chosen as the best models.

After variables for statewide and regional models were selected, we tested the assumption of linearity in the logit for continuous variables. We used a grouped, smooth scatter plot to visually assess scale of the continuous variables (Hosmer and Lemeshow 2000). If a covariate was non-linear, then we used a fractional polynomial approach to improve fit of the model (p = [−2, −1, −0.5, 0, 0.5, 1, 2, and 3]). Likelihood ratio chi-square tests using the −2 Log L value determined whether a model including transformed variables resulted in a better model fit.

RESULTS

Habitat Suitability Index Model

The best food and cover values after model adjustment varied among the statewide and regional models (Table 2). The best statewide model accounted for 31% of the variation in the population index ($P <$ 0.001; Figure 2).

Performance of the statewide model decreased when applied to individual regions except the Ouachita ($r^2 = 0.48$; Table 3). The statewide model performed worst in the Delta region ($r^2 = -0.04$). Ozark and Gulf regions were intermediate, but had poor relationships ($r^2 = 0.09$ and 0.13, respectively).

The HSI values for the statewide model ranged from 0.52 to 0.79 (Figure 1). The statewide HSI values summarized at the regional level identified the Delta region as the area of lowest suitability (0.57). The Ozark, Ouachita, and Gulf regions had average HSI values of 0.74, 0.73, 0.70, respectively (Table 3).

Habitat Suitability Index values for models tailored to each region ranged from 0.07 to 0.92. The Gulf regional model had the highest average suitability (0.82), whereas the Delta region had the lowest suitability (0.22). The average suitability values for the Ozark and Ouachita regions were similar, 0.67 and 0.68, respectively. Habitat suitability values summarized at the 1,000 ha polygon level ranged from 0 to 0.90 (Figure 3).

Models adjusted for regional variation, by altering the initial HSI values assigned to each land-cover class, improved the fit to harvest. By tailoring models

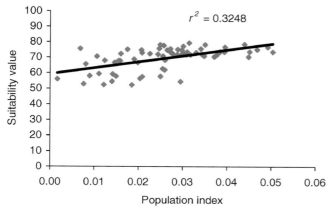

$r^2 = 0.3248$

Fig. 2. Regression of habitat suitability by the county-level harvest density for wild turkeys in Arkansas. Habitat suitability is based on 1992 satellite imagery and harvest density is an average of harvest during 1992–1997.

Table 3. Coefficients of determination (r^2) for habitat suitability models for wild turkeys and average county HSI values summarized at the regional and state level in Arkansas, 1992–1997.

Model	Statewide model r^2	Regional model r^2	Average HSI	Average regional HSI
Statewide	0.31		0.69	
Ozark	0.09[a]	0.25[a]	0.74	0.67
Ouachita	0.48[a]	0.68[a]	0.73	0.68
Gulf	0.13[a]	0.35[a]	0.70	0.82
Delta	−0.04[a]	0.10[a]	0.57	0.22

[a] Adjusted r^2 values.

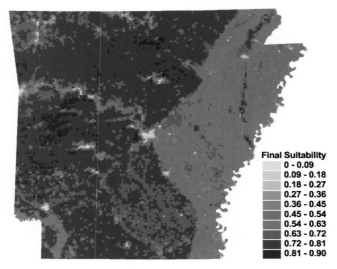

Final Suitability
- 0 - 0.09
- 0.09 - 0.18
- 0.18 - 0.27
- 0.27 - 0.36
- 0.36 - 0.45
- 0.45 - 0.54
- 0.54 - 0.63
- 0.63 - 0.72
- 0.72 - 0.81
- 0.81 - 0.90

Fig. 3. Statewide habitat suitability index values for wild turkeys in Arkansas averaged to 1,000 ha polygons.

Table 4. Parameter estimates for best predictors of a high population index of wild turkeys in Arkansas based on 1992–1997 harvest records. β is parameter estimate, χ^2 is chi-square test for H_0 when the parameter is equal to zero.

Variable	df	β	SE	χ^2	P
Statewide model (likelihood ratio χ^2 = 36.41***)					
Intercept	1	2.65	0.72	13.65	0.001
Percent com-ind-trans	1	−5.60	1.87	8.96	0.003
Percent row crops	1	−0.08	0.02	10.08	0.002
Ozark model (likelihood ratio χ^2 = 6.70**)					
Intercept	1	3.00	1.09	7.51	0.006
Percent com-ind-trans	1	−6.19	2.97	4.34	0.037
Ouachita model (likelihood ratio χ^2 = 4.17**)					
Intercept	1	−1.97	1.36	2.09	0.148
Percent evergreen forest	1	0.17	0.10	2.78	0.095
Gulf model (likelihood ratio χ^2 = 10.39**)					
Intercept	1	−3.45	1.46	5.57	0.018
Percent evergreen forest	1	0.11	0.04	6.52	0.011
Delta model (likelihood ratio χ^2 = 3.40*)					
Intercept	1	−8.81	7.08	1.55	0.213
Percent open water	1	1.11	0.96	1.33	0.250

* $P < 0.1$, ** $P < 0.05$, *** $P < 0.001$.

to specific regional characteristics, we were able to account for as much as 68% of the variation in the population index (Table 3). Both the statewide and regional models identified the Delta region as the area of lowest suitability (HSI = 0.22–0.57) and the Ouachita and Gulf regions as the highest (HSI = 0.68–0.82; Table 3). The statewide model showed comprehensive habitat suitability of 0.69; regional suitability values based on the statewide model ranged from 0.57 to 0.74 (Figure 1).

Logistic Regression Model

Only 2 variables were included in the statewide logistic regression model. The probability of a high population index (Figure 1e) was negatively associated with the percentage of Commercial-Industrial-Transportation (Com-Ind-Trans) (χ^2 = 8.96, df = 1, P = 0.028) and the percentage of land in Row Crops (χ^2 = 10.08, df = 1, $P < 0.002$) (Figure 1). The final statewide model created for logistic regression was chosen based on its AIC value of 63.86. Statewide models tested had AIC values ranging from 63.86 to 84.57. The statewide model was significant ($P < 0.05$) based on the Likelihood Ratio Statistic (Table 4):

$$ P = \frac{e^{2.6515-5.6031\times\text{Com-Ind-Trans}-0.0774\times\text{Row Crops}}}{1 + e^{2.6515-5.6031\times\text{Com-Ind-Trans}-0.0774\times\text{Row Crops}}} $$

The range of percentages for Com-Ind-Trans and row crops were 0.03–2.73 and 0.09–77.52, respectively.

The models tailored for the Ozark, Ouachita, and the Gulf region were significant based on the Likelihood Ratio Statistic ($P < 0.05$; Table 4). The lowest AIC values for the regional models compared within regions were 20.36, 17.77, 22.68, and 7.65 for the Ozark, Ouachita, Gulf, and Delta regions, respectively.

Variables retained in the logistic models differed among regions. Wild turkey abundance based on harvest in the Ozark region was inversely related to the

percentage of land in Com-Ind-Trans. Turkey abundance based on harvest was positively associated with the percentage of Evergreen Forest in the Ouachita and Gulf models, and positively associated with the percentage of Open Water in the Delta region. No interaction terms or variable transformations significantly ($P < 0.05$) improved statewide or regional model fit.

DISCUSSION

The principal question in landscape-scale habitat assessment is whether variables identified with satellite imagery can detect habitat characteristics that are biologically meaningful for wildlife. In preliminary work in southwestern New York, Glennon and Porter (1999) detected habitat attributes (e.g., linear edge) from NLCD classified land cover that appeared useful in landscape-scale habitat evaluation for wild turkeys. The application of habitat assessment using NLCD classified land cover in Arkansas was designed to expand evaluation to a statewide context and to ecological conditions that were different from New York.

To explore the use of classified land cover in habitat evaluation, we considered 2 approaches to modeling habitat suitability, and then assessed potential of each of these in light of their ability to relate habitat quality to harvest, and potentially to relative abundance of turkeys. We investigated HSI models and logistic regression. Our interpretation of performance of each of the successful models focused first on configuration and composition variables, the principal information available from satellite imagery. Second, we examined influence of degree of landform heterogeneity among the physiographic regions on model performance, and therefore the scale most appropriate for model development. Finally, we considered model performance in light of the accuracy and resolution of input data (e.g., classified land cover) and data used to develop and assess performance of the models.

Habitat Suitability Index Models

GIS-based models have the potential to work well for turkeys because their habitat requirements can be generalized to simple combinations of forested and open habitats (e.g., Dickson et al. 1978, Glennon and Porter 1999, Fleming and Porter 2001). Models that employed simple combinations of food and cover requirements were found to be the most successful in relating to harvest of wild turkeys in Arkansas. A statewide HSI model explained 32% of the variation seen in harvest, with some regional models explaining almost 70%.

Regional models were more effective at capturing variation than statewide models. This is understandable because relationships between variables in a model can differ depending upon the composition of land-cover classes within each region (Glennon and Porter 1999). Regional tailoring of habitat models allows consideration of differences in natural physiography and land use present within the regions. The Ozark and Ouachita regions are mountainous, while the Gulf and Delta share flat to rolling topography. Forest stands are predominately upland hardwoods in the Ozarks, whereas the Ouachita and Gulf regions have pine-dominated forests with similar compositions. The major land use in the Gulf is commercial forestry, and agriculture dominates the landscape in the Delta region. It is likely that there are different limiting factors to turkey abundance within each region. In the heavily forested regions, open habitat might be limiting, but where agriculture predominates, forest cover is usually the limiting habitat factor.

However, the fact that the statewide models worked as well as they did is also surprising. In general, most habitat models can only be expected to explain half of the variation in a population's abundance (Morrison et al. 1998). While habitat is important, the relative abundance of wild turkey populations is also influenced by other factors (e.g., predation, reproductive success, weather, disease, legal harvest, and poaching). Previous studies in Arkansas and Mississippi have suggested that nest predation is an important limiting factor in the Ozark and Ouachita Mountains (Seiss et al. 1990, Badyaev 1995, Thogmartin 1999, Thogmartin and Johnson 1999). Populations in northern Missouri, Kentucky, Alabama, and Virginia and West Virginia suffered high (20–40%) rates of mortality due to poaching (Wright and Speake 1975, Fleming and Speake 1976, Kurzejeski et al. 1987, Pack et al. 1999). However, illegal kill rates of 10% were considered negligible in affecting turkey populations in central and east-central Mississippi and the Ouachita Forest of Arkansas (Palmer et al. 1993, Miller et al. 1998, Thogmartin and Schaeffer 2000).

Logistic Regression Models

Several composition and 1 configuration measurement proved useful in creation of habitat models built on logistic regression. The variables selected by logistic regression relate well to our understanding of the ecology of wild turkeys, identifying commercialized areas and areas with large amounts of agriculture as limiting to turkeys. For example, Cleveland County had 0.03% of land in the Commercial-Industrial-Transportation land-cover class and 1,000 turkeys harvested/10,000 km². Pulaski County had the largest percentage of land in the Com-Ind-Trans cover class (2.73%) and had a harvest density of 200 turkeys/10,000 km². The Com-Ind-Trans cover class includes infrastructure (e.g., roads, railroads) and all highly developed non-residential areas. High Intensity Residential includes housing developments with apartment buildings or row houses where <20% of the area is vegetation. Commercial or industrial areas and areas that are used for transportation would not meet minimum food and cover requirements for wild turkeys. Alternatively, presence of these variables may be a reflection of the lack of hunting in urban and suburban landscapes.

Polk and Poinsett County had 0.09% and 77.52% of land in Row Crops, with respective turkey harvest densities of 600 turkeys/10,000 km² and 3 turkeys/10,000 km². Row crops can be an important source of food for wild turkeys, but do not provide cover year-round. There is variability associated with the amount of cover needed by turkeys, but areas with extensive agricultural fields (e.g., Delta region) provide little habitat for cover and are less suitable for wild turkeys. Landscapes that feature single crops over extensive areas are negatively associated with wild turkey abundance (Hurst and Dickson 1992). Kurzejeski and Lewis (1990) found that turkeys in northern Missouri rarely used croplands not bordered by mature timber stands. Increasing amounts of woody cover improved poult survival from 0–4 weeks posthatch, in an agriculture-dominated landscape in Iowa (Hubbard et al. 2001). Flather (1989) found a negative association between turkey densities and area in cropland and human related land-uses in the context of a landscape-scale analysis of the southern United States.

Some of the variables identified are likely surrogates for biologically meaningful variables that are not easily discerned from classified land cover. The percentage of Open Water identified in the Delta region is an example of a possible surrogate variable for bottomland hardwoods. The hardwood forest type associated with river drainages is known historically to be among the best quality habitat for wild turkeys in Arkansas (Meanley 1956). Remnants of this cover class persist along the major waterways. Bottomland hardwood should be classified in the Woody Wetland land-cover class and this type should serve as a better predictor of habitat. However, wetland areas are difficult to delineate with satellite imagery alone (Yang et al. 2001). Ancillary data sources (e.g., National Wetlands Inventory data) are often used to improve wetland detection, but are not always available. Confusion between water and wetland areas would also contribute to inaccuracies. Additional data collection in the field targeting these important, but hard to detect land-cover classes could improve variables used in model development.

Satellite Imagery and Scale

The spatial arrangement of open and forested habitats is an important factor in habitat quality for wild turkeys (Schroeder 1985, Gustafson et al. 1994). We therefore expected configuration variables to be identified as important in the Arkansas models. Research in New York has also explored the use of variables measured from NLCD satellite imagery, and identified configuration in addition to composition variables relating to measures of turkey abundance. In New York, 56% of the variation in turkey harvest was explained by amount of open area and 29% by edge (Glennon and Porter 1999). Fleming and Porter (2001) found that 47% of the variation in poult survival was explained by the Forest Core Area Standard Deviation habitat variable.

The importance of edge and core area variables did not translate to Arkansas landscapes. Edge (the interface between forest and open areas) is important for nesting habitat for wild turkeys and travel corridors for dispersal and was found to be an important habitat variable in New York (Glennon and Porter 1999, Fleming and Porter *this volume*). Thogmartin (1999) found that 9% of the forest patches in an Ouachita study site consisted entirely of edge habitat. Edge habitat was used less than expected for nesting habitat, potentially in response to increased predation in ecotones in Arkansas.

A second explanation for the lack of success of variables characterizing edge habitat in the Arkansas model may be related to the scale of the analysis. Both the scale of assessment and the population data in New York were based on township-level (approximately 10,000 ha) analysis in contrast to county-level analysis in Arkansas. Counties are large enough that they likely contain substantial variation in amount and configuration of edge. Summarizing this variation into a single value may reduce the information and obscure this relationship. For instance, the key habitat component of the Delta region is the small amount of remaining bottomland forest. Percentages of this land-cover class per county are small and therefore are not represented well when averaged to the county scale. Increases in amount of bottomland hardwoods would likely result in an increase in abundance of turkeys; however, the county HSI values would not change significantly. Consequently, HSI values at the county level cannot adequately characterize variation in the population index resulting from a rare, but important habitat component.

Harvest data used for the population index extended 4 years past the dates of satellite image collection. If the assumption of minimal land use change during this 4-year period is incorrect, the discrepancy in satellite image dates and dates of harvest data used could have negatively impacted study results. Urbanization and deforestation are land use changes that could impact suitability of turkey habitat during that period. However, due to the large scale (county-level) that landscape metrics were calculated, a small change in land use would likely not affect metric values greatly.

The overall accuracy of the 1992 classified land cover is low (44%). Combining land-cover classes with similar quality for turkeys and using an aggregate of pixels would potentially have improved the accuracy and allowed for more meaningful models. Aggregating confused land-cover classes is 1 method to overcome data shortcomings (Thogmartin et al. 2004).

Thogmartin et al. (2004) found that there were patterns in how errors were distributed and that mapping problems were associated with rare land covers (e.g., Emergent Herbaceous Wetlands). In Region 4 Open Water was most commonly confused with Emergent Herbaceous Wetlands, which was most commonly confused with Woody Wetlands. Collapsing these 3 categories might have resulted in more meaningful variable identification with logistic regression. In addition, to build predictive logistic regression models the smaller regional models would benefit from additional samples to increase predictive ability.

Although meaningful models were identified through this process, the variables identified are not useful to managers. For example, row crops and industrial areas are not target habitats for wildlife management activities. The exploration of HSI values helped to identify additional land-cover classes that could be combined for modeling wild turkey habitat. High Intensity Residential, Commercial-Industrial-Transportation, Bare Rock-Sand-Clay, and Quarries-Strip Mines-Gravel Pits should be aggregated as they have the same quality for food and cover for wild turkeys. In addition, Row Crops and Small Grains should be aggregated. When commonly confused land-cover classes identified in the southeastern United States (Region 4) are considered, Row Crops and Pasture-Hay could be aggregated to improve image accuracy.

MANAGEMENT IMPLICATIONS

Wild turkey restoration programs in most states have ended or are near completion and management objectives are shifting from restoration to managing currently established populations through habitat manipulation and harvest management. Amount and quality of available habitat will limit wild turkey populations in the future. Habitat models using remotely sensed data could be an important tool to monitor habitat composition and configuration.

Quality of the land-cover data is important to consider when building models for assessing habitat. Land-cover classes should be aggregated to reduce redundancy related to wild turkey biology and to potentially improve accuracy when commonly confused land-cover classes are combined. The expectation is that future land-cover data will have improved accuracy.

In states with a large degree of heterogeneity, assessing habitat at physiographic regions will identify more specific variables and provide better model fit. Regional models should provide more information for managers about habitat quality and priority areas for management.

The scale of assessment limits spatial detail and complexity of the models and perhaps overall utility of the approach. Improvement of quality (i.e., collection of effort information) and resolution of population data (increased sample size) would increase the predictive ability of landscape-level models. Variables averaged on a smaller scale capture more variation present on the landscape. The increase in sample size would allow for generation and testing of models with subsets of the data.

Landscape level habitat assessment at a county scale might be best used in a step-down approach to identifying important turkey habitat. After key counties are identified a more detailed assessment could be initiated using aerial photographs or traditional ground-based methods. A landscape level view can be a valuable compliment to local scale habitat information in decision making for long-term harvest goals and habitat management priority areas for wild turkeys.

ACKNOWLEDGMENTS

The Arkansas Fish and Game Commission provided support for this project. We thank M. Widner, D. Nicholson, and many District Wildlife Supervisors for the knowledge they shared about wild turkey biology in Arkanasas. K. K. Fleming, B. R. Miranda, S. A. McNulty, J. Zysik, D. C. Allen, and D. J. Leopold provided input on earlier drafts of the manuscript. Finally, we thank R. O. Kimmel and K. J. Haroldson for reviewing the manuscript before submittal.

LITERATURE CITED

Badyaev, A. V. 1995. Nesting habitat and nesting success of eastern wild turkeys in the Arkansas Ozark highlands. Condor 97:221–232.

———, W. J. Etges, and T. E. Martin. 1996. Ecological and behavioral correlates of variation in seasonal home ranges of wild turkeys. Journal of Wildlife Management 60:154–164.

Burnham, K. P., and D. R. Anderson. 1992. Data-based selection of an appropriate biological model: the key to modern data analysis. Pages 16–30 *in* D. R. McCullough and R. H. Barrett, editors. Proceedings of Wildlife 2001: Populations. Elsevier Applied Science, New York, New York, USA.

Center for Advanced Spatial Technologies (CAST). 1998. Arkansas Gap Analysis. University of Arkansas, Fayetville, Arkansas. ⟨www.cast.uark.edu/gap/⟩. Accessed 4 May 2003.

Dickson, J. G., C. D. Adams, and S. H. Hanley. 1978. Response of turkey populations to habitat variables in Louisiana. Wildlife Society Bulletin 6:163–166.

Donovan, M. L., D. L. Rabe, and C. E. Olson, Jr. 1987. Use of geographic information systems to develop habitat suitability models. Wildlife Society Bulletin 15:574–579.

Environmental Systems Research Institute 1999. ArcView GIS 3.2. Redlands, California, USA.

Flather, C. H. 1989. Recent historical and projected regional trends of white-tailed deer and wild turkey in the southern

United States. U.S. Forest Service General Technical Report RM-172.

Fleming, K., and W. F. Porter. 2001. Using a habitat-suitability approach to evaluate landscape patterns for eastern wild turkey in New York State. Proceedings of the National Wild Turkey Symposium 8:157–166.

———, and ———. *This volume.* Effect of landscape features and fragmentation on wild turkey dispersal. Proceedings of the National Wild Turkey Symposium 9:*This volume.*

Fleming, W. J., and D. W. Speake. 1976. Losses of the eastern wild turkey from a stable Alabama population. Proceedings of the Annual Conference of the Southeastern Association of Fish and Wildlife Agencies 30:377–385.

Glennon, M. J., and W. F. Porter. 1999. Using satellite imagery to assess landscape-scale habitat for wild turkeys. Wildlife Society Bulletin 27:646–653.

Gustafson, E. J., G. R. Parker, and S. E. Backs. 1994. Evaluating spatial pattern of wildlife habitat: a case study of the wild turkey (*Meleagris gallopavo*). American Midland Naturalist 131:24–33.

Hanson, G. T., and C. H. Moneyhon. 1989. Historical Atlas of Arkansas. University of Oklahoma Press, Norman, Oklahoma, USA.

Hosmer, D. W., and S. Lemeshow. 2000. Applied Logistic Regression. John Wiley & Sons, New York, New York, USA.

Hubbard, M. W., D. L. Garner, and E. E. Klaas. 2001. Factors influencing wild turkey poult survival in southcentral Iowa. Proceedings of the National Wild Turkey Symposium 8:167–172.

Hurst, G. A., and J. G. Dickson. 1992. Eastern turkey in southern pine-oak forests. Pages 265–285 *in* J. G. Dickson, editor. The wild turkey: biology and management. Stackpole Books, Mechanicsburg, Pennsylvania, USA.

Johnson, C. J., N. D. Alexander, R. D. Wheate, and K. L. Parker. 2003. Characterizing woodland caribou habitat in sub-boreal and boreal forests. Forest Ecology and Management. 180:241–248.

Kurzejeski, E. W., and J. B. Lewis. 1990. Home ranges, movements, and habitat use of wild turkey hens in northern Missouri. Proceedings of the National Wild Turkey Symposium 6:67–71.

———, L. D. Vangilder, and J. B. Lewis. 1987. Survival of wild turkey hens in north Missouri. Journal of Wildlife Management 51:188–193.

Lint, J. R. 1990. Assessment of Mark-Recapture models and indices to estimate population size of wild turkeys on Tallahala Wildlife Management Area. Thesis, Mississippi State University, Mississippi State, Mississippi, USA.

McGarigal, K., and B. J. Marks. 1995. Fragstats: spatial pattern analysis for quantifying landscape structure. U.S. Forest Service General Technical Report PNW-GTR-351.

Meanley, B. 1956. Foods of the wild turkey in the White River Bottomlands of Southeastern Arkansas. The Wilson Bulletin 68:305–311.

Miller, D. A., L. W. Burger, B. D. Leopold, and G. A. Hurst. 1998. Survival and cause-specific mortality of wild turkey hens in central Mississippi. Journal of Wildlife Management 62:306–313.

———, D. B. Leopold, G. A. Hurst, and P. D. Gerard. 2000. Habitat selection for eastern wild turkeys in central Mississippi. Journal of Wildlife Management 64:765–776.

Morrison, M. L., B. G. Marcot, and R. W. Mannan. 1998. Wildlife-habitat relationships: concepts and application. Second edition. University of Wisconsin Press, Madison, Wisconsin, USA.

Pack, J. C., G. W. Norman, C. I. Taylor, D. E. Steffen, D. A. Swanson, K. H. Pollock, and R. Alpizar-Jara. 1999. Effects of fall hunting on wild turkey populations in Virginia and West Virginia. Journal of Wildlife Management 63:964–975.

Palmer, W. E., G. A. Hurst, J. E. Stys, D. R. Smith, and J. D. Burk. 1993. Survival rates of wild turkey hens in loblolly pine plantations in Mississippi. Journal of Wildlife Management 57:783–789.

SAS Institute. 1990. SAS user's guide. Fourth edition. SAS Institute, Cary, North Carolina, USA.

Schroeder, R. L. 1985. Habitat suitability index models: eastern wild turkey. U.S. Fish and Wildlife Service Biological Report 82(10.106).

Seiss, R. S., P. S. Phalen, and G. A. Hurst. 1990. Wild turkey nesting habitat and success rates. Proceedings of the National Wild Turkey Symposium 6:18–24.

Smith, K. G., R. S. Dzur, D. G. Catanzaro, M. E. Garner, and W. F. Limp. 1998. Statewide biodiversity mapping for Arkansas. Center for Advanced Spatial Technologies, Fayetteville, Arkansas, USA.

Smith, R. M., editor. 1989. The atlas of Arkansas. University of Arkansas Press, Fayetteville, Arkansas, USA.

Thogmartin, W. E. 1999. Landscape attributes and nest-site selection in wild turkeys. Auk 116:912–923.

———, and J. E. Johnson. 1999. Reproduction in a declining population of wild turkeys in Arkansas. Journal of Wildlife Management 63:1281–1290.

———, and B. A. Schaeffer. 2000. Landscape attributes associated with mortality events of wild turkeys in Arkansas. Wildlife Society Bulletin 28:865–874.

———. 2001. Home-range size and habitat selection of female wild turkeys (*Meleagris gallopavo*) in Arkansas. American Midland Naturalist 145:247–260.

———, A. L. Gallant, M. G. Knutson, T. J. fox, and M. J. Suárez. 2004. Commentary: a cautionary tale regarding use of the National Land Cover Dataset 1992. Wildlife Society Bulletin 32:970–978.

U.S. Geological Survey. 2000. Arkansas Land Cover Data Set Metadata. U.S. Geological Survey, Sioux Falls, South Dakota, USA.

———. 2004. Accuracy assessment of 1992 National Land Cover Data. ⟨http://landcover.usgs.gov/accuracy/⟩. Accessed 26 Aug 2004.

Wigley, T. B., J. M. Sweeney, M. E. Garner, and M. A. Melchoirs. 1985. Forest habitat use by wild turkeys in the Ouachita Mountains. Proceedings of the National Wild Turkey Symposium 5:183–197.

———, ———, ———, and ———. 1986. Wild turkey home ranges in the Ouachita Mountains. Journal of Wildlife Management. 50:540–544.

Wright, G. A., and D. W. Speake. 1975. Compatibility of eastern wild turkey with recreational activities at Land Between the Lake, Kentucky. Proceedings of the Annual Conference of the Southeastern Association of Fish and Wildlife Agencies 29:578–584.

Yang, L., S. V. Stehman, J. H. Smith, and J. D. Wickham. 2001. Thematic accuracy of MRLC land cover for the eastern United States. Remote Sensing of Environment 76:418–422.

Zar, J. H. 1999. Biostatistical analysis. Fourth edition. Prentice Hall, Upper Saddle River, New Jersey, USA.

Sharon Goetz is a wildlife research biologist for the Minnesota Department of Natural Resources. She received a B.S. in biology from Coe College and an M.S. in environmental and forest biology from the State University of New York. Her research interests include the ecology of northern wild turkey populations, upland game management, and hunter attitudes.

Bill Porter began his studies of the wild turkey in southeastern Minnesota in the 1970s and in collaboration with his graduate students has been exploring questions about populations dynamics and habitat ever since. As a faculty member in Syracuse, he teaches wildlife management, winter ecology and forest ecology. He also directs research and education programs for the university's field station in the Adirondack Mountains of northern New York. He has never been allowed to forget that he once predicted that wild turkeys would not inhabit the Adirondacks.

INFLUENCE OF SILVICULTURAL TREATMENTS ON WILD TURKEY HABITAT IN EASTERN TENNESSEE

Samuel W. Jackson[1]
*University of Tennessee
Agricultural Experiment Station,
Knoxville, TN 37996, USA*

Ryan G. Basinger[2]
*University of Tennessee
Agricultural Experiment Station,
Department of Forestry, Wildlife and Fisheries,
Knoxville, TN 37996, USA*

Daniel S. Gordon
*University of Tennessee
Agricultural Experiment Station,
Department of Forestry, Wildlife and Fisheries,
Knoxville, TN 37996, USA*

Craig A. Harper
*University of Tennessee Extension,
Department of Forestry, Wildlife and Fisheries,
Knoxville, TN 37996, USA*

David S. Buckley
*University of Tennessee
Agricultural Experiment Station,
Department of Forestry, Wildlife and Fisheries,
Knoxville, TN 37996, USA*

David A. Buehler
*University of Tennessee
Agricultural Experiment Station,
Department of Forestry, Wildlife and Fisheries,
Knoxville, TN 37996, USA*

Abstract: Management of forested habitats for wild turkeys (*Meleagris gallapavo*) is critical to provide the proper vegetative requirements to improve reproductive success and survival. We investigated the effects of prescribed fire, shelterwood harvest, and wildlife retention cuts on wild turkey habitat in a mixed hardwood forest in eastern Tennessee. Vegetative response, soft and hard mast production, invertebrate availability, and crown expansion were measured. Shelterwood harvest (61–80% density), wildlife retention cut with prescribed fire (61–80%), and wildlife retention cut (41–60%) increased the density of understory vegetation. White oak (*Quercus alba*) crown expansion was greater in the shelterwood harvest (25%) and wildlife retention cut (8%) than in the control. No effects of treatments were found on herbaceous cover, acorn production, soft mast production, or invertebrate densities. Shelterwood harvest, wildlife retention cut, and wildlife retention cut with prescribed burning enhanced the nesting and brooding cover for wild turkey in the short term; however, additional treatment is needed to increase herbaceous cover and reduce density of woody understory vegetation.

Proceedings of the National Wild Turkey Symposium 9:199–207

Key words: mast production, shelterwood harvest, wild turkey habitat, wildlife retention cut.

Forest management directly influences wildlife habitat by altering forest structure, resource availability, and species composition. Understanding the effects of silvicultural practices on forest systems better enables us to successfully manage for selected wildlife habitat characteristics, including those important to wild turkey.

The eastern wild turkey depends on forested habitat for both food and cover during critical times in its life-cycle. While forested habitat is important throughout the year, it is most important in the winter months (Dickson 2001). Oak acorns are a large part of the winter diet, while other soft-mast species, such as flowering dogwood (*Cornus florida*) and blackgum (*Nyssa sylvatica*) are important when available (Hurst 1992). Other woody species, including vines (e.g., *Vitis* spp.), also provide valuable soft mast foods.

The structure of mixed hardwood stands is impor-

[1] E-mail: samjackson@utk.edu
[2] Present address: Westervelt Wildlife Services, Demopolis, AL 36732, USA

A wildlife retention cut was implemented in this stand in February 2001 (*left*). By June 2005, considerable groundcover, including Virginia wildrye, had developed and nesting and brooding cover for wild turkeys had improved dramatically over that in the adjacent control stand (*right*) only 100 yards away. (Photo Credit: Craig Harper)

tant cover for roosting, feeding, nesting, and brooding. Mixed hardwood stands can be as attractive as openings and brushy areas, provided the proper vegetative structure is in place. If managed to provide a lush herbaceous layer or shrubby conditions beneath the overstory, mixed hardwoods can provide adequate nesting and brooding cover (Davis 1992, Harper 1998). This vegetative layer also provides habitat for invertebrates and increased seed production, both critical sources of food for poults. In western North Carolina, insect availability was greater in stands containing more herbaceous cover (Harper et al. 2001). In fact, the density of preferred insects did not differ between forested areas and openings. Metzler and Speake (1985) reported poult survival in upland hardwoods was greater where more herbaceous vegetation developed. The herbaceous layer may also produce seed for both juvenile and adult wild turkeys.

Creating appropriate conditions for wild turkeys in mature mixed hardwoods can be challenging. Some research has been conducted on the effects of hardwood management on wild turkey habitat (Pack et al. 1980, Rogers 1985, Pack et al. 1988, Swanson et al. 1996, and Basinger 2002). Further, research has examined forested stand manipulation through silvicultural methods to improve habitat conditions for wild turkeys. Swanson et al. (1996) found wild turkey nesting success rates were not different between harvested and unharvested areas. Poult survival was higher in harvested areas with more ground-level vegetation.

Our objective was to study the effects of 4 silvicultural treatments with controls on wild turkey habitat characteristics in mixed hardwood in eastern Tennessee. The silvicultural treatments included: shelterwood harvest; wildlife retention cut; wildlife retention cut with prescribed fire; and prescribed fire alone. We also wanted to document the effect of the silvicultural treatments on key food sources, including soft mast production, acorn production, and invertebrate availability.

STUDY AREA

The study was conducted at Chuck Swan State Forest and Wildlife Management Area in eastern Tennessee. It was located approximately 50 miles northeast of Knoxville, Tennessee, and encompassed approximately 9,712 ha. The area was co-managed by the Tennessee Division of Forestry and the Tennessee Wildlife Resources Agency.

The primary timber type at Chuck Swan was mixed hardwoods. Predominant species included white oak, chestnut oak (*Q. montana*), black oak (*Q. velutina*), scarlet oak (*Q. coccinea*), blackgum, red maple (*Acer rubrum*), and yellow-poplar (*Liriodendron tulipifera*). There was also a large component of planted loblolly pine (*Pinus taeda*) and eastern white pine (*Pinus strobus*). The terrain at Chuck Swan was considered to be hilly with elevations ranging from 304 m above sea level to over 488 m above sea level. Temperatures ranged from a yearly average high of 20.4°C to a yearly average low of 7.9°C. The area received approximately 119 cm of rain per year (National Climatic Data Center 2001).

METHODS

We identified 4 24-acre stands on moderately productive sites for this study. All sites were on northwest aspects with slopes averaging 24 to 30%. All stands were comprised of mixed (oak-hickory) hardwoods with a small component of pine.

Treatments

We divided the 4 identified stands into 12 2-acre cells and used 5 different treatment combinations and a control. Treatments were shelterwood harvest, shelterwood harvest with prescribed fire, wildlife retention cut, wildlife retention cut with prescribed fire, and prescribed fire alone. We randomly assigned each treatment to 2 2-acre cells in each stand. We implemented treatments in 2001 and data we present in this paper represent changes in habitat from pre-treatment conditions to 3 growing seasons after treatment. We conducted the shelterwood harvest with prescribed fire treatment in accordance with the Brose et al. (1999) shelterwood-burn method. Due to the length of time between the initial harvest and the prescribed fire, we did not report the effects of this treatment in this paper.

We implemented wildlife retention cuts to kill selected overstory and midstory trees by felling or girdling trees. We applied a 50:50 mixture of Garlon 3A (Dow AgroSciences, Indianapolis, Indiana, USA) and water to girdled stems to kill the tree and to cut stems to reduce resprouting. We made cuts that would enhance understory structure and food production for wild turkeys. We did not consider economic or timber production concerns. Trees marked to be killed had less benefit to wildlife and included red maple, sourwood (*Oxydendrum arboreum*), and yellow-poplar, while leave trees included oaks, flowering dogwood, and blackgum. We established a target residual basal area of 4.7–5.6 m² per acre, an approximate 50% decrease in pretreatment basal area. In some cases, we killed a few intermediate oaks to achieve the target basal area. We did not remove trees or debris from the sites. We treated all stands in late February–March 2001.

We conducted prescribed burning to complete the uncut burned treatment and the wildlife retention cut with prescribed fire treatment during April 2001. We used the strip-fire technique to maintain a moderate to low intensity burn. According to weather data collected 61 km away in Oak Ridge, Tennessee, average temperatures on burn days ranged from 13.9 to 23.9°C and relative humidity ranged from 54 to 66%. The sites had not received any precipitation for at least 3 days prior to burning. Average flame lengths were less than 1 m, with fires burning at a fairly slow pace, less than 1.8 m per minute. We used relatively low-intensity fire to keep from damaging standing timber as much as possible.

We conducted the shelterwood harvests in early summer 2001. We marked timber based on timber production and regeneration goals. Harvest goals were residual basal areas of approximately 4.6–5.56 m² per acre, an approximate 50% reduction in pretreatment basal area. We left leave trees that were of good quality, vigorous, and with good form. Whenever possible, we left oaks as residual stems. Trees removed included American beech (*Fagus grandifolia*), red maple, sassafras (*Sassafras albidum*), and hickory (*Carya* spp.). A contract logging company conducted the harvest.

Measurements

Vegetation Measurements

We collected pre-treatment vegetation data in August and September 2000 and implemented treatments during early 2001. We collected post-treatment vegetation data in August and September 2001 and 2003. Within each treatment cell, we established 3 permanent sampling plots for vegetative measurements. To prevent edge effect and measurement overlap, we located each plot at least 30.5 m from the cell edge and at least 30.5 m from another plot.

We utilized a handheld spherical densiometer (Forest Densiometers Bartlesville, Oklahoma, USA) to estimate canopy cover. Readings were taken at points 5.5 m from plot center in each of the 4 cardinal directions.

When stationed at each direction, 4 measurements were taken, one in each cardinal direction, for a total of 16 measurements per plot.

We measured herbaceous coverage at each sampling plot. We established 3 transects, 11.3 m long, around plot center at 0, 120, and 240°. A measuring tape was stretched the length of the transect and herbaceous coverage by species was recorded.

We measured density of understory vegetation using a density board (Nudds 1977). The density board was 1.8 m tall and was divided into 4 45.7-cm sections. An observer located at plot's center visually estimated the proportion of each section obscured by vegetation at a distance of 14.9 m. We used a ranking system with 5 categories to record data: 1 = 0–20% coverage, 2 = 21–40% coverage, 3 = 41–60% coverage, 4 = 61–80% coverage, 5 = 81–100% coverage. We took density board readings directly up-slope and down-slope from plot center to calculate an average for the plot.

We recorded woody regeneration by species and height class (stems <10 cm tall; 10 cm to 1.4 m tall) using a 3.6 m radius circular plot, counting all woody stems less than 1.4 m tall. We chose these size categories to accurately measure the vegetation that provided brooding cover to turkeys.

Soft Mast Collection

We collected ripened fleshy fruit from low-growing plants once per month July through September 2001 and June through September 2002. We established 3 line transects (50 m × 2 m each) systematically within each treatment replicate and collected all ripened fruits within the transect area. Transects were spaced approximately 25 m apart and at least 5 m from the edge of each cell to prevent sampling plants impacted by an edge effect. We stored collected fruits in a freezer and then dried the samples at 40°C for 4 days (Campo and Hurst 1980). After drying, fruit was identified, counted, and weighed to quantify soft mast production for each treatment.

White Oak Sampling and Mast Collection

Because white oaks are capable of providing a more consistent annual food source for wild turkeys, we monitored individual white oaks to document their response to treatments. During September 2001, 29 white oak trees were selected and marked within the 4 stands of the study area. Selected trees occupied dominant or co-dominant positions within the canopy. Tree diameter at breast height ranged from 30 to 74 cm. We selected white oaks within the shelterwood and wildlife retention cut treatments and the controls. None were selected within treatments that were burned. The number of trees selected within the shelterwood harvest, wildlife retention cut, and control were 10, 10, and 9, respectively. Growth measurements included crown diameter (measured with a transect tape, with measurements perpendicular and parallel to slope) and were recorded in 2001 and 2002.

In addition to measuring tree characteristics, we also monitored acorn production by placing 3 mast baskets directly beneath the crown of each tree. Baskets were constructed with a mesh fabric material attached to a pipe and supported approximately 1 m above ground by 3 wooden stakes. The opening of each basket represented 1 m². We collected acorns weekly from September through December 2001 and 2002. A float test was conducted to identify sound acorns. All acorns were counted, but only sound acorns were weighed to quantify annual yields.

To determine acorn predation by wildlife (e.g., squirrels [*Sciurus* spp.] and chipmunks [*Tamais striatus*]), we placed marked acorns in baskets within each treatment. The rate of acorn predation was determined by the proportion of marked acorns removed between collection intervals.

Invertebrate Sampling

Peak hatching of wild turkeys in the southern Appalachians occurs during May and June (Pack et al. 1980, Davis 1992, Harper 1998, Norman et al. 2001). Thus, we collected invertebrates during 4 sampling periods (1 = mid-May, 2 = late May, 3 = mid-June, 4 = late June) in 2002. We sampled invertebrates using a portable vacuum sampler and 0.1 m² bottomless box with a lid (Harper and Guynn 1998) to collect invertebrates available to wild turkey poults on the vegetation and on top of the leaf litter. This method also allowed invertebrate density and biomass to be quantified per unit area.

We established 3 sampling locations systematically in each treatment and control cell in each stand. Locations were situated at least 30.5 m apart and from the edge of each replicate to prevent sampling edge habitats. We assigned bearings 0, 120, and 240° to each sampling location, representing 3 sub-samples. Subsamples were located by pacing 5 m from plot center in each direction. At each subsampling location, we placed the box on the ground to trap all invertebrates within the area. We vacuumed the vegetation and top layer of leaf litter into the sample bags. All sample bags were stored in a freezer to prevent decomposition (Murkin et al. 1996). We sorted contents in white trays where invertebrates were removed and placed in vials. Vials were opened and oven-dried for 48 hours at 60°C (Murkin et al. 1996). All invertebrates were counted, weighed, and classified to taxonomic order for each treatment.

Data Analysis

We averaged data by plot and analyzed them using Analysis of Variance (General Linear Model (GLM) procedure; SAS Institute 2000). Class variables used were stand and treatment. The GLM tested for differences within years between treatments using the stand-treatment interaction as an error term. We separated means using Tukey's mean separation technique. The Shapiro-wilk test, the W value, was used to test the normality of the data. A W of 0.90 or higher indicated normally distributed data. Some data were transformed using the natural log + 0.05 method. For data presented by year, year 2000 is the pre-treatment year and years 2001, 2002, and 2003 are the post-treatment years.

Table 1. Mean (± SE) canopy cover by year and treatment at Chuck Swan State Forest and Wildlife Management Area, Union County, Tennessee, 2000, 2001, and 2003.

Year	Treatment	% Canopy cover[a]
2000[b]	Control	96.98 (0.20) A
	Uncut Burned	97.29 (0.21) A
	Shelterwood	96.91 (0.19) A
	Wildlife Retention Burned	96.87 (0.28) A
	Wildlife Retention Cut	97.34 (0.20) A
2001[c]	Control	97.39 (0.12) A
	Uncut Burned	94.28 (0.70) AB
	Shelterwood	86.70 (1.35) C
	Wildlife Retention Burned	89.16 (1.08) BC
	Wildlife Retention Cut	92.77 (0.80) AB
2003[d]	Control	87.90 (1.15) A
	Uncut Burned	84.56 (1.42) AB
	Shelterwood	76.91 (1.71) BC
	Wildlife Retention Burned	63.78 (2.95) D
	Wildlife Retention Cut	72.68 (1.73) CD

[a] Means with the same letter are not different ($P > 0.05$).
[b] Treatment effect: $F = 0.67$, df = 4,43, $P = 0.649$.
[c] Treatment effect: $F = 13.37$, df = 4,43, $P < 0.001$.
[d] Treatment effect: $F = 16.23$, df = 4,43, $P = 0.0001$.

We separated invertebrate data means using the Least Square Means technique. An analysis of covariance was performed on invertebrate density and biomass using herbaceous cover as a covariate.

RESULTS

Canopy Cover

There was no difference in mean canopy cover prior to treatment. Means ranged from 96.87 to 97.33%. In the first year after treatment, the shelterwood had less canopy cover than the control, the uncut burned treatment, and the wildlife retention cut (Table 1). The wildlife retention cut with prescribed fire had less canopy cover than the control. By the third year post-treatment, the wildlife retention cut with prescribed fire had less canopy cover than any other treatment except the unburned wildlife retention cut (Table 1). The shelterwood and wildlife retention cut had less cover than the control or uncut burned treatment.

Herbaceous Understory

No differences between treatments were detected in mean herbaceous coverage prior to treatment ($F = 0.41$, df = 5, 42, $P = 0.838$). Mean percent coverage was 5.63–12.25%. In post-treatment year 2001, means were 2.29 to 8.3% and in year 2003, means were 4.91 to 12.92% (2001: $F = 0.98$, df = 5, 42, $P = 0.440$; 2003: $F = 0.60$, df = 5, 42, $P = 0.704$). Similarly, no differences were detected in mean herbaceous height ($F = 1.08$, df = 5, 42, $P = 0.386$). Pretreatment means ranged from 7.5 to 12 cm. In 2001, mean average height ranged from 5.9 to 10.8 cm and in 2003, means ranged from 7.7 to 19 cm (2001: $F = 2.20$, df = 5, 42, $P = 0.072$; 2003: $F = 1.87$, df = 5, 42, $P = 0.121$).

Table 2. Mean (± SE) vegetation density (1–5 rating) by treatment at Chuck Swan State Forest and Wildlife Management Area, Union County, Tennessee, 2000, 2001, and 2003.

Year	Treatment	Density board ranking[a]			
		Section 1	Section 2	Section 3	Section 4
2000[b]	Control	2.92 (0.32) A	1.79 (0.19) A	1.77 (0.23) A	1.69 (0.21) A
	Uncut Burned	2.48 (0.25) A	1.54 (0.16) A	1.31 (0.12) A	1.19 (0.12) A
	Wildlife Retention Cut	2.50 (0.32) A	1.58 (0.24) A	1.75 (0.31) A	1.83 (0.28) A
	Wildlife Ret. Burned	2.46 (0.27) A	1.77 (0.20) A	1.65 (0.20) A	1.48 (0.15) A
	Shelterwood	3.40 (0.26) A	2.20 (0.26) A	1.83 (0.17) A	1.81 (0.21) A
2001[c]	Control	2.63 (0.29) ABC	1.81 (0.20) AB	1.60 (0.15) AB	1.46 (0.14) AB
	Uncut Burned	1.71 (0.15) A	1.23 (0.11) A	1.42 (0.23) A	1.15 (0.08) A
	Wildlife Retention Cut	2.83 (0.19) BCD	1.83 (0.18) AB	1.35 (0.12) A	1.15 (0.07) A
	Wildlife Ret. Burned	1.98 (0.18) AB	1.33 (0.14) A	1.17 (0.09) A	1.10 (0.06) A
	Shelterwood	3.75 (0.21) D	3.04 (0.24) C	2.54 (0.24) C	2.48 (0.24) C
2003[d]	Control	2.27 (0.27) A	1.60 (0.19) A	1.35 (0.12) AB	1.17 (0.09) A
	Uncut Burned	2.19 (0.29) A	1.63 (0.25) A	1.27 (0.13) A	1.13 (0.09) A
	Uncut Burned	2.19 (0.29) A	1.63 (0.25) A	1.27 (0.13) A	1.13 (0.09) A
	Wildlife Retention Cut	3.44 (0.32) AB	2.48 (0.30) AB	1.75 (0.22) ABC	1.29 (0.17) A
	Wildlife Ret. Burned	4.13 (0.23) B	3.35 (0.27) B	2.10 (0.19) BC	1.40 (0.14) AB
	Shelterwood	4.06 (0.23) B	3.46 (0.29) B	2.79 (0.30) C	2.25 (0.26) B

[a] Means with the same letter are not different ($P > 0.05$).
[b] Section 1 treatment effect: $F = 1.20$, df = 4,43, $P = 0.327$; Section 2: $F = 2.08$, df = 4,43, $P = 0.087$; Section 3: $F = 0.76$, df = 4,43, $P = 0.581$; Section 4: $F = 2.07$, df = 4,43, $P = 0.089$.
[c] Section 1 treatment effect: $F = 9.17$, df = 4,43, $P = 0.001$; Section 2: $F = 14.43$, df = 4,43, $P = 0.001$; Section 3: $F = 8.42$, df = 4,43, $P < 0.001$; Section 4: $F = 10.29$, df = 4,43, $P < 0.001$.
[d] Section 1 treatment effect: $F = 4.95$, df = 4,43, $P = 0.001$; Section 2: $F = 4.89$, df = 4,43, $P = 0.001$; Section 3: $F = 4.77$, df = 4,43, $P = 0.002$; Section 4: $F = 3.76$, df = 4,43, $P = 0.007$.

Vertical Vegetation Density

There was no difference between treatments in the year prior to treatment in any section of the density board. Post-treatment, several differences were apparent (Table 2). Most important for wild turkeys, differ-

Table 3. Mean (± SE) number of stems of woody regeneration (ac) by size class and treatment at Chuck Swan State Forest and Wildlife Management Area, Union County, Tennessee, 2000, 2001, and 2003.

Year	Treatment	Stems (ac) Under 10 cm Tall[a]	Stems (ac) Over 10 cm Tall[a]
2000[b]	Control	11,840 (1,431) A	44,273 (5,832) A
	Uncut Burned	14,557 (1,851) A	40,260 (5,590) A
	Shelterwood	13,795 (2,586) A	44,579 (5,114) A
	Wildlife Ret. Burned	15,713 (1,777) A	29,566 (4,498) A
	Wildlife Retention Cut	15,299 (2,296) A	33,016 (5,007) A
2001[c]	Control	13,911 (1,558) A	24,518 (3,230) A
	Uncut Burned	42,322 (3,470) B	34,868 (4,502) A
	Shelterwood	8,755 (1,369) A	24,247 (2,774) A
	Wildlife Ret. Burned	49,247 (9,168) B	35,315 (6,051) A
	Wildlife Retention Cut	16,550 (2,196) A	35,352 (4,929) A
2003[d]	Control	9,869 (1,695) A	24,083 (2,228) A
	Uncut Burned	7,862 (890) A	19,428 (2,492) A
	Shelterwood	6,771 (811) A	22,505 (2,244) A
	Wildlife Ret. Burned	6,825 (1,548) A	25,938 (3,634) A
	Wildlife Retention Cut	6,486 (937) A	21,250 (2,546) A

[a] Means iwth the same letter are not different ($P > 0.05$).
[b] ANOVA statistics: treatment effect under 10 cm tall: $F = 0.60$, df = 4,43, $P = 0.698$; over 10 cm tall: $F = 0.97$, df = 4,43, $P = 0.450$.
[c] ANOVA statistics: treatment effect under 10 cm tall: $F = 13.44$, df = 4,43, $P < 0.001$; over 10 cm tall: $F = 1.44$, df = 4,43, $P = 0.229$.
[d] ANOVA statistics: treatment effect under 10 cm tall: $F = 0.97$, df = 4,43, $P = 0.446$; over 10 cm tall: $F = 0.41$, df = 4,43, $P = 0.839$.

ences were detected in sections 1 and 2 of the density board. The control and the uncut burned treatment contained less vegetation density than the wildlife retention cut with prescribed fire and the shelterwood.

Woody Regeneration

The number of woody regeneration stems <10 cm tall in the understory did not differ among treatments in the year prior to treatment. However, in the year immediately following treatment, the uncut burned treatment and the wildlife retention cut with prescribed fire had more woody regeneration stems under 10 cm tall than any other treatment (Table 3). The number of woody regeneration stems <10 cm tall did not differ among treatments after the second post-treatment.

Soft Mast Production

Soft mast production was highly variable within treatments. There was no statistical difference between treatments in the 2 years after treatment implementation (2001: $F = 2.07$, df = 4, 115, $P = 0.067$; 2002: $F = 0.84$, df = 4, 155, $P = 0.519$). Soft mast production was highly variable on the study site, resulting in extremely high standard errors. In 2001, mean production of soft mast ranged from 0 g/ha in the uncut burn to 243 g/ha in the control. In 2002, means ranged from 120 g/ha in the control to 19,583 g/ha in the uncut burn.

White Oak Sampling and Mast Collection

The number of acorns produced (per m² of crown area) and mass (g/m² of crown area) of acorns produced from the 29 individual white oaks monitored did not differ prior to treatment in 2001 (number: $F =$

1.11, df = 2, 24, P = 0.344; mass: F = 1.74, df = 2, 24, P = 0.195) or 2002 (number: F = 1.12, df = 2, 24, P = 0.341; mass: F = 0.97, df = 2, 24, P = 0.452). In 2001, the mean number of acorns produced ranged from 1.07 in the control to 3.23 acorns per m^2 of crown area in the wildlife thinning. Mean mass of the acorns produced ranged from 1.29 in the control to 6.98 g/m^2 of crown area in the wildlife thinning. In 2002, the mean number of acorns produced ranged from 2.93 in the control to 6.10 acorns per m^2 of crown area in the shelterwood while mean mass of the acorns produced ranged from 6.62 in the control to 14.43 g/m^2 of crown area in the wildlife thinning. The crown area of the white oaks also did not differ among treatments (2001: F = 1.38, df = 2, 27, P = 0.269; 2002: F = 0.82, df = 2, 27, P = 0.452). In 2001, mean crown area was 91.49 m^2 in the shelterwood and increased by 25% to 114.74 m^2 in 2002. Similarly, the 2001 mean crown area in the wildlife thinning was 132.8 m^2 and in 2002, it was 143.13 m^2, an increase of 8%. Predation of acorns averaged 5% in 2001 and 12.7% in 2002 across all sites (Basinger 2002).

Invertebrates

Invertebrate biomass did not differ among treatments (F = 0.39, df = 4, 44, P = 0.813). The analysis of covariance revealed a weak relationship between invertebrate density/biomass and herbaceous cover (P = 0.086). Mean density ranged from 75 invertebrates/m^2 in the uncut burn to 132.5 invertebrates/m^2 in the control. Mean invertebrate biomass was lowest in the uncut burn (0.148 g/m^2) and highest in the wildlife burn (0.200 g/m^2).

DISCUSSION

Killing trees by girdling and spraying does not happen quickly. Within the wildlife retention cuts, overstory canopy cover and residual basal area continued to decrease into the third year after treatment as the remaining treated trees died. Although reduction in canopy cover occurred more slowly in the wildlife retention cuts than the shelterwood harvests (where trees were physically removed), there was little difference in vegetation response between those treatments after 3 years. In addition, leaving standing snags and downed woody material provides habitat and food resources for a variety of wildlife. In 2003, canopy cover decreased by 10% in the control and uncut burned treatment. In the control area, we feel this difference was because of measurement variation between individual measurers as well as the possibility that there may have been a minor loss in canopy cover naturally. The uncut burned treatment likely saw an additional decline in year 3 canopy cover as a result of continued loss of midstory vegetation damaged by prescribed fire.

Herbaceous cover is important for brooding cover and forage availability. We were surprised herbaceous cover did not increase in any of the treatments. Treatment areas averaged less than 10% herbaceous coverage prior to treatment and that pattern continued

through 3 years post-treatment. Jackson (2002) reported that although new species entered the site after treatment, specifically pokeberry (*Phytolacca americana*) and fireweed (*Erechtites hieracifolia*), no significant changes in the number of species or density of particular species occurred following treatment. Naturally, various sites may respond differently, depending on site conditions, past management history, and the seedbank present.

We recognize thinning rate can influence the composition of responding vegetation; however, we feel site conditions largely determine vegetation response following initial treatment. Removing >35% of the stocking level promoted increased woody cover with an increased incidence of epicormic sprouting (Sander et al. 1983). In Pennsylvania, a lighter thinning produced more herbaceous cover (Wunz 1989). After thinning 30–70% of the basal area in 26–50 year-old Appalachian cove hardwoods, Beck and Harlow (1981) found understory vegetation increased more than 42% 3 years after cutting. Trees represented most of the increase (seed regeneration) the first year after cutting; however, an equal amount of herbaceous vegetation was produced the second year. Peak production of understory vegetation was reached in the third year and began to decline by the fourth year. Herbaceous response was increased on higher quality, mesic sites than on lower quality, xeric sites, which were more similar to our study site.

On our study sites, we believe additional treatment (e.g., prescribed fire, herbicide application) is needed to control woody stem regeneration and stimulate increased herbaceous cover. The level of basal area reduction did not influence understory composition. Basal area reduction in the wildlife retention cuts occurred slowly over 3 years post-treatment. Once full basal area reduction was realized, percent canopy cover had been gradually reduced to approximately 64–73% (Table 1). The majority of the responding vegetation was woody, from the first year post-treatment to the third year post-treatment.

When a forest canopy has been closed for many decades and prescribed fire has been suppressed, there may be a flush of less-desirable vegetation (woody sprouts from light-seeded species, such as maple and yellow poplar) following the first burn (Brose and Van Lear 1998) and the herbaceous seedbank may be reduced over time. Where woody stem density is excessive and dominates the understory, prescribed fire and/or an herbicide application may be necessary to allow herbaceous vegetation to become the dominant groundcover. Some hardwood stems, especially oaks, re-sprout quickly from existing root-stock, while problematic species (e.g., red maple, sassafras, and yellow poplar) are much more susceptible to fire, depending on season of burn (Van Lear and Watt 1992, Sutherland et al. 1997). Prescribed fire on a regular rotation (2–4 years) after the forest canopy has been opened can stimulate additional herbaceous cover (Masters et al. 1993). Increased herbaceous growth after a thinning followed by controlled burning enhanced wild turkey brood range in oak-hickory forests of West Virginia

(Pack et al. 1988). Burning or thinning alone did not produce the desired herbaceous response, nor did a controlled burn followed by thinning.

Even with little herbaceous response, we believe nesting habitat for wild turkeys was enhanced greatly by all silvicultural treatments implemented at Chuck Swan, especially the wildlife retention cut with prescribed fire and shelterwood harvest. Increased cover near ground level (Tables 2 and 3) provided the structure identified as quality nesting cover by Hillestad and Speake (1970) and Everette et al. (1985). In the southern Appalachians, the majority of wild turkey nests were located in mature mesic stands (Davis 1992, Harper 1998). Virtually all nests, however, were positioned amongst slash, dense underbrush, or other debris.

Hard mast production is naturally variable. That is compounded by the fact that individual trees may be inherently better producers than others (Beck 1977, 1989; Healy et al. 1999; Greenberg 2000). Thinning oak stands has resulted in increased acorn production, and the greatest difference in mast production between thinned stands and unthinned stands may be during years of overall poor acorn production (Healy 1997). Many years of acorn collection data, however, are required to substantiate this effort. In the short term (1–5 years post-treatment), a better gauge for potential mast production is crown size, rather than actual acorn yield. The majority of acorns are produced on large, healthy tree crowns and within a forest system (as opposed to an orchard), the only way to increase mast production is to encourage the tree's crown to expand. The average increase in crown size of white oaks on our shelterwood treatment sites increased more rapidly initially than those in the wildlife retention cuts. This was a result of the adjacent competition being removed in the shelterwood treatments, whereas the competition in the wildlife retention cuts remained alive and absorbed sunlight and nutrients for 1–2 years post-treatment before finally ceasing to produce leaves. Mast production among the white oaks selected will continue to be monitored over time to assess the effect of treatments on crown size as well as year-to-year variability and the mast-bearing potential of individual trees.

Soft mast production is also quite variable. Following the treatments that involved burning or soil scarification (shelterwood), soft mast production increased substantially, especially pokeberry. However, because of its patchy nature along the sampling transects, a statistical difference was not detected among treatments. Nonetheless, the increased availability of soft mast was noteworthy, especially considering its importance in the diet of wild turkeys (Hurst 1992).

Invertebrate abundance is an important consideration for brood survival (Everette et al. 1980, Metzler and Speake 1985); however, invertebrate abundance doesn't necessarily mean an adequate food source is available (Harper et al. 2001). Invertebrate biomass was very similar in all treatments and controls. Availability was not. Broods can forage more safely and feeding rates are higher when there is overhead protective cover (woody or herbaceous). Quality brooding cover also provides substrate for invertebrates, making them more available to poults (Rogers 1985). Invertebrates under the leaf litter are largely unavailable to poults, because the poults don't begin scratching until fall (Healy et al. 1975, Healy 1985). For this reason, only those invertebrates associated with the understory vegetation and those on top of the litter layer were sampled in our study, providing a true estimate of invertebrate availability. Interestingly, invertebrate availability on our study sites was almost identical to that found at ruffed grouse brood locations in hardwood forests of western North Carolina (18.14–20.34 mg/m^2; Fettinger 2002).

Invertebrate availability remained high throughout all sampling periods (mid-May, late May, mid-June, late June; Basinger 2003). These findings suggest invertebrates are not a limiting factor in mixed hardwood forests (regardless of treatment) and that quality brood-rearing cover is a more important consideration. If quality cover is present (understory structure), invertebrates will be available throughout the brood-rearing period. Quality cover increases invertebrate availability by placing invertebrates within reach of the poults and allows them to forage longer with less visibility to predators.

Management Implications

Silvicultural prescriptions can enhance mixed hardwood forests for wild turkeys. The main objectives should be to enhance conditions for nesting and brood rearing and increase mast production. In many stands, there is little understory vegetation present, which limits nesting and brood-rearing cover and soft mast production. Increased sunlight is needed to stimulate additional growth. Our data suggest this can be accomplished through wildlife retention cuts and shelterwood harvests. Prescribed fire alone in a closed canopy stand did not produce the desired results of increased groundcover. However, the addition of prescribed fire after a wildlife retention cut stimulated additional vegetation growth. One burn, however, is not enough to create optimal brood-rearing conditions in forested habitat that hasn't been burned in many decades. Woody sapling density can become problematic and additional fire and/or an herbicide application may be necessary. Future research on our study sites will include additional early growing-season fire and an herbicide prescription in an effort to reduce woody stems and stimulate additional herbaceous growth.

Many landowners are interested in improving their forestland for turkeys, but don't want to harvest timber. This is especially true for landowners with small acreage. A wildlife retention cut with prescribed fire is probably the best recommendation for those landowners. However, if management of private lands depends on financial return from the property, a shelterwood harvest should be considered. If a shelterwood harvest is implemented, and wildlife is a primary consideration, special attention should be given to which trees are selected for harvest. Obviously, it is beneficial to retain as many mast producers (with quality form) as possible. Likewise, both hard-mast producers (oaks, American beech) and soft-mast producers (e.g., black cherry [*Prunus serotina*], serviceberry [*Amelanchier arborea*], dogwood) should be kept in a wildlife retention cut. The most important factor, however, is identifying individual trees that are fairly consistent producers and freeing them of adjacent competition to allow their crowns to expand and produce as much mast as possible. Thinning for forestry purposes may not enhance mast production on a stand-wide basis; however, thinning can enhance mast production when non-mast producers or inherently poor producers are removed.

ACKNOWLEDGMENTS

The authors wish to thank the National Wild Turkey Federation for funding this research. The Tennessee Division of Forestry provided the research site and valuable field assistance. The University of Tennessee, Department of Forestry, Wildlife, and Fisheries provided funding and other assistance. We also wish to thank C. Greenberg, D. Hodges, L. Muller, and B. Minser for their help with the experimental design and assistance during the project. B. Miller, B. Ostby, W. Tarkington, J. Webster, and G. Snyder are also acknowledged for their assistance in the field.

LITERATURE CITED

Basinger, R. G. 2002. Initial effects of silvicultural treatments on food availability and vegetation structure for wild turkeys. Thesis, University of Tennessee, Knoxville, Tennessee, USA.

Beck, D. E. 1977. Twelve-year acorn yield in southern Appalachian oaks. U.S. Forest Service Research Note SE-244.

———. 1989. Managing mast production/capability. Proceedings of the Southern Appalachian Mast Management Workshop. University of Tennessee, Knoxville, Tennessee, USA.

Brose, P. H., and D. H. Van Lear. 1998. Responses of hardwood advance regeneration to seasonal prescribed fires in oak-dominated shelterwood stands. Canadian Journal of Forest Research 28:331–339.

———, ———, and P.D. Keyser. 1999. A shelterwood-burn technique for regenerating productive upland oak sites in the piedmont region. Southern Journal of Applied Forestry. 16(3):158–163.

Campo, J. J., and G. A. Hurst. 1980. Soft mast production in young loblolly plantations. Proceedings of the Annual Conference of the Southeastern Association of Fish and Wildlife Agencies 34:470–475.

Davis J. R. 1992. Nesting and brood ecology of the wild turkey in the mountains of western North Carolina. Dissertation, Clemson University, Clemson, South Carolina, USA.

Dickson, J. G., editor. 2001. Wild turkey. Pages 108–121 *in* Wildlife of southern forests: habitat and management. Hancock House, Blaine, Washington, USA.

Everette, D. D., Jr., D. W. Speake, and W. K. Maddox. 1980. Natality and mortality of a north Alabama wild turkey population. Proceedings of the National Wild Turkey Symposium 4:117–126.

———, ———, and ———. 1985. Habitat use by wild turkeys in northwest Alabama. Proceedings of the Annual Conference of the Southeastern Association of Fish and Wildlife Agencies 39:479–488.

Fettinger, J. L. 2002. Ruffed grouse nesting ecology and brood habitat in western North Carolina. Thesis, University of Tennessee, Knoxville, Tennessee, USA.

Greenberg, C. H. 2000. Individual variation in acorn production by five species of southern Appalachian oaks. Forest Ecology and Management 132:199–210.

Harper, C. A. 1998. Analysis of wild turkey brood habitat within the southern Appalachians. Dissertation, Clemson University, Clemson, South Carolina, USA.

———, and D. C. Guynn. 1998. A terrestrial vacuum sampler for invertebrates. Wildlife Society Bulletin 26:302–306.

———, J. K. Knox, D. C. Guynn, J. R. Davis, and J. G. Williams. 2001. Invertebrate availability for wild turkey poults in the southern Appalachians. Proceedings of the National Wild Turkey Symposium. 8:145–156.

Healy, W. M. 1985. Turkey poult feeding activity, invertebrate abundance, and vegetation structure. Journal of Wildlife Management 49:466–472.

———. 1997. Thinning New England oak stands to enhance acorn production. Northern Journal of Applied Forestry 14(3):152–156.

———, R. O. Kimmel, and E. J. Goetz. 1975. Behavior of human-imprinted and hen-reared wild turkey poults. Proceedings of the National Wild Turkey Symposium. 3:97–107.

———, A. M. Lewis, and E. F. Boose. 1999. Variation of red oak acorn production. Forest Ecology and Management 116:1–11.

Hillestad, H. O., and D. W. Speake. 1970. Activities of wild turkey hens and poults as influenced by habitat. Proceedings of the Annual Conference of the Southeastern Association of Game and Fish Commissioners 24:244–251.

Hurst, G. A. 1992. Foods and feeding. Pages 66–83 *in* J. G. Dickson, editor. The wild turkey: biology and management. Stackpole Books, Harrisburg, Pennsylvania, USA.

Jackson, S. W., and D. S. Buckley. 2002. First-year effects of shelterwood cutting, wildlife thinning, and prescribed burning on oak regeneration and competitors in Tennessee oak-hickory forests. Pages 231–237 *in* K. F. Connor, editor. Proceedings of the 12th Biennial Southern Silvicultural Research Conference. U.S. Forest Service General Technical Report SRS-71.

Masters, R. E., R. L. Lochmiller, and D. M. Engle. 1993. Effects of timber harvest and prescribed fire on white-tailed deer forage production. Wildlife Society Bulletin 21:401–411.

Metzler, R., and D. W. Speake. 1985. Wild turkey poult mortality rates and their relationship to brood habitat structure in northeast Alabama. Proceedings of the National Wild Turkey Symposium 5:103–111.

Murkin, H. R., D. A. Wrubleski, and F. A. Reid. 1996. Pages 349–369 *in* T. A. Bookhout, editor. Research and management techniques for wildlife and habitats: sampling invertebrates in aquatic and terrestrial habitats. Allen Press, Lawrence, Kansas, USA.

National Climatic Data Center. 2002. Regional climatic data for Oak Ridge, Tennessee. National Oceanic and Atmospheric Administration. ⟨http://lwf.ncdc.noaa.gov/oa/ncdc.html⟩ Accessed 20 May 2002.

Norman, G. W., J. C. Pack, C. I. Taylor, D. E. Steffen, and K. H. Pollock. Reproduction of eastern wild turkeys in Virginia and West Virginia. Journal of Wildlife Management 65:1–9.

Nudds, T. D. 1977. Quantifying the vegetative structure of wildlife cover. Wildlife Society Bulletin 5:113–117.

Pack, J. C., R. P. Burkert, W. K. Igo, and D. J. Pybus. 1980. Habitat utilized by wild turkey broods within oak-hickory forests of West Virginia. Proceedings of the National Wild Turkey Symposium 4:213–224.

———, W. K. Igo, and C. I. Taylor. 1988. Use of prescribed burning in conjunction with thinning to increase wild turkey brood range habitat in oak-hickory forests. Transactions of the Northeast Section of The Wildlife Society 45:37–48.

Rogers, R. E. 1985. Feeding activity of wild turkey poults in prescribed burned and thinned oak-hickory forests. Transactions of the Northeast Section of The Wildlife Society 42: 167–177.

Sander, I. L., C. E. McGee, K. G. Day, and R. E. Willard. 1983. Oak-hickory. Pages 116–120 *in* R. M. Burns, compiler. Silvicultural systems for the major forest types of the United States. USDA Forest Service Agricultural Handbook 445.

SAS Institute. 1990. SAS/STAT User's Guide. Version 9.0. SAS Institute, Cary, North Carolina, USA.

Swanson, D. A., J. C. Pack, C.I. Taylor, D. E. Samuel, and P. W. Brown. 1996. Selective timber harvesting and wild turkey reproduction in West Virginia. Proceedings of the National Wild Turkey Symposium 7:81–88.

Sutherland, E. K., C. T. Scott, and T. F. Hutchinson. 1997. Sapling topkill patterns after prescribed fire in an Ohio *Quercus* forest. Supplement to the Bulletin of the Ecological Society of America 78:193.

Van Lear, D. A., and J. M. Watt. 1992. The role of fire in oak regeneration. Pages 66–78 *in* D. L. Loftis and C.E. McGee, editors. Proceedings of the Oak Regeneration: Serious Problems, Practical Recommendations Symposium. U.S. Forest Service General Technical Report SE-84.

Wunz, G. A. 1989. Timber management and its effect on wild turkeys. Pages 110–120 *in* J. C. Finley and M. C. Brittingham, editors. Proceedings of workshop on timber management and its effect on wildlife. Pennsylvania State University, University Park, Pennsylvania, USA.

Samuel W. Jackson (center) is a Research Associate in the Agricultural Experiment Station at the University of Tennessee. He works in the Southeastern Sun Grant Center, which focuses on biomass utilization research. Sam earned his B.S. in Wildlife and Fisheries Management and his M.S. in Forestry at UT. He is currently pursuing a Ph.D. in Natural Resources. ***Ryan G. Basinger*** (not pictured) is the Wildlife Consulting Manager for Westervelt Wildlife Services. He earned his B.S. in Wildlife Science at Mississippi State University and his M.S. in Wildlife Science at The University of Tennessee. ***Daniel S. Gordon*** recently received his M.S. degree in forestry from the University of Tennessee, Department of Forestry, Wildlife, and Fisheries. Daniel earned his B.S. in Wildlife and Fisheries Management at UT. ***Craig A. Harper*** (left) is an Associate Professor and the Extension Wildlife Specialist in the Department of Forestry, Wildlife, and Fisheries at The University of Tennessee. Craig received his Ph.D. in Forest Resources from Clemson University, where he worked with wild turkeys in the mountains of North Carolina. He is responsible for developing wildlife-related programs for UT Extension and assisting Extension agents with matters concerning wildlife throughout Tennessee. He also remains active in research with on-going programs in forest management for wildlife, quality deer management, and applied habitat management for various wildlife species. ***David S. Buckley*** (right) earned his B.S. and M.S. degrees in biology from the University of Illinois at Chicago, and received a Ph.D. in Forest Science from Michigan Technological University in 1994. He completed a Post-Doc with the USDA Forest Service North Central Research Station from 1994 to 1998 involving an investigation of different forest management regimes on understory plants and other elements of biodiversity. David accepted a research and teaching position at the University of Tennessee within the Department of Forestry, Wildlife and Fisheries in 1998, and is currently an Associate Professor of forest ecology and silviculture. His research interests include disturbance ecology and effects of silvicultural practices on oak regeneration, understory microsites, understory plant communities, and wildlife habitat. He teaches dendrology, silvicultural practices, and forest ecology at the undergraduate and graduate levels. ***David A. Buehler*** (not pictured) has been a Professor of Wildlife Science at the University of Tennessee since 1991. His research has focused on avian-wildlife habitat relationships for a variety of game and nongame birds.

WILD TURKEY BROOD HABITAT USE IN RELATION TO PRESCRIBED BURNING AND RED-COCKADED WOODPECKER MANAGEMENT

Benjamin C. Jones[1,2]
Box 9690, Department of Wildlife and Fisheries,
Mississippi State University,
Mississippi State, Mississippi, USA 39762

James E. Inglis[3]
Box 9690, Department of Wildlife and Fisheries,
Mississippi State University,
Mississippi State, Mississippi, USA 39762

George A. Hurst
Box 9690, Department of Wildlife and Fisheries,
Mississippi State University,
Mississippi State, Mississippi, USA 39762

Abstract: Thinning and spring burning are used in pine and pine-hardwood forests to restore red-cockaded woodpecker (*Picoides borealis; RCW*) habitat; however, concerns regarding impacts on non-target species have arisen. We examined eastern wild turkey (*Meleagris gallopavo silvestris*) brood habitat on 2 areas, one managed for RCW (Caston Creek Wildlife Management Area; CCWMA), and the other under traditional pine management (Leaf River Wildlife Management Area; LRWMA). Brood habitat use differed from availability on both areas. On CCWMA, mature pine stands managed for RCW (RCWP) were selected least relative to other available habitats. Ground cover conditions created by grasses may have impeded movement and foraging of young poults. Habitats used by broods on CCWMA were pole stands, fields, and regeneration. On LRWMA, broods selected hardwood, field, and pole stands. Broods used stands that were burned ≤3 years prior on both areas. In a study of nest site selection on CCWMA, turkeys used RCWP for nesting; therefore, we recommend interspersing RCW stands with wild turkey brood habitat. Interspersion will provide nesting and brood cover in close proximity while allowing managers to meet RCW habitat goals.

Proceedings of the National Wild Turkey Symposium 9:209–215

Key words: brood, eastern wild turkey, forest management, growing season burn, habitat, *Meleagris gallopavo silvestris,* Mississippi, *Picoides borealis,* red-cockaded woodpecker.

After adopting an ecosystem management approach to forest policy, the U.S. Forest Service revised forest plans with management directions for the endangered RCW (U.S. Forest Service 1995). Current RCW range is fragmented across much of the southeastern United States and many of the largest populations occur on National Forest lands; therefore, the U.S. Forest Service has made RCW recovery a priority on >800,000 ha (Bowman et al. 1999). Although the wild turkey occurs throughout RCW range, little is known regarding impacts of RCW management on wild turkeys.

Ideal conditions for RCW are characterized by 80–100 year old pine stands, especially longleaf (*Pinus palustris*), with a low stocking level (12–18 m²/ha), sparse midstory, and open understory (Hovis and Labisky 1985, Hooper and Harlow 1986). Forest management prescriptions include thinning, hardwood

[1] Present address: Pennsylvania Game Commission, 2001 Elmerton Ave., Harrisburg, Pennsylvania, 17110, USA.
[2] E-mail: benjjones@state.pa.us
[3] Present address: Pheasants Forever, 1783 Buerkle Circle, St. Paul, Minnesota, 55110, USA.

Table 1. Forest type, age (years), acronym, and study area composition (%) for wild turkey habitats on Caston Creek (CCWMA) and Leaf River (LRWMA) Wildlife Management Areas, Mississippi, 1999–2000.

Forest type	Age	Acronym	Study site (%) CCWMA	Study site (%) LRWMA
Mature pine	30–80	PINE	4	51
Mature pine-hardwood mix	30–80	MIX	54	1
Mature hardwood	30–80	HDWD	3	21
RCW mature pine	30–80	RCWP	4	0
Pole stage	11–29	POLE	18	13
Regeneration	0–10	REGEN	4	7
Private pine-hardwood mix	30–80	PRIV	12	6
Field	NA	FIELD	1	1

midstory removal, and frequent use of prescribed fire, especially during the growing season. With regard to the wild turkey, concerns have been raised over hardwood removal and direct impacts of spring burning on nests and young poults (Sisson and Speake 1994, Bowman et al. 1999).

Wild turkey poult survival is an important factor in the species' population dynamics (Kurzejeski and Vangilder 1992). Mortality during the first 2 weeks after hatch is generally high (Vangilder 1992); however, predation losses may be reduced through provision of quality habitat (Everett et al. 1980, Metzler and Speake 1985). Structural characteristics of brood habitat have been described in detail and key components include, herbaceous understory with abundant invertebrates, protective cover for poults, and a zone of visibility for brood hens to detect predators (Porter 1992). These requirements are often met in fields, pastures or forest openings (Everett et al. 1980, Metzler and Speake 1985, Peoples et al. 1996) although appropriate management can create desirable conditions on forested sites (Healy 1985, Phalen et al. 1986, Williams et al. 1997).

Studies have reported wild turkey brood habitat across a wide range of forest types; however, none have examined habitat in relation to forest manage-

ment for RCW. We studied wild turkey brood habitat use on 2 study sites in southern Mississippi to address this issue. Caston Creek Wildlife Management Area (CCWMA) was intensively managed for RCW while LRWMA was managed under traditional pine prescriptions. Future management on LRWMA may include treatments to provide additional habitat for RCW colonies established on adjacent areas. The purpose of this research was to investigate wild turkey brood habitat use in relation to forest management practices commonly used for RCW.

STUDY AREA

Caston Creek Wildlife Management Area

Caston Creek Wildlife Management Area (11,253 ha) was within Homochitto National Forest in southwest Mississippi (Franklin and Amite counties). Soils were lower thin loess, southern Mississippi valley silty upland. Mean daily temperature was 18°C, and mean annual precipitation was 153 cm. Caston Creek was in the Homochitto River drainage, a transition zone between longleaf pine stands to the east and mixed pine-hardwood stands to the west (Frost et al. 1986). Due to physiographic location, CCWMA contained a unique combination of pine and hardwood forest (Table 1).

Habitat classifications were based on forest type, stand age, and management prescriptions. Regeneration stands (REGEN; 0–10 years) were small clearcuts or "bugspots" cut to control southern pine beetle (*Dendroctonus frontalis*) outbreaks and promote longleaf pine regeneration (U.S. Forest Service 1982). Bugspots were not planted, but allowed to regenerate naturally on a cut and leave basis. Pole-timber (POLE; 11–30 years) represented stands after complete canopy closure before trees reached mature sawtimber status. Mature pine (PINE) and mixed pine-hardwood (MIX; 30–80 years old) were managed under 2 regimes. Sawtimber stands with active RCW groups (RCWP) were

Red-cockaded woodpecker habitat is characterized by 80–100 year old pine stands with low stocking levels, sparse midstory and open understory dominated by grasses (*left*). On an area managed for RCW habitat (*right*), wild turkey broods used closed canopy (75–100%) pole stands, where herbaceous groundcover provided foraging habitat for poults while allowing the brood hen a zone of visibility to detect predators (*B. Jones*).

thinned to 11.5–14.0 m²/ha basal area. Long timber rotations (>70 years) and active hardwood mid-story removal also characterized RCWP. Mature stands without active RCW groups included pure PINE and MIX. These were well stocked (>20m²/ha) on a 35-year rotation. Mixed pine-hardwood and PINE occupied 54% and 4% of CCWMA, respectively. Mature hardwoods (HDWD) were along permanent stream drainages. Because of their location within streamside management zones, timber harvest was not implemented in most HDWD. Several private landholdings within CCWMA contained grazed pasture and hayfields (FIELD) and small areas of mixed pine-hardwood (PRIV).

Prescribed burning was carried out during winter and spring on a 2–3 year rotation. A growing season burn was any fire that occurred after 15 April. In most years, <30% of burning activities occurred during the growing season. The primarily objective of growing season burning was to maintain desirable habitat conditions for RCW.

Leaf River Wildlife Management Area

Leaf River Wildlife Management Area (16,915 ha) was located within Desoto National Forest in Perry County, southeast Mississippi. Soils were mixed loamy, clay, and sandy coastal plain materials. Mean daily temperature was 18°C, with mean annual precipitation of 153 cm. Located in the Lower Coastal Plain, LRWMA was within the historical range of longleaf pine. During this study, longleaf pine forest was the dominant cover type.

Because of differences in geographic location and forest management prescriptions, habitat types differed from those on CCWMA. Regeneration stands were harvested and planted to loblolly or longleaf pine. Unlike the small bugspots on CCWMA, average patch size of REGEN was 15 ha. Mature pine and MIX were well stocked (>20m²/ha) on 35-year rotations. In contrast to CCWMA, PINE occupied 51% whereas MIX occupied only 1%. There were no RCWP stands on LRWMA. Mature hardwoods were found along permanent and ephemeral stream drainages. Food plots (*n* = 73, FIELD) averaged 0.48 ha. Several small private landholdings within the area consisted of mixed pine-hardwood. Prescribed burn rotation during the study was 4–7 years. Most burning occurred during the dormant season, although growing season burns were used on a site-specific basis to maintain desirable conditions around gopher tortoise (*Gopherus polyphemus*) colonies.

METHODS

Data Collection

We captured turkeys using cannon nets and rocket nets from mid-January to early March 1999 and 2000. We handled animals in accordance with Institutional Animal Care and Use Committee (IACUC), Mississippi State University Protocol No. 98-012. Turkeys were placed immediately into transport boxes, then handled and processed individually. Sex and age were determined by methods described by Larson and Taber (1980). Females were equipped with patagial wing tags (Knowlton et al. 1964) and a mortality-sensitive ATS (Advanced Telemetry Systems, Isanti, Minnesota, USA) transmitter. Transmitters weighed approximately 90g and were attached "backpack" style (Everett et al. 1978). All turkeys were released at their respective capture sites.

Turkey locations were triangulated from ≥3 permanent telemetry stations (N = 307 CCWMA, N = 336 LRWMA). Stations were georeferenced using Trimble Global Positioning System units (Trimble Navigation Limited, Sunnyvale, California, USA). Signals were received using Telonics TR-2 receivers (Telonics, Mesa, Arizona, USA), Clark model H7050 headphones (David Clark Company, Worcester, Massachusetts, USA), and hand-held 4-element antennas. For each location, technicians recorded time, azimuth, turkey activity (moving or still), and a relative measure of signal strength (1 = weakest, 5 = strongest). A maximum of 12 minutes was allotted between first and last azimuths to minimize error from bird movement. Bearing error was assessed using beacons at 17 fixed locations. Each tracker recorded 15 azimuths/beacon.

Females were monitored throughout the reproductive season. If a female hatched a brood, she was located 3 times daily from hatch until 14 days after hatch. Females with young broods were monitored intensively because the first 2 weeks of life mark a critical period when mortality is greatest and survival largely depends on habitat characteristics (Everett et al. 1980, Healy 1985, Metzler and Speake 1985, Peoples et al. 1995). One location was recorded during each of 3 time periods: morning (0700–1100), midday (1101–1500), and evening (1501–1900).

Only those females with ≥1 poult alive at 2 weeks post-hatch were considered for habitat analyses. Brood presence or absence was determined by homing on females. We approached cautiously and determined presence of poults through observation of female brooding behavior or direct observation of poults. When possible, we avoided flushing the brood. Flush counts were used early in the study but were avoided after a red-shouldered hawk (*Buteo lineatus*) was observed killing a poult as it "lost-called" following a flush count. By homing on broods, we often were successful in determining brood presence or absence without flushing the brood.

Data Analysis

Telemetry data were converted to x, y coordinates in LOCATE II (Nams 2000). Location files were imported into ArcView (Version 3.2, Environmental Systems Research Institute, Redlands, California, USA). Geographic Information Systems (GIS) were developed for each study site using color infrared aerial photographs, 1:24,000 U.S. Geologic Survey 7.5-min quadrangles, U.S. Forest Service Continuous Inventory of Stand Condition (CISCS) data, and ground truthing.

Table 2. Mean home range (95% kernel) and core area (50% kernel) size for wild turkey broods on Caston Creek Wildlife Management Area (CCWMA), and Leaf River Wildlife Management Area (LRWMA), Mississippi, 1999–2000.

Site	Kernel	n	Mean (ha)	SE	Minimum	Maximum
CCWMA	95	13	155	40	23	470
	50	13	26	9	2	122
LRWMA	95	8	330	87	59	739
	50	8	55	14	11	114

We used the Animal Movement Extension (Hooge and Eichenlaub 1997) in ArcView to calculate adaptive kernel home range (95%) and core area (50%) contour intervals (Worton 1989). To determine adequate sampling (minimum locations) required for home ranges, kernel area estimates were calculated using from 4 to 32 locations. Area was then plotted against number of locations to determine sampling level at which area variation decreased and became asymptotic.

Habitat use was compared to availability at the study area scale (Johnson 1980). Availability was defined by movement potential of females with broods. We measured the linear distance each female traveled from successful nest sites to central points in respective brood home ranges (Jennrich and Turner 1969). The greatest distance traveled from a nest to a brood range was 4.45 km. This distance defined the maximum movement potential of females with poults; therefore, buffers with 4.45 km radii were placed around each successful nest site. Buffers were then merged and projected on GIS coverages to define availability. Habitat use was ascertained by the proportion of habitat types within 95% kernel home ranges. Use was compared to availability through compositional analysis (Aebischer et al. 1993). Relative ranks of habitat use were assigned by calculating pairwise differences in use versus availability for corresponding habitat log-ratios. Significance tests were used to examine differences in relative preference among ranked habitats (Aebischer et al. 1993).

Years since last burn (YSB) was calculated for stands that contained brood core areas. Time since previous burn was calculated by subtracting the year of last burn from the year of brood use. Stands that were burned during the same year as brood use were assigned a 0. Season of last burn (dormant vs. growing season) also was recorded. Because prescribed burns were not conducted on private land, YSB was not calculated for broods with core areas in PRIV and FIELD.

RESULTS

We radio-tagged and monitored 137 female turkeys. On CCWMA, 54 were captured in 1999 followed by 15 in 2000. On LRWMA, 26 were captured in 1999 and 42 in 2000. Overall, 97 nests produced 37 broods. Minimum sampling for home range estimation, as determined by location-area curves, was 16 locations/brood. Our sampling intensity exceeded the minimum for all broods that survived the 2-week post-hatch period (mean locations/brood = 30.0, SE = 1.3). Bearing error was 8.33° ± 6.03 on CCWMA and 8.17° ± 7.04 on LRWMA. Road systems on both areas allowed close access to most radio tagged turkeys. Mean distance from brood locations to telemetry stations was 195 m (SE = 10).

Home Range and Habitat Use

CCWMA

Twenty-four broods were monitored during 2 reproductive seasons. Percentage of females with ≥1 poult alive at 14 days post-hatch was 56% (10/18) in 1999, and 83% (5/6) in 2000. Thirteen broods were used for home range and habitat analysis. Mean home range size was 155 ha (SE = 40), and mean core area size was 26 ha (SE = 9) (Table 2).

Brood habitat use differed from availability ($P < 0.001$, $\chi^2_7 = 24.46$). Top ranked habitats were POLE, FIELD, and REGEN; however, relative preference did not differ among these habitats (Table 3). Mature mixed pine-hardwood stands were similar in relative preference to FIELD and REGEN. Relative to avail-

Table 3. Simplified ranking matrix of wild turkey brood habitat preference based on comparison of habitats within home ranges and availability across the study area on Caston Creek Wildlife Management Area, Mississippi, 1999–2000.

Habitat type	Habitat type[a]								Rank[b]
	POLE	FIELD	REGEN	MIX	HDWD	PRIV	PINE	RCWP	
POLE		+	+	+++[c]	+++	+	+++	+++	1
FIELD	−		+	+	+	+++	+++	+++	2
REGEN	−	−		+	+	+	+	+++	3
MIX	−−−	−	−		+	+	+	+++	4
HDWD	−−−	−	−	−		+	+	+++	5
PRIV	−	−−−	−	−	−		+	+	6
PINE	−−−	−−−	−	−	−	−		+	7
RCWP	−−−	−−−	−−−	−−−	−−−	−	−		8

[a] FIELD = privately owned pasture and hay field, REGEN = regeneration areas, MIX = mature mixed pine hardwood, HDWD = mature hardwood, PRIV = privately owned mature hardwood and hardwood regeneration, PINE = mature pine, RCW = mature pine, thinned to basal area <80 ft²/ac.
[b] 1 = greatest, 8 = least.
[c] Triple sign indicates significance at $P < 0.05$.

Table 4. Simplified ranking matrix of wild turkey brood habitat preference based on comparison of habitats within home ranges and availability across the study area on Leaf River Wildlife Management Area, Mississippi, 1999–2000.

Habitat type	Habitat type[a]						Rank[b]
	HDWD	PINE	POLE	FIELD	REGEN	MIX	
HDWD		+++[c]	+	+++	+++	+++	1
PINE	– – –	.	+	+	+	+++	2
POLE	–	–		+	+	+	3
FIELD	– – –	–	–		+	+	4
REGEN	– – –	–	–	–		+	5
MIX	– – –	– – –	–	–.	–		6

[a] FIELD = privately owned pasture and hay field, REGEN = regeneration areas, MIX = mature mixed pine hardwood, HDWD = mature hardwood, PRIV = privately owned mature hardwood and hardwood regeneration, PINE = mature pine, RCW = mature pine, thinned to basal area <80 ft²/ac.
[b] 1 = greatest, 6 = least.
[c] Triple sign indicates significance at $P < 0.05$.

able habitats, mature pine managed for RCW was selected least. Mean years since burn for brood core areas was 1.75 years (SE = 0.31). With the exception of FIELD, habitats used by broods had been burned ≤3 years prior. Season of last burn in core areas was dormant season for 7/8 broods.

LRWMA

On LRWMA, 8 broods were monitored during 2 reproductive seasons. Percentage of females with ≥1 poult alive at 14 days post-hatch was 80% (4/5) in 1999 and 50% (4/8) in 2000. Eight broods were used for home range and habitat analysis. Mean home range size was 330 ha (SE = 87), and mean core area size was 55 ha (SE = 14) (Table 2).

Brood habitat use differed from availability ($P < 0.001$, $\chi^2_5 = 20.80$). The highest ranked habitat was HDWD and the least ranked habitat was MIX (Table 4). Fields, POLE, and PINE were at a middle ranking with no difference in relative preference among them. Mean years since burn of core areas was 1.9 years (SE = 0.37) and most habitats used by broods had been burned ≤3 years prior. Season of last burn in core areas was dormant season for 7 broods and growing season for 1 brood.

DISCUSSION

Landscape scale forest management for RCW has broad implications for many wildlife species, including the wild turkey. Thinning and prescribed burning in upland pine forests open the canopy and create distinct changes in vegetation and invertebrate communities (Masters et al. 1998, New and Hanula 1998). Wild turkey broods have specific foraging and cover requirements and are especially sensitive to changes in understory structure.

Consistent with other research, broods used various forest types and openings with moderate herbaceous ground cover. Frequency of prescribed fire was an important determinant of habitat use. On CCWMA, broods used pole and mixed pine-hardwood stands that

were burned on a 2–3 year rotation. Similar forest types were not used on LRWMA where longer burning rotations promoted dense midstory and an understory that lacked herbaceous cover. In the absence of frequent burning in upland pine, most broods on LRWMA used mature bottomland hardwoods. On CCWMA, broods did not use bottomland hardwoods. Other studies in Mississippi also reported brood use of various forest types depending on fire frequency. Phalen et al. (1986) found broods used mature bottomland hardwoods on an area where pine stands were burned infrequently. In east-central Mississippi, broods used 14–20 year old pine plantations that were burned 3 years before use (Burk et al. 1990). Palmer (1990) reported that brood hens used mature pine and hardwoods that had been burned 3 years prior.

We could not assess impacts of season of burn (dormant vs. growing) on brood habitat because burn types were not adequately replicated across either study site. Sisson and Speake (1994) found spring burns did not improve habitat conditions beyond what could be attained through dormant season burning and suggested detrimental effects on nesting would outweigh potential benefits. In a study of nesting habitat, Jones (2001) suggested that if growing season fire was necessary to improve RCW habitat, relatively small burns (<300 ha) could be conducted in a mosaic across the landscape to minimize direct impacts on nesting turkeys.

Mature pine managed for RCW was the least ranked habitat for brood use on CCWMA. Ground cover consisted of grasses in the family Poaceae, predominantly broom sedge (*Andropogon glomeratus*), big bluestem (*A. gerardii*), and little bluestem (*Schizachyrium scoparium*). Although grasses provide nesting habitat (Chamberlain 1999, Jones 2001), thick ground cover conditions formed a physical barrier that impeded movement and foraging by young poults. Further, the height of grasses in RCWP (0.5–1.0 m) did not allow surveillance by brood hens. Although ground cover conditions in RCW managed pine were similar to regeneration cuts, regeneration stands were relatively small ($\bar{x}$ = 8 ha, SE = 1.1), and broods effectively foraged along their perimeter. Miller (1997) also reported turkey use along clearcut perimeters 1–2 years after establishment. Broods did not use the larger clearcut patches ($\bar{x}$ = 13.0, SE = 1.2) on LRWMA.

Similar to other methods of habitat use analysis, compositional analysis is subject to scrutiny (Bingham and Brennan 2004). We acknowledge the potential for Type I error, especially with numerous habitat types and relatively small sample sizes (<30 animals). However, few wild turkey brood habitat studies have reported sample sizes greater than our study. Further, ours is the most comprehensive examination of impacts of RCW habitat management on turkeys to date and trends in the data are apparent.

MANAGEMENT IMPLICATIONS

Our study emphasizes the importance of maintaining desirable midstory and understory conditions for wild turkey broods. Openings (predominantly privately owned fields and pasture) comprised <2% of our study sites. Creation of additional openings on these areas is unlikely; therefore most brood habitat will be provided through forest management. Prescribed burning has long been recommended and remains an essential tool for managing pine-dominated forests in the southeastern United States. Turkey broods did not use mature upland pine stands that had been thinned and burned for RCW habitat. Although ground cover is important to wild turkey poults, dense conditions in these stands may result in limited movement and foraging (Healy 1985, Palmer 1990). Pine stands managed for RCW are used by turkeys for nesting. Interspersion of RCW stands with other habitats can provide nesting and brooding cover in close proximity; however, as proportion of the landscape managed for RCW increases, broods may be forced into smaller areas with increased exposure to predators (Chamberlain 1999). Future research should ascertain the appropriate level of interspersion that will minimize negative impacts on turkeys while allowing managers to meet RCW management goals.

ACKNOWLEDGMENTS

This paper is a contribution of the Mississippi Cooperative Wild Turkey Research Project which was supported by Mississippi Department of Wildlife, Fisheries and Parks, U.S.D.A. Forest Service, National Wild Turkey Federation, and the Mississippi State University Forest and Wildlife Research Center. We thank J. Bein, D. Morrow, B. Yarbrough, B. Trunzler, J. Sykes, T. Black, A. Rinker, T. Terhune, G. Petrie, B. Holcomb, and B. Massery. Thanks to C. Tzilkowski for initial review of this manuscript.

LITERATURE CITED

Aebischer, N. J., P. A. Robertson, and R. E. Kenward. 1993. Compositional analysis of habitat use from animal radio-tracking data. Ecology 74:1313–1325.

Bingham, R. L., and L. A. Brennan. 2004. Comparison of type I error rates for statistical analyses of resource selection. Journal of Wildlife Management 68:206–212.

Bowman, J. L., D. R. Wood, F. J. Vilella, B. D. Leopold, L. W. Burger, and K. D. Godwin. 1999. Effects of red-cockaded woodpecker management on vegetative composition and structure and subsequent impacts on game species. Proceedings of the Annual Conference of the Southeastern Association of Fish and Wildlife Agencies 53:220–234

Burk, J. D., D. R. Smith, G. A. Hurst, B. D. Leopold, and M. A. Melchiors. 1990. Wild turkey use of loblolly pine plantations for nesting and brood rearing. Proceedings of the Annual Conference of the Southeastern Association of Fish and Wildlife Agencies 44:163–170.

Campo, J. J., W. G. Swank, and C. R. Hopkins. 1989. Brood habitat use by eastern wild turkeys in eastern Texas. Journal of Wildlife Management 53:479–482.

Chamberlain, M. J. 1999. Ecological relationships among bobcats, coyotes, gray fox, and raccoons and their interactions with wildturkey hens. Dissertation, Mississippi State University, Mississippi State, Mississippi, USA.

Everett, D. D., D. W. Speake, and W. K. Maddox. 1978. Multi-purpose radio transmitters for studying mortality, natality,

and movement of eastern wild turkeys. Proceedings of the International Symposium on Biotelemetry 4:155–158.

———, ———, and ———. 1980. Natality and mortality of a north Alabama wild turkey population. Proceedings of the National Wild Turkey Symposium 4:117–126.

Frost, C. C., J. Walker, and R. K. Peet. 1986. Fire-dependent savannas and prairies of the southeast: original extent, preservation status and management problems. Pages 348–357 in D. L. Kulhavy and R. N. Conner, editors. Wilderness and natural areas in the eastern United States. Center for Applied Studies, School of Forestry, Stephen F. Austin University, Nagodoches, Texas, USA.

Hayden, A. H. 1979. Home range and habitat preferences of wild turkey broods in northern Pennsylvania. Transactions of the Northeast Section of the Wildlife Society 36:76–87.

Healy, W. M. 1985. Turkey poult feeding activity, invertebrate abundance, and vegetation structure. Journal of Wildlife Management 49:466–472.

Hooge, P. N., and B. Eichenlaub. 1997. Animal movement extension to Arcview. Version 2.04. Alaska Biological Science Center, U.S. Geological Survey, Anchorage, Alaska, USA.

Hooper, R. G., and R. F. Harlow. 1986. Forest stands selected by foraging red-cockaded woodpeckers. U.S. Forest Service Research Paper SE-259.

Hovis, J. A., and R. F. Labisky. 1985. Vegetative Associations of red-cockaded woodpecker colonies in Florida. Wildlife Society Bulletin 13:307–314.

Hurst, G. A. 1978. Effects of prescribed burning on wild turkey poult food habits. Proceedings of the Annual Conference of the Southeastern Association of Fish and Wildlife Agencies 32:30–37.

Jennrich, R. I., and F. B. Turner. 1969. Measurements of non-circular homerange. Journal of Theoretical Biology 22:227–237.

Johnson, D. H. 1980. The comparison of usage and availability measurements for evaluating resource preference. Ecology 61:65–71.

Jones, B. C. 2001. Wild turkey reproductive ecology on a fire-maintained national forest in Mississippi. Thesis, Mississippi State University, Mississippi State, Mississippi, USA.

Knowlton, F. F., E. D. Michael, and W. C. Glazner. 1964. A marking technique for field recognition of turkeys and deer. Journal of Wildlife Management 56:556–562.

Kurzejeski, E. W., and L. D. Vangilder. 1992. Population management. Pages 165–184 in J. G. Dickson editor. The wild turkey: biology and management. Stackpole Books, Mechanicsburg, Pennsylvania, USA.

Larson, J. S., and R. D. Taber. 1980. Criteria of sex and age. Pages 190–197 in S. D. Schemnitz, editor. Wildlife management techniques manual. The Wildlife Society, Washington, D.C., USA.

Masters, R. E., R. L. Lochmiller, S. T. McMurry, and G. A. Bukenhofer. 1998. Small mammal response to pine-grassland restoration for red-cockaded woodpeckers. Wildlife Society Bulletin 26:148–158.

Metzler, R., and D. W. Speake. 1985. Wild turkey poult mortality and their relationship to brood habitat structure in northeast Alabama. Proceedings of the National Wild Turkey Symposium 5:103–111.

Miller, D. A. 1997. Habitat relationships and demographic parameters of an eastern wild turkey population in central Mississippi. Dissertation, Mississippi State University, Mississippi State, Mississippi, USA.

Nams, V. O. 2000. Locate II: user's guide. Pacer, Truro, Nova Scotia, Canada.

New, K. C., and J. L. Hanula. 1998. Effect of time elapsed after prescribed burning in longleaf pine stands on potential prey of the red-cockaded woodpecker. Southern Journal of Applied Forestry 22:175–183.

Pack, J. C., R. P. Burkett, W. K. Igo, and D. J. Pybus. 1980. Habitat utilized by wild turkey broods within oak-hickory forest of West Virginia. Proceedings of the National Wild Turkey Symposium 4:213–224.

Palmer, W. E. 1990. Relationships of wild turkey hens and their habitat on Tallahala Wildlife Management Area. Thesis, Mississippi State University, Mississippi State, Mississippi, USA.

———, and G. A. Hurst. 1996. Drainage systems as minimum habitat management units for wild turkey hens. Proceedings of the National Wild Turkey Symposium 7:97–104.

———, ———, and B. D. Leopold. 1996. Pre-incubationhabitat use by wild turkey hens in central Mississippi. Proceedings of the Annual Conference of the Southeastern Association of Fish and Wildlife Agencies 50:417–427.

Peoples, J. C., D. C. Sisson, and D. W. Speake. 1996. Wild turkey brood habitat use and characteristics in coastal plain pine forests. Proceedings of the National Wild Turkey Symposium 5:103–111.

Phalen, P. S., G. A. Hurst, and W. J. Hamrick. 1986. Brood habitat use and preference by wild turkeys in central Mississippi. Proceedings of the Annual Conference of the Southeastern Association of Fish and Wildlife Agencies 40: 397–404.

Porter, W. F. 1992. Habitat requirements. Pages 202–213 *in* J. G. Dickson, editor. The wild turkey: biology and management. Stackpole Books, Mechanicsburg, Pennsylvania, USA.

Ross, A. S., and G. A. Wunz. 1990. Habitats used by wild turkey hens during the summer in oak forests in Pennsylvania. Proceedings of the National Wild Turkey Symposium 6:39–43.

Seiss, R. S. 1989. Reproductive parameters and survival rates of wild turkey hens in east-central Mississippi. Thesis, Mississippi State University, Mississippi State, Mississippi, USA.

Sisson, D. C., and D. W. Speake. 1994. Spring burning for wild turkey brood habitat: an evaluation. Proceedings of the Annual Conference of the Southeastern Fish and Wildlife Agencies 48:134–139.

———, ———, and J. L. Landers. 1991. Wild turkey brood habitat use in fire-type pine forests. Proceedings of the Annual Conference of the Southeastern Fish and Wildlife Agencies 45:49–57.

Speake, D. W., T. E. Lynch, W. J. Fleming, G. A. Wright, and W. J. Hamrick. 1975. Habitat use and seasonal movements of wild turkeys in the southeast. Proceedings of the National Wild Turkey Symposium 3:122–129.

Thatcher, R. C., and P. J. Barry. 1982. Southern pine beetle. U.S. Forest Service Forest Insect and Disease Leaflet 49.

U.S. Forest Service. 1995. Final environmental impact statement for the management of the red-cockaded woodpecker and its habitat on national forests in the southern region, Volume II. U.S. Forest Service Management Bulletin R8-MB73.

Vangilder, L. D. 1992. Population dynamics. Pages 144–164 *in* J. G. Dickson, editor. The wild turkey: biology and management. Stackpole Books, Mechanicsburg, Pennsylvania, USA.

Williams, M. W., D. B. Gibbs, T. H. Roberts, and D. L. Combs. 1997. Habitat use by eastern wild turkey broods in Tennessee. Proceedings of the Annual Conference of the South-eastern Association of Fish and Wildlife Agencies 40:397–404.

Worton, B. J. 1989. Kernel methods for estimating the utilization distribution in home-range studies. Ecology 70:164–168.

Benjamin C. Jones is a habitat planning biologist with the Pennsylvania Game Commission. Jones received his Ph.D. in Natural Resources from the University of Tennessee, an M.S. in Wildlife and Fisheries Science from Mississippi State University, and a B.S. in Wildlife and Fisheries Science from Pennsylvania State University. Ben is responsible for developing habitat management plans for wildlife on public lands in Pennsylvania.

James E. Inglis is a Regional Biologist for Pheasants Forever and Quail Forever in Ohio. Jim received an M.S. in Wildlife and Fisheries Science from Mississippi State University, and a B.S. in Wildlife Science from SUNY ESF. His current responsibilities include implementing Farm Bill programs and improving wildlife habitat on agricultural landscapes. ***George A. Hurst*** (retired; not pictured) was a professor in the Department of Wildlife and Fisheries at Mississippi State University. Dr. Hurst studied wild turkeys in Mississippi for over 25 years and currently works with private landowners on various projects.

MALE RIO GRANDE WILD TURKEY HABITAT CHARACTERISTICS IN THE TEXAS PANHANDLE AND SOUTHWESTERN KANSAS

Derrick P. Holdstock[1]
Department of Natural Resources Management,
Box 42125, Texas Tech University,
Lubbock, TX 79409, USA

Mark C. Wallace
Department of Natural Resources Management,
Box 42125, Texas Tech University,
Lubbock, TX 79409, USA

Warren B. Ballard[2]
Department of Natural Resources Management,
Box 42125, Texas Tech University,
Lubbock, TX 79409, USA

John H. Brunjes[3]
Department of Natural Resources Management,
Box 42125, Texas Tech University,
Lubbock, TX 79409, USA

Richard S. Phillips
Department of Natural Resources Management,
Box 42125, Texas Tech University,
Lubbock, TX 79409, USA

Brian L. Spears[4]
Department of Natural Resources Management,
Box 42125, Texas Tech University,
Lubbock, TX 79409, USA

Stephen J. DeMaso
Texas Parks and Wildlife Department,
4200 Smith School Road,
Austin, TX 78744, USA

Jack D. Jernigan[5]
Texas Parks and Wildlife Department,
Matador Wildlife Management Area, 3036 FM 3256,
Paducah, TX 79248, USA

Roger D. Applegate[6]
Kansas Department of Wildlife and Parks,
P.O. Box 1525,
Emporia, KS, 66801-1525, USA

Philip S. Gipson
Kansas Cooperative Fish and Wildlife Research Unit,
205 Leasure Hall, Kansas State University,
Manhattan, KS, 66506, USA

Abstract: Habitat use has not been described for male Rio Grande wild turkeys (*Meleagris gallopavo intermedia*) in the northern extent of their native range. We described roost tree characteristics and compared the vegetative characteristics of diurnal habitat used for different behaviors (displaying, loafing, and foraging) by male Rio Grande wild turkeys in the Texas Panhandle and southwestern Kansas. Most (70.9%) trees used as roosts were eastern cottonwoods (*Populus deltoides*), but black locusts (*Robinia pseudoacacia*) (19.1%) and netleaf hackberries (*Celtis reticulata*) (5.7%) were also frequently used. Mean roost tree diameter at breast height (dbh), height, and height of the lowest branch was 49.9 cm, 13.6 m, and 3.4 m, respectively. Areas used for displaying were characterized by low visual obstruction and low shrub density. Areas used for loafing had greater densities of trees and large shrubs than random sites. Despite having low visual obstruction, foraging areas were not otherwise different from random sites. Spring foraging areas had less visual obstruction than summer foraging areas, with spring foraging areas similar to displaying areas and summer foraging areas similar to loafing areas. Habitat management for male Rio Grande wild turkeys should focus on protecting remaining riparian roost areas and encouraging cottonwood regeneration. Openings for displaying and brushy areas for loafing should be created or maintained in proximity to traditional roosts.

Proceedings of the National Wild Turkey Symposium 9:217–229
Key words: behavior, displaying, foraging, habitat, Kansas, loafing, *Meleagris gallopavo intermedia,* riparian restoration, roosts, Texas Panhandle.

Habitat requirements of male Rio Grande wild turkeys are not well known. The majority of Rio Grande wild turkey habitat research has taken place in South Texas or on the Edwards Plateau (Thomas et al. 1966, Beasom 1970, Haucke 1975, Baker et al. 1980, Beasom and Wilson 1992). Furthermore, research on females has far exceeded that of males. Knowledge of male turkey habitat selection, as well as current habitat management decisions in the northern portion of Rio Grande wild turkey range, are based on studies from other turkey subspecies or on Rio Grande wild turkeys in other regions. Kothmann and Litton (1975) provided the only male Rio Grande habitat study in West Texas, and they recognized that range expansion in West Texas has been facilitated by use of power line poles as roosts. Baker et al. (1980) described seasonal habitat characteristics of male Rio Grande wild turkeys in South Texas. Several other studies (Clark 1985, Lambert et al. 1990, Godwin et al. 1992, Palmer et al. 1996, Miller et al. 1999) investigated seasonal habitat use by eastern wild turkey (*M. g. silvestris*) males and found that they varied among geographic locations.

As part of a larger study, we studied habitat selection of male Rio Grande wild turkeys in the Texas Panhandle and southwestern Kansas from January 2000 through August 2002. Our objectives were to quantify male Rio Grande wild turkey roost tree characteristics and define the vegetative characteristics of areas used for displaying, loafing, and foraging.

STUDY AREA

Our study was conducted at 1 Kansas and 3 Texas study sites. The Kansas site was centered on the Cimar-ron National Grasslands in Morton County, Kansas, and adjacent Stevens County, Kansas, and Baca County, Colorado. The 3 Texas sites were centered on the Matador Wildlife Management Area (Matador) in Cottle and Motley counties, the Salt Fork of the Red River (Salt Fork) in Donley and Collingsworth counties, and the Gene Howe Wildlife Management Area (Gene Howe) in Hemphill County. Spears et al. (2002) provided a general description of the vegetative communities at each of the 4 study sites. Boundaries of each study site were determined by turkey movements. Functional study areas were approximately 25,801 ha, 9,798 ha, 6,656 ha, and 5,237 ha for Kansas, Matador, Salt Fork, and Gene Howe, respectively. Land uses at the 4 study sites included production of cattle, cotton, wheat, and grain sorghum. Oil production also occurred at the Kansas and Gene Howe sites. Grazing occurred at varying intensities on most public and private land throughout all study areas, both in uplands and in riparian areas. There were spring and autumn hunting seasons at the 3 study sites in the Texas Panhandle and on the western edge of the Kansas site and a spring-only season at the remainder of the Kansas study site.

METHODS

We captured turkeys with drop nets (Glazener et al. 1964), rocket nets (Schemnitz 1994), or walk-in traps (Davis 1994) on sites baited with whole kernel corn or milo from January through late February or early March each year. We classified turkeys as juveniles (approximately 0.5 years) or adults (≥1.5 years) based on standard methods (Pelham and Dickson 1992). For the purposes of this study, we considered a turkey an adult starting 1 January of their second year (approximately 1.5 years). We recorded sex and weight (kg), and fitted turkeys with a backpack-style radio-transmitter (AVM Instruments, Livermore, California, USA [Kansas]; Advanced Telemetry Systems, Isanti, Minnesota, USA [Matador, Salt Fork, Gene Howe]) and a butt-end aluminum leg band (National Band and Tag Company, Newport, Kentucky, USA). Transmitters (<120 g) with mortality sensors were attached using nylon overbraid harness (Advanced Telemetry Systems, Isanti, Minnesota, USA). We censored turkeys surviving <14 days post-capture due to potential capture-related mortality (Spraker et al. 1987, Nicholson et al. 2000).

The majority (94.6%) of vegetation measurements

[1] Present address: Texas Parks and Wildlife Department, Gene Howe Wildlife Management Area, 15412 FM 2266, Canadian, TX 79014, USA.

[2] E-mail: warren.ballard@ttu.edu

[3] Present address: Kentucky Department of Fish and Wildlife Resources, 1 Sportsman's Lane—Wildlife Annex, Frankfort, KY 40601, USA.

[4] Present address: US Fish and Wildlife Service, Upper Columbia Fish and Wildlife Office, 11103 E. Montgomery Drive, Spokane, WA 99206, USA.

[5] Present address: Texas Parks and Wildlife Department, Pat Mayes Wildlife Management Area, 4998 CR 2131, Detroit, TX 75436, USA.

[6] Present address: Tennessee Wildlife Resources Agency, Ellington Agricultural Center, P.O. Box 40747, Nashville, TN 37204, USA.

were made during spring and summer. We visually located turkeys using a handheld 3-element yagi antenna (AF Antronics, White Heath, Illinois, USA). We collected data at each site from 15 January 2000 until 31 August 2002 except at the Kansas site where monitoring ended on 30 June 2001 when all males were either dead or their transmitters had ceased operation. We stratified turkey locations into 4 time blocks (morning, mid-day, evening, and roost) so that each bird was sampled at different times of day throughout sampling periods (Otis and White 1999). Roost period was from dusk until dawn. Other time blocks were of equal length and varied as length of daylight changed. We used a Trimble Geoexplorer 2 or Geoexplorer 3 (Trimble Navigation Limited, Sunnyvale, California, USA) Global Positioning System (GPS) to record the coordinates of all visual turkey locations. Base stations within 250 km of each study site were used for differential correction.

Male turkey observations were categorized as 1 of 4 behaviors (roosting, displaying, loafing, or foraging). Roosting occurred when male turkeys perched in trees overnight. Displaying behavior required that ≥1 male turkey was involved in strutting in front of females, presumably for mating purposes, or in front of other males, presumably for purposes of establishing pecking order. Behavior was categorized as loafing if male turkeys were observed resting in the shade of trees or large shrubs during the day. Behavior was categorized as foraging if male turkeys were observed feeding, pecking, or scratching at the ground. Instances where turkeys were disturbed prior to observing a behavior were excluded from analyses.

We measured vegetative characteristics at sites used by male Rio Grande wild turkeys within a week of the visual observation. A 10- × 20-m quadrat oriented north and south was centered on each visually-obtained turkey location. All trees, defined as woody plants ≥10 cm in diameter, were classified by species. Diameter at breast height (dbh; cm) or diameter below the lowest trunk split, total height (m), and height of lowest branch (m) were also measured for trees in roosting plots. Trees were also classified as to whether they were used as roosts, based upon accumulations of droppings underneath. All coarse woody debris items, defined as woody debris at least 10 cm in diameter, were counted inside the quadrat.

A 20-m transect was oriented north and south through the center of the quadrat. We sampled visual obstruction ($n = 10$ per plot) on alternating sides of this transect at 2-m intervals with a modified visual obstruction pole (Robel et al. 1970). This pole was 1 m tall, 2.54 cm in diameter, and was painted with 10 alternating red and white bands (each 10 cm wide). The obstruction pole was attached to a 1-m tall observation pole with a 4-m rope or chain. We recorded the total number of bands on the obstruction pole that were visible from the top of the observation pole, which was placed perpendicular to, and 4 m from, the transect. Also, at 40-cm intervals directly below the rope or chain connecting the obstruction pole to the observation pole, we classified ground cover as grass, shrub, forb, bare ground, litter, or other to estimate percent cover of major vegetative categories within the plot.

We used a 2-m cover pole (Hagan et al. 1996) to determine the structure of the understory vegetation. Observers walked along the 20-m transect while holding the pole parallel to the ground and perpendicular to the transect at a height of 0.5 m. We classified all woody vegetation <10 cm in diameter and ≥0.5 m in height contacting the pole along the 2- × 20-m belt transect by species and recorded in the appropriate height category (0.5–1 m, 1–2 m, or 2–4 m).

For each observed turkey location for which vegetation was measured (location plots), a paired random plot was also measured. The center of the random plot was located 50 m from the visual location, in 1 of the 4 sequentially chosen cardinal directions (north, east, south, and west). Vegetative characteristics at random plots were measured using the same methods as the visual location plots.

In addition to data collected from our vegetation plots, we collected age data on black locust trees to determine approximate ages of those being used for roosts. Ring counts and diameters were measured on recently cut stumps at Gene Howe and Salt Fork. We did not have permission to cut or core live trees. We used simple linear regression to test for a linear relationship between age and diameter (Zar 1999).

In order to better determine the ranges of turkeys at each study site, we located turkeys 1–3 times per week during late winter, spring, and summer (our primary field season) and approximately once every 1–2 weeks throughout the remainder of the year using a truck-mounted dual 4-element yagi null-peak antenna system (Advanced Telemetry Systems, Isanti, Minnesota, USA) (Samuel and Fuller 1994). Triangulations consisted of ≥2 (usually ≥3) sequential bearings taken at fixed stations along roads. We used the maximum likelihood estimator method (Lenth 1981) in LOAS (Ecological Software Solutions 1999) to calculate locations from raw bearings. We triangulated test transmitters in known locations to estimate system biases for antenna calibration and bearing standard deviations (7.75° to 10.59°) for calculation of error ellipses around locations (Ecological Software Solutions 1999). Error ellipses were used to identify potential data entry or data collection errors; however, regardless of error ellipse size, each azimuth was individually investigated. If it was suspected that the turkey had moved a considerable distance between azimuths, or that the estimated location was not within the possible range of the receiver (≤3.20 km on flat terrain) for ≥1 azimuths, we discarded the location.

Roosting Habitat

We used forward stepwise logistic regression ($P < 0.20$ to enter or remove a variable; Hosmer and Lemeshow 1989) to differentiate between trees used as roosts and other trees in the roost vegetation plot that showed no sign of being used as roosts, as determined by the presence or absence of droppings underneath each tree. Diameter at breast height, height of the lowest branch, and overall tree height were characteristics considered in the logistic regression. We

Table 1. Comparison of tree characteristics using forward stepwise logistic regression (*P* < 0.20 to enter or remove a variable), and Mann-Whitney *U*-tests between male Rio Grande wild turkey roost trees (*n* = 141) and unused trees (*n* = 188) in the immediate vicinity from January 2000 through August 2002 in the Texas Panhandle and southwestern Kansas. Means are provided for comparison to the literature. Medians are provided because Mann-Whitney tests compare medians of ranked data.

Species	Variable	Mean ± SE		Forward stepwise LR[a]			Median (range)		Mann-Whitney	
		Used	Unused	Estimate	SE	P	Used	Unused	U	P
Cottonwood trees; 87.0% of cottonwood trees were classified correctly by the resulting model.										
	intercept			−8.858	1.741	<0.001				
	dbh (cm)[b]	57.76 ± 2.71	27.97 ± 1.10	0.155	0.035	<0.001	49.65 (19.70–163.50)	28.00 (10.60–47.80)	538.5	<0.001
	Height (m)	13.65 ± 0.42	8.02 ± 0.45	0.297	0.091	0.001	13.00 (6.00–26.00)	8.00 (0.00–15.00)	758.5	<0.001
	HLB (m)[c]	3.61 ± 0.23	3.05 ± 0.22	0.002	0.002	0.160	3.88 (0.00–9.00)	3.00 (0.00–7.00)	2,438.5	0.244
Black locust trees; 74.1% of black locust trees were classified correctly by the resulting model.										
	intercept			−6.143	1.582	<0.001				
	dbh (cm)	32.00 ± 2.07	17.55 ± 1.22	0.204	0.054	<0.001	30.10 (11.50–59.20)	16.80 (6.80–38.10)	735.5	<0.001
	Height (m)	14.67 ± 0.47	8.43 ± 1.03	N/A[d]	N/A	N/A	16.00 (8.00–17.00)	7.00 (1.00–22.00)	795.5	<0.001
	HLB (m)	2.48 ± 0.20	1.71 ± 0.26	0.005	0.003	0.072	2.00 (1.00–5.00)	1.00 (0.00–6.00)	923.5	<0.001
Netleaf hackberry trees; 62.5% of netleaf hackberry trees were classified correctly by the resulting model.										
	intercept			−10.744	4.492	0.017				
	dbh (cm)	21.14 ± 2.00	15.24 ± 1.66	0.218	0.129	0.092	21.50 (13.80–30.60)	13.10 (10.00–34.50)	21.0	0.012
	Height (m)	10.50 ± 0.60	7.00 ± 0.79	0.709	0.346	0.041	10.50 (7.00–12.00)	8.00 (1.00–11.00)	16.0	0.005
	HLB (m)	4.34 ± 0.52	2.82 ± 0.59	N/A	N/A	N/A	4.38 (2.25–6.00)	3.50 (0.00–6.00)	41.0	0.220
All trees; 79.5% of all trees were classified correctly by the resulting model.										
	intercept			−7.004	0.817	<0.001				
	dbh (cm)	49.88 ± 2.23	21.93 ± 0.77	0.103	0.017	<0.001	42.30 (11.50–163.50)	19.95 (6.80–86.80)	3063.5	<0.001
	Height (m)	13.63 ± 0.33	7.60 ± 0.30	0.223	0.047	<0.001	13.00 (6.00–26.00)	7.00 (0.00–22.00)	3430.0	<0.001
	HLB (m)	3.37 ± 0.18	1.82 ± 0.13	0.004	0.001	<0.001	3.00 (0.00–9.00)	1.37 (0.00–7.00)	7543.0	<0.001

[a] LR = logistic regression.
[b] dbh = diameter at breast height.
[c] HLB = height of lowest branch.
[d] N/A indicates that the variable was not selected by forward stepwise logistic regression.

also used Mann-Whitey *U*-tests (Zar 1999) to compare medians of roost tree measurements.

Diurnal Habitat

We calculated the functional study area at each study site by plotting a 99% fixed kernel home range based on all male turkey locations for each site. Both triangulations (location error x̄ = 84.7 m) and visual locations were used in the home range calculations (Kansas: *n* = 793; Gene Howe: *n* = 1,966; Salt Fork: *n* = 2,267; Matador: *n* = 2,990). We defined available habitat as the area within the respective functional study area at a study site. We manually photo-interpreted digital orthographic quadrangles to determine the percent of each general vegetation type within each functional study area. We ground-truthed our GIS coverages at the same time vegetation measurements were made.

For vegetation-type analyses, we defined vegetation types the following way: (1) wooded riparian—areas in the floodplain typically dominated by eastern cottonwoods or other large trees; (2) brushy riparian—areas in the floodplain dominated by shrubs, such as saltcedar (*Tamarisk gallica*) or Russian olive (*Eleagnus angustifolia*); (3) open riparian—areas in the floodplain dominated by grasses and occasional brush; (4) wooded upland—areas outside of the floodplain dominated by trees such as netleaf hackberry, post oak (*Quercus stellata*), gum bumelia (*Bumelia lanuginosa*), or western soapberry (*Sapindus drummondi*), including shelterbelts; (5) brushy upland—areas outside the floodplain dominated by shrubs such as honey mesquite (*Prosopis glandulo-*

sa), shinnery oak (*Q. havardii*), or skunkbush sumac (*Rhus aromatica*); (6) open upland—areas outside the floodplain dominated by grasses and occasional sand sagebrush (*Artemisia filifolia*); and (7) agricultural—anything planted, including food plots.

We assessed Rio Grande wild turkey vegetation-type selection (third-order habitat selection; Johnson 1980) by behavior, based upon male turkey visual locations, using chi-square tests (Zar 1999) and simultaneous Bonferroni confidence intervals (Neu et al. 1974). We compared the use of each of these vegetation types based upon male visual location plots with the relative availability of each vegetation type within the functional study area at each study site. This explored whether male Rio Grande wild turkeys selected for or against major vegetation types.

We studied habitat use by behavior on a study-wide scale by comparing vegetative characteristics between visual turkey locations and a random subset of all random locations from the larger, concurrent study (referred to hereafter as random locations). We used forward stepwise logistic regression (*P* < 0.20 to enter or remove a variable; Hosmer and Lemeshow 1989) to differentiate between visual locations and random locations, and Mann-Whitey *U*-tests (Zar 1999) to compare medians of vegetation variables. This explored whether vegetative characteristics differed between areas used by male Rio Grande wild turkeys and random points in areas occupied by turkeys.

We also studied habitat use by behavior on a local scale by comparing vegetative characteristics between visual turkey locations and paired random locations 50 m away (referred to hereafter as paired random locations). We used forward stepwise logistic regression ($P < 0.20$ to enter or remove a variable; Hosmer and Lemeshow 1989) to differentiate between visual locations and paired random locations, and Mann-Whitey U-tests (Zar 1999) to compare medians of vegetation variables. This explored whether vegetative characteristics differed between areas where turkeys were observed and the immediate vicinity. We considered all results significant at $\alpha = 0.05$. This research was approved by the Texas Tech University Animal Care and Use Committee (Protocol numbers 99917 and 01173B).

RESULTS

We fitted 128 juvenile and 132 adult male turkeys with radio-transmitters during our study. After censoring turkeys that survived <14 days post-capture, 107 juvenile and 115 adult males were available for analyses. We measured vegetation at 285 visual location plots (72 displaying, 71 loafing, 85 foraging, and 57 roosting) and 219 paired random plots. An additional 734 random locations from the larger, concurrent study were also used for estimating vegetative characteristics on a study-wide scale.

Roosting Habitat

Roost areas ranged from single trees to large groves (≥ 1 ha) of cottonwoods, black locusts, or mixed stands. Male turkeys were observed roosting in 100 eastern cottonwood trees, 27 black locust trees, 8 netleaf hackberry trees, 2 American elm trees (*Ulmus americana*), 2 osage orange trees (*Maclura pomifera*), and 2 western soapberry trees. Average dbh, height, and height of the lowest branch of roost trees were 49.88 cm, 13.63 m, and 3.37 m, respectively (Table 1). The formula for the probability that a tree was suitable for use as a roost was

$$p(Roost\ Tree) = \frac{e^{-7.004+0.103(\text{dbh[cm]})+0.223(\text{height[m]})+0.004(\text{height of lowest branch[m]})}}{1 + e^{-7.004+0.103(\text{dbh[cm]})+0.223(\text{height[m]})+0.004(\text{height of lowest branch[m]})}}.$$

The formula correctly classified 79.5% of the roost trees. Univariately, dbh and height were significantly greater for roost trees (Table 1).

The formulas for the probability that a tree was

suitable for use as a roost for individual species (eastern cottonwood, black locust, and netleaf hackberry, respectively) were

$$p(Cottonwood) = \frac{e^{-8.858+0.155(\text{dbh[cm]})+0.297(\text{height[m]})+0.002(\text{height of lowest branch[m]})}}{1 + e^{-8.858+0.155(\text{dbh[cm]})+0.297(\text{height[m]})+0.002(\text{height of lowest branch[m]})}},$$

$$p(Black\ Locust) = \frac{e^{-6.143+0.204(\text{dbh[cm]})+0.005(\text{height of lowest branch[m]})}}{1 + e^{-6.143+0.204(\text{dbh[cm]})+0.005(\text{height of lowest branch[m]})}},\ \text{and}$$

$$p(Netleaf\ Hackberry) = \frac{e^{-10.744+0.218(\text{dbh[cm]})+0.709(\text{height[m]})}}{1 + e^{-10.744+0.218(\text{dbh[cm]})+0.709(\text{height[m]})}}.$$

The formulas correctly classified 87.0%, 74.1%, and 62.5% of the cottonwood, black locust, and netleaf hackberry roost trees, respectively. Tree height and dbh were greater for roost trees than for other trees measured in roost vegetation plots for each individual species (eastern cottonwood, black locust, and netleaf hackberry [Table 1]). Additionally, average height of the lowest branch of roost trees was greater than that of other trees measured in roost vegetation plots for black locusts (Table 1).

Little cottonwood regeneration and moderate black locust regeneration was detected. In all, 471 of 2,344 (20.1%) vegetation plots measured in our study and the concurrent study contained cottonwood trees in the overstory. Of those, 9 (1.9%) had ≥1 cottonwood seedling or sapling in the 2- × 20-m transect that measured the understory. Additionally, 7 plots without cottonwoods in

the overstory had regeneration, indicating that roost tree replacement may be in jeopardy (Table 2). Forty-seven cottonwood seedlings or saplings were found in all plots. In contrast, 13 of the 16 (81.3%) plots with black locust trees (the second-most commonly used roost tree species in our study) in the overstory had regeneration. An additional 18 plots without black locust trees also had regeneration (Table 2). In all, 177 black locust seedlings or saplings were counted despite the fact that black locusts were present in small groves at 2 of the 4 study sites.

Eleven black locust tree stumps were available for age data. They ranged from 6.5–23.5 cm in diameter and from 23–47 years in age. A linear relationship (y = 0.8579x + 15.107; $R^2 = 0.4313$, $P = 0.028$) existed between diameter and age. The 27 black locust trees used as roosts ranged from 11.5–59.2 cm in diameter

Table 2. Regeneration (seedlings or saplings ≥0.5 m in height, <10 cm dbh) of eastern cottonwoods and black locusts measured at Rio Grande wild turkey locations from January 2000 through August 2002 in the Texas Panhandle and southwestern Kansas.

Species-Study area	Tree in overstory[a]	Regeneration[b]	Additional regeneration[c]
Cottonwoods			
Gene Howe	47	0	0
Kansas	332	4	4
Matador	73	3	0
Salt Fork	29	2	3
Total	471	9	7
Black Locusts			
Gene Howe	1	0	10
Kansas	0	0	0
Matador	0	0	0
Salt Fork	15	13	8
Total	16	13	18

[a] Total number of plots with ≥1 of the given species in the overstory.
[b] Of the plots with ≥1 of the given species in the overstory, those with regeneration (≥1 seedling or sapling).
[c] Plots with regeneration (≥1 seedling or sapling) of the given species without that species being present in the overstory.

with 6 falling within the range of the stumps available to us. However, if we can assume that the linear relationship continued at larger diameters, then the estimated range in age of black locust trees used as roosts was 27–79 years ($\bar{x} = 49$).

Diurnal Habitat

Vegetation Type

Males avoided open riparian vegetation types at Gene Howe and avoided brushy upland vegetation types at Matador when displaying. At Salt Fork, displaying males selected wooded riparian vegetation types and avoided open upland vegetation types. Across all study sites, males generally avoided open upland vegetation types for displaying (Table 3).

Males loafing at Gene Howe avoided open riparian vegetation types, while at Salt Fork, they avoided brushy upland vegetation types. In Kansas, loafing males avoided open upland vegetation types. No selection was detected at Matador. However, across all study sites, males typically avoided open upland vegetation types for loafing (Table 3).

For males foraging at Gene Howe, open riparian vegetation types were avoided. In Kansas, males selected wooded riparian vegetation types and avoided open upland vegetation types for foraging. No selection was detected at Matador or Salt Fork for foraging males; however, across all study sites, males typically avoided agricultural vegetation types and open upland vegetation types while foraging (Table 3).

Vegetative Characteristics: Visual Locations Compared to a Subset of Random Locations

The formulas for the probability that a location was suitable for a particular behavior (displaying, loafing, and foraging, respectively) were

$$p(Displaying) = \frac{e^{0.783-0.064(\%\text{visual obstruction})-0.048(\%\text{shrub})-0.019(\%\text{forb})+0.213(2-4\text{ m shrubs per }40\text{ m}^2)}}{1 + e^{0.783-0.064(\%\text{visual obstruction})-0.048(\%\text{shrub})-0.019(\%\text{forb})+0.213(2-4\text{ m shrubs per }40\text{ m}^2)}},$$

$$p(Loafing) = \frac{e^{-0.815+0.027(\%\text{litter})+0.452(2-4\text{ shrubs per }40\text{ m}^2)}}{1 + e^{-0.815+0.027(\%\text{litter})+0.452(2-4\text{ shrubs per }40\text{ m}^2)}}, \text{ and}$$

$$p(Foraging) = \frac{e^{0.127-0.048(\%\text{visual obstruction})-0.047(\%\text{shrub})+0.311(\#\text{shrub species per }40\text{ m}^2)+0.235(2-4\text{ m shrubs per }40\text{ m}^2)}}{1 + e^{0.127-0.048(\%\text{visual obstruction})-0.047(\%\text{shrub})+0.311(\#\text{shrub species per }40\text{ m}^2)+0.235(2-4\text{ m shrubs per }40\text{ m}^2)}}.$$

The formulas correctly classified 80.6%, 52.1%, and 74.1% of the displaying, loafing, and foraging locations, respectively. Univariately, displaying locations had less visual obstruction, shrub cover, and forb cover than random locations. Loafing locations had more trees, 1–2 m shrubs and 2–4 m shrubs than random locations. Foraging locations also had less visual obstruction than random locations (Table 4).

Vegetative Characteristics: Visual Locations Compared to Paired Random Locations.—

The logistic regression models contrasting visual locations for each behavior (displaying, loafing, and foraging, respectively) with paired random locations were

$$p(Displaying) = \frac{e^{0.568-0.144(\%\text{shrub})+0.103(0.5-1\text{ m shrubs per }40\text{ m}^2)-0.269(1-2\text{ m shrubs per }40\text{ m}^2)+0.139(2-4\text{ m shrubs per }40\text{ m}^2)}}{1 + e^{0.568-0.144(\%\text{shrub})+0.103(0.5-1\text{ m shrubs per }40\text{ m}^2)-0.269(1-2\text{ m shrubs per }40\text{ m}^2)+0.139(2-4\text{ m shrubs per }40\text{ m}^2)}}$$

$$p(Loafing) = \frac{e^{-0.839+0.039(\%\text{visual obstruction})-0.047(\%\text{shrub})+0.016(\%\text{bare ground})+0.138(\#\text{trees per }200\text{ m}^2)+0.134(2-4\text{ shrubs per }40\text{ m}^2)}}{1 + e^{-0.839+0.039(\%\text{visual obstruction})-0.047(\%\text{shrub})+0.016(\%\text{bare ground})+0.138(\#\text{trees per }200\text{ m}^2)+0.134(2-4\text{ shrubs per }40\text{ m}^2)}}$$

$$p(Foraging) = \frac{e^{0.271-0.035(\%\text{shrub})}}{1 + e^{0.271-0.035(\%\text{shrub})}}$$

Table 3. Chi-square analysis and simultaneous confidence intervals for vegetation types used for displaying versus availability, loafing versus availability, and foraging versus availability, respectively, for male Rio Grand wild turkeys from January 2000 through August 2002 in the Texas Panhandle and southwestern Kansas. The overall chi-square test statistic and associated *P*-value follows the study area site label.

Behavior Study Site Vegetation type	Expected proportion	Observed proportion	Bonferroni intervals Lower	Upper
Displaying				
Gene Howe (Observed: $n = 22$; $x^2_6 = 9.977$; $P = 0.126$)				
Agriculture	0.018	0.000	0	0
Open riparian	0.189	0.000[a]	0	0
Brushy riparian	0.171	0.364	0.088	0.640
Wooded riparian	0.093	0.136	0.000	0.333
Open upland	0.476	0.455	0.169	0.740
Brushy upland	0.046	0.045	0.000	0.165
Wooded upland	0.008	0.000	0	0
Kansas (Observed: $n = 8$; $x^2_4 = 8.559$; $P = 0.073$)				
Agriculture	0.064	0.000	0	0
Open riparian	0.060	0.250	0.000	0.644
Brushy riparian	0.062	0.125	0.000	0.426
Wooded riparian	0.109	0.250	0.000	0.644
Open upland	0.705	0.375	0.000	0.816
Matador (Observed: $n = 23$; x^2_6 31.523; $P < 0.001$)				
Agriculture	0.051	0.000	0	0
Open riparian	0.008	0.043	0.000	0.158
Brushy riparian	0.166	0.217	0.000	0.449
Wooded riparian	0.023	0.043	0.000	0.158
Open upland	0.139	0.304	0.046	0.562
Brushy upland	0.582	0.217[b]	0.000	0.449
Wooded upland	0.029	0.174	0.000	0.387
Salt Fork (Observed: $n = 19$; $x^2_6 = 43.017$; $P < 0.001$)				
Agriculture	0.060	0.000	0	0
Open riparian	0.132	0.158	0.000	0.383
Brushy riparian	0.018	0.053	0.000	0.190
Wooded riparian	0.052	0.368[b]	0.071	0.666
Open upland	0.236	0.053[b]	0.000	0.190
Brushy upland	0.419	0.263	0.000	0.535
Wooded upland	0.083	0.105	0.000	0.295
Pooled Study Sites (Observed: $n = 72$; $x^2_6 = 44.925$; $P < 0.001$)				
Agriculture	0.056	0.000	0	0
Open riparian	0.074	0.083	0.000	0.171
Brushy riparian	0.091	0.208	0.080	0.337
Wooded riparian	0.080	0.181	0.059	0.303
Open upland	0.484	0.292[b]	0.148	0.436
Brushy upland	0.196	0.153	0.039	0.267
Wooded upland	0.020	0.083	0.000	0.171
Loafing				
Gene Howe (Observed: $n = 11$; $x^2_6 = 45.489$; $P < 0.001$)				
Agriculture	0.018	0.000	0	0
Open riparian	0.189	0.000[a]	0	0
Brushy riparian	0.171	0.273	0.000	0.634
Wooded riparian	0.093	0.000	0	0
Open upland	0.476	0.545	0.142	0.949
Brushy upland	0.046	0.000	0	0
Wooded upland	0.008	0.182	0.000	0.495
Kansas (Observed: $n = 17$; $x^2_4 = 22.590$; $P < 0.001$)				
Agriculture	0.064	0.000	0	0
Open riparian	0.060	0.176	0.000	0.415
Brushy riparian	0.062	0.235	0.000	0.500
Wooded riparian	0.109	0.294	0.009	0.579
Open upland	0.705	0.294[b]	0.009	0.579
Matador (Observed: $n = 25$; $x^2_6 = 28.594$; $P < 0.001$)				
Agriculture	0.051	0.000	0	0
Open riparian	0.008	0.040	0.000	0.145
Brushy riparian	0.166	0.200	0.000	0.415
Wooded riparian	0.023	0.160	0.000	0.357
Open upland	0.139	0.120	0.000	0.295

Table 3. Continued.

Behavior Study Site Vegetation type	Expected proportion	Observed proportion	Bonferroni intervals Lower	Upper
Brushy upland	0.582	0.400	0.136	0.664
Wooded upland	0.029	0.080	0.000	0.226
Salt Fork (Observed: $n = 18$; $x^2_6 = 24.847$; $P < 0.001$)				
Agriculture	0.060	0.000	0	0
Open riparian	0.132	0.056	0.000	0.201
Brushy riparian	0.018	0.000	0	0
Wooded riparian	0.052	0.278	0.000	0.562
Open upland	0.236	0.333	0.034	0.632
Brushy upland	0.419	0.167[b]	0.000	0.403
Wooded upland	0.083	0.167	0.000	0.403
Pooled Study Sites (Observed: $n = 71$; $x^2_6 = 49.121$; $P < 0.001$)				
Agriculture	0.056	0.000	0	0
Open riparian	0.074	0.070	0.000	0.152
Brushy riparian	0.091	0.169	0.049	0.289
Wooded riparian	0.080	0.197	0.070	0.324
Open upland	0.484	0.282[b]	0.138	0.425
Brushy upland	0.196	0.183	0.060	0.307
Wooded upland	0.020	0.099	0.003	0.194
Foraging				
Gene Howe (Observed: n 16; $x^2_6 = 10.306$; $P = 0.112$)				
Agriculture	0.018	0.000	0	0
Open riparian	0.189	0.000[a]	0	0
Brushy riparian	0.171	0.375	0.049	0.701
Wooded riparian	0.093	0.000	0	0
Open upland	0.476	0.625	0.299	0.951
Brushy upland	0.046	0.000	0	0
Wooded upland	0.008	0.000	0	0
Kansas (Observed: $n = 20$; $x^2_4 = 18.709$; $P = 0.001$)				
Agriculture	0.064	0.050	0.000	0.176
Open riparian	0.060	0.050	0.000	0.176
Brushy riparian	0.062	0.100	0.000	0.273
Wooded riparian	0.109	0.400[b]	0.118	0.682
Open upland	0.705	0.400[b]	0.118	0.682
Matador (Observed: $n = 24$; $x^2_6 = 8.147$; $P = 0.228$)				
Agriculture	0.051	0.000	0	0
Open riparian	0.008	0.042	0.000	0.151
Brushy riparian	0.166	0.208	0.000	0.431
Wooded riparian	0.023	0.000	0	0
Open upland	0.139	0.083	0.000	0.235
Brushy upland	0.582	0.583	0.313	0.854
Wooded upland	0.029	0.083	0.000	0.235
Salt Fork (Observed: $n = 25$; $x^2_6 = 16.154$; $P = 0.013$)				
Agriculture	0.060	0.000	0	0
Open riparian	0.132	0.080	0.000	0.226
Brushy riparian	0.018	0.000	0	0
Wooded riparian	0.052	0.200	0.000	0.415
Open upland	0.236	0.280	0.038	0.522
Brushy upland	0.419	0.280	0.038	0.522
Wooded upland	0.083	0.160	0.000	0.357
Pooled Study Sites (Observed: $n = 85$; $x^2_6 = 30.010$; $P < 0.001$)				
Agriculture	0.056	0.012[b]	0.000	0.043
Open riparian	0.074	0.047	0.000	0.109
Brushy riparian	0.091	0.153	0.048	0.258
Wooded riparian	0.080	0.153	0.048	0.258
Open upland	0.484	0.318[b]	0.182	0.453
Brushy upland	0.196	0.247	0.121	0.373
Wooded upland	0.020	0.071	0.000	0.145

[a] Considered biologically significant, as indicated when the observed proportion was 0 and the expected proportion was ≥0.1.
[b] Indicates a significant difference at *P* < 0.05, as indicated when the expected proportion fell outside of the Bonferroni intervals.

Table 4. Comparison of vegetative characteristics using forward stepwise logistic regression ($P < 0.20$ to enter or remove a variable) and Mann-Whitney *U*-tests between male Rio Grande wild turkey locations and a subset of random locations from January 2000 through August 2002 in the Texas Panhandle and southwestern Kansas. Means are provided for comparison to the literature. Medians are provided because Mann-Whitney tests compare medians of ranked data.

	Mean ± SE		Forward stepwise LR[a]			Median (range)		Mann-Whitney	
Variable	Location	Random[b]	Estimate	SE	P	Location	Random	U	P
Displaying (n = 72) versus Random (n = 72); 80.6% of displaying locations were classified correctly by the resulting model.									
Intercept			0.783	0.304	0.010				
Coarse woody debris per 200 m²	2.042 ± 0.758	1.944 ± 0.438	N/A[c]	N/A	N/A	0.0 (0–50)	0.0 (0–18)	2455.0	0.584
% visual obstruction	3.903 ± 0.833	10.278 ± 1.330	−0.064	0.028	0.020	0.0 (0–33)	7.0 (0–47)	1447.0	<0.001
% grass cover	47.528 ± 3.182	45.597 ± 3.190	N/A	N/A	N/A	47.0 (1–100)	45.0 (0–98)	2491.0	0.687
% shrub cover	3.000 ± 0.792	8.542 ± 1.390	−0.048	0.033	0.140	1.0 (0–51)	4.0 (0–50)	1786.0	0.001
% bare ground cover	16.042 ± 2.041	14.431 ± 1.981	N/A	N/A	N/A	10.0 (0–72)	8.0 (0–75)	2359.0	0.352
% forb cover	11.569 ± 1.603	15.069 ± 1.467	−0.019	0.014	0.163	7.0 (0–72)	13.0 (0–52)	1948.5	0.010
% litter cover	19.778 ± 2.476	12.597 ± 1.597	N/A	N/A	N/A	16.0 (0–89)	8.0 (0–61)	2137.5	0.069
Trees per 200 m²	2.000 ± 0.487	2.222 ± 0.564	N/A	N/A	N/A	0.0 (0–21)	0.0 (0–25)	2516.5	0.763
Shrub species per 40 m²[d]	0.917 ± 0.141	1.153 ± 0.146	N/A	N/A	N/A	0.5 (0–5)	1.0 (0–6)	2248.5	0.170
0.5–1 m shrubs per 40 m²	3.750 ± 1.065	12.264 ± 5.461	N/A	N/A	N/A	0.0 (0–64)	1.0 (0–360)	2272.0	0.201
1–2 m shrubs per 40 m²	0.931 ± 0.248	1.736 ± 0.634	N/A	N/A	N/A	0.0 (0–9)	0.0 (0–43)	2310.0	0.260
2–4 m shrubs per 40 m²	0.972 ± 0.381	0.347 ± 0.114	0.213	0.152	0.161	0.0 (0–24)	0.0 (0–6)	2511.5	0.748
Loafing (n = 71) versus Random (n = 71); 52.1% of loafing locations were classified correctly by the resulting model.									
Intercept			−0.815	0.266	0.002				
Coarse woody debris per 200 m²	3.437 ± 0.775	1.972 ± 0.443	N/A	N/A	N/A	1.0 (0–41)	0.0 (0–18)	2108.0	0.092
% visual obstruction	12.272 ± 1.434	10.113 ± 1.339	N/A	N/A	N/A	10.0 (0–55)	7.0 (0–47)	2196.5	0.186
% grass cover	36.958 ± 3.065	45.183 ± 3.208	N/A	N/A	N/A	32.0 (1–93)	45.0 (0–98)	2082.0	0.074
% shrub cover	8.127 ± 1.119	8.662 ± 1.404	N/A	N/A	N/A	6.0 (0–49)	4.0 (0–50)	2367.0	0.531
% bare ground cover	14.282 ± 1.985	14.634 ± 1.998	N/A	N/A	N/A	11.0 (0–79)	8.0 (0–75)	2455.5	0.791
% forb cover	16.000 ± 1.662	14.944 ± 1.482	N/A	N/A	N/A	13.0 (0–69)	13.0 (0–52)	2456.0	0.792
% litter cover	20.690 ± 2.649	12.761 ± 1.611	0.027	0.011	0.011	12.0 (0–84)	8.0 (0–61)	2045.0	0.052
Trees per 200 m²	4.901 ± 0.679	2.254 ± 0.571	N/A	N/A	N/A	3.0 (0–22)	0.0 (0–25)	1531.0	<0.001
Shrub species per 40 m²[d]	1.549 ± 0.168	1.169 ± 0.147	N/A	N/A	N/A	1.0 (0–5)	1.0 (0–6)	2131.5	0.112
0.5–1 m shrubs per 40 m²	5.042 ± 1.078	12.437 ± 5.536	N/A	N/A	N/A	1.0 (0–46)	1.0 (0–360)	2491.5	0.906
1–2 m shrubs per 40 m²	3.606 ± 0.660	1.761 ± 0.643	N/A	N/A	N/A	1.0 (0–22)	0.0 (0–43)	1975.0	0.026
2–4 m shrubs per 40 m²	2.324 ± 0.582	0.352 ± 0.115	0.452	0.155	0.004	0.0 (0–30)	0.0 (0–6)	1764.5	0.002
Foraging (n = 85) versus Random (n = 85); 74.1% of foraging locations were classified correctly by the resulting model.									
Intercept			0.127	0.238	0.594				
Coarse woody debris per 200 m²	1.600 ± 0.440	2.035 ± 0.426	N/A	N/A	N/A	0.0 (0–27)	0.0 (0–18)	3407.0	0.522
% visual obstruction	5.844 ± 0.950	10.404 ± 1.234	−0.048	0.020	0.020	3.0 (0–52)	7.0 (0–47)	2664.5	0.003
% grass cover	42.224 ± 2.997	46.741 ± 3.047	N/A	N/A	N/A	40.0 (0–100)	49.0 (0–98)	3286.0	0.309
% shrub cover	5.212 ± 0.789	7.859 ± 1.217	−0.047	0.028	0.089	2.0 (0–35)	3.0 (0–50)	3202.0	0.201
% bare ground cover	14.447 ± 1.493	13.635 ± 1.815	N/A	N/A	N/A	11.0 (0–56)	7.0 (0–75)	3110.5	0.118
% forb cover	15.659 ± 1.697	14.929 ± 1.365	N/A	N/A	N/A	12.0 (0–74)	12.0 (0–52)	3493.0	0.710
% litter cover	15.224 ± 2.106	11.400 ± 1.401	N/A	N/A	N/A	6.0 (0–78)	6.0 (0–61)	3422.0	0.553
Trees per 200 m²	2.635 ± 0.599	2.024 ± 0.482	N/A	N/A	N/A	0.0 (0–32)	0.0 (0–25)	3364.5	0.440
Shrub species per 40 m²[d]	1.447 ± 0.165	1.129 ± 0.133	0.311	0.149	0.037	1.0 (0–6)	1.0 (0–6)	3284.5	0.307
0.5–1 m shrubs per 40 m²	6.588 ± 1.895	13.059 ± 5.188	N/A	N/A	N/A	1.0 (0–142)	1.0 (0–360)	3579.5	0.918
1–2 m shrubs per 40 m²	2.247 ± 0.606	1.565 ± 0.540	N/A	N/A	N/A	0.0 (0–34)	0.0 (0–43)	3346.5	0.407
2–4 m shrubs per 40 m²	0.812 ± 0.233	0.329 ± 0.102	0.235	0.124	0.058	0.0 (0–16)	0.0 (0–6)	3195.5	0.194

[a] LR = logistic regression.
[b] Random includes a subset of all random locatiosn from this and the larger, concurrent study.
[c] N/A indicates that the variable was not selected by forward stepwise logistic regression.
[d] Because shrub species per 40 m² is not linear, this refers to the 40 m²-belt transect used to tally shrubs of the different height classes.

The formulas correctly classified 80.6%, 62.0%, and 71.8% of the displaying, loafing, and foraging locations, respectively. Displaying locations had less visual obstruction, shrub cover, shrub species, 0.5–1 m shrubs, and 1–2 m shrubs than paired random locations. Loafing locations had more coarse woody debris, litter cover, trees, and 2–4 m shrubs than paired random locations. Vegetative characteristics at foraging locations did not differ from paired random locations (Table 5).

Male foraging locations appeared to differ between spring and summer. Spring foraging locations had less visual obstruction and litter cover than summer foraging locations (Table 6).

DISCUSSION

Roosting Habitat

Turkeys selected the largest and tallest trees from those immediately available. Overall, roost tree heights and diameters were similar to those reported for Merriam's wild turkeys (Schemnitz et al. 1985, Wakeling and Rogers 1998) and Rio Grande turkeys from other areas (Crockett 1973, Haucke 1975, Quinton et al. 1980).

Table 5. Comparison of vegetative characteristics using forward stepwise logistic regression ($P < 0.20$ to enter or remove a variable) and Mann-Whitney U-tests between male Rio Grande wild turkey locations and paired random locations from January 2000 through August 2002 in the Texas Panhandle and southwestern Kansas. Means are provided for comparison to the literature. Medians are provided because Mann-Whitney tests compare medians of ranked data.

Variable	Mean ± SE Location	Mean ± SE Random	Forward stepwise LR[a] Estimate	SE	P	Median (range) Location	Median (range) Random	Mann-Whitney U	P
Displaying (n = 72) versus Dependent Random (n = 68); 80.6% of displaying locations were classified correclty by the resulting model.									
Intercept			0.568	0.224	0.011				
Coarse woody debris per 200 m²	2.042 ± 0.758	1.559 ± 0.612	N/A[b]	N/A	N/A	0.0 (0–50)	0.0 (0–38)	2264.5	0.444
% visual obstruction	3.903 ± 0.833	10.275 ± 1.761	N/A	N/A	N/A	0.0 (0–33)	5.5 (0–85)	1605.5	<0.001
% grass cover	47.528 ± 3.182	44.529 ± 3.366	N/A	N/A	N/A	47.0 (1–100)	42.5 (0–98)	2294.5	0.522
% shrub cover	3.000 ± 0.792	9.926 ± 1.951	−0.144	0.045	0.001	1.0 (0–51)	4.0 (0–83)	1602.5	<0.001
% bare ground cover	16.042 ± 2.041	12.779 ± 1.638	N/A	N/A	N/A	10.0 (0–72)	8.0 (0–54)	2249.5	0.408
% forb cover	11.569 ± 1.603	11.382 ± 1.872	N/A	N/A	N/A	7.0 (0–72)	7.5 (0–72)	2417.0	0.897
% litter cover	19.778 ± 2.476	18.485 ± 2.182	N/A	N/A	N/A	16.0 (0–89)	12.5 (0–73)	2426.0	0.927
Trees per 200 m²	2.000 ± 0.487	1.853 ± 0.380	N/A	N/A	N/A	0.0 (0–21)	0.0 (0–13)	2401.5	0.846
Shrub species per 40 m²[c]	0.917 ± 0.141	1.456 ± 0.188	N/A	N/A	N/A	0.5 (0–5)	1.0 (0–7)	1964.0	0.044
0.5–1 m shrubs per 40 m²	3.750 ± 1.065	8.485 ± 1.991	0.103	0.038	0.006	0.0 (0–64)	1.5 (0–85)	1930.5	0.031
1–2 m shrubs per 40 m²	0.931 ± 0.248	3.162 ± 0.748	−0.269	0.091	0.003	0.0 (0–9)	0.0 (0–32)	1914.5	0.026
2–4 m shrubs per 40 m²	0.972 ± 0.381	0.868 ± 0.252	0.139	0.090	0.125	0.0 (0–24)	0.0 (0–10)	2303.5	0.547
Loafing (n = 71) versus Dependent Random (n = 70); 62.0% of loafing locations were classified by the resulting model.									
Intercept			−0.839	0.356	0.018				
Coarse woody debris per 200 m²	3.437 ± 0.775	1.771 ± 0.612	N/A	N/A	N/A	1.0 (0–41)	0.0 (0–24)	1717.5	0.002
% visual obstruction	12.272 ± 1.434	10.810 ± 1.818	0.039	0.020	0.050	10.0 (0–55)	6.0 (0–71)	2057.5	0.078
% grass cover	36.958 ± 3.065	42.914 ± 3.276	N/A	N/A	N/A	32.0 (1–93)	41.0 (0–97)	2176.5	0.203
% shrub cover	8.127 ± 1.119	10.400 ± 1.794	−0.047	0.021	0.028	6.0 (0–49)	3.5 (0–69)	2451.0	0.889
% bare ground cover	14.282 ± 1.985	12.071 ± 2.180	0.016	0.011	0.130	11.0 (0–79)	7.0 (0–95)	2124.5	0.137
% forb cover	16.000 ± 1.662	18.486 ± 1.961	N/A	N/A	N/A	13.0 (0–69)	13.5 (0–72)	2310.5	0.472
% litter cover	20.690 ± 2.649	11.929 ± 1.941	N/A	N/A	N/A	12.0 (0–84)	6.5 (0–76)	1786.0	0.004
Trees per 200 m²	4.901 ± 0.679	1.886 ± 0.492	0.138	0.046	0.003	3.0 (0–22)	0.0 (0–21)	1402.5	<0.001
Shrub species per 40 m²[c]	1.549 ± 0.168	1.357 ± 0.151	N/A	N/A	N/A	1.0 (0–5)	1.0 (0–6)	2316.0	0.486
0.5–1 m shrubs per 40 m²	5.042 ± 1.078	17.186 ± 8.366	N/A	N/A	N/A	1.0 (0–46)	1.5 (0–574)	2265.0	0.364
1–2 m shrubs per 40 m²	3.606 ± 0.660	5.900 ± 2.059	N/A	N/A	N/A	1.0 (0–22)	1.0 (0–108)	2419.0	0.786
2–4 m shrubs per 40 m²	2.324 ± 0.582	0.800 ± 0.232	0.134	0.077	0.084	0.0 (0–30)	0.0 (0–9)	1947.5	0.027
Foraging (n = 85) versus Dependent Random (n = 81); 71.8% of foraging locations were classified correctly by the resulting model.									
Intercept			0.271	0.196	0.167				
Coarse woody debris per 200 m²	1.600 ± 0.440	1.420 ± 0.428	N/A	N/A	N/A	0.0 (0–27)	0.0 (0–22)	3306.0	0.659
% visual obstruction	5.844 ± 0.950	7.494 ± 1.217	N/A	N/A	N/A	3.0 (0–52)	4.0 (0–62)	3219.0	0.470
% grass cover	42.224 ± 2.997	39.531 ± 2.893	N/A	N/A	N/A	40.0 (0–100)	34.0 (0–100)	3264.0	0.564
% shrub cover	5.212 ± 0.789	7.765 ± 1.106	−0.035	0.019	0.065	2.0 (0–35)	4.0 (0–48)	2967.5	0.125
% bare ground cover	14.447 ± 1.493	15.852 ± 1.961	N/A	N/A	N/A	11.0 (0–56)	10.0 (0–87)	3412.5	0.923
% forb cover	15.659 ± 1.697	16.667 ± 1.905	N/A	N/A	N/A	12.0 (0–74)	11.0 (0–73)	3334.5	0.727
% litter cover	15.224 ± 2.106	14.111 ± 1.956	N/A	N/A	N/A	6.0 (0–78)	8.0 (0–78)	3413.5	0.925
Trees per 200 m²	2.635 ± 0.599	2.173 ± 0.464	N/A	N/A	N/A	0.0 (0–32)	0.0 (0–17)	3326.0	0.707
Shrub species per 40 m²[c]	1.447 ± 0.165	1.531 ± 0.174	N/A	N/A	N/A	1.0 (0–6)	1.0 (0–8)	3350.5	0.766
0.5–1 m shrubs per 40 m²	6.588 ± 1.895	6.765 ± 1.562	N/A	N/A	N/A	1.0 (0–142)	1.0 (0–76)	3398.5	0.887
1–2 m shrubs per 40 m²	2.247 ± 0.606	5.037 ± 1.432	N/A	N/A	N/A	0.0 (0–34)	0.0 (0–85)	3106.5	0.278
2–4 m shrubs per 40 m²	0.812 ± 0.233	1.000 ± 0.281	N/A	N/A	N/A	0.0 (0–16)	0.0 (0–16)	3365.0	0.802

[a] LR = logistic regression.

[b] N/A indicates that the variable was not selected by forward stepwide logistic regression.

[c] Because shrub species per 40 m² is not linear, this refers to the 40 m²- belt transect used to tally shrubs of the different height classes.

The most common roost tree across all study areas was the eastern cottonwood (100 of 141). Cottonwood seedlings are a favored browse species and they are easily killed by brief moisture stress, caused either by drought or competition with encroaching saltcedar (Harlow et al. 1991). Due to these factors, the Texas Panhandle and southwestern Kansas may lose a high percentage of their turkey roost trees due to old age without sufficient regeneration to replace them. Of 471 vegetation plots with cottonwood trees in the overstory, only 9 had cottonwood saplings or seedlings in the understory. Furthermore, many of the older cottonwood trees were in various stages of decline. We suggest the above factors, as well as browse pressure from deer (*Odocoileus* spp.) and increased livestock grazing in riparian areas may be preventing cottonwood regeneration.

Though commonly used as roosts in our study (27 of 141), there has been no prior mention in the literature of turkeys using black locust as roosts. A typical black locust roost tree was about 32.0 cm dbh, 14.7 m tall, and had its first branch 2.5 m off the ground. At the Salt Fork study site, a large grove of black locust trees was used as a year-round roost. This may prove important as cattle, deer, drought, and saltcedar continue to affect the survival of highly palatable and water dependent cottonwood seedlings. Black locusts are

Table 6. Comparison of vegetative characteristics using Mann-Whitney *U*-tests between male Rio Grande wild turkey spring foraging (*n* = 29) and summer foraging (*n* = 39) locations from March 2000 through August 2002 in the Texas Panhandle and southwestern Kansas. Means are provided for comparison to the literature. Medians are provided because Mann-Whitney tests compare medians of ranked data.

Variable	Mean ± SE		Median (range)		Mann-Whitney	
	Spring	Summer	Spring	Summer	*U*	*P*
Coarse woody debris per 200 m²	1.793 ± 0.998	1.103 ± 0.437	0.0 (0–27)	0.0 (0–14)	549.0	0.838
% visual obstruction	3.448 ± 0.773	9.353 ± 1.809	2.0 (0–14)	6.0 (0–52)	365.0	0.013
% grass cover	42.966 ± 6.139	44.051 ± 3.921	33.0 (0–100)	45.0 (0–85)	533.0	0.687
% shrub cover	4.172 ± 1.150	6.487 ± 1.340	0.0 (0–21)	4.0 (0–35)	444.5	0.134
% bare ground cover	13.966 ± 3.151	11.154 ± 1.725	5.0 (0–54)	7.0 (0–56)	530.0	0.660
% forb cover	16.310 ± 3.708	18.667 ± 2.000	8.0 (0–74)	16.0 (0–47)	428.5	0.089
% litter cover	10.690 ± 3.478	14.256 ± 2.525	3.0 (0–78)	8.0 (0–71)	388.0	0.028
Trees per 200 m²	4.276 ± 1.490	1.385 ± 0.386	0.0 (0–32)	0.0 (0–9)	493.5	0.372
Shrub species per 40 m²[a]	1.276 ± 0.317	1.410 ± 0.207	1.0 (0–6)	1.0 (0–4)	487.5	0.333
0.5–1 m shrubs per 40 m²	3.621 ± 1.387	5.538 ± 1.550	0.0 (0–36)	2.0 (0–39)	459.0	0.187
1–2 m shrubs per 40 m²	1.345 ± 0.537	3.615 ± 1.224	0.0 (0–11)	1.0 (0–34)	431.5	0.097
2–4 m shrubs per 40 m²	0.414 ± 0.189	1.256 ± 0.474	0.0 (0–4)	0.0 (0–16)	473.5	0.254

[a] Because shrub species per 40 m² is not linear, this refers to the 40 m²-belt transect used to tally shrubs of the different height class.

less water dependent than cottonwoods (Harlow et al. 1991). Their seedlings are armed with spines and are less palatable than cottonwoods. Occasionally, they may be poisonous to livestock (Petrides and Petrides 1998). Increased sapling survival was apparent at our study sites as 13 of 16 plots with black locusts in the overstory showed regeneration.

Ring counts of actual roost trees were not possible because we did not have permission to cut or core trees where black locusts occurred. According to ring counts of a sample of black locusts from 2 groves, the average age of black locusts used as turkey roosts was 49 years. It should be noted that the range of trees used in the ring count regression did not contain the mean dbh for black locusts used as roosts. However, it did contain the dbh of the 6 smallest trees used as roosts. If, however, the linear relationship held for older trees, the estimated range in ages of black locusts used as roosts was 27–79 years.

Diurnal Habitat

Male Rio Grande wild turkeys displayed in a variety of different vegetation types. At the Salt Fork site, male Rio Grande wild turkeys preferred wooded riparian vegetation types. However, they showed no selection at any of the other sites. Despite the need for open areas in which to display, males avoided open upland vegetation types, illustrating their close connection with river corridors. They used areas that had lower visual obstruction and lower shrub densities than both random areas on the study-wide scale and local paired random areas. Trees were uncommon, but were present in some plots if the understory was open, particularly at Salt Fork. Most wooded displaying areas were in upland stands of trees, such as under groves of black locusts. Baker et al. (1980) reported that spring ranges for male Rio Grande wild turkeys in South Texas were in open, riparian savannahs and displaying occurred in mowed areas near brushy escape cover. Typical displaying habitat for eastern wild turkeys (Lewis 1964, Speake et al. 1975, Clark 1985, Ielmini et al. 1992) was similar to our findings except that previous studies have not reported that displaying

occurred under forest canopy. A common thread was increased use of small openings (Lewis 1964, Speake et al. 1975, Clark 1985, Ielmini et al. 1992) or edges (Holbrook et al. 1987) during spring when males were displaying.

Male Rio Grande wild turkeys also used a variety of vegetation types for loafing. They did not select for any particular vegetation type; however, they avoided open riparian and open upland vegetation types at Gene Howe and Kansas, respectively. Because single male turkeys could use anything from the shade of a single tree or large shrub to an entire cottonwood gallery, loafing vegetative characteristics varied considerably from one loafing location to the next. This was evident by the relatively low percentage of correctly classified loafing plots by logistic regression. The models classified random areas (78.9% and 77.1% for random areas on the study-wide scale and paired random areas, respectively) better than loafing areas indicating that variation in characteristics was greater among loafing areas than among random locations. For comparison, the correct random plot classifications ranged from 40.7% to 55.6% for all displaying and foraging logistic regressions. Greater densities of trees and larger shrubs were found at loafing locations than at both random areas on the study-wide scale and at local paired random areas. In general, shrubs or trees needed to be large enough to provide a canopy under which turkeys could rest and avoid the sun and yet have horizontal cover. Loafing areas for Merriam's wild turkeys had smaller Ponderosa pines, greater amounts of downed wood, greater cover between 92 cm and 184 cm, less herbaceous vegetation, greater percent canopy closure, greater distance to openings, shorter horizontal sight distances for turkey silhouettes, and greater slope than random locations (Wakeling and Rogers 1998).

Only males in Kansas showed selection for a particular vegetation type when foraging. There, they selected for wooded riparian vegetation. Foraging areas had less visual obstruction than random areas throughout turkey range. Merriam's wild turkeys avoided areas with high densities of gamble oak (*Quercus gambelii*) or rocky ground cover when foraging and foraging areas were often associated with man-made trails or roads (Wakeling and Rogers 1998).

Areas where turkeys fed did not, however, differ from the immediate surroundings. This suggested that turkeys fed opportunistically at a microhabitat scale. Further evidence for opportunistic foraging was the difference between spring and summer foraging areas. Foraging areas during spring had less visual obstruction than those during summer. Perhaps, this is due to the amount of new growth that is often present in later spring and summer. Alternatively, this may have been due to a shift in primary male behavior from displaying to loafing. Spring male turkey movements and habitat selection have been thought to be due to breeding behaviors (Watts 1968, Godwin et al. 1990, Hurst et al. 1991). Spring foraging areas were similar to displaying areas which made up about 57% of male behaviors during spring while loafing accounted for only 15% of the behavior. Summer foraging areas were similar to loafing areas which made up about 53% of male behaviors during summer, while displaying accounted for only 6%. This suggested that foraging areas may have been driven by proximity to areas suitable for displaying during spring and loafing during summer. The former is more probable than the latter as our logistic regression formula for loafing had a relatively low correct classification rate.

MANAGEMENT IMPLICATIONS

Habitat management for male Rio Grande wild turkeys in the northern extent of their native range should focus on regeneration of riparian areas for roosting. Cottonwoods were the most common tree species used for roosting, yet we found older trees to be in various stages of decline and observed little regeneration. Riparian restoration to promote increased seasonal flooding along with deferment from grazing in riparian areas may be necessary to ensure the longevity of these cottonwood belts. Planting black locusts to compensate for cottonwood decline may be a secondary method of ensuring roosting habitat.

It appeared that turkeys will readily use black locusts as roosts, even if cottonwoods are locally available. Black locust seedling and sapling survival is likely greater than that of cottonwoods as browsing by wildlife and cattle, drought, and competition for water with encroaching saltcedars all limit cottonwood regrowth (Harlow et al. 1991, Petrides and Petrides 1998). Beneficial aspects of black locusts other than their apparent use as turkey roosts include nitrogen fixing root systems, frequent use as an erosion control species (particularly in shelterbelts) (Harlow et al. 1991), and high yield of seeds that are eaten by many wildlife species (Petrides and Petrides 1998). Planting black locusts for future turkey roost trees may be a viable option if cottonwood abundance continues to decline.

A current trend in ranch management in the Rolling Plains of Texas is focusing on the removal of invasive brush species such as mesquite, redberry juniper (*Juniperus pinchotii*), and saltcedar. However, shrub cover is utilized by turkeys for summer loafing. Therefore, protection of some larger shrubs and small trees as potential loafing sites is important if managing for turkey habitat.

Openings, if small and well interspersed, are also important for displaying activities. Turkeys are tolerant of habitat management, such as moderate mechanical brush and timber control (Gore 1973, Bryant and Nish 1975, Scott and Boeker 1975, Quinton et al. 1980, Schemnitz et al. 1985), prescribed burning (Scott and Boeker 1975, Godwin et al. 1992, Palmer et al. 1996), and road development (Baker et al. 1980, Clark 1985). Therefore, openings should be created if absent or uncommon. Foraging seemed to take place in and around areas used for displaying and loafing. Therefore, supplemental foraging areas need not be created; however, the addition of small food plots may provide both foraging and displaying opportunities during spring (Gore 1973, Clark 1985).

ACKNOWLEDGMENTS

J. Bowman, E. Sobek, M. Gray, and D. Wester provided statistical assistance and logistical support. M. Butler, G. Hall, R. Houchin, and R. Huffman provided comments on the manuscript. We thank T. Barnett, B. Bedford, A. Braden, B. Buckley, J. Bullock, D. Butler, J. Davis, S. Dempsey, A. Denton, K. Derzapf, J. Doty, D. Drummond, J. Duke, C. Evans, D. Earl, D. Ferris, C. Frosch, R. Hanson, W. Hough, D. King, J. McJunkin, J. Milliken, B. Mills, J. Moon, G. Moreno, S. Pedersen, L. Robison, N. Sears, V. Spearman, K. Spears, A. Teaschner, A. Thomas, R. Ward, and N. Wilson for assistance with data collection. D. Cook, R. Cranford, D. Dvorak, T. Hinkle, G. Ibarra, D. Lucia, G. Miller, M. Miller, B. Rogers, B. Simpson, S. Sudkamp, and D. Wright, all of Texas Parks and Wildlife Department, and C. Swank, and M. Mitchener, of Kansas Department of Wildlife and Parks, assisted with turkey captures and other aspects of this study. We also thank the many private landowners who allowed us access to their properties. Texas Parks and Wildlife Department, Kansas Department of Wildlife and Parks (Federal Aid Grant W-R-54), the National Wild Turkey Federation, and the Texas State Chapter of the National Wild Turkey Federation funded this study. This is College of Agricultural Sciences and Natural Resources, Texas Tech University publication number T-9-1001.

LITERATURE CITED

Baker, B. W., S. L. Beasom, and N. J. Silvy. 1980. Turkey productivity and habitat use on south Texas rangelands. Proceedings of the National Wild Turkey Symposium 4:145–158.

Beasom, S. L. 1970. Turkey productivity in two vegetative communities in south Texas. Journal of Wildlife Management 34:166–175.

———, and D. Wilson. 1992. The Rio Grande turkey. Pages 306–330 *in* J. G. Dickson, editor. The wild turkey: biology and management. Stackpole Books, Mechanicsburg, Pennsylvania, USA.

Bryant, F. C., and D. Nish. 1975. Habitat use by Merriam's turkey in southwestern Utah. Proceedings of the National Wild Turkey Symposium 3:6–13.

Clark, L. G. 1985. Adjustment by transplanted wild turkeys to an Ohio farmland area. Proceedings of the National Wild Turkey Symposium 5:33–47.

Crockett, B. C. 1973. Quantitative evaluation of winter roost sites of the Rio Grande turkey in north-central Oklahoma. Pages 211–218 in G. C. Sanderson and H. C. Schultz, editors. Wild turkey management: current problems and programs. The Missouri Chapter of The Wildlife Society and University of Missouri Press, Columbia, Missouri, USA.

Davis, B. D. 1994. A funnel trap for Rio Grande turkey. Proceedings of the Annual Conference of the Southeastern Association of Fish and Wildlife Agencies 48:109–116.

Ecological Software Solutions. 1999. LOAS location of a signal. Ecological Software Solutions, Sacramento, California, USA.

Glazener, W. C., A. S. Jackson, and M. L. Cox. 1964. The Texas drop-net turkey trap. Journal of Wildlife Management 28:280–287.

Godwin, K. D., G. A. Hurst, B. D. Leopold, and R. L. Kelley. 1992. Habitat use of wild turkey gobblers on Tallahala Wildlife Management Area, Mississippi. Proceedings of the Annual Conference of the Southeastern Association of Fish and Wildlife Agencies 46:249–259.

———, W. E. Palmer, G. A. Hurst, and R. L. Kelley. 1990. Relationship of wild turkey gobbler movements and harvest rates to management area boundaries. Proceedings of the Annual Conference of the Southeastern Association of Fish and Wildlife Agencies 44:260–267.

Gore, H. G. 1973. Land-use practices and Rio Grande turkeys in Texas. Pages 253–262 in G. C. Sanderson and H. C. Schultz, editors. Wild turkey management: current problems and programs. The Missouri Chapter of The Wildlife Society and University of Missouri Press, Columbia, Missouri, USA.

Hagan, J. M., W. M. Vander Haegen, and P. S. McKinley. 1996. The early development of forest fragmentation effects on birds. Conservation Biology 10:188–202.

Harlow, W. M., E. S. Harrar, J. M. Hardin, and F. M. White. 1991. Textbook of dendrology. Seventh edition. McGraw-Hill, New York, New York, USA.

Haucke, H. H. 1975. Winter roost characteristics of the Rio Grande turkey in south Texas. Proceedings of the National Wild Turkey Symposium 3:164–169.

Holbrook, H. T., M. R. Vaughan, and P. T. Bromley. 1987. Wild turkey habitat preferences and recruitment in intensively managed Piedmont forests. Journal of Wildlife Management 51:182–187.

Hosmer, D. W., and S. Lemeshow. 1989. Applied logistic regression. Second edition. John Wiley and Sons, New York, New York, USA.

Hurst, G. A., D. R. Smith, J. D. Burk, and B. D. Leopold. 1991. Wild turkey gobbler habitat use and home range in loblolly pine plantations. Proceedings of the Annual Conference of the Southeastern Association of Fish and Wildlife Agencies 45:115–123.

Ielmini, M. R., A. S. Johnson, and P. E. Hale. 1992. Habitat and mortality relationships of wild turkey gobblers in the Georgia Piedmont. Proceedings of the Annual Conference of the Southeastern Association of Fish and Wildlife Agencies 46:128–137.

Johnson, D. H. 1980. The comparison of usage and availability measurements for evaluating resource preference. Ecology 61:65–71.

Kothmann, H. G., and G. W. Litton. 1975. Utilization of man-made roosts by turkey in west Texas. Proceedings of the National Wild Turkey Symposium 3:159–163.

Lambert, E. P., W. P. Smith, and R. D. Teitelbaum. 1990. Wild turkey use of dairy farm-timberland habitats in southeastern Louisiana. Proceedings of the National Wild Turkey Symposium 6:51–60.

Lenth, R. V. 1981. On finding the source of a signal. Technometrics 23:149–154.

Lewis, J. C. 1964. Populations of wild turkeys in relation to fields. Proceedings of the Annual Conference of the Southeastern Association of Fish and Wildlife Agencies 18:49–56.

Miller, D. A., G. A. Hurst, and B. D. Leopold. 1999. Habitat use of eastern wild turkeys in central Mississippi. Journal of Wildlife Management 63:210–222.

Neu, C. W., C. R. Byers, and J. M. Peek. 1974. A technique for analysis of utilization-availability data. Journal of Wildlife Management 38:541–545.

Nicholson, D. S., R. L. Lochmiller, M. D. Stewart, R. E. Masters, and D. M. Leslie, Jr. 2000. Risk factors associated with capture-related death in eastern wild turkey hens. Journal of Wildlife Diseases 36:308–315.

Otis, D. L., and G. C. White. 1999. Autocorrelation of location estimates and the analysis of radiotracking data. Journal of Wildlife Management 63:1039–1044.

Palmer, W. E., K. D. Godwin, G. A. Hurst, and D. A. Miller. 1996. Effects of prescribed burning on wild turkeys. Proceedings of the North American Wildlife and Natural Resources Conference 61:228–236.

Pelham, P. H., and J. G. Dickson. 1992. Physical Characteristics. Pages 32–45 in J. G. Dickson, editor. The wild turkey: biology and management. Stackpole Books, Mechanicsburg, Pennsylvania, USA.

Petrides, G. A., and O. Petrides. 1998. Western trees. Houghton Mifflin, New York, New York, USA.

Quinton, D. A., A. K. Montei, and J. T. Flinders. 1980. Brush control and Rio Grande turkeys in north-central Texas. Journal of Range Management 33:95–99.

Robel, R. J., J. N. Briggs, A. D. Dayton, and L. C. Hulbert. 1970. Relationships between visual obstruction measurements and weight of grassland vegetation. Journal of Range Management 23:295–297.

Samuel, M. D., and M. R. Fuller. 1994. Wildlife radiotelemetry. Pages 370–418 in T. A. Bookhout, editor. Research and management techniques for wildlife and habitats. Fifth edition. The Wildlife Society, Bethesda, Maryland, USA.

Schemnitz, S. D. 1994. Capturing and handling wild animals. Pages 106–124 in T. A. Bookhout, editor. Research and management techniques for wildlife and habitats. Fifth edition. The Wildlife Society, Bethesda, Maryland, USA.

———, D. L. Goerndt, and K. H. Jones. 1985. Habitat needs and management of Merriam's turkey in southcentral New Mexico. Proceedings of the National Wild Turkey Symposium 5:199–231.

Scott, V. E., and E. L. Boeker. 1975. Ecology of Merriam's wild turkey on the Fort Apache Indian Reservation. Proceedings of the National Wild Turkey Symposium 3:141–158.

Speake, D. W., T. E. Lynch, J. E. Fleming, G. A. Wright, and W. J. Hamrick. 1975. Habitat use and seasonal movements of wild turkeys in the southeast. Proceedings of the National Wild Turkey Symposium 3:122–130.

Spears, B. L., W. B. Ballard, M. C. Wallace, R. S. Phillips, D. P. Holdstock, J. H. Brunjes, R. Applegate, P. S. Gipson, M. S. Miller, and T. Barnett. 2002. Retention times of miniature radiotransmitters glued to wild turkey poults. Wildlife Society Bulletin 30:861–867.

Spraker, T. R., W. J. Adrian, and W. R. Lance. 1987. Capture myopathy in wild turkeys (Meleagris gallopavo) following trapping, handling and transportation in Colorado. Journal of Wildlife Diseases 23:447–453.

Thomas, J. W., C. Van Hoozer, and R. G. Marburger. 1966. Wintering concentrations and seasonal shifts in range in the Rio Grande turkey. Journal of Wildlife Management 30:34–49.

Wakeling, B. F., and T. D. Rogers. 1998. Summer resource selection and yearlong survival of male Merriam's turkeys in north-central Arizona, with associated implications from demographic modeling. Arizona Game and Fish Department, Research Branch Technical Report Number 28.

Watts, R. C. 1968. Rio Grande turkeys in the mating season.

Proceedings of the North American Wildlife and Natural Resources Conference 33:205–210.

Zar, J. H. 1999. Biostatistical analysis. Fourth edition. Prentice Hall, Upper Saddle River, New Jersey, USA.

Derrick P. Holdstock (pictured) received his Bachelor of Science degree in Environmental and Forest Biology from the State University of New York, College of Environmental Science and Forestry from Syracuse, a Master of Science degree in Secondary Science Education at Syracuse University, and a Master of Science degree in Wildlife Science from Texas Tech University. His research focused on the survival, movements, and habitat use of Rio Grande wild turkeys in the Texas Panhandle and southwestern Kansas. He currently works for Texas Parks and Wildlife Department where he recently served as the Black-tailed Prairie Dog Program Coordinator and currently serves as the Assistant Project Leader for the Panhandle Wildlife Management Areas. ***Mark Wallace*** is an Associate Professor in the Department of Natural Resources Management at Texas Tech University. He has a B.S. in forestry—wildlife science from the University of Washington, and an M.S. in wildlife ecology, and Ph.D. in wildlife and fisheries sciences from the University of Arizona. Mark's interests include integrating traditional and landscape scale habitat research, modeling plant-animal interactions and community responses to habitat changes. In particular, he is intent on finding new ways to involve our increasingly urban students into the profession and the problems facing wildlife management in the coming century.

Warren B. Ballard (pictured) is professor of wildlife sciences in the Department of Natural Resources Management at Texas Tech University. He received his B.S. in fish and wildlife management at New Mexico State University, his M.Sc. in environmental biology from Kansas State University, and his Ph.D. in wildlife science from the University of Arizona. His professional interests include predator-prey relationships and population dynamics of carnivores and ungulates. ***John H. Brunjes, IV*** received his Bachelor of Science degree in Biology from the University of North Carolina at Wilmington in and his Master of Science degree in Wildlife Ecology and Management from the University of Georgia. He recently completed his Doctor of Philosophy in Wildlife Science in the Department of Natural Resources Management at Texas Tech University. His doctoral research focused on the landscape ecology and population dynamics or Rio Grande wild turkeys. He is now a wildlife biologist with the Migratory Bird Program of Kentucky Department of Fish and Wildlife Resources. ***Richard S. Phillips*** is a doctoral candidate in Wildlife Science at Texas Tech University. His work is focused on the impacts of dispersal on population structure of Rio Grande wild turkeys in the Texas Panhandle. Richard received his bachelors degree in Biology and Human and Natural Ecology from Emory University and his masters degree from in Wildlife Science from Texas Tech. ***Brian Spears*** received his bachelors degree from the University of Arizona in Ecology and Evolutionary Biology and masters degree from Texas Tech University in Wildlife Science. Brian is a Resource Contaminants Specialist for the US Fish and Wildlife Service working on technical issues and research regarding wildlife toxicology in the Coeur d'Alene Basin, Idaho, as well as developing wetland restoration partnerships between federal agencies, the Coeur d'Alene Indian Tribe, and private land owners. He currently lives with his wife and daughter in Coeur d'Alene, Idaho. ***Steve DeMaso*** is the Upland Game Bird Program Leader for the Texas Parks and Wildlife Department in Austin, Texas. Prior to moving to Texas, he worked for the Oklahoma Department of Wildlife Conservation and served as the lead researcher on the nationally recognized Packsaddle Quail Research Project. Currently, Steve serves as Chairman of the Southeast Quail Study Group and a member of the National Wild Turkey Federation's Technical Committee. Steve is a member of the National and Texas Chapters of The Wildlife Society. Steve also served as the Program Chairman and Editor for the Proceedings of the Fifth National Quail Symposium. Steve was raised in southern Michigan and received his B.S. from Michigan State University, M.S. from Texas A&I University, and is currently pursuing a Ph.D. in the Wildlife and Fisheries Sciences Joint Program between Texas A&M University and Texas A&M–Kingsville. ***Jack D. Jernigan*** received his Bachelor of Science degree in Wildlife and Fisheries Science from Texas A&M University Texas, College of Agriculture Science. He currently works for Texas Parks and Wildlife Department where he recently served as Manager for Pat Mayse Wildlife Management Area within the Northeast Texas Ecosystem Project. ***Roger D. Applegate*** is the Small Game Coordinator for Tennessee Wildlife Resources Agency. He has a B.S. from Western Illinois University and an M.S. from the University of Illinois. He currently is serving as an Associate Editor for the Wildlife Society Bulletin. ***Philip S. (Phil) Gipson*** is leader of the Kansas Cooperative Fish and Wildlife Research Unit at Kansas State University. His principal duties include research with mammalian predators and responses of ecological systems to military training, advising graduate students, and teaching wildlife management courses. Phil received his M.S. and Ph.D. in zoology at the University of Arkansas, where he studied the dynamics of wildlife populations and predator ecology.

Wild Turkey Management:
Accomplishments, Strategies, and Opportunities
———— Grand Rapids, Michigan ————

SPATIAL DISTRIBUTION OF FEMALE RIO GRANDE WILD TURKEYS DURING THE REPRODUCTIVE SEASON

Jody N. Schaap[1,2]
2258 TAMU,
Department of Wildlife and Fisheries Sciences,
Texas A&M University,
College Station, TX 77843-2258, USA

Nova J. Silvy
2258 TAMU,
Department of Wildlife and Fisheries Sciences,
Texas A&M University,
College Station, TX 77843-2258, USA

Markus J. Peterson
2258 TAMU,
Department of Wildlife and Fisheries Sciences,
Texas A&M University,
College Station, TX 77843-2258, USA

Raymond Aguirre
Texas Parks and Wildlife Department,
Comfort, TX 78013, USA

Humberto L. Perotto-Baldivieso[3]
2126 TAMU, Department of Rangeland Ecology and Management,
Texas A&M University,
College Station, TX 77843-2126, USA

Abstract: Selection of suitable nesting habitat is commonly thought to be the catalyst for long-range movements of female Rio Grande wild turkeys (RGWT; *Meleagris gallopavo intermedia*) from their winter to reproductive ranges. However, distribution of female RGWTs across the landscape also could be an adaptation to avoid predation or competition for other resources. Thus, we hypothesized a priori that greater dispersion of female RGWTs across the landscape during the reproductive season should be linked to decreased population stability. We tested this hypothesis by comparing distances between reproductive-range centers (spatial distribution distance) for radio-marked female RGWTs on 2 study areas each in regions of declining and stable wild turkey abundance in the Edwards Plateau (EP) of Texas. During the first 2 years of the study, spatial distribution (km) in the stable region was significantly ($P < 0.001$) larger in the declining region. During the third year, one stable site had a larger ($P < 0.001$) spatial distribution than the declining sites as well as the other stable site. There was no significant ($P = 0.112$) difference between the 2 declining study sites. These data support the contention that the spatial distribution of suitable nesting sites may be as important to RGWT population stability as the mere presence of suitable nesting sites.

Proceedings of the National Wild Turkey Symposium 9:231–235

Key words: breeding, dispersal, landscape-scale, *Meleagris gallopavo intermedia*, movements, Rio Grande wild turkey, spatial distribution, Texas.

Movement of female RGWT from their winter to reproductive ranges comprises the largest portion of annual movement for RGWTs; these movements typically are larger than for other subspecies of wild turkeys (Thomas et al. 1966, Schmutz and Braun 1989, Keegan and Crawford 2001). Those studying RGWTs generally follow the lead of eastern wild turkey (*M. g. silvestris*) biologists in assuming that limited resources

induce larger ranges and longer distance movements

[1] Present address: SWCA Environmental Consultants, 7255 Langtry, Suite 300, Houston, TX 77040, USA.
[2] E-mail: JSchaap@SWCA.com
[3] Present address: Texas Agricultural Experiment Station, 1619 Garner Field Road, Uvalde, TX 78801, USA.

(Taylor 1949, Porter 1977, Exum et al. 1987, Godwin et al. 1996, Thogmartin 2001).

Badyaev et al. (1996) proposed that selection of suitable nesting habitat was the catalyst for long-distance movements of eastern wild turkeys. Numerous studies also have shown there is a tendency for female RGWTs to return to a given area to nest (Ellis and Lewis 1967, Hayden 1980, Keegan and Crawford 2001). Thus, it is possible that female RGWTs return to nesting areas because they found nesting habitat suitable previously. This fact alone, however, is inadequate to explain an individual hen's initial long-distance movement because, while suitable nesting habitat may be recognizable, it is not known what drives the initial long-distance movement or the nest-selection process. For these reasons, availability of suitable nesting sites cannot easily be quantified and subsequent preference/avoidance calculated. Consequently, while the hypothesis that long-distance movement to breeding areas is associated with selection of suitable nest sites seems plausible, it also is possible that this hypothesis is simply grounded in the expectation that because female RGWTs nest after long-distance movements, they must move a long distances to find a suitable nest site. This assumption has not been rigorously tested for wild turkeys, so it may have gained support primarily through repetition (Romesburg 1981).

If one makes the assumption that the search for suitable nesting habitat is indeed the catalyst for long-distance movements by female RGWTs, 2 logical conclusions can be drawn. One is that, in an area with abundant suitable nesting habitat, hens should not move as far as in areas with a lesser abundance of suitable nesting habitat. Another conclusion, assuming all other environmental variables are similar (e.g., habitat components, predation rates, etc.), is that if an area has more suitable nesting habitat, it should support a more stable population than regions with less suitable nesting habitat.

Data collected by Texas Parks and Wildlife Department (TPWD) biologists in cooperation with landowners and managers in the Edwards Plateau ecoregion of Texas (EP; Gould 1962) demonstrated that RGWT abundance has declined since the late 1970s in the southeastern portion of the plateau, particularly in Bandera, Kerr, and Real counties, while it remained relatively stable throughout the remainder of the EP (Figure 1). Moreover, D. A. Jones (Texas A&M University, unpublished data) demonstrated in 2001 that brood survival was significantly ($P = 0.019$) greater for a study site in the stable as compared to the declining region, while nest success was not different ($P = 0.807$).

Given this information, it follows that RGWT females in the region characterized by declining RGWT abundance should be expected to disperse a greater distance across the landscape in search of suitable nesting habitat than females in the region, which in turn should move shorter distances.

The objective of our study was to test the hypothesis that female RGWTs in the declining region disperse further during the breeding season than those in

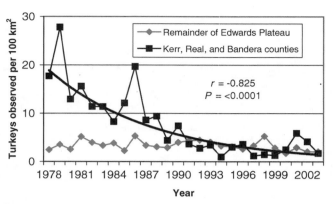

Fig. 1. Number of Rio Grande wild turkeys observed per 100 km² by Texas Parks and Wildlife Department biologists during August production surveys for Bandera, Kerr, and Real counties, Texas, and the remainder of the Edwards Plateau (EP), 1978–2004. Remainder of EP excludes counties with a mean value of <1 turkey observed per 100 km² (Taylor, Val Verde, Coke, Pecos, Kinney, Medina, Comal, Travis, Coleman, Burnet, Runnels, and Brewster counties).

the stable region. We also addressed the alternative hypothesis that RGWT hens not only seek out a nest site meeting their requirements, but also attempt to separate themselves somewhat from other breeding females, possibly as an adaptation to avoid nest predation and competition for brood resources. Specifically, we determined whether distances between reproductive-range centers for female RGWTs in the EP differed between study areas in regions of declining and stable wild turkey abundances and the direction of such differences.

STUDY AREAS

Our study areas were located in the southeastern portion of the EP in Kerr, Real, Bandera, and northern Medina counties, Texas (Figure 2). This portion of the EP is predominately classified as rangeland and is characterized by rocky limestone outcroppings, flat-to-rolling divides with rocky, but fertile soils, and an average annual precipitation of 38–89 cm (Oakes et al. 1960). Gould (1962) identified the climax vegetation community as tall and mid-size grasses including various species of bluestems (*Andropogon* spp.), gramas (*Bouteloua* spp.), and panicum (*Panicum* spp.). Mid and over-story vegetation included Ashe juniper (*Juniperus ashei*), live oak (*Quercus virginiana fusiformes*), and shinnery oak (*Q. pungens vaseyana*). In addition, important turkey roosting trees found along river bottoms included bald cypress (*Taxodium distichum*), cottonwood (*Populus deltoides*), and pecan (*Carya illnoinensis*) (Glazener 1967, Quinton et al. 1980, Reagan and Morgan 1980).

The stable and declining regions were delineated by Texas A&M University (TAMU) and TPWD personnel. Study sites were selected based on their function as winter roosting sites for RGWTs and willingness of landowners–managers to participate. We selected 2 study sites each from both the stable and declining regions (Figure 2). Stable site A (SA) was a

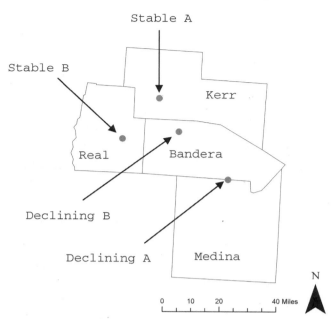

Fig. 2. Location of study sites for Rio Grande wild turkey project in the Edwards Plateau of Texas.

4,880-ha site located in the stable region in northern Kerr County, approximately 20.9 km west of Hunt, Texas. Stable site B (SB) was an 845-ha site located in Real County, approximately 9.4 km north of Leakey, Texas. Declining site A (DA) was a 4,922-ha site in the declining region of Bandera County, approximately 18.8 km west of Medina, Texas. Declining site B (DB) was a 6,100-ha site located in northern Medina County, approximately 17.0 km southwest of Bandera, Texas. Sites SA and DA were the same sites where D. A. Jones (Texas A&M University, unpublished data) conducted his study in 2001.

These study sites were in close proximity to each other (Figure 2), resulting in similar precipitation patterns, vegetation types, and topography. No vegetative differences at or near nest sites were detected between stable and declining sites (Randel 2003). The relative abundance of potential nest predators was similar on all study sites (Willsey 2003). No turkey hunting occurred on any of the study areas, but neighboring ranchers allowed turkey hunting during both the spring and fall hunting seasons (Randel 2003).

METHODS

We trapped RGWTs using modified walk-in traps (Davis 1994, Peterson et al. 2003) during winter when turkeys were gathered in flocks. During 2001, only 2 sites (1 stable and 1 declining; D. A. Jones, Texas A&M University, unpublished data) were trapped. Birds were equipped with battery-powered mortality-sensitive radio transmitters (64.2–95.0 g; Advanced Telemetry Systems, Isanti, Minnesota, USA) and aluminum leg bands unique to each individual. Each bird was aged, sexed, weighed, and had blood taken via jugular puncture for related disease and genetic studies. Radiomarked turkeys were located by homing and

triangulation from ≥3 fixed (Global Positioning System) telemetry stations (Silvy 1975, White and Garrott 1990) at random intervals and ≥3 times weekly (Swihart and Slade 1985). Locations and error polygons were estimated using LOAS software (Location of a Signal; Ecological Software Solutions, Sacramento, California, USA). Telemetry error was controlled by eliminating estimated locations with error ellipses >5 ha (Miller 1993) or estimated locations >4,827 m from the farthest telemetry station.

We focused on females during the reproductive season (16 Mar–15 Aug) to test our hypothesis. Sample size was the number of females with >10 locations for the season (Jenrich and Turner 1969, Hoffman 1991, Badyaev et al. 1996). Ranges were calculated in hectares as 95% kernels (Worton 1989), and the arithmetic mean center of each individual turkey range was found using ArcView Spatial Analyst software (Version 2.0, Environmental Systems Research Institute, Redlands, California, USA) and Animal Movement Extension (Hooge and Eichenlaub 1997).

The distances between the arithmetic centers of all radiomarked females in each population were calculated to find spatial distribution distances. Because spatial distribution distances were normally distributed, we analyzed data for each year and for each region (stable and declining) using t-tests (first year), and ANOVA and LSD tests (subsequent years) to determine if there were significant ($P < 0.05$) differences between regions and years.

RESULTS

During the first year of the study (2001), spatial distribution (km) in SA was significantly ($P < 0.001$) larger than in DA (Table 1). A similar pattern was found the second year (2002), with stable-site spatial distribution distances being roughly twice as large as those in the declining sites ($P < 0.001$, Table 1). There were no significant differences between sites in the same region, but both DA and DB had significantly ($P < 0.001$) smaller spatial distribution distances than did the stable sites. During the third year (2003), mean distribution distance in SA was again significantly ($P < 0.001$) larger than the declining sites, but also significantly ($P < 0.001$) larger than SB (Table 1). There was no significant ($P = 0.112$) differences in mean distribution distance between the 2 declining study areas or DA and SB in year 3 ($P = 0.373$), but DB was significantly ($P = 0.043$) larger than SB in that year.

DISCUSSION

The larger spatial distribution distances found in both study sites in the stable region during the first and second years, and in SA in the third year, do not support the hypothesis that female RGWTs in areas characterized by declining turkey abundance disperse further than those in areas not characterized by declining trends in abundance. Similarly, D. A. Jones (Texas A&M University, unpublished data) established that

Table 1.　Mean distance (km) between arithmetic mean centers of breeding ranges for female Rio Grande wild turkeys in 2 study areas in regions characterized by stable (SA and SB) and declining (DA and DB) turkey abundance in the Edwards Plateau, Texas, 16.

	Region											
	Declining						Stable					
	DA			DB			SA			SB		
Year	n	$\bar{x}$	SD	n	$\bar{x}$	SD	n	$\bar{x}$	SD	n	$\bar{x}$	SD
2001	21	3.85	2.04		NA		23	7.49	5.62		NA	
2002	26	3.40	2.07	9	4.11	2.65	28	8.47	4.68	10	8.01	6.55
2003	22	3.73	2.30	11	4.15	2.09	26	5.23	4.09	10	3.48	2.25

while nest success was not significantly ($P = 0.807$) different, brood rearing success was greater ($P < 0.019$) in SA than DA. Taken together, these data are consistent with the alternative hypothesis that, regardless of resource availability, there is some degree of spatial distribution required by female RGWTs during the reproductive season for there to be a stable population.

The smaller spatial arrangement of females during the reproductive season in SB appears counter to the findings in the first 2 years. It is important to note, however, the existence of a confounding factor associated with SB in the third year. This reproductive season was characterized by drought, with few females leaving hen flocks to even attempt nesting (Randel 2003).

The anomaly in year 3 for SB prompted a retrospective evaluation of the sample sizes for all study sites for that year. We calculated the percentage of females located sufficient times to create a breeding range. For DA, DB, and SA, the results were 95.65, 78.57, and 92.86%, respectively. For SB, only 34.48% of females had sufficient locations to create a breeding range. This lack of comparable sample sizes for SB in year 3 probably influenced the statistical analysis for that year.

Based on our results, we suggest that the driving force behind dispersion during the breeding season is not simply the availability of suitable nest sites (Badyaev et al. 1996). We contend that spatial distribution of females across the landscape during the reproductive season also may be an important component of population stability. Specifically, RGWT hens may not only seek out a nest site meeting their requirements, but also attempt to separate themselves from other breeding females, possibly as an adaptation to avoid nest or brood predation and/or avoid potential competition for brood resources.

Further research at a landscape level should be conducted to compare habitat characteristics between breeding ranges used by females in both regions characterized by stable and declining RGWT numbers. If these habitat characteristics are found similar, it would lend further support to the spacing hypothesis. Further, ranges that were unused by reproductive females could be analyzed for these same habitat characteristics, thereby creating a baseline habitat suitability index that could be used in future management practices.

MANAGEMENT IMPLICATIONS

Research to date suggests that RGWTs range much further than other subspecies of wild turkeys (Taylor 1949, Thomas et al. 1966, Porter 1977, Schmutz and Braun 1989, Keegan and Crawford 2001). For this reason, the traditional approach that directs management recommendations to individual landowners and managers may be misguided, at least for RGWTs. To render management recommendations relevant to landowner cooperatives operating at a landscape level, wildlife managers must better understand the habitat characteristics consistently associated with female RGWTs during the reproductive season. Currently, more accurate, reliable, and efficient geospatial analyses are available, enabling these habitat characteristics to be accurately analyzed at a landscape scale. Unoccupied areas not possessing these characteristics could be manipulated to create them, thereby increasing the area females could use during the reproductive season. The framework required to complete this task can be laid now by establishing landowner cooperatives where habitat management can be completed at a scale relevant to RGWTs.

LITERATURE CITED

Badyaev, A. V., W. J. Etges, and T. E. Martin. 1996. Ecological and behavioral correlates of variation in seasonal home ranges of wild turkeys. Journal of Wildlife Management 60: 154–164.

Davis, B. D. 1994. A funnel trap for Rio Grande turkeys. Proceedings of the Annual Conference of the Southeastern Association of Fish and Wildlife Agencies 48:109–116.

Ellis, J. E., and J. B. Lewis. 1967. Mobility and annual range of wild turkeys in Missouri. Journal of Wildlife Management 31:568–581.

Exum, J. H., J. A. McGlincy, D. W. Speake, J. L. Buckner, and F. M. Stanley. 1987. Ecology of the eastern wild turkey in an intensively managed pine forest in southern Alabama. Tall Timbers Research Station Bulletin 23.

Glazener, W. C. 1967. Management of the Rio Grande turkey. Pages 453–492 *in* O. H. Hewitt, editor. The wild turkey and its management. The Wildlife Society, Washington, D.C., USA.

Godwin, K. D., G. A. Hurst, and B. D. Leopold. 1996. Size and percent overlap of gobbler home ranges and core-use areas in central Mississippi. Proceedings of the National Wild Turkey Symposium 7:45–52.

Gould, F. W. 1962. Texas plants: a checklist and ecological summary. Texas Agricultural Experiment Station, College Station, Texas, USA.

Hayden, A. H. 1980. Dispersal and movements of wild turkeys in northern Pennsylvania. Transactions of the Northeastern Section of the Wildlife Society 37:258–265.

Hoffman, R. W. 1991. Spring movements, roosting activities, and home-range characteristics of male Merriam's wild turkey. Southwestern Naturalist 36:332–337.

Hooge, P. N., and B. Eichenlaub. 1997. Animal movement extension to ArcView. Version 1.1. Alaska Science Center—Biological Science Office, U.S. Geological Survey, Anchorage, Alaska, USA.

Jenrich, R. I., and F. B. Turner. 1969. Measurements of noncircular home range. Journal of Theoretical Biology 22:227–237.

Keegan, T. W., and J. A. Crawford. 2001. Seasonal habitat use and home ranges of Rio Grande turkeys in Oregon. Proceedings of the National Wild Turkey Symposium 8:109–116.

Miller, M. S. 1993. Rio Grande wild turkey hen survival and habitat selection in south central Kansas. Thesis, Texas Tech University, Lubbock, Texas, USA.

Oakes, H., C. L. Godfrey, and J. H. Barton. 1960. Land resource areas of Texas. Texas Agricultural Extension Service, College Station, Texas, USA.

Peterson, M. N., R. Aguirre, T. A. Lawyer, D. A. Jones, J. N. Schaap, M. J. Peterson, and N. J. Silvy. 2003. Animal welfare-based modification of the Rio Grande wild turkey funnel trap. Proceedings of the Annual Conference of the Southeastern Association of Fish and Wildlife Agencies 57:208–212.

Porter, W. F. 1977. Home range dynamics of wild turkeys in southeastern Iowa. Journal of Wildlife Management 41:434–437.

Quinton, D. A., A. K. Mantel, and J. T. Flinders. 1980. Brush control and Rio Grande turkey in north-central Texas. Journal of Range Management 332:95–99.

Randel, C. J., III. 2003. Influences of vegetation characteristics and invertebrate abundance on Rio Grande wild turkey populations, Edwards Plateau, Texas. Thesis, Texas A&M University, College Station, Texas, USA.

Reagan, J. M., and K. D. Morgan. 1980. Reproductive potential of Rio Grande turkey hens in the Edwards Plateau of Texas. Proceedings of the National Wild Turkey Symposium 3:136–144.

Romesburg, H. C. 1981. Wildlife science: gaining reliable knowledge. Journal of Wildlife Management 45:293–313.

Schmutz, J. A., and C. E. Braun. 1989. Reproductive performance of Rio Grande wild turkeys. Condor 91:675–680.

Silvy, N. J. 1975. Population density, movements, and habitat utilization of Key deer, *Odocoileus virginianus clavium*. Dissertation, Southern Illinois University, Carbondale, Illinois, USA.

Swihart, R. K., and N. A. Slade. 1985. Testing for independence of observations in animal movements. Ecology 66:1176–1184.

Taylor, W. P. 1949. Notes on the Rio Grande wild turkey in central Texas. Proceedings of the Oklahoma Academy of Science 32:110–114.

Thogmartin, W. E. 2001. Home-range size and habitat selection of female wild turkeys (*Meleagris gallopavo*) in Arkansas. American Midland Naturalist 145:247–260.

Thomas, J. W., C. Van Hoozer, and R. G. Marburger. 1966. Wintering concentrations and seasonal shifts in range in the Rio Grande turkey. Journal of Wildlife Management 30:34–49.

White, G. C., and R. A. Garrott. 1990. Analysis of wildlife radio-tracking data. Academic Press, San Diego, California, USA.

Willsey, B. J. 2003. Survival and mammalian predation of Rio Grande turkeys on the Edwards Plateau, Texas. Thesis, Texas A&M University, College Station, Texas, USA.

Worton, B. J. 1989. Kernel methods for estimating the utilization distribution in home range studies. Ecology 70:164–168.

Jody Schaap graduated from Texas A&M University in December 2000 with a B.S. in Wildlife and Fisheries Management with an emphasis in Wildlife Ecology. He earned his Master of Science from Texas A&M University in August of 2005. His research focused on population dynamics of Rio Grande wild turkeys in the Edwards Plateau of Texas. He currently works as an environmental specialist/wildlife biologist for SWCA Environmental Consultants in Houston, Texas. ***Nova J. Silvy*** is a Regents Professor with the Department of Wildlife and Fisheries Sciences at Texas A&M University. He received his B.S. and M.S. from Kansas State University and his Ph.D. from Southern Illinois University-Carbondale. Nova served as President of The Wildlife Society in 2000–2001 and received the Aldo Leopold Award in 2003. His research focus is upland game ecology. ***Markus J. Peterson*** is an Associate Professor in the Department of Wildlife and Fisheries Sciences at Texas A&M University. He received his B.S. from University of Idaho, D.V.M. from Washington State University, and M.S. and Ph.D. from Texas A&M University. Markus has a wide array of research interests ranging from ecology and management of terrestrial wildlife populations to the formation and implementation of environmental policy. ***Raymond Aguirre*** is a regulatory wildlife technician for the Texas Parks and Wildlife Department in the Edwards Plateau District. He works on a wide variety of research projects and programs associated with a diversity of wildlife species. He has worked with the Texas Parks and Wildlife Department for 29 years. ***Humberto L. Perotto-Baldivieso*** is an assistant professor in landscape ecology at the Texas Agricultural and Experiment Station in Uvalde, Texas. He received his B.S. from Universidad Mayor de San Simon (Bolivia), his M.S. and Ph.D. from Texas A&M University. His research is focused on multiple-scale analysis of ecological patterns and related processes. At the time of the research, Humberto was a graduate student in the Department of Rangeland Ecology and Management at Texas A&M University.

NESTING ECOLOGY OF RIO GRANDE WILD TURKEY IN THE EDWARDS PLATEAU OF TEXAS

Charles J. Randel[1,2]
Department of Wildlife and Fisheries Sciences,
Texas A&M University,
College Station, TX 77843, USA

Raymond Aguirre
Texas Parks and Wildlife Department,
Rt. 1 Box 76B-5,
Comfort, TX 78013, USA

Dustin A. Jones
Department of Wildlife and Fisheries Sciences,
Texas A&M University,
College Station, TX 77843, USA

Jody N. Schaap
Department of Wildlife and Fisheries Sciences,
Texas A&M University,
College Station, TX 77843, USA

Beau J. Willsey
Department of Wildlife and Fisheries Sciences,
Texas A&M University,
College Station, TX 77843, USA

Markus J. Peterson
Department of Wildlife and Fisheries Sciences,
Texas A&M University,
College Station, TX 77843, USA

Nova J. Silvy
Department of Wildlife and Fisheries Sciences,
Texas A&M University,
College Station, TX 77843, USA

Abstract: Rio Grande wild turkey (RGWT; *Meleagris gallopavo intermedia*) abundance in the southeastern portion of the Edwards Plateau (EP) of Texas has been declining for decades, whereas trends in abundance for the northwestern portion of the EP have remained stable. Our objective was to determine if nesting rates, nest success, and vegetation at nest sites differed between the 2 regions, and if differences existed, whether they could explain the decline of RGWT abundance in the southeastern EP. Vegetation variables, including height, percent coverage of bare ground, forbs, and grass as well as visual obstruction, litter depth, distance to nearest edge, tree and shrub density, and tree canopy area, were taken at nest sites and 10 m in each cardinal direction from the center of each nest to determine if these factors were associated with nest success and if they differed by region. There were no differences in nesting rates or nest success between stable and declining regions within a given year. Hens on both stable and declining regions selected nest sites with greater visual obstruction, litter depth, and litter cover than areas immediately surrounding nest sites. There were no differences detected when successful and unsuccessful nests were compared. Our results do not support the hypothesis that differences in nesting rates, nesting success, and nest-site vegetation account for the lower wild turkey abundance in the southeastern EP.

Proceedings of the National Wild Turkey Symposium 9:237–243
Key words: broods, Edwards Plateau, *Meleagris gallopavo intermedia,* nests, nesting habitat, nest rate, nest success, Rio Grande wild turkey, Texas.

Predation is the primary cause of nest failure for many avian species. This does not necessarily mean, however, that nest predation ultimately influences population dynamics. In an extensive review of the effects of predation on avian populations, Newton (1993) found little evidence to suggest predation influenced

[1] E-mail: cjrandel@sapphosenvironmental.com
[2] Present address: Sapphos Environmental, Inc., Pasadena, CA 91105, USA.

number of individuals in the breeding population for most avian species. He did, however, find that ground-nesting game birds were the exception to this rule. Similar results were found by Tapper et al. (1996) and Grant et al. (1999). Thus, nest concealment and cryptic coloring of incubating birds are critical to the nesting success for ground-nesting birds (Ricklefs 1969, Mankin and Warner 1992).

Several studies have addressed the influence of nesting rates (hens attempting nest/total marked hens) and nest success (number of nests hatching 1 poult/number of total nests laid) on eastern wild turkey (EWT; *M. g. silvestris*) populations. Nesting success was an important factor accounting for differences in EWT recruitment among years (Everett et al. 1980, Vander Haegen et al. 1988). Miller et al. (1998) found that low rates of nest initiation coupled with average nest success translated into lower recruitment of turkeys in central Mississippi. Similarly, nesting rate was a better predictor of EWT production indices (poults alive 4 weeks post hatch/females alive 1 Apr) in Virginia and West Virginia than was poult survival (Norman et al. 2001).

Some researchers have speculated that nest-site location is important to nest success and brood survival (≥1 poult surviving to 14 days). After hatching, poults begin feeding on solid foods as the yolk sac is absorbed, and need a diet much higher in protein during this period of rapid growth than do adults (Hurst 1992). Poults spend up to 24 hours in areas adjacent to the nest before moving to brood-rearing areas (Cook 1972). Lazarus and Porter (1985) suggested that wild turkeys might select nest sites based on proximity to brood-rearing habitat, with distances from the nest to brood-rearing sites decreasing as the breeding season progresses. For these reasons, vegetative characteristics near wild turkey nests probably not only influence nesting success, but also brood survival.

Less effort has been expended to determine how nesting rates and success might influence RGWT populations. Cook (1972) studied RGWTs in the EP of Texas from 1968–1971. Because nests were located through random searches (e.g., walking pastures, located by roadside maintenance crews, etc.), nesting rates could not be determined; 48.7% of 121 nests were successful. Reagan and Morgan (1980) found that 52.8% of 53 hens radio-tracked in the EP from 1973–1978 attempted to nest. Of the 53, 35.7% ($n = 19$) were successful. Nest-site characteristics were not reported by either Cook (1972) or Reagan and Morgan (1980). Other studies of RGWTs (Day et al. 1991, Keegan and Crawford 1999, Lehman et al. 2000) reported vegetation characteristics at nest sites. However, these 3 studies were outside of the historic range (South Dakota and Oregon) of RGWT and most of the vegetation characteristics associated with nests were region-specific plants.

Numbers of RGWTs began declining in the southeastern portion of the EP sometime between the studies by Cook (1972) and Reagan and Morgan (1980), while abundance in the northwestern EP remained stable (Figure 1). While Texas Parks and Wildlife De-

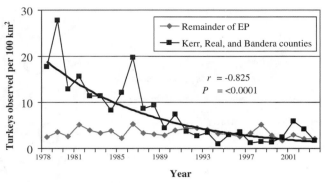

Fig. 1.   Number of Rio Grande wild turkeys observed per 100 km² by Texas Parks and Wildlife Department biologists during summer production surveys for Bandera, Kerr, and Real counties, Texas, and the remainder of the Edwards Plateau (EP), 1975–2003 (excludes counties in the EP with a mean value of <1 turkey observed per 100 km² including Taylor, Val Verde, Coke, Pecos, Kinney, Medina, Comal, Travis, Coleman, Burnet, Runnels, and Brewster counties).

partment (TPWD) personnel conducted production and harvest surveys for RGWTs within the EP, there have been few research studies conducted in this area since 1980. Insufficient long-term data exist to determine whether nesting rate, nest success, and/or vegetation at nest sites can account for declining RGWT numbers in the southeastern portion of the EP.

The objective of our study was to determine whether differences in vegetative characteristics at nest sites could account for differences in RGWT abundance trends between the northwestern (stable) and southeastern (declining) regions of the EP (Figure 1). Specifically, we determined if there were differences in: (1) nesting rates between regions of stable and declining RGWT abundances; (2) nest success between regions of stable and declining RGWT abundances; (3) vegetation characteristics at nest sites and areas surrounding the nest sites between regions of stable and declining RGWT abundances; and (4) vegetative characteristics at successful and unsuccessful nest-site locations.

STUDY AREA

Two study areas each were selected within both regions of declining and stable wild turkey abundance in the EP (Figure 2). Study areas within the stable region were located in Real and Kerr counties. The Kerr County study area (approximately 4,843 ha), was located northwest of Hunt and the Real County study area (approximately 984 ha) was north of Leakey, Texas. Both study areas within the declining region were located in Bandera County. One was northwest of Medina, and the other south of Bandera, Texas (approximately 8,858 and 2,910 ha, respectively). Livestock grazing occurred on all study areas except in Real County. The study areas near Bandera and Hunt were primarily calf-cow operations, with lease hunting as supplemental income. Turkey hunting did not occur on any study area, but surrounding ranches allowed tur-

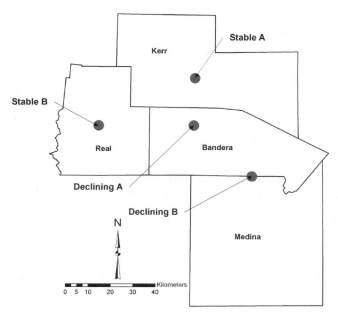

Fig. 2. Location of study sites for Rio Grande wild turkey project in the Edwards Plateau, Texas.

key hunting during both the fall and spring hunting seasons.

The EP had a precipitation range of 38.1–83.8 cm from west to east, respectively (Gould 1962). Typically, rainfall was most abundant in May, June, and September. Soils of the EP were generally shallow, ranging in textures from dark clayey and loamy to moderately alkaline silty-clay to non-calcareous clay and clay loams, on a limestone base (Natural Resources Conservation Service 1990a, 1990b, 1991a, 1991b).

Predominate climax grasses included switchgrass (*Panicum verigatum*), bluestems (*Andropogon* spp., *Bothriochloa* spp., and *Schizachyrium scoparium*), gramas (*Bouteloua* spp.), Indiangrass (*Sorghastrum natans*), wildrye (*Elymus* spp.), curly mesquite (*Hilaria belangeri*), and buffalograss (*Buchloe dacytloides*) (Gould 1962, Correll and Johnson 1970). Due to decreased fire frequency, there were dense stands of Ashe juniper (*Juniperus ashei*) interspaced with live oak (*Quercus fusiformis*) savanna (Fowler and Dunlap 1986, Miller et al. 1995).

METHODS

Trapping

We used pre-baited walk-in funnel traps (Davis 1994, Peterson et al. 2003) to capture RGWTs in the morning (0500–1100 hours) during winter, 2001–2003. We removed birds from traps using a golf club shaft modified with a shepherd's crook on the end before feeding activity decreased or intraspecific aggression occurred (typically within 30 min). After removal, we immediately placed each turkey into a darkened plywood box (1 × 1 × 0.5 m) constructed of marine grade (1.9-cm thick) plywood until it could be processed.

We physically inspected each turkey for external injuries and parasites. We collected specific information including body mass (kg), sex, and age (juvenile or adult). We fitted birds with a numbered aluminum leg band (supplied by TPWD with individual identification numbers and TPWD mailing address), and a mortality sensitive radio-transmitter (Advanced Telemetry Systems, Isanti, Minnesota, USA). We observed all released birds to determine if they ran or flew, and if individuals had to adjust to transmitters.

Monitoring

We monitored all RGWTs using standard radio-telemetric techniques (Samuel and Fuller 1996) until a transmitter failed, death, or study completion. We usually tracked each turkey 3 times per week from established georeferenced radio-telemetry receiving stations (referenced on topographical maps) on each of the 4 study areas. We determined daily locations by taking individual signals from ≥3 stations with signal directions (determined by compass) and plotting on a map to determine location polygons for each given bird.

When we located RGWT hens in the same area >3 times, we assumed nest initiation had occurred. If hens remained at the same location >6 times (2 weeks), we attempted to locate the nest. We located individual nest-site locations by walking in with a hand-held 3-element yagi antenna and tracking receiver (Advanced Telemetry Systems, Isanti, Minnesota, USA) and circling the hen. We monitored nesting hens >3 times per week with radio-telemetry to determine hatch date or cause of nest failure. We determined nest fate when hens were found off the nest >2 times in succession; we used this approach to decrease the chances of disturbing nesting hens that were feeding or watering at the time radio-telemetry locations were taken.

Nesting Rates and Success

We calculated nesting rates for juvenile females, adult females, and total females on both the stable and declining regions. We calculated nesting rate as the number of females reaching nest incubation divided by the number of females alive on 1 April of the given year (Cowardin et al. 1985). Nests were considered successful if 1 poult hatched from the nest and unsuccessful if predated or abandoned.

Vegetation Analyses

We used the point-center-quarter (PCQ) method (Cottam and Curtis 1956) to determine tree density, shrub density, and tree canopy coverage at nest locations. We took measurements distance to nearest tree (height >2 m), shrub (height <2 m), and edge (i.e., rivers, fences, and roads) in 4 quadrants centered at the nest site, and a we calculated a mean for each variable.

We used a 20 × 50 cm-quadrat frame (Daubenmire 1959), constructed of 1.3-cm diameter PVC pipe,

Table 1. Nesting rate of adult female (AF) and juvenile female (JF) Rio Grande wild turkeys on stable and declining regions in the Edwards Plateau of Texas, 2001–2003.

| | Stable | | | | | | Decline | | | | | |
| | AF | | JF | | Total | | AF | | JF | | Total | |
Year	%	n	%	n	%	n	%	n	%	n	%	n
2001	39.4	37	33.3	3	37.2*	40	64.0	26	0.0	2	57.1*	28
2002	37.5	12	18.2	21	31.4	33	50.0	17	16.7	8	43.8	25
2003	6.0	30	5.5	16	5.8*	46	15.9	28	0.0	3	14.3*	31
Total	23.4	79	12.5	40	20.8*	119	42.4	71	7.7	13	37.8*	84

* Significant difference between regions at $P < 0.05$.

Table 2. Vegetation characteristics of successful ($n = 23$) and unsuccessful ($n = 50$) Rio Grande wild turkey nest sites in the Edwards Plateau of Texas, 2001–2003.

| Characteristic | Successful | | Unsuccessful | |
	$\bar{x}$	SE	$\bar{x}$	SE
Percent cover	61.8	8.2	67.4	4.1
Cover height (m)	3.3	0.3	3.3	2.9
Robel pole (dm)	4.7	0.7	4.6	0.4
Vegetation height (cm)	13.1	5.7	9.4	2.0
Litter depth (cm)	4.4	0.7	4.3	0.3
Trees (trees/ha/100)	9.8	6.2	7.6	2.7
Canopy area (m²/10)	1.6	2.6	1.7	2.0
Edge (m)	51.4	8.3	51.6	3.7
Shrubs (shrubs/ha/10,000)	34.9	31.1	10.2	0.5

to determine percent bare ground, forbs, and grass at nest sites and 10 m from the nest site in the 4 cardinal directions. We determined percent cover using Daubenmire's (1959) 1–6 scale. Additional measurements taken within the quadrat frame were vegetation height and litter depth in the 4 corners of the quadrat frame. We averaged the measurements for data analysis.

We used a Robel range pole (Robel et al. 1970) to determine horizontal obstruction of vision (OV) at the center of the nest site and 10 m from this point in the 4 cardinal directions. We averaged measurements taken at the latter locations for data analysis.

Statistical Analysis

We analyzed vegetation characteristics by year, study region, and site (nest or 10 m away from nest) to determine if vegetation characteristics at nest sites differed from the immediate surrounding area. Because these data were non-normally distributed, we employed non-parametric approaches. We used chi-squared tests (Ott and Longnecker 2001) to determine differences between nesting rates and nesting success between study regions within and among years. We used a Kruskal-Wallis test (Ott and Longnecker 2001) to compare vegetation characteristics at nest sites within stable and declining regions among years (2001–2003). We used a Mann-Whitney U test (Ott and Longnecker 2001) to determine differences in vegetation characteristics at nest sites between stable and declining regions within years (i.e., stable 2001 vs. declining 2001), and between successful and unsuccessful nest sites. We used a Wilcoxson signed-rank test (Ott and Longnecker 2001) to determine if RGWT hens selected vegetation characteristics at nest sites that differed from those 10 m from the nest sites (surrounding area) of the same region. We used the Statistical Package for the Social Sciences statistical software (SPSS Version 11.0 2003) for all analyses.

RESULTS

We calculated nesting rates for each study region based on juvenile, adult, and all females for each of the 3 years (Table 1). Nesting rates were lower for juvenile than adult females in all years on both stable and declining regions. Overall nesting rates were highest in 2001 and lowest in 2003 (Table 1). The overall (all females; 2001–2003) nesting rate was 20.8% ($n =$

119) on stable regions and 37.8% ($n = 84$) on declining regions, with a nesting rate of 27.8% ($n = 205$) for all females (Table 1). Nesting rates were greater on the declining region in 2001 ($P = 0.017$), 2003 ($P = 0.025$), and combined (2001–2003; $P = 0.006$) than on the stable region. No statistical differences ($P = 0.061$) were detected in 2002 between stable and declining regions. The combined nesting rates for juvenile and adult females in both stable and declining regions during all years of the study were 20.8 ($n = 119$) and 37.8% ($n = 84$), respectively.

Nest success for 2001 was 47.1 and 55.6% for study areas in the stable ($n = 17$) and declining regions ($n = 18$), respectively. Nest success for 2002 was 16.7% and 15.4% on the stable ($n = 12$) and declining regions ($n = 13$), respectively. During the 2003 season, nest success was 40.0% and 25% on the stable ($n = 5$) and declining regions ($n = 8$), respectively. For the 3-year period, combined stable region nests ($n = 34$) had a success rate of 35.3%, while nests on the declining regions ($n = 39$) had a success rate of 35.9%. There was no statistical ($P = 0.355$) difference between these values.

We were unable to detect differences ($P > 0.681$) among vegetation characteristics at successful and unsuccessful nest sites (Table 2). Individual vegetation characteristics were compared between years. There was no difference found for any of the vegetation characteristics at nest sites in the stable region between years. However, when comparing data between years, within the declining region, vegetation at nest sites was shorter in 2002 ($P = 0.012$), taller in areas surrounding nest sites in 2003 ($P = 0.021$), and litter depth at nest sites was deeper in 2002 ($P = 0.022$; Table 3).

Rio Grande wild turkey hens on both stable and declining regions (subscripts s and d denote samples collected at study areas within stable and declining regions, respectively) selected nest sites with similar vegetation characteristics. However, vegetation at nest sites differed from that present 10 m away. Vegetation at nest sites had greater visual obstruction ($P_s < 0.001$, $P_d < 0.001$), shorter height ($P_s = 0.004$, $P_d < 0.001$), greater litter depth ($P_s < 0.001$, $P_d = 0.002$), less forb cover ($P_s = 0.001$, $P_d = 0.002$), less grass cover ($P_s = 0.002$, $P_d = 0.003$), greater litter cover ($P_s < 0.001$, $P_d < 0.001$), and less bare ground cover ($P_s < 0.001$,

Table 3. Mean (± SE) vegetation characteristics at nest sites (N) and surrounding areas (S) in regions of stable and declining Rio Grande wild turkey abundance in the Edwards Plateau of Texas, 2001–2003.

| | Stable | | | | | | Declining | | | | | |
| | 2001 | | 2002 | | 2003 | | 2001 | | 2002 | | 2003 | |
Characteristic	$\bar{x}$	SE	$\bar{x}$	SE	$\bar{x}$	SE	$\bar{x}$	SE	$\bar{x}$	SE	$\bar{x}$	SE
Percent cover	71.7	6.2	74.5	7.5	38.8	13.2	71.3	7.6	63.3	9.7	14.4	
Cover height (m)	0.5	0.1	0.3	0.0	2.1	1.8	3.6	3.3	0.3	0.0	0.2	0.1
Robel pole (dm)(N)	5.1	0.7	4.6	1.1	3.9	0.9	4.6	0.8	5.2	0.8	3.5	1.4
Robel pople (dm)(S)	1.6	0.3	2.2	0.7	1.9	0.4	1.7	0.3	2.6	0.8	2.1	0.2
Vegetation height (cm)(N)	12.2	4.4	10.6	7.0	10.6	4.5	9.0	5.5	7.6[a]	1.9	15.5	2.5
Vegetation height (cm)(S)	12.6	1.5	20.6	3.8	20.4	5.8	12.2	2.1	19.5	3.2	24.4[a]	6.3
Litter depth (cm)(N)	4.5	0.7	5.6	1.0	3.1	0.7	3.6	0.4	4.9[a]	0.9	3.8	0.3
Litter depth (cm)(S)	1.4	0.3	2.2	0.4	4.1	1.9	1.7	0.4	3.9	0.9	1.9	0.5
Trees (trees/ha/100)	2.2	1.0	5.3	2.6	23.1	42.4	9.3	5.9	1.8	0.6	16.9	34.8
Canopy area (m²/10)	4.2	1.0	4.4	1.3	12.8	14.5	3.9	0.6	5.4	0.9	9.8	7.1
Edge (m)	62.1[b]	6.4	51.1	11.2	46.2	7.9	47.6[b]	5.6	44.1	8.2	81.3	15.3
Shrubs (shrubs/ha/10,00)	17.7	13.8	60.7	51.9	17.0	35.4	10.7	5.6	29.3	16.8	84.7	15.6

[a] Significant difference between years within the declining region at $P < 0.05$.
[b] Significant difference between regions at $P < 0.05$.

$P_d < 0.001$) than was found 10 m away from nest sites (Table 4).

In 2001, the average distance of a nest site ($n = 35$) to the nearest edge was greater on the stable region than on the declining region ($P = 0.034$; Table 3). Due to low sample sizes during 2002 ($n = 25$) and 2003 ($n = 13$), data from nest sites were pooled for analysis. No statistical differences were detected for pooled 2002 and 2003 vegetation characteristics at nest sites between stable and declining regions.

DISCUSSION

Nesting Rates and Success

Turkeys from the declining region had nesting rates higher than hens on the stable region in all years, which was counter to our hypothesis of greater nesting rates on the stable region. Nesting rates observed on both the stable and declining regions of the EP were lower than those found by Reagan and Morgan (1980), the only other study conducted on the EP to determine nesting rates. They found that 31.3% ($n = 32$) of juvenile and 85.7% ($n = 21$) of adult hens initiated a nest (1973–1978). Overall nesting rates from both Reagan and Morgan (1980) and our study were lower than those found by Vangilder et al. (2000) for EWTs in Missouri (1989–1998; 74.4±5.6%, $n = 385$). Because nesting rates were higher on the declining region compared to the stable region during all years of the study (Table 1), it is unlikely that nesting rates alone accounted for declining turkey abundance in the southeastern EP.

Although observed nesting success in the EP was highest in 2001, overall nesting success for the 3-year study (stable = 35.3%; declining = 35.9%) was similar to that reported by Cook (1972) and Reagan and Morgan (1980) for RGWT in the EP. The highest nest success rate for the EP (48.8%) was reported by Cook (1972). Reagan and Morgan (1980) reported an overall nest success rate of 37.5%. Our results were less than those reported by Keegan and Crawford (1999) for

RGWT in Oregon (60.0%; $n = 96$), and Lehman et al. (2000) for RGWT in South Dakota (59.0%; $n = 64$), but were similar to results of Vangilder et al. (2000) for EWT in Missouri (36.2±6.1%; $n = 385$), and higher than values (combined initial and renesting) obtained by Miller et al. (1998) for EWTs in central Mississippi from 1984–1996 (27.9%; $n = 219$). Because nesting success in both stable and declining regions of the EP was similar to some previous reports from this region and for both RGWTs and EWTs elsewhere, it is unlikely that nesting success alone accounted for declining RGWT abundance in the southeastern EP.

Although Norman et al. (2001) reported that nesting rate was a better predictor of production in EWTs than nesting success, we found that neither nesting rate nor nesting success alone could account for declining RGWT abundance in the southeastern EP. For this reason, it appears that some other factor, such as differences in brood rearing success, might better explain lower recruitment into the reproductive population of the southeastern as opposed to the northwestern EP.

Table 4. Vegetation characteristics at all nest sites and surrounding areas in regions of declining and stable Rio Grande wild turkey abundance in the Edwards Plateau of Texas, 2001–2003.

| | Stable ($n = 34$) | | | | Declining ($n = 39$) | | | |
| | Nest | | Surrounding | | Nest | | Surrounding | |
Characteristic	$\bar{x}$	SE	$\bar{x}$	SE	$\bar{x}$	SE	$\bar{x}$	SE
Robel pole (dm)	4.7*	0.5	1.9*	0.3	4.7*	0.5	2.1*	0.3
Vegetation height (cm)	11.4*	3.1	16.9*	1.9	9.4*	2.9	15.5*	2.0
Litter depth (cm)	4.5*	0.5	2.4*	0.5	4.1*	0.4	2.5*	0.4
Forb cover (%)	1.0*	2.5	3.0*	0.5	1.0*	0.5	4.0*	1.0
Grass cover (%)	4.0*	1.0	21.0*	1.0	3.0*	1.0	11.0*	1.0
Litter cover (%)	67.5*	3.0	13.0*	1.0	67.5*	1.0	13.0*	1.0
Bare ground cover (%)	2.0*	1.0	11.0*	1.0	2.5*	0.5	11.0*	1.0

* Significant at $P < 0.05$.

Nest-Site Characteristics

Hens selected nest sites with greater visual obstruction, litter depth, and cover than areas immediately surrounding nest sites. Hens also appeared to avoid nesting in areas with a large percentage of grass, forbs, or bare ground as well as areas of tall vegetation on all study areas. This apparent avoidance might be related to selection of nest sites in areas with high OV, because these areas occurred within shrub dominated areas (e.g., shin oak [*Quercus havardii*] motts or dense Ashe juniper stands) having reduced amounts of grass, forbs, and bare ground. These data were similar for RGWT nests in both stable and declining regions. Our results are similar to those of other studies addressing nesting in western turkey populations. For example, nest plots of RGWT hens in northeastern Colorado were characterized by greater canopy cover, more shrubs, fewer grasses, and greater understory cover than random paired plots (Schmutz et al. 1989). Similarly, Lutz and Crawford (1987) found Merriam's wild turkey (*M. g. merriami*) hens in eastern Oregon selected nest sites with significantly higher shrub densities and OV. Thus, our findings are consistent with the notion that hens select nest sites with more dense vegetation than surrounding areas, apparently to increase concealment and to better see approaching predators (Day et al. 1991). Because hens selected nest sites with greater OV, future research should attempt to identify preferred substrates, other than "knee high" cedar (Ashe juniper; *Juniperus ashei*). With the dominance of cedar it would be helpful to understand if this is preferred or convenient nesting habitat. While cedar dominates much of the Texas Hill Country, the selection for immature "knee high" cedar by nesting RGWT provides inadequate camouflage for nest concealment from predators.

In summary, hens appeared to select certain vegetation characteristics for nest sites. Most authors studying vegetation at nests of western turkey populations have found that visual obstruction and litter depth at nest sites were correlated with nesting success (e.g., Lutz and Crawford 1987, Schmutz et al. 1989, Day et al. 1991). This was not the case in our study. We found that vegetation characteristics selected by hens appeared to remain consistent for both stable and declining regions, with the majority of differences found among years within the declining region. Because there were no differences in nest success between regions within years, but there were differences among years, it is likely that differences in nest success reflect the "boom-bust" reproductive success typical of many galliforms, rather than differences in vegetation at the nest site.

Although differences in vegetation at nest sites and the surrounding area were noted, few differences in the vegetation associated with nests were found between regions of stable and declining RGWT numbers in the EP. As reflected by similar nesting rates and nesting success for RGWT hens in both stable and declining regions of the EP, we cannot conclude that vegetative cover at nest sites was poorer in the declining region. Therefore, it is likely that the influence of other life-history stages of RGWTs, such as brood rearing, might account for the declining reproductive population in the southeastern EP.

MANAGEMENT IMPLICATIONS

Our results suggest there are reasons other than nesting vegetation, nesting rate, and nesting success that account for differing trends in RGWT numbers in the EP. Based on our results it appears the differing range management practices on each ranch were not a limiting factor to the survival and growth of turkey populations in the EP. Possible reasons for declining numbers such as brood survival, anthropogenic change/encroachment, and other potential limiting factors (i.e., invertebrate abundance and predator levels) are currently being investigated by Texas A&M University.

ACKNOWLEDGMENTS

This study was funded by the TPWD turkey stamp fund, the Texas Agricultural Experiment Station, and the Texas A&M University System. We thank the landowners and TPWD employees who assisted in the research, specifically the staff of the Kerr Wildlife Management Area for providing housing and other support. We also acknowledge field support by D. D. Marquardt (2002) and J. M. Hairston (2003).

LITERATURE CITED

Cook, R. L. 1972. A study of nesting turkeys in the Edwards plateau of Texas. Proceedings of the Annual Conference of the Southeastern Association Game and Fish Commissions 26:236–244.

Correll, D. S., and M. C. Johnson. 1970. Manual of the vascular plants of Texas. Volume 6. Texas Research Foundation, Renner, Texas, USA.

Cottam, G., and J. T. Curtis. 1956. The use of distance measures in phytosociological sampling. Ecology 37:451–460.

Cowardin, L. M., D. S. Gilmer, and C. W. Shaiffer. 1985. Mallard recruitment in the agricultural environment of North Dakota. Wildlife Monographs 92:1–37.

Daubenmire, R. F. 1959. A canopy-coverage of vegetational analysis. Northwest Science 33:43–64.

Davis, B. D. 1994. A funnel trap for Rio Grande turkey. Proceedings of the Annual Conference of the Southeastern Association of Game and Fish Agencies 48:109–116.

Day, K. S., L. D. Flake, and W. L. Tucker. 1991. Characteristics of wild turkey nest sites in a mixed-grass prairie-oak-woodland mosaic in the northern great plains, South Dakota. Canadian Journal of Zoology 69:2840–2845.

Everett, D. D., D. W. Speake, and W. K. Maddox. 1980. Natality and mortality of a north Alabama wild turkey population. Proceedings of the National Wild Turkey Symposium 4:117–126.

Fowler, N. L., and D. W. Dunlap. 1986. Grassland vegetation of the eastern Edwards Plateau. American Midland Naturalist 115:146–155.

Gould, F. W. 1962. Texas plants—a checklist and ecological summary. Texas Agricultural Experiment Station Bulletin, MS-585, College Station, Texas, USA.

Grant, M. C., C. Orsman, J. Easton, C. Lodge, M. Smith, G.

Thompson, S. Rodwell, and N. Moore. 1999. Breeding success and causes of breeding failure in curlew *Numenius arquata* in Northern Ireland. Journal of Applied Ecology 36:59–74.

Hurst, G. A. 1992. Foods and feeding. Pages 66–83 *in* J. G. Dickson, editor. Wild turkey biology and management. Stackpole Books, Mechanicsburg, Pennsylvania, USA.

Keegan, T. W., and J. A. Crawford. 1999. Reproduction and survival of Rio Grande turkeys in Oregon. Journal of Wildlife Management 63:204–210.

Lazarus, J. E., and W. F. Porter. 1985. Nest selection by wild turkeys in Minnesota. Proceedings of the National Wild Turkey Symposium 5:67–82.

Lehman, C. P., L. D. Flake, A. P. Leif, and R. D. Shields. 2000. Comparative survival and reproduction of sympatric Eastern and Rio Grande wild turkey females in Northeastern South Dakota. Proceedings of the National Wild Turkey Symposium 8:123–135.

Lutz, R. S., and J. A. Crawford. 1987. Reproductive success and nest habitat of Merriam's wild turkey in Oregon. Journal of Wildlife Management 51:783–787.

Mankin, P. C., and R. E. Warner. 1992. Vulnerability of ground nests to predation on an agricultural habitat island in east-central Illinois. American Midland Naturalist 128:281–291.

Miller, D. A., B. D. Leopold, and G. A. Hurst. 1998. Reproductive characteristics of a wild turkey population in central Mississippi. Journal of Wildlife Management 62:903–910.

Miller, R. E., J. M. ver Hoef, and N. L. Fowler. 1995. Spatial heterogeneity in eight Texas grasslands. Journal of Ecology 83:919–928.

Natural Resource Conservation Service. 1990*a*. Low stony hill. U.S. Department of Agriculture, Hondo, Texas, USA.

———. 1990*b*. Steep rocky. U.S. Department of Agriculture, San Angelo, Texas, USA.

———. 1991*a*. Loamy bottomland. U.S. Department of Agriculture, San Angelo, Texas, USA.

———. 1991*b*. Redland. U.S. Department of Agriculture, San Angelo, Texas, USA.

Newton, I. 1993. Predation and limitation of bird numbers. Current Ornithology 11:143–198.

Norman, G. W., J. C. Pack, C. I. Taylor, D. E. Steffen, and K. H. Pollock. 2001. Reproduction of eastern wild turkeys in Virginia and West Virginia. Journal of Wildlife Management 65:1–9.

Ott, R. L., and M. Longnecker. 2001. An introduction to statistical methods and data analysis. Fifth edition. Duxbury, Pacific Grove, California, USA.

Peterson, M. N., R. Aguirre, T. A. Lawyer, D. A. Jones, J. N. Schaap, M. J. Peterson, and N. J. Silvy. 2003. Animal welfare-based modification of the Rio Grande wild turkey funnel trap. Proceedings of the Annual Conference of the Southeastern Association of Fish and Wildlife Agencies 57:208–212.

Reagan, J. M., and K. D. Morgan. 1980. Reproductive potential of Rio Grande turkey hens in the Edwards Plateau of Texas. Proceedings of the National Wild Turkey Symposium 4:136–144.

Ricklefs, R. E. 1969. An analysis of nesting mortality in birds. Smithsonian Contributions to Zoology 9:1–48.

Robel, R. I., J. N. Briggs, A. D. Dayton, and L. C. Hulbert. 1970. Relationship between visual obstruction measurement and weight of grassland vegetation. Journal of Range Management 24:295–297.

Samuel, M. D., and M. R. Fuller. 1996. Wildlife radiotelemetry. Pages 370–418 *in* T. A. Bookhout, editor. Research and management techniques for wildlife and habitat. The Wildlife Society, Bethesda, Maryland, USA.

Schmutz, J. A., C. E. Braun, and W. F. Andelt. 1989. Nest habitat use of Rio Grande wild turkey. Wilson Bulletin 101:591–598.

Statistical Package for the Social Sciences, Inc. 2003. Version 11.0. Chicago, Illinois, USA.

Tapper, S. C., G. R. Potts, and M. H. Brockless. 1996. The effect of an experimental reduction in predation pressure on the breeding success and population density of grey partridges *Perdix perdix*. Journal of Applied Ecology 33:965–978.

Vander Haegen, W. M., W. E. Dodge, and M. W. Sayre. 1988. Factors affecting productivity in a northern wild turkey population. Journal of Wildlife Management 52:127–133.

Vangilder, L. D., M. H. Hubbard, and D. A. Hasenbeck. 2000. Reproductive ecology of eastern wild turkey females in the eastern Missouri Ozarks. Proceedings of the National Wild Turkey Symposium 8:53–59.

Charles J. Randel currently resides in California and works as a Wildlife Biologist for a small consulting firm. He received his B.S. from the University of Nebraska and his M.S. from Texas A&M University. His research interests are in upland game and wildlife. ***Raymond Aguirre*** is a regulatory wildlife technician for the Texas Parks and Wildlife Department in the Edwards Plateau District. He works on a wide variety of research projects and programs associated with a diversity of wildlife species. He has worked with the Texas Parks and Wildlife Department for 29 years. ***Dustin Jones*** is currently a staff ecologist with SWCA in Austin, Texas. He received his B.S. and M.S. from Texas A&M University in Wildlife and Fisheries Sciences. ***Jody Schaap*** graduated from Texas A&M University in December 2000 with a B.S. in Wildlife and Fisheries Management with an emphasis in Wildlife Ecology. He earned his M.S. from Texas A&M University in August of 2005. His research was on population dynamics of Rio Grande wild turkeys in the Edwards Plateau of Texas. He currently works as an environmental specialist/wildlife biologist for SWCA Environmental Consultants in Houston, Texas. ***Beau Willsey*** is currently working for the Florida Fish and Wildlife Conservation Commission. He received his B.S. from North Carolina State University and M.S. from Texas A&M University. ***Markus J. Peterson*** is an Associate Professor in the Department of Wildlife and Fisheries Sciences at Texas A&M University. He received his B.S. from University of Idaho, D.V.M. from Washington State University, and M.S. and Ph.D. from Texas A&M University. His research interests include the ecology and management of terrestrial vertebrate populations with an emphasis on factors influencing animal abundance, such as wildlife disease, predation, weather, habitat conditions, and human exploitation. He also has a keen interest in environmental policy formation and implementation. ***Nova J. Silvy*** is a Regents Professor with the Department of Wildlife and Fisheries Sciences at Texas A&M University. He received his B.S. and M.S. from Kansas State University and his Ph.D. from Southern Illinois University–Carbondale. Nova served as President of The Wildlife Society in 2000–2001 and received the Aldo Leopold Award in 2003. His research focus is upland game ecology.

Wild Turkey Management:
Accomplishments, Strategies, and Opportunities
———— Grand Rapids, Michigan ————

RIO GRANDE TURKEY NEST HABITAT SELECTION IN SOUTHWESTERN OREGON

Thomas W. Keegan[1,2]
Department of Fisheries and Wildlife,
Nash Hall 104, Oregon State University,
Corvallis, OR 97331, USA

John A. Crawford
Department of Fisheries and Wildlife,
Nash Hall 104, Oregon State University,
Corvallis, OR 97331, USA

Abstract: We studied nest habitat selection and characteristics of extralimital Rio Grande wild turkeys (*Meleagris gallopavo intermedia*) in southwestern Oregon to provide information about this important component of wild turkey ecology and to identify forest management strategies that will optimize preferred nesting habitat. Between March 1989 and July 1991 we identified 126 nest sites of 55 radiomarked females that were part of a recently introduced population (<10 years) and quantified habitat at 3 spatial scales in a hierarchical approach. Only regenerating mixed-conifer stands that were clearcut within 10 years were selected by nesting females (17% of observations, $P < 0.05$). Dense mature mixed conifer stands were used less than expected ($P < 0.05$) whereas meadows and dense sapling/pole conifer habitats were not used. Nest sites were characterized by dense horizontal screening (>93% from 0 to 30 cm above ground), understory vegetation >20 cm tall, and low shrubs covering 37 to 69% of nest sites. Land managers should implement forest management strategies that provide mosaics of relatively small regenerating stands, dense young conifer stands, and mixed hardwood/conifer woodland and savanna cover types with abundant understory vegetation including low shrubs to provide optimal nesting habitat for Rio Grande turkeys in the Oregon Cascade Range.

Proceedings of the National Wild Turkey Symposium 9:245–252

Key words: habitat management, *Meleagris gallopavo intermedia*, nest characteristics, nest habitat, Oregon, radiotelemetry, Rio Grande turkey.

Rio Grande turkeys were native to the southcentral Great Plains, but translocation programs resulted in population establishment in 9 western states (Wunz 1992). Variability in wild turkey movements and home ranges among geographic regions and subspecies was attributed primarily to differences in resource availability (Brown 1980). Although use of cover types indicated a high level of adaptability, turkeys were selective with respect to vegetative characteristics within cover types (Holbrook et al. 1987).

Habitat use by Rio Grande turkeys in their native range was studied extensively (e.g., Beasom 1970, Ransom et al. 1987), but few researchers described nest sites quantitatively. Habitat use by females has direct bearing on annual recruitment and maintenance of populations (Lindzey 1967) and annual recruitment is further influenced by nesting habitat because predation on females and nests may limit population growth (Ransom et al. 1987). Nest sites used by Mer-

riam's wild turkeys (*M. g. merriami*) were usually located in relatively dense understory cover or logging slash (Lutz and Crawford 1987), which provides a high level of concealment (Holbrook et al. 1987), and therefore influences predation on females and nests (Beasom 1970). Descriptions of nest sites used by extralimital Rio Grande turkeys were scarce, and we are unaware of any in the Pacific Northwest. Availability of nest habitat and proximity to habitats that provide other requirements (e.g., brood-rearing habitat and roosts) may influence turkey use of an area. Because of the importance of nesting and nest habitat to annual recruitment in wild turkey populations, we quantified nest site characteristics and investigated nesting habitat used by Rio Grande turkey females in southwestern

---

[1] Present address: Idaho Department of Fish and Game, P.O. Box 1336, Salmon, ID 83467.
[2] E-mail: tkeegan@idfg.idaho.gov

Oregon to establish a better understanding of these habitat needs and provide information for land management decisions in the Pacific Northwest.

STUDY AREA

The 675-km² study area was located in the upper South Umpqua River Basin, Douglas County, Oregon. The area was dissected with steep east-west ridges, and elevation ranged from 310 to 1,525 m. Annual rainfall from 1989 through 1991 was 6 cm below the long-term average of 102 cm (Douglas County Public Works Department, unpublished data). Temperatures during the study were within 2°C of regional 30-year mean temperatures (3°C in Jan and 19°C in Jul; National Oceanic and Atmospheric Administration 1989–1991).

Diverse edaphic and geologic conditions produced a heterogeneous association of plant cover types (Franklin and Dyrness 1973:130). Three nonforested (<10% tree cover) cover types accounted for 12% of the study area: recent clearcut (<10 yr since harvest), brushfield, and meadow-pasture. Mixed hardwood-conifer savannas (10–40% canopy cover) and woodlands (>40% canopy cover) contained >30% hardwoods, primarily Oregon white oak (*Quercus garryana*) and Pacific madrone (*Arbutus menziesii*), and occupied 9% of the area. Remaining cover types (79% of the area) were seral stages of mixed-conifer stands dominated by Douglas-fir (*Pseudotsuga menziesii*). In mixed-conifer stands, canopy closure >70% was considered dense, whereas closure <70% was classified as open. Mature, mixed-conifer stands contained overstory trees >50 cm dbh and >110 years old, and accounted for 53% of the area. Young conifer stands covered 14% of the area and were characterized by trees that were 23–50 cm dbh and 30–110 years old. Sapling-pole conifer stands (11% of the area) were <30 years old, with trees <23 cm dbh. Detailed habitat descriptions were provided by Keegan and Crawford (1997). The Oregon Department of Fish and Wildlife (ODFW) released 58 Rio Grande turkeys from Texas and Kansas on the study area in 1982 and 1983.

METHODS

Capture and Radio Telemetry

We used rocket nets to capture 36 adult and 40 yearling females during January 1989 and from December 1989 to February 1990. Individuals were equipped with 90–110-g radiotransmitters containing motion-sensitive switches; expected transmitter life was 1–3 years. All radiotagged turkeys included in analyses survived ≥2 weeks after release. At the beginning of the 1991 nesting season, 21 adult females were still carrying functional transmitters. Specific methods for capture and radiotelemetry were described by Keegan and Crawford (1999). We followed wild bird research guidelines of the American Ornithologists' Union (1988).

Habitat Quantification

We estimated characteristics of overstory (woody plants >3 m tall), midstory (woody plants >3 m tall, but beneath canopy), shrub (woody plants 1–3 m tall), and understory (woody and herbaceous plants <1 m tall) strata at randomly selected sites and nest sites with methods described by Keegan and Crawford (1997). Description of sites included quantification of the following physiographic and vegetative (overstory and midstory) variables: percent slope, aspect, elevation, percent non-forested habitat within 0.3 km, species composition, tree density, basal area, percent cover, and canopy height. Sampling of shrub and understory vegetation included quantification of tall shrub cover, understory height, understory groundcover, and horizontal screening. Nests served as focal points for sampling habitat characteristics and measurements were repeated at 2 points located 30 m from nests at random compass bearings. Measurements at nest sites typically occurred within 30 days of nest termination.

Statistical Analyses

Habitat availability was defined by a minimum convex polygon (Mohr 1947) for all annual female locations (except we excluded 2 females that moved >30 km to areas outside the South Umpqua River drainage) (Keegan and Crawford 2001). We employed Chi-square analysis to test the null hypothesis that cover types were used in proportion to availability (Neu et al. 1974, Byers et al. 1984). When null hypotheses were rejected, we calculated simultaneous confidence intervals to identify which cover types contributed to differences in use and whether use was greater or less than expected.

Initially, use and availability were analyzed within and between nest types (first or renest) and female age-classes (within constraints imposed by sample size). Preliminary analyses indicated that habitat use did not differ with nest type or female age (regardless of whether multiple nests for individual females were included). Consequently, observations were pooled accordingly for examination of habitat use.

Habitat characteristics were analyzed with a series of univariate and multivariate procedures. We combined nests (based on year, female age, or nest success) within each cover type because of small sample sizes. However, first nest attempts and renesting attempts were examined separately. We did not find differences in nest habitat characteristics based on success and pooled observations for further analyses. All data sets were examined to assess outliers, normality, multicolinearity, and homogeneity of variance-covariance matrices. We noted wide variance for several observations, but few distinct outliers were identified and inclusion of those observations did not alter results. When >2 variables were highly correlated ($r > 0.7$), we selected those variables with the greatest ecological relevance and/or management application that contributed to the most parsimonious description of relationships.

We used analysis of variance to help identify var-

Table 1. Habitats used by nesting Rio Grande turkey females (*n* = 59), Douglas County, Oregon, 1989–1991 (*n* = 133 nests).

Cover type	No. nests	Percent Available	Percent Used	Selection[a]	Nest success[b] (%)
Recent clearcut	23	6.1	17.3	+	62
Meadow-pasture	0	2.5	0	−	
Brushfield	3	3.8	2.3	0	33
Open, sapling-pole, mixed-conifer[c]	13	3.4	9.8	0	50
Dense, sapling-pole, mixed-conifer	0	8.0	0	−	
Dense, young, mixed-conifer	22	14.4	16.5	0	78
Dense, mature, mixed-conifer	36	48.9	27.1	−	69
Open, mature, mixed-conifer	6	4.3	4.5	0	40
Mixed hardwood-conifer woodland[d]	19	6.8	15.0	0	37
Mixed hardwood-conifer savanna	10	2.0	7.5	0	60

[a] 0 represents use in proportion to availability, + represents greater use than expected, and − represents less use than expected ($P \leq 0.05$).
[b] Infertile clutches incubated >30 days considered successful, excludes observer induced abandonment.
[c] In conifer cover types open defined as canopy closure <70%.
[d] Woodland defined as canopy closure ≥40%, savanna canopy closure was <40%.

iables that differed between groups (e.g., random sites and nests) and reduce the number of variables entered in multivariate procedures. Stepwise discriminant analysis (SAS 1989) was employed to select optimal sets of variables for separation of groups of observations. We then subjected the reduced variable sets selected in stepwise procedures to canonical analyses of discriminance to determine correlations between discriminating variables and canonical functions. Results of discriminant function analyses should be considered descriptive. Lack of compliance with inherent assumptions of these procedures can produce unpredictable distortion and alter resulting interpretations.

To better understand relationships of individual habitat characteristics important to wild turkeys, we compared several habitat variables with paired and unpaired *t*-tests. For example, we used paired *t*-tests to determine whether understory cover, understory vegetation height, or horizontal screening differed between nests sites (10-m diameter) and sites 30 m away from those same nests.

RESULTS

Habitat Use

Nests (*n* = 133) were located in 8 cover types (Table 1) and use of habitats by nesting females was disproportionate to availability (*P* < 0.05). Meadow-pasture and dense, sapling-pole, mixed conifer were unused, and dense, mature conifer was used less than expected (*P* < 0.05). Recent clearcut was the only cover type used more than expected (*P* < 0.05), whereas use of remaining cover types did not differ from availability. Although use of hardwood-conifer woodland and savanna stands (examined separately) did not exceed availability (*P* > 0.15), when hardwood-conifer stands were combined, use was greater than expected (*P* < 0.01).

Patterns of nest habitat use changed from year to year. During 1989, recent clearcut was most commonly used for nesting (30%); however, <13% of nests occurred in this cover type in subsequent years. Dense, mature conifer stands received the most use during 1990 (36%). Dense, young and mature conifer each

accounted for 26% of nests in 1991. Only use of recent clearcuts changed substantially when first nests and re-nests were examined separately (first nests were initiated in clearcuts in proportion to availability and re-nests were located in clearcuts more often than expected).

For all years combined, females were most successful in the 3 most frequently used cover types: dense, young conifer (78%), dense, mature conifer (69%), and recent clearcut (62%) (Table 1). Nests in brushfields, hardwood-conifer woodlands, and open, mature conifer were least likely to hatch.

Nest Site Characteristics

We completed habitat measurements at 126 nest sites during the study. Number of nests used for this analysis was less than the number included in habitat use analysis because we were unable to locate 7 nests before females left nests or died. First nest attempts (*n* = 87) accounted for 69% of all nests and we identified 39 renesting attempts (second, third, and fourth nests within a year).

As expected, overstory characteristics differed among cover types and between nest attempts (Tables 2 and 3). However, several understory variables at first nests were relatively consistent among cover types (Table 4). For example, understory vegetation height at first nests was >20 cm in all cover types. Further, horizontal screening from 0 to 30 cm was >93% and screening from 30 to 60 cm ranged from 73 to 100% at first nests regardless of cover type. High horizontal screening at nests apparently was provided by low shrubs. Low shrubs were the dominant understory component at first nest sites (37–69%) in all cover types whereas grass contributed least to ground cover estimates (2–11%). Forbs, bare ground, and woody debris each accounted for >11% of ground cover at first nests. Forbs and bare ground reached their highest coverage (25% and 22%) in dense, mature conifer. The greatest amounts of woody debris occurred in clearcuts (34%). The pattern of understory composition was similar for renesting attempts but differed in some cover types, particularly hardwood-conifer savanna (Table 5).

Table 2. Overstory and midstory habitat characteristics at Rio Grande turkey first nests (*n* = 87), Douglas County, Oregon, 1989–1991.

Variable[b]	Clearcut (n = 13) $\bar{x}$	SE	Shrub (n = 3) $\bar{x}$	SE	Open SPC[a] (n = 9) $\bar{x}$	SE	Dense YC (n = 17) $\bar{x}$	SE	Dense MC (n = 26) $\bar{x}$	SE	Open MC (n = 5) $\bar{x}$	SE	HCW (n = 9) $\bar{x}$	SE	HCS (n = 5) $\bar{x}$	SE
Overstory																
Ht (m)	15	3	7	2	15	1	27*	1	42	2	44	6	17	2	15	4
Dbh (cm)	22	7	12	4	23	1	34	1	66*	3	72	8	28	4	25	6
Basal area (m²/ha)	2	1	5	2	10	1	19	3	38	4	13	1	11	2	5	1
Density (no./ha)	82	33	262	166	258	66	181	26	111	12	35	10	213	40	170	90
Midstory																
Ht (m)	3	1	2	2	6	1	8	0.5	13	1	10	1	5	0.4	5	1
Dbh (cm)	4	1	4	4	8	1	11	1	15	1	13	1	8	1	6	2
Basal area (m²/ha)	0.2	0.1	1	1	2	0.5	4	1	11	2	3	1	2	0.4	1	0.2
Density (no./ha)	69	22	254	254	334	110	345	55	381	45	139	40	403	109	141	42
Canopy cover (%)	14	4	14	6	47	4	69	4	77	3	35	9	57	5	35	5
Elevation (m)	789	61	555	3	669	77	573	31	676	31	662	87	601	42	538	62
Slope (%)	15	2	20	8	16	2	14	2	18	2	17	4	15	3	16	3
Non-forest within 0.3 km (%)	25*	3	18	7	5	3	3	1	4	1	8	4	7	3	3	2

[a] SPC = sapling-pole conifer, YC = young conifer, MC = mature conifer, HCW = hardwood-conifer woodland, HCS = hardwood-conifer savanna.
[b] Variable means followed by an asterisk were selected by stepwise discriminant analysis when compared to randomly located sites within the same cover type.

We noted consistently greater values for understory height, low shrub cover, and horizontal screening (0–30 cm) in a comparison of nests sites to locations 30 m away from nests (*P* < 0.001). These differences were, with few exceptions, universal with respect to cover type and nest attempt. Although we did not quantify nest distribution with respect to travel lanes, we estimated that 60% of nests were <50 m from obvious travel lanes (e.g., animal or skid trail, or road).

During 3 years of study, 23 nests were located in recent clearcuts. Horizontal screening from 30 to 60 cm and amount of non-forested habitat within 0.3 km discriminated between first nest sites (*n* = 13) and randomly located sites. Differences between first nest sites and random sites accounted for 74% of canonical function variation (*P* < 0.001). Nest sites were characterized by more forested habitat within 0.3 km and more horizontal screening than at random sites. The same variables discriminated between renests and random sites in clearcuts (a situation unique to the clearcut cover type). Discrimination between renests and random sites was stronger than for first nests with 82% of canonical function variance was attributed to site differences (*P* < 0.001). Horizontal screening at all nests in clearcuts was approximately 55% greater than at random sites.

We located 21 nests in dense, young conifer stands and 4 variables allowed discrimination between first nests (*n* = 17) and random sites: understory vegetation height, overstory tree height, woody debris, and horizontal screening (60–90 cm). These variables accounted for 75% of canonical variation (*P* < 0.001). First nest sites had taller understory vegetation and overstory trees, more woody debris, and more horizontal screening from 60 to 90 cm than random sites.

Hardwood-conifer woodlands contained 15% of

Table 3. Overstory and midstory habitat characteristics at Rio Grande turkey renests (*n* = 39), Douglas County, Oregon, 1989–1991.

Variable[b]	Clearcut (n = 10) $\bar{x}$	SE	Open SPC[a] (n = 3) $\bar{x}$	SE	Dense YC (n = 4) $\bar{x}$	SE	Dense MC (n = 8) $\bar{x}$	SE	Open MC (n = 1) $\bar{x}$	SE	HCW (n = 10) $\bar{x}$	SE	HCS (n = 3) $\bar{x}$	SE
Overstory														
Ht (m)	13	3	18	0.4	32	5	46	4	42		18	1	12	1
Dbh (cm)	20	4	25	4	40	4	74	6	49		30	3	22	2
Basal area (m²/ha)	2	1	3	0.3	14	4	42	7	14		6	1	6	2
Density (no./ha)	36	8	54	12	111	25	99	21	68		86	13	107	28
Midstory														
Ht (m)	3	1	6	1	12	3	13	1	15		6*	0.4	5	0.2
Dbh (cm)	4	2	8	2	11	2	15	2	17		9	1	9	1
Basal area (m²/ha)	1	1	1	1	4	1	10	2	10		2	0.4	1	0.1
Density (no./ha)	128	59	185	44	319	68	425	69	327		256	42	104	43
Canopy cover (%)	14	7	29	8	64	11	84	3	48		46	5	38	5
Elevation (m)	709	44	645	24	693	122	742	77	495		622	38	636	7
Slope (%)	16	7	10	1	13	1	16	3	10		12	1	16	4
Non-forest within 0.3 km (%)	16*	3	0	0	1	1	5	2	0		6	1	11	5

[a] SPC = sapling-pole conifer, YC = young conifer, MC = mature conifer, HCW = hardwood-conifer woodland, HCS = hardwood-conifer savanna.
[b] Variable means followed by an asterisk were selected by stepwise discriminant analysis when compared to randomly located sites within the same cover type.

Table 4. Understory habitat characteristics at Rio Grande turkey first nests (n = 87), Douglas County, Oregon, 1989–1991.

Variable[b]	Clearcut (n = 13)		Shrub (n = 3)		Open SPC[a] (n = 9)		Dense YC (n = 17)		Dense MC (n = 26)		Open MC (n = 5)		HCW (n = 9)		HCS (n = 5)	
	$\bar{x}$	SE	$\bar{x}$	SE	$\bar{x}$	SE	$\bar{x}$	SE	$\bar{x}$	SE	$\bar{x}$	SE	$\bar{x}$	SE	$\bar{x}$	SE
Tall shrub cover (cm/10 m)	66	10	288	102	85	34	98	27	95	19	139	48	98	42	81	18
Horizontal screening (%)																
0–30 cm	96	2	100	0	97	2	94	3	93*	2	95*	3	93	3	96	3
30–60 cm	88*	3	100	0	91	4	82	4	74	5	83	9	77	7	90	6
60–90 cm	74	4	99	1	76	9	64*	6	53	5	71	11	62	9	79	9
90–120 cm	62	5	99	1	75	9	57	5	47	5	65	14	60	8	62	11
Understory ht (cm)	26	4	60	4	21	4	30*	4	30	3	40	9	35	5	37	4
Understory cover (%)																
Grass	11	5	5	3	4*	1	4	3	2	1	8	3	7	3	11	5
Forb	14	2	13	3	19	4	16	3	25	4	22	5	11	3	20	6
Bare	16	3	15	4	18	4	19	3	22	3	11	6	14	2	13	3
Low shrub	37	5	69	11	39	7	44	5	45	4	53	6	49*	7	47*	4
Debris[c]	34	5	11	1	30	6	26*	4	13*	2	16	6	28*	7	20	7

[a] SPC = sapling-pole conifer, YC = young conifer, MC = mature conifer, HCW = hardwood-conifer woodland, HCS = hardwood-conifer savanna.
[b] Variable means followed by an asterisk were selected by stepwise discriminant analysis when compared to randomly located sites within the same cover type.
[c] Dead and down woody material >1 cm diam.

all measured nest sites. Nine nests were first attempts and 10 were renesting attempts, making hardwood-conifer woodland the only cover type in which renesting attempts exceeded first attempts. Low shrub cover and woody debris discriminated between first attempts and random sites, accounting for 85% of variation in the canonical function ($P < 0.001$, but complicated by an unequal variance-covariance matrix). Low shrub and woody debris coverage at nests were 5 and 3.5 times greater than values at random sites in hardwood-conifer woodlands. Midstory tree height and horizontal screening from 0 to 30 cm discriminated between random locations and renests. Based on discriminant analysis, 76% of canonical function variance was attributable to differences between renesting locations and random sites ($P < 0.001$). Renests in hardwood-conifer woodlands were typified by increased horizontal screening and shorter midstory trees compared with random sites. Horizontal screening from 0 to 30 cm at

nests was 50% greater than at random sites (92% vs. 60%).

Relatively few females nested in hardwood-conifer savanna stands: 5 nests were first attempts and 3 were renesting attempts. A canonical function including shrub cover accounted for 85% of variation between first nest sites and random locations ($P < 0.001$). First nest sites were characterized by more low shrub cover than random locations. Understory vegetation height discriminated between random and renesting locations and 80% of canonical function variation was attributed to differences between locations ($P = 0.007$). Understory vegetation at random sites was shorter than at nest bowls.

Dense, mature conifer stands contained more nests ($n = 34$) than any other cover type, but canonical analysis provided weak discrimination (40–50%) between nests and random sites. Horizontal screening in the 0–30 cm stratum at first nests was 90% compared with

Table 5. Understory habitat characteristics at Rio Grande wild turkey renests (n = 39), Douglas County, Oregon, 1989–1991.

Variable[b]	Clearcut (n = 10)		Open SPC[a] (n = 3)		Dense YC (n = 4)		Dense MC (n = 8)		Open MC (n = 1)		HCW (n = 10)		HCS (n = 3)	
	$\bar{x}$	SE	$\bar{x}$	SE	$\bar{x}$	SE	$\bar{x}$	SE	$\bar{x}$	SE	$\bar{x}$	SE	$\bar{x}$	SE
Tall shrub cover (cm/10 m)	51	16	136	20	55	27	90	32	56		73	20	39	38
Horizontal screening (%)														
0–30 cm	96	2	100	0	88	6	93	3	93		92*	3	78	7
30–60 cm	91*	2	100	0.1	64	13	73	7	66		78	5	67	11
60–90 cm	71	6	92	4	48	13	53	6	43		57	6	48	15
90–120 cm	66	8	68	8	49	13	51	6	29		53	8	36	18
Understory ht (cm)	29	5	51*	2	19	1	31*	3	18		30	4	14*	1
Understory cover (%)														
Grass	11	6	11	5	1	0.3	3	1	41		16	5	15	8
Forb	16	4	43	4	13	2	21	4	2		14	2	5	1
Bare	16	2	11	1	19	1	16*	3	12		21	4	50	10
Low shrub	34	3	38	10	50*	5	50	6	48		44	6	22	10
Debris[c]	32	6	13	4	26	5	18	3	5		16	2	10	1

[a] SPC = sapling-pole conifer, YC = young conifer, MC = mature conifer, HCW = hardwood-conifer woodland, HCS = hardwood-conifer savanna.
[b] Variable means followed by an asterisk were selected by stepwise discriminant analysis when compared to randomly located sites within the same cover type.
[c] Dead and down woody material >1 cm diam.

72% at random locations and contributed most to discrimination. Understory vegetation at renesting locations was 2 times taller than at random sites and bare ground only occupied one-half as much area at renests. Similarly, discrimination between nest sites and random locations in open sapling/pole conifer was weak (50%), but grass cover at random sites was 3.5 times that observed at nests.

All nests were pooled for analysis of aspect use. Females nested at sites with easterly aspects (45°–135°) more often than expected ($P < 0.05$), used west and north aspects less than expected (225°–45°, $P < 0.05$), and nested on southerly aspects (135°–225°) in proportion to availability.

DISCUSSION

Nest Habitat Use

In contrast to Merriam's turkeys in the northern Cascades of Oregon (located 260 km north of the Douglas County study area; Lutz and Crawford 1987), Rio Grande turkey females nested in most available habitats and 6 of 10 cover types were used in proportion to availability. Merriam's turkey females used thinned sapling/pole conifer stands more than expected and >90% of successful nests were located in that cover type (Lutz and Crawford 1987). Only 2 of 133 Rio Grande turkey nests were located in comparable stands. Cover type use by nesting Merriam's turkeys in South Dakota was not different from availability (Rumble and Hodorff 1993), more closely resembling habitat selection patterns in our study area.

Although annual shifts in cover-type use were apparent in our study, there was no evidence of concurrent changes in nest success. Nest success was highest in the 3 most frequently used cover types, but success in all cover types was equal to or exceeded that reported in many other studies (e.g., Porter et al. 1983, Vangilder et al. 1987). High nest success in a variety of habitats led us to speculate that Rio Grande turkeys are relatively plastic with regard to nesting habitat at the cover type scale. Whereas Merriam's turkey nest location and success in northcentral Oregon seemed closely associated with a single stand condition (Lutz and Crawford 1987), Rio Grande turkey females were successful in a variety of cover types and stand conditions.

Contrary to observations of Day et al. (1991) and Schmutz et al. (1989), we did not observe a trend toward initiation of late season nests (particularly renesting attempts) in open habitats nor for females to renest in "opposite" habitats (e.g., first nest in woodland and second nest in grassland). Indeed, >50% of subsequent nest attempts (within and among years, $n = 43$) by Rio Grande turkey females were in the same cover types as previous nests. Differences between our findings and those of Day et al. (1991) and Schmutz et al. (1989) may have been a consequence of their renesting sample sizes (2 and 4). Conversely, temporal nest habitat use patterns may have reflected different plant phenology among areas. Both Day et al. (1991)

and Schmutz et al. (1989) indicated that grass-forb cover types provided increased nest cover as nest seasons progressed. In Oregon, however, cover in grass-forb associations decreased as dry conditions typically caused plant senescence by mid- to late nesting season and low shrubs provided most of the cover at nests.

Nest Site Characteristics

Although we noted considerable variation among cover types, a small number of understory variables were useful for characterizing nests. Height and density of understory vegetation (particularly low shrubs) were frequent contributors to discriminant functions. Grass and forb cover rarely were useful for discriminating between nest sites and random sites; the role of woody debris was difficult to discern.

Some structural characteristics that differentiated nests from random sites were similar for Rio Grande and Merriam's turkey females in Oregon (Lutz and Crawford 1987). Specifically, nests in both areas were characterized by relatively dense shrub cover and sparse grass and forb cover. Greater shrub cover at nest sites compared to surrounding areas and random sites also were noted by Day et al. (1991), Schmutz et al. (1989), and Rumble and Hodorff (1993). In most cover types, Rio Grande turkey females nested in relatively isolated patches (<20 m diam) of low shrubs, as indicated by shrub cover, horizontal screening, and vegetation height differentials for immediate nest sites compared to sites 30 m from nests. Rumble and Hodorff (1993) thought that nest site selection was based on areas <5 m in diameter and noted that vegetation at nests (23 cm) was taller than in surrounding areas. We noted a similar trend; average vegetation height at nests was 30 cm and decreased to <20 cm in surrounding areas. Patch size used for nesting in our study area was smaller than the ≥80 m noted by Badyaev (1995).

Horizontal screening values at nests frequently exceeded values from surrounding locations in both Oregon study areas. Screening at Merriam's turkey nests was attributed primarily to logging slash although low shrubs also contributed (Lutz and Crawford 1987), whereas low shrubs were the main source of screening at Rio Grande turkey nests and amounts of slash varied. Patterns of greater horizontal screening at Rio Grande turkey nests were consistent with observations of nests of other subspecies across the U.S. (Porter 1992, Badyaev 1995). Our estimates of horizontal cover below 60 cm were the same as those reported by Schmutz et al. (1989).

Our observation that nest success was largely unrelated to habitat characteristics agreed with results from South Dakota (Rumble and Hodorff 1993) and Colorado (Schmutz and Braun 1989) and may indicate that turkeys were not habitat-limited with respect to potential nest sites. Conversely, Badyaev (1995) found strong correlation between nest success and understory density in a wild turkey population where nest success was very low (17%). Badyaev therefore concluded nest predation was a strong influence on nest site selection and suitable nesting habitat was limited. Selection of nest sites with similar dense understory cover in our study area supports the idea that predation pressure likely influenced nest site selection to some degree, but relatively high nest success supports our contention that suitable nesting habitat was abundant.

Disproportionate use of easterly slopes for nesting may have reflected cover type distribution in southwestern Oregon where mixed hardwood-conifer stands and open sapling-pole conifer stands were more common on drier east and south facing slopes. Rumble and Hodorff (1993) did not observe disproportionate use of aspects in South Dakota.

MANAGEMENT IMPLICATIONS

Our research indicated that Rio Grande turkeys were better able to use a variety of cover types than Merriam's turkeys in the northern Oregon Cascades. High nest success in several cover types and use of most available cover types for nesting indicated that Rio Grande turkeys would persist under a variety of habitat conditions, including some apparently not conducive to Merriam's turkey populations. We speculate that, in a relative sense, Rio Grande turkeys are generalists compared with Merriam's turkeys and, therefore, recommend that managers consider available habitat and likely future land management scenarios before selecting a subspecies for translocation. Rio Grande turkeys will likely fare better than Merriam's turkeys in relatively disturbed environments in the Oregon Cascades. Esthetic and economic returns of translocation programs will be enhanced by selection of subspecies best suited to regional habitat conditions.

Although Rio Grande turkeys used a variety of cover types successfully, several management practices would enhance nest habitats. The clearcutting method of regenerating mixed-conifer stands provided nest habitat for approximately 10 years after timber harvest. Because nests were located at sites with <30% nonforested habitat within 0.3 km, relatively small clearcuts will likely receive more use than larger clearcuts. When regenerating stands developed into the dense (>70% canopy cover) sapling-pole stage they were no longer used for nesting. When compatible with other objectives, patch thinning in dense, sapling-pole stands and prescribed burning to reduce dense shrub cover in brushfields should improve stands for nesting (e.g., provide 35–55% low shrub cover). Females resumed nesting in mixed-conifer stands when stand age reached 30 years (>23 cm dbh) and continued through stand maturity. In contrast to Merriam's turkey management, moderate slash treatment may be desirable in Oregon's Rio Grande turkey range; patches of low shrub cover (<20 m diam) should be maintained for nesting cover. Conservation of mixed hardwood/conifer habitats (particularly oak woodland and savanna complexes) would maintain habitat diversity and should benefit wild turkeys and other wildlife species.

Because dense mature conifer was used less than expected for nesting, roosting (T. Keegan and J. Crawford, Oregon State University, unpublished data), brood rearing (Keegan and Crawford 1997), and year-round use (Keegan and Crawford 2001), Rio Grande turkeys will likely persist in landscapes dominated by relatively young forests (30–110 years old and 23–50 cm dbh). However, dense mature conifer was frequently used for most components of turkey life-history (ranked first or second for nest, brood, roost, and summer habitat use; Keegan and Crawford 1997, 2001, unpublished data).

Therefore, we do not recommend reducing average stand age or extensive harvest of mature timber as a means of increasing Rio Grande turkey numbers. Further, the variety of cover types used by wild turkeys in our study area suggests timber management goals should include interspersion of cover types and age classes within cover types to meet habitat needs of wild turkeys. Such interspersion stands in contrast to current landscapes composed of large expanses of even-aged conifer found in some parts of the Pacific Northwest.

ACKNOWLEDGMENTS

Research was supported by the U.S. Forest Service LaGrande Forestry and Range Science Laboratory, the National Wild Turkey Federation, Oregon State University, Idaho Department of Fish and Game, and ODFW. We thank S. R. Denney, R. A. Zalunardo, and other personnel of ODFW and the Umpqua National Forest for their assistance. We appreciate field work of P. I. Burns, N. E. Golly, and B. C. Quick. B. E. Coblentz and J. P. Loegering reviewed drafts of the manuscript. This is Technical Paper 10859 of the Oregon Agricultural Experiment Station.

LITERATURE CITED

American Ornithologists' Union. 1988. Report of committee on use of wild birds in research. Auk 105(1, Supplement).

Badyaev, A. V. 1995. Nesting habitat and nesting success of eastern wild turkeys in the Arkansas Ozark Highlands. Condor 97:221–232.

Beasom, S. L. 1970. Turkey productivity in two vegetative communities in South Texas. Journal of Wildlife Management 34:166–175.

Brown, E. K. 1980. Home range and movements of wild turkeys—a review. Proceedings of the National Wild Turkey Symposium 4:251–261.

Byers, C. R., R. K. Steinhorst, and P. R. Kraussman. 1984. Clarification of a technique for analysis of utilization-availability data. Journal of Wildlife Management 48:1050–1053.

Day, K. S., L. D. Flake, and W. L. Tucker. 1991. Characteristics of wild turkey nest sites in a mixed-grass prairie-oak-woodland mosaic in the northern great plains, South Dakota. Canadian Journal of Zoology 69:2840–2845.

Franklin, J. F., and C. T. Dyrness. 1973. Natural vegetation of Oregon and Washington. Pacific Northwest Forest and Range Experiment Station. U.S. Forest Service General Technical Report PNW-8.

Holbrook, T. H., M. R. Vaughan, and P. T. Bromley. 1987. Wild turkey habitat preferences and recruitment in intensively managed Piedmont forests. Journal of Wildlife Management 51:182–187.

Keegan, T. W., and J. A. Crawford. 1997. Brood-rearing habitat use by Rio Grande wild turkeys in Oregon. Great Basin Naturalist 57:220–230.

————, and ————. 1999. Reproduction and survival of Rio Grande turkeys in Oregon. Journal of Wildlife Management 63:204–210.

————, and ————. 2001. Seasonal habitat use and home ranges of Rio Grande turkeys in Oregon. Proceedings of the National Wild Turkey Symposium 8:109–116.

Lindzey, J. S. 1967. A look to the future. Pages 549–551 *in* O. H. Hewitt, editor. The wild turkey and its management. The Wildlife Society, Washington, D.C., USA.

Lutz, R. S., and J. A. Crawford. 1987. Reproductive success and nesting habitat of Merriam's wild turkeys in Oregon. Journal of Wildlife Management 51:783–787.

Mohr, C. O. 1947. Table of equivalent populations of North American small mammals. American Midland Naturalist 37:223–249.

National Oceanic and Atmospheric Administration. 1989–1991. Climatological data, Oregon, annual summary. National Climatic Data Center, Asheville, North Carolina, USA.

Neu, C. W., C. R. Byers, and J. M. Peek. 1974. A technique for analysis of utilization-availability data. Journal of Wildlife Management 38:541–545.

Porter, W. F. 1992. Habitat requirements. Pages 202–213 *in* J. G. Dickson, editor. The wild turkey: biology and management. Stackpole Books, Harrisburg, Pennsylvania, USA.

————, G. C. Nelson, and K. Mattson. 1983. Effects of winter conditions on reproduction in a northern wild turkey population. Journal of Wildlife Management 47:281–290.

Ransom, D., Jr., O. J. Rongstad, and D. H. Rusch. 1987. Nesting ecology of Rio Grande turkeys. Journal of Wildlife Management 51:435–439.

Rumble, M. A., and R. A. Hodorff. 1993. Nesting ecology of Merriam's turkeys in the Black Hills, South Dakota. Journal of Wildlife Management 57:789–801.

SAS Institute. 1989. SAS/STAT User's Guide. Version 6. Fourth edition. Volume 1. SAS Institute, Cary, North Carolina, USA.

Schmutz, J. A., and C. E. Braun. 1989. Reproductive performance of Rio Grande wild turkeys. Condor 91:675–680.

————, ————, and W. F. Andelt. 1989. Nest habitat use of Rio Grande wild turkeys. Wilson Bulletin 101:591–598.

Vangilder, L. D., E. W. Kurzejeski, V. L. Kimmel-Truitt, and J. B. Lewis. 1987. Reproductive parameters of wild turkey hens in north Missouri. Journal of Wildlife Management 51:535–540.

Wunz, G. A. 1992. Wild turkeys outside their historic range. Pages 361–384 *in* J. G. Dickson, editor. The wild turkey: biology and management. Stackpole Books, Harrisburg, Pennsylvania, USA.

Thomas W. (Tom) Keegan (pictured) is the Salmon Region Wildlife Manager for the Idaho Department of Fish and Game. He received his B.S. in natural resources from Cornell University, M.S. in wildlife from Louisiana State University, and Ph.D. in wildlife science from Oregon State University. His current professional interests center around upland and big game management in the western U.S. ***John A. Crawford*** (not pictured) is a professor emeritus of wildlife ecology in the Department of Fisheries and Wildlife at Oregon State University. His primary interest is the ecology and management of upland gamebirds.

Wild Turkey Management:
Accomplishments, Strategies, and Opportunities
———— Grand Rapids, Michigan ————

ROOST HABITAT SELECTION BY RIO GRANDE TURKEYS IN OREGON

Thomas W. Keegan[1,2]
Department of Fisheries and Wildlife,
Nash Hall 104, Oregon State University,
Corvallis, OR 97331, USA

John A. Crawford
Department of Fisheries and Wildlife,
Nash Hall 104, Oregon State University,
Corvallis, OR 97331, USA

Abstract: We employed a 3-level hierarchical approach to study roosting habitat of Rio Grande wild turkeys (*Meleagris gallopavo intermedia*) to increase understanding of habitat needs and provide information for managing forested landscapes in the Pacific Northwest. Roost locations ($n = 375$) were obtained year-round (Feb 1989–Jan 1991) from 76 radiomarked females that were part of a recently introduced population (<10 years) in southwestern Oregon. At the largest scale, adult females selected dense, young, mixed-conifer stands and hardwood-conifer woodlands ($P < 0.05$); 58% of roosts occurred in these cover types. Females with broods also selected hardwood-conifer woodlands ($P < 0.05$), which accounted for 35% of their roost locations. At the forest stand scale, turkeys typically roosted in trees as large as or larger than others available in the stand. The finest scale was individual roost trees, which averaged 106 years old, 50 cm diameter at breast height (dbh), and 33 m tall. Douglas-fir (*Pseudotsuga menziesii*) was the only species used more often than expected for roosting ($P < 0.05$), comprising 77% of roost trees. To accommodate wild turkey roost habitat needs, timber management plans must include an appropriate juxtaposition and balance of age classes of mixed-conifer stands over time and in relation to other habitats used by wild turkeys.

Proceedings of the National Wild Turkey Symposium 9:253–259

Key words: Meleagris gallopavo intermedia, Oregon, radiotelemetry, Rio Grande wild turkey, roost habitat, roost trees, timber management.

Rio Grande turkeys were native to the southcentral Great Plains, but translocation programs resulted in establishment of populations in 9 western states (Wunz 1992). Wild turkeys require roost sites that provide protection from predators and adverse weather conditions (Crockett 1973). Roost tree availability and proximity to habitats that provide other requirements (e.g., food and cover) influence wild turkey use of an area. Rio Grande turkeys in Texas possibly were limited by distribution of roost sites (Glazener 1967) and birds frequently roosted on man-made structures. Boeker and Scott (1969) conjectured that availability of suitable roosts may limit the range of Merriam's wild turkeys (*M. g. merriami*). Further, fidelity to roost sites (seasonal or annual) plays an important role in wild turkey ecology and management because changes to traditionally used sites can alter turkey use of an area.

Wild turkeys often roost in the largest trees within a stand (Crockett 1973, Mackey 1984), but species of trees selected for roosting differed widely among geographic regions and subspecies. Crockett (1973) in-

vestigated roost site characteristics of a native Rio Grande turkey population and several researchers examined roosts used by extralimital Merriam's turkey populations in western states (Mackey 1984, Lutz and Crawford 1987, Rumble 1992). However, we are not aware of any descriptions of roost sites used by Rio Grande turkeys outside of their native range, and particularly in the Pacific Northwest.

Because of overall habitat differences and potential differences among subspecies (Vangilder 1992), we questioned the applicability of existing information and management recommendations to the Rio Grande subspecies in forest-dominated habitats in the Pacific Northwest. We focused our research on females because of implications for annual recruitment and population trend. Our objectives were to 1) increase understanding of roost habitat use, 2) compare roost hab-

[1] Present address: Idaho Department of Fish and Game, P.O. Box 1336, Salmon, ID 83467.
[2] E-mail: tkeegan@idfg.idaho.gov

itat use by Rio Grande turkeys in the southern Oregon Cascades to that of Merriam's turkeys in the northern Oregon Cascades, and 3) provide information for managing forested landscapes in the Pacific Northwest to accommodate wild turkey populations.

STUDY AREA

The 675-km^2 study area was located in the upper South Umpqua River Basin, Douglas County, Oregon. The area was dissected with steep east-west ridges, and elevation ranged from 310 to 1,525 m. Annual rainfall from 1989 through 1991 was 6 cm below the long-term average of 102 cm (Douglas County Public Works Department, unpublished data). Temperatures during the study were within 2°C of regional 30-year mean temperatures (3°C in Jan and 19°C in Jul; National Oceanic and Atmospheric Administration 1989–1991). Diverse edaphic and geologic conditions produced a heterogeneous association of plant cover types (Franklin and Dyrness 1973:130). Three nonforested (<10% tree cover) cover types accounted for 12% of the study area: recent clearcut (<10 yr since harvest), brushfield, and meadow-pasture. Mixed hardwood-conifer savannas (10–40% canopy cover) and woodlands (>40% canopy cover) contained ≥30% hardwoods, primarily Oregon white oak (*Quercus garryana*) and Pacific madrone (*Arbutus menziesii*), and occupied 9% of the area. Remaining cover types (79% of the area) were seral stages of mixed-conifer stands dominated by Douglas-fir. In mixed-conifer stands, canopy closure ≥70% was considered dense, whereas closure <70% was classified as open. Mature mixed-conifer stands contained overstory trees ≥50 cm dbh and >110 years old, and accounted for 53% of the area. Young conifer stands covered 14% of the area and were characterized by trees that were 23–50 cm dbh and 30–110 years old. Sapling-pole conifer stands (11% of the area) were <30 years old, with trees <23 cm dbh. Detailed habitat descriptions were provided by Keegan and Crawford (1997). The Oregon Department of Fish and Wildlife (ODFW) released 58 Rio Grande turkeys from Texas and Kansas on the study area in 1982 and 1983.

METHODS

Capture and Radio Telemetry

We used rocket nets to capture turkeys during January 1989 and from December 1989 to February 1990. Age was determined by characteristics of primary feathers (Larson and Taber 1980), and individuals were equipped with 90–110-g radiotransmitters attached with a modified backpack harness (Kenward 1987:103). Transmitters had motion-sensitive switches; expected transmitter life was 1–3 years. We followed wild bird research guidelines of the American Ornithologists' Union (1988).

In January 1989, we equipped 26 adult and 19 yearling females with transmitters. Fifteen adults and 15 yearlings (considered adult during the second year)

survived to 1990. We equipped 10 more adults and 21 yearlings with transmitters during the 1989–1990 trapping season, bringing the total sample to 36 adult and 40 yearling females. All radiotagged turkeys included in analyses survived ≥2 weeks after release. On 31 January 1991, 25 adult females were still carrying functional transmitters.

We located females by triangulation from ≥3 locations or by visual observation ≥2 times/week from February 1989 through January 1991. Each female was located while roosting (1 hr after sunset to 1 hr before sunrise) at least once in each 2-week interval. Signals were generally monitored daily to identify timing of mortalities and general locations.

We randomly selected 1 active roost site/week for measurement of site characteristics; a different female was selected for each roost-site location (within a traditional 3-month season) to ensure different birds contributed to roost measurements. Roost trees were identified by visual observation of turkeys or presence of droppings under trees. We recorded sex and age composition of flocks at roost sites.

For defining female-poult flocks, we considered young birds poults until 12 weeks of age. We verified brood survival by audio or visual evidence weekly until all poults perished or until broods were integrated into autumn flocks.

Habitat Quantification

We estimated characteristics of overstory and midstory strata at randomly selected sites and roost sites with methods described by Keegan and Crawford (1997). Description of sites included quantification of the following physiographic and vegetative variables: percent slope, aspect, elevation, percent non-forested habitat within 0.3 km, species composition, tree density, basal area, percent cover, and canopy height. Individual roost trees were examined to determine species, height, height to lowest living and dead limbs, dbh, and age. Age of trees was determined from increment borings.

Statistical Analyses

Habitat availability was defined by a minimum convex polygon (Mohr 1947) for all female locations (except we excluded 2 females that moved >30 km to areas outside the South Umpqua River drainage). Non-forested (<10% tree cover) cover types (recent clearcut, brushfield, and meadow/grassland) were not used by roosting wild turkeys and therefore, not considered as available roost habitat (i.e., non-forest was disregarded and availability was recalculated based on 7 forested cover types).

We used Chi-square analysis to test the null hypothesis that cover types were used in proportion to availability (Neu et al. 1974, Byers et al. 1984). When null hypotheses were rejected, simultaneous confidence intervals were calculated to identify which cover types contributed to differences in use and whether use was greater or less than expected. Initially, use and availability were analyzed within and among years,

Table 1. Habitats used for roosting by adult (*n* = 315 locations) and female-poult (*n* = 60 locations) Rio Grande wild turkey flocks, Douglas County, Oregon, 1989–1991.

Cover type	Available (%)	Adults No. roosts	Adults Selection[a]	Females with poults No. roosts	Females with poults Selection
Open sapling/pole mixed conifer[b]	3.9	4	−	0	−
Dense sapling/pole mixed conifer	9.1	3	−	0	−
Dense young mixed conifer	16.4	129	+	15	0
Dense mature mixed conifer	55.8	93	−	22	−
Open mature mixed conifer	4.9	16	0	2	0
Mixed hardwood/conifer woodland[c]	7.7	55	+	21	+
Mixed hardwood/conifer savanna	2.3	15	0	0	−

[a] 0 indicates use in proportion to availability, + indicates greater use than expected, and − indicates less than expected (*P* ≤ 0.05).
[b] In conifer cover types, open defined as canopy closure <70%.
[c] Woodland defined as canopy closure ≥40%, savanna canopy closure was ≤40%.

traditional 3-month seasons, and female age-classes (within sample size constraints). Preliminary analyses indicated that habitat use did not differ with year or age of females. Consequently, roost habitat use was separated for 2 seasonal-social groups: females with poults <12 weeks and all other flocks of mixed sex and age composition during all seasons. Observations were pooled accordingly for analysis of habitat use.

We analyzed data sets with a series of univariate and multivariate procedures. Data sets were examined to assess outliers, normality, multicolinearity, and homogeneity of variance-covariance matrices. Although wide variability was noted for several observations, we detected few distinct outliers and inclusion of those observations did not alter results or interpretations. When ≥2 variables were highly correlated (*r* > 0.7), we selected those variables with the greatest ecological relevance and/or management application that contributed to the most parsimonious description of relationships.

We used analysis of variance to help identify variables that differed between groups (e.g., random sites and roosts). We compared several habitat variables with paired and unpaired *t*-tests to better understand relationships of individual habitat characteristics important to wild turkeys. For example, we used paired *t*-tests to test if tree dbh differed between roost sites (20-m diameter) and sites 30 m away from those same roosts.

RESULTS

Habitat Use

Analysis of roost habitat use was based on 375 locations. Adult flocks accounted for 315 locations and we located 60 roosts used by female-poult flocks. Adult and female-poult use of roost habitats were disproportionate to availability (*P* ≤ 0.005). Although adults roosted in all forested cover types, 88% of roosts were located in dense, young conifer, dense, mature conifer, and hardwood-conifer woodland (Table 1). Of cover types used frequently by adults, dense, young conifer and hardwood-conifer woodland were used more than expected and dense, mature conifer was used less than expected (*P* ≤ 0.05).

Females with poults used hardwood-conifer woodland more than expected and dense, mature conifer less than expected. More than 96% of female-poult roosts were located in the 3 cover types used extensively by adult flocks. In contrast to adults, female-poult flocks used hardwood-conifer savanna less than expected and used dense, young conifer in proportion to availability. Both social groups used dense and open, sapling-pole, conifer cover types less than expected and used open, mature conifer as expected.

Roost Site Characteristics

We quantified habitat characteristics of 99 roosts (79 adult flocks, 20 female-poult flocks) containing 565 trees. All but 1 roost selected for intensive measurement were located in 4 cover types: dense, young conifer; dense, mature conifer; open, mature conifer; and hardwood-conifer woodland.

Preliminary analyses indicated that stand characteristics at roosts in dense, and open, mature conifer were comparable. Therefore, roosts in these 2 cover types were pooled (for roost stand and roost tree characteristic analyses only). Further, with respect to roost stand characteristics within cover type, we did not observe differences among years, seasons, or social groups, so roost stand characteristics were pooled within cover type.

As expected, random site characteristics (Table 2) and roost stand and roost tree characteristics differed among cover types. Average overstory tree height in roost stands ranged from 24 m in hardwood-conifer woodlands to 37 m in mature conifer (Table 3) and tree dbh ranged from 36 cm to 58 cm. Midstory tree characteristics and densities were similar in young and mature conifer roost stands. Overstory tree density was lowest in mature conifer stands (131 trees/ha) and highest in dense, young conifer (217 trees/ha). Basal area of overstory trees ranged from 16.4 m²/ha in hardwood-conifer woodland to 38.5 m²/ha in mature conifer roost stands. The amount of non-forest habitat within 0.3 km of roosts averaged ≤6% in all cover types.

Characteristics of individual roost trees differed among cover types and between social groups. Roost trees used by adults in mature conifer stands averaged 40 m tall, 66 cm dbh, and were >150 years old (Table 4). Adults roosted in smaller trees in dense, young

Table 2. Characteristics of randomly selected forested habitats in Rio Grande wild turkey study area, Douglas County, Oregon, 1990–1991 (modified from Keegan and Crawford 1997).

Variable	Dense young conifer (n = 11)		Dense mature conifer (n = 15)		Open mature conifer (n = 2)		Hardwood/conifer woodland (n = 7)	
	$\bar{x}$	SE	$\bar{x}$	SE	$\bar{x}$	SE	$\bar{x}$	SE
Overstory								
Height (m)	22	1	50	2	43	11	16	1
Dbh (cm)	30	1	82	4	86	25	25	3
Basal area (m²/ha)	31	6	52	5	14	7	10	1
Density (no./ha)	396	70	100	12	23	1	213	31
Midstory								
Height (m)	8	1	15	1	10	2	7	1
Dbh (cm)	11	1	16	1	16	2	9	1
Basal area (m²/ha)	10	3	16	2	2	0.4	4	1
Density (no./ha)	1005	250	545	82	82	1	701	153
Canopy cover (%)	83	4	91	3	31	9	61	7
Non-forest within 0.3 km (%)	5	2	6	2	11	1	15	4
Elevation (m)	710	57	808	59	1072	74	15	2
Slope (%)	15	2	19	3	15	2	14	2

conifer and hardwood-conifer woodland stands, ranging from 28 to 31 m tall, 44 to 50 cm dbh, and 87 to 118 years old. Roost trees used by females with poults averaged 21 to 32 m tall, 39 to 50 cm dbh, and 80 to 117 years old depending on cover type. Among all cover types and social groups, the average roost tree was 33 m tall, 50 cm dbh, and 106 years old. Greater numbers of trees/roost used by adults reflected larger flocks (autumn and winter) and a tendency for poults to roost in the same tree as brood females.

Within dense, young conifer and hardwood-conifer woodland cover types, differences between roost trees used by adult and female-poult flocks were small. In mature conifer stands, female-poult roost trees were smaller (height and dbh) with living limbs closer to the ground than trees used by adults ($P \leq 0.03$). In mature conifer cover types, adult and female-poult flocks roosted in trees with smaller height and dbh than trees at randomly located sites ($P \leq 0.007$). Comparisons in dense, young conifer and hardwood-conifer woodland were mixed. Adults roosted in larger (height

and dbh) than average trees ($P \leq 0.001$) in both cover types. Heights of roost trees used by female-poult flocks did not differ from random trees in hardwood-conifer woodland or dense, young conifer ($P > 0.10$), but roost tree dbh was larger ($P \leq 0.05$).

Within cover type and social group, differences between height and dbh of roost trees compared to trees 30 m away from roost centers were inconsistent. Adult roost tree diameters were larger ($P \leq 0.03$) than surrounding trees in all cover types and roost tree height was greater in mature conifer stands ($P \leq 0.01$). Height and dbh of roost trees used by female-poult flocks did not differ ($P = 0.14$ to 0.62) from surrounding trees in roost stands.

Use of available aspects for roosting was similar for adult and female-poult flocks. Northerly aspects (315°–45°) were used less than expected by adult flocks ($P < 0.01$), but use of other aspects did not differ from availability. Although the trend of aspect use by female-poult flocks paralleled that of adults, use did not differ from availability (probably because of relatively low sample size; $n = 20$). When adult and female-poult roosts were combined, northerly aspects were used less than expected and southerly aspects were used more than expected ($P < 0.01$).

Turkeys roosted in 11 species of trees (Table 5). Adult use of tree species was disproportionate to availability ($P < 0.005$), but female-poult flocks used species as they occurred in stands ($P > 0.50$). Douglas-fir and ponderosa pine (*Pinus ponderosa*) accounted for >90% of adult roost trees, whereas 9 other species were used infrequently: sugar pine (*P. lambertiana*), incense-cedar (*Calocedrus decurrens*), white fir (*Abies concolor*), western redcedar (*Thuja plicata*), Oregon ash (*Fraxinus latifolia*), Oregon white oak, California black oak (*Q. kelloggii*), bigleaf maple (*Acer macrophyllum*), and Pacific madrone. Only Douglas-fir was used more than expected by adults ($P \leq 0.05$). Adult turkeys roosted in white fir, white oak, and madrone less often than expected and other species were used in proportion to availability.

Female-poult flocks roosted in 7 species of trees

Table 3. Structural characteristics of roost stands used by Rio Grande wild turkeys, Douglas County, Oregon, 1989–1991.

Variable	Dense young conifer (n = 42)		Mature conifer (n = 41)		Hardwood/ conifer woodland (n = 15)	
	$\bar{x}$	SE	$\bar{x}$	SE	$\bar{x}$	SE
Overstory						
Height (m)	29	1	37	1	24	1
Dbh (cm)	39	1	58	2	36	2
Basal area (m²/ha)	26	1	39	4	16	2
Density (no./ha)	217	18	131	12	163	22
Midstory						
Height (m)	11	0.4	12	1	8	1
Dbh (cm)	14	1	14	1	11	1
Basal area (m²/ha)	10	1	12	2	10	3
Density (no./ha)	546	48	563	63	797	187
Canopy cover (%)	89	2	82	3	79	3
Non-forest within 0.3 km (%)	6	1	6	2	4	1
Elevation (m)	599	22	600	22	604	24
Slope (%)	21	2	18	2	14	3

Table 4. Characteristics of roost trees used by adult and female-poult Rio Grande wild turkey flocks, Douglas County, Oregon, 1989–1991.

| Variable[a] | Dense young conifer | | | | Mature conifer | | | | Hardwood/conifer woodland | | | |
| | Adult (n = 351) | | Female-poult (n = 21) | | Adult (n = 150) | | Female-poult (n = 13) | | Adult (n = 24) | | Female-poult (n = 5) | |
	$\bar{x}$	SE	$\bar{x}$	SE	$\bar{x}$	SE	$\bar{x}$	SE	$\bar{x}$	SE	$\bar{x}$	SE
Height (m)	31	0.4	26	1.6	40	0.9	32	2.4	28	1.9	21	4.2
Dbh (cm)	44	0.7	41	2.3	66	2.0	50	5.0	50	3.2	39	6.2
Age (yr)	87	1.6	81	3.1	154	7.8	117	9.8	118	14.0	80	5.4
LLL (m)	13	0.3	10	1.2	15	0.5	11	1.1	10	1.2	7	0.6
LDL (m)	6	0.2	6	0.8	9	0.5	7	1.4	6	1.1	4	1.0
Tree/site	10	2.1	3	1.2	5	0.9	2	0.2	2	0.4	1	0.3
Bird/site	16	3.3	10	2.3	9	2.1	7	1.2	5	1.2	4	1.9

[a] LLL = lowest live limb, LDL = lowest dead limb.

with Douglas-fir accounting for 70%. We did not observe female-poult flocks roosting in 4 species used infrequently by adults (sugar pine, white oak, madrone, and ash). However, female-poult use of some alternate tree species (incense-cedar, western redcedar, white fir, black oak, and bigleaf maple) exceeded use by adults. We did not observe any turkeys roosting in western hemlock (*Tsuga heterophylla*) or red alder (*Alnus rubra*).

DISCUSSION

Habitat Use

Differences in cover types hampered direct comparisons of roost habitat use between Rio Grande turkeys in the southern Oregon Cascades and Merriam's turkeys in the northern Oregon Cascades (Lutz and Crawford 1987). However, some aspects of roost habitat use were similar for the populations. Mature mixed conifer was used frequently by both populations, but was used more than expected by Merriam's turkey flocks (75% of roosts, 14% availability) and less than expected by Rio Grande turkey flocks (30% of roosts, 56% availability). Because tree-growth patterns differed between study areas, trees in many mature mixed

Table 5. Roost tree use by adult (n = 526 trees) and female-poult (n = 39 trees) Rio Grande wild turkey flocks, Douglas County, Oregon, 1989–1991.

| Tree species | Available (%) | Adults | | Females with poults | |
		No. trees	Selection[a]	No. trees	Selection
Douglas fir	68.9	408	+	27	0
Ponderosa pine	11.2	69	0	2	0
Sugar pine	2.7	19	0	0	0
Incense cedar	4.7	14	0	2	0
White fir	4.0	8	−	1	0
Other[b]	1.9	5	0	7	0
Oregon white oak	3.3	2	−	0	0
Pacific madrone	3.2	1	−	0	0

[a] 0 indicates use in proportion to availability, + indicates greater use than expected, and − indicates less than expected ($P \leq 0.05$).
[b] Other species included bigleaf maple, California black oak, Oregon ash, and western redcedar. Red alder and western hemlock were available but unused.

conifer stands described by Lutz and Crawford (1987) were similar in size to trees in young mixed conifer stands in Douglas County. Indeed, combined use of young and mature conifer stands by Rio Grande turkeys (71%) was similar to use of mature conifer stands by Merriam's turkeys. Both populations avoided sapling/pole stands, but use of mixed hardwood-conifer forests differed. Relatively strong roost habitat selection patterns by Rio Grande turkeys contrasted with findings for Merriam's turkeys in South Dakota (Rumble 1992).

Habitat Characteristics

Comparisons of roost characteristics among studies were difficult because of differences in variables measured and geographic regions. Several differences were apparent among roosts used by Rio Grande turkeys in Oregon and Merriam's turkeys in Oregon (Lutz and Crawford 1987) and Washington (Mackey 1984). Canopy cover at Rio Grande turkey roosts (84%) was greater than reported for Merriam's turkeys (20–58%) in other areas (Lutz and Crawford 1987, Rumble 1992). Height, dbh, and lowest living limbs of roost trees used by Rio Grande turkeys were greater than reported by Mackey (1984). By contrast, Merriam's turkeys in Washington roosted in stands with greater basal area and lower canopy height (Mackey 1984) than those used by Rio Grande turkey females. Values for roost tree height and dbh in southwestern Oregon exceeded those reported for Merriam's turkeys in South Dakota (Rumble 1992). Larger trees may have been more available in our study area because of greater precipitation compared to more inland sites. Although dbh and height to lowest living limb of roost trees used by Rio Grande and Merriam's turkey female-poult flocks in Oregon were similar, adult Merriam's turkey females in Oregon roosted in larger diameter trees (Lutz and Crawford 1987) than those in our study area.

Absolute values of roost characteristics differed among areas, but some patterns of use were similar. Within some mature conifer stands, female-poult roosts used by both subspecies in Oregon were differentiated from adult roosts in that they consisted of smaller, younger trees with lowest living limbs closer to the ground. Although the same trend was evident for Rio Grande turkey female-poult flocks, the relationship was not significant in cover types other than mature conifer. We observed trends toward use of larger than average trees by Rio Grande turkeys that were consistent with reports for some Merriam's populations. However, we did not discern strong selection for the tallest trees available noted by Mackey (1984) and Lutz and Crawford (1987). Rather, relative roost tree size varied with cover type and social group. Adult flocks roosted in larger dbh trees than those available in the surrounding stand (i.e., 30 m away), but roost trees used by female-poult flocks were not different from surrounding trees. Similar trends were described by Rumble (1992).

Compared with random sites in younger cover types (dense conifer, hardwood-conifer woodland), Rio Grande turkey adults roosted in stands consisting of larger than average trees, but roost stands in mature conifer cover types contained smaller than average trees. Relatively lower tree densities in some developing younger stands may have led to development of branch structures more conducive to roosting (particularly in dense, young conifer). A different pattern of tree and stand development could explain roost tree use patterns in dense mature conifer stands; smaller trees might have branches better suited to roosting at lower heights than very large trees that had undergone high degrees of self-pruning during early stand development. Porter (1992) stressed the importance of horizontal branch structure for roosting and Rumble (1992) felt that branch structure was more important than tree diameter.

Because Rio Grande turkeys in this study did not select the largest, oldest trees available, they may be less sensitive to even-age timber management systems than Merriam's turkeys and may be able to better utilize areas with larger amounts of medium/young forest stands (<50 cm dbh and <110 years old) or stands at the lower end of our large/mature classification. Conversely, stand selection within dense, young conifer and hardwood-conifer woodland cover types indicated turkeys used older stands with lower overstory tree densities. Further, fragmentation of hardwood-conifer woodlands, as measured by forested habitat within 0.3 km, may discourage use of this frequently used roost habitat.

In contrast to Porter (1992), we observed selection of southerly aspects and avoidance of north-facing slopes for roosting. Mild winter climate in our study area may ameliorate requirements for thermoregulatory protection afforded by northeasterly slopes, but Merriam's turkeys often roosted in exposed situations (R. S. Lutz, Texas Tech University, personal communication), indicating that thermoregulatory needs may be tempered by other factors. For example, north-facing slopes in our study area often supported denser understory vegetation or deeper snow in winter that may have discouraged wild turkey use.

Tree species with relatively low branches (e.g., maple) and smaller understory species (e.g., black oak) on upslope sites probably provided easier access for

poults than taller canopy dominants. Female-poult use of tree species in proportion to availability was consistent with use of individual trees that were indistinguishable (height and dbh) from adjacent trees. Adult Rio Grande turkeys in Oregon roosted in Douglas-firs frequently (78%) and use exceeded availability. Merriam's turkeys in Washington roosted primarily in Douglas-fir (Mackey 1984), whereas Merriam's females in Oregon most often used ponderosa pine (Lutz and Crawford 1987). However, these other researchers did not report tree species use relative to availability.

MANAGEMENT IMPLICATIONS

Our research indicated that Rio Grande turkeys may be able to use a wider variety of cover types for roosting than Merriam's turkeys in the Oregon Cascades. Use of several cover types for roosting indicated that Rio Grande turkeys may persist under a variety of habitat conditions, including some not conducive to Merriam's turkey populations. We speculate that, in a relative sense, Rio Grande turkeys are generalists compared with Merriam's turkeys and, therefore, recommend that managers consider available habitat and likely future land management scenarios before selecting a subspecies for translocation. Rio Grande turkeys will likely fare better than Merriam's turkeys in relatively disturbed environments in the Oregon Cascades. Esthetic and economic returns of translocation programs will be enhanced by selection of subspecies best suited to regional habitat conditions.

Only unforested cover types and sapling/pole stands resulting from relatively recent perturbations were virtually unused for roosting. Maintaining or increasing areas of mixed hardwood/conifer habitats (particularly oak woodland complexes) would ensure availability of roost habitat as well as benefit other wildlife.

Because dense mature conifer was avoided for roosting, Rio Grande turkeys may exist in landscapes dominated by relatively young forests (30–110 years old and 23–50 cm dbh). Conversely, because wild turkeys use a variety of cover types for other life-history needs (Keegan and Crawford 1997, 2001), very large expanses of young, even-aged conifer stands typical of some areas of western Oregon may preclude use by wild turkeys. Further, we caution that average roost trees were 50 cm dbh and 106 years old and, therefore, at the upper limit of our "young" stand classification criteria. Conifer stands in this age class exceed many current harvest rotations. Lastly, dense, mature conifer received heavy use for most components of turkey life-history (ranked first or second for roost habitat, first for summer habitat [Keegan and Crawford 2001], and second for brood rearing [Keegan and Crawford 1997]). Therefore, we do not recommend reducing average stand age or extensive harvest of mature timber as a means of increasing Rio Grande turkey numbers. In order to meet the full range of habitat needs of wild turkeys and other species, timber management plans should incorporate appropriate juxtaposition and age classes of conifer stands over time and in relation to other cover types.

ACKNOWLEDGMENTS

Research was supported by the U.S. Forest Service LaGrande Forestry and Range Science Laboratory, the National Wild Turkey Federation, Oregon State University, Idaho Department of Fish and Game, and ODFW. We thank S. R. Denney, R. A. Zalunardo, and other personnel of ODFW and the Umpqua National Forest for their assistance. We appreciate field work of P. I. Burns, N. E. Golly, and B. C. Quick. This is Technical Paper 10787 of the Oregon Agricultural Experiment Station.

LITERATURE CITED

American Ornithologists' Union. 1988. Report of committee on use of wild birds in research. Auk 105(1, Supplement).

Boeker, E. L., and V. E. Scott. 1969. Roost tree characteristics for Merriam's turkey. Journal of Wildlife Management 33:121–124.

Byers, C. R., R. K. Steinhorst, and P. R. Kraussman. 1984. Clarification of a technique for analysis of utilization-availability data. Journal of Wildlife Management 48:1050–1053.

Crockett, B. C. 1973. Quantitative evaluation of winter roost sites of the Rio Grande turkey in north-central Oklahoma. Pages 211–218 *in* G. C. Sanderson and H. C. Schultz, editors. Wild turkey management: current problems and programs. University of Missouri Press, Columbia, Missouri, USA.

Franklin, J. F., and C. T. Dyrness. 1973. Natural vegetation of Oregon and Washington. Pacific Northwest Forest and Range Experiment Station. U.S. Forest Service General Technical Report PNW-8. Glazener, W. C. 1967. Management of the Rio Grande turkey. Pages 453–492 *in* O. H. Hewitt, editor. The wild turkey and its management. The Wildlife Society, Washington, D.C., USA.

Keegan, T. W., and J. A. Crawford. 1997. Brood-rearing habitat use by Rio Grande wild turkeys in Oregon. Great Basin Naturalist 57:220–230.

———, and ———. 2001. Seasonal habitat use and home ranges of Rio Grande turkeys in Oregon. Proceedings of the National Wild Turkey Symposium 8:109–116.

Kenward, R. E. 1987. Wildlife radio tagging: equipment, field techniques and data analysis. Academic Press, London, United Kingdom.

Larson, J. S., and R. D. Taber. 1980. Criteria of sex and age. Pages 143–202 *in* S. D. Schemnitz, editor. Wildlife man-agement techniques manual. Fourth edition. The Wildlife Society, Washington, D.C., USA.

Lutz, R. S., and J. A. Crawford. 1987. Seasonal use of roost sites by Merriam's wild turkey hens and hen-poult flocks in Oregon. Northwest Science 61:174–178.

Mackey, D. L. 1984. Roosting habitat of Merriam's turkeys in south-central Washington. Journal of Wildlife Management 48:1377–1382.

Mohr, C. O. 1947. Table of equivalent populations of North American small mammals. American Midland Naturalist 37:223–249.

National Oceanic and Atmospheric Administration. 1989–1991. Climatological data, Oregon, annual summary. National Climatic Data Center, Asheville, North Carolina, USA.

Neu, C. W., C. R. Byers, and J. M. Peek. 1974. A technique for analysis of utilization-availability data. Journal of Wildlife Management 38:541–545.

Porter, W. F. 1992. Habitat requirements. Pages 202–213 *in* J. G. Dickson, editor. The wild turkey: biology and management. Stackpole Books, Harrisburg, Pennsylvania, USA.

Rumble, M. A. 1992. Roosting habitat of Merriam's turkeys in the Black Hills, South Dakota. Journal of Wildlife Management 56:750–759.

Vangilder, L. D. 1992. Population dynamics. Pages 144–164 *in* J. G. Dickson, editor. The wild turkey: biology and management. Stackpole Books, Harrisburg, Pennsylvania, USA.

Wunz, G. A. 1992. Wild turkeys outside their historic range. Pages 361–384 *in* J. G. Dickson, editor. The wild turkey: biology and management. Stackpole Books, Harrisburg, Pennsylvania, USA.

Thomas W. (Tom) Keegan (pictured) is the Salmon Region Wildlife Manager for the Idaho Department of Fish and Game. He received his B.S. in natural resources from Cornell University, M.S. in wildlife from Louisiana State University, and Ph.D. in wildlife science from Oregon State University. His current professional interests center around upland and big game management in the western U.S. ***John A. Crawford*** (not pictured) is a professor emeritus of wildlife ecology in the Department of Fisheries and Wildlife at Oregon State University. His primary interest is the ecology and management of upland gamebirds.

Chapter IV

Turkeys on their Northern Range

9th National Wild Turkey Symposium

Wild Turkey Management:
Accomplishments, Strategies, and Opportunities
———— Grand Rapids, Michigan ————

NORTHERN WILD TURKEYS: ISSUES OR OPPORTUNITY

Richard O. Kimmel[1]
Farmland Wildlife Populations and Research Group,
Minnesota Department of Natural Resources,
35365 800th Avenue,
Madelia, MN 56062, USA

Wendy J. Krueger
Minnesota Department of Natural Resources,
2611 Broadway Avenue,
Slayton, MN 56172, USA

Abstract: State and provincial wildlife management agencies adjoining the Canadian/United States border are faced with public interest for expanding wild turkey (*Meleagris gallopavo*) populations northward. This manuscript reviews research on tolerance of wild turkeys for severe winter weather conditions and survival in northern climates and suggests future research necessary for northern turkey introduction programs. A survey of northern state and provincial wildlife agency biologists indicated that most agencies have successfully translocated wild turkeys north of the ancestral limit and that the most important management concerns for northern turkeys were weather, food availability, and habitat limitations. In responding to requests to move wild turkeys northward while implementing sound natural resources management policies, wildlife managers are faced with both potential issues and opportunities relating to wildlife management, ecosystem concerns, economics, and recreation.

Proceedings of the National Wild Turkey Symposium 9:263–272

Key words: management, *Meleagris gallopavo*, northern, relocation, survival, transplant, wild turkey.

State and provincial wildlife management agencies adjoining the Canadian/United States border are faced with public interest for expanding wild turkey populations northward (Glines 2003). This presents an opportunity for wild turkey managers to continue to work with the public on a successful program restoring wild turkeys not only to the species' ancestral range but also introducing the species and turkey hunting into new areas well north of the ancestral range. However, issues and unanswered questions indicate a need for careful planning and research before intensifying future wild turkey expansion efforts into northern ecosystems.

There was little discussion of expanding wild turkeys northward 20 years ago. At that time, a need for northern wild turkey research was not apparent. In the past decade we have advanced our knowledge on the tolerance of this species for winter weather (Gray and Prince 1988, Oberlag et al. 1990, Haroldson et al. 1998, Coup and Pekins 1999). However, there is a lack of information regarding wild turkey ecology in northern habitats that differ significantly from the traditional turkey range, how winter severity impacts wild turkeys at the population level, and effective management techniques for northern wild turkey populations.

At the Eighth National Wild Turkey Symposium in 2000, more than a dozen northern wild turkey bi-ologists met informally to discuss northern wild turkey management activities. The group began drafting questions for a survey of wild turkey management activities and populations in northern states and southern provinces. The results of this survey are included in this manuscript. We discussed the need for a conference focusing on northern turkey issues. The result was the Northern Wild Turkey Workshop held in January 2003 (Kimmel et al. 2003). Information from this workshop, which had more than 100 attendees and 34 presentations, is discussed.

In this manuscript, we review research on tolerance of wild turkeys for severe winter weather conditions and survival in northern climates and suggest future research necessary for northern turkey introduction programs. We provide information on current wildlife management programs from a survey of northern state and provincial wildlife agency biologists. Finally, we explore both the issues and opportunities facing wildlife managers who must balance public requests to move wild turkeys northward with implementing sound natural resources management policies.

[1] E-mail: richard.kimmel@dnr.state.mn.us

NORTHERN WILD TURKEY RESEARCH

Haroldson (1996) indicated that the northern limit of wild turkey distribution is likely determined by interactions of temperature, food availability (influenced by snow cover), and habitat quality. However, predicting impacts of weather on turkey survival is difficult, because the different weather factors are seldom in synchrony (Porter and Gefell 1996).

Turkeys can survive extreme winter weather conditions in the existing range provided the birds are able to find food (Porter et al. 1980, Haroldson et al. 1998, Hamel et al. 2003). Some wildlife agencies, especially in the northern turkey range, provide supplemental feed, such as feeders and standing-corn food plots (Austin and DeGraff 1975, Wunz and Hayden 1975, Porter et al. 1980). Supplemental winter feeding for wild turkeys has been reported as far south as Texas (Thomas et al. 1973).

Haroldson (1996) noted that supplemental foods, such as agricultural crops or livestock manure on fields, are important for survival during periods of severe winter weather in Minnesota. Austin and DeGraff (1975) found that turkeys in New York used supplemental feeds during periods where snow depths exceeded 30 cm. Porter et al. (1980) noted survival was higher in an area with corn food plots during severe winter weather conditions in Minnesota. However, Wunz and Hayden (1975) reported that turkeys starved during winter when extended periods of deep snow prevented foraging, even when supplemental food was present. More recently, Kane (2003) observed that some newly-transplanted turkeys in Minnesota starved during a winter with deep snow even when released close to standing corn food plots and feeders, apparently because they did not find the supplemental food. A relationship between survival of northern wild turkey populations and food from agricultural operations is apparent. Roberts et al. (1995) suggested mixed agricultural/forest landscapes benefit wild turkeys exposed to severe winters. Kane (2003) demonstrated a positive relationship between survival of wild turkeys north of the ancestral range and the presence of agriculture in forested landscapes. In contrast wild turkeys translocated to a heavily forested area in northcentral Wisconsin failed to survive (K. Warnke, Wisconsin Department of Natural Resources, personal communication).

Haroldson et al. (1998) assumed that availability of natural winter foods is inversely related to snow depth. Starvation of turkeys during extended periods of deep snow was observed in Pennsylvania (Wunz and Hayden 1975), Minnesota (Porter et al. 1980, Kane 2003), and Ontario (Nguyen et al. 2003). Roberts et al. (1995) suggested that winter mortality among adult females begins between 40–59 days of exposure to prolonged deep snow (>25.4 cm) in New York. Wright et al. (1996) noted that localized starvation in Wisconsin occurred during a winter with 49 consecutive days of deep snow and cold temperatures.

Low winter temperature extremes that turkeys endure in the existing range are not life threatening, provided food is available for thermoregulation (Haroldson et al. 1998). Lewis (1963) noted daily home range in Michigan varied inversely with snow depth and directly with temperature. Haroldson et al. (1998) estimated the lower critical temperature for wild turkeys is 10.9°C and the lower lethal temperature is ≤−54°C. Haroldson (1996), using predictive models to estimate metabolic responses of wild turkeys to winter weather in Minnesota, found that for every 10°C decrease in temperature below 11°C, the cost of thermoregulation increased by 60 kcal/day.

Except for the benefits of agricultural habitats, there is little clear information on natural habitats that may benefit wild turkey survival in the northern wild turkey range. Lewis (1963) and Porter (1977) provided descriptive information on winter habitat used by wild turkeys. There has been some research on winter roosting areas in Michigan (Lewis 1963), Rhode Island (Kilpatrick et al. 1988), New Hampshire (Kilpatrick et al. 1990), and Minnesota (Ermer et al. *this volume*). As suggested by Kilpatrick et al. (1990) and Ermer et al. (*this volume*), roosting areas, particularly conifers, could provide thermoregulation benefits to turkeys during periods of low winter temperatures accompanied by high winds.

Turkeys respond behaviorally to winter weather. However, no apparent physiological response to conserve body heat has been found (Haroldson et al. 2001). Porter (1977) found that turkeys in Minnesota moved to wintering areas. Turkeys in New Hampshire were observed to restrict movements and range, use shelter, and shift to supplemental food when winter severity increased (Coup and Pekins 1999). In Minnesota wild turkeys have been observed in and around barns and machinery on farms in search of food during severe winters (G. Nelson, Minnesota Department of Natural Resources, personal communication).

Winter severity increases with elevation, just as with latitude. However, there has been little research on turkey survival as related to elevation. Austin and DeGraff (1975) found lower survival rates during severe weather for wild turkeys introduced into the southern Adirondack Mountains in New York. During winters with deep snow depths, turkeys moved to lower elevations and open southern exposure slopes where snow was not as deep. Migration of turkeys to lower elevations and areas with farms has been observed during winter in South Dakota (Rumble and Anderson 1996, Lehman et al. 2003).

The impact of severe winter weather on hen condition and reproductive potential the following spring has been observed in related species (Gullion 1970). Wild turkey recruitment potentially can be impacted by winter weather. Porter et al. (1983) noted a strong correlation between winter severity and reproductive performance of females that survived to breed. Severe winter weather was associated with reduced body condition, hatching success, and recruitment. Gray and Prince (1988) reported metabolic costs for thermoregulation below the lower critical temperature were greater for female wild turkeys than for males.

It is becoming more apparent that turkeys' tolerance for human contact increases when snow conditions intensify the need for food. As human tolerance increases, the potential for agricultural depredations and urban turkey problems increases. Kulowiec and Haufler (1985) reported wild turkeys in Michigan moved to wintering areas on active farms following the first snowfall. Winter movements to ranches and farmsteads in South Dakota appeared to be influenced by availability of natural foods and snow cover (Lehman et al. 2003). Moriarty and Leuth (2003) noted that urban areas in Minnesota provide winter food and shelter for wild turkeys resulting in a fast-growing turkey population that is tolerant of human activities. Urban turkey complaints to Minnesota Department of Natural Resources staff in the Minneapolis/St. Paul area have increased from an average of 2.3 complaints/year from 1999–2001 to 15.7 complaints/year from 2002–2004 (B. Lueth, Minnesota Department of Natural Resources, personal communication). Gillespie (2003) noted urban complaints in Manitoba resulted in a trapping program to remove problem turkeys. Gruber et al. (2004) reported 12.5% of respondents to a survey (*n* = 40) reported negative human/turkey interactions in northwestern Minnesota. Landowners expressed concerns about turkeys at bird feeders, on decks, in yards close to houses, turkeys blocking traffic, and aggressive turkey behavior towards a young child.

SURVEY OF NORTHERN WILD TURKEY BIOLOGISTS

A survey (Appendix A), initially conducted in 2002 (Krueger 2003) and updated in 2004, was mailed to wildlife agency turkey biologists in the 11 states and 7 provinces along the Canadian/United States border. Follow-up phone calls and/or e-mail messages were sent to non-respondents. Responses were ultimately received from all 18 states and provinces surveyed in 2002 and 16 of 18 states and provinces in 2004.

Biologists were asked to indicate the northern boundary where wild turkeys have been established at least 5 years and identify their northernmost release site (Figure 1). Wild turkey distribution has expanded northward since 1999 (Tapley et al. 2001) and is well beyond the ancestral range identified by Schorger (1966) (Figure 1). Turkeys were found statewide in New Hampshire, New York, and Vermont. Biologists in Alberta, Manitoba, and Quebec felt that turkey distribution will not expand further north in their provinces (Table 1). In Montana, turkeys were thought to be at the northern limit, but are expanding to interior areas of the state that were not previously occupied. Nova Scotia was the only surveyed state/province without an established wild turkey population.

Of 16 states and provinces with translocation programs, all have had successful releases north of the ancestral limit, and 10 have had unsuccessful release attempts as well (Table 1). Causes of unsuccessful releases include harsh weather conditions and food limitations. Eight of the surveyed agencies monitor winter

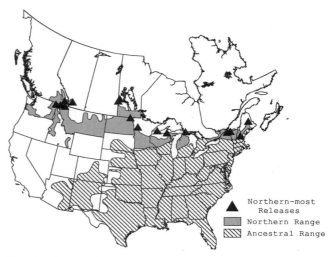

Fig. 1. Ancestral range, current range, and location of northernmost release sites obtained from a 2004 survey of northern wild turkey biologists.

weather conditions for wildlife and 7 have northern turkey research data available from within their state/province (Table 1).

The northernmost wild turkey populations (established at least 5 years) have generally originated from birds within the respective state or province (Table 2). Translocation was used to establish turkeys in 12 states/provinces, but turkey populations have also expanded into northern areas on their own. Only Manitoba and Saskatchewan do not have a hunting season on their northernmost population.

Turkey populations at the northernmost range are found in a variety of habitats, including some with minimal amounts of forested land. Agricultural habitats were reported present in all northernmost areas, and agricultural food sources (e.g., waste grain, corn silage, feedlots, manure) were most often listed as the major winter food source. Most agencies do not provide supplemental food for wild turkeys, although 5 reported having a wildlife food plot program. Only 4 agencies have not received wild turkey depredation or nuisance complaints from the northernmost range. However, most agencies indicated 'few' complaints (Table 2). Biologists listed coyotes, great-horned owls, and bobcats as major predators of northern wild turkeys.

The top 3 management concerns of surveyed biologists were weather, food availability, and habitat limitations. When asked to identify the most important limiting factor for northern wild turkeys, biologists rated weather and food equally. Other management issues/problems included winter feeding, game farm birds, depredation, and public pressure to transplant birds into questionable habitat.

Agency plans for turkey range expansion and research were also addressed in the survey (Table 3). Thirteen agencies do not have a written plan for moving turkeys northward, and 13 are not intending to release turkeys north of currently existing populations.

Table 1. Wild turkey release information, status of weather monitoring, and availability of northern turkey research data obtained from a 2004 survey of northern wild turkey biologists.

State/Province	Turkeys reached northern limit?	Successful releases north of ancestral line?	Unsuccessful releases north of ancestral line?	Agency monitor weather conditions?	Research data available?
Alberta	Yes	Yes	No	No	No
British Columbia[d]	No	Yes	Yes	No	No
Idaho	Don't know	Yes	Yes	No	Yes
Maine	Don't know	Yes	Yes	Yes (for deer)	No
Manitoba	Yes	Yes	Yes	Yes	No
Michigan	Don't know	Yes	Yes	Yes	Yes
Minnesota	No	Yes	No	Yes	Yes
Montana	Yes	Yes	Yes	No	Yes
New Hampshire	Yes[a]	Yes	No	Yes	Yes
New York	Yes[a]	Yes	No	No	No
North Dakota	No	Yes	Yes	No	No
Nova Scotia	No	No[b]	Yes[c]	No	No
Ontario	No	Yes	No	Yes	Yes
Quebec[d]	Yes	None attempted	None attempted	No	No
Saskatchewan	Don't know	Yes	Yes	No	No
Vermont	Yes[a]	Yes	No	Yes	No
Washington	No	Yes	Yes	No	Yes (limited)
Wisconsin	Don't know	Yes	Yes	Yes	No

[a] Turkeys present in entire state.
[b] No authorized releases to date.
[c] Illegal game farm releases.
[d] Did not respond to 2004 survey. Data shown is from 2002 survey.

The remaining agencies are planning limited releases, will decide on a case by case basis, or do not know the status of future northern releases. Similarly, 13 agencies do not have a policy or plan for providing winter food for wild turkeys, even though food availability was a common concern among biologists for northern turkey survival. Most agencies reported that they receive either light or moderate public pressure for northern expansion of wild turkeys. Conversely, 10 agencies reported some opposition to expansion. Seventeen agencies reported a need for more northern turkey research, but only 8 have research projects underway or planned (Table 3).

ISSUES AND OPPORTUNITIES

We classified discussion regarding wild turkey management in northern latitudes into 4 general cate-

Table 2. Information from the northernmost wild turkey populations (established at least 5 years) obtained from a 2004 survey of northern wild turkey biologists.

State/Province	Source of birds?	Expanded or transplanted?	Hunting season?	Forest type (% forest)	Agriculture present?	Food provided by agency?	Crop complaints?	Turkey/ human complaints?
Alberta	Nebraska	Transplanted	Spring only	Mixed (60%)	Yes	No	Few	Few
British Columbia[a]	Unknown	Expanded	Spring only	Conifers (80%)	Yes	No	None	None
Idaho	Unknown	Transplanted	Spring and fall	Conifers (30%)	Yes	Yes[b]	Several	Few
Maine	Within state	Expanded	Spring only	Mixed (90%)	Yes	No	Few	Few
Manitoba	Within province	Both	No	Hardwoods (50%)	Yes	No	None	Few
Michigan	Within state	Expanded	Spring and fall	Mixed (80%)	Yes	Yes[b]	Several	Few
Minnesota	Within state	Transplanted	Spring only	Mixed (20%)	Yes	Yes[b]	Few	Few
Montana	Hatchery eggs	Transplanted	Spring and fall	Mixed (98%)	Yes	No	Few	Several
New Hampshire	Within state	Expanded	Spring and fall	Mixed (95%)	Yes	No	None	None
New York	Within state	Both	Spring and fall	Mixed (50%)	Yes	No	Several	Few
North Dakota	Within state	Both	Spring and fall	Hardwoods (<5%)	Yes	Yes[b]	Few	Several
Nova Scotia	N/A	N/A	N/A	N/A	N/A	N/A	N/A	N/A
Ontario	Within province	Transplanted	Spring only	Mixed (55%)	Yes	No	Few	None
Quebec[a]	Unknown (no re-leases)	Expanded	Fall only	Mixed (20%)	Yes	No	None	None
Saskatchewan	Unknown	Transplanted	No	Conifers (un-known)	Yes	No	None	None
Vermont	Within state	Both	Spring only	Mixed (94%)	Yes	Yes[b]	Several	None
Washington	Wyoming and South Dakota	Transplanted	Spring and fall	Conifers (50%)	Yes	No	Many	Several
Wisconsin	Within state	Both	Spring and fall	Mixed (>65%)	Yes	No	Few	Few

[a] Did not respond to 2004 survey. Data shown is from 2002 survey.
[b] Food plots and/or corn seed for planting food plots was provided.

Table 3. Agency policies and plans for wild turkey expansion, providing winter food, pressures related to expansion, and future research outlook. Information was obtained from a 2004 survey of northern wild turkey biologists.

State/Province	Policy/plan for expansion?	Planning northern releases?	Policy/plan for providing winter food?	Public pressure to expand?	Opposition to expansion?	Future research planned?	Is research needed?
Alberta	No	No	No	Light	Light	No	Yes
British Columbia[a]	No	No	No	Light	None	No	Yes
Idaho	Yes	No	Yes	None	Light	No	Yes
Maine	Yes	Limited	No	Moderate	None	No	Yes
Manitoba	No	Limited	No	Light	None	Yes	Yes
Michigan	No	No	No	Moderate	Light	Yes	Yes
Minnesota	Yes	Limited	No	Moderate	Moderate	Yes	Yes
Montana	Yes	No	Yes	Light	Light	No	Yes
New Hampshire[b]	No	No	No	Light	None	Yes	Yes
New York[b]	No	No	No	None	None	Yes	Yes
North Dakota	No	No	No	Light	None	No	Yes
Nova Scotia	No	No	No	Moderate	Moderate	No	Yes[c]
Ontario	No	Unknown	No	Moderate	Light	No	Yes
Quebec[a]	No	No	No	Light	Moderate	Yes	Yes
Saskatchewan	No	No	No	None	None	No	No
Vermont[b]	No	No	Yes	None	None	Yes	Yes
Washington	No	No	Yes	Moderate	Moderate	No	Yes
Wisconsin	Yes	Case by case	Yes	Light	Light	Yes	Yes

[a] Did not respond to 2004 survey. Data shown is from 2002 survey.
[b] Turkeys occupy entire state.
[c] Research is needed if wild turkeys ever get released in Nova Scotia.

gories: (1) wildlife management opportunities and issues, (2) ecosystem considerations, (3) economic opportunities and issues, and (4) the potential for increased recreation. These categories are interrelated, and we made no attempt to discuss any one without considering the others.

Wildlife Management

Introducing wild turkeys into new areas can be an exciting challenge for wildlife management. However, some wildlife managers expressed concerns about new management demands resulting from northern turkey releases. These demands become problems for wildlife management offices that are already short of money and staff. Adding any new species, program, or hunting season requires additional attention from wildlife managers and can deplete resources needed for other important wildlife management programs. Also, questions about management of wild turkeys in northern habitats remain unanswered: what survival rates should be expected for turkeys in northern hardwood/conifer habitats, can wildlife managers alter habitats to enhance turkey survival, and is supplemental feeding required?

Expanding wild turkey populations northward provides an opportunity for wildlife managers to continue work with the public on a successful program restoring wild turkeys to their ancestral range and beyond. However, there are several issues related to expanding populations: (1) it is unknown if wildlife management techniques currently used for wild turkeys in northern habitats will be effective further north, (2) there is potential for the public to demand winter feeding programs for northern wild turkeys, (3) disease problems could result from concentrating birds at winter feeding sites, (4) there could be additional demands on limited wildlife management budgets and staff time, (5) north-

ern wild turkeys may increase depredation and urban nuisance complaints, and (6) forest management for wild turkeys may not be compatible with current management practices for existing species in northern latitudes (e.g., early succession forest management for ruffed grouse [Horton 2003]).

The Ecosystem

Ecologists, conservationists, and wildlife managers recognize that there can be ecological consequences when introducing any exotic species, such as wild turkeys, into an area where the species has not existed in the past. If we view an ecosystem as a complex system of living organisms that are interrelated, adding any new organism to this mix will alter the balance in ways that may not be immediately obvious. History has demonstrated that many exotic species have caused huge problems, even if unintended and unexpected. Elton (1958) reviews problems from various invasive species, problems he refers to as "ecological explosions." Ring-necked pheasants (*Phasianus colchicus*) have negatively impacted other North American gamebirds in a variety of different ways (Kimmel 1988). For wild turkeys we have a history of more than a half-century expanding the wild turkey range usually relatively short distances from the ancestral range and usually within North America. The only species thought to be negatively impacted at this time is the human species. However, there is concern for impacts on other species, especially as turkeys are moved into different plant associations with a different group of native wildlife. What are the costs to society to correct potential ecological problems that might result from northern turkey introductions? However, ecosystems have changed since the European settlement of North America and management for the 'pristine' presettlement condition may not be reasonable or appropriate.

Agriculture has created a stable source of winter food, which has made northern expansion of the wild turkey range possible.

A potential opportunity of expanding populations is that wild turkeys add diversity to a northern ecosystem. However, there are several issues related to expanding turkey populations and the ecosystem: (1) the potential impacts of wild turkeys on northern native flora, fauna, and their ecosystem relationships are unknown, (2) the potential for wild turkeys to alter northern ecosystems is unknown, and (3) the suitability of winter weather and non-traditional habitats for wild turkey populations is unknown.

Economics

Expanding wild turkey range may provide increased economic opportunities. Money raised by conservation/sport hunting groups can increase when conservation groups can expand into new areas. However, whether new money is generated or just shifted from one group to another is unknown. Expanding wild turkey populations northward would increase potential public interest in fundraisers and memberships for groups like the National Wild Turkey Federation (NWTF). Money raised by NWTF provides critical support for wild turkey research and management. Also, increased license revenues for wildlife management agencies are created by expanding wild turkey hunting opportunities. Baumann et al. (1990) identified significant economic inputs from spring wild turkey hunting. However, negative economic impacts from expanding wild turkeys northward may also be possible, because of increased demands on wildlife management budgets, shifting money and other resources away from native species, and potential exotic problems.

Expanding wild turkeys northward can provide the opportunity for increased revenues from conservation fundraisers and hunting seasons. However, there are issues related to turkey translocations and economics: (1) expanding wild turkeys northward could result in increased demands on wildlife management budgets for wild turkey management activities, potential depredation and urban problems, and staff time, and (2) potential wild turkey damage to ecosystems may be expensive to correct.

Recreation

Turkey hunting has expanded as wildlife managers restored wild turkeys to their original range and beyond. There are many thousands of hunters in North America looking for more turkey hunting opportunities. In spring 2004 in Minnesota, there were approximately 45,000 applicants for about half that number of spring turkey hunting permits. Hence, NWTF members and other sportsmen are asking for turkey releases north of the current population (Glines 2003).

Expanding wild turkeys northward may result in increased hunting and viewing opportunities. However, there are potential issues which include: (1) landowner tolerance of another hunting season in northern latitudes is unknown, (2) turkeys in northern latitudes may not develop or maintain populations that would withstand hunting, and (3) turkeys in northern latitudes may become exotic pests that reduce recreational opportunities for native species.

FINAL COMMENTS

The success of wildlife managers in restoring wild turkeys to their original range and then expanding that range has been impressive. Wildlife managers have successfully established populations to levels that provide hunting opportunities throughout the ancestral range. Today wild turkeys have been established in areas where they apparently never existed in the past and excited the public with hunting and viewing opportunities. It is not surprising that the public asks for more releases in areas, such as northern latitudes, where few thought turkeys would exist just a few decades ago.

Over and over again, wild turkeys have proven their resiliency to thrive in areas previously considered inadequate. Turkeys have proven that, once established in an area, they can continue to expand to places where few wildlife professionals expected them to survive. In his keynote address for the Eighth National Wild Turkey Symposium in 2000, John B. Lewis noted how the wild turkey experts of the 1970s questioned decisions to move turkeys into mixed forest/agricultural areas, which today support high wild turkey populations and successful hunting seasons. Lewis (2001) noted that turkeys adapting to agricultural habitats was one of the biggest surprises of the turkey restoration program. Today, research results indicate that food provided by agriculture may be the key to survival of turkeys in northern latitudes. It is interesting that the forest/agricultural landscapes that concerned wildlife professionals in more southern latitudes 30 years ago, might enable northern expansion of wild turkey populations in the current century. On the other hand, habitat generalists such as wild turkeys possess potential to displace native species. While negative impacts on native species have not been documented during the decades that wildlife managers have been translocating wild turkeys, a possibility for negative impacts does exist.

It is plausible that a speaker at a future National Wild Turkey Symposium may reflect on our efforts to move turkey populations further north as an opportunity that we took advantage of with great success, the beginning of an ecological disaster, or an effort that didn't succeed, wasting resource dollars and wildlife managers' energies.

ACKNOWLEDGMENTS

We thank S. Goetz, K. Haroldson, B. Penning, and P. J. Wingate for reviews of this manuscript. R. Wright provided GIS and mapmaking assistance. J. Ermer assisted with the literature review. T. Klinkner assisted with the survey of northern managers and manuscript preparation.

LITERATURE CITED

Austin, D. E., and L. W. DeGraff. 1975. Winter survival of wild turkey in the southern Adirondacks. Proceedings of the National Wild Turkey Symposium 3:55–60.

Baumann, D. P., Jr., L. D. Vangilder, C. I. Taylor, R. Engel-Wilson, R. O. Kimmel, and G. A. Wunz. 1990. Expenditures for wild turkey hunting. Proceedings of the National Wild Turkey Symposium 6:157–176.

Coup, R. N., and P. J. Pekins. 1999. Field metabolic rate of wild turkeys in winter. Canadian Journal of Zoology 77:1075–1082.

Elton, C. S. 1958. The ecology of invasions by animals and plants. University of Chicago Press, Chicago, Illinois, USA.

Ermer, J. R, K. J. Haroldson, R. O. Kimmer, C. D. Dieter, P. D. Evenson, B. D. Berg. *This volume.* Characteristics of winter roost and activity sites of wild turkeys in Minnesota. Proceedings of the National Wild Turkey Symposium 9:*This volume.*

Gillespie, M. 2003. Manitoba wild turkey status report. Pages 34–35 *in* R. O. Kimmel, W. J. Krueger, and T. K. Klinkner, compilers. Northern Wild Turkey Workshop. Minnesota Department of Natural Resources, Madelia, Minnesota, USA.

Glines, T. 2003. Desires of sportsmen and women for expanding wild turkey populations north. Page 7 *in* R. O. Kimmel, W. J. Krueger, and T. K. Klinkner, compilers. Northern Wild Turkey Workshop. Minnesota Department of Natural Resources, Madelia, Minnesota, USA.

Gray, G. T., and H. H. Prince. 1988. Basal metabolism and energetic cost of thermoregulation in wild turkeys. Journal of Wildlife Management 52:133–137.

Gruber, N. W., K. R. Geray, D. M. Bruns Stockrahm, and R. O. Kimmel. 2004. Wild turkey distribution and urban human/turkey interactions along the Red River valley in northwestern Minnesota. Summaries of wildlife research findings 2004. Minnesota Department of Natural Resources, St. Paul, Minnesota, USA. In press.

Gullion, G. W. 1970. Factors influencing ruffed grouse populations. Transactions of the North American Wildlife and Natural Resources Conference 35:93–105.

Hamel, J. P., P. J. Pekins, and M. Ellingwood. 2003. Influence of winter supplemental feeding on wild turkeys in New Hampshire. Page 10 *in* R. O. Kimmel, W. J. Krueger, and T. K. Klinkner, compilers. Northern Wild Turkey Workshop. Minnesota Department of Natural Resources, Madelia, Minnesota, USA.

Haroldson, K. J. 1996. Energy requirements for winter survival of wild turkeys. Proceedings of the National Wild Turkey Symposium 7:9–14.

———, M. R. Riggs, and R. O. Kimmel. 2001. Effects of cold on body temperature regulation of wild turkeys. Proceedings of the National Wild Turkey Symposium 8:61–67.

———, M. L. Svihel, R. O. Kimmel, and M. R. Riggs. 1998. Effect of winter temperature on wild turkey metabolism. Journal of Wildlife Management 62:299–305.

Horton, R. 2003. Turkeys vs. ruffed grouse: beyond the rhetoric. Pages 36–37 *in* R. O. Kimmel, W. J. Krueger, and T. K. Klinkner, compilers. Northern Wild Turkey Workshop. Minnesota Department of Natural Resources, Madelia, Minnesota, USA.

Kane, D. F. 2003. Winter survival of eastern wild turkeys (*Meleagris gallopavo silvestris*) translocated north of their ancestral range in Minnesota. Thesis, St. Cloud State University, St. Cloud, Minnesota, USA.

Kilpatrick, H. J., T. P. Husband, and C. A. Pringle. 1988. Winter roost site characteristics of eastern wild turkeys. Journal of Wildlife Management 52:461–463.

———, J. A. Litvatis, and G. E. Thomas. 1990. Seasonal roost site characteristics of turkeys in southeastern New Hampshire. Transactions of the Northeastern Section of the Wildlife Society 47:10–14.

Kimmel, R. O. 1988. Potential impacts of ring-necked pheasants on other game birds. Pages 253–265 *in* D. L. Hallett, W. R. Edwards, and G. V. Burger, editors. Pheasants—symptoms of wildlife problems on agricultural lands, proceedings of a symposium. 1987 Midwest Fish and Wildlife Conference.

———, W. J. Krueger, and T. K. Klinkner, compilers. 2003. Northern Wild Turkey Workshop. Minnesota Department of Natural Resources, Madelia, Minnesota, USA.

Krueger, W. J. 2003. Survey of northern turkey biologists regarding current wild turkey range and plans for continued expansion. Page 6 *in* R. O. Kimmel, W. J. Krueger, and T. K. Klinkner, compilers. Northern Wild Turkey Workshop. Minnesota Department of Natural Resources, Madelia, Minnesota, USA.

Kulowiec, T. G., and J. B. Haufler. 1985. Winter and dispersal movements of wild turkeys in Michigan's northern lower peninsula. Proceedings of the National Wild Turkey Symposium 5:145–153.

Lehman, C. P., L. D. Flake, D. J. Thompson, and M. A. Rumble. 2003. Winter survival and farmstead dependence of Merriam's wild turkeys in the southern Black Hills, South Dakota. Page 17 *in* R. O. Kimmel, W. J. Krueger, and T. K. Klinkner, compilers. Northern Wild Turkey Workshop. Minnesota Department of Natural Resources, Madelia, Minnesota, USA.

Lewis, J. B. 1963. Observations on the winter range of wild turkeys in Michigan. Journal of Wildlife Management 27:98–102.

———. 2001. A success story revisited. Proceedings of the National Wild Turkey Symposium 8:7–13.

Moriarty, J., and B. Lueth. 2003. Urban wild turkeys: are they the new problem child. Page 22 *in* R. O. Kimmel, W. J. Krueger, and T. K. Klinkner, compilers. Northern Wild Turkey Workshop. Minnesota Department of Natural Resources, Madelia, Minnesota, USA.

Nguyen, L. P., J. Hamr, and G. H. Parker. 2003. Survival and reproduction of wild turkeys in central Ontario. Page 13 *in* R. O. Kimmel, W. J. Krueger, and T. K. Klinkner, compilers. Northern Wild Turkey Workshop. Minnesota Department of Natural Resources, Madelia, Minnesota, USA.

Oberlag, D. F., P. J. Pekinds, and W. W. Mautz. 1990. Influence of seasonal temperatures on wild turkey metabolism. Journal of Wildlife Management 54:663–667.

Porter, W. F. 1977. Utilization of agricultural habitats by wild turkeys in southeastern Minnesota. International Congress of Game Biologists 13:319–323.

———, and D. J. Gefell. 1996. Influences of weather and land use on wild turkey populations in New York. Proceedings of the National Wild Turkey Symposium 7:75–79.

———, G. C. Nelson, and K. Mattson. 1983. Effects of winter conditions on reproduction in a northern wild turkey population. Journal of Wildlife Management 47:281–290.

———, R. D. Tangen, G. C. Nelson, and D. A. Hamilton. 1980. Effects of corn food plots on wild turkeys in the upper Mississippi Valley. Journal of Wildlife Management 44:456–462.

Roberts, S. D., J. M. Coffey, and W. F. Porter. 1995. Survival and reproduction of female wild turkeys in New York. Journal of Wildlife Management 59:437–447.

Rumble, M. A., and S. H. Anderson. 1996. A test of the habitat suitability model for Merriam's wild turkeys. Proceedings of the National Wild Turkey Symposium 7:165–173.

Schorger, A. W. 1966. The wild turkey: its history and domestication. University of Oklahoma Press, Norman, Oklahoma, USA.

Tapley, J. L., R. K. Abernethy, and J. E. Kennamer. 2001. Status and distribution of the wild turkey in 1999. Proceedings of the National Wild Turkey Symposium 8:15–22.

Thomas, J. W., R. G. Marburger, and C. Van Hoozer. 1973. Rio Grande turkey migrations as related to harvest regulation in Texas. Pages 301–308 *in* G.C. Sanderson and H.C. Schultz, editors. Wild turkey management: current problems and programs. University of Missouri Press, Columbia, Missouri, USA.

Wright, R. G., R. N. Paisley, and J. F. Kubisiak. 1996. Survival of wild turkey hens in southwestern Wisconsin. Journal of Wildlife Management 60:313–320.

Wunz, G. A., and A. H. Hayden. 1975. Winter mortality and supplemental feeding of turkeys in Pennsylvania. Proceedings of the National Wild Turkey Symposium 3:61–69.

Dick Kimmel (left) is a Wildlife Research Group Leader with Minnesota Department of Natural Resources, where he has been employed since 1981. He has a Ph.D. in Wildlife Management from West Virginia University. His current research interests include northern wild turkeys, urban wild turkeys, turkey songs, and turkey hunt quality. ***Wendy Krueger*** (right) received her M.S. in Wildlife Management from West Virginia University in 1995. She has worked for Minnesota Department of Natural Resources for 15 years as a research biologist, wildlife depredation specialist, and currently as an area wildlife manager. Wendy was with Minnesota's wild turkey research program from 2002–2004.

Appendix A. **Survey instrument used in 2002 and 2004 for a survey of wildlife agency turkey biologists in the 11 states and 7 provinces along the Canadian/United States border.**

NORTHERN WILD TURKEY MANAGEMENT SURVEY

Name/Title: _____

State or Province: _____

PART I—WHERE WE ARE NOW:

1) On the attached map (see page 6), draw the proven northern boundary of current wild turkey distribution in your state/province (i.e., where wild turkeys have been established at least 5 years).

2) In your opinion, does the boundary in question 1 represent the northern limit for wild turkeys to survive?
Yes ____   No ____   Don't Know ____

3) Where is the northernmost wild turkey release in your state/province? (mark on the attached map on page 6)
What is the closest town? _____

4) Have there been successful wild turkey releases (i.e., resulting in a breeding population) north of the ancestral northern limit in your state/province? (refer to ancestral range map on page 7)   Yes ____   No ____

   IF YES: Are the released turkey populations expanding on their own?   Yes ____   No ____   Don't Know ____
   Do these populations require managed food plots and/or winter feeding for survival?
   Yes ____   No ____   Don't Know ____

5) Have there been unsuccessful wild turkey releases (i.e., not resulting in a breeding population) north of the ancestral northern limit in your state/province? (refer to ancestral range map on page 7)   Yes ____   No ____

   IF YES: What were the apparent causes of the unsuccessful release(s)? (check all that apply)
   Harsh weather conditions ____   Habitat limitations ____
   Food limitations ____   Predators ____
   Other (please describe): _____

6) Does your agency monitor winter weather conditions (ex., winter severity index)?   Yes ____   No ____
   IF YES, please describe what measurements are taken. _____

7) Do you have research data available on wild turkeys transplanted north of the ancestral line in your state/province?
Yes ____   No ____

   IF YES: What type of research? (check all that apply)
   Survival/Mortality ____
   Habitat Use/Selection ____
   Movements ____
   Reproduction ____
   Other (please describe): _____
   When was the research conducted? _____
   Briefly describe results or provide a copy of a research report(s) or abstract(s) along with the survey. _____

8) Please answer the following questions based on your **Northernmost** wild turkey population that has been **established at least 5 years**:
   a) What is the latitude? _____
   b) Closest town? _____
   c) Source of birds? _____
   d) Did the turkeys expand into the area on their own or were they transplanted?   Expanded ____   Transplanted ____
      When were the turkeys first detected or transplanted? _____
   e) Is there a hunting season?   Yes ____   No ____
      If yes, when is the season?   Spring only ____   Spring and Fall ____
   f) What is the predominant forest type?   Hardwoods ____   Conifers ____   Mixed Hardwood/Conifer ____
   g) What percentage of the habitat is forest?   %Forest ____   %Other ____   (Describe): _____
   h) Is agriculture present?   Yes ____   No ____
      If yes, what types of crops? _____
   i) What are the major winter food sources for wild turkeys in the area? _____
   j) Does your agency provide food plots in the area?   Yes ____   No ____
   k) Does your agency provide food for winter feeding of wild turkeys in the area?   Yes ____   No ____
   l) How many annual complaints does your agency receive of wild turkeys damaging crops in the area?
      None ____   Few ____   Several ____   Many ____
   m) How many annual complaints does your agency receive of wild turkey/human interactions in the area?
      None ____   Few ____   Several ____   Many ____
   n) What are the major predators of wild turkeys in the area? _____

Appendix A. Continued.

9) What are **your** management concerns and/or problems in the northern wild turkey range? (check all that apply)
Habitat limitations ___
Weather conditions ___
Food availability ___
Depredation ___
Predation ___
Public pressure to transplant northward ___
Pen-raised (game farm) turkeys ___
Winter feeding ___
Turkey management diverting funds from other wildlife management programs ___
Turkeys may impact other wildlife species ___
Other (please describe): _____

10) In your opinion, what parameter(s) best describes the northern limiting factor for wild turkeys? _____

PART II—WHERE ARE WE GOING?

1) Does your agency have a written policy/plan for moving wild turkeys northward?   Yes ___   No ___

IF YES, please briefly describe or provide a copy of the policy/plan with the completed survey. _____

2) What are your agency's plans for wild turkey releases north of currently existing populations for the next 5 years?
No releases ___   Limited releases ___   As many releases as possible ___
Comments: _____

3) Does your agency have a written policy/plan for providing winter food for wild turkeys?   Yes ___   No ___

IF YES, please briefly describe or provide a copy of the policy/plan with the completed survey. _____

4) How much public pressure does your agency receive for continued northern expansion of wild turkeys?
Heavy ___   Moderate ___   Light ___   None ___

IF PRESSURE is received:
Is a formal group(s) requesting releases?   Yes ___   No ___

If yes, what group(s)? _____
Where is the public requesting birds? (location, habitat, etc.) _____

5) How much opposition does your agency receive from ecologists, wildlife managers or the public for continued northern expansion of wild turkeys?   Heavy ___   Moderate ___   Light ___   None ___

IF OPPOSITION is received, what are the reasons for **their** concerns? (check all that apply)
Habitat limitations ___
Weather conditions ___
Food availability ___
Depredation ___
Predation ___
Public pressure to transplant northward ___
Pen-raised (game farm) turkeys ___
Winter feeding ___
Turkey management diverting funds from other wildlife management programs ___
Turkeys may impact other wildlife species ___
Other (please describe): _____

6) Is there future wild turkey research planned for your state/province?   Yes ___   No ___

IF YES, what type of research? (check all that apply)
Survival/Mortality ___
Habitat Use/Selection ___
Movements ___
Reproduction ___
Other (please describe): _____
When is the project(s) expected to start? _____
Who will lead the research? _____

7) What are the research needs for northern wild turkey populations in your state/province? (check all that apply)
No research needed ___
Survival/Mortality ___
Habitat Use/Selection ___
Movements ___
Reproduction ___
Other (please describe): _____

Wild Turkey Management:
Accomplishments, Strategies, and Opportunities
———— Grand Rapids, Michigan ————

WINTER BIOENERGETICS OF EASTERN WILD TURKEYS: UNDERSTANDING ENERGY BALANCE AND SURVIVAL IN NORTHERN POPULATIONS

Peter J. Pekins[1]

Department of Natural Resources,
215 James Hall, University of New Hampshire,
Durham, NH 03824, USA

Abstract: Northern populations of eastern wild turkeys (*Meleagris gallopavo sylvestris*) extend beyond their historic northern range and are exposed to longer, more extreme winter conditions than ancestral populations. Winter mortality is a common management concern, and survival is a function of energy balance that is influenced primarily by snow depth and condition that dictate use and availability of forage, mobility, and activity. The winter bioenergetics of northern populations were examined by reviewing standard and maintenance energy requirements, forage use and nutrition, body condition, activity and behavioral adaptations, and field metabolic rate. Nutritional value of winter diets is inversely related to snow depth with ground diets dominated by acorns or corn of highest metabolizable energy. Shrub and tree/seep diets typically eaten during periods of food restriction require 3 times higher intake than ground diets to meet daily energy demands. Effective thermoregulation, substantial body fat, and low field metabolic rate (FMR) are physiological adaptations for energy conservation, particularly during periods of restricted food availability and negative energy balance. In such situations adult hens have survival advantage over juvenile hens due to more body fat and lower FMR (kJ/kg/d). Use of available supplemental food is predictable and a function of energy balance that is strongly influenced by snow conditions that reduce quantity and quality of forage. The persistence and stability of many northern populations of wild turkeys may depend on their use of supplemental food during winter. The potential for management conflict exists as biologists attempt to restrict purposeful feeding of game species.

Proceedings of the National Wild Turkey Symposium 9:273–280

Key words: behavior, bioenergetics, energy, fat, field metabolic rate, food, *Meleagris gallopavo sylvestris*, nutrition, supplemental food, wild turkey, winter.

The successful restoration of the eastern wild turkey in the northeastern United States and the Great Lakes region has produced productive and, for the most part, persistent populations that exist well beyond their historic northern range (Wunz and Pack 1992).

This range expansion occurred because of change in forest habitat, agricultural influences, active management programs, and the adaptability of wild turkeys.

---

[1] E-mail: Pete.Pekins@unh.edu

Thus, turkeys at the fringe of their northern range are exposed to longer, more extreme and variable winter conditions than historical populations. Effective management of northern populations requires knowledge and understanding of bioenergetics because winter severity, particularly prolonged, deep powder snow, is often directly related to winter mortality and geographic range (Healy 1992*b*, Kubisiak et al. 2001). The influence of winter on survival of wild turkeys can be examined from a bioenergetic perspective that extends to nutrition, activity, condition, thermoregulation, and energy balance. The intent of this paper is to summarize and demonstrate uses of winter bioenergetic data to aid management of northern populations of eastern wild turkeys.

LITERATURE REVIEW

Food Habits and Nutrition

Wild turkeys are best adapted for ground foraging that is often compromised by snow conditions in northern habitats; thus, their winter diet and intake varies regionally and temporally. Their winter diet ranges from highly variable (>20 species at least 1% volume; Korschgen 1967) to severely restricted (e.g., entirely corn; Porter et al. 1980, Timmins 2003). Ground, shrub, and tree forage have all constituted >10% of the winter diet including acorns (*Quercus* spp.), field corn, grasses and sedges, sensitive fern (*Onoclea sensibilis*), beechnuts (*Fagus grandifolia*), cherries (*Prunus* sp.), sumacs (*Rhus* sp.), ferns and mosses, and wild grapes (*Vitis* sp.). Agricultural and woodlot habitats provide greater forage diversity than forestland, particularly persistent tree and shrub fruits above snow (e.g., barberry [*Berberis* sp.], rose hips [*Rosa multiflora*], apple [*Malus* sp. and *Cratageus* sp.]). Specialized habitats such as seeps, streams, and steep slopes often provide key forages (e.g., green vegetation, invertebrates, seeds, fern spores) when mobility is restricted (Porter 1992, Wunz and Pack 1992).

Distinction between forested, agricultural, and woodlot (forested-agricultural-suburban mix) habitats is necessary to evaluate forage use and availability relative to energy balance. Acorns are considered the dominant winter food in forestland, although beechnuts are as important in certain areas and years (Korschgen 1967). The importance of beechnuts probably increases latitudinally as beech replaces oak as the dominant hard mast producing species in northern forests. Corn is as important as hard mast in agricultural areas (Porter et al. 1980, 1983; Vander Haegan et al. 1989; Healy 1992*b*). However, a key difference is that standing/waste corn usually provides a stable, concentrated forage source (Porter et al. 1980) often attracting dense, local populations (Healy 1992*a*), whereas mast availability fluctuates with annual production and snow condition. Turkeys with access to corn in agricultural habitats had higher over-winter survival than turkeys in forestland during extreme winters in Minnesota (Porter et al. 1980), Massachusetts (Vander Haegan et al. 1989), and Vermont (Hay-

den 1980). Conversely, populations receiving supplemental food in forested and woodlot habitats maintained energy balance in a severe winter in New Hampshire, whereas an agricultural population using manure had a negative energy balance (Hamel 2002). The use, influence, and dependence of northern populations on inadvertent (e.g., backyard birdfeeders, silage pits) and purposeful supplementary feeding (e.g., feeding stations) present challenges to traditional assessment of habitat carrying capacity and winter severity (Hamel 2002, Timmins 2003).

The nutritional value of 8 common winter foods was measured in mixed diets fed to captive turkeys (Decker et al. 1991). Diets were constructed to simulate 3 conditions of forage availability/snow conditions: complete access to ground forage (acorn/corn-dominated diets), moderate access to ground forage (fruiting shrub-dominated diets), and restricted access to ground forage (tree/seep-dominated diets). The digestibility of all diets was high (65–84% of gross energy, 3.1–4.0 kcal/dry g matter), intake was inversely related to dry matter content, and turkeys maintained body weight on all diets at 80% of stable intake. The ground forage diets (acorn/corn) provided highest metabolizable energy (ME) with lowest intake. Fruiting shrub diets were ranked midway on a relative nutritional scale. Although the seep diet (sensitive fern) had the lowest ME and required the highest intake, it was high in protein. A turkey would need to triple its intake (wet weight) of the shrub and tree/seep diets to provide the ME equivalent of the ground diet.

Overall, the Decker at al. (1991) study indicated that nutritional value of winter diets declines as snow depth restricts mobility and availability of preferred ground forage. Of consequence to energy balance and nutrition of northern populations is that the absolute availability and density of fruiting shrubs and seeps will vary locally, particularly given restricted mobility, yet without ground forage, gross intake must increase to maintain energy balance. Thus, although any mixed diet could theoretically meet energy needs, the relationship between food availability and mobility will largely determine the actual nutritional value available on the landscape. For example, Wright et al. (1996) reported starvation in Wisconsin when deep snow restricted movement, despite available forage within one-half mile.

Much restoration and success of northern turkey populations, especially beyond their historic range, has been linked to dairy farms because of the availability of waste corn in fields and spread manure during winter (Wunz 1992, Wunz and Pack 1992, Kubisiak et al. 2001). Ironically, new practices in manure storage have reduced spread manure on many dairy farms during winter. Recent observations indicate that turkeys are increasingly feeding in large numbers in silage pits and feeding yards that provide concentrated food sources (Timmins 2003). Turkeys transplanted in central Ontario failed to use manure in winter and Nguyen et al. (2003) suggested that habitat structure and familiarity be considered in introduction efforts.

Large flocks (>150 birds) are now common on

farms in northern New Hampshire where winter survival was near 100% despite >65 cm snow depth for 2 months (Timmins 2003). Survival of marked birds using backyard supplemental food in northern New Hampshire was also 100%, despite snow depth >50 cm for >30 days (Hamel 2002). Not surprisingly, both movement and daily energy expenditure were low for birds using supplemental food (Coup and Pekins 1999, Hamel 2002). Clearly, assessment of nutritional carrying capacity must account for behavioral adaptations by wild turkeys to exploit new food resources that are increasingly important for their energy balance and survival in northern areas where non-agricultural forage is predictably limited by snow depth. Furthermore, the tendency of wild turkeys to depredate agricultural foods when natural forage is unavailable raises management issues that should be addressed prior to translocating turkeys into new range.

Activity: Roost Sites and Movement

Eastern wild turkeys presumably select or have affinity to roost in conifers during winter (Bailey and Rinell 1967, Gray 1986, Kilpatrick et al. 1988, Vander Haegan et al. 1989). Large white pines (*Pinus strobus*) with horizontal, open branching are used most often in New England. Structure, rather than species, probably influences use on a regional basis as hemlock (*Tsuga canadensis*) is also used commonly in the northeast (Healy 1992*a*, Porter 1992). The proximity of roost trees to open water has been noted in forested areas (Kilpatrick et al. 1988, 1990), but open water is probably not a strict requirement, rather, roost trees are associated with forage in nearby seeps and streams. Similarly, roost trees in agricultural habitat are usually proximate to fields with waste corn, manure, or stored silage (Porter et al. 1980, Vander Haegan et al. 1989, Timmins 2003).

Coniferous roost sites provide energy-saving microhabitats by reducing wind speed and radiative heat loss, as shown with other galliforms such as ruffed grouse (*Bonasa umbellus*; Thompson and Fritzell 1988) and blue grouse (*Dendragapus obscurus*; Pekins et al. 1997). However, winter roosting in deciduous trees is not uncommon in the northeast (Healy 1992*a*, Coup and Pekins 1999). The necessity of coniferous roost trees, particularly in dry, low wind conditions, seems questionable given the thermoregulatory ability of eastern wild turkeys (Oberlag et al. 1990, Coup and Pekins 1999), and their use may reflect weather and/or resource conditions. The energetic value of large conifers and their proximity to forage is probably most important in northern habitats where mobility and food availability are inversely related to snow depth (Wunz and Pack 1992).

Mobility and daily movement are dictated by snow depth and condition. Powder snow hinders mobility at 15–20 cm, and >30 cm can prevent movement (Austin and DeGraff 1975, Healy 1992*a*). Starvation occurred in Pennsylvania when snow depth was >30 cm for >2 weeks (Wunz and Hayden 1975, Wunz 1981, Healy 1992*b*), in Wisconsin when deep snow persisted for 49 days (Wright et al. 1996), and in New York at 40–59 days with prolonged deep snow (Roberts et al. 1995). Close proximity of roost trees and forage is ideal during periods of restricted mobility and food availability (Porter et al. 1980, Vander Haegan et al. 1989, Wunz and Pack 1992, Roberts et al. 1995). Home range and movement decline with restricted mobility (Healy 1992*a*). Home range and daily movements of flocks accessing supplemental food in New Hampshire were only 12 ha and <500 m, respectively, in a severe winter; corresponding values in a snowless winter were about 10 times larger (Hamel 2002). To access supplemental food in deep powder snow, 1 flock created packed, single-file trails similar to those made by wintering deer to reduce their energetic cost of travel.

Body Weight and Condition

The average body weight of wild turkey hens captured during winter in Massachusetts and New Hampshire ranged from 4.0–4.4 kg for adults and 3.3–3.8 kg for juveniles (Vander Haegan et al. 1989, Coup and Pekins 1999, Hamel 2002); hens in Minnesota were considerably larger (adults: 4.2–5.7 kg; juveniles: 3.7–4.8 kg); however, they lost appreciable weight (>20%) between captures (Porter et al. 1980). Juvenile hens lose weight faster than adult hens when food is restricted. Over 18 days with limited availability of manure, juvenile hens lost 11–17% and adults 9–10% of body weight in New Hampshire (Hamel 2002). Recovery from 30% weight loss is possible with resumption of intake at moderate levels (Hayden and Nelson 1963).

Wild turkeys maintain 15–20% body fat in winter (Bailey and Rinell 1967), Coup and Pekins 1999, Hamel 2002) that is critically important during extended periods of restricted food availability. This physiological adaptation is uncommon to most northern galliforms that typically maintain about 5% body fat and rarely face winter forage restriction (Thomas et al. 1975, Bergerud and Gratson 1988).

Based on estimates calculated from total body water measured with doubly labeled water, body fat is positively related to body weight in adult hens (Hamel 2002; Equation 1):

$$R^2 = 0.59, \qquad P < 0.05;$$

body fat (g) = 571.3 × (kg body weight) − 1696.   (1)

This relationship indicates that body fat in adult hens more than doubles absolutely (about 300 to 875 g) and proportionally (9 to 19%) as body weight increases from 3.5 to 4.5 kg. Conversely, hens weighing <3.0 kg have minimal body fat. Research with captive hens indicates that body fat falls below a critical threshold of ≤5% body fat for adult hens weighing 2.5–2.7 kg (P. Pekins, University of New Hampshire, unpublished data); Hayden and Nelson (1963) suggested that hens could endure 30% weight loss and 2.0 kg (0% body fat based on Equation 1) was a critical starvation weight.

Although no similar statistical relationship was found with juvenile hens, a similar trend existed and more importantly, juvenile hens were smaller and had less body fat than adults (Coup and Pekins 1999, Hamel 2002). Average percent body fat measured in hens during 4 winters in New Hampshire ranged from 13–19% in adults and 11–14% in juveniles. The energy available from this body fat was equivalent to an estimated 13–22 days of the adult energy requirement and 12–13 days of the juvenile energy requirement (Coup and Pekins 1999, Hamel 2002). The 12–13 days of energy associated with body fat of juveniles is similar to the 2-week estimate commonly associated with onset of winter mortality during periods of complete food restriction (Healy 1992b, Wunz and Pack 1992). Because juveniles are smaller and have proportionally less body fat than adults, they are at greater risk of malnutrition and starvation. Not surprisingly, the mortality rate of juvenile hens was higher than adults in flocks with restricted food availability in Minnesota (Porter et al. 1980). These data indicate that turkeys rely on fat storage to endure periods of food restriction, and the duration of restriction causes differential mortality rates because of age-related, physiological differences.

Energy Requirements, Thermoregulation, and Existence Metabolism

The standard metabolic rate (SMR; energy expenditure of a non-stressed, inactive, post-absorptive bird at thermoneutral temperature) and thermoregulatory energy costs are baseline data required to evaluate basic temperature-energy expenditure relationships of wild turkeys, and more importantly, are essential to partition and evaluate their daily energy budget. Four studies (Gray and Prince 1988, Oberlag et al. 1990, Haroldson et al. 1998, Coup and Pekins 1999) designed to provide these data produced highly variable results: 20–30% difference in SMR and a range of −15 to 10°C for the lower critical temperature in winter (T_{lc}; temperature below which metabolic rate exceeds SMR to maintain homeostasis). However, there was similarity (<10% range in reported values) among the studies with regard to metabolic rate measured at 0 to −20°C, ambient temperatures most commonly experienced by northern populations.

Because SMR and thermoregulation are required to explain and model energy balance of wild turkeys, I chose to use data from the lab at the University of New Hampshire. The SMR values of adult and juvenile hen turkeys used in this paper were 0.461 (Oberlag et al. 1990) and 0.511 mL O_2/g/hr (Coup and Pekins 1999), respectively, with an energy equivalent of 19.6 kJ/L O_2. It was further assumed that no thermoregulatory costs were incurred by free-ranging turkeys above −10°C. The justification for using these data is described below.

Only our SMRs were similar to that of domestic turkeys (MacLeod et al. 1985) and within 10% of SMR predicted from allometric equations (Robbins 1993). Two separate studies in New Hampshire (Oberlag et al. 1990, Coup and Pekins 1999) produced similar results; food consumption of captive turkeys

was not related to T_a from −10 to 5°C (Coup and Pekins 1999) as would be predicted if turkeys were thermally stressed >−5°C, and we found that the SMR of juvenile hens was about 10% higher than that of adult hens, an age-specific result common to most metabolic studies. Further, if the fall and winter T_{lc} were well above mean seasonal T_a in northern regions, as reported by Gray and Prince (1988) and Haroldson et al. (1998), the winter energy budget would be dominated by thermoregulatory costs, an unlikely scenario for large birds (Robbins 1993, and related behavior [e.g., constant use of sheltered roosts]).

Existence metabolism (EM) is defined as the metabolism of a fed turkey that maintains body weight (±3%; Gessaman 1987), and provides an estimate of daily energy expenditure that includes thermoregulation and minimal activity. The EM of 4 juvenile hens in large cages was measured during winter by measuring their metabolizable energy intake (MEI) of grain and fecal production in 5-day periods (Coup and Pekins 1999). The mean EM was 365±17 kJ/kg/d or about 1.4 × SMR. Existence metabolism was not correlated with T_a (range of −10 to 3°C) and daily consumption was about 90 g grain. Subtracting EM from the daily energy budget of a free-ranging bird would identify additional energy costs associated with free-ranging activity and environmental influences.

Energy Balance and Field Metabolic Rate

Energy balance is achieved when daily energy (food) intake equals daily energy expenditure. Weight loss indicates negative energy balance, and the rate of weight loss is a function of the relative proportions of food and tissue energy used to meet energy expenditure. Daily energy expenditure is the sum total of energy costs associated with all phases of life, and was originally estimated with time-activity budgets developed from winter observations of free-ranging turkeys (Gray 1986); simultaneous comparison with data of captive turkeys indicated that the budgets were underestimated.

An alternative to using time-activity budgets is the doubly labeled water method which provides measurement of carbon dioxide production of free-ranging animals over extended periods (days), as well as an estimate of body condition (body fat) from measurement of total body water at capture. Carbon dioxide production is converted to its energy equivalent and referred to as FMR; partitioning of FMR into proportional costs of activity/time/energy source is possible with other data. This technique offers tremendous potential to analyze the interrelationships of weather, environmental conditions, food availability, behavior, and physiology affecting energy balance.

The ratio of FMR:SMR identifies the proportion of energy costs above minimum (SMR). Typical annual FMR:SMR ratios range from 2–3 (Robbins 1993), but seasonal ratios vary depending upon state of productivity, activity, and environmental influences. Previous winter measurements of northern galliforms (e.g., blue grouse and white-tailed ptarmigan [*Lagopus leucurus*]) yielded ratios <2.0 (Pekins et al. 1994, Thomas et al. 1994). Further, FMR:EM ratios indicate the increased activity cost associated with free-ranging turkeys versus birds with minimal activity.

The winter FMR of eastern wild turkeys was measured in 2 studies during 4 winters in New Hampshire; individual turkeys were measured for 12–26 consecutive days (Coup and Pekins 1999, Hamel 2002). The average FMRs of each winter were remarkably similar despite variable weather and snow conditions; adult hen FMR was 323–356 kJ/kg/d and juvenile hen FMR was 367–400 kJ/kg/d. Average juvenile hen FMR was 10–14% higher than adult hen FMR. The FMR:SMR ratios ranged from 1.3–1.6 for adults and 1.5–1.8 for juveniles. Although adult ratios were slightly lower, the similarity of juvenile EM (365 kJ/kg/d) and FMR (367–400 kJ/kg/d) points to the efficiency of all birds. Overall, these ratios are considered low and indicative of efficient energy conservation by free-ranging wild turkeys in variable winter conditions.

I calculated daily activity costs as a proportion of FMR by subtracting the cost of nocturnal roosting, which I considered thermoneutral (i.e., >−10°C). Roosting costs were assumed equal to resting metabolic rate, which is the metabolism of a fed bird at rest. Resting metabolic rate has not been measured in wild turkeys, but was 1.14 × SMR in sage grouse (*Centrocercus urophasianus*; Sherfy and Pekins 1994). Relative to adults, nocturnal roosting of juvenile hens is proportionally more expensive because of their higher SMR, which also elevates the cost of any activity. This effect, in large part, explains why the FMR of juvenile hens is 10% higher than that of adult hens. During 4 winters in New Hampshire, daily activity costs were similar in 3 winters (59–65%), and higher in 1 of 2 winters with unrestricted mobility (71%; Coup and Pekins 1999). Overall, daily movement isn't considered a major part of FMR (Garland 1983, Altman 1987) and will be minimal when mobility is restricted by snow; the energy cost of turkeys moving 3,400 m daily was estimated as only 6% of FMR (Hamel 2002).

Energy (food) intake can be calculated as the difference between FMR and the tissue energy associated with weight loss. The rate of weight loss can be related to body weight and body fat to predict the temporal influence of food availability on body condition. The FMR studies in New Hampshire provided the opportunity to measure individual weight loss over 12–26 days. Although most treatment groups realized energy balance by accessing supplemental food, 1 group had limited access to manure only and lost 12% body weight in 18 days. Hamel (2002) estimated that their intake (corn in manure) represented only 22% of juvenile and 36% of adult FMR, and that body fat would deplete in 14 and 21 days, respectively. It is not coincidental that if the extrapolated body weight of a juvenile hen in 14 days was <3.0 kg, that fat would deplete in a time period similar to that associated with mortality from food restriction in field and laboratory studies, and that adult hens had advantage over juveniles in this food restricted situation.

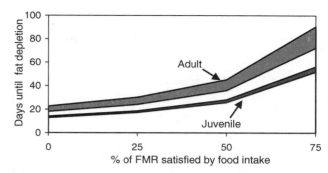

Fig. 1. The predicted number of days until fat depletes in adult and juvenile wild turkey hens when food intake during winter is varied as a proportion of the field metabolic rate (FMR). The shaded areas indicate the range of days using the average (lower bound) and largest hens (upper bound) captured in winter in northern New Hampshire (Hamel 2002).

ANALYSIS AND DISCUSSION

The combination of FMR, body weight and fat, and forage nutritional data provides an opportunity to evaluate energy balance in varied winter conditions. The age class difference in body weight, body fat, and winter mortality of hens suggests that adults have advantage over juveniles in food restricted situations. To evaluate this, I modeled the proportional contribution of body fat to FMR under variable intake regimes to predict the number of days until fat depletion. Adult and juvenile hens were assigned body weights corresponding to the average (4.1 and 3.3 kg, respectively) and heaviest body weights (4.6 and 4.1 kg, respectively) measured by Hamel (2002). Their FMRs (344 and 378 kJ/kg/d, respectively; Hamel 2002) were converted to absolute energy costs (kJ/bird) and intake energy was set at 0, 25, 50, and 75% of FMR. The body fat (g) corresponding to body weight (Equation 1; Hamel 2002) was converted to its energy equivalent (38.9 kJ/g; Dargolts 1973), and the time (days) until fat depletion was calculated by dividing total fat energy by the difference between FMR and intake energy.

This exercise (Figure 1) illustrated that despite 20% higher FMR (kJ/bird), adult hens have a distinct advantage (days until fat depletion) over juveniles whenever food is restricted, and that the advantage increased with higher food intake. Surprisingly, the large juvenile realized minimal advantage over the average juvenile in comparison to the adults (width of band). Juvenile food intake had to approach 35% of FMR to prevent fat depletion before 21 days, a delay realized by adults at 0% intake. Further, at 75% intake, adults were projected to have about 80 days of fat reserves, about 1 month more than juveniles. Considering that many northern populations occupy areas with >90 days of snow cover, the advantages of age class and food availability are apparent. Given the constraints upon energy balance and survival when food is restricted, the adaptive response by northern wild turkeys to use supplemental food sources is understandable, if not predictable.

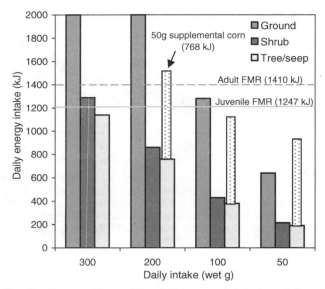

Fig. 2. A comparison of the daily energy intake by adult and juvenile wild turkey hens experiencing variable intake levels during winter. Three diets were used to simulate variable food restriction related to snow depth. Addition of 50 g of corn compensated for most of the energy deficit below the field metabolic rate (FMR) that occurred at low intake levels.

To illustrate the potential impact of supplemental feeding on energy balance during food restriction, I modeled daily energy intake as a function of the 3 diet types described previously (ground, shrub, tree/seep). I simulated food intake at 4 levels (50, 100, 200, and 300 wet g/day). Energy intake was calculated from dietary nutritional data corresponding to the diet types (dry matter and ME data; Decker et al. 1991). When intake energy was less than FMR, I simulated a dietary supplement of 50 g corn (786 kJ of ME; Decker et al. 1991). I assumed the difference between FMR and total energy intake was met by tissue energy.

This exercise illustrated a large energetic difference between a ground diet and shrub and tree/seep diets given equal intake (Figure 2). Intake approximated FMR at about 100 g for the ground diet and about 300 g for the shrub and tree/seep diets. In comparison, Decker et al. (1991) observed that captive hens maintaining body weight ate about 110 and 450 g of these diets, respectively. If intake declined to <300 g, the shrub and tree/seep diets required increasingly higher energy replacement to meet FMR; a 200-g intake level required fat energy to equal about 35% of FMR. However, addition of 50 g of corn nearly eliminated the negative energy balance of these diets at 100 g intake level (Figure 2). Although somewhat arbitrary, 50 g of corn is easily consumed by a hen based upon crop weight data (Hurst 1992) and intake rate of captive hens (Decker et al. 1991). This small amount provided >50% of FMR and represents the equivalent of >20 days of fat reserves of a juvenile hen (Figure 1). These bioenergetic data provide further evidence of the importance of agriculture, as well as the lure and impact of supplemental feeding on northern turkey populations.

SUMMARY

Eastern wild turkeys have physiological adaptations for energy conservation in northern environments including effective thermoregulation, substantial body fat, and low FMR. Nutritional status can be predicted from body weight based on a positive relationship between body weight and body fat. Adult hens have a threshold body weight of about 3.0 kg when body fat is minimal. Nutritional value of winter diets is inversely related to snow depth and intake requirements increase substantially when snow eliminates availability of ground diets high in acorns, beechnuts, or corn. The duration of food restriction is the primary factor affecting energy balance, body condition, and mortality.

The lower body fat and higher FMR of juvenile hens places them at greater risk than adult hens during periods of food restriction. Juvenile hens will deplete body fat in about 2 weeks without food and in 3 weeks with intake equal to 50% of FMR; adult hens will deplete body fat in about 20 and 40 days, respectively. High mortality of juvenile hens would limit population growth (Roberts and Porter 1996).

Because snow depth often restricts natural forage in northern regions, it is not surprising that wild turkeys access supplemental food to maintain energy balance. In agricultural areas, the potential for depredation of standing and stored crops should be considered prior to translocating wild turkeys into new range. Arguably, supplemental food could be necessary for maintaining stable northern populations of wild turkeys, particularly when and where snow limits ground forage, and agricultural forage is unavailable. This regional situation is often confounded by increased public interest in viewing and attracting wild turkeys, and near unanimous agreement of state, federal, and private biologists to discourage purposeful feeding of game species.

ACKNOWLEDGMENTS

This paper drew heavily from research of many dedicated biologists who pioneered efforts to restore wild turkeys in northern states. The authors of chapters in *The Wild Turkey, Biology and Management* provided invaluable summaries of past research. Many graduate and undergraduate students worked tirelessly on bioenergetic research at the University of New Hampshire, and their novel research efforts are principally reflected in this paper. Research at the University of New Hampshire was funded with MacIntire-Stennis research support, the New Hampshire Fish and Game Department, and the National Wild Turkey Federation. This paper recognizes the extraordinary efforts of T. Walski, wildlife biologist of the New Hampshire Fish and Game Department, who has dedicated much of his career to establish, manage, and research the wild turkey population in New Hampshire.

LITERATURE CITED

Altmann, S. A. 1987. The impact of locomotor energetics on mammalian foraging. Journal of Zoology 211:215–225.

Austin, D. E., and L. W. DeGraaf. 1975. Winter survival of wild turkeys in the southern Adirondacks. Proceedings of the National Wild Turkey Symposium 3:55–60.

Bailey, R. W., and K. T. Rinell. 1967. Events in the turkey year. Pages 73–91 *in* O. H. Hewitt, editor. The wild turkey and its management. The Wildlife Society, Washington, D. C., USA.

Bergerud, A. T., and M. W. Gratson. 1988. Survival and breeding strategies of grouse. Pages 473–577 *in* A. T. Bergerud and M. W. Gratson, editors. Adaptive strategies and population ecology of northern grouse. Volume 2. Theory and synthesis. University of Minnesota Press, Minneapolis, Minnesota, USA.

Coup, R. N., and P. J. Pekins. 1999. Field metabolic rate of wild turkeys in winter. Canadian Journal of Zoology 77:1075–1082.

Dargolts, V. G. 1973. An analysis of constants used in indirect calorimetry of birds and mammals. Soviet Journal of Ecology 4:68–74.

Decker, S. R., P. J. Pekins, and W. W. Mautz. 1991. Nutritional evaluation of winter foods of wild turkeys. Canadian Journal of Zoology 69:2128–2132.

Garland, T., Jr. 1983. Scaling the ecological cost of transport to body mass in terrestrial mammals. American Naturalist 121: 571–587.

Gessaman, J. A. 1987. Energetics. Pages 289–320 *in* B. A. Giron Pendleton, B. A. Milsap, K. W. Cline, and D. M. Bird, editors. Raptor management techniques manual. National Wildlife Federation, Washington, D.C., USA.

Gray, B. T. 1986. Bioenergetics of the wild turkey in Michigan. Thesis, Michigan State University, Lansing, Michigan, USA.

———, and H. H. Prince. 1988. Basal metabolism and energetic cost of thermoregulation in wild turkeys. Journal of Wildlife Management 52:133–137.

Hamel, J. P. 2002. Influence of winter supplemental feeding on the winter bioenergetics and reproduction of eastern wild turkeys in New Hampshire. Thesis, University of New Hampshire, Durham, New Hampshire, USA.

Haroldson, K. J., M. L. Swvihel, R. O. Kimmel, and M. R. Riggs. 1998. Effect of winter temperature on thermoregulation of wild turkeys. Journal of Wildlife Management 62: 299–305.

Hayden, A. H. 1980. Dispersal and movements of wild turkeys in northern Pennsylvania. Transactions of the Northeastern Section of The Wildlife Society 37:258–265.

———, and E. Nelson. 1963. The effects of starvation and limited rations on reproduction of game-farm wild turkeys. Transactions of the Northeast Section of The Wildlife Society 20:1–11.

Healy, W. M. 1992*a*. Behavior. Pages 46–65 *in* J. G. Dickson, editor. The wild turkey: biology and management. Stackpole Books, Harrisburg, Pennsylvania, USA.

———, 1992*b*. Population influences: environment. Pages 129–143 *in* J. G. Dickson, editor. The wild turkey: biology and management. Stackpole Books, Harrisburg, Pennsylvania, USA.

Hurst, G. A. 1992. Foods and feeding. Pages 66–83 *in* J. G. Dickson, editor. The wild turkey: biology and management. Stackpole Books, Harrisburg, Pennsylvania, USA.

Kilpatrick, H. J., T. P. Husband, and C. A. Pringle. 1988. Winter roost site characteristics of eastern wild turkeys in Rhode Island. Journal of Wildlife Management 52:461–463.

———, J. A. Litvaitis, and G. E. Thomas. 1990. Seasonal roost site characteristics of turkeys in southeastern New Hampshire. Transactions of the Northeast Section of The Wildlife Society 47:10–14.

Korschgen, L. J. 1967. Feeding habits and foods. Pages 137–198 *in* O. H. Hewitt, editor. The wild turkey and its management. The Wildlife Society, Bethesda, Maryland, USA.

Kubisiak, J. F., R. E. Rolley, R. N. Paisley, and R. G. Wright. 2001. Wild turkey ecology and management in Wisconsin. Wisconsin Department of Natural Resources, Madison, Wisconsin, USA.

MacLeod, M. G., H. Lundy, and T. A. Jewitt. 1985. Heat production by the mature male turkey: preliminary measurements in an automated, indirect, open-circuit calorimeter system. British Poultry Science 26:325–333.

Nguyen, L. P., J. Hamr, and G. H. Parker. 2003. Survival and reproduction of wild turkey hens in central Ontario. Wilson Bulletin. 115:131–139.

Oberlag, D. F., P. J. Pekins, and W. W. Mautz. 1990. Influence of season and temperature on wild turkey metabolism. Journal of Wildlife Management 54:663–667.

Pekins, P. J., J. A. Gessaman, and F. G. Lindzey. 1994. Field metabolic rate of blue grouse during winter. Canadian Journal of Zoology 70:22–24.

———, ———, and ———. 1997. Microclimatic characteristics of blue grouse *Dendragapus obscurus* roost-sites: influence on energy expenditure. Wildlife Biology 3:243–250.

Porter, W. F. 1992. Habitat requirements. Pages 202–213 *in* J. G. Dickson, editor. The wild turkey: biology and management. Stackpole Books, Harrisburg, Pennsylvania, USA.

———, G. C. Nelson, and K. Mattson. 1983. Effects of winter conditions on reproduction in a northern wild turkey population. Journal of Wildlife Management 47:281–290.

———, R. D. Tangen, G. C. Nelson, and D. A. Hamilton. 1980. Effects of corn food plots on wild turkeys in the upper Mississippi Valley. Journal of Wildlife Management 44: 456–462.

Robbins, C. T. 1993. Wildlife feeding and nutrition. Academic Press, Orlando, Florida, USA.

Roberts, S. D., J. M. Coffey, and W. F. Porter. 1995. Survival and reproduction of female wild turkeys in New York. Journal of Wildlife Management 59:437–447.

———, and W. F. Porter. 1996. Importance of demographic parameters to annual changes in wild turkey abundance. Proceedings of the National Wild Turkey Symposium 7:15–20.

Sherfy, M. H., and P. J. Pekins. 1994. The influence of season, temperature and absorptive state on sage grouse metabolism. Canadian Journal of Zoology 72:898–903.

Thomas, D. W., K. Martin, and H. LaPierre. 1994. Doubly labelled water measurements of field metabolic rate in White-tailed Ptarmigan: variation in background isotope abundances and effect on CO_2 production estimates. Canadian Journal of Zoology 72:1967–1972.

Thomas, V. G., H. G. Lumsden, and D. H. Price. 1975. Aspects of winter metabolism of ruffed grouse (*Bonasa umbellus*) with special reference to energy reserves. Canadian Journal of Zoology 53:434–440.

Thompson, F. R., and E. K. Fritzell. 1988. Ruffed grouse winter roost site selection and influence on energy demands. Journal of Wildlife Management 52:454–460.

Timmins, A. A. 2003. Seasonal home range, nesting ecology, and survival of eastern wild turkeys in northern New Hampshire. Thesis, University of New Hampshire, Durham, New Hampshire, USA.

Vander Haegen, W. M., M. W. Sayre, and W. E. Dodge. 1989. Winter use of agricultural habitats by wild turkeys in Massachusetts. Journal of Wildlife Management 53:30–33.

Wright, R. G., R. N. Paisely, and J. F. Kubisiak. 1996. Survival of wild turkey hens in southwestern Wisconsin. Journal of Wildlife Management 60:313–320.

Wunz, G. A. 1981. Evaluation of supplemental feeding of wild turkeys. Pennsylvania Game Commission, Federal Aid in Wildlife Restoration Project W-46-R-25, Final Report.

———. 1992. Wild turkeys outside their historic range. Pages 361–384 *in* J. G. Dickson, editor. The wild turkey: biology and management. Stackpole Books, Harrisburg, Pennsylvania, USA.

————, and A. H. Hayden. 1975. Winter mortality and supplemental feeding of wild turkeys in Pennsylvania. Proceedings of the National Wild Turkey Symposium 3:61–69.

————, and J. C. Pack. 1992. Eastern turkey in eastern oak-hickory and northern hardwood forest. Pages 232–264 *in* J. G. Dickson, editor. The wild turkey: biology and management. Stackpole Books, Harrisburg, Pennsylvania, USA.

Peter J. Pekins is Professor of Wildlife Ecology and Coordinator of the Wildlife Management Program at the University of New Hampshire (UNH). He received his MS in Wildlife Ecology at UNH (1981) and a PhD in Wildlife Science at Utah State University (1988). He directed UNH's long-standing bioenergetic research program focused on captive white-tailed deer and wild turkeys at the UNH Wildlife Research Facility, 1987–2004. He has conducted field and laboratory research in New England, Utah, and Norway with a multitude of species including wild turkeys, deer, moose, blue grouse, spruce grouse, sage grouse, ptarmigan, bats, black bears, coyotes, and bobcats. He has received four teaching excellence awards and an advising award at UNH, and has been the major advisor of 25 graduate students. His current research includes urban and agricultural management issues of wild turkeys, genetic tagging of black bears, and moose ecology.

9th National Wild Turkey Symposium

Wild Turkey Management:
Accomplishments, Strategies, and Opportunities
———— Grand Rapids, Michigan ————

CHARACTERISTICS OF WINTER ROOST AND ACTIVITY SITES OF WILD TURKEYS IN MINNESOTA

Jacquie R. Ermer[1]
Farmland Wildlife Populations and Research Group,
Minnesota Department of Natural Resources,
35365 800th Avenue,
Madelia, MN 56062, USA

Richard O. Kimmel
Farmland Wildlife Populations and Research Group,
Minnesota Department of Natural Resources,
35365 800th Avenue,
Madelia, MN 56062, USA

Paul D. Evenson
Midwest Computer Consultants, Inc., Box 41,
Brookings, SD 57006, USA

Kurt J. Haroldson[2]
Farmland Wildlife Populations and Research Group,
Minnesota Department of Natural Resources,
35365 800th Avenue,
Madelia, MN 56062, USA

Charles D. Dieter
Department of Biology and Microbiology, Box 2207B,
South Dakota State University,
Brookings, SD 57007, USA

Barry D. Berg
Department of Biology and Microbiology, Box 2207B,
South Dakota State University,
Brookings, SD 57007, USA

Abstract: Selection of winter microhabitats that minimize heat loss from wind and radiation can potentially reduce thermoregulatory energy requirements and increase survival of wild turkeys (*Meleagris gallopavo*). In this study we compared winter microclimatic and microhabitat characteristics of nocturnal roost sites and diurnal activity sites in an attempt to identify features of roost sites that may reduce thermoregulatory energy demands of eastern wild turkeys (*M. g. silvestris*) in Minnesota. During the winters of 1997–1999, we compared weather and habitat characteristics at 119 paired roost and activity sites of 27 radio-tagged female wild turkeys. Turkeys traveled only 396 ± 32 m ($\bar{x}$ ± SE) from diurnal activity sites to nocturnal roost sites, offering little evidence of deliberate travel to preferred roost habitats. Roost and activity sites both provided protection from wind, which averaged 12.2 km/h greater at open sites ($P < 0.001$). Wild turkeys used roost sites characterized by a higher canopy ($P < 0.001$) and, in the severe winter of 1997, larger diameter overstory trees ($P = 0.020$) and greater overstory stem density ($P = 0.018$) than at activity sites. Turkeys selected coniferous forest stands for 26.0% of their roosts, even though conifers formed <1% of the study area. However, daily selection of conifer roosts was not significantly greater ($P = 0.219$) on cold nights than warm nights. Turkeys selected upper and lower slopes for diurnal activity sites ($P < 0.001$), where they had easy access to ridgetop and valley cropland. Most activity (45.3%) and roost (47.8%) sites were located on slopes facing south to southwest. Winter roost sites in this study were better described by proximity to available food than by characteristics of favorable microclimates.

Proceedings of the National Wild Turkey Symposium 9:281–288

Key words: *Meleagris gallopavo*, microclimate, microhabitat, Minnesota, roost site, wild turkey, winter.

The historic northern distribution of wild turkeys likely was limited by winter severity, but advanced as far north as central Wisconsin and southern Minnesota during periods with mild winters (Leopold 1931). After wild turkeys were extirpated from much of their northern range in the late 1800s, Minnesota Depart-

[1] Present address: 42924 146th Street, Webster, SD 57274, USA.
[2] E-mail: kurt.haroldson@dnr.state.mn.us

ment of Natural Resources initiated a trap and trans-plant program in 1964 to reestablish and expand east-ern wild turkey (*M. g. silvestris*) range in Minnesota (Minnesota Department of Natural Resources 1983). Many release sites were north of the ancestral range (Kennamer and Kennamer 1990), exposing the birds to harsher, more prolonged winter weather than expe-rienced by historical populations.

Winter weather appears to affect survival of north-ern wild turkeys as a function of energy balance, rather than direct mortality (Haroldson 1996, Coup and Pe-kins 1999). Below the lower critical temperature esti-mated between 11°C (Gray and Prince 1988, Harold-son et al. 1998) and −16°C (Oberlag et al. 1990), wild turkey energy demands for thermoregulation increase linearly with decreasing air temperature. Because win-ter temperatures may remain below −16°C for several weeks in northern turkey range, wild turkeys must meet thermoregulatory energy demands by increasing food consumption, reducing energy expenditure, or us-ing energy reserves (i.e., body fat). Mortality rates have increased substantially when deep snow restricted food availability over a prolonged period and energy reserves were exhausted (Austin and Degraff 1975, Wunz and Hayden 1975, Porter et al. 1980, Roberts et al. 1995, Wright et al. 1996).

Selection of winter microclimates that minimize heat loss from wind and radiation to the open sky can reduce thermoregulatory energy requirements (Wals-berg 1986, Thompson and Fritzell 1988, Pekins et al. 1991, Sherfy and Pekins 1995) and potentially in-crease survival of wild turkeys. Thermoregulatory en-ergy demands of nocturnally inactive birds (e.g., wild turkeys) are greatest during winter nights when birds are resting and air temperature is lowest. Because tur-keys spend more than 50% of their time on roost dur-ing winter (Prince and Gray 1986), selection of roost microclimates may influence turkey energy expendi-tures more than selection of diurnal microclimates. Fe-male wild turkeys should benefit from microclimate selection more than males because metabolic costs for thermoregulation are greater for females than males (Gray and Prince 1988). Thompson and Fritzell (1988) determined that ruffed grouse (*Bonasa umbellus*) re-duced nocturnal energy expenditure 33% by using snow roosts and 19% by using conifer roosts that min-imized radiative heat loss.

Information is lacking on characteristics of winter roosting areas used by eastern wild turkeys in the mid-western United States. We hypothesized that if wild turkeys select favorable microclimates for winter roosting, then roost sites should differ from diurnal activity sites in microclimatic and microhabitat fea-tures. The objectives of this study were to (1) compare winter microclimatic and microhabitat characteristics of nocturnal roost sites and diurnal activity sites, and (2) identify features of roost sites that may reduce ther-moregulatory energy demands of wild turkeys at the northern periphery of their range.

STUDY AREA

The study area encompassed 90,877 ha of private and publicly owned land on and around Whitewater Wildlife Management Area in Wabasha and Winona counties in southeastern Minnesota. Elevations ranged from 180 to 450 m above sea level with steep, forested slopes separating ridgetop and valley cropland. Corn, soybeans, and alfalfa were the principal crops in the region with dairy farming as the major farm practice. The study area included 40% cultivated land, 30% de-ciduous forest, 22% grassland, 4% water and wetlands, 2% shrubland, and 2% rural or urban development. Less than 1% of the area was made up of coniferous forest and mixed coniferous-deciduous forest. Oaks (*Quercus* spp.) were the dominant deciduous forest species. Conifers were distributed in small patches (x̄ = 2.2 ha) and were dominated by red cedar (*Juniperus virginiana*) or plantations of white pine (*Pinus stro-bus*) and red pine (*P. resinosa*).

Cumulative winter (Dec-Mar) snowfall averaged 90.1 cm and winter temperature ranged from an av-erage daily high of −0.1°C to an average daily low of −11.0°C at Winona, Minnesota (Minnesota Climatol-ogy Working Group 1950–2000), which was located approximately 30 km southeast of the study area. In 51 years of measurements, daily temperature fell be-low −16°C (the lowest estimate of wild turkey lower critical temperature; Oberlag et al. 1990) an average of 31 days/winter (range 2–66 days/winter). Our study period was characterized by moderate to mild winter weather. Cumulative snowfall during 1997, 1998, and 1999 ranked twenty-first, forty-second, and twenty-ninth, respectively, and mean daily temperature ranked thirtieth, fifty-first, and forty-ninth, respectively, with a rank of one being most severe, for the 51-year period 1950–2000 at Winona, Minnesota. Snow did not ap-pear to limit mobility of wild turkeys or access to food for extended periods during the 3-year study. Winter survival rates of radiomarked birds were high (0.80 in 1997, 0.92 in 1998, 0.93 in 1999), and virtually all mortality was associated with predation (B. D. Berg, South Dakota State University, unpublished data).

METHODS

We trapped wild turkeys using rocket nets during January–March 1997 and 1998. We fitted females with a mortality-sensitive, backpack-style radio transmitter (Advanced Telemetry Systems, Isanti, Minnesota, USA) that weighed an average of 92 g (≤2.0% of body weight) and we released them at the capture site. We allowed turkeys a 7-day adjustment period post-capture before we collected habitat data (Nenno and Healy 1979).

During the 3-year study, we located diurnal activi-ty sites and nocturnal roost sites 2–3 days/week dur-ing winter (December–March) only. Each day we lo-cated both the activity and roost sites of 2–4 radio-marked birds. Because wild turkeys are grouped into small flocks during winter (Healy 1992), we randomly selected birds from different flocks to monitor each day. We treated roost and activity sites occupied by >1 radiomarked bird as one observation. We located activity sites between sunrise and 1500 hours by following the signal from radiomarked birds using a 4-element, hand-held, yagi antenna and receiver (Advanced Telemetry Systems, Isanti, Minnesota, USA) until we could visually observe the birds or their fresh tracks in the snow. We subsequently located roost sites after sunset by following a radio signal directly to the flock containing the target bird. Activity sites were located with minimal apparent disturbance to the flock, whereas we were unable to approach roost sites without flushing the flock. We used a global positioning system (GPS) receiver to determine geographic coordinates of activity and roost sites.

Weather Measurements

We measured air temperature (mercury-in-glass thermometer) and wind speed (wind meter, Dwyer Instruments, Michigan City, Indiana, USA) 1.4 m above ground level, and snow depth on the ground below roost trees at night immediately after the birds were located on their nocturnal roosts. We acknowledge that ground conditions may not have reflected those in the forest canopy where turkeys roosted, but we reasoned that turkeys may have selected their roost sites based on conditions on the ground shortly before flying into the roost. In 1998 and 1999, we also measured air temperature, wind speed, and snow depth at diurnal activity sites at night by returning to the activity site within 1 hour of measuring weather conditions at the respective nocturnal roost sites. In 1997, we measured snow depth at diurnal activity sites when the birds were located during the day and not revisited at night to measure temperature and wind. To assess weather conditions at the time when turkeys generally fly into their nocturnal roost, we measured temperature and wind speed one-half hour before sunset each sampling day in all years at randomly selected open sites (actual turkey locations could not be measured without disturbing the birds).

Microhabitat Measurements

We quantified vegetative characteristics at each roost and activity site by measuring all woody stems within a 0.025-ha circular plot (James and Shugart 1970) centered at the midpoint of nocturnal roost trees and diurnal activity, respectively. We identified species and measured diameter at breast height (dbh) using a diameter tape. We considered any woody stem ≥10.2 cm dbh to be part of the overstory, whereas we considered smaller woody stems part of the understory. From these measures, we calculated mean overstory dbh, overstory basal area, density of overstory trees, and density of understory trees. We estimated height of the top of the general canopy and percent slope with a clinometer. We estimated aspect from a downhill compass bearing. Based on the dominant overstory species, we classified vegetation as deciduous forest, coniferous forest, or grass-agriculture. We classified topographic position as upper-slope (upper 25% of slope including ridge), mid-slope, or lower-slope (lower 25% of slope including valley). We measured dis-

tance between activity and roost sites using a geographic information system.

Analyses

We used regression analysis (INSIGHT, SAS Institute 1995) to determine if distance traveled by turkeys from activity to roost sites was associated with snow depth, temperature, and wind speed. We calculated an F-statistic for each independent variable in the model, and examined plots of residuals for evidence of independence and constant variance.

We compared temperature and wind speed among activity, roost, and open sites using a randomized block design with block equal to day; means were compared using Scheffé's test (Zar 1996). We paired data collected from activity sites with roost data, and compared parameters using paired-difference t-tests (Zar 1996).

We used paired t-tests to compare snow depths between nocturnal roost sites and diurnal activity sites. We also used paired t-tests to compare microhabitat characteristics (i.e., canopy height, overstory dbh, overstory basal area, overstory density, understory density) between forested roost and forested activity sites. We determined differences among years in microhabitat characteristics at activity and roost sites using analysis of variance. Because most microhabitat measurements were related to trees, we excluded activity sites occurring in grass-agriculture vegetation in comparisons of microhabitat characteristics. However, we included all sites in comparisons of percent slope and aspect. We used chi-square tests of independence to compare topographic classes and aspect between roost and activity sites. We were unable to conduct analyses using repeated measures because of missing values due to random selection of turkeys each winter.

We used chi-square tests of independence and Fisher's exact test (Zar 1996) to evaluate the hypotheses that use of vegetative type was independent of year for both roost and activity sites and to determine if vegetative type at roost sites was independent of vegetative type at activity sites. More complex categorical modeling was not appropriate because of the number of zero counts in cells. We used the chi-square test for differences in probabilities to compare proportional use of conifer roost sites on cold versus warm nights. For this evaluation, we calculated a daily wind chill index (National Oceanic and Atmospheric Administration 2001) from temperature and wind speed at open sites one-half hour before sunset. We classified weather as cold when the wind chill index was ≤−16°C; else weather was classified as warm. We repeated this analysis using temperature alone to classify weather. We performed all statistical analyses, except the regression analyses described previously, using SAS (SAS Institute 1996) and considered differences significant at $\alpha \leq 0.05$.

RESULTS

During 3 winters, we monitored a total of 27 female wild turkeys (13 juveniles and 14 adults) from

Table 1. Mean (± SE) temperature (°C), wind speed (km/h), and snow depth (cm) at wild turkey activity (n = 119) and roost sites (n = 119), and random open sites (n = 119) in southeastern Minnesota, 1997–1999. Means with same letters across rows are not different (P > 0.05).

Year	Parameter	Activity site[a]	Roost site	Open site
1997	Temperature		-6.2 (0.68) A	-6.6 (0.57) A
	Wind speed		1.38 (0.24) A	13.25 (1.34) B
	Snow depth	24.32 (2.42) A	30.13 (1.54) B	
1998	Temperature	-1.3 (1.14) A	-3.4 (1.10) B	-3.5 (1.05) B
	Wind speed	1.79 (0.43) A	0.95 (0.28) A	9.10 (1.32) B
	Snow depth	9.03 (1.71) A	8.72 (1.62) A	
1999	Temperature	-12.1 (1.03) A	-13.9 (1.03) B	-13.8 (0.93) B
	Wind speed	3.03 (0.62) A	0.98 (0.32) A	18.87 (1.25) B
	Wind speed	3.03 (0.62) A	0.98 (0.32) A	18.87 (1.25) B
	Snow depth	21.33 (2.06) A	21.33 (2.08) A	

[a] Activity site weather was measured at night ≤1 hour after weather was measured at the paired roost site.

21 geographically separate flocks in southeastern Minnesota. Radiomarked birds were located during February–March 1997 (n = 14 birds), January–February 1998 (n = 25 birds), and December 1998–February 1999 (n = 17 birds). The actual number of radiomarked birds in the field at any time varied with trap success and mortality. We collected snow depth and habitat information from 38 paired roost and activity sites in 1997. In 1998 and 1999, we collected snow depth, temperature, wind speed, and habitat information from 39 and 42 paired sites, respectively. We also collected temperature and wind speed data from 38, 39, and 42 random open sites in 1997, 1998, and 1999, respectively.

Weather Measurements

Turkeys traveled 396 ± 32 m ($\bar{x} \pm$ SE) from diurnal activity sites to nocturnal roost sites. Distance traveled was inversely related to snow depth, described by the equation: distance = 1792.37–24.78 × snow depth. Although significant ($F_{1,117} = 12.138$, $P < 0.001$), snow depth explained <10% ($R^2 = 0.094$) of the variation in distance traveled from activity to roost sites. Temperature ($F_{1,117} = 1.718$, $P = 0.322$) and wind speed ($F_{1,117} = 0.275$, $P = 0.601$) did not contribute significantly to the model.

Temperatures did not differ between roost and random open sites in 1997 ($F_1 = 1.92$, $P = 0.174$; Table 1). However, temperature at activity sites averaged 1.9°C warmer than roost and open sites in 1998 ($F_2 = 13.70$, $P < 0.001$) and 1999 ($F_2 = 12.26$, $P < 0.001$). Mean wind speed averaged 12.2 km/h greater at random open sites than roost and activity sites in 1997 ($F_1 = 86.49$, $P < 0.001$), 1998 ($F_2 = 36.34$, $P < 0.001$), and 1999 ($F_2 = 169.16$, $P < 0.001$). Snow at roost sites averaged 5.8 cm deeper than at activity sites in 1997 ($t_1 = -2.875$, $P = 0.007$; Table 1). However, we detected no differences between snow depths at roost and activity sites in 1998 ($t_1 = 1.424$, $P = 0.164$) or 1999 ($t_1 = 0.0$, $P = 1.000$). Total snow depth at activity and roost sites measured ≥25.4 cm for 42 consecutive days in 1997, 8 consecutive days in 1998, and 25 consecutive days in 1999. Powder snow depth was generally much less than total snow depth each year due to periodic melts that formed a supporting crust (B. D. Berg, South Dakota State University, unpublished data).

Microhabitat Measurements

Wild turkeys used roost sites characterized by a significantly higher canopy than at forested activity sites in all years (Table 2). During 1997, when weather conditions were most severe, turkeys used roost sites with overstory trees having larger dbh and greater basal area than at activity sites. In comparison, overstory dbh did not differ between roost and activity sites during the more mild winters of 1998 and 1999 (Table 2). Overstory stem density was greater at roost sites than

Table 2. Mean (± SE) canopy height (m), overstory dbh (cm), overstory basal area (m²/ha), overstory and understory density (stems/ha), and slope (%) at wild turkey activity and roost sites (n = 119) in southeastern Minnesota, 1997–1999. Comparisons of all microhabitat parameters except slope excluded grass-agriculture sites.

Year	Microhabitat parameter	Activity site	Roost site	t	df	P
1997	Canopy height	11.00 ± 1.10	17.85 ± 0.80	-4.785	1	<0.001
	Overstory dbh	19.14 ± 1.47	23.64 ± 0.95	-2.451	1	0.020
	Basal area	18.37 ± 2.45	30.22 ± 1.31	-5.119	1	<0.001
	Overstory density	451.03 ± 46.42	610.32 ± 50.29	-2.522	1	0.018
	Understory density	1332.00 ± 271.37	984.52 ± 120.71	1.107	1	0.277
	Slope	26.74 ± 3.64	39.50 ± 2.91	-3.392	1	0.002
1998	Canopy height	14.35 ± 0.72	18.63 ± 1.00	-3.739	1	<0.001
	Overstory dbh	24.56 ± 1.52	26.81 ± 1.11	-1.127	1	0.269
	Basal area	22.85 ± 2.12	30.62 ± 1.79	-2.481	1	0.019
	Overstory density	417.33 ± 29.00	462.67 ± 32.30	-0.898	1	0.376
	Understory density	1320.00 ± 132.98	1165.33 ± 126.99	0.862	1	0.396
	Slope	23.18 ± 3.21	41.56 ± 2.67	-5.473	1	<0.001
1999	Canopy height	13.34 ± 1.02	18.03 ± 0.70	-4.109	1	<0.001
	Overstory dbh	22.79 ± 1.21	23.69 ± 0.96	-0.657	1	0.517
	Basal area	24.07 ± 2.43	24.59 ± 2.58	-0.157	1	0.877
	Overstory density	505.18 ± 37.66	480.00 ± 50.61	0.492	1	0.627
	Understory density	820.74 ± 96.23	672.59 ± 88.08	1.322	1	0.198
	Slope	16.21 ± 2.36	39.55 ± 2.25	-8.740	1	<0.001

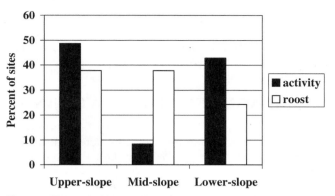

Fig. 1. Topographic location of wild turkey activity and roost sites (*n* = 119) in southeastern Minnesota, 1997–1999.

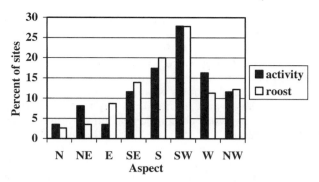

Fig. 2. Aspect of wild turkey roost (*n* = 115) and activity sites (*n* = 86) in southeastern Minnesota, 1997–1999. N = north, NE = northeast, E = east, SE = southeast, S = south, SW = southwest, W = west, NW = northwest.

activity sites only in 1997; however, understory stem density was not different between activity and roost sites in any year (Table 2).

Many microhabitat characteristics at activity and roost sites were similar among years (*P* > 0.05). However, canopy height ($F_{2,83} = 3.29$, *P* = 0.042) and overstory dbh ($F_{2,85} = 3.91$, *P* = 0.024) at activity sites differed among years, with the top of the general canopy higher and mean dbh of overstory trees larger at activity sites in 1998 than in 1997 (Table 2). At roost sites, mean dbh of overstory trees was larger in 1998 ($F_{2,85} = 3.24$, *P* = 0.044) and there were fewer overstory stems/ha ($F_{2,85} = 3.32$, *P* = 0.041) than in 1997. Understory density at roost sites in 1999 was less than in 1998 ($F_{2,85} = 4.51$, *P* = 0.014, Table 2).

Turkeys selected steeper slopes for roost sites than for activity sites (including forested and grass-agriculture sites) in all years (Table 2). For all years, selection of roost site topographic location was related to activity site topographic location ($\chi^2_4 = 12.722$, *P* = 0.013). For example, when turkeys were active at the bottom of the slope, they were more likely to roost at the bottom or middle of the slope. When turkeys were active at the top of the slope, they roosted at the top or middle of the slope. Furthermore, turkeys used upper and middle slopes more than lower slopes for roosting ($\chi^2_2 = 4.302$, *P* = 0.038), whereas they used upper and lower slopes more than middle slopes for activity ($\chi^2_2 = 33.899$, *P* < 0.001; Figure 1). We observed no difference ($\chi^2_4 = 0.113$, *P* = 0.737) among aspects between roost and activity sites. Most activity (45.3%) and roost (47.8%) sites were located on slopes facing south to southwest (Figure 2).

For all years, we located 74.0% of roost sites in deciduous forest and 26.0% in conifer forest, whereas 56.3% of activity sites were located in deciduous forest, 17.6% in conifer forest, and 26.1% in grass-agriculture vegetation. Turkey selection of roost vegetation was independent of activity site vegetation in 1997 ($\chi^2_6 = 8.108$, *P* = 0.230), 1998 ($\chi^2_2 = 1.434$, *P* = 0.488), and 1999 ($\chi^2_6 = 10.195$, *P* = 0.117). Use of vegetation type for roost sites was independent of year ($\chi^2_2 = 2.105$, *P* = 0.349). Furthermore, the proportional use of conifer roost sites was similar during nights when the wind chill index ($\chi^2_1 = 1.514$, *P* = 0.219) or temperature ($\chi^2_1 = 0.084$, *P* = 0.772) one-half hour before

sunset was above or below −16°C. In contrast, use of vegetation type at activity sites differed by year ($\chi^2_4 = 12.394$, *P* = 0.015). During the winters with deeper snow (1997 and 1999), turkeys used conifer vegetation at 23.7% and 23.8% of activity sites, respectively, versus 5.1% of activity sites during the relatively snow-free winter of 1998.

DISCUSSION

If wild turkeys selected winter roost sites at random, they might be expected to roost in the nearest tree at the end of the day. Thus, we hypothesized that the distance between diurnal activity and nocturnal roost sites would approach zero if roost site selection was random. In fact, we observed an average movement of <400 m from activity to roost sites, and that turkeys usually remained in the same topographic location. This limited degree of movement contributed little evidence that turkeys deliberately traveled to preferred roost sites. Turkey movements are restricted in 15–20 cm of powder snow, and severely restricted at 25–30 cm (Lewis 1963, Austin and DeGraff 1975, Vander Haegen et al. 1989, Wright et al. 1996). Although we observed that distance between activity and roost sites was weakly but inversely related to snow depth, powder snow reached restrictive depths infrequently during the moderate-mild winters of this study (B. D. Berg, South Dakota State University, unpublished data). We conclude that availability of preferred roost and activity habitats was not limited by deep snow during our study.

Temperatures at roost sites were slightly lower than at activity sites, but we considered this difference small and biologically insignificant. Roost and activity sites both provided significant protection from wind, which was much stronger at open sites. We acknowledge that wind speed was likely greater in the forest canopy where turkeys roosted than near the ground where we measured. Future research should focus on microclimate at the precise roost location, which has been done for other galliforms (Thompson and Fritzell 1988, Pekins et al. 1991, Sherfy and Pekins 1995).

Use of coniferous cover for winter roosting can reduce heat loss due to convection (wind) and radiation to the open sky (Walsberg 1985, Thompson and Fritzell 1988, Pekins et al. 1991). Although conifer habitat comprised <1% of our study area, 26.0% of nocturnal roost sites were in conifer stands. Despite the seasonal preference for conifer roost habitat, daily selection of conifer roosts was not significantly greater on cold versus warm nights; this was true when cold was defined by wind chill index or temperature alone. The predominant (74.0%) use of deciduous roost sites regardless of weather suggests that conifer roosts were not essential under the conditions of our study (unrestricted mobility and access to food). Winter roosting in deciduous trees by northern turkeys is common (Healy 1992, Porter 1992, Coup and Pekins 1999), although Kilpatrick et al. (1988, 1990) reported exclusive use of conifers in Rhode Island and New Hampshire. When snow limits mobility and food availability, however, selection of favorable microclimates, such as conifer roost sites, may significantly enhance winter survival. Glover (1948), Vander Hagen et al. (1989), Jansen (1992), and Coup and Pekins (1999) reported a strong preference for conifer roost sites during periods of deep snow, especially when located near foraging habitats.

We observed that turkeys in southeastern Minnesota used roost sites characterized by a higher canopy and, in the severe winter of 1997, larger dbh overstory trees and greater overstory stem density than at activity sites. Similarly, Kilpatrick et al. (1988, 1990) reported that eastern wild turkeys in Rhode Island and New Hampshire preferred to roost in areas dominated by tall, large diameter white pines. Chamberlain et al. (2000) found that adult female wild turkeys in Mississippi selected mature pine and pine-hardwood stands as roost sites. Mackey (1984) and Lutz and Crawford (1987) suggested that Merriam's turkeys (*M. g. merriami*) needed very large diameter (i.e., ≥50 cm dbh) trees for roosting. In contrast, Rumble (1992) determined that trees ≥23 cm dbh were sufficient for Merriam's wild turkeys in the Black Hills, South Dakota. A flock of eastern wild turkeys in Wisconsin used a 17-year-old conifer plantation extensively for winter roosting (Jansen 1992). These observations suggest that tall, large diameter trees may be preferred, but are not necessary for winter roost sites.

Goerndt (1983), Mackey (1984), and Rumble (1992) reported that turkeys roosted most frequently on the upper third of the slope. During our study, turkeys roosted most on upper and middle slopes, and roost sites were generally in the same topographic class as the corresponding activity site from that day. Selection of the top and bottom of slopes for diurnal activity may have reflected easier access to ridgetop and valley cropland in our study area. Most roost and activity sites in this study had a southerly aspect, which may have provided thermoregulatory benefits from incoming solar radiation during the day and protection from prevailing northwesterly winds during day and night. In addition, south-facing activity sites would permit greater mobility due to reduced snow depth (Porter et al. 1980), as we observed in the more severe winter of 1997. Eastern wild turkeys in New York (Austin and DeGraff 1975) and Rhode Island (Kilpatrick et al. 1988), and Merriam's turkeys in the Black Hills (Rumble and Anderson 1996) also preferred southerly aspects for roost sites.

MANAGEMENT IMPLICATIONS

An evaluation of thermoregulatory behavior such as winter roost selection must be conducted within the broader context of energy balance. Our data provided little evidence that turkeys selected winter roost sites characterized by favorable microclimates, even when temperatures and wind chill indices fell below −16°C, the lowest estimated lower critical temperature of wild turkey hens (Oberlag et al. 1990). Rather, turkeys in our study apparently balanced their winter energy budgets through alternate behaviors. Turkeys selected activity sites in or near habitats where food was available, allowing for increased energy intake. Nocturnal roosts were located near activity sites, reducing energy expenditure for travel. Southerly aspects, with greater sun and less wind and snow, were preferred sites for both activity and roosting.

Winter roost sites in this study were better described by proximity to available food than by characteristics of favorable microclimates. Conifer roost sites may be more important to wild turkey energy balance when snow restricts mobility and food availability, but this cannot be determined without additional research. Access to a dependable source of food is a necessary component of winter habitat, and may be the primary determinant of winter survival in northern turkey range.

ACKNOWLEDGMENTS

We thank J. Berg and J. Finnegan for assisting in data collection, J. S. Cole for housing and expertise in tree identification, and G. C. Nelson for assistance with turkey trapping. W. B. Ballard, C. S. DePerno, L. D. Flake, J. H. Giudice, M. A. Rumble, and 2 anonymous reviewers provided valuable comments to earlier versions of the manuscript. Funding and support were provided by the Minnesota Department of Natural Resources, the National Wild Turkey Federation, and South Dakota State University.

LITERATURE CITED

Austin, D. E., and L. W. DeGraff. 1975. Winter survival of wild turkeys in the southern Adirondacks. Proceedings of the National Wild Turkey Symposium 3:55–60.

Chamberlain, M. J., B. D. Leopold, and L. W. Burger. 2000. Characteristics of roost sites of adult wild turkey females. Journal of Wildlife Management 64:1025–1032.

Coup, R. N., and P. J. Pekins. 1999. Field metabolic rate of wild turkeys in winter. Canadian Journal of Zoology 77:1075–1082.

Glover, F. A. 1948. Winter activities of wild turkeys in West Virginia. Journal of Wildlife Management 12:416–427.

Goerndt, D. L. 1983. Merriam's turkey habitat in relation to grazing and timber management of a mixed conifer forest in southcentral New Mexico. Thesis, New Mexico State University, Las Cruces, New Mexico, USA.

Gray, B. T., and H. H. Prince. 1988. Basal metabolism and energetic cost of thermoregulation in wild turkeys. Journal of Wildlife Management 52:133–137.

Haroldson, K. J. 1996. Energy requirements for winter survival of wild turkeys. Proceedings of the National Wild Turkey Symposium 7:9–14.

———, M. L. Svihel, R. O. Kimmel, and R. R. Riggs. 1998. Effect of winter temperature on wild turkey metabolism. Journal of Wildlife Management 62:299–305.

Healy, W. M. 1992. Behavior. Pages 46–65 *in* J. G. Dickson, editor. The wild turkey: biology and management. Stackpole Books, Harrisburg, Pennsylvania, USA.

James, F. C., and H. H. Shugart. 1970. A quantitative method of habitat description. Audubon Field Notes 24:727–736.

Jansen, J. J. 1992. Winter factors affecting wild turkey introductions in east central Wisconsin. Thesis, University of Wisconsin, Stephens Point, Wisconsin, USA.

Kennamer, J. E., and M. C. Kennamer. 1990. Current status and distribution of the wild turkey, 1989. Proceedings of the National Wild Turkey Symposium 6:1–12.

Kilpatrick, H. J., T. P. Husband, and C. A. Pringle. 1988. Winter roost site characteristics of eastern wild turkeys. Journal of Wildlife Management 52:461–463.

———, J. A. Litvaitis, and G. E. Thomas. 1990. Seasonal roost-site characteristics of turkeys in southeastern New Hampshire. Transactions of the Northeast Section of The Wildlife Society 47:10–14.

Leopold, A. 1931. Report on a game survey of the north central states. Sporting Arms and Ammunition Manufacturer's Institute, American Game Association, Washington, D.C., USA.

Lewis, J. C. 1963. Observations on the winter range size of wild turkeys in Michigan. Journal of Wildlife Management 27:98–102.

Lutz, R. S., and J. A. Crawford. 1987. Seasonal use of roost sites by Merriam's wild turkey hens and hen-poult flocks in Oregon. Northwest Science 61:174–178.

Mackey, D. L. 1984. Roosting habitat of Merriam's turkeys in south-central Washington. Journal of Wildlife Management 48:1377–1382.

Minnesota Climatology Working Group. 1950–2000. Historical climate data/summaries. University of Minnesota, Department of Soil, Water, and Climate, St. Paul, Minnesota, USA.

Minnesota Department of Natural Resources. 1983. Minnesota's wild turkey management plan. Division of Fish and Wildlife, Minnesota Department of Natural Resources, St. Paul, Minnesota, USA.

National Oceanic and Atmospheric Administration. 2001. National Weather Service wind chill temperature index and wind chill chart. ⟨http://www.nws.noaa.gov/om/pkbwindchill/index.shtml⟩. Accessed 11 May 2005.

Nenno, E. S., and W. M. Healy. 1979. Effects of radio packages

on behavior of wild turkey hens. Journal of Wildlife Management 43:460–465.

Oberlag, D. F., P. J. Perkins, and W. W. Mautz. 1990. Influence of seasonal temperatures on wild turkey metabolism. Journal of Wildlife Management 54:663–667.

Pekins, P. J., F. G. Lindzey, and J. A. Gessaman. 1991. Physical characteristics of blue grouse winter use-trees and roost sites. Great Basin Naturalist 51:244–248.

Porter, W. F. 1992. Habitat requirements. Pages 202–213 *in* J. G. Dickson, editor. The wild turkey: biology and management. Stackpole Books, Harrisburg, Pennsylvania, USA.

———, R. D. Tangen, G. C. Nelson, and D. A. Hamilton. 1980. Effects of corn food plots on wild turkeys in the upper Mississippi Valley. Journal of Wildlife Management 44:456–462.

Prince, H. H., and B. T. Gray. 1986. Bioenergetics of the wild turkey in Michigan. Final Report. Michigan Department of Natural Resources, Wildlife Division, Lansing, Michigan, USA.

Roberts, S. D., J. M. Coffey, and W. F. Porter. 1995. Survival and reproduction of female wild turkeys in New York. Journal of Wildlife Management 59:437–447.

Rumble, M. A. 1992. Roosting habitat of Merriam's turkeys in the Black Hills, South Dakota. Journal of Wildlife Management 56:750–759.

———, and S. H. Anderson. 1996. Microhabitats of Merriam's turkeys in the Black Hills, South Dakota. Ecological Applications 6:326–334.

SAS Institute. 1995. SAS/INSIGHT user's guide. Version 6. Third edition. SAS Institute, Cary, North Carolina, USA.

———. 1996. SAS/STAT user's guide. Version 6.11. SAS Institute, Cary, North Carolina, USA.

Sherfy, M. H., and P. J. Pekins. 1995. Influence of wind speed on sage grouse metabolism. Canadian Journal of Zoology 73:749–754.

Thompson, F. R., III, and E. K. Fritzell. 1988. Ruffed grouse winter roost site preference and influence on energy demands. Journal of Wildlife Management 52:454–460.

Vander Haegen, W. M., M. W. Sayre, and W. E. Dodge. 1989. Winter use of agricultural habitats by wild turkeys in Massachusetts. Journal of Wildlife Management 53:30–33.

Walsberg, G. E. 1985. Physiological consequences of microhabitat selection. Pages 389–413 *in* M. L. Cody, editor. Habitat selection in birds. Academic, New York, New York, USA.

———. 1986. Thermal consequences of roost-site selection: the relative importance of three modes of heat conservation. Auk 103:1–7.

Wright, R. G., R. N. Paisley, and J. F. Kubisiak. 1996. Survival of wild turkey hens in southwestern Wisconsin. Journal of Wildlife Management 60:313–320.

Wunz, G. A., and A. H. Hayden. 1975. Winter mortality and supplemental feeding of turkeys in Pennsylvania. Proceedings of the National Wild Turkey Symposium 3:61–69.

Zar, J. H. 1996. Biostatistical analysis. Third edition. Prentice Hall, Upper Saddle River, New Jersey, USA.

Jacquie Ermer currently works for the U.S. Fish and Wildlife Service in North Dakota. She obtained a B.A. in Biology from Moorhead State University in Minnesota and a M.S. in Wildlife Sciences from South Dakota State University. Jacquie's interests include furbearer ecology and management and habitat restoration and management.

Kurt Haroldson (left) is a wildlife research biologist at the Farmland Wildlife Populations and Research Group of the Minnesota Department of Natural Resources. He received a B.A. in biology from Gustavus Adolphus College and a M.S. in wildlife management from the University of Missouri. Kurt's research interests include winter energetics of wild turkeys at the northern periphery of their range and wildlife responses to agricultural land retirement programs. *Richard (Dick) Kimmel* (right) supervises the Farmland Wildlife Populations and Research Group of the Minnesota Department of Natural Resources. He received a B.S. from Earlham College and a M.A. and Ph.D. from West Virginia University. His research interests include wild turkey survey and modeling techniques and habitat use. *Charles Dieter* (not pictured) is a professor of biology at South Dakota State University. He earned a M.S. in wildlife and fisheries and a Ph.D. in biological sciences from South Dakota State University. Chuck has broad interests in wetland ecology in northern prairie communities. *Paul Evenson* (not pictured) is a self-employed statistician and retired emeritus professor of statistics at South Dakota State University. *Barry Berg* (not pictured) is a resource management specialist with the South Dakota Association of Conservation Districts. Barry received a B.S. in Biology from Minnesota State University at Mankato.

Wild Turkey Management:
Accomplishments, Strategies, and Opportunities
——— Grand Rapids, Michigan ———

DEVELOPMENT OF AN ECOLOGICAL, RISK-BASED DECISION FRAMEWORK FOR RELEASING AND MANAGING WILD TURKEYS IN ONTARIO

Karen Bellamy[1]
Ontario Ministry of Natural Resources,
300 Water St., P.O. Box 7000,
Peterborough, ON K9J 8M5, Canada

J. Bruce Pollard[2,3]
Ontario Ministry of Natural Resources,
300 Water St., P.O. Box 7000,
Peterborough, ON K9J 8M5, Canada

Abstract: Ontario initiated wild turkey (*Meleagris gallopavo silvestris*) restoration efforts in 1984 and within 20 years had restored or established populations across much of southeastern and southwestern portions of the province. Within these areas, it is believed that expansion of agricultural and changing land use has extended suitable range into landscapes well beyond known historic range. There was interest in establishing wild turkey into other areas; however, expansion of turkey populations was not viewed by all groups as either desirable or appropriate. Through knowledge gained from assessment of habitat suitability, overlaying habitat information on historic distribution, factoring in land-use change, and by considering prevailing weather patterns, we developed a terrestrial ecozone framework to define the spatial extent for turkey range expansion. At present, we consider the Mixedwood Plain Ecozone to represent a biologically suitable and ecologically appropriate framework for wild turkey expansion in Ontario. Using the Mixedwood Plain Ecozone boundary, a simple risk-based decision tree was developed to deal with ecological, social, and economic risks of releasing turkeys at new locations in Ontario.

Proceedings of the National Wild Turkey Symposium 9:289–294

Key words: historic range, Mixedwood Plain Ecozone, Ontario, program framework, releases, risk-based decision tree, wild turkey.

Wild turkeys were extirpated from Ontario in the early 1900s. The known historic range of wild turkeys just prior to extirpation was documented by Allison (1976). Confirmed wild turkey records were documented in a 27,000-km² area of southwestern Ontario. This area represents only a small percentage of the approximate 917,000-km² land area of the province of Ontario.

Wild turkey restoration efforts began in 1984, and by 1987 a total of 274 birds were transferred into Ontario from 6 U.S. states. Active trap and transfer from within Ontario has contributed to the growth of Ontario's wild turkey population. In total, 4,400 birds were trapped and released at 275 sites in Ontario between 1984 and March 2004 (Malhiot 2005). The population is currently estimated at more than 80,000 birds. These birds are distributed across agricultural southern Ontario from Chatham in the west to Cornwall in the east and north to the Canadian Shield. Due to the influences of agriculture, and to some extent, milder climatic conditions, the occupied range in southern Ontario is now considerably larger than the estimated historic range.

With the success of wild turkey restoration came requests to expand wild turkey range to new areas of the province through trap and transfer. Turkey releases were requested for forested areas of the Canadian Shield in central and northern Ontario and small patch-

----

[1] E-mail: karen.bellamy@mnr.gov.on.ca
[2] E-mail: bruce.pollard@ec.gc.ca
[3] Present address: Canadian Wildlife Service, 17 Waterfowl Lane, Sackville, New Brunswick, E4L 1G6, Canada.

es of agricultural land in northern Ontario. Although it appeared that suitable habitat might have existed at some of these locations, it was not known if turkeys would survive severe winters in these areas. Other questions were also raised regarding possible impacts of turkeys on other species and potential economic and social impacts.

It was difficult to respond to requests for releases in landscapes that were significantly different or geographically isolated from that of southern Ontario. It was also desirable to be able to deal with these requests in a fair, comprehensive manner instead of on a case-by-case basis as they arose. The 1994 draft wild turkey management plan for Ontario identified turkey releases in "all suitable habitats," but did not establish any geographic boundary for turkey restoration in Ontario (Ontario Ministry of Natural Resources [OMNR]. 1994. Wild turkey management plan for Ontario (draft). OMNR, Peterborough, Ontario, Canada).

In 2003, a proposed release of wild turkeys on St. Joseph's Island near Sault Ste. Marie was challenged under Ontario's Environmental Assessment Act. Concerns were raised about potential environmental impacts including unknown ecosystem impacts of releasing wild turkeys beyond known historic turkey range, competition with other species, and the possibility that predator control might be necessary.

From a management agency perspective, there was also a need to know when wild turkey restoration in the province would be completed. Experience in other jurisdictions has found that requests for releases continued for years after restoration was deemed to be complete. Sound rationale to respond to requests for releases now and into the future was needed. Also, a landscape level framework was needed to plan future releases that would complete the wild turkey restoration in Ontario and would also provide a boundary where turkeys would be actively managed in the province.

Identifying Potential Suitable Wild Turkey Habitat in Ontario—Sudbury Experimental Release

By the late 1990s turkey populations had been restored to most areas of agricultural southern Ontario through active trap and transfer and natural range expansion. It was not known if the habitat and climatic conditions found outside of southern Ontario could support self-sustaining turkey populations. Defining the extent of suitable habitat in Ontario was viewed as a necessary step in determining future restoration efforts.

In 1999, a proposal for an experimental release of wild turkeys near Sudbury was approved to assess the potential for northern areas in the Boreal Shield Ecozone of the province to support self-sustaining turkey populations. The release site, located in a 200-km² area of mixed forest and agriculture on the Precambrian Shield near St. Charles, 30 km southeast of Sudbury, was approximately 160 km north of the existing northern range of wild turkeys in southern Ontario. Mod-

erately severe winters occurred every second year, whereas very severe winters occurred every 5 years (Nguyen 2001). An average of 67 days had >25 cm of snow and continuous snowcover was the norm between December and March. Snow depths exceeded 25 cm for 38 days during the mild winter of 1999–2000 and for 111 days during the severe winter of 2000–2001. Total snowfall was similar to some areas of the province where turkeys were well established.

In late winter of 1999, 36 turkeys (26 female, 10 male) from New York and southern Ontario were released. In March of 2000, an additional 13 hens were released. All hens were fitted with radio transmitters and monitored until the spring of 2001. Four successful broods were documented in 1999 and 2 hens with broods were seen with poults in the spring of 2000. Approximately 15 birds (including 2 hens) survived the severe winter of 2001, but there were no reports of successful nesting.

Results of the research indicate that predation had considerable impact on the survival of both adult and juvenile birds as well as nesting success (Nguyen 2001, Nguyen et al. 2003). Informal reports estimate the population in 2004 at approximately 200 birds (C. Brownson, Ontario Federation of Anglers and Hunters, personal communication). Although a low density population continues to persist in the area, little growth in the population has occurred. Results of the experimental release suggest that the habitat may be suitable for low density populations.

Identifying Ecologically Suitable Areas for Wild Turkeys in Ontario

Although the Sudbury experimental release helped to define the limits of suitable habitat for wild turkeys in Ontario, the question of where it was ecologically appropriate to release wild turkeys in the province remained unanswered.

Although other jurisdictions face similar issues, we were not aware of any framework delineating ecological boundaries specifically for the purposes of managing wild turkeys. However, we are aware of the use of a landscape level planning framework for the North American Bird Conservation Initiative (NABCI) based on ecological boundaries (Anonymous 1999).

Wild turkeys in Ontario evolved in the Mixedwood Plain Ecozone (Figure 1; as defined by the National Ecological Framework [http://www.ec.gc.ca/soer-ree/ English/Framework/NarDesc/Zone.cfm? EcozoneID=9]). Known historic range for wild turkeys in the early 1900s just prior to extirpation (Allison 1976), supports this assumption. Little is known about the historic range of wild turkeys in Ontario prior to this when populations were likely at higher levels and more broadly distributed. As agriculture spread across southern Ontario in the first half of the 20th century, it is likely that wild turkeys would also have expanded their range naturally, had they not been extirpated.

The Boreal Shield and Hudson Plains Ecozones are also found in Ontario. A number of factors includ-

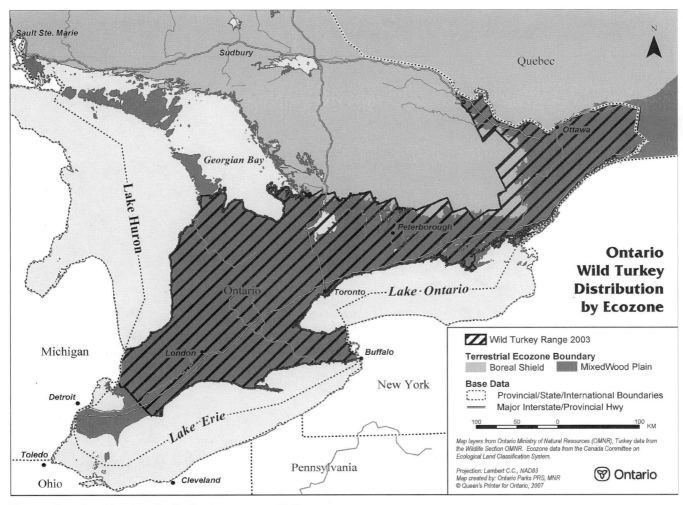

Fig. 1.   Ontario wild turkey distribution by ecozone, 2003.

ing fauna were used to define boundaries of ecoregions and ecozones within the National Ecological Framework. Ecoregions can be characterized by distinctive regional ecological factors including climate, physiography, vegetation, soil, water and fauna (Wiken 1986, Marshall and Schutt 1999).

Wild turkeys would have evolved with other species of flora and fauna within the Mixedwood Plain Ecozone. Therefore, it seems unlikely that restored wild turkey populations would interact with other species of this ecozone differently than they had 75 years earlier. Given that evolutionary processes operate over long time frames, the absence of wild turkeys from the Mixedwood Plains landscape of Ontario for 75 years is unlikely to impact or change evolutionary or ecosystem processes. Possible impacts of wild turkey releases, such as competition with, or predation on or by, other species, have been raised in Ontario as well as in other jurisdictions. Ecosystem processes such as competition and predation should be considered an appropriate component of healthy functioning ecosystems within the Mixedwood Plains Ecozone. We are not aware of any documentation suggesting ecosystem impairment as a result of restoring wild turkey populations and concluded that wild turkeys are an appro-

priate ecosystem element of the Mixedwood Plain Ecozone in Ontario.

Social and Economic Considerations Within the Turkey Management Framework

Decisions to restore wild turkey populations in certain locations almost always consider potential social and economic impacts. In Ontario, social considerations typically include increased recreational opportunities (hunting and viewing), the intrinsic value of restoring an extirpated species, and new or strengthened relationships between government and non-government partners. Economic considerations typically include potential revenue associated with new recreational opportunities, costs of management (including administration of hunts and collection of harvest data), and costs associated with potential nuisance issues and agricultural damage.

Stakeholder groups often place a wide range of values on the potential social and economic impacts of releasing or actively managing wild turkeys. Effectively dealing with these is essential to good decision making.

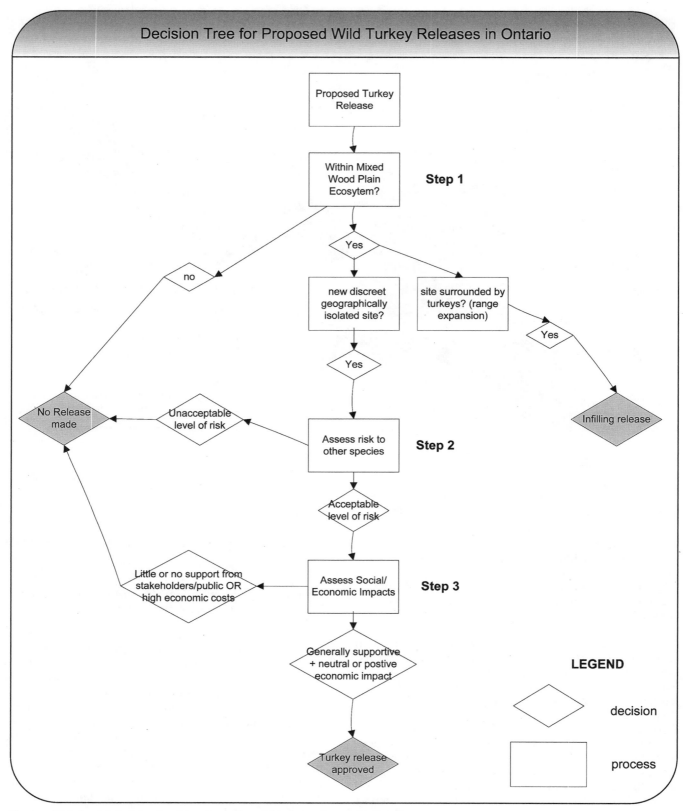

Fig. 2.   Risk-based decision tree developed for wild turkey releases in Ontario.

A Risk-Based Decision Tree for Wild Turkey Releases in Ontario

Decisions on where wild turkeys should be released and managed required consideration of ecological, social, and economic factors. With the maturation of the program, we identified a need to establish a process that managers across the province could use to guide these decisions and improve consistency and accountability. As a result, a simple risk-based decision tree was developed (Figure 2).

The mission of the OMNR is to "manage natural resources in an ecologically sustainable way to ensure that they are available for the enjoyment and use of future generations" (OMNR 2005). Given our mandate for ecological sustainability, we incorporated an ecological boundary defined by the Mixedwood Plain Ecozone into the decision tree. The ecological component of the decision process is positioned as the first step in order to ensure that OMNR's mandate of ecological sustainability is met prior to considering social and economic values. In addition to considering whether a proposed release is located within the Mixedwood Plain Ecozone, other potential ecological risks are considered including possible impacts on other species or components of the ecosystem. If the level of ecological risk is acceptable, the decision tree guides the manager to further consider social and economic risks before a final decision is made.

Informed decision making based on sound risk management practices is promoted in all areas of the provincial government (Ontario Ministry of Finance 2002). Assessing ecological, social and economic risks associated with releasing wild turkeys in Ontario is determined by evaluating the likelihood of the risk occurring, the potential impact of the risk and the reversibility of the decision. These factors are evaluated subjectively and then combined prior to deciding if the level of overall risk is acceptable or not. For example, in evaluating the risk that a turkey release may have on a rare species of insect, we would determine the likelihood that a turkey would encounter and consume the insect. In making this determination, we would consider if habitats overlapped spatially and temporally. Potential impact of the risk would consider the impact on the insect population if turkeys did eat the rare insects. This would consider the designation (e.g., globally endangered) of the insect as well as the number of locations where they are known to occur. Finally, we would evaluate the potential reversibility of a decision to release turkeys. Is the site geographically isolated in a manner that would facilitate removal of all wild turkeys if desired? A combined subjective assessment of risk is made, based on the evaluation of these 3 factors. Once risk is assessed a decision regarding the appropriate course of action is made. This action plan may incorporate strategies to manage or mitigate risks where possible.

The decision tree is designed to be used by local and provincial level resource managers and could be shared with partners to improve their understanding of decisions made regarding wild turkey releases. Although the decision tree defines a standard process to be followed across the province, local managers analyze the risk and make determinations on the acceptable level of ecological, social, and economic risk within the Mixedwood Plains Ecozone. This allows managers to use local information and values in the decision making process.

Implications for Ontario

The use of an ecological boundary has defined the wild turkey management area in Ontario. Trap and transfer and other management activities can be considered within this geographic boundary. The decision tree allows local managers to incorporate local concerns and values into decisions by determining what levels of ecological, social, and economic risk they are prepared to take. Local managers are also responsible and accountable for these decisions. The decision tree also helps improve consistency of decisions regarding wild turkey releases across the province.

At this juncture, it is not anticipated that active wild turkey management (e.g., trap and transfer) will occur outside of the Mixedwood Plain Ecozone; however, this does not preclude passive management of wild turkeys (e.g., taking advantage of possible hunting opportunities) if wild turkey populations naturally expand beyond the Mixedwood Plain Ecozone.

ACKNOWLEDGMENTS

D. Kimmel's encouragement, support, and review of the manuscript was instrumental. Many thanks to S. Goetz for reviewing and suggesting improvements to the manuscript.

LITERATURE CITED

Allison, R. M. 1976. The history of the wild turkey in Ontario. Canadian Field Naturalist 90:481–485.

Anonymous. 1999. North American Bird Conservation Initiative (NABCI): Strategy and Action Plan. ⟨http://www.bsc-eoc.org/nabcstrategy.html⟩. Accessed 11 May 2005.

Malhiot, M. 2005. 2004 Ontario wild turkey status report. Ontario Ministry of Natural Resources, Peterborough, Ontario, Canada.

Marshall, I. B., and P. H. Schut. 1999. A national ecological framework for Canada ⟨http://sis.agr.gc.ca/cansis/nsdb/ecostrat/intro.html⟩. Accessed 11 May 2005.

Nguyen, L. P. 2001. Feasibility of transplanting eastern wild turkeys (*Meleagris gallopavo silvestris*) on the Precambrian Shield in central Ontario. Thesis, Laurentian University, Sudbury, Ontario, Canada.

———, J. Hamr, and G. H. Parker. 2003. Survival and reproduction of wild turkey hens in central Ontario. Wilson Bulletin 115:131–139.

Ontario Ministry of Finance. 2002. Risk management framework for the government of Ontario. Office of the Provincial Controller, Toronto, Ontario, Canada.

Ontario Ministry of Natural Resources. 2005. Our sustainable future—Ministry of Natural Resources strategic directions. Ontario Ministry of Natural Resources, Peterborough, Ontario, Canada.

Wiken, E. B. (compiler). 1986. Terrestrial ecozones of Canada. Ecological Land Classification Series No. 19. Environment Canada, Hull, Quebec, Canada.

Karen Bellamy has held a variety of positions with the Ontario Ministry of Natural Resources over the past 25 years including involvement with Ontario's wild turkey program from 1989 to 2005. She received her B.Sc. from the University of Guelph. Her interests include wildlife management issues in southern Ontario and strategic resource management policy. Her current position with the Ontario Ministry of Natural Resources in Peterborough is Senior Policy and Planning Coordinator for Protected Areas.

Bruce Pollard is currently employed as the Atlantic Region Gamebird Management Biologist with the Canadian Wildlife Service. Prior to his recent move to the Canadian Federal government, he was employed as the Senior Avian Biologist with the Ontario Ministry of Natural Resources Wildlife Section. He earned a B.S. degree in Zoology and Botany from Brandon University and an M.S. degree in the Watershed Ecosystems program from Trent University. Professional interests include variability in waterfowl and upland gamebird production across landscapes, and natural resource policy development and implementation.

9th National Wild Turkey Symposium

Wild Turkey Management:
Accomplishments, Strategies, and Opportunities
—————— Grand Rapids, Michigan ——————

SURVIVAL AND CAUSE-SPECIFIC MORTALITY OF MERRIAM'S TURKEYS IN THE SOUTHERN BLACK HILLS

Chad P. Lehman[1,2]
Department of Wildlife and Fisheries Sciences,
South Dakota State University,
Brookings, SD 57007-1696, USA

Lester D. Flake
Department of Wildlife and Fisheries Sciences,
South Dakota State University,
Brookings, SD 57007-1696, USA

Mark A. Rumble
USDA Forest Service, Rocky Mountain Research Station,
1730 Samco Road,
Rapid City, South Dakota 57702, USA

Abstract: Merriam's turkeys (*Meleagris gallopavo merriami*) in the Black Hills feed in ponderosa pine (*Pinus ponderosa*) forest habitats during winter, but some birds centralize winter activities within or near farmsteads that provide waste grain as supplemental food. The objective of our research was to determine if female Merriam's turkeys that wintered in association with supplemental food from livestock feeding had different survival rates than birds that wintered within ponderosa pine forest. We captured and radiomarked 94 females over a 4-year period. Winter (1 Dec–31 Mar) survival of Merriam's females wintering in association with livestock feeding and farmsteads ($\hat{S}$ = 0.94, SE = 0.03) was not different from females wintering in forest habitats ($\hat{S}$ = 0.92, SE = 0.03). Annual survival of adult females (mean $\hat{S}$ = 0.67, SE = 0.09) varied among years (range = 0.54–0.83) from 2001–2003 based on Kaplan-Meier estimates. Lowest seasonal survival occurred during spring (1 Apr–30 Jun) (adult $\hat{S}$ = 0.83, SE = 0.04; yearling $\hat{S}$ = 0.64, SE = 0.13). Mammalian predators accounted for the highest percentage of mortality (47.2%). Primary mammalian predators were coyotes (*Canis latrans*) and bobcats (*Lynx rufus*) based on evidence from infrared camera photos and dorsal guard hair identification. Survival in the southern Black Hills was similar or higher than rates reported for Merriam's turkey from both its indigenous range and introduced range.

Proceedings of the National Wild Turkey Symposium 9:295–301
Key words: Black Hills, Merriam's, mortality, radiotelemetry, survival, wild turkey.

Merriam's turkeys in the Black Hills are nonindigenous. The southern Black Hills population originated with transplants from Colorado and New Mexico in 1950 and 1951 (Peterson and Richardson 1975). The Black Hills population of Merriam's turkeys supports a spring harvest of male turkeys typically ranging from 1,500 to 2,500 birds (Huxoll 2003, 2004). Merriam's turkeys in forested habitats of the Black Hills feed on ponderosa pine seed, kinnikinnick (*Arctostaphylos uva-ursi*) fruits, and grasses during winter (Rumble and Anderson 1996*a*, 1996*b*). However, many Black

Hills turkeys have centralized wintering activities (i.e., roosting, feeding, and loafing) within or near cattle feeding operations. This farmstead wintering behavior has developed in other regions of the wild turkey's range (Vander Haegen et al. 1989, Wunz 1992) and may provide some benefits to turkeys in enhanced survival and reproduction (Porter et al. 1983, Vander Hae-

[1] E-mail: Chad.Lehman@state.sd.us
[2] Present address: 13329 US HWY 16A, Custer, SD 57730, USA.

gen et al. 1988, Wunz 1992, Hoffman et al. 1996, Lehman et al. 2001). Farmsteads indirectly provide high-energy foods such as oats and corn for turkeys as waste grain from livestock feeding operations. In addition, farmsteads may provide turkeys some protection from predators during winter and the early part of spring due to the close proximity of humans.

Severe winter weather can limit northern turkey populations (Healy 1992) and food sources can be critical for survival during winter (Porter et al. 1980, Vander Haegen et al. 1988). Within South Dakota, investigators have reported winter survival and causes of mortality for eastern wild turkeys (*M. g. silvestris*) (Leif 1997, Lehman et al. 2001) and Rio Grande wild turkeys (*M. g. intermedia*) (Lehman et al. 2001). In the central Black Hills, annual survival of Merriam's females varied from 33 to 76% (Rumble et al. 2003). In Arizona, annual survival of Merriam's turkeys averaged 57% (Rumble et al. 2003) and in Montana survival averaged 45% (Thompson 1993). Spring is a period of high female mortality for Merriam's turkeys in South Dakota and southeastern Montana (Thompson 1993, Flake and Day 1996, Rumble et al. 2003). Predominant causes of wild turkey mortality in the Midwest are predation, severe weather, starvation, illegal killing, and hunting (Porter 1978, Vangilder 1995, Vangilder and Kurzejeski 1995, Wright et al. 1996, Leif 1997, Lehman et al. 2001). However, survival and cause-specific mortality information is generally lacking for Merriam's turkeys (Rumble et al. 2003). The objectives of this study were to (1) obtain survival and cause-specific mortality information on female Merriam's turkeys in the southern Black Hills, and (2) determine if birds that wintered in association with farmsteads and associated supplemental feeds had different survival rates than birds that wintered within ponderosa pine forest.

STUDY AREA

The study area was in the southern portion of the Black Hills physiographic region of southwestern South Dakota (Johnson et al. 1995). Elevations range from 930 to 1627 m above mean sea level. Three soil associations (Mathias-Butche-Rockoa, Paunsaugunt-Vanocker, and Tilford-Spearfish) characterize much of the study area's rocky ridges, rolling plateaus, drainages, canyon walls, and mountain valleys (Kalvels 1980). The study area had a continental climate with mean annual precipitation of 44.02 cm and mean annual temperature of 7.78°C (National Climatic Data Center 1971–2000). The woodland habitat was characteristic of xeric conditions, and was dominated by ponderosa pine with an understory composed of western snowberry (*Symphoricarpos occidentalis*), common juniper (*Juniperus communis*), and greater densities of Rocky Mountain juniper (*J. scopulorum*) in the western portion of the study area (Hoffman and Alexander 1987). Dominant grasses on the study area included Kentucky bluegrass (*Poa pratensis*), smooth brome (*Bromus inermis*), little bluestem (*Schizachyr-*

ium scoparium), needle and thread (*Stipa comata*), sideoats grama (*Bouteloua curtipendula*), western wheatgrass (*Pascopyrum smithii*), and blue grama (*Bouteloua gracilis*) (Johnson and Larson 1999).

METHODS

Capture and Radiotelemetry

Wild turkeys were captured in winter using cannon nets (Dill and Thornsberry 1950, Austin et al. 1972), rocket nets (Thompson and Delong 1967, Wunz 1984), and drop nets (Glazener et al. 1964) over bait. We classified females as either adult (>1 year old) or yearling (<1 year old) based on barring on the ninth and tenth primary feathers (Williams 1961) and weighed birds to the nearest 0.1 kg. Birds were fitted with 98-g backpack mounted radiotransmitters equipped with activity signals and a mercury switch mortality sensor set to activate after 8 hours of inactivity. Wild turkeys were located by triangulation and visual locations 5–6 days per week using hand-held yagi antennae.

Survival and Cause-specific Mortality

We estimated seasonal and annual survival distributions using the Kaplan-Meier product limit method (Kaplan and Meier 1958) modified for staggered entry (Pollock et al. 1989). Seasonal survival was divided into 4 time periods: (1) winter (1 Dec–31 Mar), (2) spring (1 Apr–30 Jun), (3) summer (1 Jul–31 Aug), and (4) fall (1 Sep–30 Nov). Season intervals were based on a combination of weather (i.e., seasonal variation in temperature and precipitation) and behavior patterns (i.e., nesting and brood-rearing). We estimated annual survival from 1 December–30 November of each year. Yearlings were classified as adults starting the first winter (1 Dec) following capture. Calculating survival distributions we assumed: (1) survival was unique for each radiomarked individual and independent of others, (2) individuals were unbiased and randomly selected, and (3) radiotransmitters did not affect survival.

We defined cause-specific mortality as the probability of a wild turkey dying from a mortality source in the presence of other competing mortality sources (Heisey and Fuller 1985). Necropsy of carcasses determined causes of death, and we classified mortality as mammalian predation, avian predation, weather-related starvation (emaciation or starvation resulting from deep snow cover), hunting, illegal kill, disease, car collision, and unknown. Death was attributed to predation when examination of carcasses revealed hemorrhaging accompanied by puncture wounds. Evidence such as tracks, feces, and caching of the carcass identified the mortality as mammalian predation. Sharp puncture wounds accompanied by removal of the head and neck region from the carcass identified avian predators such as great horned owls (*Bubo virginianus*) (Miller and Leopold 1992). In addition to the aforementioned sign, we used infrared cameras to verify cause of mortality in some instances. Cameras were

Table 1. Kaplan-Meier winter (1 Dec–31 Mar) seasonal survival estimates ($\hat{S}$) for females wintering in farmsteads and females wintering in forest. Estimates are for Merriam's turkey females in the southern Black Hills, South Dakota, 2001–2004.

Year	Farmstead turkeys			Forest turkeys			*Z*-value	*P*
	n	$\hat{S}$	SE	*n*	$\hat{S}$	SE		
2001	28	0.963	0.036	7	1.000	0.000	1.03	0.303
2002	20	0.950	0.049	20	0.900	0.066	0.61	0.540
2003	22	0.917	0.057	27	0.856	0.065	0.70	0.459
2004	15	0.867	0.088	19	0.947	0.051	0.79	0.430
Pooled	85	0.936	0.026	73	0.922	0.032	0.39	0.734

placed at selected nest sites while females were away from nests. Photos of predators were taken when the predator approached the nest and triggered the infrared sensor. At other mortality sites the infrared cameras were placed near the turkey carcass after the predation event and photos obtained if predators returned to the cache. Dorsal guard hairs collected from shrubs and other vegetation at mortality sites were also used to identify mammalian predators (Moore et al. 1974). We also checked 4 reference sites in cardinal directions 20 m from the nest or other predation site to determine if hair occurrence was random.

Weather-related mortalities, or birds that died from starvation, were classified during winter or early spring when carcasses had emaciated breast muscles without hemorrhaging. If hemorrhaging or emaciation were not present, then carcasses were examined for diseases at the Animal Disease and Diagnostic Laboratory at South Dakota State University by D. H. Zeman, DVM, Ph.D. Otherwise we classified the cause of mortality as unknown.

We tested for differences in survival among years and seasons using chi-square procedures described by Sauer and Williams (1989) using the program CONTRAST (Hines and Sauer 1989). This procedure was also used to compare the 3 most prominent causes of mortality within seasons. We tested the null hypothesis that survival of birds wintering in farmsteads and birds wintering in ponderosa pine forest do not differ using a *Z*-test described by Pollock et al. (1989). We did not compare mortality between adults and yearlings because of small sample sizes within the yearling age class. We censored observations when radiotransmitters failed or if contact was lost. Significant differences occurred at $P \leq 0.05$ and we used a Bonferroni approach to control the Type I experimentwise error rate for multiple comparisons.

RESULTS

Survival

We captured and radiomarked 94 females during 2001–2004. However, due to capture-related trauma we had to censor 2 females. We used 92 females ($n = 76$ adults, $n = 16$ yearlings) for analyses. Within the winter period, we were able to pool years for both farmstead wintering turkeys ($\chi^2 = 1.28$, df = 3, $P = 0.73$) and forest wintering turkeys ($\chi^2 = 3.43$, df = 3, $P = 0.33$) (Table 1). Winter survival was similar between turkeys wintering in farmsteads and turkeys wintering in forest ($Z = 0.39$, $P = 0.73$) (Table 1).

Annual survival for adult females differed among years ($\chi^2 = 9.43$, df = 2, $P = 0.009$). Survival in 2001 ($\hat{S} = 0.83$, SE = 0.06) was significantly higher than 2003 ($\hat{S} = 0.64$, SE = 0.07) and 2002 ($\hat{S} = 0.54$, SE = 0.08) (Figure 1). Average annual survival for adults for the study period was 0.67 (SE = 0.09). Average annual survival for yearlings for the study period was 0.49 (SE = 0.11). Adult seasonal survival was similar ($\chi^2 \leq 5.66$, $P \geq 0.06$) among years and we pooled seasons for the analysis (Table 2). Spring survival was the lowest among all seasons for both adult (Table 2) and yearling females (Table 3). A high percentage (53%) of spring mortality occurred while females were laying eggs or incubating nests. Seasonal survival distributions for adults differed ($\chi^2 = 11.13$, df = 3, $P = 0.01$). Spring and fall were periods of lower survival, and winter and summer periods were periods of higher survival (Table 2).

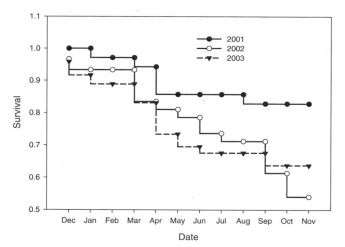

Survival

Fig. 1. Kaplan-Meier annual survival distributions (1 Dec–30 Nov) for adult Merriam's turkey females in the southern Black Hills, South Dakota, 2001–2003.

Table 2. Kaplan-Meier seasonal survival estimates ($\hat{S}$) during winter (1 Dec–31 Mar), spring (1 Apr–30 Jun), summer (1 Jul–31 Aug), and fall (1 Sep–30 Nov) for adult Merriam's turkey females in the southern Black Hills, South Dakota, 2001–2004.

Interval	*n*	$\hat{S}$	SE
Winter	158	0.932	0.020
Spring	118	0.831	0.035
Summer	91	0.956	0.022
Fall	58	0.860	0.047

Table 3. Kaplan-Meier seasonal survival estimates ($\hat{S}$) during winter (1 Dec–31 Mar), spring (1 Apr–30 Jun), summer (1 Jul–31 Aug), and fall (1 Sep–30 Nov) for yearling Merriam's turkey females in the southern Black Hills, South Dakota, 2001–2003.

Interval[a]	n	$\hat{S}$	SE
Winter 2001	6	1.000	0.000
Winter 2002	7	0.857	0.132
Winter 2003	3	0.500	0.250
Winter pooled	16	0.871	0.084
Spring 2001	6	0.667	0.192
Spring 2002	6	0.500	0.204
Spring 2003	2	1.000	0.000
Spring pooled	14	0.643	0.128
Summer 2001	4	1.000	0.000
Summer 2002	3	1.000	0.000
Summer 2003	2	1.000	0.000
Summer pooled	9	1.000	0.000
Fall 2001	4	1.000	0.000
Fall 2002	4	0.667	0.272
Fall 2003	2	1.000	0.000
Fall pooled	10	0.889	0.112

[a] Due to small sample size years were not compared and thus not pooled.

Cause-specific Mortality

Mammalian predators, primarily coyotes and bobcats, caused 47.2% of mortality to female Merriam's turkeys (Figure 2). Guard hairs found on shrubs and debris at predation sites were used to identify cause of predation at 17 sites and guard hairs were not found at reference sites. Infrared cameras were used to positively identify predators in some instances ($n = 6$). Avian predators, mostly great horned owls, caused 18.9% of mortality and weather-related starvation accounted for 7.4% (Figure 2). Other causes of mortality included fall hunting (3.8%), illegal kill (1.9%), disease (3.8%), car collisions (1.9%), and unknown (15.1%) (Figure 2). Deep snow cover in late winter of 2002 resulted in starvation of 4 females wintering in forest. Multisystemic inflammatory disease compatible with bacteria septicemia (*Escherichia coli*) caused one death, and cloacal impaction caused another death (D. H. Zeman, DVM, Animal Disease and Diagnostics Laboratory, South Dakota State University). Across seasons, most mortality factors were evenly distributed with the exception during spring when mammalian predation was noticeably higher than other seasons

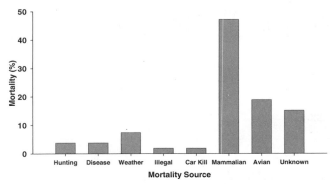

Fig. 2. Causes (%) of mortality for Merriam's turkey females ($n = 53$) in the southern Black Hills, South Dakota, 2001–2004.

(Table 4). Within winter, summer, and fall seasons cause-specific mortality rates did not differ ($\chi^2 \leq 1.22$, $P \geq 0.40$). However, during spring rates differed ($\chi^2 = 8.72$, df $= 2$, $P = 0.01$), as mammalian predation was higher than avian predation and weather-related mortality (Table 4).

DISCUSSION

In winter, female Merriam's turkeys primarily fed on ponderosa pine seeds or farmstead grains and survival was high. Although turkeys wintering in association with farmsteads have increased survival in some areas (Lehman et al. 2001), this was not evident in our study as survival rates of females that wintered in farmsteads were not higher than rates of females wintering in ponderosa pine forest. Several studies have shown a link between habitat and foods for Merriam's turkeys (Rumble and Anderson 1996a, 1996b), and this may affect their winter survival (Wakeling and Rogers 1996, Wakeling and Goodwin 1999). Merriam's females in Arizona experienced low winter survival, possibly due to lack of winter food availability (Wakeling 1991, Wakeling and Goodwin 1999). Merriam's turkeys in the central Black Hills also fed upon pine seeds in winter (Rumble and Anderson 1996a) and used pine stands with high canopy coverage (Rumble and Anderson 1996b). Turkeys in the central Black Hills also had high winter survival except for yearling females following deep snowfall events

Table 4. Seasonal cause-specific mortality rates (SE) and deaths (n) during winter (1 Dec–31 Mar), spring (1 Apr–30 Jun), summer (1 Jul–31 Aug), and fall (1 Sep–30 Nov) for Merriam's turkey females in the southern Black Hills, South Dakota, 2001–2004. Rates were calculated using the Kaplan-Meier method.

Mortality source	Season							
	Winter		Spring		Summer		Fall	
	Rate (SE)	n	Rate (SE)	n	Rate (SE)	n	Rate (SE)	n
Mammalian	0.027 (0.01)	4	0.114 (0.03)	15	0.029 (0.02)	3	0.031 (0.02)	3
Avian	0.028 (0.01)	4	0.023 (0.01)	3	0.000 (0.00)	0	0.031 (0.02)	3
Weather	0.008 (0.01)	1	0.023 (0.01)	3	0.000 (0.00)	0	0.000 (0.00)	0
Hunting	0.000 (0.00)	0	0.000 (0.00)	0	0.000 (0.00)	0	0.020 (0.01)	2
Illegal kill	0.000 (0.00)	0	0.008 (0.01)	1	0.000 (0.00)	0	0.000 (0.00)	0
Disease	0.000 (0.00)	0	0.015 (0.01)	2	0.000 (0.00)	0	0.000 (0.00)	0
Car kill	0.000 (0.00)	0	0.000 (0.00)	0	0.000 (0.00)	0	0.010 (0.01)	1
Unknown	0.014 (0.01)	2	0.015 (0.01)	2	0.010 (0.01)	1	0.031 (0.02)	3

(Rumble et al. 2003). In 2002, 3 yearlings and 1 adult wintering in forest died of starvation shortly after deep snowfall covered food resources. During this period snow cover ≥20 cm lasted about 14 days. Emaciated birds had lost 40–41% of their original body weight.

Annual survival of adult female Merriam's turkeys in the southern Black Hills averaged 67%, which is similar to that for Merriam's females in the central Black Hills ($\bar{x}$ = 68%, Rumble et al. 2003). Age-classes combined, average annual survival of Merriam's turkey females in Arizona was 57% (Rumble et al. 2003) and 45% in Montana (Thompson 1993). In Arizona, annual survival for adult females averaged 67% for the Mogollon Rim (Wakeling 1991) but reached 84% or above at some sites (Rumble et al. 2003). Adult female Merriam's turkey survival in Oregon averaged 62% but yearling female survival was only 42% (Crawford and Lutz 1984). Annual yearling female survival averaged 49% in the southern Black Hills, but sample sizes were small during this study (*n* = 16). In comparison, yearling female survival in New Mexico and Arizona was higher at 65% (Lockwood and Sutcliffe 1985) and 69% (Wakeling 1991).

In the southern Black Hills, adult survival was lowest during spring and fall, and highest during winter and summer. Spring has been a period of high female mortality apparently because of vulnerability of females nesting on the ground during the long incubation period (Speake 1980). Survival in the spring was similar to other studies of Merriam's turkeys that also showed the apparent vulnerability of females during nesting (Rumble and Hodorff 1993, Thompson 1993, Rumble et al. 2003). Mammalian predators caused most of the mortality during the spring period, and much of the mortality occurred while females were laying eggs or incubating clutches. Thompson (1993) reported 50% of all mortality of females occurred during the nesting period. In Arizona, Merriam's turkeys experienced low predation during nesting, but high predation rates during brood rearing (Wakeling 1991). Avian predators were the primary cause of mortality during brood-rearing (Wakeling 1991). We found no evidence of high female mortality in the southern Black Hills during brood-rearing. Fall survival was similar to spring survival in our study but had an even distribution of mortality factors, including predation, hunting, and unknown.

In our study, coyote and bobcat predation accounted for the highest percentage of mortality, followed by great horned owl predation. Across the Merriam's range predation by mammalian and avian predators accounts for the majority of mortality events in Merriam's turkeys (Rumble et al. 2003). Starvation associated with deep snowfall was not common in the southern Black Hills. However, in northeastern South Dakota severe winter weather caused 14% of mortality (Lehman et al. 2001). Deep snow cover on food sources in late winter and early spring can have negative cumulative effects on the physiological condition of birds (Rumble and Anderson 1996*a*, Wakeling and Rogers 1996). Fall harvest of females is slight, accounting for about 4%, and does not affect turkey pop-

ulations in the southern Black Hills. Similarly, fall hunting caused 2.6% of annual mortality in Arizona and had little affect on Arizona turkey populations (Wakeling 1991). One female (1.9%) was illegally killed by spring turkey hunters, which is a lower rate than in heavily hunted areas in the eastern United States (Healy and Powell 1999). In the southern Black Hills, cause-specific mortality rates typically did not differ within seasons with the exception of spring when mammalian predation exceeded other mortality factors. Mammalian predators were more successful in finding nesting females than avian predators and may account for the differential predation rate.

MANAGEMENT IMPLICATIONS

With the exception of adult females from some areas in Arizona (Rumble et al. 2003), survival in the southern Black Hills was similar or higher than rates reported for Merriam's turkeys from both its indigenous range (Lockwood and Sutcliffe 1985) and its introduced range (Crawford and Lutz 1984, Thompson 1993, Rumble et al. 2003). Survival was excellent for both turkeys that wintered near farmsteads and turkeys that wintered in forest. Farmstead habitats were highly utilized by Merriam's turkeys in the southern Black Hills (Lehman 2005). Farmsteads were particularly important during the winter of 2003 when there was less pine seed production. Farmsteads could be important in sustaining population levels during years of severe winter weather. Although only a small percentage (1.9%) of females were illegally killed by spring turkey hunters in this study, we recommend that illegal female harvest continue to be monitored as the number of hunters increases in the Black Hills.

ACKNOWLEDGMENTS

We thank D. Thompson, M. Rohfling, C. Sexton, and C. Kassube for field support. Cooperating landowners N. Westphal, R. (Gene) Miller, and D. Brown provided access to private lands. The USDA Forest Service Rocky Mountain Research Station provided field assistance and technical support. Funding for this research project was from the South Dakota Department of Game, Fish and Parks, Federal Aid to Wildlife Restoration Fund (Project W-75-R-132, No. 7599), National Wild Turkey Federation (National Research Projects), and the South Dakota State Chapter of the National Wild Turkey Federation (State Super Fund). Additional support was provided by South Dakota State University and McIntire-Stennis funding through the South Dakota Agricultural Experiment Station.

LITERATURE CITED

Austin, D. H., T. E. Peoples, and L. E. Williams, Jr. 1972. Procedures for capturing and handling live wild turkeys. Proceedings of the Annual Conference of the Southeastern Association of Game and Fish Commission 25:222–235.

Crawford, J. A., and R. S. Lutz. 1984. Final report on Merriam's wild turkey habitat use and movements. Oregon Department of Fish and Wildlife, Federal Aid in Wildlife Restoration Project W-79-R-2, Final Report.

Dill, H. H., and W. H. Thornsberry. 1950. A cannon-projected net trap for capturing waterfowl. Journal of Wildlife Management 14:132–137.

Flake, L. D., and K. S. Day. 1996. Wild turkey reproduction in a prairie-woodland complex in South Dakota. Proceedings of the National Wild Turkey Symposium 7:153–164.

Glazener, W. C., A. S. Jackson, and M. L. Cox. 1964. The Texas drop-net turkey trap. Journal of Wildlife Management 28:280–287.

Healy, W. M. 1992. Population influences: environment. Pages 129–143 in J. G. Dickson, editor. The wild turkey: biology and management. Stackpole Books, Harrisburg, Pennsylvania, USA.

———, and S. M. Powell. 1999. Wild turkey harvest management: biology, strategies, and techniques. US Fish and Wildlife Biological Technical Publication BTP-R5001–1999.

Heisey, D. M., and T. K. Fuller. 1985. Evaluation of survival and cause-specific mortality rates using telemetry data. Journal of Wildlife Management 49:668–674.

Hines, J. E., and J. R. Sauer. 1989. Program CONTRAST a general program of the analysis of several survival or recovery rate estimates. U. S. Fish and Wildlife Service Fish and Wildlife Technical Report 24.

Hoffman, G. R., and R. R. Alexander. 1987. Forest vegetation of the Black Hills National Forest of South Dakota and Wyoming: a habitat type classification. United States Department of Agriculture Forest Service, Research Paper RM-276.

Hoffman, R. W., M. P. Luttrell, and W. R. Davidson. 1996. Reproductive performance of Merriam's wild turkeys with suspected *Mycoplasma* infection. Proceedings of the National Wild Turkey Symposium 7:145–151.

Huxoll, C. 2003. 2003 Annual Report. South Dakota Department of Game, Fish and Parks, Report 2004–01.

———. 2004. 2004 Annual Report. South Dakota Department of Game, Fish and Parks, Report 2005–01.

Johnson, J. R., and G. E. Larson. 1999. Grassland plants of South Dakota and the Northern Great Plains: a field guide with color photographs. South Dakota State University, Brookings, South Dakota, USA.

Johnson, R. R., K. F. Higgins, and D. E. Hubbard. 1995. Using soils to delineate South Dakota physiographic regions. Great Plains Research 5:309–322.

Kalvels, J. 1980. Soil Survey of Fall River County, South Dakota. U. S. Department of Agriculture, Soil Conservation Service and Forest Service, in cooperation with the South Dakota Agricultural Experiment Station, Brookings, South Dakota, USA.

Kaplan, E. L., and P. Meier. 1958. Nonparametric estimation from incomplete observations. Journal of the American Statistical Association 53:457–481.

Lehman, C. P. 2005. Ecology of Merriam's turkeys in the southern Black Hills, South Dakota. Dissertation, South Dakota State University, Brookings, South Dakota, USA.

———, L. D. Flake, A. P. Leif, and R. D. Shields. 2001. Comparative survival and reproduction of sympatric eastern and Rio Grande wild turkey females in northeastern South Dakota. Proceedings of the National Wild Turkey Symposium 8:123–135.

Leif, A. P. 1997. Survival, reproduction and home ranges of translocated eastern wild turkeys in eastern South Dakota 1993–95. Pierre: South Dakota Department of Game, Fish, and Parks. Completion Report, Pierre, South Dakota, USA.

Lockwood, D. R., and D. H. Sutcliffe. 1985. Distribution, mortality, and reproduction of Merriam's turkey in New Mexico. Proceedings of the National Wild Turkey Symposium 5:309–316.

Miller, J. E., and B. D. Leopold. 1992. Population influences: predators. Pages 119–128 in J. G. Dickson, editor. The wild turkey: biology and management. Stackpole Books, Harrisburg, Pennsylvania, USA.

Moore T. D., L. E. Spence, and C. E. Dugnolle. 1974. Identification of the dorsal guard hairs of some mammals of Wyoming in W. G. Hepworth editor. Wyoming Game and Fish Department, Bulletin Number 14.

National Climatic Data Center. 1971–2000. Climatological Data, South Dakota, Annual Summary. National Oceanic and Atmospheric Administration, Asheville, North Carolina, USA.

Peterson, L. E., and A. H. Richardson. 1975. The wild turkey in the Black Hills. South Dakota Department of Game, Fish and Parks, Bulletin 6.

Pollock, K. H., S. R. Winterstein, C. M. Bunck, and P. D. Curtis. 1989. Survival analysis in telemetry studies: the staggered entry design. Journal of Wildlife Management 53:7–15.

Porter, W. F. 1978. Behavior and Ecology of the wild turkey (*Meleagris gallopavo*) in southeastern Minnesota. Dissertation, University of Minnesota, Minneapolis, Minnesota, USA.

———, G. C. Nelson, and K. Mattson. 1983. Effects of winter conditions on reproduction in a northern wild turkey population. Journal of Wildlife Management 47:281–290.

———, R. D. Tangen, G. C. Nelson, and D. A. Hamilton. 1980. Effects of corn food plots on wild turkeys in the upper Mississippi Valley. Journal of Wildlife Management 47:281–290.

Rumble, M. A., and R. A. Hodorff. 1993. Nesting ecology of Merriam's turkeys in the Black Hills, South Dakota. Journal of Wildlife Management 57:789–801.

———, and S. H. Anderson. 1996a. Feeding ecology of Merriam's turkeys (*Meleagris gallopavo merriami*) in the Black Hills, South Dakota. American Midland Naturalist 136:157–171.

———, and ———. 1996b. Macrohabitat associations of Merriam's turkeys in the Black Hills, South Dakota. Northwest Science 67:238–245.

———, B. F. Wakeling, and L. D. Flake. 2003. Factors affecting survival and recruitment in female Merriam's turkeys. Intermountain Journal of Sciences 9:26–37.

Sauer, J. R., and B. K. Williams. 1989. Generalized procedures for testing hypotheses about survival and recovery rates. Journal of Wildlife Management 53:137–142.

Speake, D. W. 1980. Predation on wild turkeys in Alabama. Proceedings of the National Wild Turkey Symposium 4:86–101.

Thompson, W. L. 1993. Ecology of Merriam's turkeys in relation to burned and logged areas in southeastern Montana. Dissertation, Montana State University, Bozeman, Montana, USA.

Thompson, M. C., and R. L. Delong. 1967. The use of cannon and rocket projected nets for trapping shorebirds. Bird Banding 38:214–218.

Vander Haegen, W. M., W. E. Dodge, and M. W. Sayre. 1988. Factors affecting productivity in a northern wild turkey population. Journal of Wildlife Management 52:127–133.

———, M. W. Sayre, and W. E. Dodge. 1989. Winter use of agricultural habitats by wild turkeys in Massachusetts. Journal of Wildlife Management 53:30–33.

Vangilder, L. D. 1995. Survival and cause-specific mortality of wild turkeys in Missouri Ozarks. Proceedings of the National Wild Turkey Symposium 7:21–31.

———, and E. W. Kurzejeski. 1995. Population ecology of the eastern wild turkey in northern Missouri. Wildlife Monographs 130.

Wakeling B. F. 1991. Population and nesting characteristics of Merriam's turkey along the Mogollon Rim, Arizona. Arizona Game and Fish Department, Research Technical Report 7.

———, and J. G. Goodwin, Jr. 1999. Merriam's turkey winter survival on the North Kaibab Ranger District following the Bridger Knoll complex fires. Proceedings of the Biennial

Conference of Research on the Colorado Plateau 4:123–132.

———, and T. D. Rogers. 1996. Winter diet and habitat selection by Merriam's turkeys in north-central Arizona. Proceedings of the National Wild Turkey Symposium 7:175–184.

Williams, L. E., Jr. 1961. Notes on wing molt in the yearling wild turkey. Journal of Wildlife Management 25:439–440.

Wright, R. G., R. N. Paisley, and J. F. Kubisiak. 1996. Survival of wild turkey hens in southwestern Wisconsin. Journal of Wildlife Management 60:313–320.

Wunz, G. A. 1984. Rocket-net innovations for capturing wild turkeys and waterfowl. Pennsylvania Game Commission, Pittman-Robertson Federal Aid Progress Report, Project W-46-R-21.

———. 1992. Wild turkeys outside their historic range. Pages 361–384 *in* J. G. Dickson, editor. The wild turkey: biology and management. Stackpole Books, Harrisburg, Pennsylvania, USA.

Chad P. Lehman received a B.S. in Biological Science from the University of Minnesota-Duluth (1994) and M.S. in Wildlife Science from South Dakota State University (1998). He received a Ph.D. in Biological Science from South Dakota State University (2005) and his research focused on Merriam's turkey ecology, particularly the influence of weather and habitat selection/availability on survival and reproduction. As a wildlife biologist for Custer State Park, Chad conducts research and manages habitats for game and nongame wildlife species. For hobbies, Chad enjoys hiking with his wife Michelle and son Drew, and hunting birds with his yellow Labrador Retrievers.

Mark A. Rumble received a B.S. in wildlife biology from Washington State University, an M.S. in Wildlife Science from South Dakota State University, and a Ph.D. in Zoology from the University of Wyoming. Mark has worked for the U.S. Forest Service for 27 years, and 26 years for the Rocky Mountain Research Station in Rapid City, South Dakota. His professional interest includes understanding the effects of land management on wildlife habitat with an emphasis on developing information in formats that are usable by forest and range managers.

Les Flake retired from South Dakota State University in August of 2002 after 31 years on the faculty and was appointed Distinguished Professor Emeritus. He is still advising graduate students and remains involved with several projects in South Dakota. In his free time Les enjoys visiting grandchildren, hiking in the mountains of Utah, reading, fly fishing, bow hunting, and chasing pheasants with old friends in South Dakota. Les has a Ph.D. in Zoology from Washington State University (1971) and an M.S. in Zoology from Brigham Young University (1966).

Wild Turkey Management:
Accomplishments, Strategies, and Opportunities
———— Grand Rapids, Michigan ————

FACTORS THAT INFLUENCE THE DISTRIBUTION OF WILD TURKEYS IN MICHIGAN

Steven B. Chadwick[1,2]

Michigan Department of Natural Resources, Wildlife Division,
P.O. Box 30444,
Lansing, MI 48909, USA

Abstract: Prior to European settlement, wild turkeys (*Meleagris gallopavo*) were present in Michigan south of a line from Saginaw Bay to the mouth of the Muskegon River. Habitat loss and overexploitation during settlement led to the extirpation of turkeys from Michigan in the late 1800s. Several restoration attempts followed in the early 1900s; however, it was not until the mid to latter part of the last century that restoration efforts were successful. As a result, wild turkeys currently occupy much of their ancestral range and beyond, providing Michigan residents with quality hunting and wildlife viewing opportunities on both public and private lands. The expansion of wild turkey range has led wildlife biologists to debate how far north turkeys should be introduced and actively managed. Northern range expansion in Michigan can be attributed to alteration of Michigan's native habitats and human activities that promote turkey survival throughout the year. A literature review was conducted to determine how the major limiting factors of winter weather and lack of suitable habitat influence wild turkey survival in northern regions of Michigan. These limiting factors may be overcome in some portions of the state through habitat management programs that mitigate winter loss.

Proceedings of the National Wild Turkey Symposium 9:303–306

Key words: climate, habitat, northern range, wild turkey, winter feeding.

Wild turkeys are native to Michigan. Prior to European settlement turkeys were present south of a line from Saginaw Bay to the mouth of the Muskegon River (Brewer et al. 1991). It is believed that the habitat and climate of northern Michigan were not conducive to wild turkey expansion. However, it is possible that the turkey range could have extended as far north as Oscoda County during successive years of mild winters (Kulowiec 1986).

Unregulated hunting and habitat conversion led to the extirpation of wild turkeys from Michigan around 1900 (Kulowiec 1986, Brewer et al. 1991). The first successful reintroduction of turkeys occurred in 1954 at the Allegan State Game Area (in the southwestern Lower Peninsula) with the release of 50 birds obtained from Pennsylvania (Kulowiec 1986, Brewer et al. 1991). During the years 1955–1957, additional turkeys were released in the northern counties of the Lower Peninsula. In early 1965, birds from Allegan County were moved to Menominee County in the Upper Pen-

insula (UP) along the Menominee River. A large scale restoration effort during the 1980s brought birds from Iowa, Missouri, and other states to the southern Lower Peninsula where turkeys now thrive. This restoration effort resulted in turkey populations throughout their ancestral range in Michigan and it expanded the range north to the UP (Michigan Department of Natural Resources [MDNR], unpublished data).

As a result of restoration efforts, turkeys are now present in parts of Michigan where they did not historically exist. This can be partially attributed to landscape changes (e.g., where forested land was converted to agriculture). The present distribution of turkeys also can be attributed to human activities, such as winter-

—————————————————————

[1] Present address: Crane Pond State Game Area, Michigan Department of Natural Resources, P.O. Box 158, 60887 M-40, Jones, MI 49061, USA.

[2] E-mail: CHADWICS@michigan.gov

feeding programs, which provide additional food resources in northern landscapes.

The intent of this paper was to review the current body of literature regarding turkey survival in northern landscapes to help identify the factors limiting range expansion in Michigan. This information can be used to help set management objectives throughout northern Michigan to maximize the wise use of limited turkey management resources.

WINTER WEATHER

The climate throughout most of northern Michigan is influenced by the Great Lakes, which results in moderate temperatures and heavy precipitation along the lakeshores. Areas away from the lakeshores experience a continental climate where temperatures are extremely cold during the winter months (Albert 1995). Average annual temperatures range from 4°C to 6°C throughout the region with average winter temperatures ranging from −8°C in the UP to −6°C in the northern Lower Peninsula (NLP) (ZedX 2000). Typically, over 200 cm of snow falls across much of the NLP and UP in a single season (ZedX 2000).

Moderate to severe winter conditions can have a dramatic influence on wild turkey populations by limiting survival and reducing reproduction and recruitment (Haroldson 2003). Cold temperatures and snow accumulation create conditions that increase daily energy expenditures and limit food availability. Both are critical factors affecting individual survival. An average 4.2 kg turkey requires approximately 11.3 kg of mixed diet during a 120-day winter with an average temperature >11°C. Food requirements increase by 2.4 kg for every 10°C drop in mean temperature (Haroldson 1995). A turkey can be expected to survive on little or no food for about 2 weeks, assuming 20% of its body mass is catabolizable energy available from typical body fat deposits; therefore, overwinter survival depends on fat reserves and food availability (Oberlag et al. 1990). It is assumed that Michigan's cold temperatures compound the effects of snow by increasing energy requirements by 42%, resulting in roughly a 10-day period to reach food for survival.

Turkeys can tolerate temperatures lower than those that occur on their current range with proper fat reserves and food availability (Haroldson 1995). However, deep snow (>30 cm) for prolonged periods of time limits daily movements, increases energy expenditures for travel, and prevents turkeys from reaching food sources (Austin and DeGraff 1975, Wunz and Hayden 1975). Roberts et al. (1995) found that winter mortality among adult females began after 40 to 59 days of exposure to prolonged deep snow (>25.4 cm). Therefore, snow conditions that limit food availability for extended periods may have more influence on turkey winter survival than low temperatures (Haroldson 1995).

Using 30-year average daily snow depth data (ZedX 2000), areas where 30 cm of snow persisted for 6 weeks were identified in Michigan (Figure 1). In the

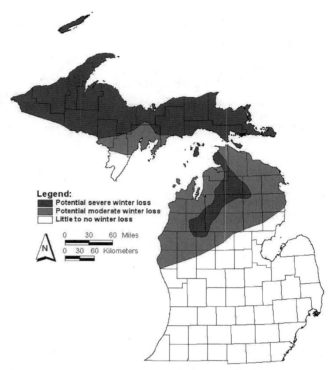

Fig. 1.   Locations of potential wild turkey winter loss based on snow depth over 30 cm (ZedX 2000) that persisted for ≥6 weeks in Michigan.

UP, snow depth and duration would limit turkey survival north of a line from Escanaba to Iron Mountain. In the NLP these conditions persisted north of a line from Rogers City through Houghton Lake and south and west to Lake Michigan at Pentwater. Based solely on winter weather conditions, there are few places in northern Michigan where wild turkeys can survive and maintain sustainable populations.

HABITAT REQUIREMENTS

Upland hardwoods and open fields (i.e., agricultural fields, pastures, old fields) have been identified as suitable turkey habitat (Porter 1980, Donovan 1985, Kulowiec 1986). Upland hardwood forests comprised of aspen (*Populus* spp.), red and sugar maple (*Acer rubrum* and *A. saccharum*), red and white oak (*Quercus rubra, Q. alba*), and American beech (*Fagus grandifolia*) provide many essential resources for turkeys and are considered a base habitat type where turkeys can spend most of the year (Porter 1980, Kulowiec 1986). Hard mast producing trees, such as oak and beech, provide high-energy foods, which become increasingly important between fall and spring (Donovan 1985).

In some northern regions, turkeys exhibit habitat selection behavior that tends to conserve heat loss and lower energy requirements during winter months (Kulowiec 1986). During severe winter weather, turkeys roost more often in conifer habitats near food and water sources (Kulowiec 1986, Kilpatrick et al. 1988, Haroldson 2003).

Active farmlands interspersed with upland hardwoods provide many additional resources critical to turkey survival and production (Porter 1980, Porter et al. 1980, Donovan 1985, Kulowiec 1986). During the winter months, when snow limits access to natural food products, turkey activity revolves around agricultural operations and wildlife food plots (Porter 1980, Kulowiec and Haufler 1985). Active agriculture operations can offset winter mortality among turkeys by providing a source of high-energy food (Porter 1980). Turkeys are able to find grain and other food items in manure spread on farm fields in the winter as well as in standing waste grain (Kulowiec and Haufler 1985).

HABITAT MANIPULATION

It is assumed that the limited amount of agriculture in some of the snow-belt regions of the NLP and areas of the south central UP may sustain a viable population of turkeys. Kulowiec (1986) reported high densities of turkeys around active agriculture in northeastern Michigan during the early 1980s, prior to large-scale winter-feeding efforts. He also suggested several habitat management options to help create sustainable turkey populations across the NLP. Conservation groups work with the MDNR and the U.S. Forest Service to promote turkey habitat projects on public and private lands. One program started by the MDNR in 1996 assists landowners in placing corn food plots on their property specifically for turkeys (MDNR. 2002. Turkey winter food plot evaluation, 1999–2002. Unpublished report, MDNR, Wildlife Division, Lansing, Michigan, USA). Locations are chosen by considering habitat features, proximity to public land, and distance from known winter deer concentration areas. An evaluation of the program in 2002 indicated that in some areas, reasonably stocked food plots fed 30–40 turkeys throughout the winter, and further funding of the program was recommended (MDNR. 2002. Turkey winter food plot evaluation, 1999–2002. Unpublished report, MDNR, Wildlife Division, Lansing, Michigan, USA).

RECREATIONAL FEEDING OF WILDLIFE

The human population in northern Michigan continues to increase as Michigan residents seek retirement homes away from urban centers. Many local residents feed wildlife throughout the year in the form of backyard bird feeders. According to national statistics, 86% of wildlife watchers said they feed wildlife, and 97% of these individuals said they feed wild birds (U.S. Fish and Wildlife Service 2002). It is assumed that the increased human population and interest in feeding wildlife in northern Michigan has resulted in more feeding sites available for turkeys during the winter.

MANAGEMENT IMPLICATIONS

After comparison of literature review information and Michigan winter weather conditions, it is apparent that a large section of the UP and NLP experience winter conditions that would limit survival of turkeys. In addition, when looking at habitat components, some portions of the UP are missing critical habitat, such as active agriculture, that provide resources to turkeys during the winter months. Placing food plots on the landscape aimed at providing food resources to turkeys has met with some success in the NLP. However, this success has not been universal; it has been localized and dependent upon private citizen involvement. There remains considerable sentiment that food plots are not completely filling in the missing habitat gaps. Furthermore, food plots may be limited due to the short growing season in the UP. In some northern areas, the only option for maintaining turkeys is by providing food resources through winter- feeding programs. This is not an acceptable practice for maintaining a naturally reproducing population.

In the face of economic hardships, it becomes important to maximize every dollar spent for resource management. It might be feasible to split Michigan into turkey management regions where weather and habitat features dictate management direction. Most of the UP experiences winter weather conditions that will not allow turkeys to survive on their own. These areas, especially along Lake Superior, are not suited to the type of agriculture that turkeys utilize for winter survival. The UP north of Highway US-2 is an area where the MDNR should not spend valuable resources specifically on turkey habitat or relocations. Also, habitat management that would be required may not be compatible with the MDNR's principles of ecosystem management, nor with the overall management direction of state and federal forests.

In contrast, the NLP and UP south of Highway US-2 may be suited to a much reduced, yet sustainable population of turkeys. Although these areas experience similar weather conditions that limit survival, there is a component of agriculture that turkeys may be able to access. In addition, food-plot programs funded through the MDNR have been attempted with some success. It may be feasible to use suggestions from Kulowiec (1986) to develop wintering areas across the NLP on private and public lands through a habitat management initiative. This may reduce the dependency on winter feeding by local residents. Any program initiated in the NLP will need to be reviewed and deemed compatible with the MDNR's principles of ecosystem management before implementation.

Some biologists consider northern turkeys to be a "bonus bird" (wildlife biologists, MDNR, personal communication). They are available for wildlife viewing and spring and fall hunting when winters are mild or residents feed them; when one or both components fail, turkey populations decrease. A much reduced, yet sustainable, turkey population might be attainable in some northern landscapes by focusing resources on habitat manipulation in landscapes where it is consistent with ecosystem management principles and where winter mortality factors could be mitigated.

ACKNOWLEDGMENTS

Thanks to M. Bailey, T. Edwards, C. Hanaburgh, and P. Lederle for reviewing drafts of this paper. Special thanks to A. Stewart for providing guidance and the opportunity to explore this interesting issue.

LITERATURE CITED

Albert, D. A. 1995. Regional landscape ecosystems of Michigan, Minnesota, and Wisconsin: a working map and classification. U.S. Forest Service General Technical Report NC-178.

Austin, D. E., and L. W. DeGraff. 1975. Winter survival of wild turkeys in the southern Adirondacks. Proceedings of the National Wild Turkey Symposium 3:55–60.

Brewer, R., G. A. McPeek, and R. J. Adams. 1991. The atlas of breeding birds in Michigan. Michigan State University Press, East Lansing, Michigan, USA.

Donovan, M. L. 1985. A turkey habitat suitability model utilizing the Michigan Resource Information System (MIRIS). Thesis, University of Michigan, Ann Arbor, Michigan, USA.

Haroldson, K. J. 1995. Energy requirements for winter survival of wild turkeys. Proceedings of the National Wild Turkey Symposium 7:9–14.

———. 2003. Weather, food, and roost cover: key factors limiting the northern distribution of wild turkeys. Page 11 *in* R. O. Kimmel, W. J. Krueger, and T. K. Klinkner, compilers. Northern Wild Turkey Workshop. Minnesota Department of Natural Resources, Madelia, Minnesota, USA.

Kilpatrick, H. J., T. P. Husband, and C. A. Pringle. 1988. Winter roost site characteristics of eastern wild turkeys. Journal of Wildlife Management 52:461–463.

Kulowiec, T. G. 1986. Habitat utilization, movements, and population characteristics of resident northern Michigan turkeys. Thesis, Michigan State University, East Lansing, Michigan, USA.

———, and J. B. Haufler. 1985. Winter and dispersal movements of wild turkeys in Michigan's northern Lower Peninsula. Proceedings of the National Wild Turkey Symposium 5:145–153.

Oberlag, D. F., P. J. Pekins, and W. W. Mautz. 1990. Influence of seasonal temperatures on wild turkey metabolism. Journal of Wildlife Management 54:663–667.

Porter, W. F. 1980. An evaluation of wild turkey brood habitat in southeastern Minnesota. Proceedings of the National Wild Turkey Symposium 4:203–212.

———, R. D. Tangen, G. C. Nelson, and D. A. Hamilton. 1980. Effects of corn food plots on wild turkeys in the Upper Mississippi Valley. Journal of Wildlife Management 44:456–462.

Roberts, S. D., J. M. Coffey, and W. F. Porter. 1995. Survival and reproduction of female wild turkeys in New York. Journal of Wildlife Management 59:437–447.

U.S. Fish and Wildlife Service. 2002. 2001 national survey of fishing, hunting, and wildlife-associated recreation. U.S. Department of the Interior, Fish and Wildlife Service, and U.S. Department of Commerce, U.S. Census Bureau, Washington, D.C., USA.

Wunz, G. A., and A. H. Hayden. 1975. Winter mortality and supplemental feeding of turkeys in Pennsylvania. Proceedings of the National Wild Turkey Symposium 3:61–69.

ZedX. 2000. Thirty-year compiled 1961–1990 Hi-Rez(TM) climatological series set for Michigan (compiled October 2000). Digital Dataset. ZedX, Inc. Bellefonte, Pennsylvania, USA. ⟨http://www.zedxinc.com/⟩. Accessed 27 Feb 2001.

Steven B. Chadwick has been with the Michigan DNR for 5 years starting as a Wildlife Technician in Lansing and more recently as a Wildlife Biologist in Southwest Michigan. Prior to working in Michigan, he held positions in Missouri and Alaska working on various field projects. Steve's interest in wild turkey management was sparked in Lansing working on statewide issues including northern range, turkey depredation on agricultural crops, and fall hunting. Steve received a B.S. in Wildlife Biology from Colorado State University.

Wild Turkey Management:
Accomplishments, Strategies, and Opportunities
——— Grand Rapids, Michigan ———

UNDERSTANDING THE ECOLOGY OF WILD TURKEYS IN NORTHERN LATITUDES

William F. Porter[1]

Faculty of Environmental and Forest Biology,
State University of New York,
College of Environmental Science and Forestry,
1 Forestry Drive,
Syracuse, NY 13210, USA

Abstract: Prior to the 1960s, conventional wisdom suggested wild turkeys (*Meleagris gallopavo silvestris*) were unlikely to thrive in the upper midwestern and northeastern United States. Two hypotheses were implicit: (1) severity of winter weather produced high mortality, thereby limiting turkey populations to more moderate climates, and (2) lack of forest cover in landscapes dominated by agriculture limited the amount of suitable habitat. This paper explores these hypotheses and the reasons for the dramatic success of the wild turkey in this region. While winter caused significant mortality, research confirmed it was access to food rather than cold temperatures that affected survival. Spring weather conditions were more important than winter to long-term fluctuations in population abundance. Forest cover in the region was sufficient and agriculture proved to be a major asset to wild turkeys because of the food it provided. Habitat suitability in this region appears to be driven by a complex interplay of proportion, configuration and spatial scale of forest and agriculture. This interplay has produced an exceptionally suitable landscape, but one that may be short lived because of large-scale societal shifts in land use.

Proceedings of the National Wild Turkey Symposium 9:307–313

Key words: agriculture, forest, habitat, landscape, nest, populations, predation, *silvestris,* spring, weather, winter.

Thirty years ago, Henry Mosby, one of the most widely recognized wild turkey biologists of the 20th century, wrote:

> "The wild turkey is much more adaptable, ecologically speaking, than was assumed 30 years ago, for it has done well in habitats and covertypes for which it did not seem well adapted in the early 1940s." (Mosby 1973: 75).

What seems especially remarkable about this statement is that exactly the same comment is often made today, and by biologists who are equally amazed at the adaptability of the species. A second generation of wild turkey biologists has witnessed a profound change in our understanding of the wild turkey, one that has helped restore the species to geographic areas beyond all expectation.

As trap and transfer of wild turkeys began to accelerate in the late 1960s, there was great uncertainty about the potential for this species in the upper Mississippi valley, the Great Lake states and the Northeast. The wild turkey evolved in southern latitudes and the only places it seemed to be doing well were areas of extensive oak forest. Consequently, its chances of success in the cold winters and highly disturbed agricultural landscapes of the northern United States appeared slim. Early releases of wild turkeys in northeast Iowa and Wisconsin had failed. While later research would show that these early releases were of the wrong subspecies to be successful in the upper Mississippi valley, the failures seemed to confirm the assessment (Dreis et al. 1973, Wigal 1973, Little 1980).

Today, the upper Midwest, Lake States, and Northeast hold more than 1.1 million wild turkeys distributed over 625,000 km² (Tapley et al. 2001). The intent of this paper is to explore 2 hypotheses implicit to the debate over biology and management of wild turkeys in northern latitudes: (1) severity of winters limits turkey populations by causing high mortality, and (2) lack of forest cover in agricultural landscapes limits suitable habitat. While the success of the species refutes these hypotheses, it is useful to draw together the lessons that research has taught us about why the wild turkey has done so well.

---

[1] E-mail: wfporter@esf.edu

STUDY AREA

The focus was the northern tier of states from Minnesota to Maine, and included Wisconsin, northern Illinois, northern Indiana, Michigan, Ohio, northern Pennsylvania, New York, Vermont, New Hampshire, Massachusetts, and southeastern Ontario, Canada. The region was noted for cold, snowy winters. Winter severity was highly variable across the region because of the influence of the Great Lakes. Coldest conditions (−35°C) occurred to the west of the Great Lakes in Minnesota and Wisconsin, with fewer days of <0°C south and east of the lakes. Accumulated snow could be ≥25 cm throughout the region with deep snow lasting 6 to 8 weeks in western portions of the region and much deeper (30 to 100 cm), but generally less persistent snow in the eastern states. Landform affects the impact of snow because ridge-and-valley topography presents south and west-facing slopes where snow depths are reduced by increased sun exposure. Thus, the rugged areas of southeastern Minnesota, southern Wisconsin, New York, Pennsylvania and New England contrast markedly with the flatlands of much of Michigan and northern Illinois, Indiana, and Ohio. The mountains of northern New York, Vermont and New Hampshire present the opposite effect on snow, capturing and holding snow depths >100 cm for 12 to 16 weeks each winter.

Land cover in the region was dominated by a mixture of agriculture and oak forest (*Quercus* spp.) to the south, and agriculture and beech-cherry-maple-hemlock forest (*Fagus grandifolia*, *Prunus* spp., *Acer* spp., *Tsuga canadensis*) to the north (Bailey 1978). As measured at the township scale (approximately 100 km²), forest cover varied from <5% where it was principally found along rivers and streams, to >95% where soil, growing season, and topographic relief preclude modern agriculture.

ASSESSING WEATHER

If winter severity affected the ability of wild turkeys to occupy northern latitudes, then we would predict reduced survival during periods of deep snow or cold temperatures. Studies conducted over the past 30 years show that turkeys are vulnerable to winter weather conditions, but not to the degree or in the manner expected.

Studies conducted during the 1970s showed turkeys could be affected by deep snow (≥25 cm). In New York, overwinter survival decreased from 75% to 50% for mild to severe winters (Austin and DeGraff 1975). In northern Pennsylvania, starvation losses were observed during periods of deep snow (Wunz and Hayden 1975). In Minnesota, winters with little snow were associated with >90% survival, while during winters of deep snow some over-wintering populations showed 90% survival and others experienced >60% mortality (Porter et al. 1980). However, studies conducted during the 1990s looked back over the previous 2 decades and found no consistent relationship between long-term population changes in wild turkeys and winter severity (Roberts et al. 1995). What explains this apparent contradiction?

The key may be found in studies of the ability of turkeys to cope with cold temperatures. Tests conducted during the 1990s showed that turkeys can survive to −40°C, and probably much lower temperatures, so long as they have food (Haroldson et al. 1998). Within the current distribution of turkeys in northern latitudes, −40°C is a rare event. Turkeys cope with cold temperatures by increasing food intake by approximately 20g/bird/day for each decrease in temperature of 10°F (Haroldson 1996, Haroldson et al. 1998).

Looking back at the field studies of the 1970s, it is clear that they were telling us more than we realized: snow and cold are not the issue, the key is food. Studies show that snow >25 cm limits mobility and that turkeys can be restricted to 25 ha, <10% of their normal home range (Porter 1977). Even with this restriction, survival can be high if there is abundant food such as provided by areas of standing corn (*Zea maize*), or if turkeys are wintering near dairy farms where manure is spread throughout the winter (Wunz and Hayden 1975, Porter et al. 1980, Vander Haegen et al. 1988). Haroldson (1996) estimated that foodplots of 1 ha of standing corn will maintain a flock of 335 turkeys for an entire winter in Minnesota (presuming they don't have to compete with white-tailed deer [*Odocoileus virginianus*]). In contrast, turkeys restricted by deep snow for more than 40 days and reliant on natural foods are likely to experience significant losses (Roberts et al. 1995).

While the primary concern about winter severity was its influence on survival, a secondary impact became evident. The effects of winter conditions extend into the nesting season. Studies in Minnesota showed that nesting success could be predicted from March weights. Females were less likely to survive to nest if they weighed <4.3 kg and those that did produced 2.6 females per nest as compared to 4.2 females per nest for females that weighed >4.3 kg (Porter et al. 1983). This finding took on added importance in the 1990s, when studies showed that annual fluctuation in turkey populations were more sensitive to nesting success than overwinter survival (Roberts and Porter 1996).

The weather factors most responsible for population dynamics of turkeys in northern latitudes proved not to be winter cold or snow, but spring temperatures and rainfall. Studies in Missouri suggested that cold spring weather delayed nesting and reduced renesting (Vangilder et al. 1987). Studies of long-term population changes in New York showed that fall population could be predicted from rainfall and heating degree days in May with 80 to 90% accuracy (Roberts and Porter 2001).

The hypothesized mechanisms by which spring weather affects turkey reproduction appear to be detectability of nests by predators and vulnerability of young to hypothermia. Moist conditions during May nesting are hypothesized to increase the efficiency with which mammalian predators can find turkey nests (Palmer et al. 1993, Roberts et al. 1995). Cold and wet conditions during May and June are thought to decrease survival of poults during the critical period after the yolk sac is expended and before poults are large enough to thermoregulate efficiently (Healy and Nenno 1985, Healy 1992).

Thus, we now have a clear picture about the weather factors important to the dynamics of wild turkeys. There seems little question that, historically, winter was a significant limitation in northern latitudes because much of the region is north of the oak, hickory and chestnut forest types (Porter and Hill 1999). Consequently, the region lacked the accessible food resources to support turkeys during winters of deep snow. However, the modifications to the regional landscape wrought by agriculture have more than offset that deficiency. The mix of forest and agriculture, especially dairy, provides a landscape that is much richer in food resources. Heavy winter losses due to winter are generally localized and thus there is no pronounced signal in the long-term, regional population trends.

The influence of spring weather, especially rainfall, appears to be more frequent and more regional in its impact. The concurrence of findings from studies from Pennsylvania, New York, Wisconsin, and Missouri on the influence of spring rain suggests that it may be fundamental to wild turkey population dynamics in northern latitudes (Wunz and Ross 1990, Porter and Gefell 1996, Rolley et al. 1998).

ASSESSING HABITAT

The implication from the test of the hypothesis that winter affects turkey populations is that it's not about snow or cold, but agriculture. In retrospect, it seems curious today that forest cover was given so much attention as a criterion in evaluating potential release sites. The origins of the perception that eastern turkeys needed extensive forest cover probably arose as biologists sought to extrapolate their experience with turkeys in the southeastern United States to the Midwest and Lake States where agriculture was so pervasive. Perhaps the most often quoted habitat characteristic was the need for 15,000 acres of forest (Mosby and Handley 1943, Kozicky and Metz 1948, Latham 1956). The interspersion of forest with open land was considered an unfavorable habitat quality (Bailey 1973) and preferred habitat was 60–80% oak forest, 10 to 15% conifer and scattered openings of <1 ha (Kozicky and Metz 1948). Bottomland hardwood areas required a ratio of 70:30 forest to open land (Holbrook and Lewis 1967, Lewis 1967).

Few areas within the ancestral range of the wild turkey in the Midwest or Lake States, as portrayed by Schorger (1966), had forest cover of this magnitude. Northern Pennsylvania, New York and New England were more likely candidates because forests had recovered from heavy clearing in the 18th and 19th centuries to reoccupy >60% of the land (Porter and Hill 1999). Other states had extensive areas of abandoned farmland on which forests were in early stages of regenerating. It was not until the 1960s that forests were

mature enough to provide for roosting habitat and mast crops important to turkeys. Still, there were some areas of forest cover in nearly every state within the region.

During the 1970s and early 1980s a series of large radiotelemetry studies demonstrated that turkeys could be successful in areas with <15% forest cover (Porter 1978, Hecklau et al. 1982, Kurzejeski and Lewis 1985, 1990). As a consequence, attempts were made to establish turkeys in areas throughout the Midwest where trees were limited to narrow river corridors and even ravines. Most of these releases met with success. By 1980 Iowa had successfully established turkeys in areas where forest woodlots were only 400 ha (1,000 acres) and Indiana, Ohio and Pennsylvania were experiencing success in areas considered non-traditional habitat (Little 1980, Clark 1985, Wunz 1985, Backs 1995). While these woodlots were sometimes surrounded by agriculture, they were still in close proximity to wooded corridors associated with drainage systems.

In the mid and late 1980s, wildlife biologists in Missouri and Indiana attempted to combine this research with recent experiences in trap and transfer in the form of habitat evaluation models. In Missouri, distinctions were made between turkey habitats of southern oak forests versus those of mixed agricultural-forest landscapes to the north (Kurzejeski and Lewis 1985). A Pattern Recognition (PATREC) model developed in Missouri introduced the idea of using empirical assessment of large geographic scale (landscape-level) land cover patterns to describe habitat in relation to wild turkey densities. The model showed highest densities of turkeys would be found in southern oak forests where the landscape was >60% oak and hickory (*Carya* spp.), or oak and pine (*Pinus* spp.) that was ≥50 years, and contained 25 to 40% semi-open or open lands. In agricultural-forest areas of northern Missouri, highest densities would be found in areas where semi-open and open land dominated 40 to 65% of the land. The model placed high value on interspersion of forest and open lands.

In Indiana, criteria for future release sites built upon the Missouri model and the Habitat Evaluation Procedures (HEP) developed by the U.S. Fish and Wildlife Service (Schroeder 1985). The Indiana model introduced the concept of habitat configuration in a landscape context, as well as amount of various covertypes (Backs and Eisfelder 1990). The criteria were qualitative descriptions of landscape patterns to be sought in potential release sites.

Studies in New York in the 1990s expanded understanding of the importance of interspersion by exploring it quantitatively. These studies employed tools in landscape analysis offered by geographic information systems. Satellite imagery was used to classify land cover for a 2,900-km² study area of southwestern New York to a resolution of 25 m². The area was a mixture of hardwood forest (44–83% coverage) and dairy-based agriculture (16–58% coverage), thus comparable to northern Missouri (Glennon and Porter 1999). Results showed that 24 to 51% of the variation in wild turkey abundance, as summarized at the township level, could be attributed to edge density, patch density, and contagion. All of these variables are measures of the amount of interspersion of forest and agriculture per unit area. The analyses suggested that higher interspersion of forest and agriculture increased habitat suitability for wild turkeys in northern latitudes. More specifically, the models pointed to the presence of dairy-based agriculture as the critical element.

Wild turkey populations fluctuate widely and are probably responding to a complex suite of factors, so the success of relatively simple models of habitat configuration suggested landscape-scale habitat evaluation was an important avenue for further exploration. In 2001, Fleming (2003) expanded the New York studies to include the entire state with the intent of better understanding the geographic scale at which wild turkeys were responding to habitat configuration. Most prior habitat assessment was done at the local level (e.g., forest stand, farm ownership, wildlife management area). Results of Glennon and Porter (1999) analyses suggested that the population response of turkeys to habitat might occur at a larger scale.

Building on the premise that long-term population dynamics were driven largely by nesting success, Fleming (2003) hypothesized that habitat played an important role in the risk of nest predation. A classic principle of wildlife biology teaches that good habitat reduces predation, but Fleming's results suggested a more complicated relationship. Geospatial statistical analysis showed that risk of nest predation was best explained by a multi-scale assessment that included information from the surrounding landscape. Variables of importance included traditional measures of cover at the nest site (10-m radius), distance to nearest edge and forest age at the patch level, and edge density at the landscape level (approximately 5-km radius). Surprisingly, >90% of variation in risk of nest predation was explained at the landscape scale and the strongest relationship was degree of fragmentation: increased risk to nest predation was related to increased edge density and decreased shape complexity. Agriculture tends to increase the fragmentation and simplify the shape of patches, suggesting that it is a detriment.

Is interspersion of forest and agriculture good for turkeys or bad? Reconciling the apparent contradiction that increased interspersion might reduce habitat suitability when earlier work suggested it improved suitability produced an interesting insight. The long-term dynamics of turkey populations in New York are characterized by densities that are generally below the long-term mean, punctuated by episodes of dramatic increase (Porter and Gefell 1996). These growth peaks are highly synchronized over large distances (>300 km; Fleming 2003), suggesting that weather is a primary influence. In years when spring weather conditions are good for nesting, the most dramatic increases occur in areas where habitat is most suitable. In New York, high suitability is associated with the ratio of forest, open and shrubland of about 1:1:1 (Fleming 2003, Porter and Gefell 1996). Roberts and Porter (2001) attributed the wide fluctuation in abundance to

variation in May rainfall and hypothesized that the mechanism was efficiency of mammalian nest predators. Avian ecologists suggest that the fragmentation of forests by agriculture may be promoting predator populations because of the associated increased breadth of buffer food species available (Donovan et al. 1997, Chalfoun et al. 2002).

We might hypothesize that while predator populations fluctuate, risk of nest predation is generally high. Good data on predator populations are rare, but there is reason to suspect that predators are abundant in most years. The abundance of individual species of nest predators may fluctuate due to changes in food supply or disease. However, in the agricultural environment, the wide array of food resources and the broad diet of most predators means they are well buffered from variations in food supplies. While disease periodically reduces the population of one species, the diversity of nest predators means that some species will always be present. Consequently, the risk of nest predation is high in most years.

The impact of these predators is not felt every year, but rather only during wet springs. Moist conditions appear to allow greater efficiency of locating nests and predation that overweighs the advantages of habitat conditions. In contrast, during dry years, the advantages of the habitat configuration so reduce the efficiency of predation that nesting success is high. Given their high reproductive potential, turkey populations explode and the largest increases occur in the most suitable habitat. Where habitat conditions are not as suitable, nesting success is not high, even in dry years. Populations in these habitats may experience increases in abundance in dry springs, but the growth is not as dramatic.

In sum, as with weather, we can reject the hypothesis that forest cover is insufficient in the upper Mississippi valley, Great Lake states, and New England. The issue is not the amount of forest, but the proportion and arrangement of that forest on agriculturally-dominated portions of the region. Similarly, it is the proportion and the arrangement of dairy-based agriculture that confers increased habitat suitability in the forest-dominated portions of the region.

Perhaps more important, the issue is not just about weather or habitat, but their complicated interaction. Weather plays a role inducing temporal change, but also has the ability to synchronize dynamics over broad regions. Habitat interacts with weather because it sets the limits on the magnitude of response by turkey populations to good weather. Landscape processes at multiple geographic scales dictate the regional patterning of habitat suitability and therefore determine the average response to good weather and the variability we see across regions. This interaction suggests that we must consider more complex models if we are to reach a deeper understanding of wild turkey ecology in northern latitudes.

LOOKING TO THE NEXT 30 YEARS

Do we finally know all we need to about the wild turkey to meet the challenges likely to face northern managers in the next 30 years? No, and for 2 reasons. First, we are just now beginning to recognize the complexity of the ecology of this species. Second, wild turkeys have benefited from a land-use trend and vegetation succession patterns that produced improving habitat conditions through the past 60 years. That trend is about to change.

Understanding the dynamics of wild turkey populations, and specifically the forces that drive change, has been a goal since biologists first began tagging birds in the 1940s. The similarity of findings pertaining to spring weather that is arising in places as distant and ecologically different as New York, Wisconsin and Mississippi suggests a common denominator in population dynamics over broad portions of the range of the eastern wild turkey. Solidifying this knowledge will be important because of its potential to allow biologists to forecast population changes. Accurate forecasts enable biologists to bring high credibility into discussions with those who question the impacts of hunting on wildlife populations, as well as those who advocate for changes in season length and bag limits.

Similarly, the relationship between wild turkeys and habitat seems to be coming into focus. Here, too, we appear tantalizingly close to some fundamental principles of wild turkey biology. In northern latitudes, and perhaps throughout the range of the eastern subspecies, the most important factor is not forest, but the interspersion of forest and agriculture. The ecology is more complex than was imagined 30 years ago because it appears to operate at multiple geographic scales.

Testing these ideas about habitat more rigorously is vital because one of the most serious threats to wild turkey abundance and hunting opportunities in the 21st century is changing land use. If we are to stem losses of habitat to industrial agriculture, transportation infrastructure, and suburban sprawl, then we need the information to effectively engage the public policy debates on land use. We need the tools to translate the impacts of local zoning, county housing-development codes, and state and federal tax-incentive programs, to specific changes in land-use and then to predicted changes in wild turkey habitat. Ultimately, we need to be able to demonstrate the consequences of these programs on wild turkey populations.

To conduct effective tests will take a coordinated effort and long-term commitment. There are 3 important challenges to overcome. First, the chief difficulty of drawing conclusive tests of hypotheses from a synthesis of published papers is the variation in methods of the studies. We need to capture a broad range of variation in the environment and the response of turkeys to it through a coordinated study of carefully orchestrated methods. Second, a primary limitation to most studies of the population dynamics of wild turkeys is the high degree of variability in the population dynamics, and the complexity of the factors affecting change (Vangilder 1992, Miller et al. 2001). Capturing the crucial information will require an efficient means of collecting data on abundance that can be sustained over decades. Finally, the challenge to understanding habitat is recognizing the geographic scale at which populations are responding. This requires close attention to collecting data at the higher spatial resolution than most states have done to date (Goetz 2002).

Henry Mosby's comments in 1973 about the surprising nature of this species were written near the end of his career and captured one of the principal messages passed on by the first generation of wild turkey biologists. Thirty years later, as we near the end of the second generation, we continue to be impressed with the adaptability of the species and how much we have learned about where its limits might be. As we look to the third generation, we wonder, will biologists in 2035 again reflect in amazement at the success of the wild turkey? Equally important, will they look back with pride at the scientific knowledge and management insight gained?

ACKNOWLEDGMENTS

Thanks to R. Kimmel who originally instigated this review paper as a summary presentation to the Northern Wild Turkey Workshop in 2003. Our ongoing dialog helped refine many of the ideas expressed in this paper. K. K. Fleming and S. D. Roberts provided the creative and analytical power to tease apart the key relationships about weather, landscape and population dynamics. C. Spilman and an anonymous reviewer helped clarify the writing.

LITERATURE CITED

Austin, D. E., and L. W. DeGraff. 1975. Winter survival of wild turkeys in the southern Adirondacks. Proceedings of the National Wild Turkey Symposium 3:55–60.

Backs, S. E. 1995. Twenty-five years of spring wild turkey hunting in Indiana, 1970–94. Proceedings of the National Wild Turkey Symposium 7:245–251.

———, and C. H. Eisfelder. 1990. Criteria and guidelines for wild turkey release priorities in Indiana. Proceedings of the National Wild Turkey Symposium 6:134–143.

Bailey, R. G. 1978. Descriptions of ecoregions of the United States. U.S. Forest Service, Ogden, Utah, USA.

Bailey, R. W. 1973. Restoring wild-trapped turkeys to nonprimary range in West Virginia. Proceedings of the National Wild Turkey Symposium 2:181–185.

Chalfoun, A. D., F. R. Thompson, and M. J. Ratnaswamy. 2002. Nest predators and fragmentation: a review and meta-analysis. Conservation Biology 16:306–318.

Clark, L. G. 1985. Adjustment by transplanted wild turkeys in an Ohio Farmland area. Proceedings of the National Wild Turkey Symposium 6:33–48.

Donovan, T. M., P. W. Jones, E. M. Annand, and F. R. Thompson, III. 1997. Variation in local-scale edge effects: mechanism and landscape context. Ecology 78:2064–2075.

Dreis, R. E., C. F. Smith, and L. E. Myers. 1973. Wisconsin's wild turkey restoration experiment. Proceedings of the National Wild Turkey Symposium 2:45–48.

Fleming, K. K. 2003. Scale-explicit spatial determinants of population structure in wild turkeys (*Meleagris gallopavo silvestris*). Dissertation, State University of New York College of Environmental Science and Forestry, Syracuse, New York, USA.

Glennon, M. J., and W. F. Porter. 1999. Using satellite imagery to assess landscape-scale habitat for wild turkeys. Wildlife Society Bulletin 27:646–653.

Goetz, S. L. 2002. Statewide habitat assessment for wild turkey in Arkansas. Thesis, State University of New York College of Environmental Science and Forestry, Syracuse, New York, USA.

Haroldson, K. J. 1996. Energy requirements for winter survival of wild turkeys. Proceedings of the National Wild Turkey Symposium 7:9–14.

———, M. L. Svihel, R. O. Kimmel, and M. R. Riggs. 1998. Effects of winter temperature on wild turkey metabolism. Journal of Wildlife Management 62:299–305.

Healy, W. M. 1992. Population influences: environment. Pages 129–143 in J. G. Dickson, editor. The wild turkey: biology and management. Stackpole Books, Harrisburg, Pennsylvania, USA.

———, and E. S. Nenno. 1985. Effect of weather on wild turkey poult survival. Proceedings of the National Wild Turkey Symposium 5:91–101.

Hecklau, J., W. F. Porter, and W. M. Shields. 1982. Feasibility of transplanting wild turkeys into areas of restricted forest cover and high human density. Transactions of the Northeast Fish and Wildlife Conference 39:96–104.

Holbrook, H. L., and J. B. Lewis. 1967. Management of the eastern turkey in the southern Appalachian and Cumberland Plateau Region. Pages 343–370 in O. H. Hewitt, editor. The wild turkey and its management. The Wildlife Society, Washington, D.C., USA.

Kozicky, E. L., and R. Metz. 1948. The management of the wild turkey in Pennsylvania. Pennsylvania Game News 19(4):3, 20–21, 26–27, 30–31.

Kurzejeski, E. W., and J. B. Lewis. 1985. Application of PA-TREC modeling to wild turkey management in Missouri. Proceedings of the National Wild Turkey Symposium 5:269–284.

———, and ———. 1990. Home ranges, movements and habitat use of wild turkey hens in northern Missouri. Proceedings of the National Wild Turkey Symposium 6:7–71.

Latham, R. M. 1956. The complete book of the wild turkey. The Stackpole Company, Harrisburg, Pennsylvania, USA.

Lewis, J. B. 1967. Management of the eastern turkey in the Ozarks and bottomland hardwoods. Pages 371–408 in O. H. Hewitt, editor. The wild turkey and its management. The Wildlife Society, Washington, D.C., USA.

Little, T. W. 1980. Wild turkey restoration in "marginal" Iowa habitats. Proceedings of the National Wild Turkey Symposium 4:45–60.

Miller, D. A., M. J. Chamberlain, B. D. Leopold, and G. A. Hurst. 2001. Lessons from Tallahalla: What have we learned for turkey management into the 21st century? Proceedings of the National Wild Turkey Symposium 8:23–34.

Mosby, H. S. 1973. The changed status of the wild turkey over the past three decades. Proceedings of the National Wild Turkey Symposium 2:71–76.

———, and C. O. Handley. 1943. The wild turkey in Virginia: its status, life history and management. Virginia Commission of Game and Inland Fisheries, Richmond, Virginia, USA.

Palmer, W. E., S. R. Priest, R. S. Seiss, P. S. Phaelen, and G. A. Hurst. 1993. Reproductive effort and success in a declining wild turkey population. Proceedings of the Annual Conference of Southeastern Association of Fish and Wildlife Agencies 47:138–147.

Porter, W. F. 1977. Home range dynamics of wild turkeys in southeastern Minnesota. Journal of Wildlife Management 41:434–437.

———. 1978. The ecology and behavior of the wild turkey (*Meleagris gallopavo*) in Southeastern Minnesota. Dissertation, University of Minnesota, Minneapolis, Minnesota, USA.

———, and D. J. Gefell. 1996. Influences of weather and land use on wild turkey populations in New York. Proceedings of the National Wild Turkey Symposium 7:75–80.

———, and J. A. Hill. 1999. Biotic resources of the northeastern United States. Pages 181–218 in M. J. Mac, P. A. Opler, C. E. Pucket Haeker and P. D. Doran, editors. Status and trends of the nation's biological resources. U. S. Department of the Interior, U. S. Geological Survey, Reston, Virginia, USA.

———, G. C. Nelson, and K. Mattson. 1983. Effects of winter conditions on reproduction in a northern wild turkey population. Journal of Wildlife Management 47:281–290.

———, R. D. Tangen, G. C. Nelson, and D. A. Hamilton. 1980. Effects of corn food plots on wild turkeys in the upper Mississippi Valley. Journal of Wildlife Management 44:456–462.

Roberts, S. D., J. M Coffey, and W. F. Porter. 1995. Survival and reproduction of female wild turkeys in New York. Journal of Wildlife Management 59:437–447.

———, and W. F. Porter. 1996. Importance of demographic parameters to annual changes in wild turkey abundance. Proceedings of the National Wild Turkey Symposium 7:15–20.

———, and ———. 2001. Annual changes in May rainfall as an index to fall turkey harvest. Proceedings of the National Wild Turkey Symposium 8:43–51.

Rolley, R. E., J. F. Kubisiak, R. N. Paisley, and R. G. Wright. 1998. Wild turkey population dynamics in Wisconsin. Journal of Wildlife Management 62:917–924.

Schorger, A. W. 1966. The wild turkey: Its history and domestication. University of Oklahoma Press, Norman, Oklahoma, USA.

Schroeder, R. L. 1985. Habitat suitability index models: eastern wild turkey. U. S. Department of Interior Fish and Wildlife Service, Biological Report 82(10.106).

Tapley, J. L., R. K. Abernathy, and J. E. Kennamer. 2001. Status and distribution of the wild turkey in 1999. Proceedings of the National Wild Turkey Symposium 8:15–22.

Vander Haegen, W. M., W. E. Dodge, and M. W. Sayre. 1988. Factors affecting productivity in a northern wild turkey population. Journal of Wildlife Management 52:127–133.

Vangilder, L. D. 1992. Population dynamics. Pages 144–164 in J. G. Dickson, editor. The wild turkey: biology and management. Stackpole Books, Harrisburg, Pennsylvania, USA.

———, E. W. Kurzejeski, V. L. Kimmel, and J. B. Lewis 1987. Reproductive parameters of wild turkey hens in north Missouri. Journal of Wildlife Management 51:535–540.

Wigal, D. D. 1973. Status of the introduced Rio Grande turkey in northeastern Iowa. Proceedings of the National Wild Turkey Symposium 2:35–44.

Wunz, G. A. 1985. Wild turkey establishment and survival in small range units in farmland and suburban environments. Proceedings of the National Wild Turkey Symposium 6:49–54.

———, and A. H. Hayden. 1975. Winter mortality and supplemental feeding of turkeys in Pennsylvania. Proceedings of the National Wild Turkey Symposium 3:61–69.

———, and A. S. Ross. 1990. Wild turkey production, fall and spring harvest interactions and responses to harvest management. Proceedings of the National Wild Turkey Symposium 6:205–207.

Bill Porter began his studies of the wild turkey in southeastern Minnesota in the 1970s and in collaboration with his graduate students has been exploring questions about populations dynamics and habitat ever since. As a faculty member in Syracuse, he teaches wildlife management, winter ecology and forest ecology. He also directs research and education programs for the university's field station in the Adirondack Mountains of northern New York. He has never been allowed to forget that he once predicted that wild turkeys would not inhabit the Adirondacks.

Wild Turkey Management:
Accomplishments, Strategies, and Opportunities
———— Grand Rapids, Michigan ————

POPULATION DYNAMICS OF TRANSLOCATED MERRIAM'S TURKEYS IN NORTH-CENTRAL WASHINGTON

Thomas C. McCall
Washington Department of Fish and Wildlife,
3860 Chelan Highway,
Wenatchee, WA 98801-1607, USA

Abstract: From the mid-1960s to the early-1990s 116 turkeys were released in Chelan and Kittitas counties in north-central Washington but these translocations were unsuccessful in establishing a population. During 2000–2002, 458 Merriam's turkeys (*Meleagris gallopavo merriami*) were again translocated to this area to determine if a successful population would establish if more birds were released, if birds were released at multiple locations and over successive years, and if birds were fed during winter. Forty females were fitted with radio-transmitters and survival, production, and movements were determined. The average annual survival of radioed females during 2000–2002 was 0.59, and 2 of 13 females were harvested illegally. The average annual production was 2.2 poults per female. The average distance moved from release sites was 5.9 km, and by 2003 radioed turkeys were using an area of 1,450 km². From 2001 to 2004, spring harvest of bearded turkeys increased 411% (28–143) and number of hunters increased 371% (161–759). The number of turkeys on winter concentration areas increased more than 10-fold (84–876). During winter most birds concentrated on feeding sites, and only 4 complaints of conflicts with turkeys were reported. Supplemental feeding was likely a significant factor for the winter survival of these turkeys. If managers want to establish turkey populations and increase hunting opportunity in northern environments with limited winter food, supplemental feeding may be a valuable management tool.

Proceedings of the National Wild Turkey Symposium 9:315
Key words: *Meleagris gallopavo merriami,* Merriam's turkey, supplemental feed, translocation, Washington.

Editor's note: This abstract was presented as a poster presentation.

Tom McCall is an assistant district biologist with the Washington Department of Fish and Wildlife. He received a B.S. degree in wildlife management from the University of Alaska and an M.S. degree in wildlife management from the University of Maine. Tom's interests include game and nongame management and research.

Chapter V

Harvest Management

Wild Turkey Management:
Accomplishments, Strategies, and Opportunities
——— Grand Rapids, Michigan ———

FACTORS AFFECTING WILD TURKEY SPRING HUNT QUALITY IN MINNESOTA

Kari L. Dingman[1,2]
Department of Biological Sciences,
Minnesota State University,
Mankato, MN 56001, USA

Richard O. Kimmel[3]
Minnesota Department of Natural Resources,
35365 800th Avenue,
Madelia, MN 56062, USA

John D. Krenz
Department of Biological Sciences,
Minnesota State University,
Mankato, MN 56001, USA

Brock R. McMillan
Department of Biological Sciences,
Minnesota State University,
Mankato, MN 56001, USA

Abstract: Increased hunting of wild turkeys (*Meleagris gallopavo*) has resulted in concerns regarding hunt quality, especially on public lands. The purpose of this study was to identify variables that influence wild turkey hunt quality in Minnesota. Spring turkey hunters from 8 permit areas in Minnesota were surveyed by mail during 2002 and 2003. The most significant factors that defined a quality spring turkey hunt in Minnesota were number of turkeys shot at, number of turkeys seen in the field, and ease of access to land for hunting. To improve and maintain the quality of spring turkey hunting, we suggest that wildlife managers strive to increase turkey numbers in order to increase the potential for hunters to see/shoot at birds, and improve access to private land.

Proceedings of the National Wild Turkey Symposium 9:319–324

Key words: hunt quality, hunter satisfaction, *Meleagris gallopavo*, Minnesota, wild turkey hunting, wild turkey.

Interest in hunting wild turkeys has grown rapidly in the past 20 years. Tapley et al. (2001) reported a 57% increase in turkey hunter numbers in North America from 1984 to 1998. Wildlife managers have responded to growing hunter interest by modifying hunting season frameworks to achieve maximum sustainable harvest (Healy and Powell 1999). However, expanding hunter densities has led to concerns about hunter interference, hunter safety, and overall hunt quality (Hawn et al. 1987, Taylor et al. 1995) leading wildlife agencies to attempt to balance hunting opportunity with hunt quality (Healy 1990, Taylor et al. 1995, Nicholson et al. 2001). Competition between hunters for turkeys and increased hunter interference could reduce hunt quality and hunter success while increasing accident rates (Kimmel 2001).

Wildlife managers seek hunting regulations that will maintain or increase hunt quality while optimizing harvest opportunities (Donohoe 1990, Nicholson et al. 2001). However, factors that influence hunt quality can differ among individuals. Thus, a range of hunter concerns needs to be identified and incorporated into management decisions that affect rules and regulations (Hendee and Potter 1971).

Minnesota has a highly structured spring wild turkey hunt where hunters apply for a limited number of permits by permit area and time period. Permit allocations are determined using a model that incorporates hunt quality factors, such as rates of hunter interference, into the permit allocation decision-making process (Kimmel 2001). However, the relationship between hunter interference rate and overall quality is poorly understood. Furthermore, alternative measures of hunt quality have not been assessed.

The purpose of this study was to identify variables that influence wild turkey hunt quality in Minnesota. An assessment of the importance of hunter interference and other hunt quality factors is essential for setting quality factors in the Minnesota model, as well as being of value to wild turkey managers from other agencies for evaluating hunting season logistics.

[1] Present address: Idaho Department of Fish and Game, 2885 North River Road, St. Anthony, ID 83445, USA.
[2] E-mail: kdingman@idfg.idaho.gov
[3] E-mail: richard.kimmel@dnr.state.mn.us

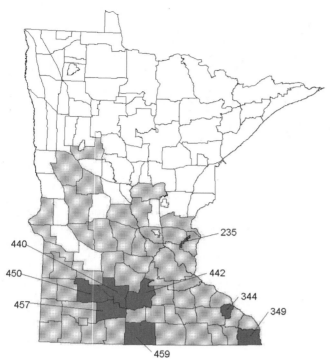

Fig. 1. Permit areas open to spring wild turkey hunting (light gray) and permit areas selected for 2002 and 2003 spring wild turkey hunter survey (dark gray), Minnesota.

METHODS

Spring turkey hunters from 8 permit areas in Minnesota (Figure 1) were surveyed by mail during 2002 and 2003. The sample of permit areas was non-randomly selected to represent a range of values within Minnesota for 3 criteria: landownership (amount of public versus private land), ease of access for hunting, and rate of hunter interference (the number of times a person is interfered with while turkey hunting). A priori estimates of hunting access and hunter interference were obtained from a statewide survey of turkey hunters in 1999 (Kimmel et al. 2000).

A random sample of wild turkey permit recipients was selected from each permit area. Samples were not equal among all permit areas based on different numbers of permits being offered for each permit area. Surveys were mailed in late May, immediately following the spring turkey hunting seasons in 2002 and 2003. Second and third mailings were sent to non-respondents in 1-month intervals. Respondents who did not hunt were excluded from analyses.

Survey questions concentrated on 4 variables that managers can attempt to manipulate. Hunters were asked to report number of days hunted, number of turkeys seen and shot at, and if they harvested a turkey. Hunters were asked to rate access to land for hunting on a 4-point scale: very easy, somewhat easy, somewhat difficult, or very difficult. We also asked if they hunted on public land and/or private land, and whether they had been denied access to private land.

Hunters were asked to report the number of times their hunt was interfered with by other hunters and by

Table 1. Percent of hunters denied access during the spring wild turkey hunting season in Minnesota, 1999, 2002–2003.

Permit area	% denied access		
	1999	2002	2003
235	3.0	0.0	0.0
344	13.3	5.7	5.2
349	38.5	28.4	23.6
440	32.5	18.7	22.0
442	31.2	24.2	21.1
450	30.0	18.8	42.1
457	83.3	67.0	17.4
459	43.8	20.8	19.1

non-hunters (hikers, mountain bikers, mushroom hunters, etc). Hunter interference was based on the respondent's perception of interference; we did not define interference for them. Lastly, hunters were asked to rate the quality of their hunt on a scale of 0 (poor) to 10 (excellent).

Statistical Analysis

For each permit area and year, we calculated the mean rates of harvest success, ease of access, and hunt quality, and proportion of hunters denied access to private land and reporting interference. Hunt quality was modeled based on various predictors using regression tree analysis (De'ath and Fabricius 2000). Regression tree analysis splits data into homogeneous groups that reduces the overall sum of squares between variables (De'ath and Fabricius 2000). Cross-validation was used to determine the appropriate size of the tree by randomly excluding a sample, developing a model, and testing the model with the excluded sample. Regression tree analysis was conducted using R 1.7.1 statistical package (Ihaka and Gentleman 1996) and the RPART library (Therneau and Atkinson 1997). Data were pooled among permit areas for regression tree analysis. Survey data from this investigation were compared to a similar survey conducted by Minnesota Department of Natural Resources (MDNR) in 1999 (Kimmel et al. 2000).

RESULTS

In 2002, there were 0 undeliverable and 1,629 usable surveys for an 88.6% response rate. In 2003, there were 15 undeliverable and 1,667 usable surveys for a 90.0% response rate. In 2002, 3% of hunters bought a license but did not hunt, compared to 2% in 2003.

Mean hunt quality ratings by permit area ranged from 6.00–7.24 in 2002 and 6.96–7.94 in 2003. Successful hunters rated hunt quality significantly higher in 2002 (successful: 8.4 ± 1.7 [mean ± SD]; unsuccessful: 6.1 ± 2.5; $P < 0.001$) and 2003 (successful: 8.7 ± 1.5; unsuccessful: 6.4 ± 2.5; $P < 0.001$). Percent of hunters denied access to private lands decreased in all 8 permit areas between 1999 and 2002 and in 6 of 8 permit areas between 2002 and 2003 (Table 1). Ease of access and hunt quality were positively correlated in both 2002 ($r_s = 0.274$, $P < 0.001$) and 2003 ($r_s = 0.283$, $P < 0.001$) (Figures 2 and 3).

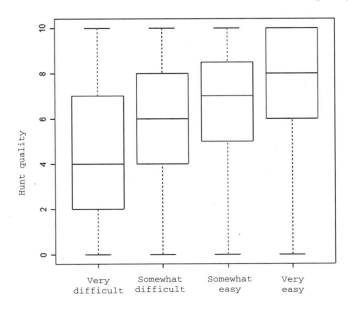

Fig. 2. Distribution of hunt quality ratings for reported ease of access to huntable land for the spring wild turkey season, Minnesota, 2002.

Hunter interference decreased between 1999 and 2002 ($P < 0.001$) and between 1999 and 2003 ($P < 0.001$) (Figure 4). Hunter interference rates also differed between 2002 and 2003 ($Q_{MH} = 7.32$, $P = 0.0068$), but the direction of change was not consistent among permit areas (Figure 4). Hunter interference was lower on private land than on public land in 2002 ($Q_{MH} = 20.22$, df = 2, $P < 0.001$) and in 2003 ($Q_{MH} = 27.52$, df = 2, $P < 0.001$).

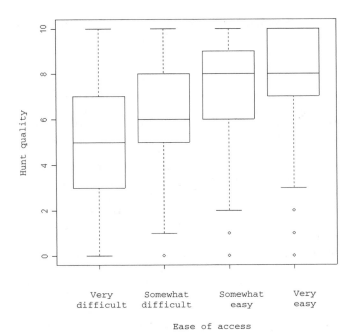

Fig. 3. Distribution of hunt quality ratings for reported ease of access to huntable land for the spring wild turkey season, Minnesota, 2003.

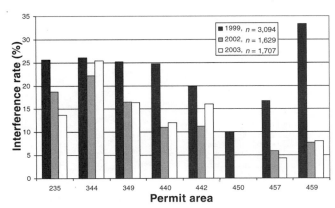

Fig. 4. Percent of hunters by permit area interfered with by other hunters during the spring wild turkey seasons, Minnesota, 1999, 2002–2003.

Hunt quality differed between hunters using public versus private land in 2002 ($Q_{MH} = 5.33$, df = 1, $P = 0.021$) and 2003 ($Q_{MH} = 7.78$, df = 1, $P = 0.005$). Hunt quality ratings were higher for hunters using private land in both years.

Factors best defining hunt quality in 2002 were number of birds shot at, number of birds seen, and ease of access (Figure 5). For individuals who did not shoot at any birds during the spring 2002 season, number of birds seen in the field was the best correlate of hunt quality. Individuals who saw fewer than 4 birds (as determined by the regression tree analysis) had a mean hunt quality rating of 4.7 while those who saw 4 or more birds had a mean hunt quality rating of 6.5. For hunters who shot at one or more birds, ease of access to huntable land was the best correlate of hunt quality. Individuals who had a difficult time finding a place to hunt had a mean hunt quality rating of 7.7 while those who had an easy time finding a place to hunt had a mean hunt quality rating of 8.7.

Factors explaining the most variation in hunt quality in 2003 were number of birds shot at, number of birds seen, ease of access, and success (Figure 6). For

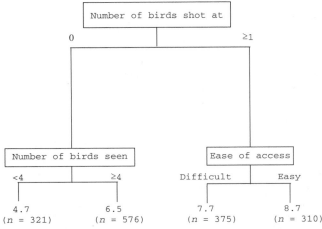

Fig. 5. Regression tree analysis of factors contributing to a quality spring turkey hunt, Minnesota, 2002. The estimates were the mean hunt quality rating of the group. Individual ratings ranged from 0 (poor) to 10 (excellent).

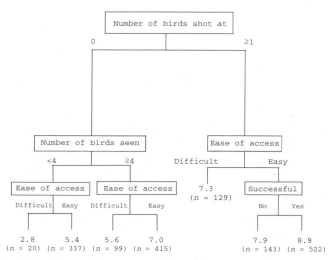

Fig. 6. Regression tree analysis of factors contributing to a quality spring turkey hunt, Minnesota, 2003. The estimates were the mean hunt quality rating of the group. Individual ratings ranged from 0 (poor) to 10 (excellent).

individuals who shot at no birds during the spring 2003 season, hunt quality was most influenced by number of birds seen while in the field and ease of access to huntable land. The mean hunt quality rating averaged 2.5 times greater for hunters who saw ≥4 birds and reported easy access to land than for hunters who saw <4 birds and reported difficult access. The mean hunt quality rating was similar for hunters who saw ≥4 birds but had difficult access and hunters who saw <4 birds but had easy access. For individuals that shot at one or more birds during the spring 2003 season, ease of access to huntable land was the best correlate of hunt quality. Hunt quality for individuals who had an easy time finding a place to hunt was further influenced by harvest success.

DISCUSSION

For this investigation, factors most closely associated with a quality spring turkey hunt in Minnesota were number of turkeys shot at, number of turkeys seen in the field, ease of access to land for hunting, and harvest success. However, when all hunt quality factors were considered simultaneously, number of birds shot at, number of birds seen, and ease of access were more strongly associated with hunt quality than harvest success.

Various authors found that success was not the only factor contributing to a quality hunt (Hawn et al. 1987, Hammitt et al. 1989, Gigliotti 2002). In our investigation, access to land and ease of obtaining a place to hunt were important criteria for establishing a quality hunt. Smith et al. (1992) observed ease of access to huntable land was a defining factor of a quality hunt. From 1999–2002, we found a decrease in the percent of hunters denied access to huntable land. Increased ease of access over time could be due to hunters developing a hunt tradition, establishing annual contacts with landowners over time, and returning to

these same areas to hunt. Also, we suspect that as years pass since turkey populations have become established, landowners may become less concerned with protecting the birds and are more likely to allow hunters on their land.

Because not all factors for wild turkey hunting can be managed, identifying the most important factors can focus management efforts to provide the best possible wild turkey hunting experience. From our research, it is assumed that hunt quality can best be maintained for Minnesota spring turkey hunting if wild turkey populations are maintained or increased and access to private land is available for hunting.

Number of turkeys seen and shot at is most likely related to turkey abundance. We did not differentiate between seeing male and female turkeys, however, and that could potentially affect the level of hunt quality, especially in a "males only" hunt. A recommendation for future surveys would be to look at the difference in hunt quality between seeing males as opposed to seeing any bird.

Managers can work to maintain or increase turkey populations by habitat maintenance and development. Habitat can be increased through land acquisition or private land programs. Minnesota has an extensive program creating Wildlife Management Areas that are open to public hunting. Management on these areas increases available habitat for wildlife, including turkeys. Habitat can be increased on private lands through various private land habitat enhancement projects and encouraging landowners to enroll land in existing land retirement programs (e.g., Conservation Reserve Program).

Number of turkeys seen and shot at is likely also related to amount of land available per hunter. Managers can influence available land per hunter via permit allocation and land access programs. Access can be improved through land acquisition and programs designed to increase access to private lands. Seventy-five percent of land in Minnesota is privately owned (Minnesota Department of Natural Resources 2000) so programs aimed at private landowners may be most effective. Examples of private land access programs are South Dakota's Walk-In Areas (Gigliotti 1999) and North Dakota's Private Land Initiative (Anonymous 2000), which work to provide access to fish and wildlife on private land. Programs that improve relationships between hunters and landowners (e.g., landowner appreciation events sponsored by a hunting organization) may foster future hunting opportunities.

In this study, rates of hunter interference were not shown to influence hunt quality for Minnesota spring turkey hunting. However, Smith et al. (1992) found hunter interference to be significant. Hunter interference is a product of hunter density, but closely related to land access. Little (1978) noted that higher hunter densities, which usually occur on public lands, result in higher interference rates that could lead to lower hunt quality ratings. Our highest hunter interference rate (26%) did occur on a permit area that was primarily public land. However, the hunt quality on that area did not differ from permit areas with little to no public land. In Wisconsin, Kubisiak et al. (1995) manipulated hunter densities to examine impacts on hunter interference and concluded that rates of hunter interference did not differ between areas with 1.5 hunters/km^2 and 0.8 hunters/km^2.

MDNR uses hunter interference as a factor to regulate the number of wild turkey permits, which could explain why hunter interference did not greatly influence hunt quality ratings. Permit numbers are regulated, but interference rates vary with little or no effect on hunt quality. Many Wisconsin Turkey Management Zones have much higher densities and higher interference rates than Minnesota but hunt quality remains high (Kubisiak et al. 1995). Hunter interference did not appear to influence hunt quality in this study with 8 permits areas ranging from 4–26% interference. However, hunter interference may affect hunt quality at interference rates >26%. Additional research is needed to quantify the relationship between interference and hunt quality over a broader range of hunter interference rates.

MANAGEMENT IMPLICATIONS

The 3 main variables determining quality spring turkey hunting in this study were number of turkeys shot at, number of turkeys seen in the field, and ease of access to huntable land. Managers should consider using these variables to assess hunt quality. In addition, managers should strive to increase turkey numbers when habitat abundance and conditions allow. Increasing turkey populations will increase the chance of hunters seeing birds and shooting potential, both of which increase the quality of the hunting experience.

Access to private land is important for hunt quality and reducing hunter interference. Since private landowners ultimately control access to most huntable land, positive relationships between hunters and landowners should be encouraged. Hunter education classes should address the importance of respecting landowners and establishing positive relationships. Also, programs aimed at increasing access to private lands should be encouraged to reduce the number of hunters denied access and maintain hunt quality.

ACKNOWLEDGMENTS

We thank J. Fieberg, MDNR Biometrician, for data analysis. D. Fulton, University of Minnesota, provided helpful advice on study design and reviewed the survey instrument. W. Krueger and T. Klinkner provided assistance with the surveys and mailings. K. Haroldson and S. Goetz reviewed manuscript drafts. Three anonymous reviewers provided useful comments and suggestions.

LITERATURE CITED

Anonymous. 2000. North Dakota Game and Fish Department private land initiative. Midwest Private Lands Working Group of the International Association of Fish and Wildlife Agencies, 14–17 May 2000, Salina, Kansas, USA.

De'ath, G., and K. E. Fabricius. 2000. Classification and regression trees: a powerful yet simple technique for ecological data analysis. Ecology 81:3178–3192.

Donohoe, R. W. 1990. The wild turkey: past, present, and future in Ohio. Ohio Department of Natural Resources, Ohio Fish and Wildlife Report 11.

Gigliotti, L. M. 1999. Hunter evaluation of the 1999 walk-in areas report, HD-5-00.SAM. South Dakota Game, Fish and Parks, Pierre, South Dakota, USA.

———. 2002. Harvest and crowding attitudes of Black Hills deer hunters. South Dakota Conservation Digest, January–February:16–19.

Hammitt, W. E., C. D. McDonald, and F. P. Noe. 1989. Wildlife management: managing the hunt versus the hunting experience. Environmental Management 13:503–507.

Hawn, L. J., E. E. Langenau, Jr., and T. F. Reis. 1987. Optimization of quantity and quality of turkey hunting in Michigan. Wildlife Society Bulletin 15:233–238.

Healy, W. M. 1990. Symposium summary: looking toward 2000. Proceedings of the National Wild Turkey Symposium 6:224–228.

———, and S. M. Powell. 1999. Wild turkey harvest management: biology, strategies, and techniques. U.S. Fish and Wildlife Service Biological Technical Publication BTP-R5001–1999.

Hendee, J. C., and D. R. Potter. 1971. Human behavior and wildlife management: needed research. Transactions of the North American Wildlife Natural Resource Conference 36:383–396.

Ihaka, R., and R. Gentleman. 1996. R: a language for data analysis and graphics. Journal of Computational and Graphical Statistics 5:299–314.

Kimmel, R. O. 2001. Regulating spring wild turkey hunting based on population and hunting quality. Proceedings of the National Wild Turkey Symposium 8:243–250.

———, A. Esala, and T. Brinkman. 2000. 1999 spring wild turkey hunter survey results. Minnesota Department of Natural Resources, Madelia, Minnesota, USA.

Kubisiak, J. F., R. N. Paisley, R. G. Wright, and P. J. Conrad. 1995. Hunter and landowner perceptions of turkey hunting in southwestern Wisconsin. Proceedings of the National Wild Turkey Symposium 7:239–244.

Little, T. W. 1978. Harvest Statistics from Iowa's five modern wild turkey hunting seasons. Iowa Wildlife Research Bulletin Number 26.

Minnesota Department of Natural Resources. 2000. Public land and mineral ownership in Minnesota. Minnesota Department of Natural Resources, Division of Lands and Minerals, St. Paul, Minnesota, USA.

Nicholson, D. S., L. S. Perrin, and E. R. Welch, Jr. 2001. Florida's special-opportunity turkey hunts: providing a unique hunting opportunity in the new millennium. Proceedings of the National Wild Turkey Symposium 8:75–81.

Smith, J. L. D., A. H. Berner, F. J. Cuthbert, and J. A. Kitts. 1992. Interest in fee hunting by Minnesota small-game hunters. Wildlife Society Bulletin 20:20–26.

Tapley, J. L., W. M. Healy, R. K. Abernethy, and J. E. Kennamer. 2001. Status of wild turkey hunting in North America. Proceedings of the National Wild Turkey Symposium 8:257–268.

Taylor, C. I., J. C. Pack, W. K. Igo, J. E. Evans, P. R. Johansen, and G. H. Sharp. 1995. West Virginia spring turkey hunters and hunting, 1983–93. Proceedings of the National Wild Turkey Symposium 7:259–268.

Therneau, T. M., and E. J. Atkinson. 1997. Technical Report Series No. 61: An introduction to recursive partitioning using the RPART routines. Department of Health Science Research, Mayo Clinic, Rochester, Minnesota, USA.

Kari L. Dingman (pictured) is a senior wildlife technician with the Idaho Department of Fish and Game. She received her B.S. in wildlife resources from University of Idaho, and her M.S. in biology from Minnesota State University, Mankato. ***Dick Kimmel*** is the Wildlife Research Group Leader for Minnesota DNR. He has worked with the wild turkey program in Minnesota since 1981. ***John D. Krenz*** studied the behavior and bioenergetics of salamanders at the University of Georgia (Ph.D. in Ecology, 1995) and now works on the ecology and evolution of vertebrates at Minnesota State University, Mankato. ***Brock R. Mc-Millan*** is an associate professor in the Department of Biological Sciences at Minnesota State University. He received in B.S. in Biology from Utah State University in 1990 and his M.S. and Ph.D. from Kansas State University in 1994 and 1999, respectively. His research interests are focused on the population ecology and behavior of mammals and birds.

Wild Turkey Management:
Accomplishments, Strategies, and Opportunities
———— Grand Rapids, Michigan ————

ATTITUDES, PREFERENCES, AND CHARACTERISTICS OF OHIO'S SPRING TURKEY HUNTERS, 1985–2001

David A. Swanson[1]
Ohio Department of Natural Resources,
Division of Wildlife, 360 East State Street,
Athens, OH 45701, USA

Robert J. Stoll, Jr.
Ohio Department of Natural Resources,
Division of Wildlife, 360 East State Street,
Athens, OH 45701, USA

W. Lloyd Culbertson
Ohio Department of Natural Resources, Division of Wildlife,
360 East State Street, Athens, OH 45701, USA

Abstract: The popularity of spring wild turkey (*Meleagris gallopavo*) hunting in Ohio increased since the first modern season in 1966. As hunter numbers increased, so have problems and issues with managing the spring hunt. Random samples of Ohio spring turkey hunters were mailed a questionnaire immediately following the 1985, 1989, 1996, and 2001 spring turkey seasons. The questionnaire responses were used to determine the attitudes, preferences, and concerns of Ohio spring turkey hunters regarding wild turkey management and turkey hunting. Over 66% (±3%) of 1985, 70% (±3%) of 1989, 80% (±3%) of 1996, and 85% (±2%) of 2001 turkey hunters reported they had spring turkey hunted in Ohio ≥2 years. As in 1989 and 1996, >95% (±2%) of turkey hunters reported using a shotgun during the 2001 Ohio spring turkey season. Use of decoys by spring turkey hunters increased from 14% (±2%) in 1989 to 67% (±3%) in 2001. The percentage of hunters hunting mostly on public land decreased from 32% (±3%) in 1989 to 19% (±3%) in 2001. The total estimated expenditures by spring turkey hunters during the 2001 season was $14.9 million compared to $5.8 million in 1996 and $2.1 million in 1989. Hunters consistently ranked uninformed hunters and overcrowded hunting conditions as the most serious problems affecting turkey hunting safety. The percentage of turkey hunters who considered disturbance by other hunters a "big" problem decreased from 26 (±3%) to 14% (±2%) between 1985 and 2001. However, almost 60% (±3%) of the 2001 turkey hunters reported they were concerned about being shot by another hunter and 38% (±3%) indicated they had another hunter sneak up on them while turkey hunting. Although most (72 ± 3%) hunters indicated they never wore hunter orange at all times, 26% (±3%) reported they always wore hunter orange when moving and 42% (±3%) always carried their harvested bird in orange covering when walking out of the woods. Public education on hunting safety was ranked the most important turkey management activity by 1996 and 2001 turkey hunters. Over 85% (±2%) of hunters ranked high gobbling activity as the primary factor contributing greatly to enjoyment of the spring turkey hunting experience, followed by killing an adult turkey (71 ± 3%) and calling turkeys (69 ± 3%). The composite Ohio spring turkey hunter was male, 49 years old, had a rural background, and a total household income >$50,000. Ohio spring turkey hunters had hunted for an average of 28 years, but had spring turkey hunted for <10 years.

Proceedings of the National Wild Turkey Symposium 9:325–330
Key words: attitudes, eastern wild turkey, hunter, *Meleagris gallopavo*, Ohio, survey.

The popularity of spring turkey hunting in Ohio increased since the first modern season in 1966. Between 1985 and 2001, the number of spring turkey hunters in Ohio increased 243% from 26,739 to 91,811 while the spring turkey harvest increased over 6-fold from 4,096 to 26,156 birds (Ohio Department of Nat-

[1] E-mail: dave.swanson@dnr.state.oh.us

Table 1. Number of licensees, hunters, success, and hunting effort (days) during the 2001 spring turkey hunting season in Ohio.

License type	No. licensees	Licensees that hunted %	Licensees that hunted 95% CL	Hunters who harvested ≥1 turkey %	Hunters who harvested ≥1 turkey 95% CL	Hunting effort (days) Total	Hunting effort (days) 95% CL	Hunting effort per hunter (days) $\bar{x}$	Hunting effort per hunter (days) 95% CL
Paid 1-bird	54,841	98	1	45	3	319,335	9,580	6	1
Paid 2-bird	11,092	99	1	62	3	88,472	2,654	8	2
Free[a]	35,311	75	3	31	3	141,192	4,236	5	2
Total	101,264	91	3	35	3	549,019	16,471	7	1

[a] Free permits were issued to hunters who were ≥66 years old.

ural Resources, unpublished data). Reasons for these tremendous increases included increased hunting opportunities resulting from expanding turkey populations and more liberal harvest regulations. Since 1993, the bag limit was increased from 1 to 2 birds, the 2-bird bag was expanded to the entire season, and all 88 counties opened to turkey hunting. As spring turkey hunter numbers increased, so have issues and problems with managing the spring hunting season.

Maintenance of wild turkey population levels has been the primary factor in formulating Ohio's spring turkey harvest recommendations (Donohoe 1990). The demands of wild turkey hunters are also important and should be incorporated into turkey management decisions (Hendee and Potter 1971). The purpose of this study was to determine the attitudes, preferences, and concerns of Ohio spring turkey hunters regarding wild turkey management and turkey hunting. Specific objectives were to determine (1) spring turkey hunter experience, pressure, and success rates, (2) expenditures for wild turkey hunting, (3) spring turkey hunter concerns regarding disturbance, overcrowding, and safety, (4) hunter opinion regarding changes in spring turkey hunting regulations and the importance of turkey management activities, (5) factors that contribute to a quality turkey hunting experience, and (6) socio-economic characteristics of Ohio spring turkey hunters.

METHODS

We mailed hunter questionnaires immediately after the 2001 spring turkey season to a random sample of paid 1-bird, paid 2-bird, and free-permit recipients. Free permits were issued to hunters who were ≥66 years old. We mailed a second questionnaire to turkey hunters who did not return their questionnaire within 2 weeks. We did not measure the nonresponse bias.

Table 2. Proportion of spring turkey hunters that hunted during one or more years in Ohio during 1985, 1989, 1996, and 2001.

Years hunted	Hunters[a] 1985 %	1985 95% CL	1989 %	1989 95% CL	1996 %	1996 95% CL	2001 %	2001 95% CL
1	37	2	30	3	20	2	14	2
2–5	51	3	53	3	52	3	42	2
6–10	9	2	11	1	18	2	24	3
≥11	3	1	6	2	9	2	20	2

[a] Percentages may not add up to 100% due to rounding errors.

Landowners, tenants, and their immediate families were not required to obtain a spring turkey hunting permit and could not be included in this survey. Thus, our estimates apply only to license buyers and hunters eligible for a free permit. In 2001, 20.6% of the total spring gobbler harvest was by license/permit exempt landowners (Ohio Department of Natural Resources, unpublished data). When possible, we compared results from the 2001 survey to those obtained from 1985 (R. Donohoe and G. Mountz, Ohio Division of Wildlife, unpublished report), 1989 (R. Stoll et al., Ohio Division of Wildlife, unpublished report), and 1996 (D. Swanson and R. Stoll, Ohio Division of Wildlife, unpublished report) surveys of Ohio spring turkey hunters.

RESULTS

For the 2001 survey, usable responses were received from 1,096 (52%) of the 1-bird permit holders, 303 (61%) of the 2-bird permit holders, and 495 (28%) of the free permittees for a total of 1,894 responses (44% overall return rate) (Table 1). Response rates to individual questions discussed below exceeded 90%.

Spring Turkey Hunter Experience, Pressure, and Success Rates

Over 98% (±1%) of 1-bird permit holders, 99% (±1%) of 2-bird permit holders, and 75% (±3%) of free permit recipients actually hunted during the 2001 Ohio spring turkey season. Turkey hunter success rates (harvested ≥1 bird) were higher for 1-bird (45 ± 3%) and 2-bird permit holders (63 ± 3%) than for free hunters (31 ± 3%). For all 3 groups combined, hunters spent 549,019 days afield in 2001 (Table 1).

Over 85% of 2001 turkey hunters reported hunting turkeys in Ohio ≥2 years, compared to 63% in 1985, 70% in 1989, and 80% in 1996 (Table 2). The estimated number of spring turkey hunters in Ohio increased an average of 15% annually since 1985 (D. Swanson and W. Culbertson, Ohio Division of Wildlife, unpublished report). In addition, the percentage of experienced hunters increased consistently since 1985, indicating the dropout rate among Ohio's spring turkey hunters is low.

About 35% (±3%) of the 2001 hunters reported never harvesting a turkey in Ohio; 17% (±2%) reported harvesting 1 bird, 40% (±3%) reported harvesting 2–10 birds, and 8% (±2%) reported harvesting >10 turkeys. Over half (53 ± 3%) of the 1996 hunters

Table 3. Hunting device, decoy use, and type of land ownership hunted by 1989, 1996, and 2001 spring turkey hunters in Ohio.

Variable	Hunters					
	1989		1996		2001	
	%	95% CL	%	95% CL	%	95% CL
Hunting device used						
Shotgun	98	1	95	1	95	1
Muzzleloader	<1	<1	1	1	1	1
Crossbow	1	<1	1	<1	1	<1
Longbow	1	1	3	1	4	1
Used decoy	14	2	49	3	67	3
Type of land hunted						
Mostly public	32	3	22	3	19	3
Mostly private	17	3	18	2	67	2
Equally public and private	51	3	60	1	14	1

had never harvested a turkey in Ohio; 17% (±3%) had harvested 1 bird, 28% (±3%) had harvested 2–10 birds, and 1.5% (±1%) had harvested >10 birds. In 1985, 70% (±3%) of the hunters reported never harvesting a turkey in Ohio; 16% (±2%) had harvested 1 bird, 14% (±2%) had harvested 2–10 birds, and 0.4% (±0.5%) had harvested >10 birds.

Most (>95 ± 1%) hunters used a shotgun when spring turkey hunting in 2001. Few hunters used a longbow, crossbow, and/or muzzleloader during the 2001 spring turkey season (Table 3).

The percentage of spring turkey hunters using a decoy increased consistently from 14% (±2%) in 1989 to 49% (±3%) in 1996 to 67% in (±2%) 2001. About 19% (±3%) of the turkey hunters hunted mostly on public land, 67% (±3%) hunted mostly on private land, and about 14% (±2%) hunted equally on public and private land (Table 3). Although the percentage of respondents hunting mostly on public land in 2001 was lower than that reported in 1989 (32 ± 3%) and 1996 (22 ± 3%), <5% of Ohio's land area is public land (Ohio Department of Natural Resources, unpublished report), illustrating the importance of public land turkey hunters.

Expenditures for Wild Turkey Hunting

The average estimated expenditure per hunter during the 3-week 2001 spring turkey season in Ohio was $162 (±$3), up 38% from the $117 average reported in 1996 and 91% more than the $85 average reported in 1989. Total expenditures by spring turkey hunters during the 2001 season was $14.9 million (±$1 million), an increase of 157% over the $5.8 million spent during the 1996 spring season and 610% more than the $2.1 million spent by hunters in 1989.

Hunter Disturbance, Overcrowding, and Hunter Safety

About 59% (±3%) of the turkey hunters believed that disturbance by other hunters was a problem, similar to the 56% (±3%) reported in 1996, 57% (±3%) reported in 1989, and 62% (±3%) reported in 1985

Table 4. Spring turkey hunter perceptions regarding disturbance by other hunters in Ohio, 1985, 1989, 1996, and 2001.

Disturbance	Hunters							
	1985		1989		1996		2001	
	%	95% CL	%	95% CL	%	95% CL	%	95% CL
No problem	38	3	43	3	44	3	41	3
Minor problem	36	3	38	3	40	3	45	3
Big problem	26	3	18	2	15	2	14	2

a Percentages may not add up to 100% due to rounding errors.

(Table 4). During the 2001 spring season, 13% (±2%) of successful hunters were disturbed by other hunters on the day of harvest. This disturbance rate was somewhat lower than in 1996 and 1989 and substantially lower than reported in 1985 (Table 4). About 16% (±2%) of 2001 unsuccessful hunters believed the major reason they failed to harvest a bird was disturbance from other hunters. This percentage was somewhat lower than reported in the 3 previous surveys (Table 4).

As in 1996 and 1989, 2001 spring turkey hunters were clearly concerned about turkey hunting safety (Table 5). Almost 95% (±1%) of the hunters completed the Ohio hunter education course. Sixty-seven percent (±3%) of the hunters read articles, attended seminars, and/or viewed films on turkey hunting safety. Although only 2% (±1%) of the hunters reported having been shot at by another hunter while turkey hunting, 58% (±3%) were concerned about being shot by another hunter and 38% (±3%) indicated they had another hunter sneak up on them while turkey hunting (Table 5). Hunters ranked uninformed hunters and overcrowded hunting conditions as the most serious problems affecting turkey hunting safety followed by wearing camouflage, shell shot size, and shotgun gauge (Figure 1).

A spring turkey hunting brochure provided to all buyers of spring turkey hunting permits recommended wearing hunter (blaze) orange when walking in the woods and wrapping an orange covering around the

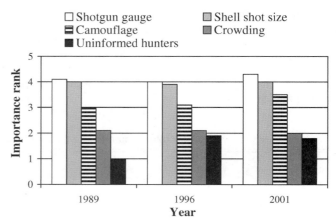

Fig. 1. Average rank of importance assigned to 5 problems affecting turkey hunting safety in Ohio by 1989, 1996, and 2001 spring turkey hunters. A rank of 5 was considered most important.

Table 5. Safety issues and concerns of spring wild turkey hunters in Ohio, 1989, 1996, and 2001.

| | Hunters | | | | | |
| | 1989 | | 1996 | | 2001 | |
Safety issue or concern	%	95% CL	%	95% CL	%	95% CL
Complete Ohio hunter education course	38	3	43	3	95	1
Read articles on turkey hunting safety	79	3	77	3	88	3
Watched films on turkey hunting safety	57	2	64	2	70	3
Attended seminars on turkey hunting safety	35	3	36	3	44	3
Concerned about being shot by another turkey hunter	66	2	60	2	58	2
Had another hunter sneak up on them	33	3	33	3	38	3

harvested bird before walking out of the woods. Although most (72% ± 3%) hunters indicated they never wore hunter orange at all times, 26% (±3%) reported they always wore hunter orange when moving and 42% (±3%) always carried their harvested bird in orange covering when walking out of the woods (Table 6). Over 25% (±3%) of the hunters reported they at least occasionally marked the tree to their backs with an item of hunter orange and 83% (±2%) reported using a flashlight when it was dark.

Spring Turkey Season Regulations and Management Activities

Most (64% ± 3%) 2001 turkey hunters did not favor increasing the bag limit from 2 to 3 birds (Table 7). A similar percentage of hunters (69 ± 3%) opposed a bag limit increase from 2 to 3 birds in 1996; 66 (±3%) opposed increasing the bag limit from 1 to 2 birds in 1989. More hunters favored expanding legal hunting hours beyond 1200 to 1400 h (58 ± 3%) compared to 1600 h (33 ± 3%) or sunset (39 ± 3%). Most (65 ± 3%) hunters favored extending the spring turkey season from 3 to 4 weeks. Over 78% (±3%) of turkey hunters favored the current regulation allowing hunters to harvest 2 birds during the entire spring season. Most (52 ± 3%) hunters believed the spring turkey season opening date of the fourth Monday in April was just right; 43% (±3%) believed the season came in too late and 5% (±1%) believed the season started too early (Table 7).

Spring turkey hunters were asked to rank 6 turkey management activities in terms of their importance to the resource. Public education on hunting safety was ranked most important followed by management efforts to secure more areas to hunt, acquiring more public land, law enforcement, habitat development on private land, and research (Figure 2). Public education on

hunter safety was ranked first in importance by 1996 turkey hunters but was ranked third in importance behind law enforcement, research, and habitat development on private land by 1989 hunters, illustrating the growing concern of spring turkey hunters regarding hunting safety.

Factors Contributing to a Quality Turkey Hunting Experience

Over 85% (±2%) of 2001 hunters ranked high gobbling activity as the primary factor contributing greatly to enjoyment of their spring turkey hunting experience, followed by killing an adult bird, and calling turkeys (Table 8). Seeing turkeys and turkey sign and hearing turkeys gobble contributed more to the enjoyment of a spring turkey hunt than harvesting a juvenile bird or low gobbling activity. Hunters ranked these 7 factors in the same order in 1996.

Characteristics of Ohio Spring Turkey Hunters

The composite Ohio spring turkey hunter was male (98 ± 1%), 49 (range = 8–90) years old, had a rural (57 ± 3%) or small town (30 ± 3%) background, and a total household income >$50,000 (43 ± 3%). This person had hunted (all game, not just wild turkeys) for 28 (range = 1–62) years, but hunted wild turkeys during spring only 2–10 years (66% ± 3%) and harvested an average of 3.4 turkeys (range = 0–35).

DISCUSSION

Since 1985, the number of spring turkey hunters and the spring wild turkey harvest in Ohio has increased annually an average of 15% and 20% (Ohio Department of Natural Resources, unpublished data).

Table 6. Frequency of hunter (blaze) orange and flashlight use by spring turkey hunters in Ohio, 2001.

| | Hunter action | | | | | | | |
| | Always | | Usually | | Occasionally | | Never | |
Safety measure	%	95% CL	%	95% CL	%	95% CL	%	95% CL
Wear hunter orange at all times during the hunt	9	2	4	1	15	2	72	3
Wear hunter orange when moving in woods	26	3	15	2	21	2	38	3
Wrap a hunter orange item in tree	7	2	7	1	11	2	75	3
Carry bird out marked with an orange covering	42	3	13	2	8	1	37	3
Use a flashlight when it is dark	49	3	17	2	18	2	17	2

Table 7. Hunter opinions regarding potential changes in spring turkey hunting regulations in Ohio, 2001.

Potential change	Hunters in favor of change (%)	95% CL
Increase bag limit from 2 to 3 birds	36	3
Expand legal shooting hours from one-half hr before sunrise to 1400 hr	58	2
Expand legal shooting hours from one-half hr before sunrise to 1600 hr	33	3
Expand legal shooting hours from one-half hour before sunrise to sunset	39	3
Extend the spring gobbler season from 3 to 4 weeks in length	65	2

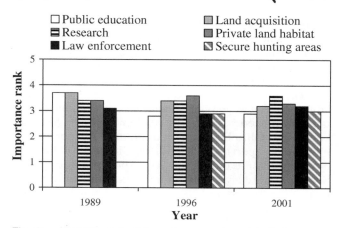

Fig. 2. Average rank of importance assigned to turkey management activities conducted by the Ohio Division of Wildlife by 1989, 1996, and 2001 spring turkey hunters. A rank of 5 was considered most important.

Factors contributing to a quality hunting experience are usually related to turkey population densities (Eichholz and Hardin 1990, Vangilder et al. 1990), whereas factors degrading the hunting experience are related to human activities (e.g., disturbance and crowded conditions) (Madson 1975, Williams and Austin 1988). Between 1985 and 2001, the percentage of Ohio hunters indicating that disturbance by other spring turkey hunters was a "big" problem decreased from 26 to 14%, the percentage of successful hunters disturbed on the day of harvest decreased from 23 to 13%, and the percentage of hunters who attributed hunter disturbance for their failure to harvest a bird decreased from 26 to 16%. The observed decline in hunter disturbance rate is likely a function of a greater number and wider distribution of wild turkeys in relation to increases in hunter numbers since 1985. However, >60% of 1989 and 1996 and 58% of 2001 turkey hunters indicated they were concerned about being shot by another turkey hunter and >30% had another hunter sneak up on them. Despite these safety concerns, little use of blaze orange was reported by spring turkey hunters in Ohio. This low use of blaze orange by Ohio spring turkey hunters parallels the findings of studies conducted in Arkansas (Cartwright and Smith 1990), Florida (Eichholz and Hardin 1990), Missouri (Vangilder et al. 1990), and Virginia (Bittner and Hale 1991).

Uninformed hunters and overcrowded hunting conditions were ranked as the most serious problems affecting spring turkey hunting safety by 1989, 1996, and 2001 hunters. Public education on hunter safety

was ranked the most important turkey management activity by 1996 and 2001 hunters. Thus, it is not surprising that hunters did not favor increasing the bag limit from 2 to 3 birds (which would probably increase hunter interest and participation), but favored expanding shooting hours beyond 1200 h and lengthening the season to 4 weeks (which would probably spread out hunting pressure and relieve overcrowding).

Although hunters indicated they would support increased opportunity via extended shooting hours and season length, these regulation changes would likely contribute to increased spring turkey harvests. Increased turkey harvests may result in decreased densities of adult male turkeys and reduced gobbling activity (Vangilder and Kurzejeski 1995). The primary factor contributing greatly to the quality of a spring turkey hunt was high gobbling activity; the opportunity to call birds was third, just behind harvesting an adult bird. These findings are consistent with those of Williams and Austin (1988), Eichholz and Hardin (1990), and Vangilder et al. (1990) who reported good turkey hunting experiences were related to turkey population densities. Thus, harvest management regulations designed to maintain good spring gobbler densities and quality hunting experiences may be more appropriate than providing additional harvest opportunity.

In addition to becoming a spring tradition for

Table 8. Turkey hunters' rankings of the amount of enjoyment certain factors contribute to a spring turkey hunting experience in Ohio, 2001.

Enjoyment factor	Importance level (% of hunters)									
	Great		Moderate		Some		Little		None	
	%	95% CL	%	95% CL	%	95% CL	%	95% CL	%	95% CL
Killing an adult bird	71	2	16	2	8	2	3	1	2	1
Killing a juvenile bird	17	2	28	3	22	3	18	2	15	2
Seeing hens with gobblers	46	3	27	3	18	2	6	2	3	1
High gobbling activity	85	3	12	2	2	1	1	<1	1	<1
Low gobbling activity	4	1	12	2	22	3	32	3	30	3
Calling turkeys	69	2	21	3	7	2	1	<1	1	<1
Seeing turkey sign	39	3	33	3	21	3	6	2	1	<1

many Ohio hunters, spring turkey season provides revenue to state and local economies. During the 3-week 2001 spring turkey season, an estimated $14.9 million was spent by hunters on items such as ammunition, food, gasoline, and lodging.

The importance of public land to the sport of turkey hunting was again demonstrated by hunters. Public land comprised <5% of the land area in occupied turkey range (Ohio Department of Natural Resources, unpublished report) yet supported almost 20% of the hunting pressure during the 2001 spring turkey season. Securing more areas to hunt and acquiring more public land were considered the second and third most important turkey management activities by 2001 hunters, providing further evidence of the importance of public land.

Crowded conditions and safety are valid concerns of Ohio spring turkey hunters. The number of non-fatal turkey hunting incidents in Ohio averaged 4 per year (range = 1–9) since 1985, but the accident rate/ 10,000 hunters declined (D. Swanson and W. Culbertson, Ohio Division of Wildlife, unpublished report). Spring turkey hunting incidents are most often the result of either mistaken-for-game or line-of-fire accidents (Vangilder et al. 1990). As the popularity of spring turkey hunting continues to grow, cooperation among individuals, conservation organizations, and the Division of Wildlife will continue to be important in preserving safe and ethical turkey hunting in Ohio.

ACKNOWLEDGMENTS

We thank the Division of Wildlife's Information Management Section for providing spring turkey hunter names and addresses for the mail questionnaire. We appreciate the time Ohio spring turkey hunters spent completing and returning their questionnaire. M. C. Reynolds, L. A. Smith, and 3 anonymous reviewers greatly improved earlier drafts of this manuscript.

LITERATURE CITED

Baumann, D. P., Jr., L. D. Vangilder, C. I. Taylor, R. Engel-Wilson, R. O. Kimmel, and G. A. Wunz. 1990. Expenditures for wild turkey hunting. Proceedings of the National Wild Turkey Symposium 6:157–166.

Bittner, L. A., and M. P. Hale. 1991. Attitudes and opinions of Virginia's spring turkey hunters towards safety issues. Proceedings of the Annual Conference of the Southeastern Association of Fish and Wildlife Agencies 45:124–132.

Cartwright, M. E., and R. A. Smith. 1990. Attitudes, opinions, and characteristics of a select group of Arkansas spring turkey hunters. Proceedings of the National Wild Turkey Symposium 6:177–187.

Donohoe, R. W. 1990. The wild turkey: past, present, and future in Ohio. Ohio Department of Natural Resources Fish and Wildlife Bulletin 11.

Eichholz, N. F., and S. B. Hardin. 1990. Turkey hunter satisfac-

tion in Florida. Proceedings of the Annual Conference of the Southeastern Association of Fish and Wildlife Agencies 44:319–327.

Hendee, J. C., and D. R. Potter. 1971. Human behavior and wildlife management: needed research. Transactions of the North American Wildlife and Natural Resources Conference 36:383–396.

Madson, J. B. 1975. The crowd goes turkey hunting. Proceedings of the National Wild Turkey Symposium 3:222–227.

Vangilder, L. D., and E. W. Kurzejeski. 1995. Population ecology of the eastern wild turkey in northern Missouri. Wildlife Monograph 130.

———, S. L. Sheriff, and G. S. Olson. 1990. Characteristics, attitudes, and preferences of Missouri's spring turkey hunters. Proceedings of the National Wild Turkey Symposium 6:167–176.

Williams, L. E., Jr., and D. H. Austin. 1988. Studies of the wild turkey in Florida. Florida Game and Freshwater Fish Commission Technical Bulletin 10.

David A. Swanson is Forest Wildlife Research Supervisor of the Ohio Department of Natural Resources (ODNR) Division of Wildlife. He coordinates statewide forest wildlife surveys and research projects and monitors the status of state endangered forest wildlife species. His research interests include population dynamics and wildlife-habitat relationships.

W. Lloyd Culbertson (pictured) is Forest Wildlife Research Technician of the ODNR Division of Wildlife. He collects and analyzes forest wildlife survey and research project data. He is heavily involved with the 4-H Shooting Sports and is a Hunter Education Instructor. ***Robert J. Stoll, Jr.*** retired in July 1999 after 29 years of service with the ODNR Division of Wildlife. During his tenure as Forest Wildlife Research Supervisor, he conducted research with ruffed grouse, wild turkey, squirrels, and white-tailed deer.

Wild Turkey Management:
Accomplishments, Strategies, and Opportunities
——— Grand Rapids, Michigan ———

COMPARISONS BETWEEN HALF-DAY AND ALL-DAY SPRING TURKEY HUNTING IN INDIANA

Steven E. Backs[1]
Division of Fish and Wildlife,
562 DNR Road,
Mitchell, IN 47446, USA

Abstract: Wildlife managers have debated whether "half-day" versus "all-day" hunting influences the probability of harvesting an adult or a juvenile wild turkey (*Meleagris gallopavo*) gobbler. Daily and hourly harvest distributions of adult gobblers were compared between 4 years of half-day hunting (1996–1999; 23,356 harvest events) and 2 years of all-day hunting in Indiana (2003 and 2004; 21,061 harvest events). The distributions of the total harvest across the 19-day season were the same for both half-day and all-day seasons. During all-day seasons, 70% of the total harvest occurred before 1000 hr, 79% by noon, 8% between 1200–1600 hr, with 13% after 1600 hr. Adults made up a slightly greater proportion (>2% points on average; e.g., 75% versus 77%) of the harvest for the all-day seasons. Our data suggest the influence of all-day hunting on adult gobbler mortality is relatively minor on a statewide basis with a 1-bird bag limit and the small differences in the proportion of the harvest that was adults may be related to factors other than extended shooting hours. Differential adult mortality may be of greater management concern under more liberal spring harvest strategies.

Proceedings of the National Wild Turkey Symposium 9:331–336

Key words: adult gobblers, harvest distribution, harvest management, hunting, Indiana, *Meleagris gallopavo*, mortality, shooting hours, spring season, time of kill, wild turkeys.

The wild turkey restoration era is essentially completed (Tapley et al. 2001) and management emphasis has shifted toward population and harvest management (Kurzejeski and Vangilder 1992). For over three decades, wild turkey populations experienced exponential growth as restoration efforts peaked and newly established turkey populations expanded into voids of available habitat (Lewis 2001). Increases in turkey numbers and their expanded distribution led to increases in open hunting range, hunter opportunities, and turkey hunter numbers (Tapley et al. *this volume*). Despite increases in turkey populations and open hunting range, hunters continually demand and expect more opportunities (e.g., more time to hunt, increased bag limits, higher success rates) and there is a desire to remove barriers to attracting new hunters, particularly youth hunters (e.g., hunting heritage movement).

Today's harvest management strategies generally evolved during decades of rapid turkey population growth and will need further evaluation as turkey population growth stabilizes and turkey hunter numbers continue to increase (Kurzejeski and Vangilder 1992, Tapley et al. *this volume*). Concerns about sustaining turkey harvest levels and hunter satisfaction have heightened as turkey habitat management on public lands has become more constrained and the negative impacts of increased urban sprawl have become more evident (Dickson 1992). Wildlife managers are now reassessing the proportion of adult gobblers taken during spring hunting seasons, sustainability of subsequent harvests, and its impact on hunt quality (Wright and Vangilder 2001, *this volume*). Natural resource agencies are cautious about increasing hunter opportunities that may subsequently be retracted due to resource or hunt-quality concerns. Wildlife managers also recognize that conservative harvest management decisions based on incomplete knowledge may unnecessarily limit hunting opportunities.

Discussions of shooting hours (half versus all-day turkey hunting) often evoke numerous opinions and perceptions among hunters, outdoor writers, and natural resource agency personnel. Shooting hours were not specifically mentioned as a factor affecting gobbler

[1] E-mail: sbacks@dnr.IN.gov

Table 1. Harvest data from 6 Indiana spring wild turkey seasons under 2 shooting-hour treatments.

	Shooting-hour treatment					
	Half-day hunting[a]				All-day hunting[b]	
	Season				Season	
	1996	1997	1998	1999	2003	2004
Season dates[c]	4/24–5/12	4/23–5/11	4/22–5/10	4/21–5/9	4/23–5/11	4/21–5/9
Total harvest[d]	4,859	5,790	6,384	6,548	10,366	10,765
Adults (%)	76	78	69	72	76	76
Harvest events[e]	4,796	5,710	6,343	6,507	10,322	10,739

[a] Half-day shooting hours = 1/2 hr before sunrise to 1200 hr.
[b] All-day shooting hours = 1/2 hr before sunrise to sunset.
[c] Seasons were 19 days with a Wednesday opening day.
[d] Total reported harvest recorded at mandatory check stations.
[e] Check station records with harvest date, time of kill, and age of bird.

density by Kurzejeski and Vangilder (1992), who cited liberal spring harvests following poor production, season length, opening dates, bag limits, and hunter density as possible factors. However, season length does infer increased hunter opportunity as do increased shooting hours. Shooting-hour restrictions are traditionally justified to protect nesting hens even though the effect of this restriction on hen mortality is unknown (Healy and Powell 2000). Presently, 33 states and 2 Canadian provinces allow all-day spring gobbler hunting while 17 states and 1 Canadian province allow half-day hunting (Perea 2005).

In 2002, all-day spring turkey hunting was implemented in Indiana after 32 years of half-day hunting. Prior to extending Indiana's shooting hours, there was a moderate amount of controversy among various resource users and natural resource managers. The gamut of concerns over extending shooting-hours included: disruption or suppression of ongoing breeding activity (e.g., reduced gobbling), an even greater proportion of the harvest occuring earlier in the season, a greater proportion of adult gobblers harvested, increased roost shooting, increased disturbance or mortality of nesting hens, and opposition by non-turkey hunting publics (e.g., mushroom hunters and dog field-trialers).

Our objective was to assess whether the lengthening of spring shooting-hours from "half-day" (half-hour before sunrise to noon) to "all-day" (half-hour before sunrise to sunset) influenced the distribution of the harvest throughout the season or the age-specific harvest on adult gobblers in Indiana.

STUDY AREA

Wild turkey populations exist in all regions of Indiana with the better quality habitat for wild turkeys generally found in the more forested regions in the southern half of the state (Backs and Eisfelder 1990). Indiana has a statewide, open-permit, spring wild turkey season with a bag limit of 1 male or bearded turkey per hunter per season (Backs 1996). The mean forest cover in the 74–90 counties open to turkey hunting during the study years ranged from 21–32%. Mean estimated hunter success during 1996–2004 was 25% (range = 23–28%) with a mean 5.3 efforts (trips)/hunt-

er/season (range = 5.0–5.5) while annual turkey harvests and hunter numbers increased 12% and 9%, respectively, during the last decade (Backs 2003, 2004a).

METHODS

Date, time of kill, and age of harvested birds were collected at mandatory check stations for each "harvest event" between 1996 and 2004 (Backs 1996, Backs and Weaver 2001). Harvest data from 1996–1999 were used for the half-day hunting treatment and the harvest data from 2003 and 2004 were used for the all-day hunting treatment (Table 1). Data from 2002, the first year all-day hunting was implemented, were excluded as a hunter-adjustment year to the new regulation. Variables within each shooting-hour treatment (half and all-day hunting) were: age class (juveniles = 1-yr-olds, adults ≥ 2-yr-olds), day killed (numerical days of the season; 1, 2, 3, . . . , 19), and time of kill (in 0100 hour intervals; 0500–1900 hr). Analysis of variance (ANOVA; Snedecor and Cochran 1980) was used to compare sample means and the Kolmogorov-Smirnov test (Conover 1971) was used to compare the similarity, goodness of fit, of sample distributions. Statistical comparisons were made using Statistix 8 (Analytical Software 2003). The age-class analysis focused on adults because the adult harvest is of principal interest in harvest management decisions (Kurzejeski and Vangilder 1992, Vangilder 1992).

RESULTS

A total of 44,417 harvest events was used to compare the daily harvest distribution between each shooting-hour treatment (Table 2). These harvest events represented 99% of the total harvest (N = 44,712) during this period. Estimated hunter success during half-day seasons ($\bar{x}$ = 24.9%) was similar to all-day seasons ($\bar{x}$ = 25.8%; $F_{1,4}$ = 0.254; P = 0.640).

The proportions of the daily harvests over the 19-day hunting season were similar for both half-day and all-day treatments (T = 0.07, n = 19, P = 1.000; i.e., similar proportions of the harvest occurred on a daily basis for both treatments; Figure 1). The proportions

Table 2. Number and percentage of wild turkeys harvested on each day of Indiana's 19-day spring hunting season for half-day (0500–1200 hr) and full-day (0500–2000 hr) hunting treatments.

| | | Shooting-hour treatment | | | | | | | | | |
| | | Half-day harvest[a] | | | | | All-day harvests[b] | | | | |
Day	Weekday	Total	Total (%)	Adults	Total adults (%)	Adults by day (%)	Total	Total (%)	Adults	Total adults (%)	Adults by day (%)
1	Wednesday	4,039	17	3,043	18	76	4,695	22	3,689	23	79
2	Thursday	2,415	10	1,772	10	73	1,925	9	1,475	9	77
3	Friday	1,955	8	1,451	8	74	1,338	6	1,010	6	75
4	Saturday	2,350	10	1,704	10	73	2,363	11	1,759	11	74
5	Sunday[c]	1,646	7	1,157	7	70	1,323	6	990	6	75
6	Monday	438	2	326	2	74	730	3	549	3	75
7	Tuesday	589	3	434	3	74	639	3	475	3	74
8	Wendesday	559	2	417	2	75	695	3	553	3	80
9	Thursday	518	2	406	2	78	629	3	479	3	76
10	Friday	1,281	5	955	6	75	644	3	498	3	77
11	Saturday	1,323	6	933	5	70	1,099	5	797	5	73
12	Sunday[c]	1,073	5	792	5	74	883	4	624	4	71
13	Monday	534	2	411	2	77	359	2	276	2	77
14	Tuesday	537	2	388	2	72	482	2	382	2	79
15	Wednesday	502	2	362	2	72	393	2	300	2	76
16	Thursday	577	2	441	3	76	517	2	400	3	77
17	Friday	898	4	636	4	71	531	3	414	3	78
18	Saturday	1,221	5	849	5	70	1,022	5	735	5	72
19	Sunday[c]	901	4	640	4	71	794	4	583	4	73
	All seasons	23,356	100	17,106	100	73	21,061	100	15,988	100	76

[a] Half-day season years = 1996–1999.
[b] All-day season years = 2003–2004.
[c] Hunt week periods; first 5 days, second week, and third week, respectively.

of the harvests that occurred during the first 5 days and the second week hunt-periods (Figure 2) were slightly greater (+3%) during all-day hunting ($F_{2,12}$ = 3.10, P = 0.082). The proportions of the adult daily harvests (Figure 3) were slightly greater (+2%) during all-day hunting ($F_{1,76}$ = 4.17, P = 0.045).

A total of 44,140 harvest events was used to compare the hourly harvest distribution between shooting hour treatments (Table 3). The distributions of the hourly total harvests (Figure 4) were similar during the morning hours (0500 through 1100 hr) for both half and all-day hunting (T = 0.02, n = 7, P = 0.980). The lower hourly proportions in the morning for all-day hunting were due to the spread of the harvest across 15 time-periods. Excluding the afternoon harvest from all-day hunting, the highest proportion of the morning harvest (57–58%) for both shooting hour

treatments occurred between 0600–0800 hr and 86–88% before 1000 hr. When all hour-periods for all-day hunting were included, 70% of the total all-day harvest occurred before 1000 hr and 79% by noon. Only 8% and 13% of the all-day harvest occurred between 1200–1600 hr and after 1600 hr, respectively.

Considering only the morning time periods (<1200 hrs) for both shooting hour treatments (Figure 5), the proportion of the adult harvest was slightly greater in the hourly periods for all-day hunting (+2%; $F_{1,28}$ = 3.21, P = 0.084). The all-day harvests that occurred in the early afternoon (8.0%; 1200–1600 hrs) and the late afternoon (12.5%; >1600 hrs) were very small compared to the 79.5% harvest occurring in the morning, but the adult proportion of the early afternoon harvest (79.8%) was greater ($F_{2,3}$ = 186, P =

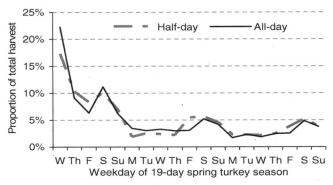

Fig. 1. Distribution of Indiana's spring wild turkey harvest by day of season for half (1996–1999) and all-day (2003–2004) hunting.

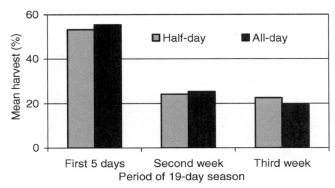

Fig. 2. Proportion of spring wild turkey harvest by weekly periods for half (1996–1999) and all-day (2003–2004) hunting in Indiana.

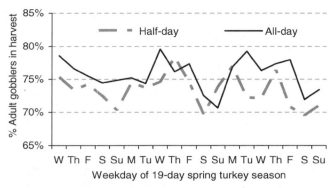

Fig. 3. Proportion of adult gobblers in the harvest by day of the spring season for half (1996–1999) and all-day (2003–2004) hunting in Indiana.

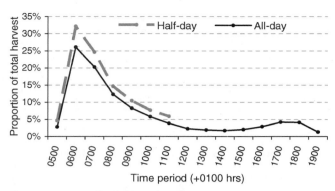

Fig. 4. Hourly distribution of the spring wild turkey harvest for half (1996–1999) and all-day (2003–2004) hunting in Indiana.

0.001) than either the morning (76.3%) or late afternoon periods (75.0%).

DISCUSSION

Daily harvest distributions through the 19-day spring seasons did not differ following extension of shooting-hours. The proportion of total harvest occurring during the third week was slightly less (3%) during years of extended shooting-hours. The proportion of the harvest taken after 1200 hr during all-day hunting was about 20%, similar to Frawley (2001). The primary differences between shooting hour treatments were that adults composed slightly greater proportions (>2%) of the all-day harvests. Differences in the proportion of adults between shooting hour treatments may have been due to a greater number of adult gobblers being available to hunters during the all-day hunting seasons and unmeasured variables of hunter selectivity. Kurzejeski and Vangilder (1992) concluded

season length, turkey population density, and hunter selectivity influenced the age structure of the harvest.

In Missouri, the proportions of juveniles to adults in the spring harvests were correlated to the poult-to-hen ratios from the previous summer brood surveys (Kurzejeski and Vangilder 1992). There were no differences ($F_{1,6} = 0.033$, $P = 0.862$) in the Indiana summer production indices (poults/adult hen) in the years prior to half-day and all-day seasons (Backs 2004b). Based on the production indices alone, it appears there was no difference in the potential number of gobblers available to hunters. However, these indices do not account for overall turkey population growth.

Accurate population estimates of wild turkeys are a persistent shortcoming facing wildlife managers, so harvest data are frequently used as an index of relative turkey population levels (Healy and Powell 2000, Cobb et al. 2001). Annual spring harvest trends suggest Indiana's wild turkey population has grown an average 12% annually during the last decade (Backs 2004a). The adult proportions of the harvest in southeast and south-central Indiana are normally greater

Table 3. Number and percentage of spring wild turkeys harvested during 1-hour intervals for 2 shooting-hour treatments in Indiana.

Interval start time	Shooting-hour treatment									
	Half-day harvest[a]					All-day harvests[b]				
	Total	Total (%)	Adults	Total adults (%)	Adults by hour (%)	Total	Total (%)	Adults	Total adults (%)	Adults by hour (%)
0500	1,070	5	877	4	82	593	3	470	3	79
0600	7,459	32	5,562	33	75	5,459	26	4,174	26	76
0700	5,721	25	4,073	24	71	4,246	20	3,181	20	75
0800	3,391	15	2,390	14	70	2,578	12	1,887	12	73
0900	2,422	10	1,746	10	72	1,727	8	1,332	8	77
1000	1,777	8	1,313	8	74	1,217	6	911	6	75
1100[c]	1,375	6	1,033	6	75	807	4	637	4	79
1200						479	2	379	2	79
1300						396	2	322	2	81
1400						362	2	285	2	79
1500[c]						432	2	345	2	80
1600						607	3	466	3	77
1700						884	4	643	4	73
1800						862	4	633	4	73
1900[c]						276	1	213	1	77
All seasons	23,215	100	16,994	100	73	20,925	100	15,878	100	76

[a] Half-day treatment (0500–1100 hrs) years = 1996–1999.
[b] All-day treatment (0500–1900 hrs) years = 2003–2004.
[c] Daily time-periods; mornign (0500–1200 hrs), early afternoon (1200–1600 hrs), late afternoon (>1600 hrs).

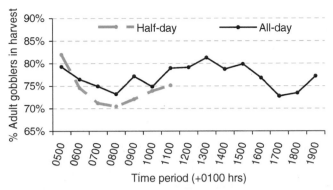

Fig. 5. Proportion of adult gobblers in the spring harvest by time period for half (1996–1999) and all-day (2003–2004) hunting in Indiana.

than other regions of the state (Backs 2003, 2004*a*). Southeast and south-central Indiana are characterized by high quality turkey habitat (Backs and Eisfelder 1990) and support the highest wild turkey population levels and harvests (Backs 1996, 2004*a*), suggesting relatively higher turkey population levels may explain the differences in the adult proportion of the all-day treatment years (2003 and 2004) rather than the extension of shooting hours. Hunter density and effort data were not available for the all-day hunting treatment years to permit the examination of hunter density and effort/mi^2 as covariates influencing the adult proportion of the harvest.

Turkey hunter preference and selection for taking adult gobblers is well documented (Vangilder et al. 1990, Kurzejeski and Vangilder 1992, Taylor et al. 1996, Healy and Powell 2000, Wright and Vangilder 2001, Swanson and Stoll *this volume*). How hunters responded to the increased opportunity of all-day hunting is speculative and based on cursory observations, but worthy of discussion.

During half-day seasons, hunters generally pursued gobblers in the first 2–3 morning hours when gobblers were actively gobbling (Kienzler et al. 1996). Once gobblers were with hens and gobbled less, many hunters either abandoned their morning hunting efforts (Hoffman 1990) or were more willing to take a juvenile gobbler (e.g., Figure 5) if the opportunity became available (Vangilder 1992). On mornings of inclement weather (e.g., raining, windy) during half-day seasons, many hunters did not bother to hunt.

During all-day seasons, hunters typically pursued the same early morning hunting strategy as in half-day seasons. Some hunters took advantage of the additional early and late afternoon hunting opportunities that coincided with another increase in gobbler activity, albeit to a lesser degree than early morning (Hoffman 1990). On mornings of inclement weather, afternoon hours provided an alternative hunting opportunity.

The afternoon time-periods, especially after 1500 hr during weekdays, may have attracted turkey hunters who previously could only hunt on weekend mornings during the half-day seasons (e.g., youth, first and third shift factory workers). Hunter mail surveys indicated a noticeably higher proportion of youth license holders

(<17 years of age) actually hunted wild turkeys in the first spring of all-day hunting compared to the previous 5 years of half-day hunting (Backs 2003).

MANAGEMENT IMPLICATIONS

The influence of all-day hunting on the distribution of harvest throughout the season and age-specific harvest of adult gobblers in Indiana's spring turkey season was minimal. There was no change in the daily distribution of the harvest and most birds were still taken during the morning hours (70% prior to 1000 hr, 80% by 1200 hr). The slightly greater take of adult gobblers (>2%) is probably related to higher relative turkey population levels and hunter selectivity rather than shooting hours. Currently, the implementation of all-day hunting provides additional and new hunting opportunities without noticeable impacts on the statewide harvest structure and estimated hunter success.

Differential adult gobbler harvest, albeit marginal under Indiana's spring season structure, may increase under more liberal harvest management strategies (e.g., >1-bird bag limit), and perhaps act synergistically with other factors to increase hunting mortality of adult gobblers (Kurzejeski and Vangilder 1992; Wright and Vangilder 2001, *this volume*). The interactions of harvest mortality variables may become more evident as turkey hunter numbers continue to grow, the growth rate of wild turkey populations level off, and the amount of suitable habitat for wild turkeys diminishes.

ACKNOWLEDGMENTS

Funding for this research was received through the Pittman-Robertson Federal Aid to Wildlife Restoration, Wildlife Research W-26-R (Job 16-G-5), Indiana. Indiana Chapters of the National Wild Turkey Federation provided supplemental support. We acknowledge C. Eisfelder, F. McNew, L. McNew, J. Mitchell, J. Pitman, and B. Plowman who commented on earlier drafts of this manuscript. Appreciation is extended to two anonymous reviewers and especially, D. E. Steffen, whose editorial suggestions regarding the data analysis were very helpful in completing the final manuscript.

LITERATURE CITED

Analytical Software. 2003. Statistix® 8: User's Manual. Analytical Software, Tallahassee, Florida, USA.

Backs, S. E. 1996. Twenty-five years of spring wild turkey hunting in Indiana, 1970–94. Proceedings of the National Wild Turkey Symposium 7:245–251.

———. 2003. Wild turkey hunter-bag check. Annual Progress Report, Pittman-Robertson Federal Aid—Statewide Wildlife Research, Project W-26-R-34; Job 16-G-5. Indiana Division of Fish and Wildlife, Indianapolis, Indiana, USA.

———. 2004*a*. Wild turkey hunter-bag check. Annual Progress Report, Pittman-Robertson Federal Aid—Statewide Wildlife Research, Project W-26-R-35; Job 16-G-5 Indiana Division of Fish and Wildlife, Indianapolis, Indiana, USA.

———. 2004*b*. Population status of wild turkeys in Indiana.

Annual Progress Report, Pittman-Robertson Federal Aid—Statewide Wildlife Research, Project W-26-R-35; Job 16-G-4, Indiana Division of Fish and Wildlife, Indianapolis, Indiana, USA.

————, and C. H. Eisfelder. 1990. Criteria and guidelines for wild turkey release priorities in Indiana. Proceedings of the National Wild Turkey Symposium 6:134–143.

————. 1996. Twenty-five years of spring wild turkey hunting in Indiana, 1970–94. Proceedings of the National Wild Turkey Symposium 7:245–251.

————, and M. T. Weaver. 2001. A device for measuring spurs to estimate the age of male wild turkeys in the spring. Proceedings of the National Wild Turkey Symposium 8:69–73.

————. 2003. Wild turkey hunter-bag check. Annual Progress Report, Pittman-Robertson Federal Aid—Statewide Wildlife Research, Project W-26-R-34; Job 16-G-5. Indiana Division of Fish and Wildlife, Indianapolis.

————. 2004*a*. Wild turkey hunter-bag check. Annual Progress Report, Pittman-Robertson Federal Aid—Statewide Wildlife Research, Project W-26-R-35; Job 16-G-5 Indiana Division of Fish and Wildlife, Indianapolis.

————. 2004*b*. Population status of wild turkeys in Indiana. Annual Progress Report, Pittman-Robertson Federal Aid—Statewide Wildlife Research, Project W-26-R-35; Job 16-G-4, Indiana Division of Fish and Wildlife, Indianapolis.

Cobb, D. T., J. L. Kalso, and G. W. Tanner. 2001. Refining population estimation and survey techniques for wild turkeys. Proceedings of the National Wild Turkey Symposium 8: 179–186.

Conover, W. J. 1971. Practical Nonparametric Statistics. John Wiley and Sons, New York, New York, USA.

Dickson, J. G. 1992. The Future. Pages 408–415 *in* J. G. Dickson, editor. The wild turkey: biology and management. Stackpole Books, Harrisburg, Pennsylvania, USA.

Frawley, B. J. 2001. 2000 Michigan Spring Turkey Hunter Survey. Michigan Department of Natural Resources Wildlife Division Report 3328.

Healy, W. M., and S. M. Powell. 2000. Wild turkey harvest management: biology, strategies, and techniques. U.S. Fish and Wildlife Service Biological Technical Publication BTP-R5001-1999.

Hoffman, R. W. 1990. Chronology of gobbling and nesting activities of Merriam's wild turkeys. Proceedings of the National Wild Turkey Symposium 6:25–31.

Kienzler, J. M., T. W. Little, and W. A. Fuller. 1996. Effects of weather, incubation, and hunting on gobbling activity in wild turkeys. Proceedings of the National Wild Turkey Symposium 7:61–67.

Kurzejeski, E. W., and L. D. Vangilder. 1992. Population management. Pages 165–184 *in* J. G. Dickson, editor. The wild turkey: biology and management. Stackpole Books, Harrisburg, Pennsylvania, USA.

Lewis, J. B. 2001. A success story revisited. Proceedings of the National Wild Turkey Symposium 8:7–14.

Perea, P. J., editor. 2005. Sign of spring: Turkey Call's 2005 spring hunt guide. Turkey Call 32:63–69.

Snedecor, G. W., and W. G. Cochran. 1980. Statistical methods. Seventh edition. The Iowa State University Press, Ames, Iowa, USA.

Swanson, D. A., and R. J. Stoll. *This volume*. Attitudes, preferences, and characteristics of Ohio's turkey hunters, 1985–2001. Proceedings of the National Wild Turkey Symposium 9:*This volume*.

Tapley, J. L., R. K. Abernethy, and J. E. Kennamer. 2001. Status and distribution of the wild turkey in 1999. Proceedings of the National Wild Turkey Symposium 8:15–22.

————, R. K. Abernethy, and J. E. Kennamer. *This volume*. Status and distribution of the wild turkey in 2004. Proceedings of the National Wild Turkey Symposium 9:*This volume*.

Taylor, C. I., W. K. Igo, P. R. Johansen, J. C. Pack, J. E. Evans, and G. H. Sharp. 1996. West Virginia spring turkey hunters and hunting, 1983–93. Proceedings of the National Wild Turkey Symposium 7:259–268.

Vangilder, L. D. 1992. Population dynamics. Pages 144–164 *in* J. G. Dickson, editor. The wild turkey: biology and management. Stackpole Books, Harrisburg, Pennsylvania, USA.

————, S. L. Sheriff, and G. S. Olson. 1990. Characteristics, attitudes, and preferences of Missouri's spring turkey hunters. Proceedings of the National Wild Turkey Symposium 6:167–176.

Wright, G. A., and L. D. Vangilder. 2001. Survival of Eastern wild turkey males in western Kentucky. Proceedings of the National Wild Turkey Symposium 8:187–194.

————, and ————. *This volume*. Mortality of Eastern wild turkey males in western Kentucky. Proceedings of the National Wild Turkey Symposium 9:*This volume*.

Steven E. Backs, Wildlife Research Biologist (1979–present), Indiana Division of Fish and Wildlife in Mitchell is the Wild Turkey and Ruffed Grouse Program Leader. He received his B.S. from Purdue University, Indiana, and M.S. from the University of Vermont, Burlington. His primary research interests are gamebird population management, gamebird habitat assessments, forest wildlife habitat management, and the influence of land use on wildlife populations.

Wild Turkey Management:
Accomplishments, Strategies, and Opportunities
——— Grand Rapids, Michigan ———

TURKEY GENDER RATIOS AND HARVEST STRATEGIES IN SOUTHEASTERN WYOMING

Mark L. Zornes[1]
Arizona Game and Fish Department, Game Branch,
2221 W. Greenway Road, Phoenix, AZ 85023, USA

Bob Lanka
Wyoming Game and Fish Department, Laramie Region,
528 S. Adams, Laramie, WY 82070, USA

Abstract: Isolated populations of introduced Merriam's turkeys (*Meleagris gallopavo merriami*) occur throughout riparian habitats in Wyoming. Anecdotal observations by Wyoming Game and Fish Department wildlife personnel indicated that isolated flocks decreased significantly as the proportion of males in the flock increased, some to the point of local extirpation. We collected winter flock classification data each January from 1997–2001 in Goshen County. Survey results in 1997 and 1998 indicated flock composition was heavily male-biased (1997–2.07:1; 1998–1.86:1). We speculated this bias resulted from habitat limitations, intraspecific competition for winter food, landowner imposed limits on gobbler harvest, and higher gobbler than hen survival rates during severe winter weather events. Beginning with the fall 1997 season, we increased harvest pressure on males by increasing fall and spring permit numbers and by instituting bearded turkey only seasons in the fall. Survey data indicated flocks were female biased (0.67:1) by 1999. In situations where turkey habitat is limited, we suggest that managers modify season structure to increase male harvest once flock classification surveys result in a gobbler:hen ratio ≥0.75:1.

Proceedings of the National Wild Turkey Symposium 9:337–341

Key words: gender ratios, gobbler harvest, hen mortality, intraspecific competition, Merriam's turkey, Wyoming.

Merriam's turkeys were first introduced to Wyoming from New Mexico in 1935 (Crump and Sanderson 1951, Zornes 2002), and to Goshen County in 1959 (Zornes 2002). Habitats used by turkeys in Goshen County more closely resemble those historically occupied by the Rio Grande subspecies (*M. g. intermedia*; Beasom and Wilson 1992).

Local Department personnel observations suggest most Goshen County turkeys are non-migratory and occupy riparian habitats near farmsteads or ranch-yards, year-round. Use of farmsteads and ranch-yards is well documented in turkeys, especially during winter (Vander Haegen et al. 1989, Wunz 1992, Hoffman et al. 1993, Lehman 2005). Farmsteads and cattle feeding sites provide a reliable source of high energy foods in the form of waste livestock grains (Vander Haegen et al. 1989, Wunz 1992, Lehman 2005) and perhaps increased protection from predators (Lehman 2005).

Hoffman et al. (1993) suggested winter flock counts provide the most potential for monitoring Merriam's turkey population trend and gender ratios. However, little has been reported in the literature concerning gender ratios in turkeys, and the impacts, if any, of male-biased ratios on flock productivity and persistence. Ratios have been assumed to be 1:1 at birth and

in modeling efforts (Suchy et al. 1983), but have not been formally documented (Weinstein et al. 1996).

Male-biased ratios were thought to have contributed to declines and accelerated the loss of isolated flocks of turkeys in eastern Wyoming (H. Harju, Wyoming Game and Fish Department, personal communication.) due to intraspecific competition. Male-biased ratios may result from greater winter mortality of Merriam's turkey hens than gobblers (Wakeling 1991, Wakeling and Rogers 1998, Rumble et al. 2003).

Local district wildlife personnel observed male-biased ratios in southern Goshen County in 1996, and initiated this project in an attempt to address our concerns. Objectives of this project were to (1) reduce gobbler:hen ratios, (2) increase turkey hunter opportunity, and (3) increase flock persistence.

STUDY AREA

Goshen County was located in the southeastern portion of Wyoming. The project area was limited to the southern half of Goshen County, south of the North

---

[1] E-mail: mzornes@gf.state.az.us

Platte River. Suitable habitat for turkeys in this portion of Goshen County was fragmented, confined to riparian areas (Driese et al. 2005), and was dominated by cottonwood (*Populus* spp.) and box elder (*Acer negundo*) tree species (Driese et al. 1997). Mast bearing shrubs and trees were limited in number and distribution (Wyoming Game and Fish Department, unpublished data). Agriculture was the dominant land use in Goshen County, both for crop (mainly corn, small grains and sugar beets) and beef cattle production (Wyoming Agricultural Statistics 2001). More than 95% of occupied turkey habitat in Goshen County was privately owned, and landowners greatly limited gobbler harvest by limiting access (Wyoming Game and Fish Department, unpublished data).

During winter, turkeys in Goshen County were restricted to narrow, linear, deciduous riparian habitats within the North Platte River drainage (Wyoming Game and Fish Department, unpublished data). Suitable habitats varied from continuous habitats along the North Platte River, to isolated, fragmented habitats along smaller tributaries. Typical ponderosa pine (*Pinus ponderosa*) summer habitats for Merriam's turkeys (Shaw and Mollohan 1992) were available to turkeys only in the extreme northwestern portion of the county (Wyoming Game and Fish Department, unpublished data).

METHODS

Season Structure Adjustment

In Goshen County, both spring and fall turkey permits were limited in number and issued via a computerized random drawing. Prior to 1997, both spring (bearded turkey only) and fall (either sex) permits were available.

Beginning with the fall 1997 season, we modified season structure to increase gobbler harvest and reduce hen harvest. We increased the number of spring and fall permits, and restricted legal take to bearded turkeys only during both seasons. We continued fall seasons to allow for additional gobbler harvest and to maintain fall turkey hunter opportunity.

In addition to increased permits, we increased gobbler harvest and hunter opportunity by increasing hunter access to private lands. Landowners in this area had concerns regarding declining turkey abundance and hunter crowding. In response to these concerns, we hosted local turkey biology seminars to increase landowner knowledge of this species and the impact of allowing additional harvest. In order to achieve greater gobbler harvest while maintaining hunter density, we split the spring season in two, and issued separate permits for each split.

We obtained harvest estimates from mail surveys sent to 100% of spring and fall turkey permit holders. Response rates averaged about 55% annually (R. Rothwell, Wyoming Game and Fish Department, personal communication).

Winter Flock Counts-Gender Ratio Estimation

To monitor impacts of season modifications on gender ratios and to assess population trend, we clas-

Table 1. Fall wild turkey harvest statistics, Goshen County, Wyoming, 1979–2001[a].

Year	Permits	Hunters	Harvest		
			Male	Female	Total
1979	76	58	20	13	33
1980	50	32	7	2	9
1981	75	58	7	7	14
1982	69	41	3	3	6
1983	85	68	17	26	43
1984	32	21	4	7	11
1985	42	34	3	16	19
1986	100	83	9	43	52
1987	50	35	13	12	25
1988	100	84	15	24	39
1989	100	89	25	17	42
1990	150	113	54	27	81
1991	150	121	51	47	98
1992	150	130	57	32	89
1993	208	141	32	22	54
1994	77	66	16	15	31
1995	73	68	22	14	36
1996	120	107	40	42	82
1997	202	153	119	0	119
1998	201	176	113	0	113
1999	200	169	101	4	105
2000	298	220	89	43	132
2001	285	213	61	65	126

[a] Data taken from 1979–2001 Wyoming Game and Fish Department Annual Reports of Small and Upland Game Harvest.

sified turkeys during the winter each year (1 Jan through 31 Jan 1997–2001) along established routes. Routes followed linear habitats along drainages and traversed the majority of mapped winter turkey habitat in Goshen County (Wyoming Game and Fish Department, unpublished data). We determined turkey gender using spotting scopes and binoculars. We classified turkeys only if they were <100 m away and could be observed for a period adequate to classify the entire flock. An estimated 75% of all observations were <50 m. We differentiated hens from yearling males by size, plumage, head characteristics, and behavior. Turkey use of waste grain at livestock feeding areas during winter facilitated data collection, because turkeys were concentrated, easily accessible, and approachable. Observer bias was reduced by using the same 2 experienced personnel for data collection during all years.

RESULTS

Season Structure Adjustment and Harvest

Increased spring and fall permits, split spring seasons, and increased hunter access resulted in an increase in gobbler harvest in both spring and fall seasons during the period 1997–2001.

In 1997 we increased fall permit numbers by 68% as compared to 1996. By 2000 we had increased fall permits by 150% (Table 1). During the 3 fall seasons with bearded-only fall harvest (1997–1999) gobbler harvest increased from a 1979–1996 average of 22 to 111. No increase in violation rate, or any significant illegal take of turkeys without beards was documented by local game wardens during these fall seasons (J. Gilbert and R. Bredehoft, Wyoming Game and Fish

Table 2. Spring wild turkey harvest statistics, Goshen County, Wyoming, 1979–2001[a].

Year	Permits	Hunters	Male harvest
1979	25	23	10
1980	25	23	15
1981	25	20	13
1982	25	24	15
1983	35	29	14
1984	38	32	13
1985	36	28	9
1986	36	26	10
1987	32	28	16
1988	50	47	28
1989	76	63	36
1990	75	63	41
1991	150	126	35
1992	150	133	51
1993	150	135	46
1994	150	104	21
1995	69	59	27
1996	75	72	46
1997	76	65	39
1998	150	140	105
1999	200	172	138
2000	403	354	231
2001	402	319	205

[a] Data taken from 1979–2001 Wyoming Game and Fish Department Annual Reports of Small and Upland Game Harvest.

Table 3. Wild turkey winter flock classification data, Goshen County, Wyoming, 1997–2001.

Year	Male	Female	Total classified	Gobblers: hen
1997	813	393	1,206	2.07
1998	859	462	1,321	1.86
1999	581	866	1,447	0.67
2000	576	789	1,365	0.73
2001	563	713	1,276	0.79

Department, personal communication). By splitting the spring season, we doubled hunter numbers and increased spring gobbler harvest by about 60% without greatly increasing hunter density (Table 2).

Winter Flock Counts-Gender Ratio Estimation

Flock classification surveys resulted in an average of 1,323 turkeys classified (Table 3). During this project, gender ratios shifted from a male bias (>2 gobblers:hen) to a female bias (<1 gobbler:hen).

Winter flock gender ratio estimates in 1997 and 1998 was consistent with previous anecdotal observations, suggesting males greatly outnumbered females in this turkey population (Table 3). Following 2 years of gobbler only hunting, the gobbler:hen ratio fell to <0.8:1.

DISCUSSION

In some states, including Wyoming, winter weather conditions act as a significant source of turkey mortality (Porter et al. 1983, Wakeling 1991, Wakeling and Rogers 1998, Rumble et al. 2003). Persistent, deep snows and cold temperatures contribute to higher mortality levels in turkeys (Healy 1992), and have been linked to reductions in reproduction the following spring (Porter et al. 1983). Starvation and predation are the primary causes of mortality during winter (Healy 1992, Wakeling and Rogers 1998). Turkeys appear to be able to cope with periods of severe cold weather if food is not limiting, but are limited by persistent snow depths >15 cm (Healy 1992).

Based on our observations and weather data from the National Oceanic and Atmospheric Administration, winter weather severity in Goshen County during all years of the project was harshest from January to

April. Blizzards during 3 of 5 years of the project dropped significant snowfall (>40 cm) with wind speeds in excess of 48 km/hr and consecutive days of very cold temperatures (<−20°C). During these events, conditions exceeded survival limits reported for turkeys (Healy 1992). Turkeys exposed to these conditions relied on livestock grains provided by ranch operators for survival. In Goshen County turkeys tended to use beef cattle feeding locations because these sites were more protected from winter weather conditions and provided an available food source. These sites differed from those reported by Vander Haegen et al. (1989) in that feed is not broadcast over an area, but is confined to livestock feeding bunks.

We observed flock behavior at cattle feeding sites, and male turkeys were observed competing with adult females and yearling turkeys for food resources. We observed adult females and yearling turkeys being excluded from feeding on livestock grains at these sites because of intraspecific competition with males. This behavior was not quantified in the results, so it is impossible to determine if females were definitely excluded at these sites. However, on 5 separate occasions we observed livestock feeding locations from sunrise to sunset and noted near total exclusion of hen-sub-adult flocks by adult gobblers at feed bunks (M. Zornes, Arizona Game and Fish Department, personal observations). Gobbler dominance and hen-subadult exclusion at feeding sites has also been observed during trapping operations in South Dakota (M. Rumble, USDA Forest Service, personal communication).

Increased gobbler harvest during our study may not totally explain the observed change in gender ratios. The dramatic decrease in the observed gobbler: hen ratio in 1999 followed only 2 years of male-only harvest. Harvest levels alone were likely not great enough to account for this entire change. Hoffman et al. (1993) suggested that males may be underrepresented in winter counts. It is possible some male flocks were using peripheral habitats and were missed during our January surveys during all years. We had no marked turkeys during this investigation; therefore, we could not evaluate this possibility. However, we do not believe this occurred because of winter weather conditions, limited habitat availability, and scarcity of alternative available food resources. If our surveys underrepresented males our results would have produced an even greater male bias. Ponderosa pine, juniper (*Juniperus* spp.), and other mast producing tree and shrub densities in this area are so low that it is unlikely sufficient mast could be obtained for turkeys to survive, regardless of variations in mast production or weather conditions.

Gender ratios garner a great deal of attention among ungulate managers (Connolly 1981, Taber et. al 1982, Timmerman and Buss 1997, O'Gara and Morrison 2004). However, little is reported concerning the effects unbalanced gender ratios may have on game bird populations. We contend male-biased ratios can have negative impact on small, isolated populations of turkeys during periods of severe weather, especially where habitat limitations exist. In similar circumstances, we believe season alterations and increased gobbler harvest can be used by managers to mitigate acceleration of flock decline and may improve flock persistence.

For us, this investigation produced more questions than answers. There is little in the literature to help managers in situations like we found ourselves, and it is our wish the wildlife research community investigate this phenomenon. Research concerning gender ratios and the affect male-biased ratios may have on flock productivity and persistence would be useful to those managing turkeys in similar habitats.

Proposed Season-Setting Criteria

We think altering season structure and increasing opportunity would be more effective if implemented before gobbler:hen ratios reach the levels seen in this project. Based on our field observations we also think it prudent for local managers to prevent excessive gobbler ratios so that hens and poults get some access to limited winter food resources. Based solely on our experience as managers, we suggest that at an observed ratio of 75 gobblers:100 hens season structure should be altered in order to increase gobbler mortality and provide additional hunter opportunity. We further suggest that gobbler:hen ratios should not be allowed to increase beyond 1:1.

ACKNOWLEDGMENTS

We wish to thank J. Gilbert for assistance with data collection. We would also like to thank all the landowners in southern Goshen County who tolerated our presence during this investigation. Thanks also to B. F. Wakeling and 3 anonymous reviewers for suggestions and contributions to this manuscript. This project was made possible through contributions from Federal Aid W-78-3.

LITERATURE CITED

Beasom, S. L., and D. Wilson. 1992. Rio Grande Turkey. Pages 306–330 in J. G. Dickson, editor. The wild turkey: biology and management. Stackpole Books, Harrisburg, Pennsylvania, USA.

Connolly, G. E. 1981. Assessing populations. Pages 287–345 in O. C. Wallmo, editor. Mule and black-tailed deer of North America. University of Nebraska Press, Lincoln, Nebraska, USA.

Crump, W. I., and H. B. Sanderson. 1951. Wild turkey trapping and transplanting. Wyoming Wildlife 15:4–11, 36–37.

Driese, K. L., B. Lanka, C. Lehman, and S. Vance. 2005. Mapping potential and occupied turkey habitat in Wyoming using geographic information systems. Wyoming Game and Fish Department, Cheyenne, Wyoming, USA.

———, W. A. Reiners, E. Merrill, and K. Gerow. 1997. A digital land cover map of Wyoming: a tool for vegetation analysis. Journal of Vegetation Science 8:133–146.

Healy, W. M. 1992. Population influences: environment. Pages 129–143 in J. G. Dickson, editor. The wild turkey: biology and management. Stackpole Books, Harrisburg, Pennsylvania, USA.

Hoffman, R. W., H. G. Shaw, M. A. Rumble, B. F. Wakeling, C. M. Mollohan, S. D. Schemnitz, R. Engle-Wilson, and D. A. Hengel. 1993. Management guidelines for Merriam's wild turkeys. Colorado Division of Wildlife Report 18.

Lehman, C. P. 2005. Ecology of Merriam's turkeys in the southern Black Hills, South Dakota. Dissertation, South Dakota State University, Brookings, South Dakota, USA.

O'Gara, B. W., and B. Morrison. 2004. Managing the harvest. Pages 675–704 in B. W. O'Gara and J. D. Yoakum, editors. Pronghorn ecology and management. University of Colorado Press, Boulder, Colorado, USA.

Porter, W. F., G. C. Nelson, and K. Mattson. 1983. Effects of winter conditions on reproduction in a northern wild turkey population. Journal of Wildlife Management 47(2):281–290.

Rumble, M. A., B. F. Wakeling, and L. D. Flake. 2003. Factors affecting survival and recruitment in female Merriam's turkeys. Intermountain Journal of Science 9:26–37.

Shaw, H. G., and C. M. Mollohan. 1992. Merriam's turkey. Pages 331–349 in J. G. Dickson, editor. The wild turkey: biology and management. Stackpole Books, Harrisburg, Pennsylvania, USA.

Suchy, W. J., W. R. Clark, and T. W. Little. 1983. Influences of simulated harvest on Iowa wild turkey populations. Proceedings of the Iowa Academy of Sciences 90:98–102.

Taber, R. D., K. Raedeke, and D. A. McCaughran. 1982. Population characteristics. Pages 279–298 in J. W. Thomas and D. E. Toweill, editors. Elk of North America: ecology and management. Stackpole Books, Harrisburg, Pennsylvania, USA.

Timmermann, H. R., and M. E. Buss. Population and harvest management. Pages 558–615 in A. W. Franzmann and C. C. Schwartz editors. Ecology and management of the North American moose. Smithsonian Institution Press, Washington, D.C., USA.

Vander Haegen, W. M., M. W. Sayre, and W. E. Dodge. 1989. Winter use of agricultural habitats by wild turkeys in Massachusetts. Journal of Wildlife Management 53:30–33.

Wakeling, B. F. 1991. Population and nesting characteristics of Merriam's turkey along the Mogollon Rim, Arizona. Arizona Game and Fish Department Technical Report 7.

———, and T. D. Rogers. 1998. Summer resource selection and yearlong survival of male Merriam's turkeys in north-central Arizona, with assorted implications for demographic modeling. Arizona Game and Fish Department Technical Report 28.

Weinstein, M., D. A. Miller, L. M. Connor, B. D. Leopold, and G. A. Hurst. 1996. What affects turkeys? A conceptual model for future research. Proceedings of the National Wild Turkey Symposium 7:135–142.

Wunz, G. A. 1992. Wild turkeys outside their historic range. Pages 361–384 in J. G. Dickson, editor. The wild turkey: biology and management. Stackpole Books, Harrisburg, Pennsylvania, USA.

Zornes, M. L. 2002. Southeast Wyoming wild turkey 2001. Pages 69–106 in Laramie Region Early and Late Migratory Birds, Small and Upland Game 2002 Job Completion Reports. Wyoming Game and Fish Department, Federal Aid in Wildlife Resoration Project W-78-3, Final Report.

Mark L. Zornes is the Small Game Biologist with the Arizona Game and Fish Department, and a former District Wildlife Biologist with the Wyoming Game and Fish Department from 1993–2002. He received a B.S. degree from Arkansas Tech University and a M.S. degree from New Mexico State University. His current professional interests and activities center around quail and blue grouse management and research in the Southwest.

Bob Lanka is the Wildlife Management Coordinator for the Laramie Region of the Wyoming Game and Fish Department, and is responsible for overseeing terrestrial game management in the southeastern part of the state. Prior to this position Bob was a WGFD district wildlife biologist in Lander, Newcastle and Cheyenne. He is currently Vice President of the Central Mountains and Plains Section of The Wildlife Society, and a former president of the Wyoming Chapter. Bob has been one of Wyoming's NWTF Technical Committee Representatives since 2002. Bob received a BS in both Wildlife Management and Range Management at Humboldt State University in 1982 and an MS in Zoology and Physiology at the University of Wyoming in 1985.

Wild Turkey Management:
Accomplishments, Strategies, and Opportunities
———— Grand Rapids, Michigan ————

GOBBLING OF MERRIAM'S TURKEYS IN RELATION TO NESTING AND OCCURRENCE OF HUNTING IN THE BLACK HILLS, SOUTH DAKOTA

Chad P. Lehman[1,2]
Department of Wildlife and Fisheries Sciences,
South Dakota State University,
Brookings, SD 57007-1696, USA

Lester D. Flake
Department of Wildlife and Fisheries Sciences,
South Dakota State University,
Brookings, SD 57007-1696, USA

Mark A. Rumble
USDA Forest Service,
Rocky Mountain Research Station,
1730 Samco Road,
Rapid City, SD 57702, USA

Dan J. Thompson
Department of Wildlife and Fisheries Sciences,
South Dakota State University,
Brookings, SD 57007-1696, USA

Abstract: Timing of wild turkey (*Meleagris gallopavo*) nesting and peaks in gobbling activity are often used in setting spring hunting season dates. The relationship between gobbling activity, hunting pressure, and nesting chronology has not been studied using hunted and nonhunted turkey populations. We tabulated gobbling activity of Merriam's turkeys (*M. g. merriami*) in Wind Cave National Park (nonhunted) and Black Hills National Forest (hunted) during spring turkey hunting seasons from 2003–2004. We also monitored female nesting activity ($n = 72$) in relation to gobbling activity. Peak incubation of nests occurred between 8 and 15 May. During the hunting period gobbling activity during early morning surveys was lower ($P = 0.001$) in the hunted population ($\bar{x} = 4.56$, SE $= 0.45$) than the nonhunted population ($\bar{x} = 7.01$, SE $= 0.52$). We observed 2 peaks in gobbling activity: one following winter break-up of flocks, and the other just before or during peak incubation. Gobbling activity was poorly predicted by measured weather and nesting chronology variables ($R^2 = 0.08$). South Dakota's spring hunting season encapsulates the second peak of gobbling activity, with most gobblers harvested (57%) during the prelaying period. Illegal harvest of females was minimal even though females were not generally nesting during peak harvest. Gobbling activity was reduced during the hunting season presumably by the negative association between gobbling and subsequent disturbance by hunters.

Proceedings of the National Wild Turkey Symposium 9:343–349

Key words: Black Hills, gobbling activity, hunting, *Meleagris gallopavo merriami*, Merriam's wild turkey, nest chronology.

Information on wild turkey nesting chronology and gobbling activity is important in setting spring gobbler hunting season dates (Healy and Powell 1999). Hunting seasons should be set to coincide with the median date of nest incubation and second gobbling

peak after most breeding has taken place (Healy and

---

[1] E-mail: Chad.Lehman@state.sd.us
[2] Present address: 13329 US HWY 16A, Custer, SD 57730, USA.

Powell 1999). This is assumed to allow hunters to cue on gobbling turkeys while protecting females from illegal or inadvertent harvest (Bevill 1975, Hoffmann 1990, Kienzler et al. 1996). Factors suggested to influence gobbling by male turkeys include weather, hunting pressure, and nesting chronology (Bevill 1975, Hoffmann 1990, Kurzejeski and Vangilder 1992, Kienzler et al. 1996, Miller et al. 1997*a*, Miller et al. 1997*b*). Some investigators have reported only 1 peak in gobbling activity (Kienzler et al. 1996, Miller et al. 1997*a*), while others have reported 2 peaks (Bevill 1975, Porter and Ludwig 1980, Hoffman 1990).

Information on nesting chronology and gobbling activity is available within the native range of the Merriam's turkey subspecies (Scott and Boeker 1972, Lockwood and Sutcliffe 1985, Hoffmann 1990). In some states, lack of quantitative data on Merriam's turkey nesting chronology and peak gobbling activity has resulted in setting season dates based on tradition rather than scientific evidence (Kennamer 1986, Hoffmann 1990). For example, gobbling and nesting chronology information has not been quantified for Merriam's turkeys in northern latitudes such as the Black Hills. Our objectives were to (1) quantify and compare gobbling activity between simultaneously hunted and nonhunted Merriam's turkey populations, (2) determine spring gobbling activity in association with nesting chronology in an introduced Merriam's turkey population considerably north of their native range, and (3) evaluate nesting chronology and weather variables as predictors of gobbling activity.

STUDY AREA

Our study area was located within the southern Black Hills of southwestern South Dakota (Johnson et al. 1995). The southern Black Hills has a continental climate with mean annual precipitation of 44.02 cm and mean annual temperature of 7.78°C (National Climatic Data Center 1971–2000). Elevations range from 930 to 1627 m above mean sea level. Woodland habitats were predominantly ponderosa pine (*Pinus ponderosa*) with an understory component composed primarily of western snowberry (*Symphoricarpos occidentalis*) and common juniper (*Juniperus communis*) (Hoffman and Alexander 1987). Dominant grasses on the study area included two exotic species, Kentucky bluegrass (*Poa pratensis*) and smooth brome (*Bromus inermis*), and native species such as little bluestem (*Schizachyrium scoparium*), needle and thread (*Stipa comata*), sideoats grama (*Bouteloua curtipendula*), western wheatgrass (*Pascopyrum smithii*), and blue grama (*Bouteloua gracilis*) (Johnson and Larson 1999).

METHODS

Capture and Monitoring

We captured Merriam's turkeys during winter using cannon nets (Dill and Thornsberry 1950, Austin et al. 1972), rocket nets (Thompson and Delong 1967, Wunz 1984), and drop nets (Glazener et al. 1964). We fitted captured turkeys with 98-g backpack-mounted radiotransmitters equipped with activity signals and a mercury switch mortality sensor set to activate after 8 hours of inactivity. We located radiomarked turkeys 6–7 days per week during spring (1 Apr–30 Jun) by triangulation and visual locations using hand-held yagi antennae.

Gobbling Activity

We followed sampling procedures outlined by previous investigators (e.g., Porter and Ludwig 1980, Kienzler et al. 1996, Healy and Powell 1999). We conducted counts of male calls, or gobbles, along 2 routes (one in the Black Hills National Forest that represented the hunted population and one in Wind Cave National Park that represented the nonhunted population) at least 2 days per week during 1 April–15 June. Each survey route (i.e., transect) included 13 listening stations at least 0.7 km apart, which were placed at the top of hills, mountains, or areas that maximized ability of researchers to count gobbles. Hunted and nonhunted stations were measured simultaneously by listening for gobbles at the same start times along transects. Gobbles per male or male group, herein referred to as gobbling activity, and number of males calling were estimated during a 4-minute period at each listening station. Transect days were the experimental units.

We did not conduct surveys on mornings with wind velocities ≥16 kmph or during rain or snow events as these conditions limit the ability to hear gobbles (Lint et al. 1995, Miller et al. 1997*a*). We monitored gobbling 40 minutes before sunrise to 65 minutes after sunrise. We alternated direction (i.e., starting point) of the route between days to negate any biases in gobbling activity associated with time of day. Additionally, we monitored a small sample (*n* = 8) of radiomarked males closely during spring to monitor movements near gobbling transects.

We partitioned gobbling activity post hoc into 3 periods based on nesting chronology for the hunted population (Black Hills National Forest Service stations): prelaying (1 April–day before initiation of first nest), laying–peak incubation (first day of nest initiation–median incubation date of first nests), and postpeak incubation (period following median incubation date of first nests–15 June). Gobbling data were collected in association to nesting chronology for 3 years on hunted transects (2001–2003).

We also partitioned gobbling activity into 3 periods post hoc based on the spring hunting season: prehunting (1 April–day before start of hunting season), hunting (first day of hunting season through last day), and posthunting (first day following end of hunting season–15 June). Gobbling data were simultaneously collected from hunted and non-hunted transects for 2 years (2003–2004).

Female Nesting Chronology

We monitored movements of radiomarked females closely during spring (1 Apr–30 Jun) to ascertain dates of nest initiation, initiation of incubation, and nest hatching. When it became apparent a nest was initiated, based on inactivity from the radiotransmitter or localized movements (Lehman 2005, Lehman et al. 2005), we attempted to locate nests using hand-held yagi antennae. If found, we marked the nest with flags on 4 sides at a distance of 10–40 m depending on density of vegetation, topography, and signal strength. We obtained 6–7 daily locations per week and recorded the Universal Transverse Mercator (UTM) coordinates of each nest.

Statistical Analysis

We used the Shapiro-Wilks statistic to test the assumption of normality, and the O'Brien statistic was used to test for equal variance. If assumption of normality was violated, we log-transformed the data (Steel et al. 1997). Before our analysis of gobbling activity data, we tested the hypothesis that number of males heard did not differ between hunted and non-hunted populations. We used two-factor analysis of variance (ANOVA) (PROC MEANS, PROC UNIVARIATE, SAS Institute 2000) to test the hypothesis that mean gobbling activity did not differ between hunted and non-hunted populations and among periods (prehunting, hunting, posthunting). Our main effects were hunted or non-hunted and hunting period. In the event of a significant main effect interaction, we compared gobbling activity between hunted and nonhunted populations within periods using paired t-tests (SAS Institute 2000). We used one-way ANOVA to test the hypothesis that mean gobbling activity did not differ among periods (main effect) based on nesting chronology for the hunted population. We used Tukey-Kramer HSD pairwise comparisons to test whether gobbling activity differed among periods.

We used mean number of days from 1 April to initiation of incubation for radiomarked females to evaluate timing of nesting among years. We used one-way ANOVA and Tukey-Kramer HSD pairwise comparisons to test the null hypothesis that timing of nesting did not differ among years. We set our initial significance level at $\alpha = 0.10$ and used Bonferroni corrections to control the Type I experimentwise error rate for multiple comparisons.

Factors Influencing Gobbling

We developed a model to predict gobbling activity using variables reported to influence gobbling in previous studies (Bevill 1975, Hoffmann 1990, Kurzejeski and Vangilder 1992, Kienzler et al. 1996, Miller et al. 1997b). We also included some additional variables (see below) that warranted evaluation. We used univariate tests (PROC UNIVARIATE, SAS Institute 2000) to determine if relationships existed between explanatory variables and gobbling activity. We considered variables with univariate tests $P < 0.30$ in forward stepwise regression (PROC REG, SAS Institute 2000) with $P = 0.15$ for variables to enter and $P = 0.20$ for variables to be removed. We evaluated residual plots for normality and tested for homogeneity of variance.

Explanatory variables we considered included: (1) number of days from 1 April to median nest incubation, (2) minimum morning temperature (°C) on date of gobbling activity count, (3) precipitation (cm) during the previous 24 hrs, and (4) change in barometric pressure the previous 16 hrs. We based median nest incubation dates on nesting data from radiomarked females. We used temperature and precipitation data collected at the field research station in Pringle, South Dakota, 2001–2004. We used barometric pressure data (mm Hg) that was collected with a micro-barograph at Jewel Cave National Park (United States Department of the Interior, Jewel Cave National Monument, Custer, South Dakota 2001–2004). The Pringle field research station was located in the center of the study area, and Jewel Cave National Park was located on the northern end of the study area.

RESULTS

Gobbling Activity

Gobbling Activity in Relation to Nesting Chronology

Gobbling activity did not differ among periods across years ($F \leq 2.30$, df = 2, $P \geq 0.12$), so we pooled annual data. Gobbling activity differed among periods ($F = 6.39$, df = 2, $P = 0.003$). Pairwise comparisons indicated that gobbling activity during post-peak incubation ($\bar{x} = 3.32$, SE = 0.42) was lower than prelaying ($\bar{x} = 5.19$, SE = 0.47) and laying-peak incubation ($\bar{x} = 5.08$, SE = 0.36) periods. Gobbling activity data were normally distributed and there was no indication of heterogeneous variance.

Two peaks of gobbling activity occurred in our study area (Figure 1). Typically, the primary gobbling activity peak occurred immediately following winter break-up of flocks in early to mid-April, and the secondary peak occurred when most females were laying or during the laying-peak incubation period (Figure 1).

Gobbling Activity and Occurrence of Hunting

Number of males heard differed ($F = 8.97$, df = 1, $P = 0.005$) between years for the nonhunted population and therefore we compared number of males heard between populations within each year. In 2003, number of males heard did not differ ($F = 1.18$, df = 1, $P = 0.28$) between hunted and nonhunted populations. In 2004, number of males heard did not differ ($F = 0.28$, df = 1, $P = 0.60$) between hunted and nonhunted populations.

Gobbling activity did not differ among periods across years ($F \leq 3.04$, df = 1, $P \geq 0.13$), so we pooled annual data. Two-factor analysis for gobbling activity indicated a significant population treatment by period interaction ($F = 2.58$, df = 2, $P = 0.08$). Therefore, gobbling activity was compared between hunted and nonhunted within each period. During the prehunting period, gobbling activity was similar (t-ratio = 0.26, df = 14, $P = 0.801$) between hunted ($\bar{x} = $

Nesting Chronology and Gobbling Activity
2001

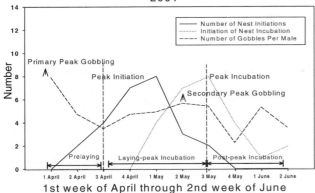

1st week of April through 2nd week of June

2002

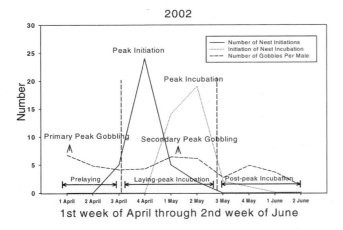

1st week of April through 2nd week of June

2003

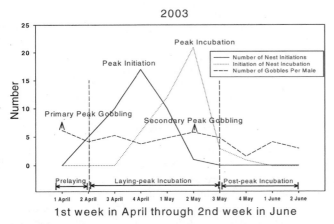

1st week in April through 2nd week in June

Fig. 1. Relationship of female nesting chronology and gobbling activity for a hunted population of Merriam's turkeys in the southern Black Hills, South Dakota, 2001–2003.

5.25, SE = 0.72) and nonhunted populations ($\bar{x}$ = 5.01, SE = 0.58) (Figure 2). During the hunting period, gobbling activity was lower (*t*-ratio = 3.55, df = 38, *P* = 0.001) for hunted turkeys ($\bar{x}$ = 4.56, SE = 0.45) compared to nonhunted turkeys ($\bar{x}$ = 7.01, SE = 0.52) (Figure 2). During the posthunting period, gobbling activity did not statistically differ (*t*-ratio = 1.43, df = 22, *P* = 0.17) between hunted turkeys ($\bar{x}$ = 2.88,

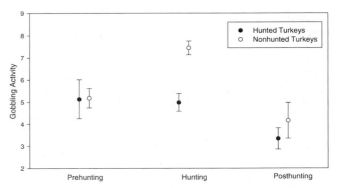

Fig. 2. Comparison of gobbling activity among prehunting, hunting, and posthunting time periods between hunted (Black Hills National Forest) and nonhunted (Wind Cave National Park) Merriam's turkeys in the southern Black Hills, South Dakota, 2003–2004.

SE = 0.48) and nonhunted turkeys ($\bar{x}$ = 4.02, SE = 0.64) (Figure 2). Gobbling activity data were normally distributed and there was no indication of heterogeneous variance.

Nesting Chronology

From 2001–2003, we captured, radiomarked, and collected nesting chronology data on 72 female Merriam's turkeys (67 adults and 5 juveniles). Nest initiation dates for first nests ranged from 11 April to 18 May. Median dates for nest initiation, incubation, and hatching for first nests were similar between years (Table 1). However, timing of nesting chronology through initiation of nest incubation differed among years (*F* = 5.37, df = 2, *P* = 0.006). Pairwise comparisons indicated that females initiated nests earlier in 2003 than in 2001 and initiation of incubation for 2002 did not differ from either 2001 or 2003. Nesting chronology data were normally distributed and there was no indication of heterogeneous variance.

Factors Influencing Gobbling

The best model contained 2 variables with number of days to median nest incubation date being entered first (*F* = 3.76, df = 1, *P* = 0.06) followed by minimum temperature second (*F* = 3.32, df = 1, *P* = 0.07). Change in barometric pressure and previous 24-hour precipitation were not entered into the model. Gobbling activity could not be modeled easily with the measured variables, and the 2-variable model accounted for less than 10% of the variance in gobbling (*R*²

Table 1. Nesting chronology of female Merriam's turkeys in the southern Black Hills, South Dakota, 2001–2003.

Year	N[a]	Days– inc[b]	SE	Median initiation date	Median incubation date	Median hatch date
2001	32	42.4	1.1	30 Apr	11 May	6 Jun
2002	36	39.1	0.8	27 Apr	9 May	5 Jun
2003	43	38.0	1.0	27 Apr	9 May	5 Jun

[a] Number of females radiomarked.

[b] Mean number of days from 1 Apr to incubation.

= 0.08). We did not have adequate information on hunter density to include in the model. Residuals from the model were normal and there was no indication of heterogeneous variance.

DISCUSSION

Kienzler et al. (1996) observed a decrease in gobbling activity once hunting season started, and their data suggested that hunting determined gobbling activity more than nesting status of females. Our results indicate that males in a nonhunted population gobble more during the hunting period than hunted males when measured simultaneously, supporting results of Kienzler et al. (1996). Gobbling activity was reduced during the hunting season presumably by the negative association between gobbling and subsequent disturbance of birds by hunters. Harvest data collected by South Dakota Department of Game, Fish, and Parks for 2002 and 2003 (Huxoll 2002, 2003) indicated about 22% of hunters harvested their birds on opening weekend. Also, harvest data indicated most harvest occurred during the prelaying period (57%). As the hunting season progresses, harvest decreases from the laying-peak incubation period (25%) to the post-peak incubation period (18%).

We observed 2 primary peaks of gobbling activity and the spring hunting season encapsulated the second peak. Similar to our findings, other studies have observed 2 peaks in gobbling activity concurrent with spring dispersal and peak initiation of incubation (Bevill 1975, Porter and Ludwig 1980, Hoffman 1990). Some studies observed only 1 peak in gobbling during the laying period or at peak incubation (Kienzler et al. 1996, Miller et al. 1997a). The first gobbling peak for males in the southern Black Hills occurred when radiomarked males and females were dispersing from wintering areas to breeding areas between late March and early April. This peak in gobbling may have been higher in late March as our data collection started 1 April. The second peak coincided with peak incubation or occurred the week before peak incubation. We found peak incubation in the southern Black Hills to be 8–10 days earlier than in Colorado as most females initiated incubation 8–15 May. In Colorado, the peak period for onset of incubation was 16–25 May (Hoffman 1990).

In our study, females had earlier initiation of incubation in 2003 than in 2001. Other studies have observed variation in nesting chronology among years (Vangilder et al. 1987, Hoffman 1990, Flake and Day 1996, Lehman et al. 2000). Nest initiation was the most influential variable in our model prediction of gobbling activity. However, very little of the variability in gobbling activity could be explained by our regression model. Patterns of gobbling activity indicated fluctuating gobbling activity throughout spring. We agree with Miller et al. (1997b) that gobbling activity appears to be influenced by a complex interaction of population and environmental conditions that may not be easily modeled. Factors that influence gobbling activity include break up of winter flocks, initiation of egg-laying, mating opportunities (Miller et al. 1997a), presence or absence of hens (Hoffman 1990), weather influences (Bevill 1973, Kienzler et al. 1996), hunting effects (Kienzler et al. 1996), and gobbler condition (Lint et al. 1995).

MANAGEMENT IMPLICATIONS

Two important goals of most wild turkey management plans are to maximize hunter opportunity for harvesting a gobbler during spring and to minimize the risk of females being illegally or accidentally harvested (Healy and Powell 1999). Gobbling is a behavioral cue that hunters use to locate turkeys during spring hunting. The current spring turkey hunting season in South Dakota encapsulates the second gobbling peak, which allows hunters to participate when males are gobbling at a higher level. Females are also nesting during the second gobbling peak and this may provide an excellent opportunity for hunters to call in and harvest males that are separated from females in early May. However, the current spring turkey hunting season in South Dakota opens the second Saturday in April, which usually occurs before most females have initiated nests. The highest proportion of harvest occurs during the prelaying period when males are courting females, and typically when Merriam's turkeys are found in large flocks. This may allow increased accidental female kill. However, illegal harvest of females during the spring turkey season accounted for only 1.9% of cause-specific mortality in the southern Black Hills (Lehman 2005). Miller et al. (1997a) suggested illegal kill was more a function of hunter density than timing of incubation. Illegal female kill in relation to hunting season dates should continue to be monitored as hunter densities increase in the Black Hills.

ACKNOWLEDGMENTS

We thank M. Rohfling, C. Sexton, C. Kassube, E. Maichak, and M. May for field support. The cooperating landowners N. Westphal, R. Miller, and D. Brown are greatly appreciated as they provided needed access to lands. Also, we thank Wind Cave National Park for providing access to lands. The USDA Forest Service, Rocky Mountain Research Station, provided field assistance and technical support. Funding for this research project was from the South Dakota Department of Game, Fish and Parks, Federal Aid to Wildlife Restoration Fund (Project W-75-R-132, No. 7599), National Wild Turkey Federation (National Super Fund), and the South Dakota State Chapter of the National Wild Turkey Federation (State Super Fund). Additional support was provided by South Dakota State University and McIntire-Stennis funding through the South Dakota Agricultural Experiment Station.

LITERATURE CITED

Austin, D. H., T. E. Peoples, and L. E. Williams, Jr. 1972. Procedures for capturing and handling live wild turkeys. Proceedings of the Annual Conference of the Southeastern Association of Game and Fish Commission 25:222–235.

Bevill, W. V., Jr. 1973. Some factors influencing gobbling activity among turkeys. Proceedings of the Southeastern Association of Game and Fish Commission 27:62–73.

———. 1975. Setting spring gobbler seasons by timing peak gobbling. Proceedings of the National Wild Turkey Symposium 3:198–204.

Dill, H. H., and W. H. Thornsberry. 1950. A cannon-projected net trap for capturing waterfowl. Journal of Wildlife Management 14:132–137.

Flake, L. D., and K. S. Day. 1996. Wild turkey reproduction in a prairie-woodland complex in South Dakota. Proceedings of the National Wild Turkey Symposium 7:153–164.

Glazener, W. C., A. S. Jackson, and M. L. Cox. 1964. The Texas drop-net turkey trap. Journal of Wildlife Management 28:280–287.

Healy, W. M., and S. M. Powell. 1999. Wild turkey harvest management: biology, strategies, and techniques. US Fish and Wildlife Biological Technical Publication BTP-R5001–1999.

Hoffman, G. R., and R. R. Alexander. 1987. Forest vegetation of the Black Hills National Forest of South Dakota and Wyoming: a habitat type classification. United States Department of Agriculture Forest Service, Research Paper RM-276.

Hoffman, R. W. 1990. Chronology of gobbling and nesting activities of Merriam's wild turkeys. Proceedings of the National Wild Turkey Symposium 6:25–31.

Huxoll, C. 2002. 2002 Annual Report. South Dakota Department of Game, Fish and Parks, Report 2003–01.

———. 2003. 2003 Annual Report. South Dakota Department of Game, Fish and Parks, Report 2004-01.

Johnson, J. R., and G. E. Larson. 1999. Grassland plants of South Dakota and the Northern Great Plains: a field guide with color photographs. South Dakota State University, Brookings, South Dakota, USA.

Johnson, R. R., K. F. Higgins, and D. E. Hubbard. 1995. Using soils to delineate South Dakota physiographic regions. Great Plains Research 5:309–322.

Kennamer, J. E., editor. 1986. Guide to the American wild turkey. National Wild Turkey Federation, Edgefield, South Carolina, USA.

Kienzler, J. M., T. W. Little, and W. A. Fuller. 1996. Effects of weather, incubation, and hunting on gobbling activity in wild turkeys. Proceedings of the National Wild Turkey Symposium 7:61–68.

Kurzejeski, E. W., and L. D. Vangilder. 1992. Population management. Pages 165–187 *in* J. G. Dickson, editor. The wild turkey, biology and management. Stackpole Books, Harrisburg, Pennsylvania, USA.

Lehman, C. P. 2005. Ecology of Merriam's turkeys in the southern Black Hills, South Dakota. Dissertation, South Dakota State University, Brookings, South Dakota, USA.

———, L. D. Flake, A. P. Leif, and R. D. Shields. 2000. Comparative survival and reproduction of sympatric eastern and Rio Grande wild turkey females in northeastern South Dakota. Proceedings of the National Wild Turkey Symposium 8:123–135.

———, ———, M. A. Rumble, R. D. Shields, and D. J. Thompson. 2005. Preincubation movements of female wild turkeys relative to nest initiation in South Dakota. Wildlife Society Bulletin 33(3):1062–1070.

Lint, J. R., B. D. Leopold, and G. A. Hurst. 1995. Comparison of abundance indexes and population size estimates for wild turkey gobblers. Wildlife Society Bulletin 23:164–168.

Lockwood, D. R., and D. H. Sutcliffe. 1985. Distribution, mortality, and reproduction of Merriam's turkey in New Mexico. Proceedings of the National Wild Turkey Symposium 5:309–316.

Miller D. A., G. A. Hurst, and B. D. Leopold. 1997*a*. Chronology of wild turkey nesting, gobbling, and hunting in Mississippi. Journal of Wildlife Management 61:840–845.

———, ———, and ———. 1997*b*. Factors affecting gobbling activity of wild turkeys in Central Mississippi. Proceedings of the Annual Conference of Southeastern Association of Fish and Wildlife Agencies 51:352–361.

National Climatic Data Center. 1971–2000. Climatological Data, South Dakota, Annual Summary. National Oceanic and Atmospheric Administration, Asheville, North Carolina, USA.

Porter, W. F., and J. R. Ludwig. 1980. Use of gobbling counts to monitor the distribution and abundance of wild turkeys. Proceedings of the National Wild Turkey Symposium 4:61–68.

SAS Institute. 2000. SAS/STAT user's guide. Version 6. SAS Institute, Cary, North Carolina, USA.

Scott, V. E., and E. L. Boeker. 1972. An evaluation of turkey call counts in Arizona. Journal of Wildlife Management 36:628–630.

Steel, R. G., J. H. Torrie, and D. A. Dickey. 1997. Principles and procedures of statistics a biometrical approach. Third Edition. McGraw-Hill Companies, New York, New York, USA.

Thompson, M. C., and R. L. Delong. 1967. The use of cannon and rocket projected nets for trapping shorebirds. Bird Banding 38:214–218.

Vangilder, L. D., E. W. Kurzejeski, V. L. Kimmel-Truitt, and J. B. Lewis. 1987. Reproductive parameters of wild turkey hens in northern Missouri. Journal of Wildlife Management 51:535–540.

Wunz, G. A. 1984. Rocket-net innovations for capturing wild turkeys and waterfowl. Pennsylvania Game Commission, Pittman-Robertson Federal Aid Progress Report, Project W-46-R-21. Harrisburg, Pennsylvania, USA.

Chad P. Lehman received a B.S. in Biological Science from the University of Minnesota-Duluth (1994) and M.S. in Wildlife Science from South Dakota State University (1998). He received a Ph.D. in Biological Science from South Dakota State University (2005) and his research focused on Merriam's turkey ecology, particularly the influence of weather and habitat selection/availability on survival and reproduction. As a wildlife biologist for Custer State Park, Chad conducts research and manages habitats for game and nongame wildlife species. For hobbies, Chad enjoys hiking with his wife Michelle and son Drew, and hunting birds with his yellow Labrador Retrievers.

Mark A. Rumble received a B.S. in wildlife biology from Washington State University, an M.S. in Wildlife Science from South Dakota State University, and a Ph.D. in Zoology from the University of Wyoming. Mark has worked for the U.S. Forest Service for 27 years, and 26 years for the Rocky Mountain Research Station in Rapid City, South Dakota. His professional interest includes understanding the effects of land management on wildlife habitat with an emphasis on developing information in formats that are usable by forest and range managers.

Leš Flake retired from South Dakota State University in August of 2002 after 31 years on the faculty and was appointed Distinguished Professor Emeritus. He is still advising graduate students and remains involved with several projects in South Dakota. In his free time Les enjoys visiting grandchildren, hiking in the mountains of Utah, reading, fly fishing, bow hunting, and chasing pheasants with old friends in South Dakota. Les has a Ph.D. in Zoology from Washington State University (1971) and an M.S. in Zoology from Brigham Young University (1966).

Dan Thompson received his M.S. in Wildlife Science in 2003 and is currently pursuing a Ph.D. at South Dakota State University. He has worked on various projects addressing wild turkey population dynamics. His research interests include large carnivore ecology and expansion, along with carnivore/human/prey interactions.

Wild Turkey Management:
Accomplishments, Strategies, and Opportunities
———— Grand Rapids, Michigan ————

A RANGE-WIDE META-ANALYSIS OF WILD TURKEY NESTING PHENOLOGY AND SPRING SEASON OPENING DATES

Darroch M. Whitaker[1,2]
Department of Fisheries and Wildlife Sciences,
Virginia Tech, Blacksburg, VA 24061, USA

James C. Pack
West Virginia Division of Natural Resources,
Wildlife Resources Section, P.O. Box 67,
Elkins, WV 26241, USA

Gary W. Norman
Virginia Department of Game and Inland Fisheries,
P.O. Box 996, Verona, VA 24482, USA

Dean F. Stauffer
Department of Fisheries and Wildlife Sciences,
Virginia Tech, Blacksburg, VA 24061, USA

Scott D. Klopfer
Conservation Management Institute, Virginia Tech,
1900 Kraft Drive, Suite 250, Blacksburg, VA 24061, USA

Abstract: Timing of nesting is an important consideration when setting opening dates for spring male-only wild turkey (*Meleagris gallopavo*) hunts. We conducted a meta-analysis in which we used mean dates of incubation initiation from 58 studies to evaluate *a priori* models hypothesized to predict turkey nesting phenology across the species' range. Models were based on geographic setting, climate, and management activities, and had weak to moderate explanatory power (Range R^2_{adj} = 0.12–0.55). We developed 2 *post hoc* models to better predict mean incubation date, and used one of these to generate a range-wide map predicting timing of nest incubation. A second model selection exercise focused solely on the eastern subspecies of wild turkey, and our best model of incubation date included population status and a cubic term for latitude (n = 41, R^2_{adj} = 0.80). Lastly, we compared incubation initiation dates to opening dates for spring male-only hunting in each jurisdiction. Of 34 states and provinces for which we obtained data, 25 opened spring hunting >2 weeks prior to the mean date of incubation initiation, and 18 of these also allowed fall either-sex hunting. This finding is noteworthy because extended fall seasons and spring hunting during the pre-nesting period can lead to additive and unsustainable levels of female kill.

Proceedings of the National Wild Turkey Symposium 9:351–360

Key words: breeding phenology, incubation initiation, *Meleagris gallopavo*, meta-analysis, nesting, range-wide, spring hunting, wild turkey.

Research has indicated that opening spring male-only wild turkey hunting before most females have begun nesting can lead to high rates of illegal female kill, potentially reducing poult recruitment and depressing populations (e.g., Kimmel and Kurzejeski 1985, Vangilder and Kurzejeski 1995, Norman et al. 2001*b*). Further, some researchers report that males gobble more or are more susceptible to calling after females have begun nesting (Bevill 1974, Hoffman 1990, Miller et al.

1997*a*). These facts suggest that opening dates for spring gobbler seasons should coincide with the initiation of incubation by females (Healy and Powell 2000). However, managers often are pressured to set early opening dates for seasons, as many hunters believe that male tur-

[1] Present address: Biology Department, Acadia University, Wolfville, NS, Canada, B4P 2R6.
[2] E-mail: darroch.whitaker@acadiau.ca

keys call and display more aggressively early in the breeding season and thus may be more responsive to calling. Consequently, accurate knowledge of nesting and gobbling phenology is important for managers setting opening dates for spring gobbler hunting, as opening seasons too early can have negative consequences for turkey populations, while opening seasons too late may lead to reduced hunt quality and dissatisfaction among hunters.

Researchers have studied timing of breeding by wild turkeys at numerous localities across their range, and several authors have investigated factors leading to variation in nesting phenology between years (e.g., Porter et al. 1983, Vangilder and Kurzejeski 1995, Miller et al. 1998, Norman et al. 2001*a*). However, there has been no effort to quantitatively describe or predict spatial patterns in the timing of breeding by wild turkeys across their range. Perhaps the simplest model to predict breeding phenology would be latitude alone. Expanding on this, Hopkins' law of bioclimatics predicts spring phenology based on latitude, longitude, and elevation, and may be a more useful geographic predictor (Hopkins 1938, McCombs 1997, McCombs et al. 1997). Alternatively, factors relating to the progression of seasonal change, particularly those relating to climate or the phenology of development of plant and animal foods, might also serve as good predictors of timing of breeding. Finally, inclusion of biological or management information on the turkey population may also improve models.

Here we present a meta-analysis to improve our understanding of range-wide patterns in the timing of nesting by wild turkeys. We used existing field studies to obtain estimates of the mean date of Initiation of Nest Incubation (INI) at numerous locations across North America, and evaluated factors such as climate and geographic setting as predictors of nesting phenology. We also used our database to evaluate the extent to which states and provinces had timed the opening of spring seasons to coincide with the onset of nesting and thereby reduce exposure of non-incubating hens to risk of illegal kill.

METHODS

We compiled a comprehensive database on wild turkey breeding phenology from published studies, Federal Aid in Wildlife Restoration (Pittman-Robertson) reports, state and federal reports, and through a request to turkey biologists for unpublished data. We then searched each study for an estimate of the interannual mean date of incubation initiation by female turkeys or for raw data sufficient to calculate one. We attempted to standardize the data extracted from each report to the maximum extent possible. We converted calendar dates to the Day of the Year (DoY), calculated as the cumulative number of days since January 1, thereby quantifying breeding phenology on a continuous and standardized numeric scale. We took into account the extra day in February during leap years. Interannual means were calculated as the average of

annual means, rather than the average of individual nesting dates. We considered only incubation initiation dates for first nests (vs. renests), and discarded a study if we were unable to obtain a mean date estimated solely from first nest attempts. If authors reported hatching dates we back-calculated the incubation initiation date by assuming a 28-day incubation period (Eaton 1992). If the date of initiation of egg-laying was reported, we added 1 day for each egg plus 2 additional days, the typical interval between the initiation of laying and incubation (Schorger 1966, Eaton 1992).

In some cases, authors reported median incubation initiation dates, but did not report means or provide the raw data necessary to calculate means. We expected that median incubation initiation dates typically would occur earlier than mean incubation dates, as the distribution of nest initiation dates is often slightly right-skewed for wild turkeys (e.g., Roberts 1993, Kienzler et al. 1995; D. H. Jackson, W. H. Bunger, and T. W. Little, Iowa Department of Natural Resources, unpublished report). To evaluate the necessity of a correction factor to estimate mean nesting dates from median dates, we carried out a Wilcoxon signed rank test (Sokal and Rohlf 1995) of the difference between pairs of mean and median incubation initiation dates from studies for which both parameter estimates were reported or could be calculated. Then, in the event that the difference between mean and median incubation initiation dates differed from zero, we would use the median value of the within-study differences as a correction factor to estimate mean incubation initiation dates for studies reporting only median nesting dates.

We appended a number of covariates to each mean incubation initiation date (Table 1). We recorded whether the research was conducted on an established population or newly-translocated individuals (Status). We recorded the location of each study area in latitude and longitude coordinates (decimal degrees). We estimated elevation for each study as the midpoint between the highest and lowest points on the study area. A Relative Phenologic Index (RPI), which predicts the net delay in spring phenology for a site, was calculated for each study site based on its latitude, longitude, and elevation (Hopkins 1938, McCombs 1997, McCombs et al. 1997). For this we used a reference point at sea level, south of the southernmost study site, and west of the westernmost site (26°00′N, 123°00′W, elevation = 0 m). The RPI for each study site relative to this reference point was calculated by assuming a 4-day delay in growing season phenology for each 1° increase in latitude northwards, each 5° increase in longitude eastwards, and each 122 m increase in elevation (Hopkins 1938). For each study area we obtained 30-year averages (1971–2000) of 3 climatic variables: mean annual snowfall (cm), median date of the last spring frost (DoY date), and median length of the annual frost-free period (Environment Canada 2002, National Oceanic and Atmospheric Administration 2004). In most cases we took values for climate normals from the nearest weather station (within <0.25° latitude and longitude); when multiple stations were approximately

Table 1. List of variables included in models to explain variation in the timing of the mean date of Initiation of Nest Incubation (INI) by wild turkeys.

Variable	Description	Units
Elev	Elevation midpoint of the study area	m
Frostfree	Median annual period between the last spring frost and first fall frost	Days
Hunt	Whether or not the population was open to spring gobbler hunting	Y or N
INI	Mean date of Initiation of Nest Incubation at a location (response variable)	Day of Year
LastFrost	Median date of the last frost each spring	Day of Year
Lat	Latitude of the study area	Decimal Degrees
Long	Longitude of the study area[a]	Decimal Degrees
RPI	Relative Phenologic Index, predicting phenologic delay based on Hopkin's (1938) Bioclimatic Law (reference point = 26.00°N, 123.00°W, elevation = 0 m)	Days
Status	Whether the population was established (E) or represented first-year translocated birds (NT)	E or NT
Snowfall	Mean annual snowfall at a given location	cm

[a] Though sometimes designated as a negative value for locations in the western hemisphere (i.e., west of the Greenwich prime meridian, longitude 0°), for our analyses longitude was always specified as a positive value.

equidistant or were located within a study area values of climate normals were averaged.

We developed a series of *a priori* linear models to explain variability in the timing of incubation initiation across the range of wild turkeys. We did not include geographic variables in models specifying climatic variables; climate is strongly influenced by location and so inclusion of both would likely lead to overfitting or multicolinearity. The response variable was incubation initiation date (INI), and we fit models using JMP statistical software (Version 4.0.4; SAS Institute, Cary, North Carolina, USA). To assess model fit we inspected a residual plot and carried out a goodness-of-fit test on our most complex model (Burnham and Anderson 2002). Models were then evaluated and ranked using information-theoretic model selection techniques (Burnham and Anderson 2002). This approach favors models having greater explanatory power and penalizes models based on complexity, helping to identify the most parsimonious model(s). For reference and to gain an appreciation of the explanatory power of our models, we included a null model (i.e., intercept only) in the set of candidate models. Models within the set were evaluated based on Akaike's Information Criterion adjusted for small sample size (AIC_c), AIC_c differences (Δ_i), explanatory power (R^2_{adj}), and Akaike weights (ω_i). We ordered models from largest to smallest ω_i, and then to identify a 95% confidence set of best models sequentially summed ω_i until $\Sigma \omega_i \geq 0.95$.

We applied our best model to a Digital Elevation Map (DEM) encompassing the contemporary range of wild turkeys to create a map of predicted mean incubation initiation dates. The DEM base map was obtained from the USGS global digital elevation database (GTOPO30; USGS EROS Datacenter, Sioux Falls, Missouri, USA), which has a resolution of 30 arc-seconds (approx. 1 km). The range of wild turkeys is highly fragmented, particularly in western North America, but is expanding rapidly. Consequently, we did not restrict model application to the extant species range, but rather applied it across all of southern Canada, the contiguous United States, and northern Mexico. To illustrate any spatial patterns of systematic error we plotted residual errors for each observation on the map.

Of the 5 subspecies, eastern wild turkeys (*M. g. silvestris*) occupy the largest and most contiguous range, and have been most frequently studied. We carried out a second model selection exercise, similar to that described above, but in this case restricted our dataset to eastern wild turkeys. As above, a set of *a priori* models were developed based on factors we suspected might be important within the range of this subspecies, and mean incubation initiation date was the response variable. Data were insufficient to model other subspecies individually.

To assess the extent to which opening dates for spring gobbler hunting seasons are synchronized with initiation of nesting we compared mean incubation initiation dates to spring 2004 opening dates for hunting in each state or province. In cases where we obtained >1 estimated incubation initiation date for a jurisdiction we took the average of the differences between the incubation initiation dates and the opening date of hunting. We accounted for the fact that 2004 was a leap year in our calculations, and considered the location of study sites for states having different opening dates in different management regions.

RESULTS

Our final dataset comprised interannual mean incubation initiation dates from 58 locations in 33 states plus Ontario (Figure 1). We were able to obtain estimates of both mean and median incubation initiation dates from 18 studies. Median incubation initiation dates occurred 1.5 days earlier than mean incubation initiation dates ($P = 0.033$), and we used this difference as a correction factor for 10 studies reporting only median nesting dates. Studies included all 5 subspecies of wild turkey, and mean incubation initiation dates ranged from 14 April in coastal Georgia to 7 June for newly translocated turkeys in central Ontario (DoY 104–158; mean = DoY 129 [9 May]). Elevation midpoints of study sites ranged from 4–2,630 m. The 7 sites having elevations >1,200 m were located in the western United States (AZ, CO, NM, OR, SD, WY), while sites below 120 m elevation were concentrated in the Southeast (FL, GA, MS, NC, SC, TX, VA).

All of our *a priori* models had some ability to

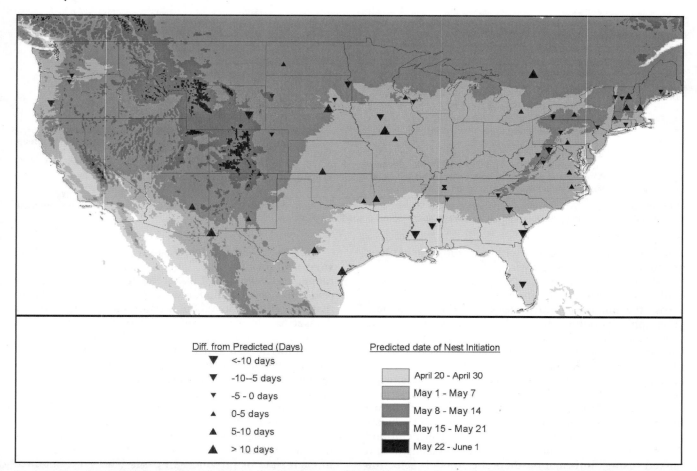

Fig. 1. Predicted Initiation of Nest Incubation (INI) dates for established wild turkey populations, developed by applying the model 16 (Table 3) to a Digital Elevation Model (DEM) of North America. Triangles represent the locations of studies used in our meta-analysis; negative Differences from Predicted (i.e., residual errors) indicate that the actual INI date at that location was earlier than predicted.

predict mean incubation initiation date across the range of wild turkeys, and all models in the 95% confidence set (models 1–5) accounted for >50% of variation in INI date (Table 2). Latitude, longitude, and elevation, and interactions between latitude and both longitude and elevation all appeared to be important predictors of mean incubation initiation date. Population status (established or newly translocated) was an important predictor of incubation initiation date, with newly translocated turkeys typically nesting 10–15 days later than established populations. Presence or absence of spring hunting appeared to explain some variability in mean incubation initiation date, though most studies of nonhunted populations were of recently translocated birds. Climatic variables we tested accounted for up to 25% of the variation in mean incubation initiation date. Our model specifying the Hopkins RPI index (model 8) also had some explanatory power (R^2_{adj} = 0.26). However, the coefficient for RPI indicated that it provided a >5-fold overestimate of phenologic delays for wild turkeys (β_{RPI} = 0.18 ± 0.040).

Based on results from our *a priori* model fitting and selection, we developed 2 *post hoc* models combining explanatory power, ecological insight, and parsimony (models 16 and 17; Table 3). Both models in-

cluded population status, and the model including latitude, longitude, and elevation accounted for approximately half of the variation in mean incubation initiation date (model 16; R^2_{adj} = 0.49). We applied this model to a DEM of North America to create a map predicting the timing of mean incubation initiation for established populations across the range of wild turkeys (Figure 1). The second *post hoc* model (model 17) included median date of the last spring frost and population status, and was able to account for much of the variation in mean incubation initiation date (R^2_{adj} = 0.47).

Our database included estimated incubation initiation dates for 41 populations of eastern wild turkeys. Model selection indicated that, after controlling for population status, a cubic polynomial term for latitude was the best predictor of the timing of incubation initiation for eastern wild turkeys (Table 4; Figure 2). Length of the frost-free period and date of the last spring frost also were good predictors of incubation initiation date (Table 4).

Comparing nesting dates to 2004 spring gobbler season opening dates indicated that of 34 states and provinces for which we obtained data, all but one (CT) opened their hunting season earlier than the mean in-

Table 2. Fit of *a priori* models conceived to explain range-wide variation in the timing of Initiation of Nest Incubation (INI) by wild turkeys (*n* = 58).

No.	Model (*a priori*)	SSE	*K*	AIC_c	Δ_i	R^2	R^2_{adj}	ω_i
1	INI = 58.0 + 1.12(*Lat*) + 0.30(*Long*) − [0.090(*Lat* − 39.02) × (*Long* − 88.80)] + ϵ	2229.9	5	222.8	0.0	0.55	0.52	0.41
2	INI = 69.73 + 0.97(*Lat*) + 0.24(*Long*) − 0.00059(*Elev*) − [0.065(*Lat* − 39.02) × (*Long* − 88.80)] − [0.00080(*Lat* − 39.02) × (*Elev* − 572.38)] + ϵ	2052.9	7	223.1	0.3	0.59	0.55	0.35
3	INI = 59.78 + 1.11(*Lat*) + 0.28(*Long*) + 0.00060(*Elev*) − [0.088(*Lat* − 39.02) × (*Long* − 88.80)] + ϵ	2225.5	6	225.2	2.4	0.55	0.52	0.12
4	INI = 108.11 + 0.59(*Lat*) + 0.0058(*Elev*) + {*Status*: [NT or E] ± 7.57} + ϵ^a	2393.1	5	226.9	4.1	0.52	0.49	0.05
5	INI = 58.47 + 1.22(*Lat*) + 0.25(*Long*) + 0.00079(*Elev*) − [0.076(*Lat* − 39.02) × (*Long* − 88.80)] − [0.00022(*Lat* − 39.02) × (*Elev* − 572.38)] − [0.00014(*Long* − 88.80) × (*Elev* − 572.38)] − [0.000042(*Lat* − 39.02) × (*Long* − 88.80) × (*Elev* − 572.38)] + ϵ	1996.5	9	227.0	4.2	0.60	0.54	0.05
6	INI = 101.40 + 0.68(*Lat*) + 0.0011(*Elev*) − [0.0015(*Lat* − 39.02) × (*Elev* − 572.38)] + ϵ	2533.3	5	230.2	7.4	0.49	0.46	0.01
7	INI = 94.57 + 0.84(*Lat*) + 0.0051(*Elev*) + {*Hunt*: [N or Y] ± 3.18} + ϵ^b	3101.3	5	241.9	19.1	0.37	0.34	0.00
8	INI = 110.77 + 0.18(*RPI*) + ϵ	3622.3	3	246.2	23.4	0.27	0.26	0.00
9	INI = 93.98 + 0.82(*Lat*) + 0.0046(*Elev*) + ϵ	3523.9	4	247.0	24.2	0.29	0.26	0.00
10	INI = 144.51 − 0.095(*Frostfree*) + ϵ	3704.5	3	247.5	24.7	0.25	0.24	0.00
11	INI = 108.89 + 0.17(*LastFrost*) + ϵ	3709.0	3	247.6	24.8	0.25	0.24	0.00
12	INI = 96.78 + 0.81(*Lat*) − 0.032(*Long*) + 0.0050(*Elev*) + ϵ	3516.3	5	249.2	26.4	0.29	0.25	0.00
13	INI = 96.29 + 0.82(*Lat*) + ϵ	3962.2	3	251.4	28.6	0.20	0.19	0.00
14	INI = 124.84 + 0.044(*Snowfall*) + ϵ	4279.9	3	255.9	33.1	0.14	0.12	0.00
15	INI = 128.46 + ϵ (null model)	4946.4	2	262.1	39.3	0.00	0.00	0.00

[a] *Status* is a categorical variable: If *Status* = NT, then add 7.57 days. If status = E, then subtract 7.57 days.
[b] *Hunt* is a categorical variable: If *Hunt* = N, then add 3.18 days. If Hunt = Y, then subtract 3.18 days.

cubation initiation date (Table 5). Four northeastern states opened seasons during the week preceding the mean incubation initiation date (ME, NY, PA, and VT), and another 4 states (MA, NH, WI, and WV) opened seasons 8–14 days prior to the INI date. On average, the remaining 25 jurisdictions (74%) opened hunting 28 days prior to the mean incubation initiation date, with 3 opening hunting ≥40 days prior (FL, SC, and TX).

DISCUSSION

Through our review of existing field studies, we were able to construct a database of estimates of the timing of nesting by wild turkeys across most of the species' range. Using this, we identified geographic and climatic factors that related to regional variability in turkey nesting phenology. Managers may find the associated models and figures useful when making decisions regarding opening dates for spring hunting seasons. If the figures are deemed too general, readers can use the formulae and estimates presented in Tables 3–5

to obtain more precise estimates for a locality (see Table 1 for details on measurement units).

Our best models accounted for 50–80% of the variation in timing of incubation by wild turkeys (Tables 2–4). We presume that there were other important drivers of nesting phenology that we could not test, such as vegetation cover (e.g., Lazarus and Porter 1985, Day et al. 1991, Vander Hagen et al. 1991). Another potentially important factor is the effect of hunting on timing of nesting. However, because very few studies we reviewed were of unhunted wild turkey populations, our test of this relationship was inconclusive. We also expect that some portion of the residual error in our models resulted from inaccuracy in estimation of mean incubation initiation dates during field studies. Though we made every effort to standardize the data extracted, studies we reviewed used a variety of methods to measure reproductive phenology. Further, 60% of the estimates we obtained were derived from ≤3 years monitoring, and many studies were based on small numbers of individual turkeys in any one year. Since reproductive phenology is highly variable across

Table 3. *Post hoc* models explaining range-wide variation in the timing of Initiation of Nest Incubation (INI) by wild turkeys (*n* = 58). Values for AIC differences (Δ_i) were calculated based on the best model in the *a priori* set (Table 2).

No.	Model (*post hoc*)	SSE	*K*	AIC_c	Δ_i	R^2	R^2_{adj}
16	INI = 116.53 + 0.57(*Lat*) − 0.091(*Long*) + 0.0070(*Elev*) + {*Status*: [NT or E] ± 7.83} + $\epsilon^{a,b}$	2332.6	6	227.9	5.1	0.53	0.49
17	INI = 115.90 + 0.16(*LastFrost*) + {*Status*: [NT or E] ± 7.46} + ϵ^a	2515.6	4	227.4	4.6	0.49	0.47

[a] *Status* is a categorical variable: If *Status* = NT, then add the indicated number of days. If status = E, then subtract the indicated number of days.
[b] See also Figure 1.

Table 4. Fit of *a priori* models explaining variation in the timing of Initiation of Nest Incubation (INI) by the eastern subspecies of wild turkeys ($n = 41$).

No.	Model (*a priori*)	SSE	K	AIC$_c$	Δ_i	R^2	R^2_{adj}	ω_i
18	INI = 126.88 + 0.15(*Lat*) + 0.0044(*Lat* − 39.27)² + 0.036(*Lat* − 39.27)³ + {*Status*: [NT or E] ± 5.56} + ε[a,b]	665.7	6	128.7	0.0	0.82	0.80	0.81
19	INI = 159.18 − 0.15(*Frostfree*) + {*Status*: [NT or E] ± 7.80} + ε[a]	858.4	4	133.8	5.1	0.76	0.75	0.06
20	INI = 101.11 + 0.28(*LastFrost*) + {*Status*: [NT or E] ± 7.88} + ε[a]	871.7	4	134.4	5.7	0.76	0.75	0.05
21	INI = 92.49 + 1.04(*Lat*) − 0.0022(*Elev*) − [0.0025(*Lat* − 39.27) × (*Elev* − 351.79)] + {*Status*: [NT or E] ± 6.28} + ε[a]	766.5	6	134.5	5.8	0.79	0.76	0.05
22	INI = 80.35 + 1.32(*Lat*) + {*Status*: [NT or E] ± 6.10} + ε[a]	925.9	4	136.9	8.2	0.74	0.73	0.01
23	INI = 81.13 + 1.14(*Lat*) + 0.11(*Long*) − 0.0054(*Elev*) − [0.036(*Lat* − 39.27) × (*Long* − 82.27)] − [0.0030(*Lat* − 39.27) × (*Elev* − 351.79)] − [0.00034(*Long* − 82.27) × (*Elev* − 351.79)] − [0.000040(*Lat* − 39.27) × (*Long* − 82.27) × (*Elev* − 351.79)] + {*Status*: [NT or E] ± 6.66} + ε[a]	614.4	10	138.3	9.6	0.83	0.79	0.01
24	INI = 80.97 + 1.28(*Lat*) + 0.0023(*Elev*) + {*Status*: [NT or E] ± 6.23} + ε[a]	912.3	5	138.9	10.2	0.75	0.73	0.01
25	INI = 86.43 + 1.10(*Lat*) + 0.042(*Long*) − 0.0017(*Elev*) − [0.015(*Lat* − 39.27) × (*Long* − 82.27)] − [0.0024(*Lat* − 39.27) × (*Elev* − 351.79)] + {*Status*: [NT or E] ± 6.33} + ε[a]	759.8	8	140.2	11.5	0.79	0.75	0.00
26	INI = 111.99 + 0.22(*RPI*) + {*Status*: [NT or E] ± 7.94} + ε[a]	1020.5	4	140.9	12.2	0.72	0.70	0.00
27	INI = 82.24 + 1.27(*Lat*) − 0.010(*Long*) + 0.0023(*Elev*) + {*Status*: [NT or E] ± 6.30} + ε[a]	912.1	6	141.7	13.0	0.75	0.72	0.00
28	INI = 129.39 + 0.048(*Snowfall*) + {*Status*: [NT or E] ± 8.33} + ε[a]	1381.1	4	153.3	24.6	0.62	0.60	0.00
29	INI = 63.0 + 1.65(*Lat*) + ε	1608.8	3	157.1	28.4	0.55	0.54	0.00
30	INI = 63.01 + 1.65(*Lat*) − 0.00017(*Elev*) + ε	1608.7	4	159.6	30.9	0.55	0.53	0.00
31	INI = 127.78 + ε (null model)	3601.9	2	187.8	59.1	0.00	0.00	0.00

[a] *Status* is a categorical variable: If *Status* = NT, then add the indicated number of days. If status = E, then subtract the indicated number of days.
[b] See also Figure 2.

individuals and between years (see below), long-term monitoring and large samples are required to obtain a reliable estimate of the interannual mean incubation initiation date.

Inclusion of interaction terms between latitude and longitude and latitude and elevation yielded models that more fully accounted for variation in mean INI date (Table 2; models 1, 2, 3, 5, and 6). However, elevation of study sites increased from east to west, leading to a poor ability to discriminate statistically

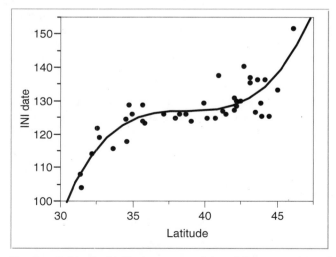

Fig. 2. Cubic fit of latitude as a predictor of the mean date of incubation initiation for established populations of eastern wild turkeys (see Table 4, model 18).

between effects of elevation and longitude, likely accounting for the observed interaction between latitude and longitude. The interaction between latitude and elevation, which suggests turkeys nest later as elevation increases in the South, but earlier at higher elevations in the North, is counterintuitive. It may be that, due to severity of conditions at higher elevations, turkeys on northern sites made greater use of lowlands and riparian areas (e.g, Schmutz and Braun 1989). If this was the case, our method of estimating study area elevations as the midpoint between the highest and lowest points would overestimate the mean elevation at which turkeys occurred on northern sites. Consequently, we suspect that these interactions were spurious and chose to base our *post hoc* model relating INI date to geographic setting (model 16; Figure 1) or the first order model (model 12).

Our map of nesting dates (Figure 1) should have value as a predictor of nesting phenology, though 2 caveats are necessary. Accuracy of estimated incubation initiation dates can be gauged for localities proximate to the study sites used to develop the model, but many areas are distant from any of these study sites. Greater uncertainty must be associated with these unverified estimates. Also, examination of the map reveals some pattern in the spatial distribution of errors, in that the model generally predicted early in the Southwest and late in the Southeast. We urge that individuals using this map pay attention to patterns in the surrounding residual errors when estimating nesting dates.

Table 5. Mean date of initiation of nest incubation, opening dates for 2004 spring gobbler season, and information on fall turkey hunting for each of 34 jurisdictions for which we obtained nesting data.

State or province	n[a]	Mean INI date (DoY)[b]	Spring opening date (DoY)[c]	Difference (days)	Fall hunting[d]
Alabama	1	4/28 (118)	4/1 (92)	26	MO
Arizona	1	5/19 (139)	4/23 (114)	25	ES
Arkansas	1	5/7 (127)	4/3 (94)	33	MO
Colorado	2	5/12 (132)	4/10 (101)	31	ES
Connecticut	1	5/6 (126)	5/5 (126)	0	ES
Florida	1	4/19 (109)	3/6 (66)	43	MO
Georgia	2	4/20 (110)	3/20 (80)	30	NFH
Iowa	2	5/10 (130)	4/12 (103)	27	ES
Kansas	1	5/10 (130)	4/14 (105)	25	ES
Maine	1	5/6 (126)	5/3 (124)	2	ES
Massachusetts	1	5/10 (130)	4/26 (117)	13	ES
Minnesota	1	5/8 (128)	4/14 (105)	23	ES
Mississippi	3	4/24 (114)	3/20 (80)	34	ES
Missouri	1	5/5 (125)	4/19 (110)	15	ES
New Hampshire	3	5/16 (136)	5/3 (124)	12	ES
New Jersey	1	5/7 (127)	4/19 (110)	17	ES
New Mexico	2	5/22 (142)	4/15 (106)	36	ES
New York	3	5/9 (129)	5/1 (122)	7	ES
North Carolina	2	5/5 (125)	4/10 (101)	24	NFH
North Dakota	1	5/15 (135)	4/10 (101)	34	ES
Oklahoma	1	5/5 (125)	4/6 (97)	28	ES
Ontario	2	5/17 (137)	4/25 (116)	21	NFH
Oregon	2	5/2 (122)	4/15 (106)	16	ES
Pennsylvania	2	5/7 (127)	5/1 (122)	5	ES
South Carolina	1	5/2 (122)	3/15 (75)	47	NFH
South Dakota	4	5/11 (131)	4/10 (101)	30	ES
Tennessee	2	5/2 (122)	4/3 (94)	28	ES
Texas	2	5/9 (129)	3/27 (87)	42	ES
Vermont	2	5/8 (128)	5/1 (122)	6	ES
Virginia	2	5/6 (126)	4/10 (101)	25	ES
Washington	1	5/4 (124)	4/15 (106)	18	ES
West Virginia	4	5/6 (126)	4/26 (117)	9	ES
Wisconsin	1	5/7 (127)	4/14 (115)	12	ES
Wyoming	1	5/4 (124)	4/10 (101)	23	ES

[a] Number of studies used to calculate mean nesting date.
[b] 15 days were subtracted from mean incubation initiation dates for newly translocated populations.
[c] 2004 was a Leap Year, so DoY corresponding to calendar dates is 1 greater than for non-Leap Years.
[d] NFH = No Fall turkey Hunting, ES = Either Sex fall hunt, MO = Male Only fall hunt.

Our modeling efforts were most successful when restricted to the eastern subspecies of wild turkey. This may be due in part to the reduced variability in environmental factors such as elevation, moisture, and vegetation types within the region occupied by this subspecies. We also had more complete and even data coverage for eastern wild turkeys than for other subspecies. Our best model included a cubic polynomial term for latitude and a term for population status (Table 4). This indicated that, while relatively constant around 5–9 May in the Mid-Atlantic States, incubation initiation date increased sharply from south to north in both the Southeast and Northeast (Figure 2). Reasons for this pattern might include the transition from coastal plain to more mountainous terrain in the Southeast, and the rapid increase in the prevalence of persistent snow cover in the Northeast. Median date of the last spring frost and median length of the frost-free period also were good predictors of timing of incubation for this subspecies. Interestingly, neither elevation nor longitude emerged as important predictors of nesting phenology for eastern turkeys, possibly because this subspecies occupies a narrower range of these features than does the species as a whole. It may also be the

case that the smaller size of eastern mountains means that most turkeys inhabiting mountainous terrain can still make extensive use of lowlands, thereby avoiding any effect of elevation on nesting phenology (e.g., Fleming and Porter 2001).

There is considerable interannual variation in mean nest initiation dates for turkeys, with ranges of 19–28 days being observed in studies spanning ≥ 5 years (e.g., Vangilder and Kurzejeski 1995, Hubbard 1997, Miller et al. 1998, Thogmartin and Johnson 1999, Norman et al. 2001a). This variability in breeding phenology has been related to metrics of winter severity, including mean March temperature, number of subfreezing days, and snow depth (Vangilder and Kurzejeski 1995, Norman et al. 2001a). Thus, though photoperiod cues physiological pathways that prepare turkeys for breeding, there is still considerable plasticity in timing of reproduction. Presumably this behavioral flexibility is beneficial in turkey restoration efforts, as even when individuals are translocated over large distances they soon modify their breeding phenology to coincide with conditions at the release site.

Even with this flexibility in breeding phenology, our analyses indicated that newly translocated turkeys typically delayed nesting by 10–15 days (Tables 2–4). Of note, this effect was evident in a study comparing reproduction between translocated and established turkeys inhabiting the same area during the same years; on average, translocated individuals nested 10 days later than local birds (Benner 1989; but see Lehman et al. 2001). Three studies we reviewed followed individual turkeys for >1 breeding season after translocation. Weaver (1989) monitored 1 individual in consecutive years, and it nested 24 days earlier during its second year post-translocation. The 2 remaining studies pooled second year post-release turkeys with additional newly translocated individuals during the second year of monitoring, potentially weakening any trend in timing of breeding relative to time since release. However, both studies reported that mean nesting dates occurred earlier in the second year of study (Nguyen 2001, Shields 2001). Thus, there is some evidence that delayed breeding of translocated turkeys is limited to the year of release. Combining this observation with the facts that relocated populations all nested late regardless of the direction of translocation, and that established turkeys exhibit considerable variability in nesting phenology, we doubt that delayed nesting resulted from translocated turkeys being inflexible in their nesting phenology and poorly adapted to local seasonal cues (e.g., photoperiod). Rather, we suspect delays resulted from proximate factors such as increased time spent searching unfamiliar areas for breeding sites or mates, disrupted dominance hierarchies, or poor physical condition due to inexperience with the distribution and variety of local foods (e.g., Porter et al. 1983, Badyaev et al. 1996).

Finally, though the influence of daily weather on gobbling rates is relatively well understood, there is still uncertainty as to the effects of a number of important ecological and management factors on patterns of gobbling by male turkeys (Hoffman 1990, Kienzler et al. 1995, Miller et al. 1997b, Norman et al. 2001b). We originally designed this study to include analyses of gobbling phenology and interactions between gobbling, hunting, and nesting. However, our review of existing studies yielded only a handful of reliable estimates of gobbling chronology, few of which were accompanied by information on nesting, so we were forced to abandon this topic. However, our review made clear the need for research comparing gobbling chronology to nesting phenology, and comparing gobbling behavior between hunted and unhunted turkey populations.

Timing of Opening Dates for Spring Hunting

Setting season opening dates to coincide with the initial peak in gobbling may lead to high levels of illegal female kill (Kimmel and Kurzejeski 1985, Vangilder and Kurzejeski 1995, Miller et al. 1997b, Healy and Powell 2000, Norman et al. 2001b). This is a critical concern for managers, as harvests of even 10% of females can depress turkey populations (Healy and Powell 2000), and harvests are typically greatest during the opening days of spring seasons (Miller et al.

1997b, Norman et al. 2001b; J. Pack, West Virginia Division of Natural Resources, unpublished data). Because female wild turkeys are less vulnerable to harvest following initiation of incubation, the onset of nesting behavior is recommended as a biological benchmark for setting opening dates for spring gobbler seasons (Healy and Powell 2000, Norman et al. 2001b). However, only 1 state for which we obtained estimates of nesting chronology delayed hunting until the mean incubation initiation date, and only 26% of states met the less conservative criterion of delaying hunting until the onset of laying by most females (approx. 2 weeks preceding mean incubation initiation date) (Table 5). Fall and spring harvests of female turkeys may be additive in their impact on populations (Vangilder and Kurzejeski 1995, Rolley et al. 1998, Pack et al. 1999), so jurisdictions having restricted (e.g., male-only) or no fall turkey hunting seasons can perhaps afford to be more liberal in regulating spring harvests. However, 18 of 25 states (72%) that opened spring hunting >2 weeks prior to the mean incubation initiation date also allowed fall either-sex turkey hunting (Table 5).

While our comparison of opening dates and timing of nesting suggests that many management agencies do not consider nesting phenology and related illegal harvest issues when setting spring wild turkey hunting seasons, a number of other factors must also be taken into account. Other steps can be taken to limit harvests, for example restricting bag limits or the number of licenses available, and non-biological factors, including hunt quality and social and political expectations, are important considerations. For example, it is desirable to offer hunting opportunities during periods when males are gobbling vigorously and responsive to calling (Norman et al. 2001b). Consequently, managers must strive to set season opening dates that achieve a balance between the desire to maximize both quality and quantity of hunting opportunities, and the need to ensure harvest sustainability (e.g., Wright and Vangilder 2000). Towards this end, there is a need for research to improve our understanding of temporal patterns in gobbling propensity, effects of hunting and social factors on gobbling behavior, and seasonal trends in the susceptibility of males to calling. Further, greater knowledge of the interactive effects of breeding phenology and timing of spring hunting seasons on female kill, and the consequences of such loss of females for populations, is necessary for informed wild turkey management. In light of current limits to our understanding of these factors, it is apparent that many states, particularly those also allowing extended fall either-sex turkey hunting, are accepting higher risks when setting opening dates for spring gobbler seasons. Managers in these jurisdictions should carefully monitor wild turkey populations, as these may suffer from reduced female survival and consequently impaired population growth or even population decline, ultimately affecting harvests and hunt quality.

ACKNOWLEDGMENTS

We are grateful to the numerous individuals and agencies that contributed data and reports for this investigation. Financial support for this project was provided through Super Fund or Target 2000 monies contributed by several state chapters of the National Wild Turkey Federation, including Connecticut, Maryland, Massachusetts, New Hampshire, New Jersey, New York, Pennsylvania, Rhode Island, Virginia, and West Virginia, as well as Ontario. We thank the Technical Committee members, state chapter leaders, and volunteers from cooperating states for their support of this project. This work represents the continuation of a review of northeastern wild turkey breeding phenology initiated by a subcommittee of the Northeast Wild Turkey Technical Committee, including M. J. Casalena, B. Erikson, B. Long, G. Norman, J. Pack, B. Tefft, and R. Sanford. We extend special thanks to J. Cardoza, Chair of the Northeast Wild Turkey Technical Committee, for his leadership and support of this project. Additional advice and comments which improved the study were provided by P. Devers, L. Flake, J. McGhee, D. Steffen, and an anonymous reviewer. The Biology Department at Acadia University supported D. Whitaker during preparation of this paper.

LITERATURE CITED

Badyaev, A. V., T. E. Martin, and W. J. Etges. 1996. Habitat sampling and habitat selection by female wild turkeys: ecological correlates and reproductive consequences. Auk 113: 636–646.

Benner, J. M. 1989. Comparative survival and reproductive ecology of resident and introduced eastern wild turkey on Natchez Trace Wildlife Management Area, Tennessee. Thesis, Tennessee Tech University, Cookeville, Tennessee, USA.

Bevill, W. V. 1974. Some factors influencing gobbling activity among wild turkeys. Proceedings of the Southeast Association of Fish and Wildlife Agencies 27:62–73.

Burnham, K. P., and D. R. Anderson. 2002. Model selection and multimodel inference: a practical information-theoretic approach. Second edition. Springer-Verlag, New York, New York, USA.

Day, K. S., L. D. Flake, and W. L. Tucker. 1991. Characteristics of wild turkey nest sites in a mixed-grass prairie-oak-woodland mosaic in the northern great plains, South Dakota. Canadian Journal of Zoology 69:2840–2845.

Eaton, S. W. 1992. Wild turkey (*Meleagris gallopavo*). Pages 1–28 *in* A. Poole, P. Stettenheim, and F. Gill, editors. Birds of North America No. 22. Academy of Natural Sciences, Washington, D.C., USA.

Environment Canada. 2002. Canadian climate normals or averages, 1971–2000. Environment Canada home page. ⟨http://www.ec.gc.ca/envhome.html⟩. Accessed 15 Feb 2003.

Fleming, K. K., and W. F. Porter. 2001. Using a habitat suitability approach to evaluate landscape patterns for eastern wild turkey. Proceedings of the National Wild Turkey Symposium 8:157–166.

Healy, W. M., and S. M. Powell. 2000. Wild Turkey harvest management: biology, strategies, and techniques. U.S. Fish and Wildlife Service, Biological Technical Publication BTP-R5001–1999.

Hoffman, R. W. 1990. Chronology of gobbling and nesting activities of Merriam's wild turkeys. Proceedings of the National Wild Turkey Symposium 6:25–31.

Hopkins, A. D. 1938. Bioclimatics: a science of life and climate relations. U.S. Department of Agriculture, Washington, D.C., Miscellaneous Publication 280.

Hubbard, M. W. 1997. Behavior and survival of nesting wild turkeys in southern Iowa. Dissertation, Iowa State University, Ames, Iowa, USA.

Kienzler, J. M., T. W. Little, and W. A. Fuller. 1995. Effects of weather, incubation, and hunting on gobbling activity in wild turkeys. Proceedings of the National Wild Turkey Symposium 7:61–67.

Kimmel, V. L., and E. W. Kurzejeski. 1985. Illegal hen kill—a major turkey mortality factor. Proceedings of the National Wild Turkey Symposium 5:55–65.

Lazarus, J. E., and W. F. Porter. 1985. Nest habitat selection by wild turkeys in Minnesota. Proceedings of the National Wild Turkey Symposium 5:67–82.

Lehman, C. P., L. D. Flake, A. P. Leif, and R. D. Shields. 2001. Comparative survival and reproduction of sympatric eastern and Rio Grande wild turkey females in northeastern South Dakota. Proceedings of the National Wild Turkey Symposium 8:123–135.

McCombs, J. W. 1997. Geographic information system topographic factor maps for wildlife management. Thesis, Virginia Tech, Blacksburg, Virginia, USA.

———, S. Klopfer, D. Morton, and J. Waldon. 1997. An alternative approach to land cover mapping in complex terrain. GAP Analysis Program Annual Bulletin 6:36–39.

Miller, D. A., G. A. Hurst, and B. D. Leopold. 1997a. Factors affecting gobbling activity of wild turkeys in central Mississippi. Proceedings of the Southeastern Association of Fish and Wildlife Agencies 51:352–361.

———, ———, and ———. 1997b. Chronology of wild turkey nesting, gobbling, and hunting in Mississippi. Journal of Wildlife Management 61:840–845.

———, B. D. Leopold, and G. A. Hurst. 1998. Reproductive characteristics of a wild turkey population in central Mississippi. Journal of Wildlife Management 62:903–910.

National Oceanic and Atmospheric Administration. 2004. Climatography of the United States No. 20: station climatological summaries. National Oceanic and Atmospheric Administration, National Climatic Data Center home page. ⟨http://www.ncdc.noaa.gov/oa/ncdc.html⟩. Accessed 15 Feb 2003.

Nguyen, L. P. 2001. Feasibility of transplanting eastern wild turkeys (*Meleagris gallopavo silvestris*) on the Precambrian Shield in central Ontario. Thesis, Laurentian University, Sudbury, Ontario, Canada.

Norman, G. W., J. C. Pack, C. I. Taylor, D. E. Steffen, and K. H. Pollock. 2001a. Reproduction of eastern wild turkeys in Virginia and West Virginia. Journal of Wildlife Management 65:1–9.

———, D. E. Steffen, C. I. Taylor, J. C. Pack, K. H. Pollock, and K. Tsai. 2001b. Reproductive chronology, spring hunting, and illegal kill of female wild turkeys. Proceedings of the National Wild Turkey Symposium 8:269–280.

Pack, J. C., G. W. Norman, C. I. Taylor, D. E. Steffen, D. A. Swanson, K. H. Pollock, and R. Alpizar-Jara. 1999. Effects of fall hunting on wild turkey populations in Virginia and West Virginia. Journal of Wildlife Management 63:964–975.

Porter, W. F., G. C. Nelson, and K. Mattson. 1983. Effects of winter conditions on reproduction in a northern wild turkey population. Journal of Wildlife Management 47:281–290.

Roberts, S. D. 1993. Survival and reproduction of wild turkeys in south-central New York. Thesis, State University of New York, College of Environmental Science and Forestry, Syracuse, New York, USA.

Rolley, R. E., J. F. Kubisiak, R. N. Paisley, and R. G. Wright. 1998. Wild turkey population dynamics in southwestern Wisconsin. Journal of Wildlife Management 62:917–924.

Schmutz, J. A., and C. E. Braun. 1989. Reproductive performance of Rio Grande wild turkeys. Condor 91:675–680.

Schorger, A. W. 1966. The wild turkey: its history and domestication. University of Oklahoma Press, Norman, Oklahoma, USA.

Shields, R. D. 2001. Ecology of eastern wild turkeys introduced to minimally forested agricultural landscapes in northeastern South Dakota. Thesis, South Dakota State University, Brookings, South Dakota, USA.

Sokal, R. R., and F. J. Rohlf. 1995. Biometry; the principles and practice of statistics in biological research. Third edition. W. H. Freeman and Company, New York, New York, USA.

Thogmartin, W. E., and J. E. Johnson. 1999. Reproduction in a declining population of wild turkeys in Arkansas. Journal of Wildlife Management 63:1281–1290.

Vander Haegen, W. M., M. W. Sayre, and J. E. Cardoza. 1991. Nesting and brood-rearing habitat use in a northern wild turkey population. Transactions of the Northeast Section of the Wildlife Society 48:113–119.

Vangilder, L. D., and E. Kurzejeski. 1995. Population ecology of the eastern wild turkey in northern Missouri. Wildlife Monographs No. 130.

Weaver, J. E. 1989. On the ecology of wild turkeys reintroduced to southern Ontario. Thesis, University of Western Ontario, London, Ontario, Canada.

Wright, G. A., and L. D. Vangilder. 2000. Survival of eastern wild turkey males in western Kentucky. Proceedings of the National Wild Turkey Symposium 8:187–194.

Darroch Whitaker (pictured) completed his Ph.D. with the Department of Fisheries and Wildlife Sciences at Virginia Tech in 2003. His doctoral research was conducted through the Appalachian Cooperative Grouse Research Project, and focused on the habitat ecology of ruffed grouse across the Appalachian region. At present he is a postdoctoral fellow at Acadia University (Nova Scotia), where he is studying the effects of industrial forestry on the spatial ecology of songbirds. ***Jim Pack*** received an M.S. in wildlife science from Virginia Tech. At present he works for the West Virginia DNR, and has been involved in wild turkey research and management for over three decades. He has a keen interest in the ecology of forest wildlife, particularly with regards to habitat management and harvest regulation, and has been a strong supporter of science-based wildlife management. ***Gary Norman*** received a B.S. from West Virginia University and M.S. from Virginia Tech. He worked for the West Virginia Department of Natural Resources (WVDNR) for 7 years and has been employed with the Virginia Department of Game and Inland Fisheries since 1987. Gary currently serves as Forest Game Bird Project Leader and is responsible for statewide research, conservation, and management programs for ruffed grouse and wild turkey. Gary's research efforts have centered on population dynamics of wild turkey and ruffed grouse. He coordinated a 5-year study of wild turkey hens with the West Virginia DNR and served as coordinator for the 8-state Appalachian Cooperative Grouse Research Project. He is currently working on a cooperative study of wild turkey gobblers and gobbling with the WVDNR. ***Dean Stauffer*** completed his Ph.D. at the University of Idaho in 1983, where he studied the habitat ecology of blue and ruffed grouse. He joined the Department of Fisheries and Wildlife Sciences at Virginia Tech in 1983 and currently is a professor of wildlife sciences. While at Virginia Tech he has supervised numerous graduate students, received awards for his academic contributions to the university, and made important contributions to the Wildlife Society including serving as an associate editor for the Wildlife Society Bulletin and chair of the education working group. ***Scott Klopfer*** completed his M.S. on the use of GIS in land management at the Department of Fisheries and Wildlife Sciences of Virginia Tech in 1997. Since that time he has worked for the Conservation Management Institute, were he serves as director of the GIS and Remote Sensing Division. His work there is directed towards facilitating the implementation of spatial data and GIS technologies in natural resource management. He has also maintained an active involvement with the graduate program at Virginia Tech, and assists numerous students with their research.

9th National Wild Turkey Symposium

Wild Turkey Management:
Accomplishments, Strategies, and Opportunities
———— Grand Rapids, Michigan ————

SURVIVAL OF EASTERN WILD TURKEY MALES IN THE EASTERN MISSOURI OZARKS

Michael W. Hubbard
Missouri Department of Conservation,
P.O. Box 180,
Jefferson City, MO 65102, USA

Larry D. Vangilder[1]
Missouri Department of Conservation,
Resource Science Center,
1110 South College Avenue,
Columbia, MO 65201, USA

Abstract: From 1988 to 2000, we monitored 487 radiomarked male wild turkeys (*Meleagris gallopavo silvestris*) on 2 study areas (South Study Area [SSA] and Peck Ranch Conservation Area [PRCA]) in the eastern Missouri Ozarks. We estimated annual survival and cause-specific mortality rates, including spring harvest for juvenile and adult males. On the SSA (primarily United States Forest Service Property) access was unlimited while on PRCA (primarily Missouri Department of Conservation lands) public access was controlled. Annual survival was higher for juvenile males than for adults. Annual survival for juvenile and adult males was not different between study areas and was 0.595 and 0.368, respectively, on SSA and 0.569 and 0.372, respectively, on PRCA. Human-caused mortality (legal and suspected illegal kill) was 14.1% and 40.8% for juvenile and adult males on SSA and 19.0% and 27.2% for juvenile and adult males on PRCA. For adult males on both study areas, human-caused mortality increased beginning in 1998, which corresponded with an increase in the spring hunting season from 2 to 3 weeks. However, increased mortality appeared to occur during the first 2 weeks of the season and not during the third. Population modeling suggests that spring turkey harvest on public land in the eastern Missouri Ozarks is approaching a level that may result in a decline in spring turkey hunting quality (high proportion of adult males in the population and harvest).

Proceedings of the National Wild Turkey Symposium 9:361–366

Key words: eastern wild turkey, harvest, male, *Meleagris gallopavo silvestris,* Missouri, mortality, Ozark, radio-telemetry, spring turkey season, survival.

Wild turkey populations have been restored across large portions of the Midwest in the last 50 years. At the same time, interest in the pursuit of the birds for sport hunting has also increased (Wright and Vangilder 2000) making the need for accurate information on the harvested segments of the populations necessary for state agencies to effectively manage their wild turkey resources.

Since restoration efforts began, numerous studies have documented survival and mortality of female wild turkeys (Roberts et al. 1995, Miller et al. 1998, Hubbard et al. 1999). However, mortality information on male wild turkeys is limited (Wright and Vangilder 2000) and the influence of various harvest strategies on male wild turkey survival is unknown.

To better understand wild turkey population dynamics, we studied the survival and mortality of east-ern wild turkey males in the eastern Ozarks of Missouri from 1989–2000 on 2 study areas.

STUDY AREA

Our study was conducted at 2 sites in the eastern Missouri Ozarks (Vangilder et al. 2000). The SSA was approximately 40,000 ha and was located south of U.S. Highway 60 in Shannon, Oregon, and Carter counties. Over 80% of the study area was located within the Winona and Van Buren ranger districts of the Mark Twain National Forest. The area was typical of the Missouri Ozarks and was composed mainly of oak (*Quercus* spp.) and hickory (*Carya* spp.) forest with a

[1] E-mail: Larry.Vangilder@mdc.mo.gov

small amount of agricultural land isolated in bottomland corridors.

The PRCA (9,187 ha) was located in Carter County. Approximately 4,280 ha of the area was enclosed by a woven wire fence and public access was controlled. The area was predominated by forest (86.4%), but also had some semi-open areas (9.8%). The area also contained 100 1–10-ha open areas (3%) that were in agricultural crops and perennial grasses. These open areas were located mainly within the controlled access portion of the area. Telemetry data was collected from an area approximately 30,000 ha in size as defined by turkey movements.

Forested areas at both study sites were composed mainly of scarlet oak (*Q. coccinea*; 26%), white oak (*Q. alba*; 25%), black oak (*Q. velutina*; 20%), shortleaf pine (*Pinus echinata*; 7%), and post oak (*Q. stellata*; 6%). The study areas had a mean annual rainfall of 112 cm and a mean annual temperature of 13.3°C. For a complete description of the study sites, see Vangilder (1996) and Schroeder and Vangilder (1997).

METHODS

We captured wild turkeys with cannon and rocket nets from November through March, 1988–2000. We used the methods of Pelham and Dickson (1992) to determine the age and sex of all turkeys captured. We released turkeys within 4 hr at their original capture site. All turkeys captured were fitted with 100-g backpack style mortality mode transmitters (Telonics, Mesa, Arizona, USA, LB-400) and 2 numbered aluminum patagial tags (National Band and Tag Company, Newport, Kentucky, USA, 890N-4 Zip, size 4). We determined the age of males (juvenile or adult) according to Pelham and Dickson (1992).

We monitored male turkeys ≥4 days per week except during the spring turkey season when turkeys were monitored daily. If a turkey had been killed, an immediate attempt was made to determine the cause of death. Cause of death was classified as predation, illegal kill, legal harvest, suspicious loss, or crippling loss. Death was classified as a suspicious loss if humans were implicated but the evidence was not definitive. We defined total human-caused mortality as legal harvest, illegal kill, and suspicious loss. In Missouri, all hunters were required to register harvested turkeys at mandatory check stations where transmitters and hunter information were recovered.

Spring turkey season was 2 weeks in length with a bag limit of 1 male turkey or turkey with visible beard per week from 1989–1997. From 1998–2000, spring turkey season was liberalized to 3 weeks in length with a bag limit of 2 male turkeys or turkeys with visible beard during the season provided that only one could be killed during the first week and, during the second 2 weeks, only 1 could be killed per day.

We estimated annual survival from 15 March to 14 March of the following year using the Kaplan-Meier product-limit estimator (Pollock et al. 1989), which allows staggered entry of animals with program

Table 1. Annual Kaplan-Meier survival estimates ($\hat{S}$) of wild turkey males on the South Study Area in the central Missouri Ozarks, 1990–2000.

Year	Adult				Juvenile			
	($\hat{S}$)	SE	n^a	n^b	($\hat{S}$)	SE	n^a	n^b
1990–91	0.455	0.112	22	9	—^{c}	—	—	—
1991–92	0.109	0.042	11	6	—^{c}	—	—	—
1992–93	0.600	0.120	6	10	—^{c}	—	—	—
1993–94	0.423	0.074	10	19	—^{c}	—	—	—
1994–95	0.412	0.084	21	14	0.454	0.075	5	20
1995–96	0.400	0.073	18	18	0.625	0.069	16	31
1996–97	0.325	0.065	27	17	0.629	0.096	22	16
1997–98	0.308	0.105	27	6	0.600	0.268	5	2
1998–99	0.313	0.130	8	4	—^{c}	—	—	—
1999–00	—^{c}	—	—	—	0.538	0.129	16	8
Mean	0.372	0.031^d	9^e		0.569	0.066^d	5^e	

^{a} Number at beginning of interval.
^{b} Number at end of interval.
^{c} Not enough data to estimate survival.
^{d} Standard error estimates from program CONTRAST (Hines and Sauer 1989).
^{e} Number of years.

STAGKAM (T. G. Kuloweic, Missouri Department of Conservation, Columbia, Missouri, USA). We reclassified juvenile turkeys as adults on 15 March of the year following capture.

We used program CONTRAST (Hines and Sauer 1989) to calculate standard error estimates for annual survival across years and to test differences in point estimates of human-caused mortality during spring turkey season. Human-caused mortality during spring turkey season and its associated standard errors were calculated using a ratio estimate as described in Vangilder and Kurzejeski (1995).

RESULTS

Annual Survival

Survival information from 1989–1990 was not included due to possible transmitter effects. We monitored 487 male wild turkeys during this study. Annual survival for juvenile ($\chi^2 = 0.078$, df = 1, $P = 0.781$) and adult males ($\chi^2 = 0.098$, df = 1, $P = 0.754$) was not different between study areas and was 0.595 and 0.368, respectively, on SSA and was 0.569 and 0.372, respectively, on PRCA. Across all years of the study, juvenile male survival was higher than adult survival on both SSA ($\chi^2 = 7.370$, df = 1, $P = 0.007$; Table 1) and PRCA ($\chi^2 = 6.609$, df = 1, $P = 0.010$; Table 2).

Mortality During Spring Turkey Season

Human-caused mortality during spring turkey season across all years was 14.1% and 40.8% for juvenile and adult males on SSA and 19.0% and 27.2% for juvenile and adult males on PRCA. From 1990–1997, of males alive at the beginning of spring turkey season on SSA, 14.0% of juveniles and 34.7% of adults were killed by humans (legal and illegal harvest and suspicious loss; Table 3). From 1998–2000, of males alive at the beginning of spring turkey season on SSA, 14.3% of juveniles and 67.9% of adults were killed by

Table 2. Annual Kaplan-Meier survival estimates (Ŝ) of wild turkey males on the Peck Ranch Conservation Area in the central Missouri Ozarks, 1990–2000.

Year	Adult (Ŝ)	SE	n^a	n^b	Juvenile (Ŝ)	SE	n^a	n^b
1990–91	0.305	0.051	26	25	0.800	0.103	9	12
1991–92	0.458	0.119	25	8	0.533	0.364	12	1
1992–93	0.533	0.163	9	5	—c	—	2	0
1993–94	0.667	0.146	5	7	0.625	0.171	10	5
1994–95	0.114	0.044	10	6	—c	—	2	0
1995–96	0.333	0.272	6	1	0.485	0.246	11	2
1996–97	—c	—	3	0	0.714	0.106	1	13
1997–98	0.291	0.087	28	8	0.486	0.132	12	7
1998–99	0.200	0.089	11	4	0.298	0.057	4	19
1999–00	0.600	0.114	5	11	0.819	0.086	18	17
Mean	0.368	0.065d	9e		0.595	0.046	11e	

a Number at beginning of interval.
b Number at end of interval.
c Not enough data to estimate survival.
d Standard error estimates from program CONTRAST (Hines and Sauer 1989).
e Number of years.

Table 3. Human-caused mortality [number, (percent)] for radio-marked juvenile (JV) and adult (AD) wild turkey males during the spring hunting seasona on the South Study Area in the central Missouri Ozarks, 1990–2000.

Year	Age	n^b	Legal harvest	Illegal and suspicious loss	Total
1990	JV	0	0 (0.0)	0 (0.0)	0 (0.0)
	AD	21	5 (23.8)	2 (9.5)	7 (33.3)
1991	JV	0	0 (0.0)	0 (0.0)	0 (0.0)
	AD	7	3 (42.9)	1 (14.3)	4 (57.1)
1992	JV	0	0 (0.0)	0 (0.0)	0 (0.0)
	AD	6	1 (16.7)	0 (0.0)	1 (16.7)
1993	JV	0	0 (0.0)	0 (0.0)	0 (0.0)
	AD	9	0 (0.0)	0 (0.0)	0 (0.0)
1994	JV	8	0 (0.0)	1 (12.5)	1 (12.5)
	AD	17	3 (17.6)	2 (11.8)	5 (29.4)
1995	JV	16	6 (37.5)	0 (0.0)	6 (37.5)
	AD	14	3 (21.4)	2 (14.3)	5 (35.7)
1996	JV	22	0 (0.0)	0 (0.0)	0 (0.0)
	AD	28	7 (25.0)	4 (14.3)	11 (39.3)
1997	JV	4	0 (0.0)	0 (0.0)	0 (0.0)
	AD	22	8 (36.4)	2 (9.1)	10 (45.5)
1998	JV	0	0 (0.0)	0 (0.0)	0 (0.0)
	AD	8	4 (50.0)	0 (0.0)	4 (50.0)
1999	JV	13	1 (7.7)	1 (7.7)	2 (15.4)
	AD	4	3 (75.0)	0 (0.0)	3 (75.0)
2000	JV	1	0 (0.0)	0 (0.0)	0 (0.0)
	AD	16	9 (56.3)	3 (18.8)	12 (75.0)
Total (2-wk season, 1990–1997)	JV	50	6 (12.0)	1 (2.0)	7 (14.0)
	AD	124	30 (24.2)	13 (10.5)	43 (34.7)
Total (3-wk season, 1998–2000)	JV	14	1 (7.1)	1 (7.1)	2 (14.3)
	AD	28	16 (57.1)	3 (10.7)	19 (67.9)
Overall	JV	64	7 (10.9)	2 (3.1)	9 (14.1)
	AD	152	46 (30.3)	16 (10.5)	62 (40.8)

a A 2-wk season with a 2-bird bag limit and only 1 bird per week was in effect from 1990–1997. A 3-wk season with a 2-bird limit with 1 bird the first week and 1 bird a day in the second and third weeks was in effect from 1998–2000.
b Number alive beginning the first day of spring turkey season.

Table 4. Human-caused mortality [number, (percent)] for radio-marked juvenile (JV) and adult (AD) wild turkey males during the spring hunting seasona on the Peck Ranch Conservation Area in the central Missouri Ozarks, 1989–2000.

Year	Age	n^b	Legal harvest	Illegal and suspicious loss	Total
1989	JV	0	0 (0.0)	0 (0.0)	0 (0.0)
	AD	28	5 (17.9)	0 (0.0)	5 (17.9)
1990	JV	0	0 (0.0)	0 (0.0)	0 (0.0)
	AD	21	5 (23.8)	1 (4.8)	6 (28.6)
1991	JV	7	0 (0.0)	0 (0.0)	0 (0.0)
	AD	26	2 (7.7)	1 (3.8)	3 (11.5)
1992	JV	0	0 (0.0)	0 (0.0)	0 (0.0)
	AD	6	1 (16.7)	0 (0.0)	1 (16.7)
1993	JV	10	2 (20.0)	0 (0.0)	2 (20.0)
	AD	8	2 (25.0)	0 (0.0)	2 (25.0)
1994	JV	0	0 (0.0)	0 (0.0)	0 (0.0)
	AD	8	3 (37.5)	1 (12.5)	4 (50.0)
1995	JV	9	0 (0.0)	0 (0.0)	0 (0.0)
	AD	3	0 (0.0)	1 (33.3)	1 (33.3)
1996	JV	1	0 (0.0)	0 (0.0)	0 (0.0)
	AD	4	0 (0.0)	0 (0.0)	0 (0.0)
1997	JV	8	2 (25.0)	0 (0.0)	2 (25.0)
	AD	24	5 (20.8)	1 (4.2)	6 (25.0)
1998	JV	4	2 (50.0)	0 (0.0)	2 (50.0)
	AD	8	4 (50.0)	0 (0.0)	4 (50.0)
1999	JV	17	2 (11.8)	2 (11.8)	4 (23.5)
	AD	5	2 (40.0)	0 (0.0)	2 (40.0)
2000	JV	7	2 (28.6)	0 (0.0)	2 (28.6)
	AD	17	8 (47.1)	1 (5.9)	9 (52.9)
Total (2 wk season, 1990–1997)	JV	35	4 (11.4)	0 (0.0)	4 (11.4)
	AD	128	23 (18.0)	5 (3.9)	28 (21.9)
Total (3 wk season, 1998–2000)	JV	28	6 (21.4)	2 (7.1)	8 (28.6)
	AD	30	14 (46.7)	1 (3.3)	15 (50.0)
Overall	JV	63	10 (15.9)	2 (3.2)	12 (19.0)
	AD	158	37 (23.4)	6 (3.8)	43 (27.2)

a A 2-wk season with a 2-bird bag limit and only 1 bird per week was in effect from 1989–1997. A 3-wk season with a 2-bird limit with 1 bird the first week and 1 bird a day in the second and third weeks was in effect from 1998–2000.
b Number alive beginning the first day of spring turkey season.

humans (Table 3). From 1989–1997, of males alive at the beginning of spring turkey season on PRCA, 11.4% of juveniles and 21.9% of adults were killed by humans (Table 4). From 1998–2000, of males alive at the beginning of spring turkey season on PRCA, 28.6% of juveniles and 50.0% of adults were killed by humans (Table 3).

Not enough juvenile males were alive at the beginning of spring turkey season on either study in most years to allow analysis (see Tables 3 and 4); therefore, only adult males were used to compare mortality estimates between study areas and before and after spring turkey season liberalization. Across all years of the study, human-caused mortality during spring turkey season was lower for adult males on PRCA (0.356 ± 0.022) than on SSA (0.511 ± 0.045; χ^2 = 9.563, df = 1, P = 0.002). Across both study areas, human-caused mortality during spring turkey season was lower for adult males before 1998 (0.278 ± 0.026) than

Table 5. Timing of adult male wild turkey loss by week [number, (percent)] on the South Study Area in the central Missouri Ozarks, 1990–2000.

| Year | n^b | Harvest mortality[a] or suspicious loss | | |
		First week	Second week	Third week
1990	21	7 (33.3)	0 (0.0)	—
1991	7	2 (28.6)	2 (28.6)	—
1992	6	0 (0.0)	1 (16.7)	—
1993	9	0 (0.0)	0 (0.0)	—
1994	17	4 (23.5)	1 (5.9)	—
1995	14	5 (35.7)	0 (0.0)	—
1996	28	8 (28.6)	3 (10.7)	—
1997	22	6 (27.3)	4 (18.2)	—
1998	8	3 (37.5)	1 (12.5)	0 (0.0)
1999	4	2 (50.0)	1 (25.0)	0 (0.0)
2000	16	10 (62.5)	1 (6.3)	1 (6.3)
Total (2-wk season)	124	32 (25.8)	11 (8.9)	—
Total (3-wk season)	28	15 (53.6)	3 (10.7)	1 (3.6)

[a] A 2-wk season with a 2-bird bag limit and only 1 per week was in effect from 1990–1997. A 3-wk season with a 2-bird limit with 1 the first week and 1 a day the second and third weeks was in effect from 1998–2000.
[b] Number alive beginning the first day of spring turkey season.

Table 6. Timing of adult male wild turkey loss by week [number, (percent)] on the Peck Ranch Study Area in the central Missouri Ozarks, 1989–2000.

| Year | n^b | Harvest mortality[a] or suspicious loss | | |
		First week	Second week	Third week
1989	28	4 (14.3)	1 (3.6)	—
1990	21	4 (19.0)	2 (9.5)	—
1991	26	2 (7.7)	1 (3.8)	—
1992	6	0 (0.0)	1 (16.7)	—
1993	8	2 (25.0)	0 (0.0)	—
1994	8	2 (25.0)	2 (25.0)	—
1995	3	1 (33.3)	0 (0.0)	—
1996	4	0 (0.0)	0 (0.0)	—
1997	24	5 (20.8)	1 (4.2)	—
1998	8	1 (12.5)	2 (25.0)	1 (12.5)
1999	5	1 (20.0)	1 (20.0)	0 (0.0)
2000	17	5 (29.4)	4 (23.5)	0 (0.0)
Total (2-wk season)	128	20 (15.6)	8 (6.3)	—
Total (3-wk season)	40	7 (17.5)	7 (17.5)	1 (2.5)

[a] A 2-wk season with a 2-bird bag limit and only 1 per week was in effect from 1989–1997. A 3-wk season with a 2-bird limit with 1 the first week and 1 a day the second and third weeks was in effect from 1998–2000.
[b] Number alive beginning the first day of spring turkey season.

after 1998 (0.589 ± 0.043; χ^2 = 38.298, df = 1, $P <$ 0.001).

Although human-caused mortality during spring turkey season increased after the season was liberalized (beginning in 1998), the increased mortality did not occur during the additional (third) week on SSA (Table 5) or PRCA (Table 6). Only 3.6% and 2.5% of the total human-caused mortality occurred during the additional week on SSA and PRCA, respectively.

DISCUSSION

Annual Survival

Annual survival of juvenile males during this study (PRCA, 0.595; SSA, 0.569) was slightly higher than in western Kentucky (0.533; Wright and Vangilder *this volume*). Annual survival of adult males during this study (PRCA, 0.368; SSA, 0.372) was also higher than in western Kentucky (0.275), but similar to the rate reported in Georgia (0.36; Ielmini et al. 1992). The observed survival rate was lower than that reported in Wisconsin (0.51; Paisley et al. 1996). In Wisconsin (Paisley et al. 1996) and Mississippi (Godwin et al. 1991), no difference in juvenile and adult male survival was observed. However, in our study and in studies in Georgia (Ielmini et al. 1992) and Kentucky (Wright and Vangilder *this volume*), juvenile survival was higher than adult male survival because of differential mortality during the spring turkey season.

Mortality During Spring Turkey Season

Wright and Vangilder (*this volume*) reported that 59.8% of adult males and 22.7% of juvenile males were killed during spring turkey season in western Kentucky. In our study, 40.8% of adult males on SSA and 27.2% on PRCA, were killed during spring turkey season. For juvenile males, 14.1% and 19.0% on SSA

and PRCA, respectively, were shot during spring turkey season. Thus, mortality rates during spring turkey season for juvenile males in this study were similar to those reported in western Kentucky, but for adult males, the mortality rates during spring turkey season in this study were lower.

Mortality rates during spring turkey season on our study areas increased after the season was liberalized in 1998. Rates of mortality for adult males during spring turkey season went from 34.7% to 67.9% on SSA, and from 21.9% to 50.0% on PRCA. The rates observed after liberalization were similar to those reported by Wright and Vangilder (*this volume*).

The increased mortality after liberalization did not occur during the additional week of the season. However, estimated hunting success increased after the liberalization. The success rate of hunters in the eastern Missouri Ozarks averaged 48 birds/1000 trips (maximum = 53 birds/1000 trips) before the season was liberalized in 1998 but had increased to 81 birds/1000 trips by 2000 (M. W. Hubbard and L. D. Vangilder, Missouri Department of Conservation, unpublished data). The increased success rate was probably due to the increased number of days in the season as well as the change in the structure of the bag limit. Prior to 1998, only 1 bird could be taken per week of the season. Beginning in 1998, only 1 bird could be taken the first week, but 2 birds could be taken during the second 2 weeks provided only one bird could be taken per day.

We observed significantly higher mortality rates during spring turkey season on SSA (0.511) where access was unlimited than on PRCA (0.356) where hunter access was limited on the central portion of the study area. The South Study Area was mostly comprised of land owned by the Mark Twain National Forest, while PRCA was mostly owned by the Missouri Department of Conservation and access was limited on about 4,280 ha.

Wright and Vangilder (*this volume*) observed high mortality rates of adult males during spring turkey season on a study area in western Kentucky which was >90% private land. In this study, we also observed high mortality rates of adult males during spring turkey season (after liberalization), but our study areas were >80% heavily hunted public land.

MANAGEMENT IMPLICATIONS

Vangilder and Kurzejeski (1995) observed that as simulated harvest rates of male turkeys during the spring season increased, the proportion of adult males in the prehunt population and in the harvest decreased. At harvest rates greater than 30%, the proportion of adult males in the prehunt population and harvest dropped below 25 and 69%, respectively. They felt that harvest rates beyond 30–35% would begin to impact turkey hunting quality (as defined by a high proportion of adult males in the population and harvest). The spring harvest rates observed during this study after 1998 appear to be high enough to impact turkey hunting quality. However, we believe the harvest rate on surrounding private lands is lower than that observed on public land. In Missouri, greater than 30% of hunters report hunting on public land (Vangilder et al. 1990) although <5% of Missouri's land area is in public ownership open to hunting. Thus, hunting pressure appears to be much higher on public than on private land. In the eastern Ozarks region, the information used to evaluate Missouri's spring turkey season shows no change in harvest, hunting success, or adult male spur length distribution indicating the spring harvest has not surpassed sustainable levels (J. Beringer, Missouri Department of Conservation, unpublished data).

We believe that further increases in the harvest rate on heavily hunted public land in the eastern Missouri Ozarks will decrease turkey hunting quality. Unlike in western Kentucky where high harvest rates are probably sustained by rapid population growth and expansion (Wright and Vangilder *this volume*), population growth in the eastern Missouri Ozarks stabilized in 1987 (L. D. Vangilder, Missouri Department of Conservation, unpublished data). In stable populations, we recommend a spring harvest rate of no more than 40% of the male population which translates to a spring harvest rate of about 30% for juvenile males and 60% for adult males. This recommendation assumes that juvenile males are much less vulnerable to harvest than adult males because the juveniles that survive their first spring season become the adults available for harvest in future years. If the proportion of juveniles in the harvest is relatively stable across years and is lower than 30%, then exploitation rates of the male segment of the population is probably sustainable.

ACKNOWLEDGMENTS

We would like to thank D. W. Murphy, D. A. Granfors, J. D. Burk, P. C. Freeman, and G. E. Sullivan for coordinating the fieldwork for this study. We also thank the numerous highly dedicated technicians that made this study possible. We are also appreciative of the cooperation and input of the wildlife management staff at the Peck Ranch Conservation Area. The Eleven Point Ranger District of Mark Twain National Forest (United States Forest Service) allowed the use of their land for one of the study areas and also provided housing for research technicians. Partial funding for this project was provided by the National Wild Turkey Federation (NWTF), the George Clark Missouri State Chapter of NWTF, and the St. Louis Chapter of the Safari Club International. This study was also supported by the Federal Aid in Wildlife Restoration Act, under Pittman-Robertson Project W-13-R.

LITERATURE CITED

Godwin, K. D., G. A. Hurst, and R. L. Kelley. 1991. Survival rates of radio-equipped wild turkey gobblers in east-central Mississippi. Proceedings of the Annual Conference of the Southeastern Association of Fish and Wildlife Agencies 45: 218–226.

Hines, J. E., and J. R. Sauer. 1989. Program CONTRAST—a general program of the analysis of several survival or recovery rate estimates. U.S. Fish and Wildlife Service Technical Report 24.

Hubbard, M. W., D. L. Garner, and E. E. Klaas. 1999. Factors influencing wild turkey hen survival in southcentral Iowa. Journal of Wildlife Management 63:731–738.

Ielmini, M. R., A. S. Johnson, and P. E. Hale. 1992. Habitat and mortality relationships of wild turkey gobblers in the Georgia Piedmont. Proceedings of the Annual Conference of the Southeastern Association of Fish and Wildlife Agencies 46: 128–137.

Miller, D. A., L. W. Burger, B. D. Leopold, and G. A. Hurst. 1998. Survival and cause-specific mortality of wild turkey hens in central Mississippi. Journal of Wildlife Management 62:306–313.

Paisley, R. N., R. G. Wright, and J. F. Kubisiak. 1996. Survival of wild turkey gobblers in southwestern Wisconsin. Proceedings of the National Wild Turkey Symposium 7:39–44.

Pelham, P. H., and J. G. Dickson. 1992. Physical characteristics. Pages 32–45 *in* J. G. Dickson, editor. The wild turkey: biology and management. Stackpole Books, Harrisburg, Pennsylvania, USA.

Pollock, K. H., S. R. Winterstein, C. M. Bunck, and P. D. Curtis. 1989. Survival analysis in telemetry studies: the staggered entry design. Journal of Wildlife Management 53:7–15.

Roberts, S. D., J. M. Coffey, and W. F. Porter. 1995. Survival and reproduction of female wild turkeys in New York. Journal of Wildlife Management 59:437–447.

Schroeder, R. L., and L. D. Vangilder. 1997. Tests of wildlife habitat models to evaluate oak-mast production. Wildlife Society Bulletin 25:639–646.

Vangilder, L. D. 1996. Survival and cause-specific mortality of wild turkeys in the Missouri Ozarks. Proceedings of the National Wild Turkey Symposium 7:21–31.

———, M. W. Hubbard, and D. A. Hasenbeck. 2000. Reproductive ecology of eastern wild turkey females in the eastern Missouri Ozarks. Proceedings of the National Wild Turkey Symposium 8:53–59.

———, and E. W. Kurzejeski. 1995. Population ecology of the eastern wild turkey in northern Missouri. Wildlife Monographs 130.

———, S. L. Sheriff, and G. S. Olson. 1990. Characteristics, attitudes, and preferences of Missouri's spring turkey hunters. Proceedings of the National Wild Turkey Symposium 6:167–176.

Wright, G. A., and L. D. Vangilder. 2001. Survival of eastern wild turkey males in western Kentucky. Proceedings of the National Wild Turkey Symposium 8: 187–194.

———, and L. D. Vangilder. *This volume.* Survival and dispersal of eastern wild turkey gobblers in western Kentucky. Proceedings of the National Wild Turkey Symposium 9:*This volume.*

Mike Hubbard (right) supervises the Mangement Evaluation and Support section of the Missouri Department of Conservation's (MDC) Resource Science Division. He is also an adjunct assistant professor of Fisheries and Wildlife Sciences at the University of Missouri-Columbia. He received his B.S. in Fisheries and Wildlife Biology from the University of Missouri-Columbia, and his M.S. and Ph.D. from Iowa State University (ISU) where he worked on pheasant and wild turkey population dynamics. Mike did postdoctoral work at ISU on landscape influences on white-tailed deer/motor vehicle accidents. He came to MDC in 1999 as a wildlife research biologist with responsibility for wild turkey research and management. He wrapped up a 10-year research project on wild turkey population dynamics in the southern Missouri Ozarks before moving to his current position in February 2003. Mike's interests include population dynamics, landscape influences on survival, reproduction, and movement of animals, and the analysis of habitat selection and preference of animals. *Larry D. Vangilder* (left) is Chief of the Missouri Deparment of Conservation's (MDC) Resource Science Center. He directs the activities of 40 resource scientists who gather information to help make better policy and management decisions. He is also an adjunct associate professor of Fisheries and Wildlife Sciences at the University of Missouri-Columbia. He has a B.S. and M.S. in Fisheries and Wildlife Biology from the University of Missouri-Columbia and a Ph.D. in Zoology from the Ohio State University. He also held post-doctoral positions with the Savannah River Ecology Laboratory and with Patuxent Wildlife Research Center through Cornell University. He started with the MDC in 1985 as a wildlife research biologist with responsibility for wild turkey research and management and research in forest ecosystems. In 1999 Larry became a Research Supervisor in the Wildlife Research Section. He moved to his current position in January 2003. His interests include animal population dynamics and forest ecosystems. He has been involved in the development of the Missouri Ozark Forest Ecosystem Project since its inception.

Wild Turkey Management:
Accomplishments, Strategies, and Opportunities
———— Grand Rapids, Michigan ————

SURVIVAL AND DISPERSAL OF EASTERN WILD TURKEY MALES IN WESTERN KENTUCKY

George A. Wright[1]
Kentucky Department of Fish and Wildlife Resources,
149 Needmore Road,
Princeton, KY 42445, USA

Larry D. Vangilder[2]
Missouri Department of Conservation,
Resource Science Center,
1110 South College Avenue,
Columbia, MO 65201, USA

Abstract: From 1995 to 2002, we monitored 526 radiomarked male wild turkeys (*Meleagris gallopavo silvestris*) in western Kentucky to obtain estimates of survival, cause-specific mortality, harvest rates, and dispersal distance. Average annual survival rates differed between juvenile and adult males and averaged 0.53 and 0.28, respectively. This difference in annual survival rates was due to the difference in the magnitude of human-caused mortality between juveniles and adults. Human-caused mortality during the spring turkey season averaged 59.8% for adult males, but only 22.7% for juvenile males. Annual natural mortality rates (with human-caused mortality censored) were 0.24 and 0.29 for juvenile and adult males, respectively. Annual human-caused mortality rates (with non-human-caused mortality censored) for juvenile and adult males were 0.29 and 0.61, respectively. Seasonal survival rates outside the spring turkey season (1 Dec–10 Apr and 10 May–30 Nov) were >0.80 and did not differ between age classes. Median dispersal distance from trap sites was greater for juvenile males (2,773 m) than for adult males (2,094 m). Our data, along with the results of population modeling, suggest that the observed level of adult gobbler harvest cannot be sustained unless recruitment remains high or hunter success rates decline.

Proceedings of the National Wild Turkey Symposium 9:367–373

Key words: Eastern wild turkey, harvest, hunting, male, spring turkey season, survival.

Eastern wild turkey restoration occurred in Kentucky from 1978 through 1998. As a result, the state-wide turkey population increased from a few hundred birds to over 200,000. As turkey populations increased, spring turkey seasons were liberalized. By 1995, the entire state was open to spring turkey hunting, and by 1998, the spring season had been liberalized to 3 weeks and a 2-bird bag limit with all-day hunting. The number of turkey hunters also increased dramatically and reached 76,000 in 2002 with a spring harvest of 29,000 males. A limited fall either-sex gun hunt was initiated in 1998. Because of the great popularity of turkey hunting, pressure to provide even more hunting opportunity is constant.

To manage wild turkey populations for quality spring turkey hunting (a high percent of adult males in the population and in the harvest), information on male survival, cause-specific mortality, harvest rates, and dispersal is necessary. This information is essentially lacking for most of the eastern wild turkey range. To better understand the population dynamics and human-caused mortality of wild turkey males, we initiated a 7-year radiotelemetry study in 1995.

In this paper we report on all 7 years of the study and update the 4 years of information presented by Wright and Vangilder (2001).

STUDY AREA

The study was conducted in parts of 3 western Kentucky counties: Caldwell, Hopkins, and Christian. The study area was about 777 km², of which approximately 50% was forested. Private land comprised 90% of the area. The public land in the study area consisted of 2 state wildlife management areas, Pennyrile and Jones–Kenney, which comprised 8,093 ha. Open lands were dominated by fescue pasture and crop fields (alfalfa, corn, beans, milo, and tobacco). Forest stands were dominated by oak (*Quercus* spp.) and hickories (*Carya* spp.). Elevation ranged from 110 to 205 m. Annual total precipitation averaged 119.4 cm and average annual temperature was 14.3°C.

[1] Deceased.

[2] E-mail: Larry.Vangilder@mdc.mo.gov

METHODS

Beginning fall 1995, we trapped male turkeys annually from 1 September to 15 March using rocket nets. Turkeys were marked with aluminum butt end leg bands (National Band and Tag Company, Newport, Kentucky, USA, 1242, size 24). A 100-g backpack-style mortality mode transmitter (Telonics, Mesa, Arizona, USA, model LB-400) was attached using 4.7-mm shock cord. Rubber bands were used to keep the transmitters snug on juvenile males (Taylor 1995). We determined the age of males (juvenile or adult; Williams 1981) and released them at their capture site. Turkeys that did not survive >14 days after being radiomarked were not included in the study.

We monitored birds ≥4 times/week during the year, except during spring turkey season and the 10-day modern gun deer season when birds were monitored daily. Attempts were made to determine cause immediately after receiving a mortality signal. If the turkey had been killed, the cause of death was determined. Cause of death was classified as predation, illegal kill, legal harvest, crippling loss, or other. The category 'other' included deaths for which the cause was unknown, accidental deaths, deaths from disease or parasites, and deaths caused by vehicles. Where possible, cause of predation was determined from evidence at the mortality site. Hunters were required to check birds at mandatory check stations. Check station operators recovered the transmitter and recorded the hunter's name, address, phone number, and location of kill.

Annual and seasonal survival distributions were estimated using the Kaplan–Meier product-limit estimator modified for staggered entry (Pollock et al. 1989) using program STAGKAM (T. G. Kuloweic, Missouri Department of Conservation, Columbia, Missouri, USA). Censored observations were handled as suggested by Vangilder and Sheriff (1990). The log-rank test (Pollock et al. 1989) was used to test for differences in survival distributions between juvenile and adult males. Summary statistics for the log-rank test and the 3 chi-square tests (Pollock et al. 1989) were calculated using a SAS program.

Seasonal intervals were winter (1 Dec–10 Apr), spring hunting (11 Apr–9 May), and summer–fall (10 May–30 Nov). Birds were considered to be juveniles until the second December after hatching. Spring turkey hunting seasons were 17 Apr–30 Apr (2 weeks) with a 1300 hr closure in 1996; 14 Apr–4 May (3 weeks) and a 1300 hr closure in 1997; 13 Apr–3 May (3 weeks) and all-day hunting in 1998; and 12 Apr–2 May, 17 Apr–7 May, 14 Apr–4 May, 15 Apr–5 May with all-day hunting in 1999, 2000, 2001, and 2002, respectively. All seasons (1996–2002) had a 2-bird bag limit (1 per day).

Annual natural mortality (survival) was estimated by censoring human-caused deaths. Annual human-caused mortality (survival) was estimated by censoring deaths resulting from causes other than those associated with humans.

Differences in point estimates of survival or mortality were tested using program CONTRAST (Hines

Table 1. Human-caused mortality [number (%)] for radio-marked juvenile (JV) and adult (AD) males during 7 spring turkey seasons in western Kentucky, 1996–2002. The number alive is the number of males alive beginning the first day of the spring turkey season for each year. Illegal harvest represents males killed during the spring turkey season but not checked at mandatory check stations.

			Cause of death			
Year	Age	Number Alive	Legal harvest	Illegal harvest	Crippling kill	Total loss
1996	JV	31	6 (19.4)	2 (6.5)	0 (0.0)	8 (25.8)
	AD	28	12 (42.9)	2 (7.1)	2 (7.1)	16 (57.1)
1997	JV	56	11 (9.6)	0 (0.0)	0 (0.0)	11 (19.6)
	AD	40	19 (47.5)	1 (2.5)	1 (2.5)	21 (52.5)
1998	JV	32	10 (31.3)	1 (3.1)	1 (3.1)	12 (37.5)
	AD	79	52 (65.8)	3 (3.8)	2 (2.5)	57 (72.2)
1999	JV	59	9 (15.3)	0 (0.0)	1 (1.7)	10 (16.9)
	AD	40	15 (37.5)	2 (5.0)	4 (10.0)[a]	21 (52.5)
2000	JV	34	5 (14.7)	0 (0.0)	2 (5.9)	7 (20.6)
	AD	76	40 (52.6)	0 (0.0)	4 (5.3)	44 (57.9)
2001	JV	44	9 (20.5)	1 (2.3)	0 (0.0)	10 (22.7)
	AD	46	22 (47.8)	2 (4.3)	1 (2.2)	25 (54.3)
2002	AD	34	19 (55.9)	1 (2.9)	1 (2.9)	21 (61.8)
Total	JV	256	50 (19.5)	4 (1.6)	4 (1.6)	58 (22.7)
	AD	343	179 (52.2)	11 (3.2)	15 (4.4)	205 (59.8)

[a] Includes 1 adult shot and crippled during the season but recovered just after the season closed.

and Sauer 1989). Estimates and their associated standard errors were input into the program and an overall chi-square test was calculated.

To examine the relative importance of the various mortality sources, the number of deaths for each cause was converted to a percent of the total number of deaths.

Dispersal distance was determined using ArcMap (Version 9.0, Environmental Systems Research Institute, Redlands, California, USA) by comparing the UTM coordinate of the site where a bird was trapped with the UTM coordinate of the site where a bird died or disappeared. The Kruskal-Wallis Test (Conover 1971) was used to test whether dispersal distances were larger for juvenile or adult males.

RESULTS

The maximum number of radiomarked males at risk ranged from 56 in 1997–1998 to 65 in 1998–1999 for juvenile males and from 34 in 1995–1996 to 88 in 1999–2000 for adult males. The maximum number of birds at risk on opening day of the spring hunting season ranged from 34 in 2002 to 111 in 1998 (Table 1).

Survival distributions differed between juvenile and adult males for each of the 6 years ($P < 0.047$; Figure 1). The average survival distributions of juvenile and adult males show that most of the mortality of males occurs during the spring turkey hunting season and that mortality of adult males is greater than that of juveniles (Figure 1).

Annual survival rates ranged from 0.484 to 0.577 for juvenile males and from 0.191 to 0.355 for adult males (Table 2). Annual survival rate estimates for

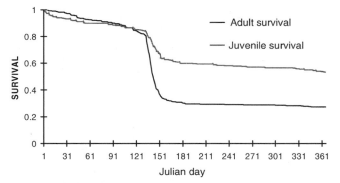

Fig. 1. Average survival distributions of juvenile and adult male turkeys in western Kentucky, 1995–2000.

adult males were significantly lower than for juvenile males ($\chi^2 = 76.41$, df = 1, $P < 0.001$).

Winter survival (1 Dec–10 Apr) ranged from 0.772 to 0.941 for juvenile males and from 0.735 to 0.874 for adult males (Table 2). Summer/fall (10 May–30 Nov) survival ranged from 0.778 to 0.941 for juvenile males and from 0.716 to 0.941 for adult males (Table 2). Seasonal survival rate estimates during winter ($\chi^2 = 1.44$, df = 1, $P = 0.230$) and summer/fall ($\chi^2 < 0.01$, df = 1, $P = 1.000$) did not differ between juvenile and adult males.

Annual natural mortality rate estimates (with human-caused mortality censored) ranged from 0.075 to 0.380 for juvenile males and from 0.218 to 0.475 for adult males (Table 3). Annual human-caused mortality rate estimates (with non-human-caused mortality censored) ranged from 0.212 to 0.401 for juvenile males and from 0.546 to 0.738 for adult males (Table 3). Annual natural mortality rate estimates did not differ between juvenile and adults ($\chi^2 = 2.273$, df = 1, $P = 0.132$); however, annual human-caused mortality was

Table 3. Natural and human-caused mortality rate estimates [estimate (SE)] for radio-marked juvenile (JV) and adult (AD) males in Western Kentucky, 1995–2001. The natural mortality rate was estimated by censoring deaths not due to natural causes. The human-caused mortality rate was estimated by censoring deaths not due to human causes. The overall estimates and their associated standard errors were generated from program CONTRAST (Himes and Sauer 1989).

| | | Mortality | |
Year	Age	Natural	Human-caused
1995–1996	JV	0.194 (0.042)	0.284 (0.046)
	AD	0.253 (0.078)	0.677 (0.055)
1996–1997	JV	0.333 (0.071)	0.212 (0.067)
	AD	0.218 (0.061)	0.546 (0.056)
1997–1998	JV	0.075 (0.034)	0.401 (0.051)
	AD	0.271 (0.074)	0.738 (0.044)
1998–1999	JV	0.380 (0.054)	0.219 (0.051)
	AD	0.475 (0.075)	0.539 (0.071)
1999–2000	JV	0.266 (0.049)	0.320 (0.050)
	AD	0.266 (0.063)	0.596 (0.052)
2000–2001	JV	0.166 (0.063)	0.330 (0.071)
	AD	0.272 (0.095)	0.557 (0.083)
Overall	JV	0.236 (0.021)	0.294 (0.023)
	AD	0.293 (0.031)	0.609 (0.025)[a]

[a] Human-caused mortality of adults was significantly greater than that of juvenile males ($P < 0.001$).

significantly greater for adult males than for juvenile males ($\chi^2 = 84.62$, df = 1, $P < 0.001$).

Legal harvest accounted for a higher percentage of the deaths of adult males (58.5) than for juvenile males (39.6; Table 4). In addition to the 14 birds killed and not checked during spring turkey hunting seasons, 18 birds were killed illegally outside spring turkey season. Of the 416 birds that died during the study, 32 (8%) were known to be the result of illegal kill. Eight more birds disappeared under suspicious circumstances and were thought to have been poached (these birds were censored in the survival analyses). No birds were lost during any of the 7 10-day modern-gun deer sea-

Table 2. Seasonal and annual survival rate estimates [estimate (SE)] for radio-marked juvenile (JV) and adult (AD) males in western Kentucky, 1995–2001. Seasonal intervals were winter (1 Dec–10 Apr) and summer/fall (10 May–30 Nov). The overall estimates and their associated standard errors were generated from program CONTRAST (Hines and Sauer 1989).

| | | Season | | |
Year	Age	Winter	Summer/Fall	Annual
1995–1996	JV	0.862 (0.058)	0.910 (0.033)	0.577 (0.045)
	AD	0.774 (0.070)	0.889 (0.062)	0.241 (0.044)
1996–1997	JV	0.841 (0.045)	0.778 (0.068)	0.526 (0.067)
	AD	0.833 (0.054)	0.898 (0.048)	0.355 (0.048)
1997–1998	JV	0.941 (0.040)	0.941 (0.030)	0.554 (0.049)
	AD	0.861 (0.036)	0.836 (0.066)	0.191 (0.034)
1998–1999	JV	0.772 (0.047)	0.804 (0.050)	0.484 (0.049)
	AD	0.735 (0.059)	0.716 (0.080)	0.242 (0.044)
1999–2000	JV	0.775 (0.064)	0.818 (0.045)	0.500 (0.046)
	AD	0.874 (0.034)	0.821 (0.058)	0.296 (0.041)
2000–2001	JV	0.867 (0.047)	0.853 (0.061)	0.559 (0.069)
	AD	0.766 (0.053)	0.941 (0.057)	0.322 (0.066)
Overall	JV	0.843 (0.021)	0.851 (0.020)	0.533 (0.023)
	AD	0.807 (0.021)	0.850 (0.025)	0.275 (0.019)[a]

[a] Annual survival of adults was significantly less than that of juvenile males ($P < 0.001$).

Table 4. The number of deaths by cause for radio-marked juvenile (JV) and adult (AD) males in western Kentucky, 1995–2000. The percent of total deaths (all years combined) by cause for juvenile and adult males is shown parenthetically in the bottom row.

| | | Cause of mortality | | | | | |
Year	Age	Predation	Legal	Illegal	Crippling	Other	Total
1995	JV	7	6	3	0	3	19
	AD	4	12	8	2	1	27
1996	JV	15	11	1	0	2	29
	AD	7	19	3	1	2	32
1997	JV	3	10	3	1	0	17
	AD	13	53	3	3	0	72
1998	JV	11	11	0	1	10	33
	AD	18	16	2	4	2	42
1999	JV	4	6	1	3	5	19
	AD	11	40	2	5	5	63
2000	JV	6	11	2	2	1	22
	AD	13	22	4	1	1	41
Total	JV	46 (33.1)	55 (39.6)	10 (7.2)	7 (5.0)	21 (15.1)	139
	AD	66 (23.8)	162 (58.5)	22 (7.9)	16 (5.8)	11 (4.0)	277

sons during this study. Of the losses due to predators (n = 112), the type of predator could be attributed for 72 of them. Of these, bobcats (*Lynx rufus*) accounted for 44.4%; coyotes (*Canis latrans*), 25.0%; great-horned owls (*Bubo virginianus*), 18.1%; and red fox (*Vulpes vulpes*), 13.9%. Some of the kills attributed to coyotes could have been the result of coyotes scavenging kills made by other predators.

Of 256 juvenile males alive the first day of 6 spring turkey seasons, 19.5% ($\bar{x}$ = 20.1%, range = 14.7–31.3%) were legally harvested (Table 1). Of 343 adult males alive the first day of 7 spring turkey seasons, 52.2% ($\bar{x}$ = 50.0%, range = 37.5–65.8%) were legally killed (Table 1). Illegal kill during spring turkey season (killed but not checked at mandatory check stations) and crippling losses accounted for 1.2% and 1.6%, respectively, of the juvenile males and 3.2% and 4.4%, of the adult males, respectively (Table 1). Total human-caused mortality during the 7 spring turkey seasons accounted for 22.7% and 59.8% of the juvenile and adult males (Table 1).

During the 7 archery turkey seasons (3–3.5 months) no radiomarked males were killed. During Kentucky's fall firearms turkey seasons (2–6 Dec 1998; 1–5 Dec 1999; 29 Nov–3 Dec 2000; 28 Nov–2 Dec 2001), 1.4% (4 [3 legal harvest, 1 crippling loss]/276) of the males alive at the beginning of the season were killed.

The harvest of juvenile males varied from 0.103/km^2 of forest in 2000 to 0.213/km^2 of forest in 2002. The harvest of adult males varied from 0.311/km^2 of forest in 1996 to 0.505/km^2 of forest in 2002. Estimates of the prehunt population for each year were derived by dividing the spring harvest per km^2 of forest for each age class by the proportion killed during the spring turkey season (see Table 1). Prehunt population size of juvenile males ranged from 0.286/km^2 of forest in 1998 to 0.908/km^2 of forest in 1999. Prehunt population size of adult males ranged from 0.527/km^2 of forest in 1998 to 0.817/km^2 of forest in 2002.

Permit sales for the 3 counties were available for 1996–2002. The number of permits sold in the 3 counties ranged from 0.954/km^2 of forest in 1996 to 1.55/km^2 of forest in 2002. Permit sales in the 3 counties provide a minimum estimate of hunter numbers because permit buyers from other counties also hunt in the 3-county area. In addition, landowners may hunt without a permit and hunters over 65 are exempt from buying a turkey permit. Based on the number of turkeys shot by landowners and hunters over 65, we estimate the density of hunters to be at least 20% higher than the minimum figures given above.

Birds caught as juvenile males died significantly further from their trap site (median = 2,772 m) than did adult males ($\bar{x}$ = 2094 m; χ^2 = 34.4062, df = 1, P < 0.0001). Ninety-nine percent of juvenile males dispersed less than 12,998 m, while 99% of the adult males dispersed less than 7,610 m. One juvenile male dispersed 20,736 m. As an example, patterns of dispersal from 1 trap site where more than 10 juvenile and 10 adults were caught are shown in Figure 2.

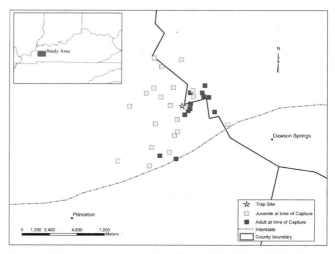

Fig. 2. Dispersal, based on location of deaths, of 21 male turkeys caught as juveniles and 12 male turkeys caught as adults from a trap site in western Kentucky.

DISCUSSION

Mean annual survival of adult males in our study (26.2%) was lower than the 51% reported in Wisconsin (Paisley et al. 1996), the 36% reported in Georgia (Ielmini et al. 1992), and the 37% reported for 2 study areas in the Missouri Ozarks (Hubbard and Vangilder *this volume*). Mean survival of juvenile males in this study (55%) was slightly lower than in the Georgia study (63%) and in the Missouri Ozarks on 2 study areas (60% and 57%). The combined annual survival rate for juvenile and adult males in a Mississippi study was 46% (Godwin et al. 1991). In our study, the overall annual survival for juveniles (55.2%) was much higher than for adult males (26.2%) because of the different mortality rates between juveniles (22.7%) and adults (59.8%) during the spring turkey season. Studies in Wisconsin (Paisley et al. 1996) and Mississippi (Godwin et al. 1991) found no difference in juvenile and adult male survival during the spring turkey season. However, studies in Georgia (Ielmini et al. 1992), Missouri (Lewis 1980, Hubbard and Vangilder *this volume*), and Kentucky (Wright 1998) showed that adults were more vulnerable than juveniles during the spring turkey season.

In our study, seasonal survival rates of juvenile and adult males outside the spring turkey season were ≥0.80. Vangilder (1996) also reported high seasonal survival rates for radiomarked adult males outside the spring season (≥0.75) in the eastern Missouri Ozarks.

Natural mortality rates (human-caused deaths censored) for juvenile (20.1%) and adult males (24.7%) did not differ. Speake (1980) reported a 10.9% annual rate of mortality for males from predation across 7 years and 3 study areas using pooled monthly mortality rates (percent method).

Because of the large difference in vulnerability between juvenile and adult males to spring harvest, the human-caused mortality rate of juvenile males was much lower (0.30) than that of adult males (0.65).

Of the 416 deaths during the study, 69 (27%) were caused by predation. Legal harvest accounted for 54%

of the overall mortality. In the eastern Missouri Ozarks, Vangilder (1996) reported that 51% of adult male mortality was caused by predation while 30% of the deaths were the result of legal harvest. In Mississippi, 71% of the total mortality of males was the result of legal harvest (Godwin et al. 1991).

The average harvest rate (58%) of adult males in this study was higher than any other recorded in the literature. In Wisconsin, Paisley et al. (1996) reported harvest rates of males that averaged 30 to 37%. Because the proportion of adult males in the spring harvest was declining and production had been poor, they concluded that at these levels of harvest, the adult male population was being overexploited. In Georgia, Ielmini et al. (1992) reported that 45% of the radio-marked males were killed on a wildlife management area. Ielmini et al. (1992) also felt the opportunity to kill a 'trophy' male was limited because most of the adult males killed were 2-year-olds. In Mississippi, Godwin et al. (1991) found the harvest rate of males ranged from 37 to 58%. In the Missouri Ozarks on 2 study areas, 27% and 41% of adult males were killed during spring turkey season while only 19% and 14% of juvenile males were killed (Hubbard and Vangilder *this volume*). Hubbard and Vangilder (*this volume*) believed that any further increases in spring harvest would impact turkey hunting quality.

Because of our relatively large sample size and daily monitoring during spring turkey season, we were better able to detect crippling losses and birds killed and not checked during the spring turkey season (Table 1). Adult males were more likely to be lost to crippling (4.4% of those alive opening day of spring turkey season) than juvenile males (1.6%). In some years, unusually high predation shortly after spring turkey season suggests that crippling losses are probably higher than indicated above. Williams and Austin (1988) reported that 3 of 35 (8.6%) radiomarked males were lost to crippling during the 16-day spring turkey season in Florida. Two of 74 known mortalities occurring during spring turkey season in Mississippi were classified as crippling losses (Godwin et al. 1991). Six mortalities occurring during spring turkey season in Wisconsin that were classified as apparent predation kills could have been caused by crippling (Paisley et al. 1996).

In Missouri, after the 1994 spring turkey season, about 8% of the respondents to a survey reported shooting at a male and not retrieving it (Vangilder and Sheriff 1996). In West Virginia, after the 1995 spring season, 9% of the hunters reported crippling a male (Pack et al. 1996). On average, from 1983–1993, 8% of West Virginia spring turkey hunters reported crippling a male (Taylor et al. 1996). In Virginia, from 1987–1992, an average of 6% of the respondents to a survey reported crippling a male (Norman and Steffen 1992). During a 1989–1991 turkey hunter survey in Wisconsin, 9% of hunters reported hitting but not recovering turkeys they shot at (J. F. Kubisiak, Wisconsin Department of Natural Resources, unpublished data). In a 1998 turkey hunter survey in Kentucky, 27.3% of hunters reported shooting at 1 or more birds and not recovering them (G. A. Wright and L. Garri-

son, Kentucky Department of Fish and Wildlife Resources, unpublished data).

In our study, adults were more likely to be killed and not checked (3.2%) than juveniles (1.6%). On a Mississippi study area, Gribben (1986) reported a 95% check-in rate for harvested males. On 2 study areas in the eastern Missouri Ozarks, 1.9 and 2.5% of the radio-marked males shot during spring turkey season were not checked at mandatory check stations (Vangilder 1996). Hubbard and Vangilder (*this volume*) reported that 8 and 4% of the males killed during the spring turkey season were the result of illegal and suspicious loss.

Males taken illegally accounted for 32 (8%) of the 416 birds that died during this study. An additional 8 birds that mysteriously disappeared were suspected of being killed illegally. Most studies of male turkeys reported little or no illegal losses to hunting (Godwin et al. 1991, Paisley et al. 1996, Ielmini et al. 1992). However, Vangilder (1996) reported that 15% of the deaths of radiomarked males on 2 study areas in the eastern Missouri Ozarks were caused by illegal kill.

In Wisconsin, in an experimental wild turkey management zone, 7.2 hunters/km^2 of forest resulted in a harvest rate of 0.323 or 1.3 birds shot/km^2 of forest (Paisley et al. 1996). On our study area, in 2002, when harvest was greatest, about 1.9 hunters/km^2 of forest were associated with an average harvest rate of 0.227 for juvenile males and 0.598 for adult males and a total harvest of 0.213 juvenile males/km^2 of forest and 0.505 adult males/km^2 of forest. Total harvest for both juvenile and adult males combined was 0.718/km^2 of forest. In the eastern Missouri Ozarks from 1990–1997, about 1.0 hunter/km^2 of forest resulted in a harvest rate of 0.300 for adult males and a total harvest of 0.2 adult males/km^2 of forest (L. D. Vangilder, Missouri Department of Conservation, unpublished data). These comparisons among states suggest no consistent relationships among hunter density, harvest rates, and harvest densities.

Juvenile males clearly dispersed further, on average, than did adult males. During our study, juvenile males tended to leave the area where they were trapped in late fall or in early spring. The difference in dispersal rate suggests that juvenile males from other areas replace adult males as they die.

Vangilder and Kurzejeski (1995) reported the results of a simulation model with varying levels of spring harvest on the male segment of the turkey population. They found that when 45% of the males were killed, annual survival rates were 0.26 for adult males and 0.40 for juvenile males (see Vangilder and Kurzejeski 1995; Table 19). Their model assumed adult males were twice as vulnerable to spring harvest as juvenile males. They did not, however, report for a 45% harvest of males what proportion of the adult or juvenile male population was killed. We re-ran the simulations using parameter estimates identical to those used in Vangilder and Kurzejeski (1995) and calculated what proportion of the prehunt population of adult and juvenile males were killed. At a 45% harvest of males, 63 and 32% of the adult and juvenile male prehunt population was killed. In our study, 60 and 23% of the adult and juvenile male prehunt population was killed. Annual survival rates were 0.28 and 0.53 for adult and juvenile males. Thus, a 45% level of harvest in the model corresponds well with the adult harvest rates (model, 63%; this study, 60%) and adult survival rates (model, 26%; this study 28%) observed in this study. However, at a 45% level of harvest in the model, juvenile male harvest rates are higher (model, 32%; this study, 23%) and juvenile survival rates are lower (model, 40%; this study, 53%) than those observed in this study. This comparison suggests that in western Kentucky, adult males are more than twice as vulnerable to spring harvest than are juvenile males.

MANAGEMENT IMPLICATIONS

A comparison of the results of this study with the Missouri model (Vangilder and Kurzejeski 1995) suggests that the spring turkey harvest in the study area cannot be increased without causing a decline in the quality of turkey hunting. By far, the greatest factor affecting the male population is the spring turkey season. The current 3-week season (2-bird bag limit) with all-day hunting cannot be liberalized without having a negative impact on the male population and the quality of spring turkey hunting. We believe the high levels of adult male harvest observed in our study are being sustained only because the wild turkey population is still expanding rapidly after restoration. The low vulnerability of juvenile males along with their high survival rate outside spring turkey season results in a high rate of recruitment to the adult population. We believe when population growth stabilizes and annual reproduction begins to fluctuate, the observed level of adult male harvest will not be sustainable without a substantial decrease in the proportion of adult males in the population and in the harvest. Adult males currently make up about 70% of the spring harvest in Kentucky. If harvest continues at the present rate after population growth stabilizes, we expect the proportion of adults in the spring harvest to decline and the total spring harvest to exhibit greater fluctuations because the total harvest will be more reflective of the previous year's reproduction. If the harvest of juvenile males increases, fewer of them will be available to disperse to other areas and replace adult males that have died.

Crippling losses and illegal kills are taking far too many birds. Public relations and turkey hunter education need to stress the importance of these factors. Thousands of additional males could be available to turkey hunters if these factors could be reduced. It is estimated that 4,500 adult and 1,100 juvenile males were lost to crippling and illegal kills during the 2002 spring turkey season in Kentucky. In western Kentucky, illegal kills outside of season are having a minor impact on the male wild turkey population.

ACKNOWLEDGMENTS

Special thanks to wildlife technicians B. J. Morse, S. L. Wright and conservation officer C. E. Gillespie for their assistance with the field work. Thanks to the many landowners and hunters who made this study possible, especially M. A. Hamby and R. E. Murphy. M. W. Hubbard helped improve the manuscript. L. W. Burger wrote the SAS program for the log-rank tests. This research was supported by funding from the Federal Aid in Wildlife Restoration Act under Pittman-Robertson Project W-45-D, the National Wild Turkey Federation (NWTF) and the Kentucky Chapter of the NWTF.

LITERATURE CITED

Conover, W. A. 1971. Practical nonparametric statistics. John Wiley and Sons, New York, New York, USA.

Godwin, K. D., G. A. Hurst, and R. L. Kelley. 1991. Survival rates of radio-equipped wild turkey gobblers in east-central Mississippi. Proceedings of the Annual Conference of the Southeastern Association of Fish and Wildlife Agencies 45: 218–226.

Gribben, K. J. 1986. Population estimates for the wild turkey in east-central Mississippi. Thesis, Mississippi State University, Mississippi State, Mississippi, USA.

Hines, J. E., and J. R. Sauer. 1989. Program CONTRAST—a general program of the analysis of several survival or recovery rate estimates. U. S. Fish and Wildlife Service, Fish and Wildlife Technical Report 24.

Hubbard, M. W., and L. D. Vangilder. *This volume.* Survival of eastern wild turkey males in the eastern Missouri Ozarks. Proceedings of the National Wild Turkey Symposium 9:*This volume.*

Ielmini, M. R., A. S. Johnson, and P. E. Hale. 1992. Habitat and mortality relationships of wild turkey gobblers in the Georgia Piedmont. Proceedings of the Annual Conference of the Southeastern Association of Fish and Wildlife Agencies 46: 128–137.

Lewis, J. B. 1980. Fifteen years of wild turkey trapping, banding, and recovery data in Missouri. Proceedings of the National Wild Turkey Symposium 4:24–31.

Norman, G. W., and D. E. Steffen. 1992. 1992 Virginia gobbler season survey. Virginia Department of Game and Inland Fisheries, Verona, Virginia, USA.

Pack, J. C., W. K. Igo, C. I. Taylor, G. H. Sharp, and J. E. Evans. 1996. 1995 spring gobbler survey. West Virginia Division of Natural Resources, Wildlife Resources Section and West Virginia Chapter of the National Wild Turkey Federation. Wildlife Resources Section Bulletin 96–1.

Paisley, R. N., R. G. Wright, and J. F. Kubisiak. 1996. Survival of wild turkey gobblers in southwestern Wisconsin. Proceedings of the National Wild Turkey Symposium 7:39–44.

Pollock, K. H., S. R. Winterstein, C. M. Bunck, and P. D. Curtis. 1989. Survival analysis in telemetry studies: the staggered entry design. Journal of Wildlife Management 53:7–15.

Speake, D. W. 1980. Predation on wild turkeys in Alabama. Proceedings of the National Wild Turkey Symposium 4:86–101.

Taylor, C. I. 1995. Survival of wild turkey hens in the New River Valley, Summers County, West Virginia. Proceedings of the New River Symposium 12:97–107.

————, W. K. Igo, P. R. Johansen, J. C. Pack, J. E. Evans, and G. H. Sharp. 1996. West Virginia spring turkey hunters and hunting, 1983–93. Proceedings of the National Wild Turkey Symposium 7:259–268.

Vangilder, L. D. 1996. Survival and cause-specific mortality of wild turkeys in the Missouri Ozarks. Proceedings of the National Wild Turkey Symposium 7:21–31.

————, and E. W. Kurzejeski. 1995. Population ecology of the eastern wild turkey in northern Missouri. Wildlife Monographs 130.

————, and S. L. Sheriff. 1990. Survival estimation when the fates of some animals are unknown. Transactions of the Missouri Academy of Science 24:57–68.

————, and ————. 1996. Turkey hunter information survey—1996. Missouri Department of Conservation, Federal Aid in Wildlife Restoration Project W-13-R-50, Study 14. Final Report.

Williams, L. E., Jr. 1981. The book of the wild turkey. Winchester Press, Tulsa, Oklahoma, USA.

————, and D. H. Austin. 1988. Studies of the wild turkey in Florida. Florida Game and Freshwater Fish Commission, Technical Bulletin 10.

Wright, G. A. 1998. Turkey hunting data. Kentucky Department Fish and Wildlife Resources, Federal Aid in Wildlife Restoration Project W-45-30, Annual Report.

————, and L. D. Vangilder. 2001. Survival of eastern wild turkey males in western Kentucky. Proceedings of the National Wild Turkey Symposium 8:187–194.

George A. Wright (left) served in the U.S. Navy from 1961 through 1969. He received his B.S. in Wildlife Management from Tennessee Technological University in 1972, and his M.S. in Wildlife Management from Auburn University in 1975. He was employed by the Kentucky Deparment of Fish and Wildlife Resources (KDFWR) from 1974 through 2002 and as the state's first turkey program coordinator from 1978 through 2003. He supervised modern-day turkey restoration efforts in Kentucky, which lasted from 1978 to 1998, and watched the turkey population in Kentucky grow from almost none to 230,000 birds. George used turkeys trapped in Mississippi and turkeys obtained from Missouri through a river otter trade to build his own supply source, transplanting them into prime locations with good natural habitat and with landowners who promised to protect them. The transplants took root and soon he was trapping turkeys in state and transplanting them all over Kentucky. After restoration efforts were essentially complete, George concentrated his efforts on research: understanding the impacts of spring harvest on gobblers. George used his great turkey trapping skills to catch and put radio transmitters on almost 600 gobblers over the course of 5 years in and around Caldwell County, Kentucky. George A. Wright, the undisputed architect of Kentucky's wild turkey restoration, management, and research program who retired from the KDFWR in 2002 after 27 years, suffered a massive heart attack while turkey hunting with his wife in Mexico in March 2005 and died a few days later in a Nashville hospital. He was 62. *Larry D. Vangilder* (right) is Chief of the Missouri Deparment of Conservation's Resource Science Center. He directs the activities of 40 resource scientists who gather information to help make better policy and management decisions. He is also an adjunct associate professor of Fisheries and Wildlife Sciences at the University of Missouri–Columbia. He has a B.S. and M.S. in Fisheries and Wildlife Biology from the University of Missouri–Columbia and a Ph.D. in Zoology from the Ohio State University. He also held post-doctoral positions with the Savannah River Ecology Laboratory and with Patuxent Wildlife Research Center through Cornell University. He started with the Missouri Department of Conservation in 1985 as a wildlife research biologist with responsibility for wild turkey research and management and research in forest ecosystems. In 1999 Larry became a Research Supervisor in the Wildlife Research Section. He moved to his current position in January 2003. His interests include animal population dynamics and forest ecosystems. He has been involved in the development of the Missouri Ozark Forest Ecosystem Project since its inception.

A YOUTH TURKEY SEASON IN MISSOURI: IMPLICATIONS TOWARDS RECRUITMENT AND RETENTION

Jeff Beringer[1]
Missouri Department of Conservation, 1110 South College Avenue, Columbia, MO 65201, USA

Joshua J. Millspaugh
Department of Fisheries and Wildlife Sciences, University of Missouri, 302 Anheuser-Busch Natural Resources Building, Columbia, MO 65211, USA

Ronald A. Reitz
Missouri Department of Conservation, 1110 South College Avenue, Columbia, MO 65201, USA

Michael Hubbard
Missouri Department of Conservation, P.O. Box 180 Jefferson City, MO 65102, USA

Abstract: Responding to declines in hunter recruitment and retention, the Missouri Department of Conservation has provided a 2-day wild turkey (*Meleagris gallopavo*) youth hunt that occurs on the weekend one week prior to the regular season. We assessed recruitment (the number of new participants) and retention (the number of returning participants each year) of youth turkey hunters in Missouri from 1996–2004. Sales of youth tags increased from 6,168 in 1996 to 9,950 in 2000, 13% per year. After the initiation of a special youth hunt, the number of turkey tags sold increased about 18% per year between 2000 and 2004. From 1996–2000, about 6,700 turkey hunters were recruited compared with 12,300 from 2001–2004. The number of turkey hunters recruited from 2001–2004 represents about 10% of all Missouri turkey hunters. Since the inception of the youth turkey season, about 60–65% of recruited youths hunted at least one more year and about 25–30% hunted in 5 consecutive years. Based on hunter attitude data, 84% of youths hunted during the special youth season in 2005. In contrast to other youth activities, such as baseball which has seen national declines of about 41% over the same period and 5% declines for youth fishing, recruitment and retention of youth turkey hunters has increased in Missouri. While turkey permit sales to adult hunters have remained stable, permit sales to youth hunters have increased. We believe the special youth hunting season has resulted in an increased interest in turkey hunting by Missouri youth.

Proceedings of the National Wild Turkey Symposium 9:375–380

Key words: hunter attitude, hunter recruitment, *Meleagris gallopavo*, retention, wild turkey.

State agencies routinely monitor hunter participation and attitudes through license sales and surveys of hunters. Trends in hunter numbers allow agencies to forecast budgetary needs, measure support for management programs, and adjust harvest strategies. Revenue from hunting license sales and taxes paid on hunting equipment are important for a variety of habitat management activities for game and nongame species, critical habitat acquisition, and education programs that promote conservation of wildlife species and their habitats. Hunter attitude surveys enable agencies to gather input and opinions of user groups (e.g., youth) regarding various issues.

Recently, participation in hunting activity has de-

clined (Duda 1993). Nationally, the number of hunters has decreased 18% since 1975, but trends in some regions suggest stable to slightly increasing participation (United States Fish and Wildlife Service 1997). Hunting participation in Missouri has decreased for small game hunting, but has been stable to slightly increasing over the past 10 years for turkey hunting (Missouri Department of Conservation 2003). The average age of Missouri turkey hunters has, however, increased from 36 to 42 years since 1978 (J. Beringer, Missouri Department of Conservation, unpublished data) sug-

---

[1] E-mail: Jeff.Beringer@mdc.mo.gov

gesting our clientele are aging faster than we are recruiting new hunters. A recent bright spot in permit sales and participation in Missouri has been sales of youth deer and turkey permits. Since the creation of a reduced-cost permit for youth in 1999 and a separate youth turkey season in 2001, participation by youth turkey hunters has increased substantially. The Missouri youth deer and turkey permit costs $17.00 and entitles the holder to harvest 1 spring male turkey or turkey with a visible beard, 1 autumn turkey of either sex, and 1 deer of either sex. The special youth-only spring turkey season occurs on the weekend 9 days prior to the traditional Monday opening day.

We describe youth hunter participation during spring turkey seasons following the creation of a low-cost youth deer and turkey permit coupled with seasons designated for youth-only participation. We attempt to determine if the permits and season have resulted in more youth participation (recruitment) and whether these youth continue to hunt turkeys in subsequent years. Further, we describe success rates and attitudes of youth hunters to better understand the parameters that may increase youth participation in, and satisfaction with, youth turkey hunting.

METHODS

We obtained youth spring turkey hunting data from 1996–2004 from the Missouri Department of Conservation point-of-sale (POS) database which records license sales and an associated unique hunter identification number (conservation number). Youth hunters in Missouri eligible to purchase a youth permit are aged 6–15 yrs. We determined annual recruitment and retention rates of youth turkey hunters using birth dates and conservation numbers to track individual hunters throughout our study period. We defined recruitment as the number of new youths (≤15 yr) that purchased a youth deer and turkey permit prior to the end of the spring turkey season in each year. Missouri survey data suggest that 85% of youth turkey permit buyers actually hunt turkeys. We compared recruitment rates before and after 2001 (the year a special youth hunt was established) using a *t*-test.

We quantified retention in two ways. First, using conservation numbers, we tallied the number of youths that hunted during subsequent years (e.g., how many youths that hunted in 1998 hunted in at least 1, 2, 3, 4, 5, and 6 years). This provided us with information about overall retention. Second, we recorded the youth hunters in each year, treating them as a cohort related to recruitment, and tallied their return in succeeding years (e.g., how many youths that hunted in 1998 hunted in 1999, 2000, 2001, 2002, 2003, and 2004). This second method to assess retention allowed us to better understand youth participation patterns by year.

To assess the impact of regulation changes on permit sales to youth we calculated the annual rate of change for youth sales before the low cost permit was created (1996–1998), after the low cost permit was created but before the youth season (1999–2000), and after the youth season was created (2001–2004).

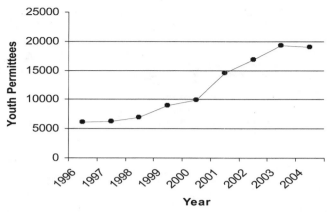

Fig. 1. The number of youth permittees in the spring turkey youth season, by year.

To compare attitudes of youth and adult turkey hunters in Missouri, we analyzed results of available spring post-season harvest surveys for the years 2000 (pre-youth season) through 2004, stratified by permit type (youth deer and turkey and resident spring turkey permittees). In these surveys, we contacted 8,000 purchasers of spring turkey permits. The number of youth hunters contacted has varied over time, but has been about 900 for the past two years. Post-season harvest surveys are used to obtain estimates of harvest and hunting pressure, number of trips on public and private land, and perceptions of interference by other hunters. These estimates may be biased as harvest estimates derived from surveys are often higher than those reported by check stations. However, trends in survey estimates closely follow those of actual check station data. While it is possible that nonresponse bias exists, no follow-up analyses were conducted to determine the effects of nonresponse on our survey estimates.

We also compared youth and adult responses to a 2004 Turkey Hunter Attitude Survey. We conducted this survey to measure turkey hunter attitudes toward potential spring and fall turkey regulation changes. We used POS databases for spring 2004 and fall 2003 to randomly select 8,000 adult and 2,000 youth turkey hunters for the survey. We received useable responses from 5,250 adults and 1,136 youth. We compared responses for the two groups using contingency tables and chi-square tests.

RESULTS

The number of youth permittees (from POS database) in the spring turkey season increased every year, except 2004 (Figure 1). From 1996 to 2004, the number of permittees increased more than three-fold to near 20,000 permittees. The youth permit was first available in 1999 and 1,276 permits were sold. The greatest increase in youth license sales, with 4,544 new youth permittees occurred in 2001 when a special youth turkey season was created. Our analysis further indicated that significantly more youths purchased a license in 2001 and beyond than did before 2001 (*t* = −7.464, *P* < 0.001, df = 7).

Table 1. Number of youth license buyers in Missouri that purchased a spring turkey hunting license in multiple years, 1996–2003.

Number of additional years license purchased	Year license purchased							
	1996	1997	1998	1999	2000	2001	2002	2003
≥1	3237	4732	5355	6714	7496	10090	11501	10301
≥2	2600	3930	4293	5739	5916	7490	7331	
≥3	2159	3230	3437	4276	4513	4787		
≥4	1820	2662	2609	3217	2931			
≥5	1490	2078	1706	2087				
≥6	1164	1533	1361					
≥7	894	978						
≥8	558							

Overall retention numbers of youth turkey permittees declined by about 20–30% per year (Table 1). That is, about 70–80% of youths hunted at least one additional year; of those that participated at least once about 70–80% participated twice and so on (Table 1). However, the first year of the study, we observed lower retention when only 52.4% of those participating hunted at least one additional year. The 2003 data indicate a similar trend, but this may change as youth have additional opportunity (years) to purchase a license. Otherwise, overall retention numbers were consistently between 70–80%.

The number of youth purchasing a permit during subsequent years declined about 10–20% per year (Table 2). That is, about 80–90% of youths hunted the following year. Thus, retention from year to year remained high for youth turkey hunters. It is likely these numbers are slightly biased as some nonresident youth might graduate to an adult tag but not purchase one because they no longer receive a price break. These nonresident youth may have purchased a resident permit for their resident state but we were unable to obtain this information. Youth that purchased adult permits in Missouri were tracked through their conservation number.

Annual rates of change for permit sales to youth hunters was 6.2% per year from 1996–1998 (before the low cost permit was created) 20.1% from 1999–2000 (after the low cost permit was created but before the youth season) and 18.8% from 2001–2004 (after the youth season was created).

Table 2. Retention of individual Missouri youth that purchased a spring turkey hunting license at least once during subsequent years, by year.

Year	Year							
	1996	1997	1998	1999	2000	2001	2002	2003
1997	2590							
1998	2198	3843						
1999	1947	3427	4465					
2000	1771	3090	3959	5622				
2001	1503	2584	3379	4895	6405			
2002	1377	2256	2956	4242	5553	8751		
2003	1314	2066	2641	3786	4909	7528	10481	
2004	1221	1877	2302	3128	3989	6088	8351	10301

Table 3. Proportion (±SE) of youth resident deer and turkey and adult hunters hunting the first, second, and third weeks of the 2000–2004 Missouri spring turkey seasons.

Year	Week 1		Week 2		Week 3	
	Youth	Adult	Youth	Adult	Youth	Adult
2000[a]	78.6	86.4	64.9	75.1	43.5	49.2
	(3.3)	(0.6)	(3.9)	(0.7)	(4.0)	(0.8)
2001	59.8	84.0	38.2	73.4	28.9	49.6
	(3.9)	(0.6)	(3.8)	(0.8)	(3.6)	(0.9)
2002	57.3	84.2	40.4	77.1	21.3	51.5
	(3.7)	(0.6)	(3.8)	(0.7)	(3.1)	(0.9)
2003	54.1	84.8	36.6	74.4	25.1	50.2
	(2.3)	(0.6)	(2.2)	(0.7)	(2.0)	(0.8)
2004	50.9	83.9	35.6	75.8	25.1	53.8
	(2.3)	(0.6)	(2.2)	(0.7)	(2.0)	(0.8)

[a] No special youth season.

The percentage of respondents that said they hunted the first, second, and third weeks, respectively, decreased during the regular season (Table 3); however, about 30% of youths harvested birds during the special early youth season. In 2001 a youth season was introduced that preceded the regular season. As a result, the percentage of youth hunting the regular season declined, but appeared to have stabilized in 2003 and 2004. Surveys indicated that, since the inception of the youth weekend, most harvest occurred during that time period (Table 4). Youth participation was 84%, 87%, 87%, and 83% for 2001, 2002, 2003, and 2004, respectively.

Prior to the youth season implemented in 2001, youth harvest patterns were similar to adults with the top harvest days being the Monday opener (about 25% of the total harvest), and either the next day or the first Saturday after the opener (usually contributing 7% to 11% of total harvest). Since 2001, the first day of youth weekend has been the top harvest day for youth, followed by the second day of youth season.

Youth permit buyers typically hunted fewer days than adult resident permit buyers. The mean number of days hunted annually, since 2000, has remained relatively consistent, with 3.61 (SE = 0.24) to 3.71 (SE = 0.14) days for youth permit buyers, and from 5.70 (SE = 0.07) to 5.88 (SE = 0.07) days for adult respondents (resident spring permittees).

Success rates for youth hunters increased with the advent of the youth weekend. The percentage of youth harvesting a bird increased an average of about 9% with success rates ranging from a low of about 23% in 2000 (no youth season), to 33% in 2001 and 2002,

Table 4. Proportion (±SE) of turkey harvest by youth deer and turkey hunters taken on the first and second day of youth spring turkey seasons in Missouri, 2001–2004.

Year	Harvest (%)		
	First day of youth weekend	Second day of youth weekend	Cumulative
2001	47.9 (3.9)	12.2 (2.6)	60.1 (3.8)
2002	44.9 (3.8)	30.6 (3.5)	75.5 (3.3)
2003	39.7 (2.2)	29.1 (2.1)	68.8 (2.1)
2004	45.3 (2.3)	17.5 (1.7)	62.8 (2.2)

Table 5. Percent hunter success (±SE) for youth deer and turkey and adult resident spring turkey hunters in Missouri, 2000–2004.

Year	One turkey harvested		Two turkeys harvested	
	Youth success	Adult success	Youth success	Adult success
2000[a]	22.3 (3.4)	29.1 (0.8)	0.7 (0.7)	13.7 (0.6)
2001	30.6 (3.6)	29.0 (0.8)	0.6 (0.6)	12.4 (0.6)
2002	31.7 (3.6)	27.6 (0.8)	1.2 (0.8)	11.2 (0.5)
2003	30.9 (2.1)	28.3 (0.8)	0.8 (0.4)	10.2 (0.5)
2004	31.5 (2.1)	29.0 (0.8)	0.7 (0.4)	12.0 (0.5)

[a] No special youth season.

and 32% in 2003 and 2004 (Table 5). However, youths are still not as successful as older hunters with resident permittees reporting an average success rate of 38–41% for the season.

Youth were less likely to report a problem with interference from other hunters than adult hunters, with about 70–75% of youth reporting "no problem" compared to 60–64% of adults. Adults reported having "somewhat of a problem" and "little problem" more often than youth hunters (Table 6).

In general, response patterns from the 2004 Turkey Hunter Attitude Survey indicated that youth were more accepting of liberalizing turkey regulations to allow more opportunity. We asked hunters if they supported or opposed changing the current check station system to a telephone checking system. Youth responses were different than adult's ($\chi^2 = 69.66$, df = 2, $P < 0.001$). Most adult hunters (60.4%, SE = 0.7) supported this change, while 46.8% (SE = 1.5) of youth supported it. Some youth hunters (37.8%, SE = 1.4) still had a desire to check their turkey at a check station whereas 27.8% (SE = 0.6) adults did.

Support for all day hunting in the spring was high in both the youth and adult groups, although youth hunters displayed more support for this change ($\chi^2 = 13.94$, df = 2, $P < 0.001$). Most hunters were in support of extending the current closure (1300 hr) to sunset; 78.6% (SE = 1.2) youth and 76.1% (SE = 0.6) adult hunters supported all day turkey hunting.

DISCUSSION

The creation of a special youth spring turkey hunting season in 2001 resulted in a substantial increase in youth participation. We have not observed similar increases in sales of permits to adult hunters. During every year except 2004 we noted an increase in youth participation. Given recent concerns over hunter recruitment and retention, our data suggested that special youth tags and seasons might boost turkey hunter numbers. In contrast, Enck et al. (1996) suggested that making it easier or less expensive to buy licenses or have opportunities to go afield may have little influence on recruitment and retention. We believe that for youth, special opportunities are paramount given the competing interests and rapid paced lifestyle of today's youth.

Retention of youth spring turkey hunters is consistently high from year to year, with about 70–80% returning annually. While youths not continuing to hunt are not considered retained, their hunting experience might cause them to consider themselves hunters. Purdy et al. (1989) found that very few hunters who discontinued hunting did not consider themselves hunters 5 years later. While this group may not contribute financially, they still may support hunting from a social or political standpoint. Retention rates of youth turkey hunters were higher than those reported for other youth activities such as baseball and soccer which had 41% and 10% declines, respectively, since 1990 (Sporting Goods Manufacturer Association 2001). Participation by youth in fishing declined 5% during the same time period (United States Fish and Wildlife Service 2002).

Most youths hunt during the special youth spring turkey hunting season, and we observed an increase in success of youth hunters after the establishment of the special season. However, their overall success is still lower than adults. Clearly our data indicated that youths take advantage of the early hunting opportunity available to them. They apparently recognize this as a special and unique opportunity. The special season not provides an opportunity for youths, but it also provides a chance for adults to accompany and teach youths about turkey hunting while not detracting from their own hunting time. The availability of this hunt not only increased participation, but increased actual success rates of youth hunters.

More youths were in support of turkey season liberalizations and check stations than adults. These findings may have important implications for maintaining youth interest in hunting activities. We suggest liberalizations when they are within the biological parameters for populations established by the agency. Such

Table 6. Percentage (±SE) of resident youth and adult hunters reporting problems with interference while spring turkey hunting in Missouri, 2000–2004.

Year	Degree of Problem							
	Great		Some		Little		None	
	Youth	Adult	Youth	Adult	Youth	Adult	Youth	Adult
2000[a]	3.4 (1.5)	3.9 (0.3)	9.4 (2.4)	13.4 (0.6)	15.4 (2.9)	22.3 (0.7)	70.5 (3.7)	59.3 (0.8)
2001	1.2 (0.9)	3.9 (0.3)	8.6 (2.2)	12.9 (0.6)	14.8 (2.8)	21.2 (0.7)	73.5 (3.4)	61.2 (0.8)
2002	3.0 (1.3)	3.9 (0.3)	8.3 (2.1)	12.9 (0.6)	11.9 (2.5)	21.7 (0.7)	76.2 (3.3)	60.5 (0.8)
2003	3.4 (0.8)	3.3 (0.3)	8.3 (1.3)	13.4 (0.6)	16.2 (1.7)	21.8 (0.7)	69.4 (2.1)	60.4 (0.8)
2004	1.5 (0.6)	2.8 (0.3)	8.3 (1.3)	11.8 (0.5)	13.3 (1.6)	20.3 (0.7)	74.6 (2.0)	63.9 (0.8)

[a] No special youth season.

liberalizations may create enthusiasm and thus additional participation and possibly retention. The support of check stations might indicate the importance of social interactions among youth hunters. We suspect that successful youths are interested in sharing the results of their success with others at check stations. A youth hunting survey conducted by Responsive Management (2003) suggested that traditional management programs geared towards wildlife harvest and management are not as important to youth satisfaction as are factors such as interacting with family and friends. In contrast, adults seem to be more in favor of remote checking (telechek), possibly due to their time constraints. We suggest that states without check stations consider the social benefits of meeting places for hunters. For example, stations where successful hunters weigh their bird and record harvests might promote an important social gathering place.

Our evaluation points to several recommendations when considering implementation of a special youth turkey season. First, we suggest the season be limited to youth-only participants. We observed the greatest increase in youth permit sales in Missouri following creation of a special youth only season. We suggest that timing be set to coincide with the first peak of turkey gobbling and prior to initiation of continuous incubation. Setting seasons around these time periods may boost success and opportunities for youths to harvest a bird. However, success was not the only motivation for retention; we observed that retention rates were not improved despite improved success rates for youths. Second, we suggest weekend season openers for special youth turkey hunting seasons. Traditional weekday openers were established to reduce interference among hunters and minimize accidents. However, they are not accommodating to youths. Our data suggests that interference was not an issue with the majority of youth turkey hunters, and weekend hunts would minimize conflicts with schooling.

ACKNOWLEDGMENTS

Funding for this study was provided by the Missouri Department of Conservation. F. Lowry performed most of the POS database queries.

LITERATURE CITED

Duda, M. D. 1993. Factors related to hunting and fishing in the U.S. Phase I: Literature review. United States Fish and Wildlife Service, Harrisonburg, Virginia, USA.

Enck, J. W., G. F. Mattfeld, and D. J. Decker. 1996. Retaining likely dropouts from hunting: New York's Apprentice Hunter Program. Transactions of the North American Wildlife and Natural Resources Conference 61:358–366.

Missouri Department of Conservation. 2003. Annual hunting and fishing permit distribution and sales summary. Administrative Services Division, Missouri Department of Conservations, Jefferson City, Missouri, USA.

Purdy, K. G., D. J. Decker, and T. L. Brown. 1989. New York's new hunters: influences on hunting involvement from beginning to end. Department of Natural Resources, Cornell University, Human Dimensions Research Unit Publication 89-3, Ithaca, New York, USA.

Responsive Management. 2003. Factors related to hunting and fishing participation among the Nations youth. Prepared for the United States Fish and Wildlife Service. Responsive Management, Harrisonburg, Virginia, USA.

Sporting Goods Manufacturers Association. 2001. The SGMA Report 2001: Teen and pre-teen participation trends, 1990–2000. West Palm Beach, Florida, USA.

United States Fish and Wildlife Service. 1997. 1996 national survey of fishing and hunting and wildlife-associated recreation. United States Department of Interior, and United States Department of Commerce, Bureau of the Census, Washington, D.C., USA.

———. 2002. 2001 national survey of Fishing, Hunting, and Wildlife-Associated recreation. United States Department of Interior, and United States Department of Commerce, Bureau of the Census, Washington, D.C., USA.

Jeff Beringer is a resource scientist with the Missouri Department of Conservation (MDC). He received his B.S. from the University of Wisconsin-Stevens Point and M.S. from the University of Tennessee. His primary interests are deer, turkey, and ruffed grouse research and management. He and his 2 boys enjoy hunting and fishing whenever possible.

Joshua (Josh) Millspaugh is an assistant professor of wildlife conservation at the University of Missouri. Prior to joining the MU faculty, Josh was a postdoctoral researcher in the School of Fisheries at the University of Washington (UW). He received his Ph.D. in wildlife science from UW, his M.S. from South Dakota State University, and his B.S. from SUNY College of Environmental Science And Forestry. Josh's research currently focused on design and analysis of radiotracking studies, large-mammal ecology and management, and the refinement and use of hormone assays in wildlife conservation.

Ron Reitz is a Resource Scientist with the Missouri Department of Conservation. He has a B.S. and an M.S. in Forestry from Southern Illinois University Carbondale. His professional interests include social science research and survey methodology and design.

Mike Hubbard is currently the program leader for the Management Evaluation unit of the Resource Science Division for the Missouri Departement of Conservation (MDC). He obtained a B.S. in Fisheries and Wildlife management from the University of Missouri-Columbia. He acquired an M.S in wildlife biology, a Ph.D. in animal ecology, and held a post-doctoral position at Iowa State University. He has been involved in research focusing on numerous gamebirds, songbirds, small mammals, white-tailed deer and habitat-space use questions. He started with MDC in 1999 as a wildlife research biologist with responsibility for wild turkey research and management and research in forest systems. His interests include animal population dynamics, habitat use and hunter recruitment.

Index